FIGHTING WITH ALLIES

AMERICA AND BRITAIN IN PEACE AND WAR

ROBIN RENWICK

Biteback Publishing

This edition published in Great Britain in 2016 by
Biteback Publishing Ltd
Westminster Tower
3 Albert Embankment
London SE1 7SP
Copyright © Robin Renwick 1996, 2016

Originally published in Basingstoke in 1996
by Palgrave Macmillan and in New York by Times Books.

ISBN 978-1-84954-979-0

10 9 8 7 6 5 4 3 2 1

A CIP catalogue record for this book is available from the British Library.

Set in Sabon by Adrian McLaughlin

Printed and bound in Great Britain by
CPI Group (UK) Ltd, Croydon CR0 4YY

CONTENTS

LIST OF PLATES

Cover photograph: Roosevelt and Churchill on board HMS *Prince of Wales* in Placentia Bay, Newfoundland, in August 1941 at the conference that decided the Atlantic Charter. Also in the picture Averell Harriman, Admiral King and General George Marshall. © Getty Images

Rear-Admiral Sir George Cockburn in Washington; 24 August 1814. (Corbis Images)

Ambassador Joseph Kennedy, John F. Kennedy and Joseph Kennedy Jr in London; 1938. (Corbis Images)

Franklin D. Roosevelt and Winston Churchill fishing at Shangri-La; May 1943. (Franklin D. Roosevelt Presidential Library and Museum)

Franklin D. Roosevelt and Winston Churchill in the White House grounds; 24 May 1943. (Franklin D. Roosevelt Presidential Library and Museum)

Franklin D. Roosevelt, Winston Churchill and Joseph Stalin in Tehran; 29 November 1943. (Franklin D. Roosevelt Presidential Library and Museum)

Harry Truman, Winston Churchill and Joseph Stalin at Potsdam; July 1945. (Corbis Images)

Portrait of Montgomery by Eisenhower. (UK Government Art Collection)

Harry Truman, Clement Attlee, Dean Acheson and George Marshall in Washington; December 1950. (Abbie Rowe, National Park Service, Harry S. Truman Library & Museum)

ACKNOWLEDGEMENTS

INDISPENSABLE SOURCE MATERIAL is to be found in the Prime Ministerial, Cabinet and Foreign Office documents in the Public Record Office in Kew, in the collection Foreign Relations of the United States (FRUS) published by the State Department, in the US presidential libraries, at the Margaret Thatcher Foundation and in the memoirs and diaries of those principally involved in these events. A unique resource in more recent times has been the evidence submitted to and the conclusions of the Iraq inquiry.

In writing about the UK/US relationship over the past twenty years, I have been grateful for the insights of those of my former colleagues and of many of the senior military figures involved. The opinions expressed are my own, but my thanks are due especially to:

Frank Berman
Christopher Collins
Sherard Cowper-Coles
Paul Drayson
Christopher Elliott
Robert Fry
Robert Gates
Jeremy Greenstock
Charles Guthrie
Richard Haass
Roderic Lyne
Stanley McChrystal
David Manning
Christopher Meyer

Ray Odierno
David Omand
Colin Powell
Jonathan Powell
David Richards
John Sawers
Nigel Sheinwald
Richard Shirreff
Kevin Tebbit
Simon Webb

My thanks are due also to James Stephens and Olivia Beattie at Biteback Publishing, and to Marie-France Renwick for her help with the illustrations, and to the staff of the House of Lords library.

FOREWORD

*We, my dear Crossman, are Greeks in the American Empire.
You will find the Americans much as the Greeks found the
Romans – great big, vulgar, bustling people, more vigorous
than we are.*

—HAROLD MACMILLAN, 1943

WE HAVE ONLY Richard Crossman's word for it that Macmillan said this
and Crossman was never the most reliable of witnesses. But there were
plenty of later occasions on which Macmillan talked in similar terms and
this was among the British a near-conventional way of thinking at the time.
To some, it still is. We find the same plaintive and patronising echo in a
piece of doggerel inspired by the Anglo-American negotiations at the end
of the Second World War, which resulted in the setting up of the World
Bank and the International Monetary Fund:

> In Washington Lord Halifax
> Once whispered to J. M. Keynes,
> It's true they have the money bags,
> But we have all the brains.

In the same year, similar sentiments were expressed in more official language in a Foreign Office paper on relations with the United States:
'If we go about our business in the right way we can help to steer this
great unwieldy barge, the United States of America, into the right harbour.
If we don't, it is likely to continue to wallow in the ocean, an isolated
menace to navigation.'[1]

When Winston Churchill tried and failed, towards the end of the Second World War, to alert the United States to Stalin's plans for the subjugation of Eastern Europe, in exasperation he exclaimed to General Alan Brooke, Chief of the Imperial General Staff: 'There is only one thing worse than fighting with Allies, and that is fighting without them!' He firmly believed that the United States could be relied upon to do the right thing in the end, 'having first exhausted the available alternatives'.

The 'special relationship', real or supposed, that has existed between Britain and the United States since the Second World War has been the subject of much analysis and editorialising, often telling us more about the opinions of the author than the facts of the case.

This is not another attempt at interpretation. It is, for the most part, a narrative: an effort to describe what happened and why, and how it appeared at the time, and in retrospect, to the principal actors on both sides, though I have offered some observations along the way.

An earlier version of this book was published by Macmillan and Times Books shortly after I left my post as British ambassador in Washington in 1995. A couple of wars and two decades later, plus the British decision to exit the European Union, and with the tectonic plates shifting on both sides of the Atlantic, it is time to update this story and to consider how meaningful the relationship is today, raising some important questions about the role Britain envisages itself playing in future in world affairs. There are many who believe that there is today far less to the relationship than meets the eye and that the accompanying rhetoric is no more than a sop to the British for the loss of real influence. The country is felt to have paid a high price in blood and treasure for having been first in support of the United States in Iraq and Afghanistan. These episodes are dealt with in some depth, given the importance to the future of the relationship of the lessons to be drawn from them.

It certainly cannot be taken for granted, least of all today. The opening pages are a reminder that there is nothing automatic about the especially close relationship between Britain and the United States, which had its origins in the destroyers for bases agreement signed by Churchill and Roosevelt in September 1940. Before that, it did not exist at all.

For all his magnificent rhetoric, Churchill knew that, without the direct participation of the United States, the war was unwinnable. When he heard of the attack on Pearl Harbor and Roosevelt told him 'we are all in the same boat now', his reaction that same evening was 'so we had won after all'. With the US in the war 'up to the neck and in to the death … we should emerge, however mauled and mutilated, safe and victorious'. With the Americans now as allies, on 25 February 1942, Churchill, having already informed Roosevelt about the *Ultra* intercepts of German communications, wrote to tell him that the British could read US diplomatic traffic as well, a practice that was now being discontinued. He ended by asking that his letter should be burned.[2]

———————

What follows is not based on my own experiences, except in relation to the Falklands Crisis, Bosnia and Northern Ireland, but of course it is influenced by them. As counsellor in the British embassy in Washington in the 1980s, I was involved in the effort to secure American support for Britain in the Falklands War. As Margaret Thatcher observed in her memoirs, without the Sidewinder missiles made available to us by the US Secretary for Defense, Cap Weinberger, we would not have been able to re-take the Falklands.[3] Calling with the ambassador, Sir Nicholas Henderson, to get the support of Senator Joe Biden, nowadays Vice-President, we were greeted with the words: 'Forget all the crap about self-determination, we are going to support you because you are British!'

There has by now been a full release of documents on both sides of the Atlantic about the Thatcher/Reagan period, revealing just how torrid some of the exchanges were about the Falklands and what many will find the surprising degree to which Margaret Thatcher was prepared to compromise because of the imperative need to retain American support. In the middle of the crisis, Alexander Haig confessed to the President and others that, as Thatcher suspected, he had indeed been trying to engineer a 'camouflaged transfer of sovereignty to Argentina' in his efforts to avoid a military showdown in the South Atlantic.[4]

On returning a few years later as British ambassador to the United States, I banned use in and by the embassy of the term 'special relationship', not because I doubted that the relationship was special – in defence, nuclear and intelligence cooperation it undoubtedly is – but because it carried with it too much emotional baggage on the British side, plus the delusion that the United States might somehow be expected to agree with us, come what may.

As one of my successors in Washington, David Manning, observed: 'We sometimes get trapped into thinking that the special relationship is as special for them as it is for us.' In Whitehall, it seemed at times to carry with it a belief that, because we are older than the United States, we are wiser too – an idea the Americans have always found amusing. The relationship generally seemed to me to be viewed more sanely through American eyes. We should, I felt, leave it mostly to them to refer to the relationship as special, as successive US presidents have continued to do.

I returned to Washington in the warm afterglow of the successful US/ UK military cooperation in the liberation of Kuwait. In the ensuing period, the Bosnia crisis provoked sharp transatlantic differences and one of the most serious disagreements between the British and American governments since Suez. Starting as a humanitarian mission, the Europeans committed peace-keeping forces in the absence of a peace to keep. The United States, with no desire to get involved in the Balkans or to commit any troops themselves, attempted for a while to engage in the impossible task of leading from behind. As ambassador in Washington, my most important task was to help to contain and overcome these differences and to persuade the Americans to show the leadership that eventually was displayed in the action taken against the Serbs and the Dayton Accords in the autumn of 1995.

This account deals with the political relationship between governments – not with the myriad ties of language, literature, family and history that also make up what really is special about the relationship. A belief in 'shared values' remains a constant refrain in discussion of the relationship, regularly referred to in statements by President Obama, as with every one of his predecessors. The British may be surprised at the adoption by the American Bar Association of Magna Carta (they financed the memorial at Runnymede), given that it was signed by a bunch of barons several hundred years before the US Declaration of Independence. Yet they consider that it embodies principles, above all *habeas corpus*, fundamental to US law today. The founders of the Republic considered that they were fighting the British for their rights as Englishmen and a more advanced form of parliamentary democracy, which existed in Britain but scarcely elsewhere in Europe. The firm belief in the US is that in two world wars, the Cold War and other instances, the US and Britain have indeed been defending shared values.

Beyond what some will regard as these nebulous beliefs, the relationship today is underpinned by the fact that Britain and the United States are by far the largest investors in each other's countries, with investments which, combined, are worth well over a trillion dollars. This phenomenon is a development mainly of the past three or four decades. The major US banks to date have run their operations in Europe, the Middle East and Africa from London, though, post-'Brexit', they will have to make some major adjustments. A vast array of US corporations have chosen to establish themselves or to expand their operations in Britain as the most convenient way, for reasons of language and ease of operating, to access the European common market, giving some serious economic ballast to the relationship of a kind that did not exist in the distant days of the 1930s. The continuance of US investment on anything like this scale will, however, depend on what new trade agreements can be reached with the EU, pending which many future investment decisions will be delayed.

The Alliance periodically is the subject of obituary notices in the press – another near-constant feature of the relationship. Yet it has shown a Lazarus-like tendency to survive and to weather successive changes of administration in Britain and the United States over the past seventy-five years, including that from Bill Clinton to George W. Bush, whose Secretary of State, Condoleezza Rice, felt that 'if you cannot count on the Brits, you are really alone'. According to Barack Obama: 'Through the grand sweep of history … there is one constant – the rock-solid alliance between the United States and the United Kingdom.'[5] Beyond the hyperbole, however, Obama has been more distant and less engaged with America's allies than any of his recent predecessors.

The relationship with the United Kingdom has undergone profound changes, of which the most profound of all has been the increasing disparity of power, accentuated by a series of ever deeper cuts in Britain's defence capabilities. The US does not want the UK's relevance to diminish, but has seen that as the path we may be on.

This book is published at a time when many on this side of the Atlantic, in Asia and the Middle East have felt that the United States under President Obama and in response to the botched intervention in Iraq and the fourteen-year war in Afghanistan has sought to become more detached from world crises, or half-heartedly engaged, an increasingly 'reluctant sheriff', leaving it, for instance, to Angela Merkel to negotiate with Vladimir Putin over Ukraine, with no direct US involvement and, initially, more concerned to stay out of than to engage seriously in dealing with the crisis in Syria.

This was indeed the Obama doctrine of caution and 'restraint', as set out in his May 2014 speech at West Point and in his April 2016 interview with *The Atlantic*. The US, he made clear, did not want to go on acting as the world's policeman and had a 'hard-earned humility' about its ability to determine outcomes in other countries. The so-called Islamic State or ISIS initially was dismissed by him as a 'junior varsity team' which posed no real danger to the United States and, following the overly aggressive and ill-considered actions of George W. Bush, he has appeared in almost any circumstances not to want to see US troops actively engaged abroad – a conclusion reached by his own former defense secretaries. Having drawn publicly a 'red line' against the use of chemical weapons by the Syrian regime, he has claimed to be proud of the moment when he decided to take no action when they did so, despite being told by the 'Washington establishment' that his own credibility and that of the United States was at stake. Putin's adventurism in Ukraine and Syria is seen by him as weakening, not strengthening, Russia, with Ukraine regarded by him as a former Russian client state and core interest, 'which is going to be vulnerable to military domination by Russia whatever we do'.[6] As President, Obama has seen his job as being to get the United States out of wars, and to avoid getting too deeply entangled in situations in, for instance, Syria or Ukraine, that could risk the US getting involved in another one.

The Obama administration has achieved what is hoped to be a fifteen-year nuclear agreement with Iran, highly controversial in the US and the Middle East, but supported by the Western allies. But the West manifestly has been cynically out-manoeuvred by Putin in Ukraine and Syria. Hillary Clinton is firmly of the opinion that 'super-powers don't get to retire'[7] and that the US must show leadership in dealing with crises, whether in Ukraine, with ISIS or in the South China Sea. Donald Trump, in contrast, represents a throwback to the days of 'America first', even going so far as to suggest that, regardless of its treaty obligations, the US might be selective about which allies are worth defending against Russian aggression, depending on the contribution they are making themselves.

The Ukraine crisis has demonstrated that Western Europe is more than ever dependent on the United States for its security, but also that the Europeans remain extremely resistant to making any greater efforts for their own defence. The US currently accounts for 75 per cent of all NATO countries spending on defence, as against 50 per cent during the Cold War. The outgoing British ambassador to the US has suggested that other NATO members need to consider whether it is right, or likely to be sustainable, to ask the US to go on indefinitely bearing so disproportionate a part of the burden of European defence. There is at present little sign of them doing so.

Another predominant theme of the 2016 US presidential election has been the aggressively protectionist attitudes of Trump and Bernie Sanders, causing Hillary Clinton to back away from support of the Trans-Pacific Trade Partnership that she helped to initiate. The prospects for the proposed Transatlantic Trade and Investment Partnership currently look bleak, given the resurgence of protectionism in the US and in France and Germany.

Obama has justified his own extreme caution about US military involvement by denouncing Allied 'free riders', who, he contends, clamour for US leadership without being prepared to do much themselves. The British and French have been exceptions to this rule, yet were blamed by him for having done little to stabilise Libya following the overthrow of Gaddafi, a task he chose to regard as one for the Europeans rather than the US. This was in response to criticism in the US of his own failure to act more decisively, in particular in the fight against ISIS.

Obama's Defense Secretary, Robert Gates, and the head of the US Army, General Ray Odierno, both voiced their alarm at the shrinkage in UK defence capabilities resulting from the coalition government's defence cuts in 2010, reducing the size of the British Army to 82,000, the Royal Navy to nineteen combatant surface ships and the frontline capabilities of the RAF, while massively increasing the aid budget, which, unlike defence, was ring-fenced against future cuts. The concern is understandable, given that Britain's army, navy and air force today have scarcely more than half the frontline strength they had at the time of the Falklands War. The current US Defense Secretary, Ashton Carter, declared that it would be 'a great loss to the world when a country of that much history and standing for so much to so many people around the world takes actions which seem to indicate disengagement'.[8]

It is hardly surprising that the experience of two military interventions in the past decade should have made the British public and politicians very cautious about further military ventures. The vote in the House of Commons in August 2013 against taking any action in response to the killing by the Syrian regime of 1,400 of its own citizens by nerve gas in Damascus, in flagrant violation of international law, appeared to be regarded in Westminster as of little long-term consequence. It was not seen like that by Britain's principal allies, coming as a very unpleasant shock to the US Secretary of State, John Kerry, and the Obama national security team, with a knock-on effect on Obama's own resolution in dealing with the problem, and to the French, who had agreed to participate in a retaliatory strike on the Republican Guard headquarters from which the nerve gas attack had been launched. The Syrian regime has continued ever since to use chlorine gas against its opponents.

The subsequent inability of the British government for several months to secure a majority in the House of Commons for action against so-called Islamic State in its main centres in Syria dismayed the United States and France. The chief of defence staff, General Houghton, described this as 'letting down our allies',[9] which was indeed how they saw it. The Defence Secretary, Michael Fallon, regarded it as 'morally indefensible' for Britain, which is directly threatened by them, to leave it to others to deal with ISIS in Syria. The vote in Parliament in December 2015 authorising the RAF to extend the campaign against ISIS targets from Iraq to Syria re-aligned the country with its key allies.

Britain also was absent from the efforts made by Angela Merkel, supported by François Hollande, to stabilise the situation in Ukraine. These developments led a raft of US pundits to question whether Britain any longer has the will to play a leading role in world affairs and the chief of defence staff to wonder whether the country today still has the 'courageous instinct' crucial to its ability to make a difference in the world.

What consequences are the shrinkage of Britain's defence capabilities, particularly of the army, the controversy over Iraq and under-resourcing of the British forces in Iraq and Afghanistan likely to have for the US/UK relationship over time? It would be absurd to suggest that these will not be significant, or that the relationship is as important to the US today as it was in the past. Obama has declared that he told David Cameron that if he wished to preserve the 'special relationship', he would have to commit to spending 2 per cent of GDP on defence.[10] The British Army, which hitherto was able to commit an armoured division in any major conflict, would not be able to deploy such a force today. Yet, with Britain still spending more on defence than all but the US, China, Russia and Saudi Arabia, and planning to operate a new aircraft carrier (though not until 2020), the capability will remain to support the US militarily in any crisis in which British interests also are involved, provided the political will exists to do so and the US displays sufficiently intelligent leadership to be worth supporting.

This book is intended to provide some historical perspective and to serve as a reminder that at the end of the Cold War there was a fashionable tendency to question whether NATO was going to have much of a future role. Anglo-American cooperation was vital in ensuring that NATO was re-configured to play a crucial part in Bosnia, Kosovo, Libya and Afghanistan, while the security of the Baltic states, with their large Russian minorities, depends today on Article V of the North Atlantic Treaty and not much else. Ideas that the European Union would develop a common defence policy 'which might in time lead to a common defence' have proved largely illusory, leading the French to decide to re-join the NATO integrated military structure and the President of the European Commission, Jean-Claude Juncker, to declare in October 2015: 'If I look at the common European defence policy, a bunch of chickens would be a more unified combat unit.' Attempts to revive the idea of a 'European army' will carry little conviction in the absence of any real determination to increase Europe's defence capabilities.

The decision in March 2009 by President Nicolas Sarkozy to end the more than four-decade boycott of the NATO military command decreed by De Gaulle in 1966 failed to attract all the attention it deserved. For this major shift by France has resulted in far closer US/French defence cooperation than in the past, in particular in the fight against ISIS, and a vast increase in intelligence-sharing (codenamed Lafayette), bringing the three major Western military allies into a closer alignment with each other. This has changed the dynamic across the Atlantic, with the US Defense Secretary declaring that, currently, he is in closer contact with the French Defence Minister than with any of his other international counterparts. Far from concerning the British, this Franco-American rapprochement is positive for Britain's own relationship with its two key military allies.

If British political leaders of whatever complexion wish to continue to claim to play a role in world affairs, as most of them still purport to want to do, they are going to need to give priority to preserving the capability of Britain's armed forces to act in support of their allies when required. In dealing with some future crisis, Britain is likely again to be asked to participate in operations alongside the United States, or risk not having it dealt with at all and the Americans concluding that, absent any effort from the European allies, they should revert to a more 'America first' calculation of US interests. An underlying reason for Obama's caution over engagement in Syria has been the fact that the crisis there is seen by him as far more of a threat to Europe than to the United States, which indeed it is.

———————

There are other reasons for US concern about their traditionally closest ally. Americans favoured self-rule for Scotland, but reacted with surprise to the proposition that Scotland should be allowed to vote on whether to remain a member of the United Kingdom. Obama made a direct appeal to the United Kingdom to stay united. Hillary Clinton greeted the outcome with relief as, otherwise, the United Kingdom would have been 'diminished'.

The British Labour Party, with its Atlanticist tradition stretching back to the days of Clement Attlee and Ernest Bevin, is seen as having reverted to a degree of anti-Americanism and non-alignment well beyond that seen under Michael Foot. While that will affect its electability, and thereby may prove self-correcting, it marks a clear break from the bipartisan consensus in foreign policy that existed hitherto. The gap between the United States, whether Republican or Democrat, and the Labour Party under its current leadership is as wide as the Atlantic.

The United States shares many of Britain's reservations about the European Union and would never begin to consider any surrender of sovereignty itself. It regards the EU as a highly bureaucratic, overregulated, low-growth economic zone. The EU is taken very seriously in terms of trade negotiations, less so in other respects. The Obama administration, on coming into office, announced a 'pivot to Asia'. Successive US presidents have approached the ritual meetings with the presidents of the European Commission and of the EU with all the enthusiasm of a visit to the dentist. Their confidence in the project has not been helped by the *Alice-in-Wonderland* economics of Greece as a member of the eurozone and Europe's struggles in dealing with ISIS-sponsored terrorism and the massive inflow of refugees and migrants it currently is experiencing. There is a sense, not only in the United States, of Europe in relative decline, and of the European institutions, faced with these huge challenges, as short of ideas as to what to do.

The United States historically, however, has counted on Britain to exert its influence in Europe to help ensure that the European Union is more outward-looking, less protectionist and more committed to the transatlantic partnership than, in its view, would otherwise be the case. The Americans are no less scathing than the British about the difficulty of dealing with the EU institutions. Few present-day American leaders would claim to be able to calculate whether, for Britain, the loss of control over its own laws is more than offset by membership of the European Union and whether the EU is in fact reformable. But, in general, they have seen it as clearly in *America's* interests for Britain to remain in the EU and as potentially prejudicial to the vast US investments in Britain if it were to leave.

It came as no surprise, therefore, to hear President Obama inject himself into this debate by declaring on 7 June 2015: 'We very much are looking forward to the United Kingdom staying part of the European Union because we think its influence is positive not just for Europe, but also for the world.' During his visit to the UK a few weeks before the referendum, Obama delivered a further lecture about the need for Britain to remain in Europe, adding, ill-advisedly, that if a Brexit Britain sought a separate trade agreement with the US, it would be 'at the back of the queue'. This is in fact unlikely, under a future administration, to prove to be the case, given bipartisan support in Congress for an agreement with Britain, which does not, however, mean that one is likely to be able to be concluded any time soon.

A raft of former US foreign policy and defence officials led by George Shultz declared that

> the United Kingdom has played a key role in strengthening the transatlantic relationship. But we are concerned that should the UK choose to leave the EU, the UK's place and influence in the world would be diminished and Europe would be dangerously weakened … The special relationship between our two countries would not compensate for the loss of influence that the UK would suffer if it was no longer part of the EU … in foreign policy, defence and international trade matters.[11]

Donald Trump, on the other hand, hailed the Brexit vote ('They took their country back'), regarding the outcome as representing a vindication of his own populist brand of politics. Obama, shifting hastily into reverse, declared that the 'special relationship' would endure, with both the UK and the EU remaining indispensable partners for the United States.

A constant thread throughout this book is the chronicling of the decades-long efforts that successive US administrations made to propel the frequently reluctant British into a closer relationship with Europe, where British involvement was seen as being important to and wholly positive for the United States. The outcome of the referendum on British membership of the European Union, therefore, is bound to have a profound effect on the future relationship across the Atlantic.

Britain's departure from the EU will not put an end to the specially close relationship with the United States, certainly not in the domains of defence and intelligence. There may indeed be an autumnal glow, as the incoming US administration, Democrat or Republican, will want to be seen as starting off on close terms with America's closest and generally most dependable ally. Beyond all the romanticism about it, the relationship has been and will continue to be based on the solid foundation of common interests, which is why it has endured so long. Hillary Clinton is a firm believer in it, though clear-sighted about it. Those who believe that, along with much else, it would not survive a Trump presidency, if there is one, will find that they are mistaken about that and have forgotten about the separation of powers, intended by the Founding Fathers to shackle any President and particularly any potentially maverick one. The next President can be expected to greet the new British Prime Minister with the usual talk about the 'specialness' of the relationship and, up to a point, he or she will mean it.

The exit from the EU, however, will alter its nature. In the near term, some further US investment in Britain will be held back until there is clarity about future access to the European market. Britain outside the EU eventually is likely to be able to secure favourable access to the US market, but will be perceived as having far less influence in Europe and, consequently, in Washington, on matters other than defence, rendering this country still a very important ally but a less positive factor for the United States in Europe than it was before.

PROLOGUE

ON 24 AUGUST 1814, Rear-Admiral Sir George Cockburn sat down to dinner at the White House. He was an uninvited guest. The table had been laid for President Madison. At around 3 p.m. that afternoon, with the streets of the capital choked with soldiers and refugees, Dolley Madison had fled the White House, having at the last moment found a wagon to carry off the silver, her favourite velvet curtains, papers, books, a clock and, cut from its frame, the full-length portrait of George Washington by Gilbert Stuart. Left behind were most of her clothes and other belongings. President Madison and his companions, fleeing in a ferry across the Potomac and from the Virginia shore, saw

> columns of flame and smoke ascending throughout the night ...
> from the Capitol, the President's house and other public edifices, as
> the whole were on fire ... If at intervals the dismal sight was lost to
> our view, we got it again from some hilltop or eminence where we
> paused to look at it.[1]

Admiral Cockburn, meanwhile, ate the meal still on the table and drank to 'Jemmy's health, which was the only epithet he used whenever he spoke of the President', one citizen reported. He took as mementoes an old hat of the President's and the cushions from Dolley Madison's chair, about which he made 'pleasantries too vulgar ... to repeat'. His marines with their torches then set a fire in each of the windows, so that 'the whole building was wrapt in flames and smoke'. That night and the following day the British burned the Library of Congress and all the other public buildings of the capital. Cockburn told the onlookers: 'You may thank old Madison for this; it is he who has got you into this scrape ... We want to catch him and carry him to England for a curiosity.'[2]

————

The causes of the war of 1812 were straightforward. Britain would not permit neutral shipping to trade with continental Europe under Napoleon and the Royal Navy was in a position to enforce this blockade. The British position, claimed Madison, rested not on law but on 'a mere superiority of force' and the 'comparative state of naval armaments'.

The British Minister in Washington, Anthony Merry, had done little to improve relations. When first invited to dinner by Madison, Merry ousted the wife of the Treasury Secretary, Mrs Gallatin, from the head of the table, insisting that she must give up her seat to his wife who, in his view, had precedence. At the President's New Year reception, Merry felt slighted at the attention paid to an emissary of the Bey of Tunis and after five minutes left in a huff. Madison found Merry's conduct 'truly extraordinary, in this age and in this country'.

British seizures of American merchantmen and the impressment of some of their sailors into the Royal Navy increased. Madison's negotiator in London, James Monroe, future President of the United States and author of the Monroe Doctrine, tried to exert a calming influence. With Spain hostile and Napoleon rampant, he told President Jefferson that 'it is important for us to stand well with some power' and that, for the duration of the war, Britain's 'very existence ... depended on an adherence to its maritime pretensions'.[3]

On 22 June 1807, in Hampton Roads, near Norfolk on the American coast, HMS *Leopard* attacked the American frigate *Chesapeake*, which had refused to submit to a boarding party sent to seize some deserters. Twenty-one American sailors were killed or injured and one deserter hanged. With the administration lacking the naval power required to confront the British, Jefferson and Madison responded with the Embargo Acts, interrupting trade, especially with Britain. The British Foreign Secretary, Canning, sent George Rose to Washington to negotiate with Madison. But Rose came, as Henry Adams remarked, 'not to conciliate, but to terrify. His apology was a menace.' Rose in turn was unimpressed by Congress, which, he considered, proved 'the excess of the democratic ferment ... the dregs having got up to the top'.[4]

As the US Treasury Secretary, Gallatin, had predicted ('I prefer war to a permanent embargo'), the restrictions on trade caused great resentment and were largely ignored in New England, dependent on trade with Britain and Canada. Canning sneered at their ineffectiveness while Madison tried in vain to plug the myriad loopholes. In 1809 the embargo was lifted but then was reimposed when the British Cabinet repudiated an agreement with Madison reached by the British Minister in Washington, David Erskine. Jefferson expressed his outrage at Canning's 'unprincipled rascality'. But the British remained determined to prevent American trade with the European continent.

Erskine was succeeded by Francis Jackson, famous for his order given some years earlier to the British fleet to destroy Copenhagen. Within a month Mrs Jackson was reporting that her husband, 'being accustomed to treat with civilized Courts and governments of Europe, and not with savage Democrats, half of them sold to France, has not succeeded in his negotiation'. She found the Washington cuisine detestable: 'no claret, champagne and Madeira indifferent'. President Madison, outraged by Jackson's insufferable arrogance, informed him that 'no further communication will be received from you'.

In August 1810, the French Foreign Minister told the Americans that France would withdraw its own discriminatory measures against American commerce. In fact Napoleon had no intention of doing so ('it is evident that we should commit ourselves to nothing'), but Madison sought to use this offer to put pressure on the British. The embargo against Britain was reimposed. British warships reappeared off New York, intercepting merchantmen and impressing seamen. In November 1811, the War Hawk Congress was told by Madison that 'anything was better' than the existing state of Anglo-American relations. The new British Minister, Foster, reported that the administration preferred war to its 'present embarrassments'. Britain was given one last chance to withdraw the Orders in Council restricting neutral trade. At the same time Congress declined to vote the funds necessary to strengthen the American Navy. The British were accused of fomenting treason in New England and conspiring to promote the break-up of the Union. In June 1812, Congress voted for war.

The war soon turned into a disaster. The French continued their own attacks on American shipping. New England was disaffected. The American forces were extraordinarily ill-prepared. General Hull's invasion of

Canada ended in a humiliating surrender. The British blockaded the East Coast, though the Americans took heart from individual naval exploits, including the destruction by the USS *Constitution* of the British frigate *Java*. Madison observed that 'rage and jealousy' in England against America 'accounted for the gigantic force she is bringing against us on the water'.

Admiral Cockburn, later described by Napoleon, whom he escorted to Saint Helena, as 'rough, overbearing, vain, choleric and capricious', destroyed Fredericktown and Georgetown on the Maryland shore. Dolley Madison wrote of 'the fears and alarms' that circulated in Washington, while Cockburn sent her word that he intended soon to make his bow in her drawing room. The *Chesapeake* was beaten in a duel off Boston harbour, memorable in American naval history for Captain James Lawrence's famous order, 'Don't give up the ship!', before he died of wounds.

In the north, the British were driven out of the area around Detroit but subsequent American reverses, wrote Madison, 'were as unexpected as they have been distressing'. The Americans were ejected from York (now Toronto), which they burned, and the British controlled both banks of the Niagara. The Foreign Secretary, Castlereagh, rejected Russian mediation, saying that he considered the Anglo-American war 'a sort of family quarrel, where foreign interference can only do harm'. By 1814, with Napoleon defeated and New England in near revolt, Gallatin reported from London that 'a continuation of the war might prove virtually fatal to the United States'.[5] Gallatin suggested that the United States should soften its position on impressment, which, with the ending of the European war, should become only a theoretical issue anyway.

On 17 August, a British fleet carrying 4,000 troops under General Ross anchored thirty-five miles south-east of Washington. Madison's incompetent Secretary for War, Armstrong, still insisted that the British objective was Baltimore. General Winder's militia was defeated outside the capital, at Bladensburg. Madison escaped across the Potomac. Cockburn and Ross entered Washington in triumph. Having burned every public building except the Patent Office, the British returned to their ships. Madison, on his return, found the White House 'in ashes, not an inch but its cracked and blackened walls remained'. Smoke was still rising from the ruins of the Capitol.

Three weeks later, Fort McHenry, south of Baltimore, beat off a determined British attack. It was this episode that gave the new nation its national anthem. Francis Scott Key, a Washington lawyer sent by Madison to arrange an exchange of prisoners, observed 'by the dawn's early light' that 'our flag was still there', proving that the British bombardment had failed. In the north, a British attack towards Albany was repulsed. The British, Madison warned, still were aiming 'a deadly blow at our growing prosperity, perhaps at our national existence'.

The British and American negotiators by now were meeting at Ghent. Fourteen thousand British troops, under the Duke of Wellington's brother-in-law, Sir Edward Pakenham, were bound for New Orleans. His courage was undoubted but, as Wellington observed, 'Pakenham may not be the brightest genius'. In a textbook example of military folly, he led his red-coats in a frontal assault on the heavily defended ramparts of the city. The defence was organised by General Andrew Jackson. The result was a massacre, the British suffering over 2,000 casualties and the Americans sixty-two. Sir Edward, urging on his men, was among the first to be killed. His body was returned to England, pickled in a hogshead of rum.

The battle, though it did wonders for American morale, had been fought in vain, for on Christmas Eve 1814, the peace treaty had been signed at Ghent. The British had abandoned their demands for the creation of an Indian buffer state, south of the Great Lakes, between the United States and Canada. When the Prime Minister, Lord Liverpool, urged Wellington to take over the command in North America, he declined, declaring the conquest of the United States impossible. He advised the British Cabinet to settle on the basis of the status quo before the war; Gallatin gave identical advice to Madison. With the defeat of Napoleon the main cause of the conflict – the enforcement of the British blockade – had disappeared.

Another of the American negotiators, John Quincy Adams, expressed the hope that this would be the last peace treaty between Britain and the United States. And so it was to prove.

For the Americans, despite the dissidence in New England, the war of 1812 was a further important stage in the building of the nation. To the British it seemed just another episode in a long history of colonial and European wars. Nathaniel Hawthorne, visiting Britain a generation later, was dismayed to find no one who could remember the Battle of New Orleans.

There followed through the nineteenth century a number of episodes that were to have an important bearing on Anglo-American relations. In 1822, President Monroe recognised the Latin American states asserting their independence from Spain. In October 1823, Canning proposed that the United States should join Britain in condemning any attempts by Spain to reassert its authority, but also promising non-intervention themselves. Canning boasted that thereby he 'had called in the New World to redress the balance of the Old'. Monroe consulted Jefferson, who replied: 'Our first and fundamental maxim should be never to entangle ourselves in the broils of Europe, and our second never to suffer Europe to intermeddle with Cis-Atlantic affairs.' America, he said, had interests different from those of Europe: 'She should therefore have a system of her own, separate and apart from that of Europe.' Jefferson added that 'Great Britain is the nation which can do us the most harm of anyone, or all on earth'. Britain's friendship, therefore, was worth cultivating, but the priority must be to establish the American system.[6]

The Secretary of State, John Quincy Adams, did not want to appear to be travelling in Canning's wake or to give up the possibility of annexing Cuba. On 2 December 1823, Monroe proclaimed to Congress his own version of the principle of non-interference by the European powers in the American hemisphere. The United States, declared Monroe, had no intention of interfering in the struggles between the Europeans. America would in turn consider 'any attempt on their part to extend their system to any portion of this hemisphere as dangerous to our peace and safety'. This, he explained, was not intended to apply to existing colonies. But the intent was clear: the American continent was henceforth to be considered as not subject to future colonisation by the European powers. This was not what Canning had in mind: 'How could America be closed to future British colonization, when America's geographical limits are actually unknown?'

Canadian–American relations remained tense and marked by violent incidents until the border settlement of 1842. The dispute over the border between Oregon and British Columbia was settled four years later on the basis of the 49th parallel. This settlement of territorial claims did not result in any great cordiality of relations. George Mifflin Dallas, who arrived as the American envoy in London in 1856, proudly disclaimed any belief in 'all the balderdash about mother country, kindred and so forth'. Not surprisingly, he did not get on well with Palmerston. Sir Henry Bulwer, his counterpart in Washington, sought through public speeches to 'cure this anti-English disease at its source'. While admiring the American government, he found the people who lived under it to be 'of a wild, adventurous and conquering character'.

Not all Americans were so ill-disposed. In 1858, as British and French expeditionary forces approached the coast of China, they were bombarded by the shore batteries to such effect that several British vessels were disabled and would have been sunk but for the intervention of Josiah Tattnall, commander of a supposedly neutral American squadron that also was in the vicinity. He intervened to shield the British ships from the Chinese batteries and towed them to safety. When asked to account for his action, Tattnall replied: 'Blood is thicker than water.'

———————

In 1860, the British Minister in Washington, Lord Lyons, was unimpressed by the Republican candidate in the presidential election: 'a Mr Lincoln, a man unknown, a rough Westerner, of the lowest origin and little education'.[7]

A few months later, in her speech from the throne in February 1861, Queen Victoria noted that 'serious differences have arisen among the states of the North American Union'. Palmerston was not alone in being suspected of hoping that these might lead to a dissolution of the Union. The US Secretary of State, Seward, had told the Duke of Newcastle that if he joined the administration it would become his duty to insult England, and that he meant to do so. But, restrained by Lincoln and anxious that the British should not support the Confederates, he became more accommodating. The Foreign Secretary, Lord John Russell, declared that Britain was not involved in any way in the Civil War 'and, for God's sake, let us if possible keep out of it'. The Confederate envoys sought recognition, which to their indignation was denied them.

But the seizure on the high seas in November 1861 from the British vessel *Trent* of two Confederate Commissioners, Mason and Slidell, by Captain Wilkes of the US Navy precipitated a crisis. Palmerston opened a Cabinet meeting by throwing his hat on the table and telling his colleagues: 'I don't know whether you are going to stand this, but I'll be damned if I do.'[8] Seward managed to obtain the release of the commissioners.

Confederate hopes were pinned on Lancashire's dependence on cotton from the southern states, but this made no difference to the British policy of non-recognition. The northerners were outraged by the construction in British yards of warships for the South. The war steamer *Alabama*, built at Cammell Laird's, sank nearly sixty northern vessels in two years.

By 1864, Lord Lyons believed that 'three-fourths of the American people are eagerly longing for a safe opportunity of making war with England'. Seward, meanwhile, was arranging the purchase from Russia of Alaska and proclaiming his certainty that the whole of North America, sooner or later, would be 'within the magic circle of the American Union'. Queen Victoria wrote in her diary of the danger of war with America 'as soon as she makes peace: of the impossibility of our being able to hold Canada, but we must struggle for it'. This fear accelerated the granting of dominion status to Canada in 1867, with a system of government based as much on the American as on the English model. In an attempt to re-establish a better relationship with the United States after the Civil War, Britain agreed to pay £15.5 million in compensation for the damage caused by the *Alabama*.

———

Sir Lionel Sackville-West, serving as the British Minister in Washington in the 1880s, attributed 'the whole anti-British spirit in America … almost wholly to the Irish'. The Secretary of State, James Blaine, was an ardent Anglophobe. In a thinly disguised portrait of him in his novel *Democracy*, Henry Adams wrote:

> A certain secret jealousy of the British Minister is always lurking in the breast of every American Senator, if he is truly democratic; for democracy, rightly understood, is the government of the people, by the people, for the benefit of senators, and there is always a danger that the British Minister may not understand this political principle as he should.[9]

Sackville-West was a popular figure in Washington, though his daughter burst into fits of giggles when President Chester Arthur, an unhappy widower, proposed to her one evening after dinner at the White House. But, in September 1888, Sackville-West received a letter purporting to come from a US citizen of British origin, asking how to vote in the presidential election. Having nothing better to do on a rainy afternoon, he replied, advising his correspondent to vote for President Cleveland. The Republican press published his letter, under the heading: 'The British Lion's Paw Thrust Into American Politics'. When Lord Salisbury proved reluctant to withdraw him, Sackville-West was given his passports and required by Cleveland to leave.[10]

After the defeat of Home Rule in 1886, the Irish problem continued to throw a shadow on relations. Cleveland was very conscious of the amount of public support that could be won by 'twisting the lion's tail'. It was thanks to his efforts that the Venezuela dispute brought Britain and the United States for the last time within measurable distance of war.

In Britain no more than one in ten MPs, as James Bryce later told Theodore Roosevelt, 'even knew there was such a thing as a Venezuelan question'. The demarcation of the boundary with British Guyana was certainly not thought worth a war with the United States.

But Cleveland returned as President on a rising tide of American self-assertion. In 1895, his Secretary of State, Richard Olney, accused Britain, by maintaining its claims on Venezuelan territory, of violating the Monroe Doctrine. Olney's note, one of the most remarkable ever addressed to a British government, stated baldly: 'Today the United States is practically sovereign on this continent.' Olney added that 'the United States' infinite resources combined with its isolated position render it master of the situation and practically invulnerable as against any or all other powers'. Lord Salisbury, who had other things on his mind – the colonial rivalry with France and the increasingly impetuous behaviour of the Kaiser – replied that 'no statesman, however eminent, and no nation, however powerful, are competent to insert into the code of international law a novel principle which was never recognised before, and which has not since been accepted by the Government of any other country'.[11]

On 17 December 1895, President Cleveland, in a message to Congress, stated that the United States itself would adjudicate the boundary between Venezuela and British Guyana and would thereafter resist as wilful aggression any attempt by Britain to assert claims on what it determined to be Venezuelan territory. This strong language swept Congress and the country off its feet. The ensuing explosion of jingoism horrified Henry James.

In Britain, the reaction was one of amazement and incredulity. America at the time had two second-class battleships and twelve cruisers to Britain's forty-four battleships and forty-one cruisers. But on 3 January 1896, the Kaiser despatched his telegram of congratulations to Kruger on having repelled the Jameson Raid. In such circumstances, war with the United States over the Venezuelan border was deemed unthinkable. Joseph Chamberlain stated that 'war between the two nations would be an absurdity as well as a crime … The two nations are … more closely allied in sentiment and in interest than any other nations on the face of the earth.'[12] Cleveland had proposed an inquiry into the border, in which the British agreed to cooperate. By the time the decision was issued in 1899, public interest in the matter was practically dead.

———

The next phase of American history belonged not to Cleveland but to Theodore Roosevelt. While Cleveland played the anti-British card, Roosevelt came into office with entirely different predispositions. On 2 December 1886, at St George's Church, Hanover Square, Teddy Roosevelt married his second wife, Edith. The church, almost deserted, was penetrated by a London fog. Roosevelt's best man, Cecil Spring-Rice, was a young British diplomat whom he had met on the voyage across the Atlantic. Roosevelt and his family made fun of 'good, futile, pathetic Springy', also known as 'Spwing-Wice of the Bwitish Legation'. His combination of courtliness and inquisitiveness caused them to compare him to the White Rabbit in *Alice in Wonderland*. But their friendship was to endure throughout Roosevelt's presidency and, thereafter, seriously to complicate Spring-Rice's relations with Woodrow Wilson. Spring-Rice introduced Roosevelt to the Savile Club and society in London. Roosevelt in turn introduced him to his enormous circle of acquaintances in America and to the arts of political wire-pulling.

But it was to another Englishman that Roosevelt looked for intellectual inspiration. In March 1895 Rudyard Kipling was not yet thirty, but already he was the world's most famous writer. Roosevelt found him 'bright, nervous, voluble', though displaying at times a truculence towards America that required 'very rough handling'. Taking Kipling to visit the Smithsonian, Roosevelt thanked God in a loud voice that he had 'not one drop of British blood in him'. When Kipling mocked the self-righteousness of a nation that had extirpated its native population 'more completely than any modem race has done', Roosevelt made the glass cases of the museum 'shake with his rebuttals'.[13]

In 1889, Senator Henry Cabot Lodge wrote: '[O]ur relations with foreign nations today fill but a slight place in American politics.' But by this time, as James Bryce observed in *The American Commonwealth*: 'The Republic is as wealthy as any two of the greatest European nations, and is capable, if it chooses, of quickly calling into being a vast fleet and a vast army. Her wealth and power has in it something almost alarming.' Bryce was to serve as the British ambassador in Washington from 1907 until succeeded by Spring-Rice in 1913. American energies, which had been absorbed in the opening up of the West, were starting to be turned outwards. It was Joseph Chamberlain who, in 1898, began to speak publicly of the need for an 'Anglo-Saxon alliance'. Chamberlain, a self-made man married to Mary Endicott, daughter of President Cleveland's Secretary of War, felt a particular affinity for the United States. But, as Henry Adams put it, 'the sudden appearance of Germany is the grizzly terror which ... frightened England into American's arms'.

On the American side, Admiral Mahan, in *The Influence of Sea-Power upon History* and in his other writings, sought to convince the Anglo-Saxon world of its fundamental identity of interests as well as of the supreme importance of naval power. By 1906, the American Navy was second only to the British. Neither Theodore Roosevelt nor Secretary of State John Hay felt an alliance to be possible. But, Roosevelt observed: 'The settlement of the Alaskan boundary settled the last serious trouble between the British Empire and ourselves ... I feel very differently towards England from the way I feel towards Germany.' Even Richard Olney of the Venezuela ultimatum by now was writing: 'There is a patriotism of race as well as of country.'

One cause of the *rapprochement* was the benevolent neutrality of the British government and the pro-American public sentiment manifested in Britain when the sinking of the USS *Maine* in Havana harbour led to war between the United States and Spain over Cuba. In the Philippines, Admiral Dewey defeated the Spanish fleet in Manila Bay. Ambassador Hay reported from London that Britain wanted the United States to retain the Philippines. In return, the US government resisted pressure to side with the Boers against the British in South Africa.

On 22 November 1898, at Rottingdean in Sussex, Kipling completed his poem 'The White Man's Burden', which he hastened to send across the Atlantic to Theodore Roosevelt. The poem, subtitled 'The United States and the Philippine Islands', was intended to influence the debate in the Senate on what was to be done with the Philippines:

> Take up the White Man's burden –
> Send forth the best ye breed –
> Go bind your sons to exile
> To serve your captives' need;
> To wait in heavy harness
> On fluttered fold and wild –
> Your new-caught, sullen peoples,
> Half devil and half child ...
> Take up the White Man's burden –
> The savage wars of peace
> Fill full the mouth of Famine
> And bid the sickness cease;
> And when your goal is nearest
> The end for others sought,
> Watch Sloth and heathen Folly
> Bring all your hope to nought ...
> Take up the White Man's burden
> And reap his old reward:
> The blame of those ye better,
> The hate of those ye guard

Roosevelt sent Kipling's work to Henry Cabot Lodge, describing it as 'rather poor poetry, but good sense from the expansionist viewpoint'. Cabot Lodge liked it: 'I think it is better poetry than you say.' The poem was published in New York the day before the Senate vote.

Roosevelt continued to correspond with Kipling until his death. In 1904, he described his frame of mind as 'a good deal like that of your old Viceroy'. Admiral Mahan wrote that in the Spanish territories, the American Empire ought to act like the British, with the interests of the native people uppermost. Echoing Kipling, Mahan warned that 'the inhabitants may not return love for their benefits – comprehension or gratitude may fail them'. This he ascribed to their being 'still in race childhood'.[14]

From the outbreak of the war in Europe, Kipling made desperate appeals to Roosevelt to persuade his countrymen to join the crusade against the Germans: 'The Allies are shedding their blood (and the butcher's bill is a long one) for every ideal the United States stands for.' Kipling despised Woodrow Wilson and warned Roosevelt of the influence exerted by the eight million Germans 'within your borders'. The United States, he claimed, had 'grown up and thriven for 142 years under the lee of the British fleet'.

This was too much for Teddy Roosevelt:

> As a matter of fact for the first ninety years the British Navy, when, as was ordinarily the case, the British government was more or less hostile to us, was our greatest danger. I am not condemning Great Britain. In those good old days the policies of the United States and Great Britain toward one another and toward much of the outside world, were sufficiently alike to give a touch of humor to the virtuous horror expressed by each at the kind of conduct of the other which most closely resembled its own.[15]

1

'YOU MUST NOT SPEAK OF US AS COUSINS'

You must not speak of us ... as cousins, still less as brothers;
we are neither. Neither must you think of us as Anglo-Saxons,
for that term can no longer be rightly applied to the people of
the United States ... there are only two things which can establish
and maintain closer relations between your country and mine:
they are community of ideals and of interests.
—PRESIDENT WILSON TO KING GEORGE V, 1918[1]

ON THE OUTBREAK of war in 1914, President Woodrow Wilson made his position clear:

> The United States must be neutral in fact as well as in name ... we
> must be impartial in thought as well as in action, must put a curb
> upon our sentiments as well as upon every transaction that might be
> construed as preference of one party to the struggle before another.[2]

Wilson was determined that America should not be drawn into the internecine conflict in Europe. The people of the United States, he pointed out,
were drawn from many nations and chiefly from the nations now at war.
Over eight million of America's population of 105 million in 1914 had been
born in Germany or had at least one German parent. The Irish-Americans,
some four million and a half at the start of the war, also had no love for
the British. Americans did not feel themselves threatened by the renewal of
quarrels in Europe. The United States had never had to form any serious

alliance, except tactically with the French during the War of Independence. 'Thanks to the width of the ocean', Teddy Roosevelt wrote to Rudyard Kipling, 'our people believe that they have nothing to fear from the present contest, and that they have no responsibility concerning it.'[3]

Yet the majority of Americans still traced their ancestry back to British roots and, particularly on the east coast, sympathy for Britain was strong. J. P. Morgan acted as the agent for British purchases of munitions and vital raw materials. As the Allies were, effectively, subjecting Germany to a blockade, US trade with Germany was insignificant while exports to Britain and France rose to nearly $3 billion.

The President's closest confidant and envoy, Colonel Edward House, found him 'singularly lacking in appreciation of the importance of this European crisis. He seems more interested in domestic affairs.'[4] But, in January 1915, Wilson accepted House's suggestion that he should seek to act as a channel of confidential communication through which the warring nations could explore the possibilities for peace. Encouraged by the German ambassador in Washington, Count Bernstorff, to believe that Germany might agree to evacuate and indemnify Belgium, House set sail for Europe.

In London he was charmed by the Foreign Secretary, Sir Edward Grey. 'If every belligerent nation had a Sir Edward Grey at the head of its affairs, there would be no war.'[5] But Grey did not believe Bernstorff's account of the German position and it soon turned out that he was right. Indeed, Dr Arthur Zimmermann, on behalf of the German Foreign Office, came close to suggesting to House that Germany needed to be indemnified for the loss of life they had suffered in invading Belgium! The Germans did, however, suggest that if Britain lifted the blockade, they might no longer need to occupy Belgium.

The Americans also wanted the blockade eased or ended. When German sympathisers chartered an American vessel, the *Wilhelmina*, and loaded it with food for Hamburg, the ship was intercepted and the cargo seized by the British. Wilson's Secretary of State, William Jennings Bryan, and Colonel House canvassed the idea of a *modus vivendi* whereby, if the Germans would cease submarine warfare, the Allies should permit food shipments to Germany.

This found favour with neither side. In May, the Cunard liner, *Lusitania*, which had brought House across the Atlantic, was torpedoed off the southern coast of Ireland. The *Lusitania*, it transpired subsequently, was carrying some munitions, but 124 American passengers were killed. Theodore Roosevelt demanded that the United States should protect its neutral rights by force. President Wilson responded by describing America as being 'too proud to fight. There is such a thing as a nation being so right that it does not need to convince others by force that it is right.'[6]

The British ambassador in Washington, Cecil Spring-Rice, close friend of Teddy Roosevelt, strongly disliked Woodrow Wilson, whom he found a remote and forbidding figure. There was, he believed, nothing to be done with 'this hardened saint'. He wrote in exasperation to Balfour that he had served in Russia, Berlin, Constantinople and Persia, 'but I have never known any government so autocratic as this'. This did not mean that the President acted without consulting the popular will, 'but his interpretation of the oracle is his own secret'.[7] As Lloyd George, at the time Minister of Munitions, observed, Wilson was 'so studiously unpleasant to both sides' that each suspected him of being particularly hostile to them.[8]

The intensely patriotic Spring-Rice, author of 'I Vow to Thee My Country' ('I vow to thee, my country – all earthly things above – Entire and whole and perfect, the service of my love'), became understandably overwrought at the tendency of the President and the State Department to apportion blame equally between the two sides, as if the Germans had not violated Belgian neutrality – described by the German Chancellor as a 'scrap of paper' – and were not occupying a large part of northern France. Spring-Rice found it trying to his nerves to have to coexist in Washington through two and a half years of war with Bernstorff. When, on Wilson's behalf, Colonel House showed him an American 'indictment' of the actions of the British government in enforcing the blockade, Spring-Rice exploded: 'I suppose you know that the record will forever stand that when the laws of God and Man were violated, there came no protest from America.'[9] Wilson considered demanding his recall.

Nevertheless, on Wilson's behalf, House intensified his efforts to prepare some form of mediation between the combatants. Understanding, as he put it, that 'blockade of Germany was essential to the victory of the Allies, but the ill-will of the United States meant their certain defeat', Sir Edward Grey devoted infinite pains to the management of Colonel House. Grey was to write in his memoirs of 'a certain intimacy, if it may be called so, of attraction and repulsion, which has made the relations between Britain and the United States at once more easy and more difficult, more cordial and more intractable, than those between any two other countries'.[10] But Britain was becoming increasingly dependent on American support. In 1915, the British government was obliged to ask J. P. Morgan to raise a half-billion-dollar loan as the only way to finance Britain's vital American trade.

Basing himself on their earlier conversations, in September 1915 Grey wrote to House with a proposal calculated to appeal to Woodrow Wilson. In his letter, Grey floated the idea of a League of Nations committed to enforcing disarmament and the peaceful settlement of disputes. 'Would the President propose that there should be a League of Nations binding themselves to side against any Power which broke a treaty ... or which refused, in case of dispute, to adopt some other method of settlement than that of war?'[11] When, in May 1916, Wilson himself proposed his scheme for a world organisation, he undoubtedly was convinced that the idea was his own, which to a large extent it was, as Grey had proposed it in full knowledge of Wilson's convictions.

House was more sympathetic than Wilson to the cause of the Allies, but suffered from the conviction that he could mediate anything. Having failed to persuade the British government to lift the blockade of Germany in return for an end to submarine warfare, he now made a more ambitious proposal designed to fulfil Wilson's dream of becoming the world's peacemaker, while seeking to impose penalties on those who thwarted his efforts. In February 1916, he agreed with Grey a memorandum that stated:

> Colonel House told me that President Wilson was ready, on hearing from France and England that the moment was opportune, to propose that a Conference should be summoned to put an end to the War. Should the Allies accept this proposal, and should Germany refuse it, the United States would probably enter the war against Germany. Colonel House expressed the opinion that, if such a Conference met, it would secure peace on terms not unfavourable to the Allies; and if it failed to secure peace, the United States would [Wilson inserted a second 'probably' here] leave the conference as a belligerent on the side of the Allies, if Germany was unreasonable.[12]

House indicated that Wilson favoured the restoration of Belgium and the return of Alsace-Lorraine to France, though Germany might have to be compensated outside Europe. Grey said that any such proposal would have to be agreed with the French and other Allies and he doubted if this was the moment to approach them.

Back in Washington, House saw Spring-Rice and told him that the United States would end up taking part in the war because, he believed, the Germans would reject Wilson's offer. The ambassador remained sceptical about the chances of the United States entering the war. Wilson approved the memorandum and waited impatiently for word from the British. Grey's colleagues in the War Cabinet were unimpressed. They did not reject the memorandum, but there was no willingness to proceed on the basis proposed. Grey played for time. While Wilson wanted to know whether the British were serious about peace, the War Cabinet wanted to know whether the United States was serious about entering the war. In reality, as the ardently pro-British US ambassador in London, Walter Page, warned House, the British saw no scope for mediation. In their view, 'this German military caste caused all the trouble and there can be no security in Europe as long as it lives in authority'.[13]

Britain's reputation in America, meanwhile, suffered a severe blow with the suppression of the Easter Rising by Irish nationalists in Dublin. Sir Roger Casement, sent to Ireland by the Germans to foment insurrection, was hanged for treason, notwithstanding pleas for clemency from the US Senate. The British government further annoyed Wilson by blacklisting US firms suspected of trading with Germany.

On 27 May, Wilson infuriated the Allies by saying of the war: 'with its causes and objects we are not concerned'.[14] His Secretary of State, Robert Lansing, expressed privately his concern that the President

> does not seem to grasp the full significance of this war or the principles at issue ... The violations of American rights by both sides seem to interest him more than the vital interests as I see them. That German imperialistic ambitions threaten free institutions everywhere apparently has not sunk very deeply into his mind.[15]

House, disappointed in London and still more so in Berlin, prophesied an eventual peace of exhaustion – a victory, as Churchill put it, almost indistinguishable from defeat.

As the presidential election approached, Teddy Roosevelt, the one leading figure openly advocating intervention on the side of the Allies, had so little support that he did not attempt to secure the Republican nomination. Wilson won the election with the slogan: 'He kept us out of the War'. The Republican candidate, Hughes, had to declare himself equally firmly of that persuasion and was in fact supported by the German-American League.

Britain was struggling to finance not only its own war spending, but also much of that of its European allies and by this stage was critically dependent on American loans. From the Treasury, John Maynard Keynes warned the Cabinet that 'any feeling of irritation or lack of sympathy' from the American public would endanger vital financial operations. Policy towards the United States, he suggested, 'should be so directed as not only to avoid any form of reprisal or active irritation but also to conciliate and please'.[16] The Chancellor of the Exchequer, Reginald McKenna, warned that President Wilson would soon be in a position, if he wished, to dictate his own terms. David Lloyd George, Minister of Munitions, challenged these despondent conclusions: 'If victory shone on our banners, our difficulties would disappear.'[17] He regarded both McKenna and Keynes as defeatist. The Americans, Lloyd George argued, would go on making loans available so long as they saw it as in their commercial interest to do so. They did not want the British government to discontinue its American purchases.

In November 1916, however, when J. P. Morgan had tried to sell $1 billion of UK Treasury bonds on the US market, Wilson urged the Federal Reserve to caution US banks against buying foreign Treasury bills. The object was to force Britain to accept the President's mediation by cutting off supplies. In December, Wilson invited the belligerents to state their respective war aims, hoping 'they would not prove irreconcilable'. To the alarm even of Colonel House, Wilson further suggested that the aims of both sides in the war were 'virtually the same'.[18] Keynes, who was a conscientious objector, became quite hopeful that American pressure might bring an end to the war. 'Maynard', wrote Virginia Woolf, 'thinks we may be on the verge of ruin, and thus of peace; and possibly Wilson intends to cut off our supplies.'[19] In February 1917, Keynes calculated that the reserves would not last more than another four weeks. The British government did not know how much longer it would be able to continue purchasing essential supplies.

By this time Lloyd George had taken over from Asquith as Prime Minister. 'At the beginning of 1917', he wrote in his memoirs, 'the entry of the United States into the War seemed more remote and improbable than at any time since the first outbreak of world hostilities.'[20] On 22 January, President Wilson made his 'Peace without Victory' speech to Congress, advocating general disarmament, civil and religious liberty and freedom of the seas. It contained not the slightest hint that America might enter the war.

Salvation for the British came from the German military commanders, who succeeded in persuading the Kaiser to resume unrestricted submarine warfare. All shipping around the British Isles, whether neutral or not, would be subject to attack. The aim was to cut off Allied supplies from the United States – not realising that, in the view of some British officials, 'finance was about to accomplish the same result'. On 21 February, Richard Sperling of the Foreign Office observed that 'we should have found it impossible to get the action of the Federal Reserve Board reversed if the German Government had not, as usual, been more stupid than ourselves in our dealings with the US'.[21] President Wilson broke off diplomatic relations with Germany. Spring-Rice, who had been obliged to endure nearly three years of American neutrality, even at this stage took a negative view of the likelihood of American intervention. He predicted: 'It would be unpopular to send a large force abroad in case of war, and I think this would be wholly out of the question.'[22]

British naval intelligence under Admiral 'Blinker' Hall, meanwhile, had intercepted and decoded a telegram from the German Foreign Minister, Arthur Zimmermann, to the German Minister in Mexico (they also succeeded in decoding House's reports to President Wilson). Zimmermann proposed that if the United States went to war, an alliance should be forged between Germany, Mexico and Japan and that Mexico should be encouraged to re-conquer its lost territory in Texas, New Mexico and Arizona. Publication of the telegram in the American press produced a furious public reaction.[23] Still, it was not until three American ships had been sunk by U-boats that, on 2 April, the President at last told Congress that the United States must accept the status of belligerent which had been thrust upon it: 'The world must be made safe for Democracy.' On 6 April 1917, the United States finally entered the war.

As Lloyd George commented, the United States 'had clung to their neutrality with almost incredible patience and persistence. Had it been possible, they would have stood aside from the conflict to the end.'[24] The Germans were undismayed. They had confidence in their submarine attacks. Their calculation was that 'America had no army and before it could raise and train an army there would be no ships to carry it to Europe'.[25] With Russian resistance apparently close to collapse, the Americans appeared unlikely to arrive in time or in sufficient numbers to give effective help to the Allies. At the outbreak of the war, the US Army numbered a mere 210,000 men. A few months earlier, the British had suffered 60,000 casualties in a single day on the Somme.

By July 1917, thirty-six American destroyers had been moved to British ports and placed under British command to combat the U-boat threat. They made a crucial difference to the defence of the sea lanes in the Atlantic. Yet, politically, Wilson still wanted to keep his distance, saying of Britain: 'I hope to see the relationship less close after the war.' He added: 'England and France have not the same view with regard to peace that we have by any means. When the war is over we can force them to our way of thinking, because by that time they will, among other things, be financially in our hands.'[26]

The first American troops – George Marshall among them – arrived in France in June 1917. But for months they played no part in the war, as General Pershing adamantly rejected Allied demands to feed them into the front line. The French and the British commander, Field Marshal Haig, wanted the American troops to be 'amalgamated' with British and French forces. Pershing replied that

> it is impossible to ignore our national viewpoint. The people themselves would not approve, even though the President should lean that way. We cannot permit our men to serve under another flag except in an extreme emergency and then only temporarily ... No people with a grain of national pride would consent to furnish men to build up the army of another nation.

Haig, engaged in desperate battles in Flanders, complained that Pershing did not understand the urgency of the situation or the exhaustion of the Allies, while he hankered after a 'great self-contained American army'. Pershing did not believe that the decisive battles of the war would be fought until 1919 and his intention was indeed that US forces should fight as an American army, and under American command.

The Americans, however, were providing invaluable financial assistance. In September, Lord Reading and Keynes were sent across the Atlantic to negotiate further loans. Keynes was not a success with the Americans. 'Rude, dogmatic and disobliging', he made a 'terrible impression' in Washington. 'The only really sympathetic and original thing in America is the niggers, who are charming,' he informed Duncan Grant.[27] But Reading succeeded in getting the loans.

Winston Churchill, as Minister of Munitions, organised with Edward Stettinius of the US War Department and his deputies, Bernard Baruch and Robert Lovett, the procurement of war material in the United States. In return, 'we ransacked our cupboards to find anything the American troops in France required'.[28] More prescient than his colleagues, in March 1918, Churchill wrote to the War Cabinet:

> The immense political and military advantages of drawing American manhood into the War, and of their partially filling the gap caused by the diminution of our own forces, ought to out-weigh all other considerations ... Quite apart from the imperious military need, the inter-mingling of British and American units on the field of battle and their endurance of losses and suffering together may exert an immeasurable effect on the future destiny of the English-speaking peoples.[29]

At this stage Pershing's forces had scarcely been engaged in the fighting in France, and Pershing himself still believed that the decisive battles of the war would not be fought until 1919. But, following the collapse of Russian resistance and the armistice signed at Brest-Litovsk, the German High Command was able to concentrate all its resources on the Western Front. In March 1918, Ludendorff launched his great offensive. The British suffered 150,000 casualties as Haig used his last reserves to stem the German advance.

Lloyd George asked Lord Reading, now ambassador in Washington, to tell President Wilson that the military situation was 'undoubtedly critical and if America delays now she may be too late'. As Ludendorff intensified his efforts to drive a wedge between the British and French armies, Pershing at last was convinced that the 'extreme emergency' he had envisaged was now upon him. On 26 March, he told Marshal Foch and Clemenceau: 'Infantry, artillery, aviation, all that we have are yours.' Pershing instructed the US First Division: 'You are going to meet a savage enemy, flushed with victory. Meet them like Americans.'

On 11 April, Haig issued his desperate Order of the Day to the British troops withstanding the German advance: 'With our backs to the wall, and believing in the justice of our cause, each one of us must fight on to the end.' As the British managed to contain the German advance, Luden-dorff switched his main attack to the south in a final and almost successful attempt to achieve a decisive breakthrough. At the end of May, the US 2nd and 3rd Divisions distinguished themselves in the battles at Chateau Thierry and Belleau Wood on the River Marne, barring the way to Paris. On 6 June, at Belleau Wood, the US Marines suffered over 1,000 casualties in the bloodiest day's fighting in the history of the Marine Corps.

By mid-July, the tide had turned. Pershing by this time had sufficient forces to form the US First Army and to insist that it should take over a sector of its own. Washington was told that he would need an additional two million men for the decisive victories he expected to win in the summer of 1919. With the British and French armies at the end of their reserves, and the Germans equally exhausted, victory for the Allies depended on the American reinforcements, by now arriving in France at a rate of 200,000 a month.

By September 1918, more than a million American troops were engaged – Douglas MacArthur and Harry Truman among them – as Pershing led the US First Army into action. In the Battle of the Argonne they inflicted severe casualties on the Germans, while also suffering severely themselves. Above all they demonstrated that the Allies now had seemingly inexhaustible reserves of manpower while the Germans had reached the end of their manpower resources. On 25 September, Churchill reported: 'The United States in response to our appeals are sending men to Europe far in advance of their general munitions programme.' He pledged to supply them with artillery and ammunition. No British minister, Churchill pointed out, had ever had as great a volume of business to conduct with the United States as he did in 1918.

Lloyd George and others still took a rather patronising view of US military efforts, noting that most of their artillery had to be supplied by the

British and French. On the American side, George Marshall was infuriated that the United States – the world's largest steel producer – had failed to equip its troops in time with tanks. But the balance of power was changing before everyone's eyes. General Jan Smuts, Prime Minister of South Africa and member of the Imperial War Cabinet, warned Lloyd George that 'it may well be with the indefinite continuation of the war, we shall become a second or third class power, and the leadership, not only financially and militarily, but in every respect will have passed on to America and Japan'.[30]

Eventually, the number of Americans in France reached nearly two million, with a firm intention to increase that number, if necessary, to three million in 1919. Through superhuman efforts, Britain and its dominions at this time had four and a half million men in the field. In the last six months of the war, the British suffered 800,000 casualties.

In October 1918, German resistance collapsed. Hoping to get better terms from the United States than from Britain and France, the Germans surrendered on the basis of President Wilson's peace proposals – the 'fourteen points' – made public in January 1918, calling for an end to secret diplomacy and its replacement by open covenants, openly arrived at. Wilson also sought absolute freedom of navigation and an adjustment of colonial claims, weighing the interests of the population concerned with the rights of the governing powers. The French Prime Minister, Georges Clemenceau, remarked of the fourteen points: 'The Lord God had only ten.' Britain rejected Wilson's demand for freedom of the seas as a challenge to Britain's sea power and right of blockade. Colonel House threatened that if the proposals were not accepted, the United States would build a larger navy than Britain. Lloyd George replied that Britain would spend her last guinea to keep a navy superior to that of the United States or any other power.

Keynes commented that Wilson by now controlled the realities of power, with Europe dependent on America for manpower, food and finance. 'Never had a philosopher held such weapons wherewith to bind the princes of this world.'[31] Keynes further pointed out the advantage to Britain of a general debt cancellation: Britain held a lot of bad debts from its European allies, while the United States held a lot of good debts from Britain. If these obligations were not reduced, Britain would be exposed to 'future pressure by the United States of a most objectionable description' and its ability to invest abroad would be crippled. Keynes did not believe that this tribute would continue to be paid for more than a few years. But his proposal to commute a large proportion of the intra-Allied debts, not surprisingly, was rejected by the US administration.

Wilson decided to lead the American delegation to the peace conference himself, staying in Europe for over six months, and thereby losing control over the situation at home. Wilson, as A. J. P. Taylor observed, 'arrived in Europe with the firm conviction that all statesmen were wicked except himself'. Lloyd George and Clemenceau found him insufferably sanctimonious. They had little enthusiasm for most of his ideas but paid lip service to them to secure his support or acquiescence in matters of key concern to them, including German reparations. Wilson argued that the new world order must be free from all taint of imperialism and balance of power politics.

But at home the US Senate did not share these high ideals: it was more interested in asserting the United States' exclusive sphere of interest in the Americas, as defined in the Monroe Doctrine. Britain and France were less dependent on America once the fighting was over. Germany was forced to agree to pay financial reparations to the Allies and to accept the occupation of the Rhineland by Allied forces. Keynes resigned from the British delegation in protest at the financial terms imposed on Germany, which he forecast were bound to damage Germany's chances of economic recovery after the war. In *The Economic Consequences of the Peace*, he portrayed Wilson as playing Blind Man's Bluff in the company of Clemenceau and Lloyd George. Towards the end of the conference, Lloyd George, concerned at the harshness of some of the terms the Allies were about to impose, tried to express his concerns to Wilson, but found it harder to 'debamboozle the old Presbyterian than it had been to bamboozle him'.[32]

When after these long months of absence Wilson returned to the United States, he campaigned across the country for the League of Nations. On 2 October 1919, he suffered a stroke and for months thereafter lay helpless in the White House. Henry Cabot Lodge denied him the two-thirds majority in the Senate required to ratify US participation in the League.

In July 1919, George Marshall participated in the Victory Parade in London. For eight miles he had the ride of his life as his borrowed horse tried to kick spectators, rearing and prancing sideways as he tried to keep his place in the column. As they entered Admiralty Arch, the horse reared and fell over backwards. Marshall rolled clear of the flailing hooves and managed to remount and regain his place in the parade, despite having broken a bone in his hand. Churchill, dismayed by the passage of the Eighteenth Amendment, reviewing the American troops, exclaimed to Marshall: 'What a magnificent body of men never to take another drink!'[33]

———————

The First World War marked the decisive shift in the balance of power between Britain and the United States. In 1860, Britain had produced 50 per cent of the world's iron and steel. Twenty years later, it still exceeded the United States in manufacturing output. The crowds cheering Queen Victoria's Diamond Jubilee celebrations in 1897 had no doubt that Britain and its empire represented the world's preeminent power. The Royal Navy was over twice the size of any of its rivals. Britain had by far the largest merchant marine. London indisputably was the world's greatest financial centre. The United States by then was ahead in industrial output, with a population nearly twice the size of Britain's, but its armed forces were tiny. Though already a Great Power, as Professor Paul Kennedy has observed, it was not yet part of the Great Power system.[34]

All that changed in 1914–18. The United States lost 117,000 men in the war, rescuing Europe from its quarrels. Britain suffered 750,000 dead and was financially exhausted. In 1917, looking forward to victory the next year, Lloyd George assured the Imperial War Cabinet that the British Empire 'will easily then be the first Power in the world'.[35] By 1919, the much greater economic power of the United States could no longer be gainsaid. Colonel House sensed British resentment and antagonism towards the United States: 'while the British Empire vastly exceeds the United States in area and population and while their aggregate wealth is perhaps greater than ours, yet our position is much more favourable'.[36] The two countries still saw themselves as rivals and the key to their rivalry was the question of naval power.

2

'WE WILL GET NOTHING FROM THE AMERICANS BUT WORDS'

THE WAR OVER, in 1920 Sir Auckland Geddes was appointed British ambassador in Washington. He was not the first, nor was he a particularly good choice. Sir Auckland was felt to have a particular affinity for North America, having been Professor of Anatomy at McGill University in Canada and because his wife came from Staten Island. He had served as Minister for Manpower during the latter part of the war and, subsequently, as President of the Board of Trade. Geddes had a reputation for arrogance. President Wilson, when consulted, commented: 'I instinctively dislike what I hear of this man, but I have no ground on which I can object.' Wilson feared that America was on the verge of a commercial war with the British Empire.

Geddes, on his arrival in America, found much anti-British sentiment. Ireland was embroiled in the struggle for independence. Supporters of Sinn Féin threatened to kidnap or murder Geddes and his family. There was friction over colonial markets, naval armaments and the repayment of war debts. In private, Geddes showed his disdain for American politicians and parties, describing President Warren Harding as a party hack and the Republican Party as chauvinistic and devoted to 'America *über alles*'.

In January 1921, Geddes unwisely confided to American correspondents in Paris that Britain and America were 'drifting towards war'. The American press, not surprisingly, printed this information, which Curzon, then Foreign Secretary, was obliged to deny. Geddes was unrepentant: 'I do not at present foresee an Anglo-American war, but I do picture a deadly struggle disguised as peace.' He saw no reason, he added, why Britain should not win such a struggle in fifteen or twenty years. In April, he wrote to Curzon: 'I regret to inform you that the Secretary of State [Hughes] is, in my opinion, abnormal mentally and subject to attacks of very mild mania.' This led Curzon to remark to Lloyd George that he, Curzon, suspected that it was Geddes who was suffering from a mild form of mania.[1]

Geddes, however, was benefiting from the effects of Prohibition. On George Washington's birthday in 1922, he entertained the entire United States Congress and their wives at the embassy. The members of Congress suggested that this should become an annual event. This unprecedented attendance was explained by the fact that the embassy, being extra-territorial, was not 'dry'.

One of President Harding's friends, recognising his predicament in these difficult times, sent him six bottles of the finest liqueur brandy from France. The case was intercepted by the New York Customs and seemed likely to provide the material for a first-class political scandal until a quick-witted aide in the White House told the customs officers that the case was incorrectly labelled. It had been intended as a gift from the President to the British ambassador. The case duly arrived at the embassy with the President's name crossed out and that of Geddes in its place. Enquiries were made at the White House to see if the President's staff could throw any light on the matter. One of the President's aides explained that a mistake had been made: they would have a car round to collect the case. But Geddes decided instead to keep the brandy and used it subsequently to celebrate his children's weddings.[2]

A main cause of tension was the unresolved naval rivalry between Britain and the United States. The Royal Navy still was larger than that of the United States and well ahead of that of Japan, but the United States was determined to achieve parity with Britain and knew that it now had the wealth to outbuild Britain in the naval race. The Americans were concerned about growing Japanese strength in the Pacific and it was their objective to put an end to the alliance between Britain and Japan. In November 1921, President Harding convened the Washington Conference to consider the level of naval armaments. Secretary Hughes proposed the establishment of a 5:5:3 ratio of ships between America, Britain and Japan and proceeded to list the names of twenty-three ships that he said the Royal Navy must give up. Admiral Beattie, the First Sea Lord, reacted furiously to this impertinence, but was overruled by Lloyd George, who by now was convinced that Britain could not afford a naval race with the United States. The British also were obliged to agree not to renew the alliance with Japan.

The Washington Treaty covered capital ships over 10,000 tonnes. It did not cover cruisers, destroyers and submarines. In 1927, President Calvin Coolidge convened another conference of the world's major sea powers. The British, concerned about the protection of their global trade, claimed the right to seventy cruisers. Winston Churchill, then Chancellor of the Exchequer, told the Cabinet that no doubt it was right in the interests of peace to go on talking about war with the United States as 'unthinkable'. But, he added,

> everyone knows that this is not true. However foolish and disas-
> trous such a war would be ... we do not wish to put ourselves in
> the power of the United States. We cannot tell what they might
> do if at some future date they were in a position to give us orders
> about our policy, say, in India, or Egypt, or Canada, or on any
> other great matter behind which their electioneering forces were
> marshalled.

In the following year, Sir Maurice Hankey, Secretary of the Cabinet, complained that Britain had conceded to the United States over the League of Nations, the Japanese alliance, the Washington Treaty on naval forces, the debt settlement and Ireland, 'always making concessions and always being told that the next step would change their attitude'. Yet the Americans in response were more overbearing and suspicious than ever.[3]

In 1930, at yet another naval conference in London, agreement was reached that the 5:5:3 ratio agreed for capital ships should now apply to cruisers as well. The Prime Minister, Ramsay MacDonald, obliged the Admiralty to accept a ceiling of fifty cruisers, thus averting an Anglo-American arms race.

The next cause of tension was in the Far East. In 1931, the Japanese invaded Manchuria. The US Secretary of State, Henry Stimson, tried to get Britain to join him in condemning Japanese aggression. President Herbert Hoover told Stimson that he could take any measures to resist Japanese aggression – so long as they did not entail the use of force. The British government declined to get involved.

Another main source of friction was finance. Until 1914, Britain was the financial centre of the world. The pound sterling, set at a fixed price in terms of gold, was the main trading currency. But in 1919, Britain, her reserves depleted, was forced to abandon the gold standard. To help finance the war, most of Britain's vast American assets had been sold. America, which had been a net debtor before the war, emerged as a large net creditor after it. The United States had loaned nearly $12 billion to the Allied countries, including $4.7 billion to Britain alone. The British in turn had lent just over $11 billion to their allies.

The British once again proposed that all war debts should simply be cancelled. The Americans did not agree. They insisted on repayment. 'They hired the money, didn't they?' declared President Coolidge. Montagu Norman, Governor of the Bank of England, concluded that confidence in London as a financial centre would collapse if Britain failed to pay these debts. In January 1923, he and Stanley Baldwin, Chancellor of the Exchequer, reached agreement with the US administration after difficult negotiations in Washington. They agreed that Britain would repay the debt in instalments over the next sixty-two years. The agreement was unpopular at home but did restore Britain's international credit.

In 1925, Winston Churchill, as Chancellor of the Exchequer, announced that Britain would return to the gold standard, whereby sterling once again was made convertible into gold. Otherwise, he remarked, the rest of the British Empire would have done so, not on the basis of sterling, but of the dollar.

There followed the Wall Street Crash in October 1929 and the Depression. The United States' gross domestic product declined by 30 per cent between 1929 and 1933. In 1931, the Labour government in Britain did its best to counter the effects of the slump by keeping interest rates low and increasing welfare payments.

The result was a mounting budget deficit. J. P. Morgan advised that before they could raise money in the USA, the British government would have to show a plan to bring expenditure within its means. This placed the Labour Cabinet in a classic dilemma. Montagu Norman recommended an austerity package, including a substantial cut in unemployment insurance. Ramsay MacDonald said that this 'represented the negation of everything that the Labour Party stood for', yet saw no alternative but to agree. Half his Cabinet dissented and in August 1931 the Labour government resigned.

The *Daily Herald* denounced the 'virtual ultimatum from New York bankers' which had brought this about. MacDonald formed a national government including the Conservatives and Liberals. The new Cabinet implemented the expenditure cuts and a loan to support sterling was raised in America. But further loans proved impossible to raise. In September, the national government gave up the struggle and Britain abandoned the gold standard. Douglas Dillon, starting his career in Wall Street at the time, realised that this was the end of an era. Britain no longer commanded the world financial markets: 'they were just another player in the game'.[4]

In 1930, faced with the recession, Congress passed the Smoot-Hawley Act, raising US tariffs to protect domestic industries and thereby intensifying the world depression. The results were foreseen at the time. A thousand economists petitioned Hoover to veto the Bill. Instead he signed it into law. Britain in turn raised tariffs in 1932 on most of her imports, while agreeing to keep them lower for countries within the empire, thus consolidating the system of Imperial Preference. These advantages were extended to other trading partners who relied mainly on sterling and the City to finance their trade within the sterling era.

In 1933, Britain was obliged to default on the payment to America of the war debts, as it could no longer afford to settle them in gold. In an effort to improve international economic cooperation, the British government convened a conference in London. But it was torpedoed by Franklin Roosevelt, who made clear that the United States would not support any permanent stabilisation of world currencies until the American economy was back on its feet.

Relations between America and Britain by this stage were marked mainly by bitterness and recrimination. In 1927, the Foreign Office commented that 'we have treated them too much as blood relations, not sufficiently as a foreign country'.[5] Successive British governments believed they had discovered that no great faith could be placed in the United States, particularly when its presidents had so little control over Congress. They saw US policy as one of deliberate withdrawal from world affairs. In 1932, the Prime Minister, Stanley Baldwin, complained: 'we will get nothing from the Americans but words'. Sir Robert Vansittart, head of the Foreign Office, said:

> [W]e have been too tender, not to say subservient, with the US for a long time past ... It is still necessary, and I desire as much as ever, that we should get on well with this untrustworthy race. But we shall never get very far: they will always let us down.[6]

This pattern of rivalry rather than cooperation was no less evident in other ways through the decade leading up to the outbreak of the Second World War. In 1928, taking Wilsonian diplomacy to its ultimate extreme, the US Secretary of State, Frank Billings Kellogg, negotiated with the French Prime Minister the Kellogg-Briand Pact, under which sixty-three countries solemnly renounced the use of war as an instrument of national policy. 'The United States,' wrote Denis Brogan, 'which had abolished the evils of drink by the eighteenth amendment, invited the world to abolish war by taking the pledge. The world, not quite daring to believe or doubt, obeyed.'[7]

In the first volume of his War Memoirs, Churchill describes the contorted and ineffectual European diplomacy of these crucial years, hindered by the lack of any effective involvement by the United States. Many in America argued that the United States never should have been sucked into European quarrels in 1917. In 1935, Congress passed the Neutrality Act, which banned the export of arms to any belligerent country in time of war. The object was to preserve the United States from any of the entanglements that had led to its involvement in the Great War. In the following year, Congress added a ban on loans to belligerents. Belligerents wishing to purchase permitted goods must pay for delivery and ship them themselves.

In October 1935, when Italian forces invaded Abyssinia, sanctions were imposed, albeit half-heartedly, by the members of the League of Nations. US non-participation in the League was a major complicating factor. There was no prospect of the United States joining in the application of sanctions, though in accordance with the Neutrality Act an embargo was imposed on the supply of arms to both Italy and Abyssinia. The US administration took the line that trade should not exceed 'normal peace-time levels'. But it had no legislative powers to carry this policy into effect. The US Secretary of State, Cordell Hull, would have liked to restrain oil exports to Italy. But the 'moral embargo' was largely ineffective. As US oil exports to Italy trebled, Cordell Hull explained: 'A moral embargo is effective only as to persons who are moral.' Neville Chamberlain, as Chancellor of the Exchequer, used US inactivity as an argument for a policy of appeasement. Echoing Baldwin, he said: 'It is always best and safest to count on nothing from the Americans except words.' The British, for their part, turned down further pleas to join the United States in condemning Japanese aggression in China.

In January 1938, Roosevelt, concerned about Hitler's increasingly threatening behaviour following the reoccupation of the Rhineland, put forward a proposal for a peace conference to be held under the auspices of the United States. But Neville Chamberlain, by now Prime Minister, had an 'almost instinctive contempt for the Americans'.[8] Without consulting his Foreign Secretary, Anthony Eden, who was on holiday in France, he made clear that he preferred to proceed with his own talks with Mussolini and Hitler in which, as Eden remarked, he had 'dogmatic faith'.

Eden thought it a mistake to have rejected Roosevelt's approach. He did not expect it to succeed, but at least it showed a more active interest on the part of the United States, and it was this episode, plus Chamberlain's determination to pursue his own negotiations with the dictators, that led to Eden's resignation as Foreign Secretary.

In February 1938, Hitler marched into Austria and started threatening Czechoslovakia. Roosevelt, like many others, was relieved when Chamberlain returned from Munich but, thereafter, he became increasingly doubtful that any agreement with Hitler would be honoured and began pressing for American rearmament.

In March 1939, Hitler seized the remainder of Czechoslovakia. In April, Roosevelt sent a message to Hitler and Mussolini, urging them not to undertake further aggression for ten 'or even twenty-five years'. That summer, King George VI paid the first visit by a reigning British monarch to the United States. The King and Queen got a warm reception in Washington and New York. They were entertained at the Roosevelt family home at Hyde Park with beer and hot dogs. In the event of war, Roosevelt said, he would try to provide practical help, including patrolling part of the Atlantic.[9]

In September, when war did come, Roosevelt's reaction was very different from that of Woodrow Wilson: 'I cannot ask that every American remain neutral in thought,' he said. 'Even a neutral cannot be asked to close his mind or conscience.' Winston Churchill, recalled to the Admiralty, was delighted to receive a letter from Roosevelt suggesting that they should 'keep in touch personally with anything you want me to know about'.[10] It was an invitation that was to lead to over a thousand messages being exchanged between them over the next five years.

But neutrality remained America's policy. In November, Roosevelt persuaded Congress to amend the Neutrality Acts to end the arms embargo. This, he pointed out, was in the interests of US manufacturers. Britain was able to purchase armaments, but had to pay cash and arrange collection ('cash and carry'). In December, the United States joined in a protest by the American republics to Britain and Germany against the naval action off the River Plate that led to the sinking of the *Graf Spee*. Churchill kept writing to Roosevelt, but with little response. 'The United States', he commented, 'was cooler than in any other period.'[11]

In the United States, the German–American *Bund* was at the height of its activity. So was the America First Committee, dedicated to ensuring that the United States did not repeat the 'mistake' of 1917. At this stage, according to the polls, fewer than 10 per cent of Americans were ready to enter the war. On Christmas Day 1939, Churchill wrote to Chamberlain that Roosevelt 'is our best friend, but I expect he wants to be re-elected and I fear that isolationism is the winning ticket'.[12]

3

'IN THE LONG HISTORY OF THE WORLD THIS IS A THING TO DO NOW'

IN JANUARY 1940, Roosevelt wrote to thank Churchill for his 'tremendously interesting account' of the action against the *Graf Spee*, but also to warn that the stopping and searching by the Royal Navy of American merchant ships was causing fierce public criticism. He wondered whether the benefit to Britain and France was worth the annoyance caused to the United States. This, he acknowledged, was liable to be the reaction in a nation 3,000 miles away from the fact of war.[1]

On 10 May, the German Army invaded the Low Countries and northern France. Allied forces were soon in headlong retreat. At 6 o'clock that evening Neville Chamberlain resigned, the debate over the inability of British forces to prevent the German invasion of Norway having shown that he had lost the confidence of much of his own party in the House of Commons. As Winston Churchill became Prime Minister, Ed Murrow, reporting for CBS, observed that Churchill came into office with the 'tremendous advantage of being the man who was right'.

It is possible to define fairly precisely in time the beginning of the creation of the special relationship. Churchill had a very different attitude from Chamberlain to cooperation with the United States. He had an American mother, Jenny Jerome, and, unlike Chamberlain, he both knew and understood America well. Twice between the two world wars he had restored his finances with lecture tours and the syndication of articles in the US press. In December 1931, visiting Bernard Baruch in New York, Churchill's career and his life very nearly came to an end at the hands of a cab driver on Fifth Avenue as he looked the wrong way crossing the road. But, despite these personal ties, he still was viewed in America with some suspicion. He was remembered for his opposition to the restrictions placed on the size of the Royal Navy and his ardent championship of the empire. Thanks to the gossip relayed by his ambassador, Joseph Kennedy, Roosevelt believed that the new Prime Minister was 'drunk half of his time'.[2]

Kennedy had been a valued member, reassuring to business, of Roosevelt's first administration as head of the Securities Commission. Thereafter he remained an important but politically uncomfortable ally, who saw himself as representing pro-business Democrats *vis-à-vis* the more ardent exponents of the 'New Deal'. Roosevelt always distrusted his restless ambition. Denied the Treasury, it was Kennedy himself who suggested that he should be appointed to the London embassy. The President at first resisted but then, in March 1938, agreed because, he told Henry Morgenthau, 'Kennedy is too dangerous to have around here'. Roosevelt wondered how on earth Kennedy would get on in London, claiming to regard the appointment as 'the greatest joke in the world'.[3]

Conceived as a means of rewarding Kennedy while keeping him out of the way, Roosevelt's gambit failed. The energetic and opinionated ambassador soon regarded himself as an honorary member of Chamberlain's Cabinet. He shared Chamberlain's dread of war and Communism. He was far from alone in believing that it would be the height of folly for America to involve itself in Europe's affairs. Roosevelt at the time was just as committed to neutrality as his ambassador was. In Kennedy's case, these sentiments were passed on to the German ambassador.

After a year in London, Kennedy started telling those willing to listen to him that a little Fascism was no bad thing. The Munich agreement was greeted by him with tremendous relief. Democracies and dictatorships, he said publicly, had to learn to live together. The White House distanced itself from these remarks. With presidential ambitions of his own and a lot of friends in the press, Kennedy was never particularly loyal to Roosevelt and the President soon became even more distrustful of him. Kennedy discomfited the punctilious Chamberlain by addressing him in public as 'Neville'. As Marian Frankfurter reported: 'Chamberlain's Adam's apple would work up and down three or four times and then he would emit a forced "Joe".'

When war came, the State Department was informed by the ambassador that Britain was fighting 'for her possessions and her place in the sun just as she has in the past … Democracy as we conceive it in the United States will not exist in Britain or France after the War.' The British were warned that a long war would bankrupt them: the best course was to make peace. Even Chamberlain by this time was tired of Kennedy. Winston Churchill, hearing of Kennedy's predictions of defeat, said: 'Supposing, as I do not for one moment suppose, that Mr Kennedy were correct in his tragic utterances, then I for one would willingly lay down my life in combat rather than, in fear of defeat, surrender to the menaces of these most sinister men.'

Joseph Kennedy by now had made himself detested on all sides. Noting his reappearance in London in March 1940 after a visit to the United States, the Foreign Office correctly reported that the ambassador had returned 'not because he wants to or because the President or State Department have the slightest degree of confidence in him, but in order to get him out of the way'. Even the remarkably insensitive Kennedy himself by this time had noticed that 'a certain coolness had developed towards me in those circles, official and otherwise, whose main use for America was to embroil her in the War'.[4]

––––––––––

While still at the Admiralty, Churchill had asked Roosevelt if a British aircraft carrier could call at an American port to enable aircraft being purchased by Britain in the United States to be shipped uncrated and ready to fly. Roosevelt told Arthur Purvis, head of the British purchasing mission in the United States, that this could not be done under the Neutrality Act. But the President himself proposed a way to circumvent the Act. The aircraft carrier should call at Newfoundland. The aircraft could then be flown to the Canadian border where, to comply with US law, they would have to be *pushed* across the border, then flown on to Newfoundland. This extraordinary expedient was duly put into effect.

On 15 May 1940, Churchill telegraphed to Roosevelt:

> If necessary, we shall continue the war alone, and we are not afraid
> of that. But I trust you realise, Mr President, that the voice and
> force of the United States may count for nothing if they are withheld

too long. You may have a completely subjugated Nazified Europe
established with astonishing swiftness and the weight may be more
than we can bear.

Although to date virtually all his hopes of American assistance had been
disappointed, Churchill, in the House of Commons, in defiant statements
talked of carrying on the struggle 'until, in God's good time, the New
World with its power and might steps forth to the rescue and the liberation of the Old'. For Churchill knew that without American help, Britain
was lost. The enormous supplies that were required and could not immediately be paid for could come from no other source.

As the British Expeditionary Force risked being cut off by the German
attacks towards the Channel ports, on 17 May Kennedy brought Churchill
a negative response from Roosevelt to the Prime Minister's first request
for the loan of fifty American First World War destroyers moth-balled in
US shipyards ('I am not certain that it would be wise for that suggestion
to be made to Congress at this moment'). Churchill replied that he did
not need to tell the President about the gravity of what had happened in
France. Britain in turn must expect to be attacked 'and we hope to give
a good account of ourselves'. But if American assistance was to play any
part, 'it must be available soon'.

Churchill was exasperated by US inaction. His ambassador, Lord
Lothian, knew that there was little faith in Washington in Britain's ability
to withstand a German attack. On 20 May, Churchill told Roosevelt that

> our intention is, whatever happens, to fight on to the end in this
> Island ... Members of the present Administration would likely go
> down in the process should it result adversely, but in no conceiva-
> ble circumstances will we consent to surrender. If members of the
> present Administration were finished and others came in to par-
> ley amid the ruins, you must not be blind to the fact that the sole
> remaining bargaining counter with Germany would be the Fleet,
> and, if this country was left by the United States to its fate, no one
> would have the right to blame those then responsible if they made
> the best terms they could for the surviving inhabitants.
>
> Excuse me, Mr President, putting this nightmare bluntly. Evi-
> dently I could not answer for my successors, who in utter despair

and helplessness might well have to accommodate themselves to the German will.

'However,' Churchill added, 'there is happily no need at present to dwell upon such ideas. Once more thanking you for your good-will.'

———————

There followed the evacuation from Dunkirk of 300,000 British troops without most of their weapons and equipment. Anxious to do what he could to help in this extremity, George Marshall, as US Chief of Army Staff, told Purvis that he intended to declare substantial quantities of munitions 'surplus' and, therefore, available to the British. As the Germans approached Paris at midnight on 10 June, Churchill, working at the Admiralty, listened to the broadcast of a speech by Roosevelt at the University of Virginia: 'we will extend to the opponents of force the material resources of this nation'. Churchill's response to this 'message of hope' was to renew, again unsuccessfully, his request for destroyers.

Churchill redoubled his efforts to persuade the French government to fight on, if necessary from the French territories overseas. On 13 June, when Churchill met the French Prime Minister, Paul Reynaud, at Tours, the French said that they could not carry on unless they got a pledge of immediate assistance from the United States. On his return to London, Joseph Kennedy brought Churchill Roosevelt's reply to an earlier plea from Reynaud. Roosevelt said that his administration would do all in its power to supply the Allies with the war material they required and encouraged Reynaud to continue the fight even if that meant withdrawal to North Africa.

An elated Churchill told the War Cabinet that this message 'came as near as possible to a declaration of war'. Roosevelt, he suggested, 'could hardly urge the French to continue the war … if he did not intend to enter the war to support them'. The War Cabinet agreed that Churchill should tell Reynaud that Roosevelt's message could only mean that the United States intended to enter the war. Churchill expected Britain in turn to be attacked 'perhaps within a fortnight, but before that the United States of America would be in the war on our side'.[5]

Churchill had urged Roosevelt to make his message public, but was told that the Secretary of State, Cordell Hull, was opposed. Churchill warned Roosevelt that the French were 'very nearly gone'. Churchill, in desperation, told Reynaud that if France continued to resist, an American declaration of war 'must inevitably follow'.

This bore no relation to the state of affairs in Washington. On 14 June, Kennedy told Churchill that Roosevelt's message could not be published. That night Roosevelt told Churchill that his message to Reynaud 'was in no sense intended to commit and did not commit the Government to military participation in support of Allied governments'. Churchill tried once more to bring home to Roosevelt all that was at stake. Only a public declaration that the United States would if necessary enter the war might save France. As for Britain:

> Although the present Government and I personally would never fail to send the Fleet across the Atlantic if resistance was beaten down here, a point may be reached in the struggle where the present Ministers no longer have control of affairs and when very easy terms could be obtained for the British Island by their becoming a vassal state of the Hitler Empire. A pro-German Government would certainly be called into being to make peace, and might present to a shattered or a starving nation an almost irresistible case for entire submission to the Nazi will.
>
> The fate of the British Fleet, as I have already mentioned to you, would be decisive on the future of the United States, because if it were joined to the Fleets of Japan, France and Italy and the great resources of German industry, overwhelming sea-power would be in Hitler's hands. He might of course use it with a merciful moderation. On the other hand, he might not. This revolution in sea-power might happen very quickly, and certainly long before the United States would be able to prepare against it.
>
> If we go down you may have a United States of Europe under the Nazi command far more numerous, far stronger, far better armed than the New World.

Churchill's telegram continued: 'I know well, Mr President, that your eye will already have searched these depths, but I feel I have the right to place on record the vital manner in which American interests are at stake in our battle and that of France.'

Despite the lack of any effective response to these appeals, Churchill, in a message to the prime ministers of the dominions, expressed his personal conviction that

> the spectacle of the fierce struggle and carnage in our Island will draw the United States into the war, and even if we should be beaten down by the superior numbers of the enemy's Air Force it will always be possible ... to send our fleets across the oceans, where they will protect the Empire and enable it to continue the war and the blockade, I trust in conjunction with the United States, until the Hitler regime breaks under the strain.[6]

Churchill telegraphed to Roosevelt that they were now faced with the imminent collapse of French resistance. The successful defence of Britain would be 'the only hope of averting the collapse of civilisation as we define it. We must ask, therefore, as a matter of life or death, to be reinforced with these destroyers.' In a further message to the President, Churchill said that

> when I speak of the United States entering the war I am, of course, not thinking in terms of an expeditionary force, which I know is out of the question. What I have in mind is the tremendous moral effect that such an American decision would produce, not merely in France but also in all the democratic countries of the world.

On the following day the French government, now under Marshal Pétain, sued for peace.

While the Americans still rejected British pleas for the destroyers, they proposed instead Anglo-American staff talks as a gesture of support. Churchill at first opposed the idea, telling his Foreign Secretary, Viscount Halifax, that the main topic of such talks on the American side was bound to be the 'transfer of the British fleet to trans-Atlantic bases'. That would be 'bound to weaken confidence here at the moment when all must brace themselves for the supreme struggle'.[7]

At the end of June, Lord Lothian urged Churchill to make a further broadcast to influence American opinion. Churchill rejected the suggestion. He was now convinced that only the force of events would influence the Americans. 'Up till April they were so sure the Allies would win that they did not think help necessary. Now they are so sure we shall lose that they do not think it possible.' Lothian was told to impress on Roosevelt that if Britain were successfully invaded and some quisling government forced to make peace, the only bargaining counter would be the fleet:

> Feeling in England against United States would be similar to French bitterness against us now. We have really not had any help worth speaking of from the United States so far. We know President Roosevelt is our best friend, but it is no use trying to dance attendance upon Republican and Democratic Conventions. What really matters is whether Hitler is master of Britain three months from now.

Only deeds, not words, would impress the Americans. 'No one is downhearted.'[8]

On 2 July, as Britain prepared for invasion, Lothian saw Roosevelt. The President wanted talks on what would happen if the French fleet passed into German hands. Asked if American opinion would support the forcible seizure of these ships, the President said: 'Certainly.' Churchill already had decided to solve the problem for him. On the following day, British warships under Admiral Somerville appeared off Oran. The French fleet was invited to join the British in the fight against Germany. When this ultimatum was rejected, Admiral Somerville opened fire for nine minutes on the French fleet. Its capital ships were disabled and over 1,000 French sailors killed.

This spectacular display of ruthlessness and the determination to survive had its effect in Washington. Harry Hopkins, several months later, told Churchill's Private Secretary, Jock Colville, that Oran had helped to convince Roosevelt, despite Joseph Kennedy's defeatist opinions, that Britain would indeed continue the fight, if necessary alone.[9]

In view of the extent of Britain's dependence on the United States for war supplies, Churchill now agreed, reluctantly, to an exchange of information about the British ASDIC anti-submarine detection system and other technical secrets. On 30 July, he was told by Lothian that 'this is the moment to press the President about the destroyers'. Churchill warned that Britain could not withstand the current rate of losses to German submarines for long.

On the following day, Churchill cabled again in desperation: 'Mr President, with great respect, I must tell you that in the long history of the world, this is a thing to do now.'

There remained serious doubts in Washington, including on the part of the Chiefs of Staff, that Britain could hold out. Joseph Kennedy continued to express his own scepticism on that score. But Roosevelt was advised, among others by Dean Acheson, that he need not go to Congress for special legislation but could act independently, as Commander-in-Chief. He told Churchill that Britain could have the destroyers, but there would have to be a *quid pro quo*. The United States wanted 99-year leases on eight British possessions in the Americas on which the United States could build air and naval bases to strengthen its own defences.

The British Cabinet initially was horrified at these demands and considered such a bargain to be out of the question. Churchill was extremely reluctant to give a 'blank cheque on the whole of our trans-Atlantic possessions'.[10] But Britain had no choice. Two of the leases were counted as a 'gift': the others were made part of the deal Roosevelt needed to carry with him political opinion in America.

On 6 August, Churchill received a further telegram from Roosevelt wanting reassurance that, if Britain were overrun, the British fleet would continue to fight, and would neither be surrendered nor sunk. Churchill told the Foreign Secretary, Lord Halifax, that they must not discuss the question of what to do with the fleet in the event of invasion. Lothian was told that the British government could never agree to compromise their freedom of action, 'nor tolerate any such defeatist announcement, the effect of which would be disastrous'.[11]

On 14 August, Roosevelt told Churchill that he would supply the destroyers, subject to Britain making available the bases. Once the destroyer deal went through, Churchill told the War Cabinet, the United States would have taken 'a long step towards coming into the War on our side'. On 20 August, Churchill reported the agreement to the House of Commons: 'Undoubtedly this process means that these two great organisations of the English-speaking democracies, the British Empire and the United States, will have to be somewhat mixed up together for mutual and general advantage.'

King George VI was less enthusiastic, writing to his friend, Lord Halifax, that he did not feel happy. 'Everything was done in their interests, no give and take ... I hope the Americans will not try to bleed us white over the dollar asset question ... they cannot wish to make us bankrupt. At least I hope they do not want to.'[12]

Roosevelt still wanted assurances about the fleet. On 31 August, Churchill telegraphed to confirm that his statement in Parliament on 4 June that Britain would never surrender or scuttle her fleet represented 'the settled policy of Her Majesty's Government ... I must, however, observe that these hypothetical contingencies seem more likely to concern the German Fleet, or what is left of it, than our own.' On 2 September 1940, the 'Destroyers for Bases' deal finally was signed. It marked the beginning of the development of a unique relationship.

4

'YOUR BOYS ARE NOT GOING TO BE SENT INTO ANY FOREIGN WARS'

ON SUNDAY 22 September 1940, Churchill received a message from Roosevelt that the German invasion of Britain would begin at 3 p.m. that afternoon. Churchill, who had been living through such alarms every week since June, was sceptical. If the Germans did manage to land, he told his luncheon guests, 'we shall show them no quarter'. It transpired that the message had been garbled. The country about to be invaded was not Britain, but French Indo-China, by the Japanese.[1]

Roosevelt continued to do all he could to facilitate British purchases of aircraft and other war material. But he still had no thought in his mind of entering the war. There was growing support for Britain in the United States. The reports of Ed Murrow and other US correspondents on the Battle of Britain were making a tremendous impact on American opinion. But the America First campaign continued. There was a feeling that, whatever the horrors of Nazism in Europe, Hitler could not pose a threat to the United States.

Joe Kennedy, meanwhile, had been continuing his own campaign to keep America out of the war. Kennedy predicted that when Churchill finally succeeded in drawing the United States into the conflict, 'he'll reach for that brandy, charge his glass, lift his hand on high and say, "I have discharged my duty. Victory is ours! This is my crowning achievement! God save the King!"' To Kennedy's embarrassment, in May the British police arrested a cypher clerk in his embassy, Tyler Kent, who considered Roosevelt's policy to be contrary to the interests of the United States. He was found to have passed to the Germans copies of the entire Roosevelt–Churchill correspondence up to that date. In July, Neville Chamberlain recorded in his diary that he 'saw Joe Kennedy, who says everyone in the USA thinks we shall be beaten before the end of the month'.[2]

Kennedy's views were not held by other members of his embassy. If the British survived the war, wrote the American military attaché, 'they will be bankrupt but entitled to almost unlimited respect'.[3]

President Roosevelt by this time regarded Kennedy as being 'entirely out of hand and out of sympathy'. He feared that Kennedy might declare for his Republican opponent, Wendell Willkie. Willkie supported Roosevelt's policy of giving material help to Britain. But he and other Republican Party spokesmen argued throughout the election campaign that Roosevelt would embroil the United States directly in the war. No less an authority than Dr George Gallup was convinced that the constant reiteration of this theme had brought Willkie 'within easy striking distance of victory'.

Kennedy's return to the United States in October was eagerly awaited by the press, which had been led to believe that he might declare for Willkie. When he was persuaded instead by Roosevelt to make a broadcast in his favour, the Democratic National Committee claimed that Kennedy had 'smashed into smithereens Wendell Willkie's brutal charge that President Roosevelt is planning to send our boys to England'. It was in Boston, with Joe Kennedy present, that Roosevelt made a speech so convincingly isolationist that Willkie protested: 'That hypocritical son of a bitch! This is going to beat me!' It included Roosevelt's famous pledge: 'Your boys are not going to be sent into any foreign wars.'[4]

The election over, Kennedy confided to an American journalist, who printed his remarks, that democracy was 'finished' in England. After a stormy meeting with Roosevelt at Hyde Park, Kennedy resigned as ambassador in London. He intended, he said, to devote himself to 'the greatest cause in the world today ... That cause is to help the President keep the United States out of the war.'

———————

Having won the election, Roosevelt was confronted by a message from Churchill describing Britain's predicament in detail. Churchill was prompted to write by Lothian and Purvis, who were both conscious that Britain could no longer meet the 'cash and carry' requirements for American supplies. It was the last service rendered by Lord Lothian to his country. Appointed to the Washington embassy by Chamberlain in August 1939, Lothian had been just as firmly identified with the policy of appeasement. But he became popular in America, not least because of his free and easy relationship with the press. Having helped Churchill draft his letter, Lothian dismayed both Roosevelt and the Chancellor of the Exchequer by informing the press on his return to New York: 'Well, boys, Britain's broke. It's your money we want!'[5]

In his letter to Roosevelt, Churchill explained that while the danger of direct invasion had somewhat receded, Britain was in mortal danger from the losses of merchant shipping to submarines. This could be countered if the United States took over some of the burden of escorting the shipping. Above all, Britain was no longer able to pay in dollars or gold for munitions and other supplies from the United States.

Roosevelt read and re-read this letter while cruising on an American warship, the *Tuscaloosa*, in the Caribbean, accompanied by his closest confidant, Harry Hopkins. Anticipating the problem, Roosevelt already had begun to suggest that 'we must find some way to lease or even lend these goods to the British'. On 17 December, at a press conference on his return to Washington, he declared that 'the best immediate defense of the United States is the success of Britain in defending itself'. There followed his inspired metaphor: 'Suppose my neighbour's home catches fire, and I have a length of garden hose...' On 30 December, he declared: 'We must be the great arsenal of democracy.'

Thus was conceived the Lend-Lease Bill, described by Churchill as 'the most unsordid act in the history of any nation'. The United States undertook to lend Britain the war material, and other supplies so desperately needed, against repayment to be arranged after the war. To tide things over until the Bill passed, the British were obliged to hand over to the United States the gold reserves accumulated in Cape Town and to sell assets in the United States. Churchill resented bitterly the US insistence on taking over the gold at Cape Town, which he regarded as humiliating. He drafted a telegram to Roosevelt ('It is not fitting that any nation should put itself entirely in the hands of another') but, mollified by the President's New Year address, decided not to send it.[6]

———————

Two days after Churchill sent his letter to Roosevelt, Lord Lothian died, as a Christian Scientist, refusing all medical treatment. Churchill at first wanted Lloyd George to succeed him, but then settled on Lord Halifax, whom he was determined to remove from the Foreign Office. As Foreign Secretary at the time of Munich, Halifax was even more closely identified than Lothian with Chamberlain's policies and was not at all anxious to go to Washington, which he described as an 'odious thought'. 'I have never liked Americans, except odd ones,' he told Baldwin. 'In the mass, I have always found them dreadful.'[7]

In January 1941, the reluctant ambassador arrived in the Chesapeake Bay on the battleship *King George V*. To show his solidarity with Britain at war, Roosevelt sailed out on the presidential yacht to welcome him. Halifax reported to the King that he found Americans 'very much resemble a mass of nice children – a little crude, very warm-hearted and mainly governed by emotion'. He considered them to be semi-educated and 'dangerously afraid of public opinion'. He told Sumner Welles, Under-Secretary in the State Department, that he did not think that the Baltic peoples deserved much consideration. An early visit to a fox hunt aroused the ire of the American press. He claimed to be unable to understand the American system of government, which he was in the habit of likening to 'a disorderly day's rabbit shooting'. In an effort to project a more democratic image, the ambassador was persuaded to attend a match of the Chicago White Sox. Presented with a hot dog, which he found not much to his taste, he attempted to hide it under his seat. The press took pictures of the unfinished hot dog, with unfortunate public relations consequences.[8]

The Foreign Office wondered whether Halifax would ever recover from these setbacks. But in fact he did so. The tide began to turn for him when he was pelted with eggs by a crowd of isolationist women in Detroit. The ambassador was quoted as saying that Americans were fortunate: 'in Britain we get only one egg a week'. The comment in fact came from his press secretary, but Halifax thereafter enjoyed a more benign press and established good relationships with Roosevelt's key advisers. Much of the real business of state, however, continued to be conducted direct between the President and Prime Minister.

Roosevelt followed up his New Year address by sending Harry Hopkins to see Churchill and investigate the situation in Britain. Hopkins arrived with a number of prejudices. He was capable, as Churchill noted, of being very disagreeable and saying hard and sour things. But Churchill appreciated his strength of character and, above all, his proximity to the President, and Hopkins soon became the first of a series of distinguished Americans to be exposed to Churchill's force of personality and charm. At their first meeting, Churchill launched into a bitter attack on Ambassador Kennedy, who shortly afterwards was replaced. Churchill took Hopkins everywhere and showed him everything, including him in meetings with his military commanders and other key advisers.

On 14 January, Hopkins wrote to Roosevelt from Claridge's: 'The people here are amazing from Churchill down and if courage alone can win – the result will be inevitable ... This island needs our help now, Mr President, with everything we can give them.' Taken by Churchill to Scapa Flow, the frail and exhausted Hopkins nearly fell into the sea, then tried to find somewhere to rest on the deck of a destroyer – only to be hauled to his feet by a petty officer who advised him not to sit on the depth charges. Hopkins spent three weekends with Churchill and voted Chequers the coldest house he had ever visited. Although Churchill seemed to thrive there in his boiler suit, Hopkins seldom took off his overcoat. His favourite haunt was the downstairs bathroom – the only room, he claimed, where the central heating was detectable. He would go there to read his papers, but even there was still clad in his overcoat.

By this stage he had spent twelve long evenings with Churchill. He reported that Churchill had 'an amazing hold on the British people of all classes ... No matter how fierce the attack may be, you can be sure that they will resist it.' But he was appalled by their lack of the means to do so. The Lend-Lease Bill passed the Senate in March. Hopkins, on his return, was given the responsibility for coordinating assistance to Britain. Averell Harriman, at the time Chairman of the Union Pacific Railroad, was sent to do the same in London. His instructions from Roosevelt were to 'recommend everything that we can do, short of war, to keep the British Isles afloat'. Churchill continued to use his friendship with Hopkins to good effect. When he did not want to address the President direct, he tried his ideas out on Hopkins first.[9]

From the outset, Churchill had devised other ways of getting the Americans engaged in a *de facto* alliance against the Germans. On the day he became Prime Minister, Churchill asked his friend, the Canadian industrialist William Stephenson, to coordinate British intelligence operations in the United States. Churchill saw it as Stephenson's task to establish an entirely new degree of intelligence cooperation with the United States. Roosevelt agreed that there should be the 'closest possible marriage' between the FBI and British intelligence. Stephenson went to see J. Edgar Hoover, who said that he was under instructions from the State Department not to collaborate with Britain in any way that might conceivably be interpreted as infringing or compromising US neutrality. If Stephenson could get this rescinded by the White House, Hoover would be ready to cooperate provided no other US government department, including the State Department, knew about it. Through an intermediary, Stephenson persuaded Roosevelt to send a confirmatory message to Hoover.

Stephenson established himself in the Rockefeller Center in New York, nominally in charge of the British Passport Control Office. One of his priorities was to prevent interference with US munitions supplies to Britain in the New York docks. In July 1940, the White House decided to ask a distinguished Republican veteran of the First World War, Colonel William 'Wild Bill' Donovan, to go to Britain to investigate fifth-column activity and the country's chances of withstanding a German attack. Stephenson and Lothian arranged for Donovan to see Churchill and to meet the King and Queen. On his return to Washington, Donovan campaigned against the defeatist views of Joe Kennedy, reporting that British morale was high and pressing for the release of the First World War destroyers.[10]

In the early days of their collaboration, Hoover and the FBI could not have been more cooperative, permitting Stephenson to recruit a large network of operatives and acting on the information Stephenson was able to provide about the efforts of Axis sympathisers and of the Italian, German and Vichy French embassies. But the rapid expansion of Stephenson's activities caused deep alarm to the Assistant Secretary of State, Adolf Berle, who observed that Stephenson was rapidly developing 'a full size secret police and intelligence service'. Legally, he added, the British were on 'almost impossible ground; they are in fact spies'. Hoover disregarded this memorandum and in 1941, with Hoover's help, Stephenson's office was formally registered as that of British Security Co-ordination. Stephenson, for his part, proved adept at utilising the generally pro-British US press to expose the activities of German sympathisers.

At the end of 1940, Donovan made a long visit to the Middle East, organised by the British. In May 1941, Stephenson told London that he was 'attempting to manoeuvre Donovan into accepting the job of co-ordinating all US intelligence'. He had an ally in the White House in the author Robert Sherwood, who wrote many of Roosevelt's speeches. Stephenson continued to supply Donovan with intelligence to 'build up his candidacy' for the position he wanted to help him achieve. At the end of May, the chief of British Naval Intelligence, Admiral Godfrey, and his assistant, Commander Ian Fleming, arrived in Washington also to argue the case for a single directorate of intelligence. In June 1941, these efforts were rewarded when Donovan was asked by Roosevelt to coordinate oversees intelligence. 'You can imagine how relieved I am', reported Stephenson, 'after three months of battling and jockeying for position in Washington that our man is in a position of such importance to our efforts.'[11]

Ian Fleming stayed on in Washington for a few weeks to offer advice to Donovan, but the real influence on Donovan remained that of Stephenson. While Stephenson played a major role in helping establish the first major US overseas intelligence operation – apart from signals intercepts by the War Department – this did affect his relations with Hoover and the FBI. As Kim Philby records, the reason for Hoover's resentment was that 'Stephenson was playing politics in his own yard, and playing them pretty well'. Stephenson's promotion of a new and rival US intelligence agency was bound to arouse Hoover's suspicions, despite the FBI's limited role in external operations. Stephenson believed that, initially, if Donovan had not been able to rely on British assistance, his organisation could not have survived. After Pearl Harbor, Donovan's organisation was transformed into a new body under the US Chiefs of Staff, known henceforth as the Office of Strategic Services (OSS). Among its earliest recruits were David Bruce and Allen Dulles. J. Edgar Hoover, in Philby's view, 'never forgave Stephenson for the part he played as mid-wife and nurse to OSS'.[12]

––––––––––

The British and Americans by now were engaged in exchanges of scientific information, the pooling of some military intelligence, security cooperation between the FBI and Stephenson, and preliminary staff talks as well as in regular discussions of all Britain's military requirements. It was in this period, before the entry of the United States into the war, that a pattern of cooperation was established which has endured to the present day. Averell Harriman was co-opted by Churchill exactly as Hopkins had been. He reported that he was with the Prime Minister at least one day a week and usually at weekends as well. 'He likes to take me on his trips to the devastated cities – so I can report to the President, but also, I am sure, so the people can see an American around.' Harriman's special relationships included an affair with the Prime Minister's daughter-in-law, Pamela, married to Randolph Churchill. Harriman's presence was reinforced by that of a much more congenial American ambassador, John G. Winant.

The British were unable to provide effective protection to convoys all the way across the Atlantic. In April, ten out of twenty-two ships were lost in one convoy. On 10 April, Harriman told Roosevelt that 'England's strength is bleeding. In our own interest, I trust that our Navy can be directly employed before our partner is too weak.'[13] On the following day, Roosevelt told Churchill that the United States would patrol the Western Atlantic, though the direct responsibility for convoy protection would remain with the British. This action Churchill regarded as a 'long step towards salvation'. Detailed plans were worked out between the British and American naval staffs.

On 15 June, Churchill warned Roosevelt that a massive German attack on Russia was imminent. It was launched one week later. In July, Hopkins reappeared on his second visit to London. The American military were questioning the wisdom of the British continuing to devote so many of their military resources to the fighting in North Africa, rather than concentrating their efforts on withstanding an invasion of the United Kingdom. Hopkins was invited to attend meetings of the British Cabinet. This demonstration of trust, however, had its limits. As Sir Alexander Cadogan, head of the Foreign Office, recorded on one occasion: '[W]e had to get rid of him before the end on the grounds that we were going to discuss home affairs, and then discussed – America and the Far East!'[14]

In July 1941, it was agreed that the Prime Minister and the President should hold their first meeting at Placentia Bay in Newfoundland. Hopkins proposed to Roosevelt that he should visit Moscow to see Stalin beforehand. Hopkins undertook the hazardous journey from Scotland to Archangel in an

RAF Catalina. He was greatly impressed by Stalin, who was confident that the German offensive would grind to a halt in the Russian winter. Hopkins gave a lyrical description of his meetings with the Soviet leader ('a smile that can be cold but friendly, austere but warm') to the *American* magazine.[15]

He returned to Britain in time to embark with Churchill on the *Prince of Wales* at Scapa Flow. On the voyage across the Atlantic, he was able to give invaluable advice about the meeting with Roosevelt and future assistance to Russia.

At Placentia Bay on 9 August, Churchill went aboard the USS *Augusta*. He was greeted by the President, standing with the aid of his son, Elliott. On the Sunday morning, 10 August, Roosevelt and his senior military advisers joined Churchill and his team in an emotional service on the deck of the *Prince of Wales*. It was, as Churchill said, 'a great moment to live'. As he also wrote in his war memoirs: 'Nearly half of those who sang were soon to die.' Four months later, the *Prince of Wales* was sunk by Japanese dive-bombers off Singapore.

The unity of the morning did not survive into the afternoon. Roosevelt insisted before the conference that no embarrassing questions were to be raised about the entry of the United States into the war. He needed to be able to say that the military and naval conversations in no way had involved any future commitments between the two governments.

Roosevelt had proposed drawing up a joint declaration of principles and Churchill gave an outline of what might be said. Roosevelt wanted the reference to open trade to be accompanied by the words 'without discrimination'. Churchill could not agree, given the preference accorded to and by the dominions. When Sumner Welles insisted, Churchill 'could not help mentioning the British experience in adhering to Free Trade for eighty years in the face of ever-mounting American tariffs'. Roosevelt resisted Churchill's demand that the United States should give a clear warning that further aggression by Japan could lead to war with the United States.[16]

By 12 August, agreement had been reached on a joint declaration – the Atlantic Charter. This stated that Britain and the United States sought no territorial aggrandisement; territorial changes must be freely agreed by the people concerned. After the 'final destruction of the Nazi tyranny', they looked forward to a peace based on self-determination, freedom of the seas and abandonment of the use of force. Churchill and the *Prince of Wales* were escorted back to Iceland by American destroyers.

Churchill had succeeded in his main objective, which was to achieve a 'remarkable demonstration of Anglo-American solidarity'. The Americans had agreed to take over patrolling of the Atlantic west of Iceland. But Roosevelt watered down the warning he had agreed with Churchill to send to the Japanese. Churchill had his own reservations about the pledge of self-determination, which he told his Secretary of State for India, Leo Amery, would only apply in cases where a transfer of territory or sovereignty arose. A year later he telegraphed to Roosevelt that its 'proposed application to Asia and Africa requires much thought'. He did not see how it could possibly apply to the British colonial territories in Africa.

Churchill told the War Cabinet that he had got on intimate terms with the President. Roosevelt had told him that he would 'wage war, but not declare it'. But the British Chiefs of Staff reported that their American counterparts were thinking in terms of the defence of the Americas and had not formulated any joint strategy for the defeat of Germany in the event of their entry into the war. Churchill was very disappointed by Roosevelt's statements after the conference that it had brought the United States no closer to war and that no secret commitments had been entered into. These, he told Hopkins, had undermined the confidence Churchill had been able to inspire on his return. He doubted if Hitler would provoke an incident severe enough to bring the United States into the war and added that he did not know what would happen if England were still fighting alone in 1942.[17] Hopkins told Roosevelt that not only Churchill but the entire British people believed that ultimately the United States would join the conflict on some basis.

On 31 October, an American destroyer on convoy duty in the North Atlantic was torpedoed and all her crew lost. But, as with the *Lusitania*, this did not bring the United States to a declaration of war. Churchill told the War Cabinet on 12 November of the difficulties Roosevelt faced with Congress. Roosevelt, he said, was a great leader. It was in his power to make war without declaring it. The Americans had made immense credits and resources available to Britain, and they were escorting the Atlantic convoys. Yet, as he had told Halifax on his appointment to succeed Lord Lothian in Washington, it was not possible to *win* the war without American participation. Certainly, without it, there could be no worthwhile peace.

The full extent of the assistance the United States at this stage was providing to Britain still was a closely guarded secret. Henry Brandon, making his first and extremely hazardous crossing of the Atlantic on a British merchant vessel, describes the sense of relief and amazement he felt to awake one morning and see eight American destroyers on the horizon, as they took over the escort of the convoy in mid-Atlantic. It provided him with his first journalistic scoop.[18]

On 20 October, Churchill had assured Roosevelt that if the United States found itself at war with Japan, Britain would join in 'within the hour'. But he still believed that a firm enough warning from the Americans would deter the Japanese from an attack on Dutch and British possessions in the Far East. Churchill 'had long dreaded being at war with Japan without or before the United States'.[19]

Churchill was dining with the US ambassador, John Winant, and Averell Harriman at Chequers on Sunday 7 December when, after the main 9 o'clock news, they thought they heard a few sentences about Japanese attacks on American ships at Hawaii. The butler confirmed that they had heard correctly: the Japanese had attacked the Americans. As Winant described it, they looked at one another incredulously. Winant got through to the White House. Roosevelt confirmed the news to Churchill: 'We are all in the same boat now.' Churchill grasped at once the full import of the news:

> Now at this very moment I knew the United States was in the War, up to the neck and in to the death. So we had won after all! ... we should emerge, however mauled and mutilated, safe and victorious ... I went to bed and slept the sleep of the saved and thankful.[20]

5

'THE PRIME MINISTER OF GREAT BRITAIN HAS NOTHING TO HIDE FROM THE PRESIDENT OF THE UNITED STATES'

THE NEXT MORNING, as soon as he woke, Churchill decided at once to go to see Roosevelt. On 10 December, the *Prince of Wales* and *Repulse* were sunk by the Japanese off Singapore. Four days later, Churchill left for Washington on the *Duke of York*. His main concern was whether he could persuade the President that, notwithstanding the US losses in the Pacific, the first priority must be the defeat of Germany. During the voyage, the British Chiefs of Staff prepared a paper, presented by Churchill to Roosevelt, urging that the main objective for 1942 should be to secure the whole of the North African coastline. An invasion of continental Europe should follow in 1943.

Churchill disembarked at Hampton Roads and flew to Washington to meet the President on 22 December. He stayed at the White House for the next three weeks. He saw Roosevelt for several hours each day and they lunched together, with Hopkins as a third. Dinners were more social occasions, the President making the cocktails himself. On the way in to dinner, Churchill would propel Roosevelt in his wheelchair. Churchill occupied the north-east suite, next to that of the President. 'As we both, by need or habit, were forced to do much of our work in bed, he visited me in my room whenever he felt inclined, and encouraged me to do the same.' Hopkins stayed across the passage. He told many times the story

of Roosevelt being wheeled to his guest's room and entering as Church-
ill emerged from the bathroom, 'stark naked and gleaming pink from his
bath'. As Roosevelt made to withdraw, Churchill protested: 'The Prime
Minister of Great Britain has nothing to hide from the President of the
United States.' The story, unfortunately, is one Churchill himself denied.
He always had, he claimed, at least a bath towel wrapped around him!
And the President, he added, would have known that it was not strictly
true that they had no secrets from one another.[1]

Churchill installed his map room next to his bedroom. The normally
tranquil upstairs hall in the White House was filled with British officials
carrying red leather despatch cases. As Churchill knew that Roosevelt
went to bed early, he would pretend to do so himself, then continue his
discussions with Hopkins.

On 23 December, they gave their first joint press conference. It was held
in the Oval Office, with the reporters clustering around the President's
desk. Henry Brandon describes the scene:

> [T]here was FDR in the flesh, with his broad, fetching smile, his
> cigarette in its famous long holder cockily held in the corner of
> his mouth, the embodiment of self-confidence, urbanity, joy of life
> and American power. No one, if anyone existed who did not already
> know, would have guessed that he was an invalid who had to get
> about in a wheelchair.

Churchill climbed on a chair so the reporters could see him: they all broke
into applause. To the inevitable question 'how long will it take to win the
war?' Churchill replied: 'If we manage it well, it will only take half as long
as if we manage it badly.' By the end of the press conference, Brandon
observes, Churchill had taken an important body of prisoners – the White
House press corps. Brandon felt that he had been present at the first making of the special relationship and also its personification.[2]

The traditional Christmas tree was set up in the grounds of the White
House. Roosevelt and Churchill made brief speeches from the balcony
to an enormous crowd. Churchill spoke of how, though far from his
family, 'yet I cannot truthfully say that I feel far from home'. On Boxing
Day, Churchill addressed both Houses of Congress: 'Here we are together
defending all that to free men is dear.' He could not help reflecting,

he said, that if his father had been American and his mother British, instead of the other way around, 'I might have got here on my own.' If the Allies had remained together after the First War, he added, the present calamity could have been avoided.

———————

Churchill left Washington having gained satisfaction on two essential points. The Americans agreed that Germany was the preponderant Axis power and the European theatre, therefore, decisive. And Roosevelt appeared to agree that US forces might be committed to the North African campaign. General Marshall agreed on the priority that needed to be given to the European theatre. But he and the US Chiefs of Staff were by no means convinced about Churchill's 'peripheral' strategy, which Marshall suspected was designed to protect British interests in the Mediterranean and the empire. Marshall was afraid that the President might concede too much to the Prime Minister. But he himself felt that among his military colleagues at this stage there was 'too much anti-British feeling on our side ... Our people were always ready to find Albion perfidious.'[3] On Churchill's departure, Hopkins retired to the navy hospital, exhausted.

During this visit to Washington, Churchill revealed to Roosevelt the extent to which the British government's Code and Cypher School at Bletchley had succeeded in breaking German cyphers. Along with the work on 'Tube Alloys' (see below), it was the most closely guarded secret of the war.[4] On 25 February 1942, Churchill revealed another British secret to Roosevelt. This was that the British also could read the US diplomatic cyphers. 'From the moment that we became allies, I gave instructions that this work should cease.' Roosevelt was urged to burn the letter to him about this!

As Bradley Smith, a leading US scholar of the relationship, observed: 'Never before had sovereign states revealed their vital intelligence methods and results even to their closest allies.'

During his stay in Washington, Churchill appointed Field Marshal Sir John Dill to liaise with Marshall and the US Chiefs of Staff. Dill was not a Churchill confidant. The Prime Minister had replaced him with Alan Brooke as Chief of the Imperial General Staff. Cautious and reserved, Dill did not seem an obvious choice to deal with the Americans. But Marshall installed him as his near neighbour in the US officers' quarters at Fort Myer and they formed an extraordinary friendship. Asked on one occasion what his job was, Dill confessed that he did not know, but 'at least he provided neutral ground on which the American Army and Navy could meet'.

Dill was astonished not only by the prosperity but also by the peacefulness of America: 'Never have I seen a country so utterly unprepared for war.' At dinner at the British embassy, he got into an argument with the Secretary for War, Henry Stimson, about the possibilities for offensive action on the European mainland. Dill did not believe that the Americans at this stage had the slightest conception of the kind of war the British had been fighting for the past two years.

———————

Britain at this point was at the nadir of its military fortunes, with Rommel on the offensive in North Africa, the Japanese seizing Malaya, Singapore and Hong Kong, and shipping losses at their worst in the North Atlantic. Roosevelt sought to cheer Churchill about these setbacks but, prompted by the State Department, this also was the moment he chose to send Churchill a message about India. Recapitulating the constitutional development of the United States up to the War of Independence, he suggested that a representative group should be chosen to decide a future constitution that might 'cause the people of India to forget past hard feelings and to become more loyal to the British Empire'. As one of Roosevelt's advisers, Robert Sherwood, observed, the only part of the message with which Churchill agreed was the President's admission that this was 'none of my business'. As negotiations with the Indian leaders broke down, Roosevelt suggested that this was because of the British refusal to concede self-government. This message, reported Hopkins, who was with Churchill at the time, was wrathfully received.[5]

Foreshadowing the major differences that were to develop between them on this subject, on 18 March Roosevelt wrote to Churchill:

> I know you will not mind my being brutally frank when I tell you
> that I think I can personally handle Stalin better than either your

Foreign Office or my State Department. Stalin hates the guts of all your top people. He thinks he likes me better, and I hope he will continue to do so.

In April, Marshall and Hopkins were sent to London to convince Churchill of the need to open a second front in Europe to take some of the pressure off the Russians. Roosevelt proposed an immediate decision to prepare for the invasion of northern France and the capture of Antwerp in 1943.

Hopkins said that if public opinion in America had its way, the weight of the American effort would be directed against Japan. If the plight of Russia necessitated earlier action, the Americans favoured an attempt in 1942 to seize Brest or Cherbourg. The decisive theatre would be northern France. The US Chiefs of Staff regarded plans to seize North Africa as a dangerous diversion.

Churchill remained attached to operations in North Africa. These he saw as the best way in which British and American forces could be brought into action together against the Germans in 1942. While Churchill agreed in principle to the American plan for a second front in 1943, Marshall realised that his acceptance was partly tactical. Marshall did not take to Brooke, who in turn thought the American a good organiser, but a bad strategist. 'In many respects he is a very dangerous man, while being a very charming one.'

Brooke thought Marshall simply failed to understand the difficulty of sustaining an invasion force against German counter-attacks after the initial landing. The British pointed to the lack of landing craft. The two and a half divisions the Americans could hope to produce by September 1942 would be 'no very great contribution'. Marshall warned that the alternative to his plan was a Pacific First strategy. Churchill's military adviser, General Ismay, thought in retrospect that the British should have explained more frankly that they were not prepared again to contemplate losing 60,000 men in a single day's fighting in France, as they had in July 1916. Each time he stood in the House of Commons, Churchill said, he saw 'the faces not there' of those who had died in Flanders. Roosevelt remained concerned that a Russian collapse could render a frontal assault on France well-nigh impossible.[6]

In mid-1942, Churchill made his second visit to Washington. On 19 June, he flew to meet Roosevelt at his home on the Hudson, Hyde Park. The President welcomed him with great cordiality, and,

> driving the car himself, took me to the majestic bluffs over the Hudson River on which Hyde Park, his family home, stands. The President drove me all over the estate, showing me its splendid views. In this drive I had some thoughtful moments. Mr Roosevelt's infirmity prevented him from using his feet on the brake, clutch or accelerator. An ingenious arrangement enabled him to do everything with his arms, which were amazingly strong and muscular. He invited me to feel his biceps, saying that a famous prize-fighter had envied them. This was reassuring; but I confess that when on several occasions the car poised and backed on the grass verges of the precipices over the Hudson I hoped the mechanical devices and brakes would show no defects. All the time we talked business, and though I was careful not to take his attention off the driving, we made more progress than we might have done in formal conference.[7]

Churchill told Roosevelt that the British Chiefs of Staff had been unable to come up with a plan for a cross-Channel landing in September that could lead to anything other than disaster. They should look instead to North Africa.

There was another matter Churchill needed to raise privately with the President. In the summer of 1939, on the eve of the outbreak of war, Albert Einstein had written to warn Roosevelt of the potential military applications of atomic energy. Informed of the research being conducted at the Cavendish laboratory in Cambridge, at the same time Churchill, advised by Professor Lindemann (later Lord Cherwell), wrote to the Secretary of State for Air to alert him to the 'immense amount of energy which might be released from uranium by the recently discovered chain of processes which take place when this particular type of atom is split by neutrons. At first sight this might seem to portend the appearance of new explosives of devastating power.' He was concerned that Hitler might use the threat of a new secret weapon for propaganda purposes and noted that this research could not lead to practical results for several years. To consider the possible military applications, the British established the Maud Committee, bringing together their most distinguished nuclear scientists (Thomson, Chadwick, Cockcroft and Blackett). In the United States, a similar committee was established under Roosevelt's chief scientific adviser, Vannevar Bush.

In the autumn of 1940, the first serious exchange of militarily useful scientific information took place when Sir Henry Tizard and Cockcroft visited Washington. In view of Britain's dependence on the USA for war supplies, Tizard was instructed to tell the Americans *'everything* that Britain was doing in the scientific field'. This included the latest work on radar, jet engines and anti-submarine warfare. The US Office of Scientific Research was later to claim this to have been 'the most valuable cargo ever brought to the shores of the United States'.[8]

Part of that cargo was the progress of the work in Britain on nuclear fission, explained by Cockcroft. In June 1941, the Maud Committee reported that, having started with 'more scepticism than belief', they now were convinced that it would be possible to make an effective uranium bomb of enormous explosive power and which would release large quantities of radioactive material which would make places near the explosion dangerous to human life for a long period. The British realised that they could not devote sufficient financial resources to all the possible avenues for research. The committee recommended further exchanges with the Americans to ensure that work was carried forward on both sides of the Atlantic, irrespective of where the first uranium separation plant was located.

The Ministry of Defence still believed it unlikely that an atomic weapon would be of any use in the Second World War. Vast resources would be required for an uncertain result. The Ministry proposed that laboratory and design work should continue in Britain, but development of a full-scale plant should rather be considered in Canada or the United States. Research work was approaching the point at which large-scale government funding would be required for further development.

Dr Charles Darwin, head of the British scientific office in Washington, was consulted by Vannevar Bush. Dr Bush suggested that atomic weapons should be regarded not just as a matter for coordinated research between Britain and the United States but, in effect, as a joint project. Colonel Moore-Brabazon, the British Minister of Aircraft Production, emphasised the potential importance of nuclear fission as a new source of energy. If a bomb proved practical, he suggested, America and Britain, policing and controlling the world, would have an overwhelming military superiority.

Lindemann reported to Churchill: 'I am quite clear that we must go forward.' He wanted the separation plant to be built in Britain or Canada for

> whosoever possesses such a plant should be able to dictate terms
> to the rest of the world. However much I may trust my neighbour,
> and depend on him, I am very much averse to putting myself completely at his mercy and would therefore not press the Americans
> to undertake this work: I would just continue exchanging information and get into production over here without raising the questions
> of whether they should do it or not.

Churchill responded that: 'Although personally I am quite content with the existing explosives, I feel we must not stand in the path of improvement.'[9] But the experts concluded that a full-scale separation plant could not be built in Britain because of the risk of air attack. The British still hoped it might be possible to carry the work forward in Canada, giving them greater control over the project.

The Maud Committee report was passed to Vannevar Bush in October 1941. Bush told Roosevelt of the British conviction that a uranium bomb could be made. Influenced by the Maud report and the progress of research in the United States, Bush's committee concluded in November that a fission bomb of enormous destructive power was indeed technically feasible. Roosevelt received the report nine days before the Japanese attack on Pearl Harbor.

Within six months, the US effort far outstripped the British in terms of resources. Churchill had agreed in December to a full exchange of information. The British now realised that they risked being left behind if the work were not pursued jointly. At his meeting with Roosevelt at Hyde Park in June 1942, Churchill urged that they should pool all their information, work together on equal terms and share the results equally between them.[10]

6

'THE ONLY WAY IN WHICH WE COULD POSSIBLY LOSE THIS WAR'

ON THEIR RETURN to Washington, Roosevelt gave Churchill the news of the surrender of the British forces in Tobruk, with 30,000 troops taken prisoner. This was a devastating blow to the Prime Minister, who felt that the garrison should have continued its resistance. The response from Roosevelt was: 'What can we do to help?' Churchill asked for Sherman tanks, then just coming into production. Though these were badly needed for the US Army, the request was granted. He also was promised an American armoured division for North Africa. Brooke considered that the bold decisions taken by the President in this crisis were decisive in cementing the personal confidence between Roosevelt, the Prime Minister and their military advisers. At Fort Jackson, Churchill watched US forces exercising. General Ismay thought that to put these inexperienced troops up against the Germans would be murder. 'You are wrong,' said Churchill. 'They are wonderful material and will learn very quickly.'[1]

Churchill believed, correctly, that Roosevelt was now more attracted by his North African plan than were his military advisers. Dill reported that the US Chiefs of Staff feared that large-scale operations in the Mediterranean would preclude any landing in France in 1943. Admiral King, head of the US Navy, regarded his real enemy as the Japanese. Marshall saw North Africa as a diversion and at this point even he suggested that the United States instead should 'turn to the Pacific for decisive action against Japan'. He and King denounced the North African plan as 'both indecisive and a heavy drain on our resources'. But Roosevelt obliged them to admit that as yet they had no clear plans for offensive action in the Pacific, and further suggested that their recommendations should be removed from the official records so that it would not appear in later years that 'we had proposed what amounted to the abandonment of the British'.[2]

On 18 July, Hopkins, Marshall and King arrived in Britain to try to reach agreement with Churchill. 'A queer party', Brooke noted in his diary. 'Hopkins is for operating in Africa, Marshall wants to operate in Europe, and King is determined to stick to the Pacific.' But their instructions from Roosevelt, if a cross-Channel operation were ruled out, were to 'determine upon another place for US troops to fight in 1942'. Roosevelt had told them that he was opposed to an all-out effort in the Pacific against Japan, as that would increase the chance of complete German domination of Europe and Africa, whereas 'defeat of Germany means defeat of Japan'.[3]

Hopkins reported to the President some lively exchanges. He and Marshall annoyed Churchill by insisting on conferring with General Dwight Eisenhower and General Mark Clark, who were in London to liaise with the British military commanders, before they met the Prime Minister. 'The Prime Minister threw the British Constitution at me with some vehemence. As you know, it is an unwritten document so no serious damage done. Winston is his old self and full of battle.' Marshall failed in a further attempt to get the British to agree to a cross-Channel attack, being told by Professor Lindemann that he was 'arguing against the casualties on the Somme'. Churchill remained convinced that an unsuccessful invasion of France was 'the only way in which we could possibly lose this war'.[4] Eisenhower was despondent, suggesting that this might go down as 'the blackest day in history'. He feared that without the early opening of a second front, the Soviet Union might be knocked out of the war; a landing in France would then become impossible.

Marshall was reduced to devising what he regarded as the 'least harmful diversion'. He pointed out that sending American troops to North Africa probably would render a 1943 cross-Channel attack impossible. But it was agreed that the Americans should aim to occupy French North Africa and ultimately join forces with the British Eighth Army – Operation Torch. Despite the misgivings of his military commanders, Roosevelt declared himself happy with the outcome.

Marshall still suspected that the British were as much concerned with preserving the empire as defeating the Germans and what Eisenhower described as a 'trans-Atlantic essay contest' raged for the next two months, with Marshall initially suggesting that the operation should be confined to landings in Morocco – as far away as possible from the real military action in North Africa. The Canadians and British, meanwhile, staged a raid on the French Channel port of Dieppe, in which the Canadians suffered 66 per cent casualties.

In August, Churchill made his first visit to Moscow. At his suggestion, Roosevelt sent Harriman with him. Churchill told Stalin that there would be no second front in Europe in 1942, but there would be American landings in North Africa. Harriman gave Churchill staunch support, though, he observed, it was 'very rough sledding'. Churchill reported to Roosevelt that the Russians had swallowed 'this bitter pill', and by the end of their meeting Stalin was showing a bit more enthusiasm for operations to throw the Germans out of the Mediterranean.

The British proposed that Eisenhower should be appointed to command Torch, with the British commander, General Harold Alexander, as his deputy. Churchill arranged a weekly lunch at No. 10 with Eisenhower, Mark Clark and Eisenhower's Chief of Staff, Bedell Smith, who also frequently were invited to Chequers. Roosevelt wanted the initial landing to be by US troops alone, with British air and sea support. He thought this would reduce the likelihood of resistance by the Vichy French, who were continuing to declare their intention of defending French North Africa against the Anglo-Saxons. Churchill argued passionately for a landing to be made at Algiers, and not just at Casablanca and Oran. Montgomery, meanwhile, was beating off Rommel's final effort to break through to Cairo.

On 23 October, Montgomery launched his own attack at Alamein. By 5 November, the German forces were outmanoeuvred and outgunned, and Rommel was in full retreat, with 20,000 German prisoners taken. As Churchill commented: 'Before Alamein, we never had a victory. After Alamein, we never had a defeat.'

———————

On 5 November, Eisenhower arrived in Gibraltar. Three days later the Americans landed in French North Africa, supported by the Royal Navy and the RAF. There was quite fierce resistance by French forces still loyal to Marshal Pétain at Oran and Algiers. To put an end to this,

General Clark reached an agreement with Pétain's deputy, Admiral Darlan, and allowed him to remain as High Commissioner of French North
Africa. Churchill had deep misgivings about this and it was regarded
as an outrage by the Free French Forces fighting with the Allies. But
Roosevelt continued to display his intense distrust of de Gaulle, writing
to Churchill: 'I have heretofore enjoyed a quiet satisfaction in leaving him
in your hands.'

The Foreign Office pointed out that Darlan's record was odious: 'We
are fighting for international decency and Darlan is the antithesis of this.'
Churchill told Roosevelt that this could be only a 'temporary expedient
… We must not overlook the serious political injury which may be done
to our cause.' Eisenhower insisted that, without Darlan, he would have to
undertake a complete military occupation of North Africa. General Marshall defended Eisenhower, saying that the agreement was necessary to
save American lives. Publicly loyal to his allies, Churchill insisted to the
House of Commons that Eisenhower was right, 'and even if he was not
quite right I should have been reluctant to hamper or impede his action'.
Stalin had fewer inhibitions. Not only Darlan, he suggested, should be used
against the Germans but, if necessary, 'the Devil himself and his grandma'.[5]
On 24 December, this disagreement was overtaken as Darlan was assas-
sinated by a French monarchist opposed to Pétain.

On 14 January 1943, Roosevelt and Churchill met in Casablanca, where
they were joined by Eisenhower and Alexander, who reported that Montgomery was about to take Tripoli. Roosevelt had warned his advisers that
when they got to Casablanca, they would find that the British would have
a plan and stick to it. Admiral King noted that whenever he brought up a
subject, 'the British had a paper ready'. Brooke indicated that, 'if not this
year', he could definitely contemplate a cross-Channel invasion in 1944.
The British Chiefs of Staff did not believe that a cross-Channel invasion
could succeed in 1943. Marshall questioned Churchill's plan for an invasion of Sicily as he remained opposed to 'interminable operations in the
Mediterranean'. From time to time he had to calm down Admiral King,
prone to outbursts against the 'godamned British'. Yet, between Roosevelt
and Churchill, according to Harold Macmillan, appointed to liaise with
Eisenhower in Algiers, 'there was a lot of bezique, an enormous quantity
of highballs, talk by the hour and a general atmosphere of extraordinary
goodwill'.[6]

Churchill pledged that when Germany was defeated, Britain would make a full contribution to the fight against Japan. Although the Commonwealth shortly would have twelve divisions in North Africa to the United States' four, Churchill proposed that Eisenhower should retain command, with Alexander as his deputy. This was Brooke's idea:

> We were carrying out a move which could not help flattering and pleasing the Americans ... We were pushing Eisenhower up into the stratosphere, where he would be free to devote his time to the political and inter-allied problems, whilst we inserted under him one of our own commanders to deal with the military situations and to restore the necessary drive and co-ordination which had been so seriously lacking.[7]

After ten days, the Chiefs of Staff at last reached agreement to drive the Germans out of Tunisia and then invade Sicily. Churchill persuaded the President to accompany him to Marrakesh. Over dinner, they sang songs together. Next morning Roosevelt, visiting him to say goodbye, found Churchill still in bed. 'I jumped up and put on my zip, and nothing else except slippers, and in this informal garb I drove with him to the airfield.'[8]

———

In March, the Foreign Secretary, Anthony Eden, visited Washington. He noted that the President from time to time urged the British government to give up Hong Kong as a 'gesture of goodwill'. Eden observed that Roosevelt had suggested other similar gestures on the part of the British, for example over India. He remarked to Hopkins that he had not heard the President propose any similar gestures on the part of the United States. Eden got on well with Roosevelt but, like others, found the Secretary of State, Cordell Hull, difficult to deal with and hostile in his attitude to de Gaulle and the Free French.[9]

In Tunisia, the campaign did not go well for the inexperienced American forces. In mid-February, a counter-attack by Rommel through the Kasserine Pass caught the Americans badly unprepared. But under General Omar Bradley, their performance rapidly improved. On 7 May, the British First Army entered Tunis supported by elements of the US Second

Corps. A quarter of a million prisoners were taken. On the flight back to Algiers, Macmillan and Eisenhower looked down on a huge Allied convoy proceeding unhindered towards Egypt. 'There, General,' said Macmillan, 'are the fruits of your victory.' Eisenhower replied: 'Ours, you mean, ours.'

In May 1943, Churchill sailed across the Atlantic on the *Queen Mary*, with a large number of German prisoners also on board. As he neared the American coast, he telegraphed to Roosevelt: 'Since yesterday we have been surrounded by the United States Navy, and we greatly appreciate the high value you evidently set on our continued survival.' Hopkins met him at Staten Island. Churchill was whisked off to his old rooms in the White House.

In his meeting with Roosevelt, Churchill recalled the striking change in the situation since their last meeting, when they had received the news of the fall of Tobruk. He said that he would never forget the manner in which the President had sustained him at that time, and the Sherman tanks that had been handed over so generously. The first objective, he argued, was in the Mediterranean. The great prize there was to get Italy out of the war. Roosevelt agreed that a cross-Channel attack could not take place on a large scale until 1944, but was unconvinced about an Italian campaign. In Maryland, at the President's retreat at 'Shangri-La', Churchill spent half an hour watching Roosevelt stick stamps in his album. Both tried to catch trout, with no success. 'Evidently he had the first quality of an angler, which is not to measure the pleasure by the catch.'[10]

Marshall warned Roosevelt that American and British war aims differed. 'Their military objectives were conditioned upon political aspects of guaranteeing their postwar position – above all in the Mediterranean.' The British, he said, were 'traditionally expert at meeting the letter while avoiding the spirit of their commitments'. An Allied occupation of Italy, in Marshall's view, would be 'more of a liability than an asset', tying up large numbers of troops and aircraft needed for cross-Channel operations. If the British wanted to get involved in the Balkans, they should do so on their own.[11]

The meetings in the Federal Reserve Building between the British and American Chiefs of Staff, Ismay noted, at first were marked by 'an unmistakable atmosphere of tension'. As General Brooke walked with him to one of the meetings, Marshall said that he still found it hard not to look on the North African strategy with a jaundiced eye. Brooke asked what

strategy he would have preferred. 'Cross-Channel operations for the liberation of France and advance on Germany; we should finish the war quicker.'
Brooke replied: 'Yes, probably, but not the way we hope to finish it!'[12]

Churchill observed that 'at first the differences seemed insuperable and
it looked like a hopeless breach ... After a serious crisis of opinions ... an
almost complete agreement was reached about invading Sicily.' Brooke
agreed to plans for an invasion of France in May 1944. To his dismay,
Churchill then crashed in where angels feared to tread, insisting that after
Sicily the Allies should invade southern Italy 'and gain touch with the
insurgents of the Balkan countries'. This mention of the Balkans made
Marshall bristle.

Churchill noted also the 'very stern mood' in Washington about de
Gaulle. At lunch at the British embassy there was discussion of the need
for a 'Supreme World Council', more effective than the League of Nations,
to help keep the peace after the war.[13]

––––––––––

The other issue of overriding importance to the British was the resumption of cooperation on nuclear research, codenamed 'Tube Alloys'. A year
before, Churchill had discussed the project with Roosevelt at Hyde Park.
His whole understanding, Churchill recorded, was that everything was
on the basis of fully sharing the results as equal partners. But in January
1943, the Americans had interrupted the exchange of information on
the most sensitive processes. For the Americans now were making rapid
progress themselves and the programme increasingly was under the control of the War Department. Vannevar Bush had concluded that since the
Americans were doing 90 per cent of the work, and several processes
were entirely American, no more should be shared with the British than
necessary and this was approved by Roosevelt. The British and Canadians were told that no further information was to be given to them on the
electromagnetic method, the production of heavy water or fast neutron
reaction. In other areas the release of information would be subject to the
authority of General Leslie Groves of the US Army Corps of Engineers.

Sir John Anderson, in charge of the project in Britain, told Churchill
that this had come as a bombshell and was intolerable. The Americans
still wanted input from British nuclear physicists like James Chadwick and

Rudolf Peierls, but on a highly restricted basis. Anderson noted that the pretext for the restrictions was secrecy, 'but one cannot help suspecting that the United States military authorities who are now in complete control wish to gain an advance upon us and feel that having benefited from the fruits of our early endeavours they will not suffer unduly by casting us aside'. Churchill raised this with Roosevelt at Casablanca and was given 'the most satisfactory personal assurances'.[14]

Following this exchange, in February Hopkins asked Churchill to let him have full details of the history of the 'Tube Alloys' project. Churchill sent him two long cables recording all Anglo-American dealings since the first exchange in 1940. Churchill expressed the conviction that this record proved that, on the grounds of fair play, he could justify his request for restoration of the policy of joint work in atomic research and development. He added that urgent decisions about the British programme depended on the extent to which collaboration was restored. In March he told Hopkins that cooperation was still at a standstill and if a full exchange of information on nuclear fission were not resumed, Britain would be compelled to go ahead separately. That, he added, would be a 'sombre decision'.

Anderson reported that the Americans had secured complete control over Canadian uranium and heavy water supplies. The Americans were applying resources the British could not match to the work on 'Tube Alloys' and were making increasingly rapid progress. Anderson concluded that the pilot plant would have to be built in the United States. While academic research could be continued in Britain, the British design team would have to be transferred to America. Otherwise the pioneer work done in Britain would be a dwindling asset and 'unless we capitalise quickly, we shall be rapidly out-stripped. We now have a real contribution to make to a merger. Soon we shall have little or none.'

On 26 May 1943, to the relief of his colleagues in London, Churchill reported Roosevelt's agreement that a full exchange of information on 'Tube Alloys' should be resumed. Churchill thanked Hopkins for his help in persuading Roosevelt that the enterprise must be considered a joint one, given that 'this weapon may well be developed in time for the present war' and that it fell, therefore, within the general agreement covering the interchange of research and invention secrets.[15]

To Churchill's distress, Roosevelt still declined to press his advisers to agree to plan the invasion of Italy. Instead it was agreed that Churchill should go with a reluctant Marshall to discuss the possibilities with the commanders in the field. Churchill and Marshall set off for North Africa in the Prime Minister's plane. Churchill had regarded Marshall as a 'rugged soldier and a magnificent organiser and builder of armies', but discussing how to deal with Stalin, he now began to understand that Marshall had statesmanlike qualities too. The aircraft was struck by lightning en route to Gibraltar, but no harm was done. From Gibraltar, they flew on to Algiers to meet Eisenhower and Alexander.

Marshall had reluctantly accepted that no large force could be landed in France before May 1944. Brooke argued that the Allies, therefore, must seek to strain and disperse German resources. Churchill pointed out that the Allies had thirty-six divisions available in the Mediterranean, most of them British. On 30 May, he kept Eisenhower up all night as he argued for the invasion of Italy. Brooke saw a sleepless Eisenhower the next day and smiled at his distress, having himself suffered repeatedly from this kind of treatment from Churchill. Brooke met Eisenhower privately to say that only the Soviet Army could produce decisive results in 1943. The British and Americans must do all they could to divert German forces from the Russian front. Montgomery then presented his plan for the invasion of Sicily. Famous for his lack of tact, he displayed a patronising attitude towards the Americans. 'It is most distressing that the Americans do not like him', Brooke wrote in his diary, 'and it will always be a difficult matter to have him fighting in close proximity to them.'[16]

7

'MY GOD! NOW THEY'VE STARTED SHOOTING'

THERE WERE BY now signs that the Italian Commander-in-Chief, Marshal Badoglio, was ready to break with Mussolini, and the British increasingly were convinced that an invasion could knock Italy out of the war. Churchill argued that if the Germans made strong efforts to defend Italy, that would draw forces away from the Russian front. To allay American suspicions, Churchill continued to emphasise that he was not advocating intervening in the Balkans. By the time Churchill left Algiers, he believed that Eisenhower accepted the advantages of invading Italy, but Marshall continued to insist that a decision should be deferred until Sicily was captured.

Roosevelt remained convinced that he knew how to deal with Stalin and that he would be able to get on better with him if Churchill were not present. In May 1943, the former US ambassador to the Soviet Union, Joseph Davies, was sent to Moscow to propose a meeting between Stalin and the President in Alaska. Averell Harriman was instructed to tell the Prime Minister that, in Roosevelt's view, it would be easier for him to break the ice with Stalin if they met on their own.[1] Hopkins, who could judge what Churchill's reaction would be, laughed as he wished Harriman the best of luck in this mission. Churchill lost no time in doing everything he could to prevent a Stalin–Roosevelt *tête-à-tête*, promptly drafting a counter-proposal for a preliminary conference of the British, Russian and American Foreign Ministers to prepare for a summit meeting. Roosevelt, no longer confident that he could persuade Stalin to meet him anyway, agreed to Churchill's suggestion, which eventually was accepted by the Russians.

For the invasion of Sicily and southern Italy, the British had eight and the United States six divisions available. Of the naval forces, 80 per cent were British. The landings in Sicily on 10 July 1943 were the greatest amphibious operation ever attempted and the island was captured by mid-August. The operations in the Mediterranean were the last in which the British and Americans were involved as, militarily, equal partners.

As Churchill reported to General Smuts, the Americans remained concerned about becoming involved too deeply in the Mediterranean. The US Chiefs of Staff were sticking to their original decision that no reinforcements from the United States should be sent to the Mediterranean theatre. They did not believe that the conquest of Italy would threaten Germany. Instead, they wanted all efforts against Germany to be centred on the shortest route across the English Channel.

Roosevelt agreed to a further meeting with the Prime Minister in Quebec. Among others, Churchill took with him Orde Wingate, who had distinguished himself in the jungle fighting in Burma, and Wing Commander Guy Gibson, fresh from leading the successful attack by the Royal Air Force on the Ruhr dams. On the voyage across the Atlantic on the *Queen Mary*, Churchill each day studied with the British Chiefs of Staff the issues they were to discuss with the Americans – above all the plans for the invasion of France, codenamed Overlord. The planning for the operation had been conducted under the British General F. E. Morgan. Morgan and his advisers recommended a landing in Normandy rather than in the area of Calais. The hope was that the port of Cherbourg could be captured early in the operation and that Allied armoured forces would be able to deploy rapidly in the open country south of Caen. But the Channel tides had a play of more than twenty feet and enormous quantities of supplies would have to be landed on the beaches. 'The fools or knaves who had chalked "Second Front Now" on our walls for the past two years had not had their minds burdened by such problems,' Churchill observed.[2]

He knew that he had to convince the Americans that he was serious about Overlord. The US Secretary of War, Stimson, who saw Churchill in London in July, came away convinced that the British still were haunted by the ghosts of Passchendaele and Dunkirk, and were not in their hearts committed to a cross-Channel invasion. Churchill spoke of his nightmare of seeing the Channel choked with Allied corpses. The Americans believed that although the Prime Minister invariably gave his support to Overlord in principle, he steadfastly refused to accept it as a scheduled fact, preferring to believe that German power could be worn down by attrition to the point of collapse, whereupon the Anglo-American forces in the United Kingdom could perform a triumphal march from the Channel to Berlin with no more than a few snipers' bullets to annoy them.[3]

Having arrived in Quebec on 11 August, on the following day Churchill and his daughter, Mary, travelled to stay with Roosevelt at Hyde Park. It was so hot that Churchill, 'unable to sleep and hardly to breathe', watched the dawn from a bluff overlooking the Hudson River.

While there, Roosevelt and Churchill approved a memorandum on 'Tube Alloys' which formally placed the research and manufacture of the atomic bomb in the United States, but as a joint project with no secrets withheld from either side. Despite the agreement with Roosevelt in May, and frequent reminders to Harry Hopkins, there had been no confirmation from the Americans of the renewal of cooperation. Sir John Anderson observed that, if the worst came to the worst, Britain would have to go ahead on its own. In a first justification of the British nuclear deterrent, he wrote: 'We cannot afford after the war to face the future without this weapon and rely entirely on America should Russia or some other power develop it.' In prior discussions in London, Churchill managed to convince the US Secretary for War, Stimson, and Vannevar Bush that the British were not interested in gaining an unfair commercial advantage through their access to US technology. But Anderson was still worried that, on their return to Washington, Stimson and Bush would be told that 'like other visitors to our misty shores, they had been taken in by our hypocritical cunning and carried away by our brilliant Prime Minister'.[4]

But Roosevelt at last had decided on Hopkins's advice that he must honour his undertakings to Churchill. He instructed Dr Bush to 'renew in an inclusive manner the full exchange of information with the British'. Anderson was sent to Washington on 1 August to negotiate the terms of an agreement to be signed by Churchill and Roosevelt. This noted the crucial importance of early completion of the project; that this would be more speedily achieved if British and American research were pooled; and that it would be 'an improvident use of war resources' to duplicate plants on both sides of the Atlantic. They agreed that the weapon would not be used against third parties without each other's consent, nor would information about it be communicated to third parties without mutual agreement. The British solemnly foreswore any commercial advantages. A joint policy committee, including a Canadian representative, was to be set up in Washington. The agreement formally was signed in Quebec on 19 August 1943.

Over dinner at Hyde Park on 14 August, with Harriman also present, Churchill expressed his hope that the 'fraternal association' between Britain and the United States would be perpetuated in peacetime. Eleanor Roosevelt feared that this might be misunderstood by other nations and weaken the concept of a new world organisation. But Churchill argued that any hope for the United Nations, which he and Roosevelt hoped to see established after the war as a new and more effective League of Nations, would lie in the leadership given by the United States and Britain.

As the United States had the command in the Mediterranean, Churchill wanted General Brooke to have the command of Overlord and told Brooke so early in 1943. But as the year advanced and the immense scale of the invasion took shape, Churchill became conscious of the overwhelming preponderance of American troops that would have to be employed after the original landings, which the British and US forces would undertake with roughly equal numbers. At Hyde Park he offered to accept General Marshall as Overlord Commander, with the Mediterranean being entrusted to a British commander.

On 17 August, Roosevelt and Harry Hopkins arrived in Quebec for the formal summit conference. The British and American Chiefs of Staff agreed that the target date for Overlord should be 1 May 1944 and that, *vis-à-vis* operations in the Mediterranean, the priority must go to Overlord.

The Americans wanted more effort devoted to operations from Burma to help China. Roosevelt and Marshall agreed to the appointment of Admiral Louis Mountbatten, Chief of Combined Operations, as commander in south-east Asia.

They may well have done so with some misgivings. Mountbatten seized on a pause in the tense and difficult discussions between the British and American Chiefs of Staff to ask if he could give a demonstration of a special mixture of ice that his scientists had discovered called Pykrete. His idea was that North Atlantic ice floes, reinforced with this material, might serve as aircraft carriers.

The staff brought in two blocks of ice, about three feet high, one of ordinary ice, the other of Pykrete. The US Air Force General Hap Arnold split the ordinary ice with a blow of an axe, but when he struck the Pykrete he let go with a cry of pain, his elbow badly jarred. Mountbatten then drew a pistol from his pocket to demonstrate the strength of Pykrete against gunfire. He fired first at the ordinary ice, which shattered into a thousand pieces. Then he fired at the Pykrete, from which the bullet ricocheted, narrowly missing Air Marshal Portal. A member of the staff outside, Churchill observes, aware of some of the disagreements inside the room, was reported to have exclaimed: 'My God! Now they've started shooting!'[5]

Another jarring note in the conference was the performance of Cordell Hull, with whom, Churchill reported, Eden had an 'awful time', mainly over Hull's aversion to the Free French. But the Combined Chiefs of Staff had reached an agreement that Churchill and Roosevelt approved. Eisenhower was to launch the invasion of southern Italy across the Straits of Messina in September. The Americans in turn obtained a firm British commitment to Overlord.

After a short rest in Canada, Churchill travelled by train to Washington, arriving at the White House on 1 September. He had deliberately prolonged his stay in order to influence the Americans over Italy. While in Washington, he attended several US Cabinet meetings or their equivalents. 'The Prime Minister's sleeping arrangements', noted Sir Alexander Cadogan, 'have now become quite promiscuous. He talks to the President till 2 a.m. and consequently spends a large part of the day hurling himself violently in and out of bed, bathing at unsuitable moments and rushing up and down corridors in his dressing gown.'[6]

Roosevelt encouraged Churchill to accept an honorary degree at Harvard. The ceremony took place on 6 September and Churchill saw it as a perfect occasion for a public declaration of Anglo-American unity and amity. The United States and Britain could not stop, he said:

> We must go on. It must be world anarchy or world order ... You
> will find in the British Commonwealth and Empire good comrades
> to whom you are united by other ties besides those of state policy
> and public need. To a large extent they are the ties of blood and
> history. Naturally I, a child of both worlds, am conscious of these.

Law, language, literature – these are considerable factors. Common conceptions of what is right and decent, a marked regard for fair play, especially to the weak and poor, a stern sentiment of impartial justice, and above all the love of personal freedom, or, as Kipling put it 'Leave to live by no man's leave underneath the law' – these are the common conceptions of both sides of the ocean among the English-speaking peoples.

This gift of a common tongue, he added, was a priceless inheritance 'and it may well some time become the foundation of a common citizenship. I like to think of British and Americans moving about freely over each other's wider estates with hardly a sense of being foreigners to one another.'

Churchill went on to speak about the combined Chiefs of Staff Committee which, he observed, disposed of all Allied resources and in practice used British and American troops, ships, aircraft and munitions as if they were the resources of a single state. Naturally, there were divergences of view, but they were thrashed out between men who trusted one another until 'after a few days, the President and I find ourselves furnished with sincere and united advice. This is a wonderful system. There was nothing like it in the last war. There never has been anything like it between two Allies.'

Churchill added:

Now in my opinion it would be a most foolish and improvident act on the part of our two Governments, or either of them, to break up this smooth-running and immensely powerful machinery the moment the war is over. For our own safety, as well as for the security of the rest of the world, we are bound to keep it working and in running order after the war – probably for a good many years, not only until we have set up some world arrangement to keep the peace, but until we know that it is an arrangement which will really give us that protection we must have from danger and aggression, a protection we have already had to seek across two vast world wars.

Whatever form a new system of world security might take, 'nothing will work soundly or for long without the united effort of the British and American peoples'.

In fact, before speaking at Harvard, Churchill had put to Roosevelt the idea of maintaining the Combined Chiefs of Staff Committee for, say, ten years after the war. This would involve no treaty but would have such advantages to both sides that it might become permanent. Churchill envisaged a continuing interchange of officers, weapons and training. Roosevelt listened sympathetically, but no conclusion was reached.

On 9 September, the news came in of the surrender to the Allies of the Italian fleet. On the following day, Roosevelt left Washington for Hyde Park. He invited Churchill to use the White House not only as a residence but also for any conferences he might wish to hold, either with his own advisers or with the US Chiefs of Staff. Churchill duly presided over a meeting of the Combined Chiefs of Staff at the White House on 11 September. As he observed, this 'seemed to be an event in Anglo-American history'. Dill reported to Brooke on Churchill's exploit: 'However, as you will see, no harm was done.'[7]

A major source of disagreement remained policy towards de Gaulle. Roosevelt described him as 'our mutual headache' and opposed the formation of any government or committee that might appear to pre-empt the choice of the French people. He revealed such a mounting hostility to de Gaulle that Churchill feared for the future of Allied relations with the Free French.

Meanwhile, the invasion of Italy had begun. The Allied invasion force ran into stiff German resistance and for some time its position was precarious. Churchill felt that the risks of the military operations in Italy were being increased by rigid insistence of the US Chiefs of Staff on the priority to be given to Overlord.

As the Italians effectively withdrew from the war, the British sent small forces to occupy the islands of Leros and Kos in the eastern Aegean. Churchill also wanted to seize Rhodes. On 7 October, he telegraphed to assure Roosevelt once again that he had no wish to send an army into the Balkans, but he asked for US support for an attack on Rhodes. General Marshall was determined not to permit any diversion of resources. Churchill was pained to receive from the President a telegram that he had sent to Eisenhower, which practically amounted to the refusal of all help. Roosevelt said that he did not want to force on Eisenhower 'diversions which limited the prospects for success in difficult operations in Italy'. He also was against any diversion of forces or equipment that might prejudice Overlord. Churchill responded immediately with an offer to go to Eisenhower's headquarters with the British Chiefs of Staff. He also asked General Marshall to meet them there.

He sent this message despite the misgivings of his own generals. Brooke thought that Churchill was magnifying the importance of the capture of Rhodes out of all proportion to its real military significance. He had 'set his heart on capturing this one island even at the expense of endangering his relations with the President and the Americans and the future of the Italian campaign'.[8]

Roosevelt replied that he understood the difficulties the British forces faced in the eastern Aegean but he had to give priority to success in Italy. He was against any Balkan campaign or a precarious amphibious operation against Rhodes without any means to follow through. Roosevelt declined to have Marshall join in what would in effect be a meeting of the Combined Chiefs of Staff in North Africa in which the President himself could not participate.

Churchill had to cancel his journey. The Germans, meanwhile, were reinforcing their troops in southern Italy to fight a major battle south of Rome. Churchill concluded that if he had to submit, it was wasteful not to do so with the best grace possible: 'when so many grave issues were pending I could not risk any jar in my personal relationship with the President'. He acknowledged that in view of the German reinforcements in Italy, the Allies could not undertake an attack on Rhodes. But he feared that without help, the fate of the British garrison on Leros was sealed. Alexander was told to 'try to save what we can from the wreck'. Churchill commented: 'The American staff had enforced their view: the price had now to be paid by the British.' The British brigade on Leros was attacked by German parachutists and forced to surrender. This episode, Churchill wrote, gave rise to 'the most acute difference I ever had with General Eisenhower'.[9]

While the Germans poured reinforcements into southern Italy, the Allies were sending eight of their best divisions back to England to prepare for Overlord. On 24 October, the Prime Minister telegraphed to General Marshall that he felt in his marrow the withdrawal of the two best British divisions 'from the very edge of the battle of Rome in the interests of distant Overlord. We are carrying out our contract, but I pray God it does not cost us dear.' Marshall replied that he believed that Eisenhower had adequate troops to fight in Italy, given the overwhelming Allied superiority in aircraft. In November, Churchill secured a delay in the withdrawal of landing craft from the Mediterranean to Britain. Churchill contended that there was no question of going back on Overlord. 'The utmost I asked for was an easement, if necessary, of two months – i.e. from some time in May 1944 to some time in July.'[10]

8

'THIS IS MUCH THE GREATEST THING WE HAVE EVER ATTEMPTED'

FOLLOWING THE QUEBEC Conference, Churchill and Roosevelt intensified their efforts to get Stalin to agree to a meeting of the three heads of government. On 20 October 1943, Churchill telegraphed to Eden in Moscow that the plans for Overlord seemed to him to have very grave defects. Unless there was a German collapse, Hitler could concentrate forty to fifty divisions against the invading force. Churchill did not think the Allies should cross the Channel with less than forty divisions available by the sixtieth day and then only if the Italian front were in strong action against the enemy: 'I do not accept the American argument that our metropolitan airforce can flatten everything out in the battle zone or on its approaches.' He warned against being committed to a 'lawyers' bargain' to undertake the invasion in May, 'for the sake of which we may have to sacrifice the Italian front and Balkan possibilities' and yet have insufficient forces to maintain the invasion of France.

As his worries increased about the Italian campaign, Churchill telegraphed again to Eden:

> The reason why we are getting into this jeopardy is because we are moving some of our best divisions and a large proportion of vital landing craft from the Mediterranean in order to build up for Overlord, seven months hence. This is what happens when battles are governed

> by lawyers' agreements made in all good faith months before, and
> persisted in without regard to the ever-changing fortunes of war.

Churchill said that he would not allow the campaign in Italy to be 'cast
away and end in a frightful disaster, for the sake of crossing the Channel
in May'. Three days later, he reassured Eden that there was no question
of abandoning Overlord, but there might have to be some postponement.
Eden had a difficult time with the Russians in consequence.

Eden was in Moscow for a conference with Molotov and the US Secretary of State, Cordell Hull, to prepare for a summit meeting. Hull insisted
on making the journey himself even though he was seventy-two years
old, in very poor health and had never before flown in an aeroplane.
Robert Murphy, serving at the time as the US representative in Algiers,
was astonished to find Hull 'almost mystical in his approach'. His utter
certainty that it would be possible to establish a lasting friendship with
Stalin after the war led him to make a utopian presentation to Congress
on his return: 'There will no longer be need for spheres of influence, for
alliances, for balance of power, or any of the other special arrangements
through which, in the unhappy past, the nations strove to safeguard their
security or to promote their interests.'[1]

On 26 September, Churchill had written to Hopkins that there was a lot
of talk in the press about Marshall becoming Commander-in-Chief with
authority over all the forces in the West. Churchill reminded Hopkins that
the agreement was that Marshall should command Overlord: he would not
have authority over other operations. Churchill told Dill in Washington
that he would never agree to putting both Overlord and the Mediterranean command under a US Commander-in-Chief: 'Such an arrangement
would not be conformable to the principle of equal status which must be
maintained among the great Allies.' The British, he pointed out, had done
far more of the fighting and had suffered much higher casualties in the
Mediterranean than the Americans.

Churchill urged on Roosevelt the need to concert their plans for Overlord before a summit with the Russians. But, Churchill commented, 'there
was emerging a strong current of opinion in American government circles
which seemed to wish to win Russian confidence even at the expense of
co-ordinating the Anglo-American war effort'.[2] Churchill pointed out to
Roosevelt that the Russians ought not to be vexed if they concerted their

plans for 1944 on fronts where no Russian troops would be involved. 'My dear friend, this is much the greatest thing we have ever attempted, and I am not satisfied that we have yet taken the measures necessary to give it the best chance of success.'

Roosevelt suggested that they might meet in North Africa and should invite Molotov to join their meeting. Roosevelt also proposed that Stalin should be invited to send a Russian military representative to sit in at the British–American military staff conferences. The idea of including a Soviet representative in these meetings filled Churchill with alarm, as he told Roosevelt on 27 October:

> He would simply bay for an earlier Second Front and block all other discussions. Considering they tell us nothing of their own movements, I do not think we should open this door to them ... I regard our right to sit together on the movements of our own two forces as fundamental and vital. Hitherto we have prospered wonderfully, but I now feel that the year 1944 is loaded with danger. Great differences may develop between us and we may take the wrong turning ... The only hope is the intimacy and friendship which has been established between us and between our High Staffs. If that were broken I should despair of the immediate future ... I am more anxious about the campaign of 1944 than about any other in which I have been involved.

Churchill insisted that the British and American Chiefs of Staff must work out their plans before meeting the Russians. But Roosevelt still was saying that 'it would be a terrible mistake if Uncle Joe thought we had ganged up on him on military action'. He continued to want Molotov and a Russian military representative to be present in Cairo. Churchill replied: 'His Majesty's Government cannot abandon their rights to full and frank discussions with you and your officers about the vital business of our inter-mingled armies. A Soviet observer cannot possibly be admitted to the intimate conversations which our own Chiefs of Staff must have.'

The danger was averted by Roosevelt's invitation to Chiang Kai-shek also to be present in Egypt. This caused the Russians to decline. On 22 November 1943, Churchill went to the airport to welcome Roosevelt on his arrival in Cairo. The British and American Chiefs of Staff met in a hotel opposite the Pyramids. The President was closeted in conferences with Chiang Kai-shek. Roosevelt, in spite of Churchill's arguments, promised the Chinese amphibious operations across the Bay of Bengal. Churchill told the British Chiefs of Staff that this was out of the question. But it was not until after their return from Tehran that he was able to prevail on Roosevelt to retract his promise.

Churchill's memorandum for the conference noted the divergences of view between the British and American Chiefs of Staff. His paper was intended as an indictment of what he saw as the mismanagement of operations in the Mediterranean. It complained about the diversion of British forces from Italy to the United Kingdom, the failure to support the partisans in Yugoslavia and the abandonment of the eastern Aegean, which he attributed to the shadow of Overlord. The decision to give priority to that operation, he contended, had been maintained with inflexible rigidity. This would continue to enfeeble the Mediterranean campaign and prejudice the position in the Balkans.

The Americans made their proposal for one overall Supreme Commander in charge of all Allied forces in the West. The British Chiefs of Staff opposed the idea and on the following day Churchill put in his own paper rejecting the proposal. 'The principle which should be followed as far as possible between Allies of equal status is that the command in any theatre should go to the ally who has the largest forces deployed or about to be deployed there.'[3] He handed the paper to Roosevelt before they left for Tehran.

None of these differences affected their personal relations. On Thanksgiving Day, 25 November, Roosevelt invited Churchill and his daughter, Sarah, to join him at dinner in his villa. Two enormous turkeys were brought in to be carved by the President:

> We had a pleasant and peaceful feast ... Speeches were made of warm intimate friendship. For a couple of hours we cast care aside ... Dance music – from gramophone records – began to play. Sarah was the only woman present, and she had her work cut out, so I danced with 'Pa' Watson [Roosevelt's trusted old friend and aide] to the delight of his chief, who watched us from the sofa.[4]

Roosevelt said that Thanksgiving was a family festival. Britain and America formed a family more united than ever before. According to the US record, 'the Prime Minister responded in his usual masterful and inspiring manner'. But in the military talks, the US Chiefs of Staff felt certain that whenever Churchill started talking about Rhodes or 'veering towards the right' from northern Italy, he was resuming his advocacy of strategic diversions in the Balkans and away from northern France. They prepared themselves for battles in Tehran in which the Americans and Russians would form a united front.

———————

On their arrival in Tehran, Molotov insisted that, for reasons of security, President Roosevelt should move to a villa inside the Soviet embassy compound. Churchill was a couple of hundred yards away in the British Legation.

In his memoirs Churchill noted that it had become a legend in America that he strove to prevent the cross-Channel landings and to lure the Allies into an invasion of the Balkans. In fact it was now agreed that Overlord should be launched in May or June or at the latest in early July and that the Allied forces in southern Italy must be supported in their efforts to capture Rome. Churchill claimed that he was not opposed at this time to a landing in the South of France, but he preferred an attack from northern Italy through the Ljubljana Gap towards Vienna. He argued that operations in the Eastern Mediterranean could bring Turkey into the war on the side of the Allies:

> This was the triple theme which I pressed upon the President and Stalin on every occasion, not hesitating to repeat the argument remorselessly. I could have gained Stalin, but the President was oppressed by the prejudice of his military advisers ... Our American friends were comforted in their obstinacy by the thought that 'at any rate we have stopped Churchill entangling us in the Balkans'.[5]

In a private meeting with Stalin, Roosevelt referred to his support for self-government in the colonial territories in Asia. But he cautioned Stalin against bringing up the problems of India with Churchill. Stalin agreed that this was undoubtedly a sore subject.

The first plenary session was held at the Soviet embassy on 28 November, with Roosevelt presiding. He welcomed the Russians as 'new members of the family circle'. He said that he believed that the three nations represented could work together in close cooperation not only for the duration of the war but for generations to come.

Roosevelt described the plans for Overlord. He told Stalin that the English Channel was a disagreeable bit of water that was unsafe for military operations before the month of May. Churchill interjected that the British people had every reason in the past to be thankful that the Channel was such a disagreeable bit of water. Churchill said that it was planned to land a million men in France in May to July 1944. The initial force for Overlord would consist of nineteen American and sixteen British divisions. After the initial battles, the reinforcements would have to come from the United States. The main bottleneck remained the shortage of landing craft.

Churchill sought, unsuccessfully, to get Russian support for Allied operations in the Eastern Mediterranean. Roosevelt wanted no delay to Overlord. Stalin observed that Italy was not a suitable jumping-off ground for the invasion of Germany. Churchill concluded the meeting by saying that, 'although we were all great friends, it would be idle for us to delude ourselves that we saw eye to eye on all matters'.

The formal conferences between Roosevelt, Stalin and Churchill were interspersed with conversations over lunch and dinner. Churchill observed to Stalin that Britain had declared war because of Poland. But he had given no pledges about frontiers. He wanted Stalin to tell him what was necessary for the defence of Russia. Churchill suggested that Poland 'might move westwards', at the expense of Germany.

On the morning of the second day, as he knew that Stalin and Roosevelt had already had a private conversation, Churchill suggested that he and the President might lunch together before the second plenary. Roosevelt declined, sending Harriman to explain that he did not want Stalin to know that he and Churchill were meeting privately. Roosevelt instead had a further meeting with Stalin and Molotov.[6]

In the conference, Stalin asked who would command Overlord. Roosevelt explained that this had not yet been decided, though General Morgan had done much of the planning.

Stalin was adamant that Overlord must not be delayed beyond May. Churchill replied that he did not consider that the possibilities in the

Mediterranean should be cast aside merely to save a month or so in the launching of Overlord. He reminded Stalin of the conditions necessary for the success of the invasion. To reduce the German forces available to counter it, the Allies had to tie down German divisions in Italy.

In the staff talks, Marshal Voroshilov asked General Brooke point blank if he attached the same importance to Overlord as General Marshall. Brooke said that he did, but added that he knew how strong the German defences in northern France were and that, under certain circumstances, Overlord could fail. Stalin posed a direct question to Churchill: 'Do the Prime Minister and British staff really believe in Overlord?' Churchill said that provided the conditions laid down were fulfilled, 'it will be our stern duty to hurl across the Channel against the Germans every sinew of our strength'.[7]

One of the methods Roosevelt used to try to gain Stalin's confidence was to distance himself ostentatiously from Churchill, as he reported to Frances Perkins:

> Winston got red and scowled, and the more he did so, the more Stalin smiled. Finally, Stalin broke out into a deep, hearty guffaw, and for the first time in three days I saw light. I kept it up until Stalin was laughing with me, and it was then that I called him 'Uncle Joe'. He would have thought me fresh the day before, but that day he laughed and came over and shook my hand. From that time on our relations were personal … The ice was broken and we talked like men and brothers.[8]

30 November was Churchill's sixty-ninth birthday. It started badly. The fact that Roosevelt was in private contact with Stalin and staying at the Soviet embassy, and that he had avoided seeing Churchill alone since they left Cairo, 'in spite of our hitherto close relations and the way in which our vital affairs were interwoven', led Churchill to seek a personal interview with Stalin. He told him that the idea that Churchill and the British Chiefs of Staff wanted to stop Overlord and operate instead in the Balkans was false. Overlord depended on the availability of landing craft. He would have to talk Roosevelt out of his commitment to operations in the Bay of Bengal. There were more British troops than Americans in the Mediterranean and they must remain in action against the enemy. Overlord would

certainly take place provided the Germans did not bring into France larger forces than the Americans and British could gather there. Stalin said that he would attack in the spring: Germany would have no troops for France. In the conference, General Brooke said that the US and British Chiefs of Staff were recommending Overlord for May, in conjunction with an operation in southern France. Roosevelt said that they would shortly appoint a Supreme Commander.

Churchill claimed the right to be the host at dinner that night. His was the longest established of the three governments. 'I might have added, but did not, that we had been longest in the war.' And it was his birthday. This last argument was conclusive. On Churchill's right sat Roosevelt, on his left, Stalin. 'Together we controlled a large preponderance of the naval and three-quarters of all the air forces in the world, and could direct armies of nearly twenty millions of men, engaged in the most terrible of wars.'

Hopkins made a speech in which he said that he had made a long and full study of the British constitution, which was not written, and of the War Cabinet, whose powers were not defined. As a result of his study he had learned that the British Constitution and the powers of the War Cabinet were 'just whatever Winston Churchill wants them to be at any given moment'. This was greeted with general hilarity, though Churchill denied it. When Roosevelt proposed the health of General Brooke, Stalin implied that Brooke had failed to show friendship towards the Red Army. Brooke made a tough and dignified reply, mollifying Stalin and delighting Churchill: 'I went to bed tired out and content, feeling that good had been done. It certainly was a happy birthday for me.'[9]

At a further meeting on 1 December, Stalin said that he was not prepared to deal with the Polish government in exile. He would like to see Germany split up after the war. Roosevelt agreed, but Churchill said that if the various provinces of Germany were split up, they would still want to reunite.

By the conference's end, the exhausted Roosevelt was finding Churchill's tireless advocacy of his own projects taxing of his patience. The Americans, for their part, had attained one of their main objectives at Tehran: Stalin had promised that the Soviet Union would declare war on Japan the moment Germany was defeated.

On their way back, Churchill and Roosevelt stopped briefly in Cairo to review the results of their discussions with Stalin. Churchill continued to agonise about the invasion of Normandy. A million Americans were to be thrown in and 500,000 to 600,000 British: 'Terrific battles were to be expected, on a scale far greater than anything that we had experienced before.' Roosevelt left for Tunis to tell Eisenhower of his appointment as Supreme Commander of Overlord. He warned Eisenhower that in London he would be surrounded by the full panoply of the British government and the powerful personality of Churchill, who still believed, in Roosevelt's view, that only through the failure of a frontal attack across the Channel could the Allies lose the war. In his broadcast on Christmas Eve, Roosevelt described Stalin as combining 'relentless determination with a stalwart good humour ... I believe that we are going to get along very well with him – and the Russian people – very well indeed.'

9

'EVEN SPLENDID VICTORIES AND WIDENING OPPORTUNITIES DO NOT BRING US TOGETHER ON STRATEGY'

ON HIS RETURN to England to prepare for the invasion of Normandy, Eisenhower became a regular visitor to Chequers, dining and watching films with Churchill and talking often until the small hours. For the British ground forces commander in northern Europe he wanted Alexander, but accepted Montgomery when Churchill insisted on keeping Alexander in Italy. By 1944, his relations with Churchill were such that he could disagree violently with the Prime Minister on issues of strategy without this affecting their personal friendship.

He got on even better with his courageous and attractive English driver, Kay Summersby, who became his near-inseparable companion throughout the war. According to Harry Truman, Eisenhower told General Marshall of his intention to leave his wife and marry Miss Summersby, only to receive a crushing reply. In her book, *Past Forgetting*, written when Eisenhower was dead and she was dying, Summersby describes their unconsummated affair.

Eisenhower had dozens of major and hundreds of minor disagreements with Churchill and the British Service Chiefs during the war, threatening on one occasion to resign unless he was given command over the strategic air forces. This provoked a clash with Air Chief Marshal Sir Arthur Harris, who, as Brooke noted, 'told us how he might well have won the war if it had not been for the handicap imposed by the existence of the two other Services'. But the US and British headquarters staff were interlocking – at officer level, there were 1,600 Americans and 1,229 British – and Eisenhower made clear that he would tolerate no denigration of British efforts by the Americans.

At the beginning of 1944, Churchill still was deeply worried about the wisdom of a cross-Channel attack, saying to Eisenhower: 'When I think of the beaches of Normandy choked with the flower of American and British youth ... I have my doubts.' Churchill himself recalls that although now committed to Overlord: 'I was not convinced that this was the only way of winning the war ... The fearful price we had had to pay in human life and blood for the great offensives of the First World War was graven on my mind.' But Churchill was encouraged by Montgomery's optimism about the chances of success. Montgomery had insisted that the initial assault must be by five divisions and on a broader front than the three-division landing envisaged in earlier plans. On 11 March, Churchill wrote to reassure Marshall that he was 'hardening very much on this operation'. As the time of the invasion approached, he became his usual inspirational self. Churchill wanted to observe the landings from a British cruiser. When Eisenhower objected, Churchill replied that four-fifths of the naval forces involved were British and no one could prevent him embarking on a British ship. It was only when the King intervened that Churchill gave way.[1]

On the eve of the invasion, Churchill had a stormy meeting with de Gaulle. Brought from Algiers to be told of the invasion plans, de Gaulle said that the administration of liberated France should have been settled long before. Churchill advised him to visit Washington, which he declined to do. Churchill reminded him that the British and Americans were about to risk the lives of scores of thousands of men to liberate France. If there was a split between him and the United States, Churchill would almost certainly side with the Americas. De Gaulle replied that he quite understood that if the United States and France disagreed, Britain would side with the Americans. On this note their meeting ended.[2]

It was to Eisenhower that it fell to take the most difficult military decision of the entire war – whether to proceed with the invasion on which the liberation of Europe depended, despite adverse weather conditions, on Tuesday 6 June. Montgomery's advice was unequivocal: 'I would say – Go!'

Montgomery had command over the Allied invasion force, including the US First Army under General Bradley. On the left flank of the Allied landings, Montgomery had hoped to take Caen on the first day but still had not done so by the end of June. As the Germans concentrated their armour in front of Caen, the hoped-for break-out in that sector was never achieved. Montgomery succeeded in defeating a series of German counter-attacks. But he was loath to engage in repeated frontal assaults, declaring that his strategy was to hold the German armoured divisions on his left flank while Bradley broke out on the right.

By this point the Allies had thirty divisions ashore – half of them American, half British and Canadian. Eisenhower was pinning his hopes for a break-out on Bradley. But what he asked for was an all-out attack along the entire Allied line. Brooke concluded that Eisenhower had only the very vaguest conception of war. He appeared to have 'some conception of attacking on the whole front, which must be an American doctrine'. Eisenhower correctly observed that there was nothing so wrong that a good victory would not cure.

On 27 July, Montgomery reported that the main enemy army strength was deployed on his front, but the Americans were making rapid progress to the West. Eisenhower recorded that 'without the great sacrifices made by the Anglo-Canadian armies in the brutal, slogging battles for Caen and Falaise these spectacular advances made elsewhere by the Allied forces could never have come about'. General Bedell Smith doubted if Overlord could have been accomplished without Montgomery: 'it was his sort of battle'. By early August, Bradley and Patton had achieved the break-out that led on 24 August to the liberation of Paris.[3]

Churchill still had his doubts about the invasion of southern France (Anvil). Many of the troops would have to come from the Allied forces in Italy. Churchill and Alexander still wanted to aim for an offensive towards Vienna from northern Italy through the Ljubljana Gap. The British Chiefs of Staff argued that the diversion of forces to southern France would hamstring Alexander's operations in Italy. Eisenhower considered that Allied resources did not permit them to sustain two major campaigns in the European theatre.

Churchill appealed to Roosevelt. He wanted to help Eisenhower. 'But we do not think this necessarily involves the complete ruin of all our great affairs in the Mediterranean, and we take it hard that this should be demanded of us.'

The President's reply, as Churchill commented, was prompt and adverse. He was determined to stick to the strategy agreed at Tehran. Stalin favoured Anvil and Roosevelt declared that he could not abandon the operation without consulting him. The Allies would still have sufficient forces to maintain pressure on the Germans in northern Italy. Roosevelt insisted that three US and two French divisions should be withdrawn from Italy for the invasion. He was opposed to any plans for an attack through the Ljubljana Gap and would not agree to the employment of any US forces for that purpose. He would, he said, never survive a setback to Overlord if it were known that forces had been diverted to the Balkans.[4]

Roosevelt suggested at one point that they should lay their respective cases before Stalin. Stalin, commented Churchill, seemed likely to prefer that central and southern Europe should fall naturally under his control. Churchill replied that he was 'deeply grieved' by Roosevelt's telegram. The decision to proceed with the invasion of southern France and to abandon a major offensive in Italy was in his 'humble and respectful opinion, the first major strategic and political error' of the war.

On 5 August, Churchill was still arguing with Eisenhower that the forces for the invasion of southern France should be switched to Brittany. Eisenhower argued so long and patiently that he was 'practically limp' by the time Churchill left and observed that, although he had said 'no' in every language, the Prime Minister simply returned to the charge. This he did again on the following day, writing to Harry Hopkins: 'I am grieved to find that even splendid victories and widening opportunities do not bring us together on strategy.' He described himself as 'bowing to the United States' Chiefs of Staff under recorded protest and the over-riding of our views'. Hopkins, unsurprisingly, regarded it as impossible at this stage to switch the invading forces to Brittany, a reply confirmed by Roosevelt on 8 August. Churchill replied to the President: 'I pray God you may be right.'

————————

On 18 May, the Soviet ambassador in London called at the Foreign Office to discuss the suggestion Eden had made to the Russians that they should temporarily regard Romanian affairs as mainly their concern, while leaving Greece to the British. The Russians were prepared to accept this, but wanted to know if the Americans had been consulted. Churchill reported the suggestion to Roosevelt in a message on 31 May, emphasising that the agreement would apply only to wartime conditions.

Cordell Hull was horrified. Churchill observed to Halifax in Washington that the Russians would anyway have to deal with the Romanians and Bulgarians, as their armies were approaching their territory. Roosevelt accepted the military realities, but opposed Churchill's idea because the tendency for influence to extend beyond the military field would be strengthened by an agreement of the type proposed. Churchill was not prepared to take no for an answer. The British, he argued, would have to take firm action to help establish a democratic government in Greece.

On 13 June, Roosevelt replied, reluctantly acquiescing but adding that they 'must be careful to make it clear that we are not establishing any post-war spheres of influence'. Eden confirmed to the Russians British acceptance of this 'division of responsibility'. Roosevelt declared himself disturbed that the British had only raised the matter with him after it had been put to the Russians. Churchill, in reply, referred to a message Roosevelt had sent to Stalin about Poland 'of which as yet I have heard nothing from you'. In Greece and Yugoslavia, he added, he was struggling to bring order out of chaos. 'I am keeping you constantly informed, and I hope to have your confidence and help within the sphere of action in which initiative is assigned to us.'

Churchill now decided to visit Italy. In mid-August, near the island of Ischia, he encountered an enormous US troop convoy sailing for the landings on the Riviera: 'All the ships were crowded with men, and as we passed along their lines they cheered enthusiastically. They did not know that if I had had my way they would be sailing in quite a different direction.'[5] Churchill witnessed the landings in the bay of St Tropez from a British warship. The invading forces met little resistance and advanced rapidly up the Rhone Valley. Churchill still was unconvinced of the value of the operation. It had not, he believed, helped Overlord. It drew no enemy forces down from Normandy. It was, rather, Eisenhower's forces that had drawn the Germans away from Anvil. Once the final decision was taken, Churchill claimed to have given the operation his full support 'though I had done my best to constrain or deflect it'.

On 17 August, Churchill telegraphed to Roosevelt about Greece. The Greek people, he said, must have the opportunity to decide between a monarchy and a republic once tranquillity had been restored: 'I do not expect you will relish any more than I do the prospect either of chaos or street fighting or of a tyrannical Communist government being set up.' Churchill intended to send several thousand British troops to Athens as soon as the Germans withdrew. Roosevelt agreed to this plan. Churchill was determined to help the Papandreou government establish itself against the Communists.

On 28 August, Churchill again complained to Roosevelt about the 'great weakening of our armies in Italy', due to the landings in southern France. He considered that this was responsible for Alexander's inability to push the Germans out of the Po Valley. As a result 'the right-handed drive to Vienna was denied to us and, except in Greece, our military power to liberate the eastern part of South Eastern Europe was gone'.

At the same time, Churchill was sending urgent messages to Roosevelt about the Russian refusal to permit American or British aircraft to help the Polish insurrection in Warsaw. He persuaded the President to join him in sending a joint appeal to Stalin. Stalin replied, rejecting any assistance to 'the group of criminals who have embarked on the Warsaw adventure in order to seize power'. Churchill tried to persuade Roosevelt to send a further joint message, but the President refused: 'I do not consider it would prove advantageous to the long-range general war prospects for me to join with you in the proposed message to Stalin.' On 5 September, he told Churchill that the problem of relief for the Poles in Warsaw had 'unfortunately been solved by delay and by German action, and there now appears to be nothing we can do to assist them'.

———————

On the same day, Churchill sailed from the Clyde in the *Queen Mary* for a further meeting with Roosevelt in Quebec. He wanted to discuss how Britain could contribute to the war against Japan:

> What I feared most at this stage of the war was that the United States would say in after-years, 'we came to your help in Europe and you left us alone to finish off Japan'. We had to regain in the field of battle our rightful positions in the Far East and not have them handed back to us at the peace table.[6]

The meeting between the Prime Minister and the President had been preceded by another of equal importance. In the British Treasury, Keynes, from an early stage of the war, was worried about the acute balance of payments difficulties Britain and other countries would face after it and the danger that these could generate a new wave of protectionism. He devised the idea of a Clearing Union to help ease the necessary adjustments. Simultaneously, US Treasury Secretary Morgenthau's deputy, Harry Dexter White, with similar preoccupations, was developing the idea of a Stabilisation Fund and an International Bank. Their respective ideas began to be exchanged in July 1942. The British side accepted the basic structure of the White plan.

In September 1943, Keynes visited Washington for the crucial discussions with the Americans. He and White were soon engaged in an 'open clash of will and personality'. Keynes at times infuriated the Americans with his barbed and disparaging remarks and displays of intellectual virtuosity, causing White on one occasion to address him with bitter irony as 'Your Royal Highness'.[7] White was so sympathetic to the Soviet Union that he was regarded by the KGB as, with Alger Hiss, the principal Soviet agent of influence in Washington. Yet, to Keynes, he appeared a far more conservative economist. Despite their personal clashes, White and Keynes had a respect for one another, but White represented the stronger power. At the end of their conference, Keynes complained at the Americans' refusal to initial the documents ('I doubt if anyone has ever seen Harry White's initials'). But they had reached agreement on the Bank and the Fund.

In July 1944 the product of their discussions was endorsed by the other major nations in the conference at Bretton Woods in New Hampshire. In Roy Harrod's words: 'The International Monetary Fund and the International Bank were the products of English and American brains, with valuable help from the Canadians.' The British would have preferred their headquarters not to be in America, but were told by Dean Acheson that they would have to give way on this if the legislation was to get through Congress.

Meeting Roosevelt in Quebec on 13 September 1944, Churchill reluctantly acknowledged the success of Anvil. He pointed out that Britain and the dominions still had as many divisions engaged in France and Italy as the Americans. He offered the participation of the British Far East fleet in operations against Japan. He also wanted the RAF to participate in the bombing of Japan despite the refuelling difficulties that would entail. He reported to Attlee that the conference had opened in a 'blaze of friendship'.

Churchill raised again his ambitions for Alexander's army to break out towards Vienna, emphasising the 'rapid encroachment of the Russians into the Balkan peninsula and the dangerous spread of Soviet influence there'. But as Roosevelt made clear to Robert Murphy at the time, he took a different view of Soviet intentions. He was confident that a permanent Soviet–American understanding could be reached. He urged Murphy to bear in mind that the primary US postwar objective was Soviet–American cooperation, without which world peace would be impossible, and he wanted the occupation of Germany to be arranged in such a way as to convince the Russians that the United States really desired to cooperate with them.

Churchill had misgivings about the ambitions of Henry Morgenthau, the US Treasury Secretary, to restrict German industry after the war. He remembered the damage inflicted on the German economy by reparations after the First World War. The idea of trying to 'pastoralize' Germany seemed to him impractical.[8]

Churchill travelled on from Quebec with his wife and daughter Mary to visit Roosevelt at Hyde Park. Churchill and Roosevelt had a further discussion about the atomic bomb. The British by now were very much junior partners in 'Tube Alloys', rechristened by the Americans the Manhattan Project, the entire industrial development of which was taking place in the United States. As more British nuclear scientists moved to America, work on the project in Britain virtually closed down. Professor Chadwick, head of the British atomic energy mission in Washington, was supposed to be the only British nuclear scientist with full knowledge of all aspects of the Manhattan Project, though a British scientific team, including the atom spy Klaus Fuchs, by now were working at the most sensitive facility of all at Los Alamos. Chadwick had succeeded in winning the confidence – not easily given – of General Groves, who managed the project for the War Department. The British still were not convinced that a nuclear weapon could be produced by mid-1945, an attitude Groves regarded as defeatist.

Churchill reported to his colleagues in London that he and Roosevelt had initialled at Hyde Park an agreement establishing the basis for indefinite collaboration after the war. A telegram went back: 'Well done indeed.' The aide-memoire agreed between them at Hyde Park stated that full collaboration between the United States and Britain in developing 'Tube Alloys' for military and commercial purposes should continue after the defeat of Japan 'unless and until terminated by joint agreement'. The suggestion that the world should be informed about 'Tube Alloys', with a view to an international agreement concerning its control and use, was not accepted. Churchill and Roosevelt agreed that the project should be carried forward in the greatest secrecy. Conscious of the immense difficulty of finally defeating the Japanese through an invasion of Japan, they further agreed that when a bomb was finally available, 'it might perhaps, after mature consideration, be used against the Japanese, who should be warned that this bombardment will be repeated until they surrender'.

Churchill left Hyde Park satisfied. But none of those responsible for the project in Washington were aware of this agreement until April 1945, after Roosevelt died. They had to ask the British to let them know what was in it. President Roosevelt's copy eventually was found years later in the files of his naval aide. Someone, seeing the title 'Tube Alloys', had concluded that it dealt with naval supplies.[9]

————

Churchill now decided to visit Moscow to see Stalin. He did not consider that Romania and Bulgaria merited any special sacrifices, but he was concerned about Poland and Greece. In the main, he noted, these feelings were shared by the Americans, 'but they were very slow in realising the upsurge of Communist influence'. Roosevelt encouraged Churchill to meet Stalin. As the questions discussed would be of concern to the United States, he instructed Averell Harriman to participate as his observer.

Churchill was still asking Roosevelt to consider diverting two or three American divisions to the Italian front. In reply, Roosevelt pointed out that in Italy their combined efforts to date had cost them nearly 200,000 battle casualties, 90,000 of them American. Eisenhower, meanwhile, was fighting the decisive battle of Germany with divisions that had been in continuous combat since they landed in Normandy in early June.

Meeting Stalin in Moscow on 10 October, Churchill got straight down to business. He proposed that they should settle affairs in the Balkans. The Russian Army was in Romania and Bulgaria. He suggested that the Russians should have 90 per cent predominance in Romania, Britain should have 90 per cent of the say in Greece, and that there should be a 50/50 split in Yugoslavia and Hungary. Churchill wrote these percentages out on a scrap of paper. He realised that it might be thought rather scandalous if they were seen to have 'disposed of these issues so fateful to millions of people in such an off-hand manner'. He proposed that they should burn the paper. Stalin said that Churchill should keep it.[10]

Churchill tried in vain to get Stalin to accept the need for a broad-based Polish government, including the government in exile in London, as well as Stalin's own puppet regime.

———————

To forestall a Communist takeover in Greece, Churchill pressed ahead with plans for British forces to occupy Athens and its airfield as the Germans withdrew. On 3 December 1944, Communist supporters clashed with the Athens police and the Greek civil war began. The British commander, General Scobie, ordered the Communists to evacuate Athens. On learning that the Communists had captured most of the police stations in the capital, murdering many of their occupants, Churchill ordered Scobie and the 5,000 British troops he had despatched to Athens to open fire as necessary. It was, he observed, 'no use doing things like this by halves'.

On 5 December, Churchill told Scobie that he should neutralise or destroy all Communist bands approaching the city. He must seek to act with the authority of Papandreou and his colleagues:

> Do not, however, hesitate to act as if you were in a conquered city where a local rebellion is in progress ... We have to hold and dominate Athens. It would be a great thing for you to succeed in this without bloodshed if possible, but also with bloodshed if necessary.

The British actions were strongly criticised in the American press and by the State Department, which was urging non-interference by outside powers in the politics both of Italy and of Greece. Churchill told Roosevelt what he thought of this public rebuke. Within a few days, the American press had got hold of Churchill's message to Scobie. The leak came from the State Department.

US newspapers were suggesting that British troops were killing Greek patriots who had been fighting the Germans and were using lend-lease weapons for the purpose. A furious Churchill telephoned Hopkins on 10 December about a decision by Admiral King not to permit American ships to transfer war supplies to the British forces in Greece. Churchill was aware that his telephone call was insecure. But even if it was overheard, he told Hopkins, what could be worse than supplies being cut off and an open breach between Britain and the United States? Hopkins got the order rescinded.[11] There was great indignation in Whitehall at this holier-than-thou attitude on the part of the Americans, who were not themselves in a position to do anything about Greece.

Churchill told Hopkins: 'I consider that we have a right to the President's support in the policy we are following.' But, on 13 December, Roosevelt expressed his concern 'as a loyal friend and ally'. He wanted to help, he said, but there were limitations imposed by the traditional policies of the United States and the adverse reactions of public opinion. For these reasons it had not been possible for the US government to support the British action.

Roosevelt claimed to be distressed at this state of affairs but, as Churchill commented, this did not give him any practical help. Churchill replied, pointing out how serious it would be if the British withdrew and the result was a massacre and a Communist regime in Athens: 'the fact that you are supposed to be against us has added, as I feared, to our difficulties and burdens'.

Hopkins warned Churchill that US opinion was deteriorating rapidly. The President would have to state unequivocally his determination to do all he could to seek a free and secure world. Churchill noted sardonically that they all were agreed on this aim, but the question was whether it could be achieved by allowing the Communists to seize power in Athens. A major bone of contention was the US suspicion that Churchill's main interest was in trying to re-establish the monarchy. Churchill observed that within two years the State Department, overwhelmingly supported by US opinion, would itself be making strenuous efforts to defeat the Communist insurrection in Greece. That Greece escaped the fate of Czechoslovakia, in Churchill's view, was due to the British action in December 1944.[12]

Churchill flew with Eden to Athens on Christmas Day to deal with the situation there himself. He convened a meeting of the Greek political leaders, including the Communists. They settled on a regency under the Archbishop, pending a referendum, and persuaded the King of Greece to acquiesce. Roosevelt wished him success in resolving the Greek problem 'which seems very promising as a result of your journey'. Churchill continued to complain about the portrait being painted in the American press of the Communists as champions of democracy fighting against the British backing the royal cause.

10

'IKE AND I WERE POLES APART WHEN IT CAME TO THE CONDUCT OF THE WAR'

FROM D-DAY ON, sharp disagreements, exacerbated by the difference of personalities, developed between Eisenhower and Montgomery, a singularly insubordinate commander, over strategy throughout the subsequent fighting in northern Europe.

The two could hardly have been more dissimilar. Eisenhower was gregarious; Montgomery liked isolation. Montgomery handed down his directives while Eisenhower waited for general agreement among his staff. Eisenhower was modest, or at any rate affected to be. Montgomery's self-satisfaction and condescension irritated the Americans intensely.

Their very first encounter had not been auspicious. When the chain-smoking Major-General Eisenhower visited Montgomery's headquarters in southern England in May 1942, he lit a cigarette, only to be told abruptly to stop smoking. Kay Summersby recorded Eisenhower's fury as he travelled back in his car.[1] Yet his official report described Montgomery as decisive, extremely energetic and able.

More fundamentally, they disagreed about strategy and tactics. Eisenhower's military theory was straightforward. He was an advocate of the direct approach, favouring attack all along the line and putting his faith in the sheer overwhelming power of the American military machine. The British had neither the manpower nor the material resources to overwhelm the Germans and had learned in 1914–18 that it was near suicidal for them to adopt that approach. Eisenhower was accused of having a mass production mentality and, indeed, he came from a mass production society. As Montgomery wrote: 'Ike and I were poles apart when it came to the conduct of the War.' Montgomery was, in theory, responsible to Eisenhower, but constantly appealed to Brooke.

As Montgomery's 21st Army Group drove along the northern coast towards Belgium, he kept telling Eisenhower that one really full-blooded thrust towards Berlin could end the war. Eisenhower was preoccupied with serious supply problems. Montgomery wanted to be given control over the US First Army and a near monopoly of supplies to enable him to advance to Antwerp and the Ruhr. Eisenhower continued to insist on two main thrusts.

On 23 August, Eisenhower visited Montgomery's headquarters at Condé to be given a patronising lecture on strategy. Montgomery told Eisenhower that he should not 'descend into the land battle'. To appease Montgomery, Eisenhower promised him a degree of operational control over the US First Army, thereby infuriating Bradley and Patton. In response to Bradley's protests, Eisenhower rescinded his decision, to Montgomery's disgust.

By this time the Americans had twenty-two divisions in France, the British and Canadians seventeen. The Americans now felt, Brooke wrote, that they possessed the major forces at sea, on land and in the air 'in addition to the vast financial and industrial advantages they have had from the start'.[2] They naturally wanted the decisive say in the running of the war.

In public, Eisenhower continued to lavish praise on Montgomery and to defend him from charges of having been too cautious in front of Caen. But as Patton advanced beyond the Meuse, Montgomery renewed his protests that there were not enough supplies for two offensives. At a meeting in Brussels on 10 September, Montgomery launched into a tirade against Eisenhower's plans. Eisenhower considered that it was fantasy to talk of marching to Berlin with an army, most of whose supplies were still being landed on the beaches. Eisenhower wrote in his diary: 'Monty's suggestion is simple, give him everything, which is crazy.'[3]

Eisenhower continued to believe that Montgomery underestimated German resistance and that a single thrust, especially beyond the Rhine, would be subject to counter-attacks on the flanks that could destroy the leading Allied forces. Until Antwerp was secured, the Allies could not bring forward adequate supplies to sustain an army beyond the Rhine. Like

Eisenhower, Montgomery's Chief of Staff, Freddie de Guingand, well-liked by the Americans, doubted whether there would be a collapse of German morale. In the end it took the combined efforts of over a hundred Russian divisions, Montgomery's and Bradley's armies, Alexander's Italian offensive and eight months of continuous air bombardment to force German capitulation. After the war, de Guingand drily observed that he had to doubt that Montgomery could have brought about the same result with the 21st Army Group alone. His conclusion was that Eisenhower was right.

Eisenhower agreed to plans for the airborne landing at Arnhem because he wanted to get a bridgehead across the Rhine before the momentum of the offensive was lost. He took responsibility for the ensuing military disaster, though he added that what this demonstrated was the folly of the idea of one full-blooded thrust to Berlin. He kept reminding Montgomery of the imperative need to secure the approaches to Antwerp for supply purposes. Brooke concluded that Montgomery's strategy for once was at fault. 'Instead of carrying out the advance on Arnhem, he ought to have made certain of Antwerp in the first place. Ike nobly took all the blame on himself as he had approved Montgomery's suggestion to operate on Arnhem.'[4]

Eisenhower understood Montgomery's great qualities. He regarded him as having no superior in his ability to conduct a set-piece battle. But he had by now reached the limits of his patience. On 13 October, he told Montgomery that if he regarded the plan of campaign as unsatisfactory, the issue would have to be settled in the interest of future efficiency. If Montgomery felt that Eisenhower's directives were such as to endanger the success of operations, the matter would need to be referred to 'higher authority for any action they may choose to take, however drastic'.[5] Montgomery hastened to reply that Eisenhower would hear no more from him on the subject of command, signing his letter: 'Your ever devoted and loyal subordinate'.

In mid-December, the Germans launched their counter-offensive in the Ardennes. Montgomery was given command of all the forces north of the Ardennes, including the US First Army, to coordinate a counter-blow. At Bastogne, the US 101st Airborne Division was surrounded. Called on to surrender by the Germans, its commander, General McAuliffe, gave a famous reply ('Nuts!').

On 28 December 1944, Brooke wrote in his diary: 'Monty has had another interview with Ike. I do not like the account of it. It looks to me as if Monty, with his usual lack of tact, has been rubbing into Ike the results of not having listened to Monty's advice!' On the following day, Montgomery wrote to Eisenhower: 'One commander must have power to direct and control the operations; you cannot possibly do it yourself.'

Bradley and Patton threatened to resign rather than serve under Montgomery. At this stage Marshall intervened, instructing Eisenhower to make no concessions whatsoever. On 31 December, Eisenhower wrote to Montgomery: 'For my part I would deplore the development of such an unbridgeable gap of convictions between us that we would have to present our differences to the Combined Chiefs of Staff.' De Guingand warned Montgomery that Eisenhower was on the verge of asking for him to be replaced by Alexander. Montgomery cabled back: 'Very distressed that my letter may have upset you and I would ask you to tear it up.'[6]

Eisenhower was furious because an attack Montgomery had promised on 1 January 1945 was delayed and German divisions were switched south to stop Bradley's counter-attack. On 3 January, the US First Army, temporarily under Montgomery's command, began its attack. The Germans were driven out of the salient. Montgomery held a press conference to explain how he had won the Battle of the Bulge and saved the Americans. He added that the GIs made great fighting men – when given proper leadership. In fact, the US forces had done the great bulk of the fighting and the Americans believed that far more German prisoners could have been taken if Montgomery had launched his offensive earlier.

Colville noted that Montgomery's 'triumphant, jingoistic and exceedingly self-satisfied' performance had given great offence. Churchill described Montgomery's statement as 'most unfortunate'. It had a patronising tone and completely overlooked the fact that the United States had lost perhaps 80,000 men and the British 2,000–3,000. 'Through no fault of our own we have been very little engaged in this battle.' Eisenhower told him that the anger of his generals was such that he would hardly dare to order any of them again to serve under Montgomery.[7]

Churchill sought to undo what he could of the damage. He told Roosevelt that the British government had complete confidence in Eisenhower and felt acutely any attacks made on him. He congratulated Roosevelt on the extraordinary gallantry shown by the US forces at Bastogne. He referred to criticisms in the US press that British forces had been kept out of the battle, assuring the President that they were ready to respond to Eisenhower's commands. On 18 January, Churchill said in Parliament: 'I have seen it suggested that the terrific battle which has been proceeding since December 16 on the American front is an Anglo-American battle. In fact, however, the United States troops have done almost all of the fighting, and have suffered almost all the losses.'

Roosevelt and Churchill, meanwhile, were getting nowhere with their attempts to persuade Stalin to accept the return to Poland of the government in exile in London. The three leaders agreed to meet at Yalta in the Crimea. Churchill told Hopkins that if they had spent ten years on research, they could not have found a worse place in the world. He claimed that it was 'good for typhus', but felt that he could survive it with an adequate supply of whisky. Roosevelt at first opposed the idea of a prior meeting with Churchill in Malta. He said that he would have to go on by air on the same day to keep his date with Stalin. There would be no time, therefore, for talks with Churchill or British–American staff talks. Churchill protested that they must settle their military plans together before they went on to Yalta. On 21 January 1945, Hopkins flew to London to discuss the differences that had arisen over Greece, Poland and Italy. He and Churchill had very frank conversations in some of which, Hopkins reported, Churchill was volcanic in his remarks. Roosevelt was persuaded to agree to a prior meeting with Churchill in Malta.

The staff talks were marked by further disagreements about strategy. Eisenhower was planning two simultaneous attacks across the Rhine, one by US forces into southern Germany and one by Montgomery's army group in the north. The British Chiefs of Staff argued that the northern advance, under Montgomery, would be much more important and should not be weakened for the sake of the attack in the south. Churchill commented that General Bradley attributed to Montgomery much of the pressure that was brought to bear. The Americans were not to be moved and Eisenhower's view prevailed.

On the morning of 2 February, the USS *Quincy*, with the President on board, entered Valletta harbour. Churchill watched the scene from HMS

Orion. As the American cruiser steamed slowly past, he and the President waved to each other. 'With the escort of Spitfires overhead, the salutes, and the bands of the ships companies in the harbour playing "The Star-Spangled Banner" it was a splendid scene.'[8]

They lunched together on the *Quincy*. Eden noted that the President gave the impression of failing powers. That evening, they reviewed the report of the Chiefs of Staff on Eisenhower's plans for crossing the Rhine. Churchill told Roosevelt that they ought to occupy as much of Austria as possible as it was 'undesirable that more of Western Europe than necessary should be occupied by the Russians'. The impatient Eden found the dinner no more successful than lunch. He complained to Hopkins that they were going into a decisive conference without having agreed 'how to handle matters with a Bear who would certainly know his mind'.[9] The Prime Minister and President then flew in their respective planes on to the Crimea. As Roosevelt was carried from his plane on arrival, Churchill was alarmed to see him looking so frail and ill. Hopkins later told Halifax that he doubted if, at Yalta, the President had heard more than half of what went on around the table.[10]

On 4 February, Stalin called on Churchill to talk about the war in Germany and Russian operations on the Eastern Front. On the following day, the three leaders discussed the future zones of occupation in Germany. At this meeting, to Churchill's alarm, Roosevelt said that the United States would take all reasonable steps to preserve peace, but not at the expense of keeping a large army in Europe, 3,000 miles from home. He did not believe that American troops would stay in Europe much more than two years.[11] Churchill did not see how, if the Americans left, Britain could occupy most of the western part of Germany – a task far beyond the country's strength. Stalin wanted to discuss various schemes for the dismemberment of Germany.

But the main issue was Poland. It was discussed at seven of the eight plenary meetings. Poland had been the most urgent reason for the Yalta Conference and was to prove the first cause of the breakdown of the wartime alliance. Churchill and Roosevelt continued to press for a coalition between the Polish government in exile in London and the Soviet-sponsored Lublin government. They agreed to the Soviet proposal that the eastern boundary of Poland should be the Curzon line and that, in compensation, Poland should receive additional territory in the west at the expense of Germany. As Stalin promised elections in Poland, Roosevelt declared that the differences between the Western Allies and the Russians seemed to be largely a matter of words. Churchill commented that the Polish communiqué agreed at Yalta laid down in general terms a policy that, if carried out in good faith, might have preserved the wartime alliance. But Stalin never had any intention of carrying it out in good faith.

At Yalta, at a crucial moment in the conference, Hopkins passed a note to Roosevelt that 'the Russians have given in so much at this Conference that I do not think we can let them down. Let the British disagree if they want to.' This was on the issue of war reparations. Roosevelt told Stalin privately that, after the war, he thought Hong Kong should be given back to the Chinese or internationalised as a free port. He knew, he said, that Churchill would have a strong objection to this proposal. Hopkins was exalted by Yalta: '[W]e really believed in our hearts that this was the dawn of the new day we had all been praying for.' The main reservation in his mind was that they could not foretell what might ensue if anything happened to Stalin.[12]

On the way home on 15 February, Churchill had a last meeting with Roosevelt at Alexandria. Churchill explained plans for atomic weapons research in Britain after the war. 'This was the last time I saw Roosevelt. We parted affectionately. I felt he had a slender contact with life.'

As the weeks passed after Yalta, it became clear that Stalin was doing nothing to carry out the agreement about broadening the Polish government to include non-Communists or any representatives of the Polish government in exile that had been formed in London. At this critical time, Churchill observed, Roosevelt's health and strength had faded. In his long telegrams, Churchill thought he was talking to his trusted friend and colleague as he had done over the years. In reality, 'I was no longer being fully heard by him.'[13]

On 6 March, the Russians imposed a Soviet-nominated government in Romania. This was to prove the pattern of things to come. Churchill acknowledged to Roosevelt that he was hampered in his protests by the fact that he had recognised that Russia should have the predominant voice in Romania and Stalin had not interfered when the British were doing battle with the Communists in Athens.

On 13 March, Churchill telegraphed to Roosevelt that at Yalta they had agreed to take the Russian view of Poland's frontier:

> Poland has lost her frontier. Is she now to lose her freedom? ... I do not wish to reveal the divergence between the British and the United States Governments, but it would certainly be necessary to make it clear that we are in the presence of a great failure and a true break-down of what was settled at Yalta.

Roosevelt replied, claiming that there was no divergence, though he did not agree that they were as yet confronted with the breakdown of the Yalta agreement.

In his exchanges with Roosevelt, Churchill had the feeling that 'except for the occasional flashes of courage and insight, the telegrams he was sending us were not his own'. Churchill expressed the hope that the numerous telegrams he felt obliged to send were not becoming a bore to the President. He told Eden that they could not press the case against Russia beyond where they could carry the United States. 'We can now see the total hiatus which existed between the fading of President Roosevelt's strength and the growth of President Truman's grip on the vast world problem.'[14]

11

'THE GREATEST AMERICAN FRIEND WE HAVE EVER KNOWN'

ON 25 MARCH 1945, in a meeting at Montgomery's headquarters, Churchill told Eisenhower that he thought the Allied forces ought to make a definite effort to beat the Russians to Berlin and hold as much of eastern Germany as possible 'until my doubts about Russia's intentions had been cleared away'. Churchill wanted Eisenhower to start thinking less about the Germans and more about the Russians. With the full backing of his political masters in Washington, who believed firmly in the possibilities for postwar cooperation with the Soviet Union, Eisenhower resisted such a switch. Militarily, he was preoccupied with the need finally to eradicate the resistance of the *Wehrmacht* in the German redoubts in the Alps.

The diversion of Allied efforts from the race to Berlin to dealing with German resistance in the south was to become one of the great controversies of the war. Six months earlier, Eisenhower had agreed with Montgomery: 'Clearly Berlin is the main prize.' But, in March 1945, Bradley advised Eisenhower that taking Berlin would cost 100,000 casualties – 'a pretty stiff price for a prestige objective' – when, as Bradley pointed out, Allied forces would still have to withdraw as Berlin had been placed within the occupation zone assigned to the Russians.[1]

The future zones of occupation had been worked out with the Russians in the European Advisory Commission in London and endorsed by the heads of government at Yalta. The eastern limits of the British and American zones were based on an underestimate of how far the US and British forces would advance by the time of German capitulation and a corresponding overestimate of the Soviet advance. It was a remarkable example of negotiators giving away at the conference table territory to be gained at great sacrifice by their armies in the field. While the agreement guaranteed the Western Allies occupation rights in Berlin, it failed adequately to guarantee unrestricted access to the city. If the eventual lines of demarcation had been based on the territory actually occupied by the Western and Soviet armies, a large difference would have been made to the postwar history of Germany.

Montgomery was suspected by the Americans of wanting to ride into Berlin on a white charger. By this stage, Eisenhower noted: 'Montgomery had become so personal in his efforts to make sure that the Americans – and me, in particular – got no credit, that, in fact, we hardly had anything to do with the war, that I finally stopped talking to him.'[2] Bradley was ordered to make the main thrust south of Berlin, towards Dresden, and the Ninth Army was taken away from Montgomery and assigned to Bradley for this purpose.

On 28 March, Eisenhower sent a cable direct to Stalin to inform him of his plans and ask about Russian intentions. Stalin agreed enthusiastically that Dresden was the best place for a meeting between the Allied and Soviet armies, adding that Berlin had lost its former strategic significance. He claimed that the Red Army planned to allocate only secondary forces to capture the city. In fact the Red Army had begun a massive redeployment to attack Berlin with over a million soldiers.

Churchill objected both to the manner and the content of Eisenhower's message. He told Roosevelt that he had no intention to lower the prestige of Eisenhower in his dealings with the Russians. But the British were concerned at a procedure – Eisenhower's telegram to Stalin – which appeared to leave the dispositions of the British Army, which, though only a third the size of the American forces, nevertheless amounted to over a million men, to be settled without reference to any British authority. 'I say quite frankly that Berlin remains of high strategic importance ... I therefore consider that from a political stand-point we should march as far east into Germany as possible.'

The British feared that Stalin was making a dupe of Eisenhower. Montgomery warned Brooke: 'I consider that we are about to make a terrible mistake.' The British Chiefs of Staff protested to Marshall. Marshall was upset that they should display such a lack of trust in Eisenhower after all his success in the advance across Europe. Eisenhower pointed out that the

Russians were, anyway, much closer to Berlin and that an Allied advance there would be through difficult and heavily defended terrain. He was determined to concentrate his forces to effect a junction with the Russians south of Berlin as the quickest way to end the war. The British, he complained, wanted him to turn aside from that objective.

On 31 March, Churchill telegraphed to Eisenhower: 'Why should we not cross the Elbe and advance as far eastward as possible? This has an important political bearing.' This upset Eisenhower 'quite a bit'. He replied that he intended Montgomery to cross the Elbe, but towards Lubeck, not Berlin, so as to keep the Russians out of Denmark.

The British realised that nothing they could say or do would change Eisenhower's mind. There was only one thing worse than fighting with allies, Churchill commented to Brooke, and that was fighting without them. He now sought to heal the bruises, telling Roosevelt that he wished to place on record 'the complete confidence felt by His Majesty's Government in General Eisenhower'. Churchill sent a copy of this message to Eisenhower, adding, however: 'I deem it highly important that we should shake hands with the Russians as far to the East as possible.' On 6 April, Montgomery told Eisenhower that he did not agree that Berlin did not have much value: 'I consider that Berlin has definite value as an objective and I have no doubt whatever that the Russians think the same.' But Marshall told the British Chiefs of Staff that only Eisenhower was in a position to know how to conduct the campaign. The British had little choice but to agree. Churchill told representatives of the dominions that the resources in men and material commanded by the United States were 'vastly superior to our own'. The British Commonwealth could only hold its own 'by our superior statecraft and experience'.[3]

In the light of subsequent events, Eisenhower tried in various ways to rewrite the historical record, claiming, much later, that he had told Roosevelt in January 1944 that he anticipated trouble with the Russians but Roosevelt would not listen. In fact all the contemporary evidence is that Eisenhower, like Roosevelt, entertained unrealistic hopes about the possibilities for postwar cooperation with Stalin – provided the British did not get in the way.

Yet when, on 13 April, Churchill received the news of Roosevelt's death the previous evening, he felt as if he had suffered a physical blow. In his tribute in the House of Commons, he spoke of the 1,700 messages that had passed between them, of their nine meetings and the 120 days of close personal contact, much of it spent privately with Roosevelt and members of their families. 'There never was a moment's doubt, as the quarrel opened, upon which side his sympathies lay.' It was in this speech that Churchill described Lend-Lease as the

> most unselfish and unsordid financial act of any country in all history. For us, it remains only to say that in Franklin Roosevelt there died the greatest American friend we have ever known, and the greatest champion of freedom who has ever brought help and comfort from the New World to the Old.[4]

Eden attended Roosevelt's funeral in Washington. On 16 April, Eden and Halifax paid their first call on the new President. Truman had been furnished by the Secretary of State, Edward Stettinius, with a note that stated: 'Mr Churchill's policy is based fundamentally on cooperation with the United States.' The British government, he added, had been showing increasing apprehension about Soviet intentions. There was a shared concern about implementation of the Yalta agreement, but Churchill was inclined to press this with the Russians with 'unnecessary rigidity as to detail. The British ... are deeply conscious of their decline from a leading position to that of the junior partner of the Big Three.'

It was, the new President stated, his intention to continue on exactly the same lines as Roosevelt. Eden reported to Churchill that he was favourably impressed. He found Truman honest and friendly. 'His references to you could not have been warmer. I believe we have in him a loyal collaborator and I am much heartened by this first conversation.'

Truman was ready to join in Churchill's representations to Stalin against the establishment of a puppet government in Poland. Churchill was reassured: 'My appreciation is that the new President is not to be bullied by the Soviets.'

On 24 April, Churchill asked Eisenhower about his plans to advance to Prague. On 30 April, he telegraphed to Truman that the liberation of Prague by US forces might make the whole difference to the postwar situation in Czechoslovakia. Otherwise the country would go the way of Yugoslavia. Eisenhower's plan, however, was to halt his troops on the Czech border. While he did so, the Red Army occupied Prague.

Before Roosevelt's death, Churchill had warned: 'We must always be anxious lest the brutal tone of the Russian messages does not foreshadow some deep change of policy for which they are preparing.' On 18 April, he telegraphed to Truman that the occupation zones had been decided hastily at Quebec in September 1944, when it was not foreseen that Eisenhower's armies would make such deep inroads into Germany. But the zones, he acknowledged, could not be altered except by agreement with the Russians. On 30 April, Churchill argued that the Western Allies must take a strong stand with the Russians over Austria, otherwise they would find it difficult to exercise any influence there in the future. Truman agreed and also supported Churchill in his determination to ensure that Alexander's forces should keep Trieste out of Tito's hands.

On 4 May, Churchill telegraphed to Eden in San Francisco that terrible things had happened during the Russian advance to the Elbe. Under the arrangements which the British and American staffs had agreed between them at Quebec, the Americans now would be obliged to withdraw in some places over a hundred miles to the west. Once this Russian advance took place, Poland would be completely engulfed and swallowed up. In Churchill's view, the Allied armies ought not to fall back to the occupation line until they were satisfied about Poland. 'All these matters could only be settled before the United States armies in Europe were weakened.' If not, there would be no prospect of a satisfactory solution and little of preventing a Third World War.[5]

The German surrender came on 7 May. Churchill expressed to Truman his appreciation of Eisenhower's great qualities: 'Let me tell you what General Eisenhower has meant to us. In him we have had a man who set the unity of the Allied armies above all nationalist thoughts.'

———

Harry Hopkins took a quite different view of Soviet intentions. When he visited Moscow on Truman's behalf in May 1945, Stalin said that the Soviet Union wanted a friendly Poland, but Britain wanted to revive a *cordon sanitaire* around the Soviet Union. Hopkins said that neither the government nor the people of the United States had any such intention.

The United States desired a Poland friendly to the Soviet Union and in fact wanted to see friendly countries all around the Soviet borders. Stalin replied that if that were so, they could easily come to terms about Poland. Hopkins did mention certain fundamental rights that, when impinged upon or denied, caused concern in the United States.[6]

Churchill's concern at this stage was to arrange a further meeting of the three Great Powers. He hoped that Truman would pass through London on the way. But, Churchill noted, very different ideas were being pressed on the new President in Washington.

The sort of mood and outlook that had been noticed at Yalta had been strengthened. The United States, it was argued, must be careful not to let herself be drawn into any antagonism with Soviet Russia. This, it was thought, would stimulate British ambition and would make a new gulf in Europe. The right policy, on the other hand, should be for the United States to stand between Britain and Russia as a friendly mediator, or even arbiter, trying to reduce the differences about Poland or Austria and make things settle down into a quiet and happy peace, enabling American forces to be concentrated against Japan.

Churchill was confirmed in this impression when Truman declared that he and Churchill ought to go to the meeting separately, so as to avoid any suspicion of 'ganging up'.

On the previous day, in his first mention of the 'Iron Curtain', Churchill had written to Truman that he was profoundly concerned about the European situation. Half the US air forces in Europe had already begun to move to the Pacific. The press was full of the withdrawal of American troops. As for the Russians: 'an iron curtain is drawn down upon their front. We do not know what is going on behind.'[7] It seemed to Churchill vital for the Allies to see where they were with the Russians before weakening their armies further or withdrawing to the zones of occupation.

On 22 May, Truman replied that he had asked Joseph Davies to see Churchill before the tripartite conference. Davies had been US ambassador in Moscow before the war and was known to be sympathetic to the regime. He had written a book about his mission that Churchill regarded as an apologia for the Soviet system.

Churchill, nevertheless, received Davies at Chequers. What Davies proposed was that Truman should meet Stalin first somewhere in Europe before he saw Churchill. Churchill expressed his amazement at this suggestion.

He would, he said, not agree in any circumstances to what seemed to be an affront to Britain after its service in the cause of freedom from the first days of the war. He objected to the implicit idea that the new disputes now developing with the Soviet Union lay between Britain and Russia.

In his account of this conversation, Davies claimed to have asked Churchill sardonically whether he and Britain had made a mistake in not supporting Hitler against the Soviet Union. Whatever Churchill's greatness, Davies reported to Truman, he was 'first, last and all the time a great Englishman, more interested in preserving England's position in Europe than in preserving the peace'. Admiral Leahy, Truman's Chief of Staff, commented that 'this was consistent with our staff estimate of Churchill's attitude throughout the war'.[8]

Distrusting Davies, Churchill wrote to Truman on 27 May, making clear his opposition to any prior meeting between Truman and Stalin: '[I]t must be understood that the representatives of His Majesty's Government would not be able to attend any meeting except as equal partners from its opening.' There would be plenty of opportunities for private talks with Stalin in the course of the meeting. 'The Soviet Government have a different philosophy, namely Communism, and use to the full the methods of police government, which they are applying in every state which has fallen a victim to their liberating arms.' The Prime Minister objected to the notion that the US position was that Britain and Soviet Russia were 'just two foreign powers, six of one and half a dozen of the other'. The freedom of Poland was a matter for which the British people had gone to war and it and other issues could not be set aside in a desire to placate the Russians. Faced with these objections, Truman withdrew from the idea of a prior meeting with Stalin.

Stalin agreed to a meeting at Potsdam, which, in view of the forthcoming British elections, Churchill invited Clement Attlee also to attend. Churchill wanted the meeting to take place before US forces withdrew from the positions they occupied well to the east of the agreed line of demarcation between the Soviet, British and American occupation zones. On 4 June, Churchill told Truman again that he viewed with profound misgivings the withdrawal of the US Army to the line of occupation, 'thus bringing Soviet power into the heart of Western Europe and the descent of an iron curtain between us and everything to the eastward'. On 12 June, Truman replied that the tripartite agreement about the occupation of

Germany, approved by Roosevelt and Churchill, made it impossible to delay the withdrawal of American troops from the Soviet zone in order to press the settlement of other problems. On 1 July, the US and British armies began their withdrawal to their allotted zones.

From Washington, Halifax reported to Churchill that he was sure he would find Truman anxious to work closely with him. But he judged that American tactics with the Russians would be to display at the outset confidence in Russia's willingness to cooperate. Halifax warned that the Americans would be more responsive to arguments about economic reconstruction in Europe than to 'balder pleas about the risks of extreme Left Governments or the spread of Communism'. They were nervous about the portrayal of Europe as the scene of a clash of ideas in which Soviet and Western influences were likely to be hostile and conflicting. 'At the back of their minds there are still lingering suspicions that we want to back Right-Wing Governments or monarchies for their own sake.' They were expecting to play, or at any rate to present themselves as playing, a moderating role between the British and the Russians. A few years later, Churchill noted, it was Britain and Europe that were being urged to play a 'moderating role' between the United States and the Soviet Union.

Churchill met Truman in Berlin and was impressed with his 'gay, precise, sparkling manner and obvious power of decision'. On 18 July, he lunched alone with the President. Churchill spoke of the 'melancholy position' of Britain, which had spent most of its foreign investments to sustain itself alone against Germany and now emerged from the war with an external debt of £3 billion. Truman declared that the USA owed Britain an immense debt for having held the fort at the beginning: '[T]his justifies us in regarding these matters as above the purely financial plane.' Churchill said that he had told the British electorate that they were living to a large extent on American imported food, for which at present they could not pay: 'We should have to ask for help to become a going concern again.' The President said that he would do his best, but there would be difficulties in his own country.

Churchill also made clear that he wanted, in whatever guise, a continuation of the wartime system of joint use of each other's military facilities. Truman seemed to agree, as long as this could be presented in a way that did not appear to be an exclusive alliance. Churchill went on to mention his long-cherished idea of keeping the organisation of the Combined Chiefs of Staff in being, at any rate until the world calmed down. Truman sounded positive about this. Churchill felt that he was dealing with a man of exceptional character and ability, self-confidence and determination.

On the day before his meeting with Truman. the US Secretary for War, Henry Stimson, called on Churchill and showed him a paper on which were written the words 'babies satisfactorily born'. What this meant, Stimson explained, was that the experiment at the test site in New Mexico had succeeded and the atomic bomb was a reality. Devastation within a one-mile circle was absolute. 'Here then', wrote Churchill, 'was a speedy end to the Second World War and perhaps to much else besides.'

Truman conferred with Churchill. Until then, they had been obliged to envisage prolonged air bombardment of Japan followed by an invasion with very large armies. They had expected desperate resistance with heavy loss of American and British lives, 'for we were resolved to share the agony'. There never was, Churchill recalls, a moment's discussion as to whether the atomic bomb should be used or not. British consent in principle to its use had been given on 4 July before the test in Mexico took place. The official decision now lay with Truman, who had the weapon: 'But I never doubted what it would be nor have I ever doubted that he was right.'

The immediate question was what to tell Stalin. The United States no longer needed his aid to defeat Japan. The President said that he would simply tell him that the Americans had an entirely novel form of bomb that they thought would have a decisive effect on the Japanese will to continue the war.

The Potsdam Conference opened on 17 July. Much of the discussion again was about Poland. As Churchill put it: 'Frustration was the fate of this final conference of "the Three".' When it came to his turn to host a dinner, Churchill proposed the toast of 'the Leader of the Opposition', adding 'whoever he may be'. On 24 July, after the plenary meeting had ended, Churchill watched Truman go up to Stalin and talk to him alone with their interpreters. Stalin seemed delighted at the news of a new bomb of extraordinary power. Churchill was sure that he had no idea of the significance of what he was being told.[9] Truman shared that impression. Both were wrong. The Russians had been kept informed of the Manhattan Project by their atom spies, including Klaus Fuchs at Los Alamos.

Two days later, Churchill and the Conservative Party were defeated in the British elections. This came as almost as much of a surprise to Churchill as it did to the Russians and Americans. Churchill's personal popularity in Britain remained immense. But after the terrible trials of the war, the British people dreamed of, and believed they were voting for, a new and different world. As the votes were counted, Churchill learned that 'the power to shape the future would be denied me'. Over lunch his wife observed that, after the strain of leading Britain through the war, the loss of office might prove to be a blessing in disguise. 'At the moment', Churchill replied, 'it seems quite effectively disguised.'

Towards the end of his life, Harry Hopkins wrote: 'I know no person in his right mind but that he believes that if this nation ever had to engage in another war Great Britain would be fighting on our side.' He believed that the British had

> saved our skins twice – once in 1914 and again in 1940. Many Brit-
> ishers do not make it particularly easy for those of us who want to
> see a close working relationship with Great Britain. When the Prime
> Minister said that he was not selected to be the King's Minister to
> liquidate the Empire, every isolationist in America cheered him ...
> There is constant friction between our business interests and we
> think – and I have no doubt with some good reason – that Great
> Britain would take an unfair advantage of us in trade around the
> world. It is footless [sic] to ignore the fact that the American people
> simply do not like the British colonial policy.

His conclusion, nonetheless, was:

> If I were to lay down the most cardinal principle of our foreign pol-
> icy, it would be that we make absolutely sure that now and forever
> the United States and Great Britain are going to see eye to eye on
> major matters of world policy. It is easy to say that. It is hard to
> do, but it can be done and the effort is worth it.

But, reflecting the hopes of a new world which caused such serious differ-ences at the end of the war, Hopkins added: 'The Russians undoubtedly like the American people ... They trust the United States more than they trust any power in the world.' The Soviet government were 'going to see to it that their borders are protected from unfriendly states and I, for one, do not blame them for that'.[10]

12

'ALLIES OF A KIND'

THE WAR AGAINST Japan was far from over. In his book *Allies of a Kind* Christopher Thorne describes the cooperation, but also near-constant friction and disagreements between the British and Americans over the conduct of the war in Asia.[1]

A main underlying cause of friction was the US conviction that they represented the world's greatest anti-colonial power and that this must not be sullied by too close an association with the British. They regarded Churchill, with reason, as a dyed-in-the-wool Victorian imperialist and the overriding war objective of the British as being to reconstitute their colonial empire in Asia.

In March 1942, Roosevelt had urged on Churchill the idea of setting up a temporary government in India, representing all groups and interests, to work out an eventual new constitution. Within the British Cabinet, the Labour Deputy Prime Minister, Clement Attlee, had put it to Churchill that his strong views on India 'were not widely shared'. Churchill told the Viceroy, Lord Linlithgow, that due to the American outlook, it was not possible 'to stand on a purely negative attitude'.[2]

A senior Labour member of the War Cabinet, Sir Stafford Cripps, was sent out to talk to Gandhi and the other Indian leaders, including the Muslim leader, Muhammad Ali Jinnah. Encouraged by Roosevelt's representative, Louis Johnson, Cripps went a long way further than Churchill would have wanted, offering a completely Indian executive, apart from the Viceroy and Commander-in-Chief, and full dominion status at the end of the war, but found Gandhi and the Congress party demanding a full and immediate transfer of power, including control over defence, and resistant to any idea of self-determination or a right to secede for the Muslims.

In April, Roosevelt sent a further message to Churchill attributing the deadlock to Britain's refusal to grant immediate self-government. This, as Hopkins reported, was 'wrathfully received' by Churchill, who told Roosevelt that, if pressed too hard on a matter that concerned the empire and the successful conduct of the war in Asia, he would have to think of 'retiring into private life'. Faced with this reaction from Churchill, and the absence of any undertaking from Gandhi to support the war against Japan, Roosevelt backed away, declaring subsequently that he did not think that India was yet ready for independence and that 'this country must not get into a serious dispute with Great Britain'.[3]

Roosevelt, however, did not give up hope entirely. At the Tehran Conference in November 1943, he told Stalin that, at a future time, he would like to talk to him about India, where he felt that the best solution would be reform from the bottom, 'somewhat on the Soviet line'. The senior US diplomat, Chip Bohlen, however, who was present in Tehran, reported Stalin's view at the time as being that 'because of the British military contribution ... there should be no reduction in the British Empire'.[4]

———————

For Churchill, the fall of Singapore to the Japanese, with very little resistance, in February 1942 marked the nadir of Britain's war effort and fortunes, preceded as it had been by the sinking of the battleships *Prince of Wales* and *Repulse*, the fall of Hong Kong and surrender in Malaya. By May, Macarthur had been forced to abandon the Philippines (declaring 'I shall return'). In June, the US Navy confirmed Admiral Yamamoto's alleged fears about awakening a sleeping tiger* by sinking four Japanese aircraft carriers in the crucial battle of Midway.

Relations between the military commanders were not helped by the appointment of General 'Vinegar Joe' Stilwell, as the US commander in

---

* Yamamoto, who organised the attack on Pearl Harbor, never actually said or wrote this, but did foresee that Japan's dominance in the Pacific might be short-lived. He botched the Battle of Midway by failing to concentrate his far superior forces. Understandably cross with Yamamoto, the Americans killed him in a targeted attack on his plane in April 1943.

south-east Asia. Stilwell also served as military adviser to General Chiang Kai-shek. Stilwell was convinced, with reason at the time, that the British had no appetite for any offensive operations (nor did they have the capacity to conduct any) and were interested only in the defence of India. Washington had to insist that, even if he would not join in singing 'God Save the King', he must at least stand up when it was played![5]

Stilwell regarded Field Marshal Wavell, Commander-in-Chief in India, as a long way past his best, as did a good many others at the time. In 1942, when Wavell explained to him the impossibility of launching an offensive against the Japanese in Burma and asked what Stilwell proposed to tell Chiang Kai-shek, Stilwell reportedly replied: 'I shall tell him the bloody British won't fight.'[6] Stilwell kept demanding that the British should do more to try to re-open the Burma road to China and canvassed what the British regarded as wildly unrealistic notions of training thirty or more divisions of General Chiang Kai-shek's Kuomintang troops to fight the Japanese.

Stilwell bitterly resented Churchill's influence on Roosevelt, which he held responsible for the failure to back his plans to carry the fight to the Japanese in northern Burma. Churchill's opinion was that he could not think of a worse place to fight the Japanese.

It was not only with the British that Stilwell did not get on. 'The Limeys', he complained, had completely hypnotised the President, who was a 'rank amateur in military matters'. Roosevelt later was referred to by him as a 'flighty fool' and 'double-crossing bastard'.[7] Stilwell did get some Chinese troops involved in fighting in northern Burma. But there also was friction with the US Air Force commander, Claire Chennault, whose handful of pilots were flying supplies from India to China over the 'hump' of the Himalayas and harassing their Japanese counterparts. In the end there followed a definitive falling out with Chiang Kai-shek, who Stilwell had taken to referring to by his codename, 'Peanut'.

The Americans, however, remained convinced that the overriding British objective being to hold on to India, they were resolved to neglect China and assistance to the anti-Japanese forces there. Madame Chiang Kai-shek was for a time a favourite of Roosevelt and the Americans insisted on Chiang's attendance at the Cairo conference in November 1943, at which, according to the head of the Foreign Office, 'Winston fell for Madame Chiang.'[8] This did not, however, affect his scepticism as to how much China would contribute to the war against Japan.

In accordance with his general anti-colonialist stance, Roosevelt kept expressing the hope (including to Chiang Kai-shek) that, after the war, Hong Kong would be handed over to China 'as a gesture of goodwill'.[9]

By the later stages of the war, the Americans had developed their own doubts about the Generalissimo, who clearly was more interested in fighting the Communists than the Japanese, and ceased to believe that China could make much of a contribution to the defeat of Japan. They pursued for a while the forlorn hope of a reconciliation between the Kuomintang and the Communists to fight the Japanese, sending emissaries to Mao Tsetung in Yan'an. Senior US figures had convinced themselves that Mao's followers were not really Communists, even though they said they were, but 'agrarian reformers', a conclusion all the more surprising as Mao in his book, *New Democracy*, had emphasised his adherence to Communist principles as part of a worldwide movement.

Anglo-American differences over China, however, had ceased to be of any importance until the recognition of the Communist regime by the Attlee government in 1949, upsetting the Americans, who withheld recognition until after the Kissinger/Nixon opening to China in 1971–72. The British policy was to recognise reality. 'Are we to refuse to recognise facts,' enquired Attlee, 'however unpleasant they may be?'[10]

The main issue in the war in Asia, however, was the fact that the British did not have the military resources to do much fighting in the theatre. Churchill was as frustrated as the Americans about this, deploring 'our lack of enterprise and drive'[11] and becoming an ardent supporter of Orde Wingate's Chindit operations behind enemy lines in Burma, which did show aggressive intent. To impress the Americans, Wingate was taken with him to the Quebec conference in August 1943, following which the relatively junior admiral and member of the royal family, Louis Mountbatten, was appointed as Commander-in-Chief for South East Asia. Mountbatten was a favourite of Churchill, despite his responsibility for the failed raid on Dieppe, but was accompanied by the vastly more experienced General Pownall as his Chief of Staff to 'keep him on the rails'.[12]

Mountbatten's plans for a seaborne attack to re-capture Rangoon in 1944 were vetoed by the Chiefs of Staff in London, who, understandably, were not prepared to divert landing craft from Europe. Chindit operations resumed in March 1944, when Wingate was killed in an air crash. His courage was undoubted, but his eccentricities had extended on occasions to addressing orders to his troops with no clothes on.

It was not until the battles at Kohima and Imphal in the spring of 1945, as the Japanese strove to break through into Assam and were defeated in ferocious close-quarter fighting by the 'forgotten' Fourteenth Army of General Sir William Slim, that the British earned the respect of the American commanders in Asia. They had the highest regard for Slim, who went on to capture Mandalay in March and Rangoon in May, satisfying Churchill's ambition to see Britain's earlier humiliations at the hands of the Japanese 'avenged in battle'.

In July 1945, Mountbatten, visiting MacArthur's headquarters in Manila, found that he had met his match in the Supreme Allied Commander. He had, he recorded in his diary, 'a long and interesting conversation with Mac-Arthur. Or, to be more precise, I listened to a fascinating monologue, and found the same difficulty trying to chip in as I have no doubt most people find in trying to chip in to my conversation.' He found MacArthur 'a rather shy and sensitive man, who regards compliance with the needs of publicity a duty [sic]'. A British liaison officer with MacArthur took a different view. 'He is shrewd, selfish, proud, remote, highly-strung and vastly vain. He has imagination, self-confidence, physical courage and charm, but no humour about himself, no regard for truth and is unaware of these defects.'[13]

Having succeeded in the all-important effort to persuade Roosevelt and Marshall to commit to a 'Germany first' strategy, it was an article of faith for Churchill, supported by his Cabinet colleagues and the British Chiefs of Staff, that Britain must contribute directly to the final defeat of Japan. The British found that MacArthur did not at all share Roosevelt's anti-colonial sentiments and wanted to see Britain's Asian colonies restored as a factor of stability in Asia after the war, advising them to get military units into position to receive Japanese surrenders 'as possession is nine tenths of the law'.[14] Nor did he take seriously Stilwell's plans in China. In his Pacific campaign, MacArthur had proved himself to be the greatest of the Allied commanders, but the British figured very little in his universe.

Admiral Ernie King, head of the US Navy, had never taken 'Germany first' too literally, with far more US naval strength deployed in the Pacific than the Atlantic and not rating highly the contribution the British could make. Nor, to Churchill's amusement, did the US Navy take the President's anti-colonial rhetoric seriously, as they prepared to entrench themselves permanently in a string of bases across the Pacific, of which he approved. When Churchill offered to send to the Pacific a British fleet, which arrived there in December 1944, the offer was no sooner made than accepted by Roosevelt. The British also undertook to contribute to the long-range bombing of Japan, negotiating bases at Okinawa for the purpose, and were planning, with the Australians and Canadians, to contribute three army divisions to an eventual invasion of Japan.

The issue on which there was no difference whatsoever between the two governments was that of using the atomic bomb to put an end to Japanese resistance. The ferocious fighting at Okinawa had shown what could be expected when Allied troops reached the mainland. The casualties attending an invasion were expected to be very high and the resistance extended. As has been seen, this was not a decision over which Truman or Churchill, supported by Attlee, displayed any hesitation at all.

13

'I MUST ALWAYS KNOW WHAT IS IN THE DOCUMENTS I SIGN'

ALTHOUGH HE HAD accompanied Churchill to Potsdam, the new Prime Minister, Clement Attlee, had made little impression on the other delegations, though Truman had informed him as well as Churchill of the successful testing of the atomic bomb. He had as much difficulty emerging from Churchill's shadow as Truman did from that of Roosevelt. But they had many of the same qualities and Attlee in due course was to belie Churchill's unkind description of him as 'a modest little man, with much to be modest about'.

After the election, Attlee returned to Potsdam accompanied by Ernest Bevin, now Foreign Secretary. The US Secretary of State, James Byrnes, commented that Britain's stand in the conference was not altered in the slightest, so far as the Americans could observe, by the change of government. Bevin disconcerted the Americans by taking a very tough line with the Russians. Stalin was upset that Churchill had not been re-elected. If Attlee made no impact at the conference, he did at least make a good impression on Truman, who wrote later: 'Attlee had a deep understanding of the world's problems, and I knew there would be no interruption in our common efforts.'[1]

Following the nuclear attacks on Hiroshima and Nagasaki, Japan surrendered on 14 August. One week later, Truman signed a document prepared by Leo Crowley, head of the Foreign Economic administration, terminating the Lend-Lease agreement.

Britain, in the words of Hugh Dalton, Chancellor of the Exchequer, was now in a desperate plight. Keynes described the country as facing a 'financial Dunkirk', without the financial resources necessary to cover essential imports. Attlee was appalled by the President's action in terminating Lend-Lease without warning or discussion. He had formed a high opinion of Truman's character and set great store by the relationship that seemed to have developed between them. Yet the first the British government heard of Truman's decision was in a bulletin on the BBC News. Truman himself later confessed his mistake: 'Crowley ... taught me this lesson early in my Administration – that I must always know what is in the documents I sign.'[2]

The only course of action available to Attlee was to seek alternative forms of help from the United States. Between 1939 and 1945, US manufacturing output tripled, while Britain's overseas assets were liquidated and exports fell by two-thirds. They came nowhere near covering essential imports. Keynes believed that Britain had an overwhelming case for requesting more financial aid. Her economic difficulties were due to the war effort, which had been in the common interest. But when Keynes arrived in Washington, he found that a grant or interest-free loan was out of the question. The American people and government still regarded the Russians as allies and believed that they could work with them if the British did not interfere. There was no sign of the kind of understanding of the world situation that, two years later, was to produce the Marshall Plan.

The British Cabinet awaited the outcome of Keynes's negotiations with acute anxiety. The entire reconstruction and demobilisation programme depended on them. Eventually Keynes and Sir Edward Bridges, head of the Treasury, were able to obtain a loan of $3.75 billion, repayable at 2 per cent over fifty years. There was a public outcry and most of the Conservative Party abstained in the vote on acceptance of the loan. In reality, there was no alternative but to accept the loan on American conditions, which included the proviso that, within a year, Britain must make sterling convertible into dollars on demand.

This crisis was followed immediately by a dispute over the exchange of atomic energy information, which put a further strain on the friendship between Attlee and Truman. When Truman told Attlee in Potsdam that the Americans were ready to use the atomic bomb to force Japanese capitulation, Attlee did not object: his information was that, otherwise, the Japanese would have gone on fighting, at great cost to Allied lives.

When he heard of the devastating effects of the attack on Hiroshima, Attlee sent a telegram to Truman urging 'a joint declaration of our intention to utilise the existence of this great power, not for our own ends, but as trustees for humanity'.

In September 1945, Attlee suggested to Truman that Britain and America must use their lead in this field to secure 'that better ordering of human affairs which so great a revolution at once renders necessary and should make possible'. In November, Attlee flew to Washington for discussions with Truman and the Canadian Prime Minister, Mackenzie King, 'in the light, the terrible light, of the discovery of atomic energy'.[3] The undeclared purpose of his visit was to try to allay American suspicions about the character of a British socialist government. On 13 November, Attlee addressed a joint session of Congress, emphasising the attachment of the British Labour Party to individual freedoms, while presenting his party's economic programme in as reassuring terms as possible.

Attlee's objectives were to get the United States to declare its readiness to give up its monopoly of the atomic bomb and place control of it with the United Nations as soon as the development of international confidence permitted and, second, to ensure that the wartime Anglo/American atomic collaboration under the Quebec Agreement continued. Roosevelt and Churchill had agreed at Hyde Park in September 1944 that collaboration in developing 'Tube Alloys' for military and commercial purposes should continue after the defeat of Japan 'unless and until terminated by joint agreement'. But General Groves advised Truman against agreeing to any public undertakings. Truman assured Attlee that information about atomic energy would continue to be exchanged, but insisted that public references to cooperation in this field should be in very general terms.

Attlee left Washington believing that the US government agreed that there should continue to be full collaboration with Britain and Canada on nuclear projects. But in February 1946, with the British declaring their intention to build a plant to produce plutonium for 'eventual industrial or military application', the Americans refused a British request for an exchange of information. Senator McMahon introduced a Bill terminating virtually all communication with foreign states about atomic energy. Attlee expressed his concern in a series of messages to Truman. He warned Averell Harriman that if the Bill became law, Britain would build its own atomic plant for military use.

As he received no reassuring reply, Attlee instructed the British ambassador in Washington, Lord Inverchapel, formally to assert Britain's right under the Quebec Agreement and his own agreement with Truman of the previous November to request data to be supplied for the construction of an atomic plant in Britain. In April, this request was refused. Attlee told Truman that he was greatly disturbed. The wartime arrangements for collaboration between the two countries in this area had meant that technological and engineering information had accumulated in US hands. Truman argued that the Quebec Agreement applied only to the exchange of basic scientific information. It did not bind the United States to give Britain in the postwar period assistance in the construction and operation of atomic plants. He added that if Britain were to create an atomic energy plant, this would damage the development of the United Nations.

Attlee reminded Truman of the genesis during the war of Anglo-American cooperation in this field, pointing out that the refusal of the United States to provide information amounted to a dissolution of their partnership with Britain and Canada. Truman did not reply. In his memoirs he said that he could not do so because of the McMahon Act, which he signed into law in August. Senator McMahon said subsequently that if he had been informed by the administration of the history of atomic collaboration between Britain and the United States, he would not have pressed for a Bill in so restrictive a form. The result, as Attlee recorded, was that 'we had to go ahead on our own'. Attlee had now been let down twice by Truman – first over the sudden termination of Lend-Lease and now over atomic cooperation. Attlee chose charitably to conclude that: 'It was not Truman's fault. Congress was to blame.'[4]

Attlee and Bevin were determined to go ahead with the development of a British nuclear weapon. 'If we had decided not to have it,' said Attlee, 'we would have put ourselves entirely in the hands of the Americans. That would have been a risk a British Government should not take.' NATO did not yet exist. At the time, 'nobody could be sure that the Americans would not revert to isolationism'.[5] In reality there also was a feeling that Britain must possess the atomic bomb in order to deter any nuclear armed enemy and a conviction that, unless it did possess such weapons, Britain would cease to be a major power.

When in 1949 Dean Acheson became Secretary of State, he felt guilty about the way Britain had been treated over atomic energy. Britain had developed a great deal of technical knowledge and by now was well on the way to producing her own bomb. The Russians exploded their first nuclear weapon, thereby, commented Acheson, 'exploding also a good deal of Senatorial nonsense about our priceless secret heritage'.[6] But in February 1950, the British atomic scientist, Klaus Fuchs, who had worked on the Manhattan Project in the United States during the war, was arrested and charged with giving information to the Russians. Britain tested her first nuclear weapon in 1952. Not until the mid-1950s was Anglo-American cooperation in the nuclear field fully re-established.

In March 1946, Truman invited Churchill to travel with him to his home state, Missouri, to give the address at Westminster College, Fulton. Though Truman did not know it, Churchill shared the general doubts at the time as to whether Truman would prove to be a worthy successor to Roosevelt. Truman hardly knew Churchill – they had been together for only a short time at Potsdam – but he had a reverential attitude towards a man he considered to be the 'first citizen of the world'.

As the party travelled by train to Missouri, Truman and his cronies whiled away the time playing the President's favourite game, poker. Churchill joined in, with little success. 'The truth emerged quickly', reports Clark Clifford: 'Churchill was not very good at the game.' The President's travelling companions conspired to limit his losses.

Secretary Byrnes read a draft of Churchill's speech before they left Washington and briefed the President on its contents. The President said that he would not read the full text, so as to be able to say that he had not endorsed or approved it in advance. But when the final version was distributed on the train, Truman found that he could not resist reading it. It was a brilliant and admirable statement, he told Churchill, and would create 'quite a stir'.

But it presented Truman with a dilemma. He was not ready to endorse Churchill's view that the West was entering an era of confrontation with Moscow. Still hoping to keep channels of communication open to the Russians, the President instructed Clifford to put into his introductory speech some positive words about Stalin.[7]

Churchill's theme was that the United States now stood at the pinnacle of its power, with an awe-inspiring responsibility for the future: 'From Stettin in the Baltics to Trieste in the Adriatic, an iron curtain has descended across the Continent.' The people of Eastern Europe now found themselves 'in the Soviet sphere, and are all subject, in one form or another, not only to Soviet influence, but to a very high and in some cases increasing measure of control from Moscow'. Churchill did not believe that Soviet Russia wanted war: 'What they desire is the fruits of the war and the indefinite expansion of their power and doctrine ... I am convinced that there is nothing they admire so much as strength and there is nothing for which they have less respect than for weakness, especially military weakness.' Churchill had sounded the same kind of warnings about Hitler's Germany, he added, but the world had not paid much attention.

Churchill's other great theme was the need for Anglo-American cooperation to meet the challenge:

> Neither the sure prevention of war, nor the continuous rise of world organization will be gained without what I have called the fraternal association of the English-speaking peoples. This means a special relationship between the British Commonwealth and Empire and the United States ... Fraternal association requires not only the growing friendship and mutual understanding between our two vast but kindred systems of society, but the continuance of the intimate relationship between our military advisers, leading to common study of potential dangers, the similarity of weapons and manuals of instructions, and to the interchange of officers and cadets at technical colleges. It should carry with it the continuance of the present facilities for mutual security by the joint use of all Naval and Air Force bases in the possession of either country all over the world.

It was the repeated use by Churchill of the phrase 'special relationship' in the Fulton speech that established it in the public consciousness in Britain. It never gained the same currency in America. What had gained near-universal acceptance, however, was the conception of Britain as the United States' closest ally.

That evening, back with Truman on the train, Churchill described it as the most important speech of his career. Churchill wanted to accelerate the process by which the United States would assume leadership in the postwar world, while preserving a role for Britain as the United States' special partner.

The initial reaction in the United States to the speech was mixed, with most editorial comment hostile. The *Wall Street Journal* rejected Churchill's call for a closer relationship with Britain, writing that: 'The United States wants no alliance, or anything that resembles an alliance, with any other nation.'

Truman was far from ready to endorse Churchill's message. He continued to hope that some sort of agreement with Stalin would be possible. It was for this reason that he told reporters that he had not read the speech in advance. To the relief of the Americans, Churchill did not contradict him. To distance the administration from the speech, Truman instructed Dean Acheson not to attend a reception for Churchill the following week in New York. Byrnes declared that the United States was no more interested in an alliance with Britain against the Soviet Union than in an alliance with the Soviet Union against Britain. Truman sent Stalin a message emphasising that he still hoped for better relations and invited him to make a similar speech in Missouri. The future, as Clark Clifford commented, was not as apparent to Truman as it was to Churchill. Truman still hoped that the Cold War could be avoided. But by December, as Churchill wrote to Thomas Dewey, 'if I made the Fulton speech today, it would be criticised as consisting of platitudes'.[8]

It was not only with Churchill that there were differences over policy towards Russia. Attlee's biographer, Kenneth Harris, refers to the 'incompetence of an American foreign policy which in the last months of the war had suffered from Roosevelt's belief that if he could sufficiently dissociate himself from Britain's long term foreign policy commitments, and muzzle Churchill, he could do business on a basis of trust with Stalin'.[9] This attitude was continued under Truman's Secretary of State, Byrnes. Byrnes was 'a difficult man to like', given to patronising his colleagues, and Bevin did not like him at all. He considered Byrnes too willing to concede far more to the Soviet Union than was wise or safe.

American hostility to British imperialism was coupled with the conviction that Britain was too weak to be much of a factor in world politics. Harry Hopkins, sent by Truman to Moscow before Potsdam, reported to him that whereas Britain's interests could bring her into conflict with those of the United States, those of Russia would not. Admiral Leahy,

Truman's military adviser at Potsdam, told him that Britain was prostrate economically. The Americans took a dim view of the Labour government's nationalisation programme.

Attlee, for his part, was delighted with Churchill's speech at Fulton: he considered the Americans still to be naive in their attitude towards Stalin. But in September 1946, the US Secretary of Commerce, Henry Wallace, made a speech attacking the idea of getting tough with Russia. He warned Americans against letting 'British balance of power manipulation' determine whether America became embroiled in another war: 'To make Britain the key to our foreign policy would, in my opinion, be the height of folly.' The United States, he argued, had no business in the political affairs of Eastern Europe. This was too much for Truman. Wallace – the nearest thing to a socialist in the US government – was sacked.

14

'THE PATIENT IS SINKING WHILE THE DOCTORS DELIBERATE'

WALLACE HAD HIS British counterpart in Richard Crossman. The objective of Labour policy, he argued, should be to prevent the division of the world into two blocs, instead of tying Britain to the United States. Attlee and Bevin had to contend with systematic criticism from the virulently anti-American 'Keep Left' group within the Labour Party. Facing a continuing economic haemorrhage, beset by fuel and other shortages through the winter, the British government cast around for ways of reducing its overseas commitments.

Greece at this time remained largely an area of British responsibility. The Communists refused to participate in the elections of March 1946 and a three-year civil war ensued in the northern mountains with Communist groups supported from Bulgaria and Yugoslavia. Turkey, meanwhile, was confronted by demands from Stalin that Russia must be permitted to participate in the defence of the Straits, that is, have the right to station forces in Turkey.

On 21 February 1947, the British ambassador in Washington, Lord Inverchapel, contacted the State Department to arrange to present two notes. These stated that Britain's resources already were strained to the utmost. They announced the decision of the British government to remove its forces from Greece and Turkey and to terminate economic assistance to both countries on 31 March. Thus the first great passing of the baton took place. General Marshall had succeeded Byrnes as Secretary of State. Dean Acheson remained Under-Secretary. Acheson was alarmed at the situation in Greece and Turkey and by the speed with which Britain planned to withdraw.

Acheson and Marshall persuaded Truman that the United States must step into the breach with both economic and military support. Truman met Senator Vandenberg and the other Congressional leaders and warned them that if the USA did not act, Greece and Turkey would be unable to withstand the pressures being directed against them. On 12 March, Truman addressed a joint session of Congress: 'I believe that it must be the policy of the United States to support free peoples who are resisting attempted subjugation by armed minorities or outside pressures.'

The world, he argued, faced a choice between freedom and totalitarianism. Totalitarian regimes undermined the foundations of international peace and hence the security of the United States. James Reston suggested that the speech was comparable in importance to the Monroe Doctrine and indeed it became known as the Truman Doctrine.[1] The United States took over Britain's responsibility in the Eastern Mediterranean, except for Cyprus, and did so with success. The insurrection in Greece was contained and progressively defeated as, following Tito's break with Stalin, the Greek Communists lost support from Yugoslavia.

Acheson realised that it was not only Greece and Turkey that were desperately going to need American assistance to survive. General Marshall returned from talks with Bevin and Molotov in Moscow convinced that the Russians intended to try to exploit the economic suffering in Western Europe as they had in the Balkans. The economic recovery of Europe had been far slower than expected. As Marshall put it on 28 April: '[T]he patient is sinking while the doctors deliberate.' With Acheson, the main author of the Marshall Plan was Will Clayton, Under-Secretary of State for Economic Affairs. He reported that the USA had grossly underestimated the destruction of the European economy by the war. The Europeans could not pay for the essential imports needed to feed their people and rebuild their economies.

On 5 June 1947, General Marshall made his great speech at Harvard. It was intended, as Acheson said, to win over the critics of the Truman Doctrine both at home and abroad. The aim, Marshall said, must be to achieve 'the revival of a working economy in the world so as to permit the emergence of political and social conditions in which free institutions can exist'. Before the United States could proceed with its efforts to help start the European world on its way to recovery, there must be some agreement among the Europeans about their requirements and the part they could play themselves.[2]

The British embassy in Washington decided parsimoniously not to report the speech by telegram. They sent it back to the Foreign Office by sea-mail instead. But Acheson had briefed the British correspondents in Washington, asking them to direct the speech to Bevin's attention. Bevin, listening to the BBC correspondent's broadcast, realised immediately the importance of what was being proposed. He contacted the French Foreign Minister, Georges Bidault. Two weeks later they met Molotov to discuss how the Europeans might devise a recovery plan. Molotov made clear that the Russians did not intend to cooperate, Bevin and Bidault then invited other Western European countries to send representatives to a conference in Paris.[3]

In July, reluctantly honouring the terms of the American loan, Britain ended exchange controls and made sterling freely convertible. Holders of sterling seized the opportunity to convert into dollars, forcing the British government to suspend convertibility within five weeks. This costly experiment itself helped to use up most of the funds remaining from the US loan.

By September, the committee of European governments set up by Bevin had completed its work, asking for American loans totalling $29 billion. Truman reduced the amount to $17 billion over four years and sent the proposal to Congress. While the Bill was being debated, the Communists seized power in Czechoslovakia and the Foreign Minister, Jan Masaryk, died in sinister circumstances. When the Bill was finally approved by Congress in March, Churchill called it 'a turning point in the history of the world'.

———————

In his first-hand account of *The Birth of NATO*, Sir Nicholas Henderson, who participated in the British negotiating team at the time, notes how reluctant the Americans still were in 1948 to enter into any new alliance committing them to the defence of Western Europe in the face of Soviet threats. He describes the persistent opposition the British negotiators encountered from two of the most important officials in the State Department and leading experts on the Soviet Union, George Kennan and

Chip Bohlen. It was Kennan who, in the 'Long Telegram' from Moscow, sent in March 1946, had sought to alert the Truman administration to the nature of the Soviet regime and Stalin's expansionist designs. But Kennan, who changed his views more than once over the succeeding years, feared the consequences of increasing Soviet paranoia and of the division of Europe into two hostile blocs. Bohlen and Bob Lovett, Acheson's successor as Under-Secretary, were more concerned about Congress, and to retain America's freedom of action. This made the negotiations in the early part of 1948 extremely hard going. Throughout this period it was Bevin who had to take the initiative.[4]

After the breakdown in December 1947 of discussions with the Russians on the future of Germany, Bevin told Marshall that there would have to be some understanding, though not a formal alliance between the principal Western countries, to convince the Soviet Union that it could advance no further. In the first instance, Bevin set about trying to form a union of the Western Europeans. He realised that the Americans were likely to refuse to enter into a binding commitment, but he also knew that Western Europe could not stand on its feet without American support. Bohlen was warning against anything that might complicate getting the Marshall Plan through Congress.

The fall of Czechoslovakia helped to change American minds. On 12 March, without consulting his officials, Marshall told Bevin that he was ready to discuss 'the establishment of an Atlantic security system'. A successful outcome to the negotiations between the five Western European countries (Britain, France and the Benelux) was an 'essential pre-requisite to any wider arrangement in which the United States might play a part'.

On 17 March, the five European governments signed the Brussels Treaty under which they undertook to come to each other's assistance in the event of external aggression. Responding to the Communist takeover in Prague, Truman told Congress of his intention to keep US forces in Germany 'until the peace is secured in Europe'. But in discussions with the British delegation in Washington – which included in its ranks Donald Maclean – the Americans remained reluctant to consider anything that would commit future American governments or require Congressional approval. Bevin was disturbed by Lovett's pessimism and nervousness about Congress, attitudes in which he was still being encouraged by Kennan and Bohlen. The continuing presence of US forces in Germany should suffice, they contended, without the need for a new treaty. Kennan looked forward to changes in Europe that eventually, he believed, might permit a general unification of the continent. As for Lovett, it was at the time a Herculean task to squeeze from him any positive contribution at all.[5]

On behalf of the Europeans, Sir Oliver Franks, who had succeeded Inverchapel as ambassador in Washington, played a crucial role in the negotiations. Shortly after his arrival in Washington, Sir Oliver was asked by a local radio station what he would like for Christmas. Franks, a man of austere tastes, demurred for a while before replying. On Christmas Eve the station reported the results of its enquiries. The French ambassador replied: 'Peace throughout the world.' The Soviet ambassador declaimed: 'Justice for all oppressed peoples.' There followed the polite voice of Sir Oliver Franks saying that he would like a small box of candied fruit.

But in the discussions with the State Department, Franks was formidably effective. The British found an important ally in Jack Hickerson, head of the European Bureau. He favoured extending the Brussels Treaty into a North Atlantic Pact.

The world, by this time, had come to the verge of war. The Western Allies, concluding that they would never get Stalin's cooperation in establishing a unified, democratic Germany, started to create a new West German state in their areas of occupation. On 24 June 1948, the Russians blocked the autobahn and all other routes into Berlin. Truman considered forcing a way through. But Marshall concluded that Berlin could be supplied by air. If the Russians acted against the airlift, that would lead to war. Marshall asked Bevin to allow US bombers, which had been withdrawn after 1945, to return to British bases. Three B-29 bomber groups arrived in Britain. B-29s had dropped the first nuclear weapons on Japan and it was widely assumed that these squadrons too had a nuclear capability. At the height of the Berlin crisis, no difficult questions were raised. US Air Force General Leon Johnson later observed of the return of the USAF to Britain: 'Never before in history has one first-class Power gone into another first-class Power's country without an agreement. We were just told to come.'[6]

It was not until October 1951, shortly before leaving office, that Attlee reached a formal agreement with Truman, subsequently confirmed by Churchill and Truman in January 1952, that the use of the bases in an emergency was accepted to be 'a matter for joint decision by the two governments in the light of the circumstances prevailing at the time'.

Meanwhile, the laborious negotiations in Washington continued. They were now condemned to succeed, but the Americans continued to resist the binding language in the Brussels Treaty, under which the five European powers had undertaken to afford any of them who was attacked 'all the military and other aid and assistance in their power'. By December the presidential elections were over and, in response to the Berlin blockade, public opinion in America had moved strongly in favour of a pact. There remained differences over the duration of a treaty, with the British favouring fifty and the Americans and Canadians twelve to twenty years.

Acheson now returned to the State Department as Secretary of State. In his inaugural address, President Truman declared: 'If we can make it sufficiently clear, in advance, that any armed attack affecting our security would be met with overwhelming force, the armed attack might never occur.' But there still were difficulties with Congress, These centred on the wording of Article V of the proposed treaty. Senators Connally and Vandenberg objected to the treaty committing the parties to assist each other 'by taking forthwith such military or other action' as might be necessary to deter an attack. This, Connally argued, would mean 'letting European nations declare war and letting us fight'.

Acheson found himself in the awkward position of having to mediate between the European governments and the Senate. He consulted Franks about ways of meeting the Senate's concerns, without losing the treaty. Acheson proposed to substitute the words 'as it may deem necessary' in relation to the action each party was committed to take in the event of an attack for the original 'as may be necessary'. Although this was a clear weakening of the text, Franks thought it tolerable, provided a clear reference to military action remained.[7] The final text of Article V provided that: 'The Parties agree that an armed attack against one or more of them in Europe or North America shall be considered an attack against them all.' They agreed that if an armed attack occurred, each of them would 'assist the Party or Parties so attacked by taking forthwith ... such action as it deems necessary, including the use of armed force, to restore and maintain the security of the North Atlantic area'.

While this language clearly was weaker than the commitment in the Brussels Treaty, it was sufficient because of the continued presence of large numbers of US troops in Europe and thanks to the subsequent development of the integrated military structure of the Alliance, which did more than anything else to ensure that an attack on any of its European members would indeed have the character of an attack on all. Senators Connally and Vandenberg themselves suggested that the treaty should have an indefinite duration, provided that after a time parties should have the right to withdraw. Twenty years was set as the minimum duration of the treaty.

On 4 April 1949, the treaty was signed in Washington. Truman said that if such a treaty had existed in 1914 and 1939, he believed that it would have prevented the acts of aggression that had led to two world wars. The treaty, he hoped, would 'create a shield against aggression and the fear of aggression'.

This display of firmness had its immediate as well as its long-term effect. Stalin abandoned the blockade of Berlin. The political development of West Germany was assured. Although others, especially the Canadians and the French, played an important part, this was the greatest and most enduring success for Anglo-American diplomacy. Yet, in August 1948, the US ambassador in Britain, Lewis Douglas, observed

> an undercurrent of feeling here against the U.S. both in and out of government ... At times their attitude towards U.S. borders on the pathological ... Anglo-American unity today is more firmly established than ever before in peacetime. But Britain has never before been in a position where her national security and economic fate are so completely dependent on and at the mercy of another country's decisions. Almost every day brings new evidence of her weakness and dependence on the U.S. This is a bitter pill for a country accustomed to full control of her national destiny.[8]

In 1949, the Labour government was forced into a major devaluation of sterling, Bevin went to Washington to get American support. The Treasury Secretary, Snyder, was unsympathetic, asking, according to Paul Nitze:

> Why didn't the UK get a hold of itself, and why didn't its people do some work for a change, and why don't you cure these productivity problems in the United Kingdom and why don't you get off your butts ... I think that was the general sense of his remarks!

This so irritated Bevin that he held forth for five minutes in defence of

Britain and why Snyder was wrong. According to Nitze, who was struggling to take a note, there were

> just words, no sentences of any kind ... But one was left with a realisation of the tremendous contribution to world history that Britain had made by its standing alone against [Hitler] and the sacrifices England had made on its own behalf but also the impact of that upon the rest of the world. The degree of honour and respect to which England was entitled by virtue of that tremendous contribution.

When Bevin had finished, Nitze saw to his amazement that Snyder had tears in his eyes. The Treasury Secretary promised to do what he could to help.[9]

15

'THE JEWS ARE A RELIGION, NOT A NATION OR A RACE'

WHILE THE ABRUPT termination of Lend-Lease and difficulties over the exchange of atomic information imposed some strain on the relationship, by far the most serious dispute between the Attlee government and the Truman administration was over Palestine. To the Foreign Office, Britain's interests in the Middle East dictated support for the Arabs. This was deemed necessary to secure vital oil supplies as well as to maintain the position of Britain as, still, the predominant external power in the region. The British Chiefs of Staff believed that, in the event of war, the Arabs would drive the Jews into the sea. In their view, to support Zionist ambitions would achieve nothing for Britain and put vital Western interests at stake. To some extent these views were shared by the State Department. But they were not shared by President Truman. He was sympathetic to Zionist aspirations partly, though not solely, because of his preoccupation with domestic politics and concern to win the Jewish vote.

Bevin shared in full the views of officials in the Foreign Office. He was in the habit of stating that 'the Jews are a religion, not a nation or a race'. In their attitude towards Palestine, Bevin and Attlee were outside the mainstream of sentiment in the Labour Party, which was sympathetic to Jewish aspirations. Attlee and Bevin were inclined to regard Truman's Zionism as simply a response to political pressure and in that respect they were wrong. Acheson described Truman's Zionist sympathies as stemming from conviction. But, as Truman also explained to a group of Arab ambassadors: 'I have to answer to hundreds of thousands who are anxious for the success of Zionism. I do not have hundreds of thousands of Arabs among my constituents.'[1]

When Attlee became Prime Minister in July 1945, he found a letter written by Truman to Churchill expressing the hope that Britain would lift the restrictions on Jewish immigration into Palestine. The Foreign Office told Bevin that the State Department was advising Truman to resist domestic pressure to support unlimited Jewish immigration. But in August 1945, Truman urged Attlee to grant an additional 100,000 immigration certificates.

In reply Attlee argued that the Jews were not using all the certificates already available to them, that Arab consent had to be obtained for future immigration, that the Muslims in India could be roused by inconsiderate treatment of the Arabs and that the Jews in camps in Europe should not be regarded as a special case. Not surprisingly, this did not go down well with Truman and to try to deal with him, Attlee proposed an Anglo-American Court of Inquiry. In May 1946, this recommended the immediate grant of 100,000 immigration certificates. Its other recommendations, however, were not so favourable to the Zionists. It ruled out as impractical an early attempt to establish a Jewish state in Palestine and it called on the Jewish Agency, representing Zionist interests, to cooperate in suppressing terrorism.

Truman, however, seized on the recommendation to allow in 100,000 immigrants. Without warning Attlee or waiting for the State Department's advice, Truman announced publicly that he endorsed the recommendation about Jewish immigration.

Attlee responded angrily. He said that the US administration would be asked to share any military and financial responsibilities that arose from acceptance of the report and that large-scale immigration would not begin until Jewish armed units had been disbanded. Truman admitted that the United States was not prepared to assume any obligations that could require the use of military force. In June, at the Labour Party conference, Bevin publicly rejected the granting of 100,000 extra immigration certificates, adding inexcusably that the Americans wanted Jews to go to Palestine because 'they did not want too many Jews in New York'.[2]

Opinion in Britain was outraged by the activities of the Jewish terrorist organisations. Attlee continued to oppose the establishment of a Jewish state in Palestine: 'It is really no good suggesting that we have no obligation to the Arabs as well as the Jews.' In July 1946, an Irgun terrorist gang destroyed the King David Hotel in Jerusalem. The British proposed the creation of semi-autonomous provinces, Jewish and Arab, with a strong central trustee government which could supervise immigration and control the religious centres.

Under pressure from American Zionists, Truman rejected this plan, preferring a scheme for the partition of Palestine. By this time, commented Acheson, Attlee had 'deftly exchanged the United States for Britain as the most disliked power in the Middle East'.[3] On 4 October (Yom Kippur), shortly before the midterm Congressional elections, Truman announced that he would continue to press for the admission of 100,000 Jews and that the United States would support partition.

Attlee was appalled. Truman's intervention was held to have ruined Bevin's attempt to persuade the Zionist leaders to settle for autonomy. Attlee had asked Truman to postpone his statement, but Truman ignored his request. Attlee replied indignantly:

> I have received with great regret your letter refusing even a few hours grace to the Prime Minister of the country which has the actual responsibility for the government of Palestine in order that he could acquaint you with the actual situation and the probable result of your actions. This may well include the frustration of our patient efforts to achieve a settlement and the loss of still more lives in Palestine.[4]

This exchange marked the lowest point in relations between Attlee and Truman.

American opinion, however, was solidly behind the President. In November, Bevin returned from a visit to the United States convinced that no support for the British position could be expected from the Americans and that it was time for Britain to surrender the Mandate whereby Britain was saddled with the task of administering Palestine. The Jews and Arabs were equally intransigent and the British Cabinet was divided, with several of its members, including Aneurin Bevan and Hugh Dalton, urging support for a Jewish state.

Bevin considered that support for partition would destroy the British position in the Middle East. The Jews would not accept autonomy. It was not possible to impose a solution. Bevin told Attlee: 'I am at the end of my tether.'

In February 1947, the Cabinet decided that Britain should hand the problem over to the United Nations. Bevin said that he was not prepared to sacrifice any more British lives in trying to sustain an impossible burden. He continued to oppose partition, arguing that: 'The existence of a Jewish State might prove a constant factor of unrest in the Middle East.' Attlee announced that Britain would abandon the Mandate and withdraw from Palestine when it expired.

In November, a majority in the United Nations voted for partition, including the United States and the Soviet Union. Britain abstained. As the end of British control approached, both Jews and Arabs sought to strengthen their military position. The day after the expiry of the Mandate, on 16 May 1948, the Jews proclaimed the existence of a Jewish state, which immediately was recognised by the United States. Russia followed suit. Britain delayed recognition. Egyptian planes bombed Tel Aviv and armies from Lebanon, Syria, Iraq and Egypt invaded Palestine. In the ensuing fighting, the British Chiefs of Staff turned out to be totally wrong in their prediction that the Arabs would drive the Jews into the sea. On the contrary, they more than held their ground, thereby establishing the State of Israel.

Attlee said publicly that President Truman had been ill-advised to rush into recognition of Israel. By abandoning the Mandate rather than agree to partition, Britain had sought to safeguard its position with the Arabs. But this 'solution' was certainly not one that added anything to Britain's prestige. Attlee failed to understand Truman's attitude to the problem. He did not realise until much too late that US policy would be decided not by the State Department, but by the President. These differences over policy towards the Middle East were to become a near-permanent feature of Anglo-American relations.[5]

16

'I THINK IT IMPROBABLE THAT THE AMERICANS WOULD BECOME INVOLVED'

IN DECEMBER 1949, the British Foreign Office asked the War Office for an assessment of the dangers of war in Korea. The War Office replied that the North Korean objective undoubtedly was to overrun the South, but an invasion seemed unlikely: they would probably proceed by subversion. If an invasion did take place,

> I think it improbable that the Americans would become involved. The possession of South Korea is not essential for Allied strategic plans, and though it would obviously be desirable to deny it to the enemy, it would not be of sufficient importance to make it the cause of World War III. Meanwhile, we must ... hope for the best.[1]

The author of this report, Major Ferguson Innes, did not lack confidence. Unfortunately, he was wrong on all counts.

On 24 June 1950, Dean Acheson left Washington for a quiet weekend at his farm in Virginia. No sooner had he gone to bed than he was woken up to be told that North Korean forces had launched a massive attack across the 38th parallel and were driving the South Korean Army back towards Seoul. A UN Security Council resolution condemning the attack and demanding North Korean withdrawal was passed the next day, in the absence of the Soviet delegate, the infamous Jacob Malik, who was boy-cotting the council in protest at the failure to admit Communist China.

US armed forces were at the lowest point of their postwar run-down. Yet Truman and Acheson decided immediately that the aggression must be resisted. As Acheson commented: 'A doctrine that later became fashionable with presidents, called "keeping all options open" (apparently by avoid-ing decisions), did not appeal to Harry S. Truman.'[2] George Kennan told the British ambassador, Oliver Franks, that the symbolic significance of South Korea's preservation was tremendous, especially in Japan. Truman promised US air and naval support for the South Korean forces.

A further UN resolution was passed calling on member nations to ren-der South Korea such assistance as might be necessary to repel the armed attack. By 30 June, General MacArthur had visited the front, witnessed the rout of the South Korean Army and advised that the offensive could not be stopped without the commitment of US ground forces, to which Tru-man agreed. Acheson asked the British government to consider urgently what forces it might send to support the United Nations. Franks reported that US opinion was solidly behind Truman in wanting to call the Sovi-ets' bluff and not let the North Koreans get away with it. The Americans were convinced that the North Korean attack could not have taken place without Soviet connivance and encouragement.

Franks was a close friend of Acheson. He was an admirer of Truman and Marshall. Acheson, he noted, 'came to believe that the United States had an appointment with destiny, from which there was no way out but for the nation to lead and bend its whole energies to ordering the world'.[3] The US leaders saw the invasion of South Korea as part of the pattern of Soviet behaviour, following the Czech coup, the subjugation of Eastern Europe and the Berlin blockade. They were determined to meet the chal-lenge, as they had over Berlin.

And so were Clement Attlee and Ernest Bevin. The British Cabinet agreed on 27 June that it was the clear duty of the British government, with the other members of the United Nations, to help the South Koreans – even though this would impose a serious additional strain on the British economy.[4] In 1950, Britain's status as the third of the Big Three was not in doubt. It was not until April 1951 that Aneurin Bevan, Harold Wilson and John Freeman resigned from Attlee's government because the cost of rearmament was deemed by Hugh Gaitskell, Chancellor of the Exchequer, to necessitate the imposition of prescription and other charges for health care. The resignations came on the domestic issue – health care charges – not on that of the Korean War.

The British Cabinet noted, however, that it was not proven that the North Koreans were acting on orders from Moscow: there might be advantage in trying to isolate the conflict and deal with it as an act of aggression committed by the North Koreans on their own initiative. They worried that the Americans might provoke the Chinese into attacking Hong Kong.[5] The British had doubts as to how far the Russians and Chinese were pursuing a joint strategy and did not want a confrontation with China.

The British Far East fleet was ordered to join US naval forces in support of the South Koreans. Parliament was strongly behind the government, with only Tom Driberg and a handful of other left-wing Labour MPs protesting against British involvement. Michael Foot in *Tribune* declared that for Britain not to participate in UN action would be an act of appeasement.

The British ambassador in Moscow, Sir David Kelly, judged that the North Korean attack was certainly launched with Soviet knowledge and almost certainly at Soviet instigation. The Soviet Union probably had hoped for a walkover. The attack was intended to exploit a favourable local situation, not to provoke a general conflict. US military intervention had not been expected and the Russians would not want to find themselves entangled directly with the United States.

The Foreign Office assumed that US intentions were to clear the territory up to the 38th parallel. The British Chiefs of Staff warned that if US ground forces proved insufficient to restore the situation in Korea, the Americans might suggest dropping an atomic bomb on North Korea. The Chiefs of Staff noted that they were agreed 'from the military point of view that the dropping of an atomic bomb on North Korea would be unsound. The effects of such action would be worldwide, and might well be very damaging. Moreover it would probably provoke a global war.'

The Chiefs of Staff also registered 'strong military objections' to sending British land and air forces to Korea. Like Acheson, they saw the North Korean aggression as a further deliberate move in the Cold War by the Russians. The army and air force might be needed to deal with a still more serious crisis in Europe. They also pleaded manpower constraints, though the RAF at this time still had 120 squadrons of aircraft and the army had very large forces in Germany, the Middle East, Malaya and Hong Kong. But in the House of Commons on 5 July, Attlee, supported by Churchill, made clear that Britain would play its part: 'Surely, with the history of the last twenty years fresh in our minds, no one can doubt that it is vitally important that aggression should be halted at the outset.' National Service was extended to two years and social expenditure had to be cut to make way for rearmament.

As the South Korean Army was driven back, the British Chiefs of Staff were doubtful whether the United States would be able to keep a foothold in the peninsula. The war, they noted, 'cannot fail to be long, arduous and expensive in life and material'. If the UN forces were driven out, they suggested, 'we may well be faced with the situation that the Koreans as a whole will urge us not to return'. The people who would mainly suffer from 'liberation', they claimed, would be the South Koreans. In the event of evacuation, they urged an air offensive against North Korea. This, they acknowledged, might not succeed, but

> we shall be no worse off. We assume there will be no question of using the atomic bomb in Korea. The weapon must, in our view, be kept in reserve for use in the proper place in the event of a major war with Russia. Anyway there are no suitable objectives for it in North Korea.[6]

The British Chiefs of Staff feared becoming engulfed in Korea, while the Russians might strike elsewhere. The Americans considered that, whatever other crises might have to be faced, the immediate challenge was to stop the Communist aggression in South Korea.

On 23 July, Sir Oliver Franks advised that the decision whether to send British land forces to Korea would be crucial to the future relationship with the United States:

> Underneath the thoughts and emotions engendered at times by difficulties and disagreement between us and them there is a steady and unquestioning assumption that we are the only dependable ally and partner. This derives from our position in the world over past decades, our partnership with them in two world wars and their judgement of the British character. The Americans in Korea will be

> in a tough spot for a long time. They look round for their partner ...
> The second reason is that despite the power and position of the
> United States, the American people are not happy if they feel alone
> ... For these reasons I should expect the reaction of the United
> States Administration to a negative decision by us to be deep and
> prolonged ... I believe that because of the rational and irrational
> elements in the American mind about this for them unparalleled
> undertaking to act as a policeman in the world, a negative decision
> would seriously impair the long term relationship.[7]

Under pressure from Bevin and Attlee, the British Chiefs of Staff agreed, with great reluctance, that a brigade should be despatched to help. The American forces already in Korea struggled meanwhile to blunt the Communist offensive and hold on to the Pusan perimeter. At the end of August, the British 27th Brigade arrived to join them. Despatched in a hurry from Hong Kong, they were woefully ill-equipped for fighting in Korea. They were rushed into the line on 12 September.

While the North Korean advance was stopped at Taegu, General MacArthur was planning the greatest of all his military coups. Instead of trying to fight his way north from the Pusan perimeter to Seoul, he devised instead a wildly ambitious plan to land the First Marine Division at Inchon, outflanking completely the North Korean invasion forces and threatening them from the rear. MacArthur was virtually alone in favouring this operation. It was considered too risky by the Joint Chiefs of Staff, the US Navy and the local commanders, but MacArthur would brook no dissent. At the decisive staff meeting at his headquarters in Tokyo, MacArthur, brushing all objections aside, gave an inspired defence of his plan, ending in a dramatic hush: 'I can almost hear the ticking of the second hand of destiny ... We shall land at Inchon and I shall crush them.'[8]

And so it proved. On 15 September the landings took place, with brilliant success. Seoul was retaken and the North Korean forces north of the Pusan perimeter began a precipitate retreat.

Having won this great victory, MacArthur had no intention of stopping at the 38th parallel. His aim was to break the military power of Kim Il Sung's regime. The State Department at first argued that only South Korean forces should enter North Korea. Acheson joined the US Chiefs of Staff in replying that it was militarily absurd to march up to and stop at a surveyor's line. MacArthur was authorised to carry the fight to North Korea – provided there was no Soviet or Chinese military intervention.

The British government agreed that North Korean military power must be broken and that this meant carrying the fight to the North. The Foreign Secretary, Ernest Bevin, was a strong supporter of reunifying Korea under UN auspices.

But the British were becoming uneasy about the Chinese. They wanted the Allies to make clear that the occupation of North Korea would be temporary. They would have preferred British forces not to cross the 38th parallel, but accepted that they could not be held back while others advanced.

Bevin did not think the Russians or Chinese would intervene. MacArthur responded angrily to a British proposal that a buffer zone should be established south of the Yalu: 'The widely reported British desire to appease the Chinese Communists by giving them a strip of North Korea finds its historic precedent in the action taken at Munich on 29 September 1938.' General Bradley sought to reassure the British: 'We all agree that if the Chinese Communists come into Korea, we get out.'[9]

On 3 October, Zhou Enlai had told the Indian ambassador in Peking, Panikkar, that if the United Nations' forces crossed the 38th parallel, China would intervene. The US administration did not believe this report. Panikkar was distrusted in Washington as a Communist fellow-traveller. The first South Korean forces reached the Yalu on 26 October. On the same day they were attacked by forces that clearly were Chinese. So, a few days later, were the Argyll and Sutherland Highlanders.

MacArthur ordered the bombing of the Korean end of the bridges across the Yalu. The order was countermanded by Acheson and the Pentagon: for the State Department, Dean Rusk said that the Americans were committed to prior consultation with the British. As MacArthur prepared an offensive to deal with the enemy forces south of the Yalu, General Matthew Ridgway in the Pentagon pointed out that MacArthur's two armies advancing within reach of the eastern and western coasts of Korea were widely separated, leaving both of their flanks uncovered. Both armies suddenly were attacked by large Communist forces that had occupied the mountainous terrain south of the Yalu between the two wings of the Allied advance. The victor of Inchon was taken completely by surprise.

On 28 November, Truman was told by Bradley that 'a terrible message had come in from General MacArthur … The Chinese have come in with both feet.' The bad news from Korea had turned 'from rumours of resistance into certainty of defeat'.[10] Truman, Marshall and Acheson agreed that all-out war with China must be avoided. The United States' allies, including Britain, continued to oppose bombing the Yalu bridges or targets across the border. Attlee declared that Britain had 'no quarrel with the Chinese'. Acheson feared that if the USA bombed Chinese airfields, that could bring Russia into the war. MacArthur demanded reinforcements, including Chiang Kai-shek's army from Formosa – a request that was refused. All the military commanders were frustrated at the inability to attack targets on and beyond the Yalu. MacArthur fulminated against this 'enormous handicap, without precedent in military history'. As Chinese forces poured across the Yalu, the Allied retreat became a near rout.

In a press conference on 30 November, Truman said that the USA would take whatever steps were necessary to meet the military situation. Asked whether that would include the atomic bomb, Truman said: 'That includes every weapon we have.' Pressed to say whether this meant that there had been active consideration of the use of the atomic bomb, Truman said: 'There has always been active consideration of its use.'

By this stage, on 13 November 1950, the overseas policy committee of the British Cabinet already had concluded that it was no longer practicable, without risking a major war, to occupy North Korea and place it under UN control. They doubted if UN forces could reach the northern frontier without air attacks on Manchuria. 'Korea was of no strategic importance to the democratic powers; and further operations there should now be conducted with a view to preventing any extension of the conflict and avoiding any lasting commitment in the area.'[11] The Chiefs of Staff favoured a shorter line of defence, along the 40th parallel. Bevin was anxious to prevent the US government from being led by their military advisers into policies that would provoke further intervention by China. He feared that MacArthur would press his demands to bomb beyond the Yalu. Bevin had stoutly defended the British commitment in Korea to the Labour Party conference. But the Americans, faced with the imminent danger of defeat on the battlefield, were increasingly impatient at the hand-wringing of their allies.

In the parliamentary debate immediately following Truman's statements on 30 November, Bevin was forced to confess that he knew little of American intentions. For the Conservatives, Rab Butler spoke of 'the horror that many of us would feel' at the use of the atomic bomb in 'circumstances which were not such that out own moral conscience was satisfied that there was no alternative'. Attlee agreed with Butler. Churchill warned that

> the United Nations should avoid by every means in their power becoming entangled inextricably in a war with China ... the sooner the Far Eastern diversion ... can be brought into something like a static condition and stabilised, the better it will be ... For it is in Europe that the world cause will be decided ... it is there that the mortal danger lies.

Attlee ended the debate by announcing that he would fly to Washington to see Truman.

17

'ALL THE PASSION OF A WOODCHUCK CHEWING A CARROT'

ACHESON DID NOT find the Prime Minister's visit a particularly welcome one:

> December opened by bringing us a Job's comforter in Clement Attlee, the British Labour Prime Minister. He was a far abler man than Winston Churchill's description of him as a sheep in sheep's clothing would imply, but persistently depressing. He spoke, as John Jay Chapman said of President Charles W. Eliot of Harvard, with all the passion of a woodchuck chewing a carrot. His thought impressed me as a long withdrawing, melancholy sigh. The fright created in London when the British press misconstrued and exaggerated the unfortunate answers President Truman gave to questions at his press conference on November 30, 1950, propelled him across the ocean.

Acheson already had put out a statement to 'clarify' the President's remarks. He also had sought to reassure Oliver Franks, but Attlee still wanted to come – largely, Franks explained, for domestic political reasons.

One episode can hardly have helped to reassure Attlee during his visit. On 6 December, Acheson was told by the Pentagon that the US early

warning radar system in Canada had picked up formations of unidenti-
fied objects heading south-east on a course that could bring them over
Washington in two or three hours. US interception and defence forces were
alerted. Acheson was asked to inform but not consult the Prime Minister.
Acheson told Oliver Franks, who asked if the President was cancelling his
planned meeting with Attlee. Acheson said that he was not. Franks wondered about the purpose of his message. Acheson suggested fair warning
and the opportunity for prayer. The objects, fortunately, disappeared. It was
suspected that they were geese.[1]

Britain remained the United States' most important ally. The British
continued to worry about the constant tension in US policy between the
Pacific and the Atlantic. They had no doubt where MacArthur's sentiments lay. As his biographer, William Manchester, wrote: 'He hated an
entire continent: Europe.' Conscious of the vulnerability of Hong Kong
and determined to avoid becoming bogged down in a land war in Asia,
the British continued to oppose a confrontation with China.

In Korea, the military situation was desperate. Briefing Truman before
the meeting, General Bradley envisaged a withdrawal to beachheads in the
Seoul-Inchon and Pusan areas, from which the UN forces might have to
be evacuated. When Attlee and Truman met with their respective Chiefs
of Staff, Field Marshal Slim asked whether it was intended to hold the
beachheads or withdraw from them. General Marshall said that MacArthur had not been told to withdraw, but that the safety of his troops must
be his first consideration.

Acheson agreed on the need to avoid an all-out war with China, but
reacted sharply to British pressure for negotiations. This was, in Acheson's
view, the worst possible moment to negotiate. He regarded British views
on China as based on political and commercial self-interest and sought
to remind the British sharply of what was at stake in the struggle against
Communism in Asia. When the British proposed admitting China to the
UN, the Americans were adamantly opposed.

Marshall remonstrated that in these discussions Franks gave the impression that 'we had to proceed on the assumption that we were licked in
Korea'. Marshall rejected this view: '[I]t should not be treated as a fore-
gone conclusion that we are out of Korea.'

In his second meeting with Attlee, on the presidential yacht *Williamsburg*, Truman made clear that he would not agree to voluntary withdrawal:

'We must fight it out. If we failed, we should at least fail honorably.' Attlee replied: 'We are in this with you and we stand together.' But he saw it as a mistake to regard the Chinese as instruments of the Soviet Union. Rather, the aim should be to detach the Chinese from the Russians. The British expressed anxiety about their interests in Hong Kong, Malaya and Singapore if China were attacked.

Acheson agreed that the central opponent was not China but the Soviet Union. But, he replied, it would be a serious mistake to believe that the American people would follow a leadership that proposed a vigorous policy against aggression in Europe while accepting defeat in Asia. To cut and run would not be acceptable. The Chinese might be able to push the UN forces out, but that remained to be seen. There was a great difference between getting out and being forced out.[2]

In a further discussion over dinner at the British embassy on 6 December, Attlee raised the 'difficult and delicate' question of General MacArthur's conduct of the war and the absence of any Allied say in the decisions he took. According to the British, Acheson said that this raised the question 'whether any Government had any control over General MacArthur, a point on which he desired to express no view'.[3] Marshall and Bradley said that a war could not be run by a committee. Truman said that since all involved had entrusted the unified command to the United States and they continued to supply so preponderantly the means and men to carry on the war, they would have to go on exercising that responsibility. Acheson pointed out that the Prime Minister had been discussing the conduct of the war for three days with the President and all his key advisers. 'The President capped this bluntly by stating that we would stay in Korea and fight. If we had support from others, fine; if not, we would stay on anyway.'[4]

At this, what Acheson regarded as a second try by Field Marshal Slim and Air Marshal Arthur Tedder to get the United States to consider disengaging from Korea, rather than fighting a long war of attrition against large Chinese forces, sputtered out. On the following day, Bradley responded sharply to ideas that the Chinese should be treated diplomatically when they were attacking American and British forces. They were pouring troops into Korea, 'yet if we drop one bomb across the Yalu, they say we are making war'. Slim replied that if the Soviet Air Force intervened, 'we should have to say goodbye'. By the end of these very fraught meetings, there was slightly better news from Korea, with the US commanders estimating that they could eventually contain the Chinese advance.

———————

Acheson observed that Attlee's objective was to get Britain admitted to some participation in any future decision to use nuclear weapons. 'Mr Attlee's method of discussion was that of the suave rather than the belligerent cross-examiner … Framing his statements to draw Presidential agreement with his exposition, he soon led the President well onto the fly-paper.'

On the last day of the talks there was what Acheson described as 'one of those close calls that lurk in summit meetings'. Truman took Attlee off for a private word in his study. When they emerged, the President said they had agreed that neither would use nuclear weapons without consulting the other. This was in accordance with the agreement reached by Churchill and Roosevelt during the war. But following the passage of the McMahon Act, in January 1948 the British had been coerced into accepting a *modus vivendi* that superseded the earlier agreements and did not contain that crucial provision, now deemed unacceptable to the US Senate.

Acheson pointed out that the President alone had the duty and power under US law to authorise use of the atomic weapon if he believed it to be necessary in defence of the country. Congress would not accept any change in that respect.

> All agreed with this, albeit Mr Attlee a little sadly … The President pulled out the slide at the left of his desk. Oliver [Franks] left his chair and knelt between mine and Attlee's to write on it. 'I think that this is the first time', said the President, 'that a British ambassador has knelt before an American President.' Franks produced a paragraph for the communiqué that was far from satisfactory from the British point of view. The President expressed the hope that circumstances would never call for use of the atomic bomb. He added that it was 'his desire to keep the Prime Minister at all times informed of developments which might bring about a change in the situation.[5]

In the US memorandum for the record, of which the sole copy was retained in Secretary Marshall's office, the President recalled that the British and American governments

> had always been partners in this matter and that he would not consider the use of the bomb without consulting with the United Kingdom. The Prime Minister asked whether the agreement should be put in writing, and the President replied that it would not be in writing, that if a man's word wasn't any good it wasn't made any better by writing it down. The Prime Minister expressed his thanks.[6]

Attlee, optimistically, reported to Bevin that they had been treated as partners, 'unequal no doubt in power but still equal in counsel'.[7]

Acheson ended this, his first summit conference, with an ungranted prayer that he might be spared another, but satisfaction at the gap between Attlee's brief and what he had obtained. In fact, the summit prevented an open split developing between Britain and the United States. It had helped to damp down the furore in Britain caused by Truman's remarks and worries about MacArthur's intentions. But the British left Washington still worried that the Americans appeared to be considering a limited war against China.

Oliver Franks did not believe that the Americans ever seriously considered the use of atomic weapons in Korea. In fact, however, following the Chinese intervention, thought was given at the military planning level to possible targets. Acheson commented on 7 December that the British would demand consultation on any planned use of nuclear weapons. He would try to march in step with the British, but without constraining the President's ultimate freedom of action. The Joint Chiefs warned US commands that 'the current situation in Korea has greatly increased the possibility of general war'. Commanders were told to take such action as was feasible to increase readiness, without creating an atmosphere of panic. Opinion in the USA was running strongly in favour of tougher action to deal with the Chinese. On 24 December, MacArthur submitted a list of twenty-six targets in North Korea and China that he considered suitable for nuclear attack.

But the administration shared the British desire to limit the war. Acheson told the National Security Council on 12 December that the discussions with Attlee had demonstrated how important a close relationship with Britain remained, 'since we can bring US power into play only with the cooperation of the British'. While this was a large exaggeration, there was no doubt about the importance the administration attached to the continued support of its principal ally.

Truman and Acheson paid a political price for heeding the advice of the Allies. British opposition to attacks on military targets in China or on the bridges across the Yalu caused fury in MacArthur's headquarters at a time when Allied forces were under intense military pressure in the field. The Republicans were demanding that the administration should retaliate against China, or else withdraw. A sharp divide developed between the political and military leaders, with not only MacArthur but Bradley and the Joint Chiefs urging air strikes against Chinese military targets and lines of supply beyond the Yalu.

By this stage, Brigadier Basil Coad, commanding the British 27th Brigade, was painting a grim picture of the state of his forces and the difficulties of operating with the Americans. He was told to stick it out. By the New Year a second and much better equipped British brigade, the 29th, had arrived and was engaged immediately in repelling mass Chinese attacks, heralded by trumpets, in 'Happy Valley', north of Seoul.

General Sir Robert Mansergh, commanding British forces in Hong Kong, reported at this time that: 'I doubt whether any British really think that the war in Korea will be brought to a successful conclusion.' He criticised the US Army as unwilling to leave the roads and, therefore, prone to let itself be outflanked. 'The British troops, although sympathetic to the South Koreans in their adversity, despise them and are not interested in this civil war.'[8] MacArthur, for his part, was convinced that the opportunity of military victory was being denied him and the lives of his troops imperilled by feeble allies.

At Christmas 1950, General Matthew Ridgway arrived to take command of the Eighth Army in Korea, under MacArthur's overall control. Few field commanders have ever made such a difference, so rapidly, to the performance of the troops under their command. Ridgway rallied the Allied forces, organised them for defence in depth across the narrow waist of the Korean peninsula and brought superior fire-power to bear on the mass Chinese attacks. The difficulty of the choices facing Truman was reduced as the US military commanders became convinced that they could contain the Chinese offensive. On 26 January, MacArthur told Brigadier Coad that on the Yalu, the Chinese might be able to support a million men under arms; at Pyongyang, this fell to 600,000 and by the 38th parallel to 300,000. Air Vice-Marshal C. A. Bouchier reported to London: 'The myth of the magical millions of the Chinese in Korea has been exploded. In the last United Nations offensive, the Americans have learned how easy it is to kill the Chinese and their morale has greatly increased.' In March, Seoul was retaken by the Allies.

At the turn of the year, MacArthur had been told that the administration now was committed to fighting a limited war for limited objectives. They were convinced that Korea was the wrong place to precipitate a general war.

The British military attaché, Brigadier A. K. Ferguson, foresaw difficulties in maintaining morale, given the ill-defined nature of the military task. But Ridgway by now had a tested, tough and confident army, which he was convinced could deal with anything short of massive Soviet military intervention. As the Allied armies fought their way back north towards the 38th parallel, Truman wanted to start discussing a peace based on that position. MacArthur, increasingly publicly, disagreed. As his biographer, William Manchester, observed, he simply could not bear to end his career in stalemate. He detested the British who, he believed, were conspiring against him. The distrust was mutual. On 9 April, Field Marshal Slim, Chief of the Imperial General Staff, told his colleagues that, in this opinion, General MacArthur personally wanted war with China. The American Chiefs of Staff, he believed, were scared of MacArthur and might be pushed by him into authorising massive air attacks beyond the Yalu.

The British Foreign Secretary telegraphed to Franks in Washington:

> Our principal difficulty is General MacArthur. His policy is different from the policy of the UN. He seems to want a war with China. We do not. It is no exaggeration to say that by his public utterances, he has weakened public confidence in this country and in Western Europe in the quality of American political judgement and leadership. Here we seem to have a case of a commander publicly suggesting that his policy is not the stated policy of his government,

not subject to the control of his own government, and whom his own government is, nevertheless, unwilling and unable to discipline.[9]

In fact, Truman already had decided that MacArthur would have to be dismissed: 'I could no longer tolerate his insubordination.' The final straw was MacArthur's message to a Congressman: 'As you have pointed out, we must win. There is no substitute for victory.' On 7 April, Bradley told Truman that MacArthur had shown repeatedly that he was not in sympathy with the decision to try to limit the conflict to Korea: it was necessary to have a commander more responsive to control from Washington.

On 11 April, MacArthur was dismissed and replaced by Ridgway. He returned to ticker-tape parades, his great address to Congress ('old soldiers never die, they just fade away'), Senate hearings and a hero's welcome in the United States. In Britain the feeling was one of immense relief.

18

'THE TIMELY USE OF ATOMIC WEAPONS SHOULD BE CONSIDERED'

THE BRIEFS FOR Attlee's visit to Washington in the most critical phase of the Korean War were prepared by the head of the American Department in the Foreign Office, Donald Maclean. Serving in the British embassy in Washington from 1944 to 1948, he had been one of the few officials there with access to the files about 'Tube Alloys' and was a junior member of the British negotiating team in the discussions leading to the establishment of NATO. Maclean had been recruited by Soviet intelligence while at Cambridge before the war, together with Kim Philby, Guy Burgess and Anthony Blunt. Appointed to Cairo as the youngest Counsellor in the Foreign Service, Maclean, after two days of heavy drinking with his friend Philip Toynbee, destroyed a flat belonging to two girls in the American embassy. This unusual behaviour caused him to be recalled to London, but did not prevent him from being put in charge of relations with North America.

In March 1951, in a comment on Anglo-American relations, Maclean wrote: 'There is a good deal of disquiet here about American leadership, particularly fear that their fire-eating in the Far East and generally will land us unnecessarily in war.' This caused no surprise, as such attitudes were common currency in the Foreign Office at the time. A few days later Sir Oliver Franks, visiting London, had a meeting with the Permanent Under-Secretary in the Foreign Office in which there was an anguished discussion of the decline of the 'special relationship'. Not long afterwards, Maclean minuted that 'Americans have for some time had a steady diet of "punishing the aggressor", "fighting communism" etc.', and wondered when they would come up with a comprehensible policy in China and Korea.

By this time the US/UK Venona project targeting KGB communications had revealed the existence of a spy, codenamed 'Homer', in the British Foreign Service, as well as the activities of Klaus Fuchs. On 25 May 1951, the Foreign Secretary, Herbert Morrison, approved a recommendation that Maclean should be interrogated. That evening Maclean and Guy Burgess defected to Russia, via France.

Burgess had just been sent home in disgrace by Oliver Franks for various escapades, including being stopped three times in one day for speeding by the Virginia police, causing the Governor of Virginia to protest vigorously to the ambassador. Burgess shared a house in Washington with Philby, who, as the senior representative of MI6 (the Secret Intelligence Service), was aware of the investigation into 'Homer'. Burgess was instructed by Philby to warn Maclean, but it was not Philby's intention that Burgess also should defect. Philby's last words to Burgess were: 'Don't you go as well.'

In Washington, the State Department at first found it very difficult to get any answers from the Foreign Office about the disappearance of Burgess and Maclean, though MI5 had forewarned the FBI – in a message seen by Philby – that Maclean was about to be questioned. On 7 June, testifying to the Senate about the dismissal of MacArthur, Dean Acheson was asked about reports that two British diplomats had defected. Acheson was obliged to reply that he had only just heard of this from a broadcast. On the same day, the US embassy reported that the Foreign Office claimed to have no information about the intentions of Burgess and Maclean. It was not until 11 June that Sir Percy Sillitoe, head of MI5, visited Washington to confirm to Edgar Hoover and the FBI that Burgess and Maclean had disappeared and must be presumed to have been Soviet agents. Hoover was scathing about the failure to intercept them or to inform the FBI of their disappearance before he learned of it from the press.

It was not the British but the Americans who forced the recall of Philby, who still had his supporters in the British Secret Intelligence Service (SIS), unwilling to believe that their wartime comrade was a spy. General Bedell Smith, head of the CIA, informed the head of SIS that he was no longer prepared to deal with his representative in London. Philby had found Bedell Smith to have a 'cold, fishy eye and a precision tool brain ... Bedell

Smith, I had an uneasy feeling, would be apt to think that two and two made four rather than five.'[1]

These spectacular defections caused enormous strains, yet they did not destroy the Anglo-American intelligence partnership. The special nature of the relationship that had been built up during the war was reaffirmed and codified after it. SIS had been virtually present at the creation of the CIA and, Philby and subsequent inquisitions notwithstanding, the ties between them remained much closer than between any other services. But the core of the relationship remained the continuing exchange of signals intelligence intercepts between the Government Communications Head-quarters in Cheltenham and the US National Security Agency, established during their wartime collaboration.

The fall-out at the time was serious. The nuclear spies, Nunn May and Klaus Fuchs, Philby, Burgess and Maclean all had done much damage to the Allied cause, as another member of SIS, George Blake – recruited by the Russians while in captivity during the Korean War – also was to do. But the Americans were suffering from their own spy cases, notably that of Alger Hiss, a far more influential figure in the State Department than Maclean had been in the Foreign Office and a member of the US delega-tion at Yalta. Philby's closest friend in the CIA, James Angleton, chief of the agency's counter-espionage service, was so horrified by Philby's treachery that he became obsessed with the notion that other senior members of SIS and the CIA were Soviet moles. The Soviet KGB defector Oleg Gordievsky notes that the most enduring damage done by Philby and the 'Cambridge Comintern' to the Anglo-American intelligence community was to lead Angleton, Peter Wright of MI5 and a minority of intelligence officers on both sides of the Atlantic into a 'wilderness of mirrors, searching in vain for the chimera of a still more vast but imaginary Soviet deception'.[2]

Many in the CIA were outraged by the Philby case and what they regarded as a tragi-comic performance by the British in their handling of the subsequent investigation. Both sides continued to suffer from cases in which Soviet agents compromised the other's operations, including much later that of Aldrich Ames, who may have compromised Gordievsky. Yet the collaboration in this field was so ingrained, and felt to be so useful, as to withstand the most severe tests. Within two years the British were rendering the CIA invaluable assistance with the operation that led to the overthrow of the Mossadeq regime in Iran (Chapter 19).

Meanwhile in Korea, in the days following the dismissal of MacArthur, the First Battalion of the British Gloucestershire Regiment was fighting a desperate battle on the Imjin River against an overwhelming Chinese attack. The Gloucesters received no air support and artillery had to be withdrawn. Only one officer and thirty-nine men escaped. Sixty-three men were killed and the rest, many of them wounded, were taken prisoner. The Chinese, however, suffered fearful casualties in this and other encounters, and the assault on the Imjin was to prove their last full-scale offensive of the war.

A war of attrition continued for the next two years, while the North Koreans turned the peace talks in Panmunjom into a propaganda farce. Tens of thousands more casualties were suffered as Ridgway's forces continued to hold at bay seven Chinese armies and two North Korean Army corps. In the South, the British press and soldiers were horrified at the treatment of its own people by the corrupt and dictatorial government of Syngman Rhee. Holding, apparently, the British government responsible for the dismissal of MacArthur, Rhee stated publicly that the British and other Commonwealth troops had outlived their welcome in South Korea. But the British, like the Americans, who continued to bear the brunt of the fighting, hung on grimly. The Commonwealth Division with units from Britain, Canada, Australia, New Zealand and South Africa won an outstanding reputation over the next two years. RAF pilots flew with the American air squadrons, learning at first hand the extraordinary scale of US military resources. While undergoing training on Sabre jets in the United States, Flight Lieutenant John Nicholls of the RAF found that there were more aircraft at Nellis Air Force Base than in the whole of RAF Fighter Command.[3]

By this stage the war had reached a violent stalemate. Ridgway's successor in Korea, General Van Fleet, now commanding the Allied troops in Korea, believed that he could break through and roll up the enemy line, but only at a heavy cost in casualties. The North Koreans continued to spin out the negotiations in Panmunjom while heavy fighting continued. The war had become unpopular in the United States. General Mark Clark, who succeeded Ridgway, as overall commander, took just as jaundiced a view of Syngman Rhee and his rigged elections as the British did.

On 29 March 1952, his popularity affected by the war, Truman announced that he would not stand for re-election. In April, Eisenhower asked to be relieved of his command in NATO to run for President.

Eisenhower promised, if elected, to go to Korea and he did so before his inauguration. He acknowledged the unlikelihood of winning a decisive victory, but said that the United States would see it through. Advised by MacArthur to bomb China, Eisenhower said that he would have to look at the understandings with the Allies.

In January 1953, the United States tested successfully the first nuclear artillery shell. In March the Joint Chiefs of Staff produced a study which suggested: 'The efficacy of atomic weapons in achieving greater results at less cost of effort in furtherance of US objectives in connection with Korea points to the desirability of re-evaluating the policy which now restricts the use of atomic weapons in the Far East.' It added that, in view of the implications of committing larger ground forces, 'the timely use of atomic weapons should be considered against targets affecting military operations in Korea'. On 19 May, the Joint Chiefs recommended air and naval operations against China, including the use of nuclear weapons. There should be no gradual escalation of force, they argued, but a dramatic surprise attack.[4]

Eisenhower's Secretary of State, John Foster Dulles, visiting India, told Nehru that a warning should be conveyed to Chou En Lai. If a peace agreement were not reached soon at Panmunjom, the United States would begin to attack targets north of the Yalu. Dulles added that the Americans had recently carried out successful tests of atomic artillery shells.

At one of the first National Security meetings of the Eisenhower presidency, Dulles spoke of the need to make the idea of nuclear weapons more acceptable and to counter the Soviet success to date in 'setting atomic weapons apart from all other weapons as being in a special category. It was his opinion that we should try to break down this distinction.' Eisenhower suggested the Kaesong area of North Korea as 'providing a good target for this type of weapon'. In March, Eisenhower and Dulles agreed that, somehow, the taboo that surrounded the use of atomic weapons needed to be destroyed. Eisenhower said that although there were not many good targets, he felt that the use of tactical nuclear weapons would be worth the political cost if a major victory could be won in Korea.[5]

While it is impossible to say if Eisenhower really would have considered authorising the use of nuclear weapons in the event of further massive Chinese attacks on Allied ground forces in Korea, there is no doubt that the attitude of the Allies, led by the British, was a major limiting factor. The American warnings and the development of tactical nuclear capabilities did appear, however, to make the desired impression on the North Koreans. After nearly two years of stalemate, the talks in Panmunjom suddenly began to make progress.

On 27 July 1953, the armistice was signed. General Mark Clark bitterly regretted becoming 'the first US commander in history to sign an armistice without victory'. Like most of the other senior military, he believed that the USA should have bombed beyond the Yalu.

Of the 1,319,000 Americans serving in Korea, over 33,000 were killed and over 100,000 wounded. Britain, Canada, Australia and New Zealand suffered 1,263 losses and 4,817 wounded. Hundreds of thousands of North and South Koreans and Chinese were killed.

Many Americans, including the military, were exasperated by the prevarication and scruples of allies who made a relatively small military contribution. But that contribution was politically very significant. The war in Korea was very much an American show. But British participation was important to the United States. It also was important in sustaining US support for NATO. Korea was the first major war to be waged in the nuclear age – an attempt to apply limited force to achieve limited objectives. Allied troops, who found the war infinitely frustrating, chafed under the restrictions imposed by their political masters. Nor did they enjoy fighting to make the world safe for Syngman Rhee. But they succeeded in their objective, which was to defeat North Korean aggression. The support the US administration got from Attlee and Bevin, despite the reservations of the British Chiefs of Staff, was crucial to the development of postwar Anglo-American relations. But fears of the costs of being entangled in a land war in Asia remained. It was for military as well as political reasons that the British, subsequently, refused to become involved in US efforts in Vietnam.

19

'WHAT COULD BE MORE EARTHY THAN COAL OR STEEL?'

IN MAY 1950, Acheson visited Paris on his way to London for a meeting of the North Atlantic Council. Acheson's presence in Paris, he wrote later, 'in view of what occurred, convinced Bevin of a Franco-American conspiracy against him'.

The French Foreign Minister, Robert Schuman, explained privately to Acheson the plans he had been developing with Jean Monnet to place all French and German production of coal and steel under a joint high authority, which would be open to the participation of other European countries. As Acheson observed, the more the Americans examined the plan, the more they were impressed by it. Its genius lay in its practical common-sense approach: 'What could be more earthy than coal and steel...? This would end age-old conflicts. It was not exclusive but open to all European nations who wished to participate.'

Two days later, Acheson met Bevin in London. He found him in a distressing condition, recovering from major surgery and taking sedative drugs 'that made him doze off, sometimes quite soundly, during the discussion'. Informed by the French of the Schuman Plan, an angry Bevin accused Acheson of conspiring with Schuman. Acheson acknowledged that he had been stupid in failing to foresee Bevin's rage at not being consulted from the outset and the difficulties Schuman's plan posed for the Labour government's strategy of nationalised control over coal and steel. Despite all Acheson's arguments, Britain made 'her great mistake of the post-war period by refusing to join in negotiating the Schuman Plan'. Acheson welcomed the plan publicly as a most important development, designed to further a *rapprochement* between Germany and France and progress towards the economic integration of Western Europe, which were objectives favoured by the United States government: 'In this way we did our best to back the launching with a fair breeze. But Bevin was still growling.'

When Schuman and Acheson arrived in London, Bevin complained about the lack of consultation. When Schuman formally invited the British to join with the Benelux countries, France, Germany and Italy in working out the treaty establishing the European Coal and Steel Community, the British refused. British GNP at this time was the second largest in the world, having only recently ceased to equal that of France and West Germany combined, and the British government did not want to be bound by the decisions of a joint European authority. It wanted to be able to pursue its own plans for the coal and steel industries. 'Important but secondary', commented Acheson, 'was the national policy of special ties with the Commonwealth and the United States', as well as the traditional determination of the British to go their own way. Britain, Bevin told Schuman, could never become an entirely European country.

On the eve of the Korean War, the State Department had prepared a paper which concluded: 'No other country has the same qualifications for being our principal ally and partner ... The British and with them the rest of the Commonwealth, particularly the older dominions, are our most reliable and useful Allies, with whom a special relationship should exist.' But, the paper noted, the British were inclined to make the relationship more overt than the United States felt desirable. They reacted strongly to being treated as just another European power. Acheson was not pleased:

> It was not the origin that bothered me, but the fact that the wretched paper existed. In the hands of trouble-makers it could stir up no end of a hullabaloo, both domestic and international ... Of course a unique relation existed between Britain and America – our common language and history ensured that.

But, Acheson argued, unique did not mean affectionate. Sentiment, he bizarrely suggested, was reserved for America's oldest ally, France.

Acheson's real problem was that 'my own attitude had long been, and was known to have been, pro-British'. His annoyance about the paper

was not caused by doubt about the genuineness of the special relationship, or about the real identity of Britain and American interests
in Europe and elsewhere ... My annoyance came from the stupidity
of writing about a special relationship, which could only increase
suspicions among our allies of secret plans and purposes and [just
as important to Acheson – give the Mayor Thompsons, McCarthys
and others] proof that the State Department was the tool of a foreign power. So all copies of the paper that could be found were
collected and burned.

The European Coal and Steel Community Treaty was signed by the Six
in April 1951. Exasperated by British resistance to schemes for European
economic integration, both David Bruce, then US ambassador in Paris,
and Averell Harriman felt that the United States had been 'too tender with
the British since the War'.

   During the remainder of his stay in London, Acheson dined with the
King and Queen, whom he greatly admired. Arriving at Chequers for
lunch with the Attlees on a miserable spring day, the Achesons found the
house 'noticeably colder than the outdoors'. Bevin tried to warm himself
by huddling in the fireplace. Acheson resorted to 'the far more reliable
device of straight gin'. As they entered the dining room, Mrs Attlee thought
it stuffy and had the Wrens who were serving lunch open the windows.
'As they did so, the curtains stood out.' The American female guests kept
on their fur coats.[1]

––––––––––

The Conservative victory in the British elections in October 1951 brought
Winston Churchill and Anthony Eden back to power. Acheson and Eden
attended the sixth General Assembly of the United Nations in Paris. At
first, they got on well. 'Eden and I worked easily together, agreed on basic
matters, where he was a resourceful and strong ally.' There were to be
plenty of disagreements later. Eden, Acheson noted, was more cautious
in departing from traditional policies, 'quite understandably, as he had
been far more deeply involved in making them'. For the Russians, Vyshin-
sky, Stalin's prosecutor in the show trials of the 1930s and now Soviet
representative at the United Nations, contributed a series of aggressive

diatribes, the effect of which he attempted to soften by appearing with a captive dove.

When, in January 1952, Churchill returned to Washington as Prime Minister, Acheson viewed his arrival with mixed feelings. 'Official visits were never relaxing and always time-consuming affairs. On both counts, Mr Churchill usually topped the list.' The House of Representatives demanded full and complete information about any agreements, commitments or understandings reached during the discussions. 'Curiously enough, while among our allies the French consistently caused us trouble ... the more forthright British were suspected of dominating us.'

But Truman was determined that Churchill should return home in a good mood. This, Acheson noted, did not require concessions or changes in US policy, but 'long, intimate and frank discussions conducted with respect and good will. The impression we hoped he would leave behind was that Britain was doing and would do its share. In this he was brilliantly successful.'

Matters on which the Truman administration disagreed with the Attlee government included policy towards the Soviet Union, China, European integration and nationalism in Iran and Egypt. Even Acheson, however, was somewhat in awe of Churchill. Truman often spoke of Churchill as the greatest public figure of the age. To Acheson, this was an understatement: 'He used all the artifices to get his way, from wooing and cajolery through powerful advocacy to bluff bullying ... the old lion seemed to be weakening, though still formidable and quite magnificent.'

Churchill was given an extraordinary reception, including six formal meetings with the President. After dinner on the President's yacht on the Potomac, Churchill asked Acheson if he did not feel that 'around the table this evening there was gathered the governance of the World – not to dominate it, mind you, but to save it?'[2]

Acheson complained that confidences given to the British government were being relayed to Commonwealth governments, which then protested that the Americans should be dealing with them direct. Churchill was deeply sceptical about Schuman's proposed European Defence Community, but agreed not to oppose it. Sharp differences remained over Iran, where Acheson considered the visitors drawn to courses high in debating appeal and short on practicality. A discussion with Eden became sufficiently heated on this point for Acheson to have to apologise afterwards.

Acheson also considered that the British were mishandling the situation in Egypt, where anti-British sentiment was running strong and clashes between British and Egyptian troops in the Canal zone were shortly to take place. The Pentagon, Acheson observed, wanted Britain to remain responsible for the defence of the Suez Canal and the Middle East, while noting her declining capability to perform the mission. Lord Cherwell painted a dark picture of Britain's economic and financial state and the thinness of her reserves.

On 17 January, Churchill returned from Canada to address a joint session of Congress. British and American staff officers and the previous British government had agreed that NATO naval forces in the Atlantic should be placed under an American commander. When this part of the communiqué was shown to Churchill, he tore it to shreds. As the Prime Minister's emotional outburst on the subject rolled to its conclusion, a note came from Oliver Franks across the table, warning Acheson to be 'very, very careful'. Acheson found a face-saving formula.

After the meetings, *Newsweek* published a well-founded article about a clash of personalities between Eden and Acheson. Acheson attempted to mend fences. In the subsequent four-power meetings with Schuman and Adenauer, Acheson commented, Eden 'could be counted on to end up on the side of the angels, which I tended to identify with my own. If sometimes it took him a little time to get there, he was well worth waiting for.'[3]

On one crucial issue, Churchill had been disappointed. He returned to office convinced that he could restore the wartime atomic collaboration between Britain and the United States. He intended, he said, to 'arrange to be allocated a reasonable share of what they have made so largely on our initiative and substantial scientific contribution'. Lord Cherwell believed that Churchill was living in the past on this subject: Britain would only be taken seriously by the Americans when it had produced its own nuclear weapon.[4] Churchill's pleas for the renewal of cooperation got nowhere. On 3 October 1952, the first British atomic bomb was exploded at Monte Bello in Australia.

20

'NEVER HAD SO FEW LOST SO MUCH SO STUPIDLY AND SO FAST'

IN THIS PERIOD, writes Denis Greenhill from the vantage point of the British embassy in Washington at the time, 'handicapped by its economic problems, the British Government had the task of trying to make a controlled descent from a position of world power. The Middle East was an area in which British power had far exceeded that of the US.'[1]

The Americans believed that the British were clinging to outmoded colonialist ambitions that conflicted with their own supposedly more liberal views. There also was a very sharp element of straightforward commercial rivalry. Roosevelt in 1944 had felt it necessary to urge Churchill to accept his assurances 'that we are not making sheep's eyes at your oil fields in Iraq or Iran'. Churchill replied that the British had no thought of trying to horn in on American interests in Saudi Arabia.

For the Iranians, the British-controlled Anglo-Iranian Oil Company had become a symbol of foreign exploitation. For the British, it was vital to the security of their oil supplies. The Labour government, despite its own record on state ownership, was infuriated when the Iranian Prime Minister, Dr Mossadeq, nationalised the company in April 1951. This placed them in serious domestic difficulty, with Churchill accusing the Labour Party of failing to defend British interests and of a policy of 'scuttle'.

Acheson considered that the British had brought this on themselves. George McGhee, Assistant Secretary for Near East Affairs in the State Department, had urged them to make concessions that, the Americans believed, might have averted nationalisation. In Saudi Arabia the Arabian-American

Oil Company (ARAMCO) had announced a new contract based on a 50 per cent division of the profits with the Saudi government. This was the model that, the Americans contended, should have been followed by Anglo-Iranian. About their performance Acheson commented: 'Never had so few lost so much so stupidly and so fast.' In the view of the United States, the British, having precipitated a crisis by their own inflexibility, were now looking to the Americans to get them out of it. The British regarded the histrionic, pyjama-clad Mossadeq with contempt. But in America initially he attracted some anti-imperialist sympathy for the underdog.

In London the Foreign Secretary, Herbert Morrison, was advocating the use of force to recover Anglo-Iranian's assets. As British warships patrolled off Abadan, Acheson warned Oliver Franks against military action.

Truman and Acheson tried in vain to mediate. Acheson feared that Britain 'might drive Iran to a Communist *coup d'état*, or Iran might drive Britain out of the country. Either would be a major disaster. We were deeply concerned.' Anglo-Iranian by this time was making what Acheson regarded as reasonable negotiating offers, which were rejected by Mossadeq. But, with its employees given one week to decide whether to work for the nationalised company, Anglo-Iranian threatened to shut down operations. Acheson thought this would be a disaster. 'It would face us with the possibility of an economic collapse in Iran, a Communist coup and the loss of Iran to the West.' If British personnel were withdrawn, he argued, they might never be able to return.

As HMS *Mauritius* appeared off Abadan to protect British personnel at the refinery, Mossadeq claimed that the first shot fired would signal the start of a Third World War. Convinced that both sides were 'pressing their luck to the point of suicide in the game of Russian roulette', Acheson, Harriman, McGhee and others held a crisis meeting on the fourth of July holiday in Washington with Franks.

Franks, who had just returned from London, left them in no doubt how seriously and angrily the British government and public regarded Iranian actions. He doubted whether the British government could or should resist the popular sentiment that Mossadeq's seizure of British assets should be met by force. Acheson was convinced that British military intervention at Abadan would trigger Soviet intervention in northern Iran, from which after the Second World War the Russians had only been persuaded with difficulty to withdraw. There would be uproar in the United Nations, with the Americans obliged to side against Britain.

Acheson proposed that, to stop the drift towards military intervention, Averell Harriman should go to Tehran to try to get negotiations started again. The British ambassador in Tehran, Francis Shephard, opined publicly that there 'was not much point' to the visit. Acheson regarded Shephard as an 'unimaginative disciple of the "whiff of grapeshot" school of diplomacy'. Morrison also expressed doubts, but Truman despatched Harriman anyway.[2]

He got a torrid reception in Tehran, as the Communists organised a violent demonstration against him, and he found Mossadeq almost impossible to negotiate with. Far from taking two steps forward and one back, reported Vernon Walters, who accompanied Harriman as his military aide, Mossadeq's method was to take one step forward and two back. Harriman, however, was as critical as Acheson of the British 'colonial mindset' and their failure to understand the growth of nationalism in underdeveloped countries. Eventually, Harriman thought he had achieved a breakthrough, as Mossadeq appeared to agree to negotiations if the British accepted the principle of nationalisation.[3]

Harriman flew to London to convince the British, who offered to send a senior business envoy, Sir Richard Stokes, to negotiate. Franks told Acheson that he thought Harriman's mission had been a godsend. But on arrival Stokes and Harriman found Mossadeq completely intransigent. On a visit to inspect the refinery at Abadan, Harriman insisted on travelling separately from the British and pronounced the accommodation for the Iranian workers 'shocking for housing of employees of a large Western oil company'. The British offered transfer of the ownership of the refinery and a 50/50 division of the profits, but Mossadeq refused to accept British management. Harriman's patience with Mossadeq had worn out. It was, he concluded, impossible to deal with him. The talks broke down. Having urged the young Shah to take a more active interest in the nationalisation controversy, Harriman left for Washington.

In September 1951, Mossadeq announced that if the British did not come to terms, he would expel the British technicians working for Anglo-Iranian. At a Cabinet meeting in London on 27 September, the Labour Foreign Secretary, Herbert Morrison, argued the case for the use of force in response to Mossadeq's behaviour. Showing greater wisdom than his successors, Attlee vetoed the suggestion. Truman and Acheson, he pointed out, had made clear that a policy of force would not have their support: 'We could not afford to break with the United States on an issue of this kind.'[4]

Herbert Morrison flew to Washington for talks with Acheson. Denis Greenhill helped to organise his visit. 'It was difficult not to feel sorry for him, but also not to feel a little ashamed. He was clearly exhausted but totally out of his depth ... he was no match for Acheson and there was no compatibility.' Acheson commented that Morrison 'knew nothing of foreign affairs and had no feel for situations beyond the sound of Bow bells. Perhaps to compensate for a sense of insecurity, he accentuated a natural abrasiveness of temperament.'[5]

Acheson remarked on the irony of a Labour Foreign Secretary arguing furiously against nationalisation, at any rate in Iran. In New York, Mossadeq elicited more public sympathy than the British representative at the UN, Gladwyn Jebb. But when he came to Washington, Acheson in turn was to discover that negotiating with Mossadeq was 'like walking in a maze and every so often finding oneself at the beginning again'.

By this time the Labour government had lost the election. Morrison gave way to Anthony Eden, whom Acheson found a 'signal improvement, except on Iran'. In November 1951, US efforts to mediate were broken off, with Acheson still believing that a deal could have been made if the British had been more forthcoming.

There is not much evidence to suggest that he was right. Acheson himself acknowledged that the Americans were slow to realise that Mossadeq was motivated by a determination to eradicate completely British influence in Iran.

The British were successful, with the help of the Royal Navy, in preventing the Iranians from selling oil, which, in the British view, belonged to Anglo-Iranian. Acheson still wanted negotiations. But Mossadeq continued 'whirling like a dervish' and Eden saw no need for haste. Iran's economy, he believed, was too primitive to collapse and Communist rule was not the only alternative to Mossadeq. Acheson made further proposals to London and was incensed at the reply. 'The Ambassador [Oliver Franks] did an excellent job of calming me down and cooling me off in his incomparable quiet and humorous way.'

But in Eden's absence Churchill now proposed to Truman that they should make a joint approach to the Iranians. This was done, substantially on the basis earlier proposed by Acheson, but it was rejected by Mossadeq.

By this time London was convinced not only that no agreement could be reached with Mossadeq, but also that he was not as secure politically as he might appear.

Truman still hoped that something might be achieved before the end of his term of office. US purchases of Iranian oil had been discouraged. To pressurise the British, Acheson issued a statement that decisions whether to purchase Iranian oil must be left to individual judgement and appraisal of the legal risks involved. Acheson told Eden that Iran was on the verge of an explosion in which Mossadeq would break relations with the United States, after which nothing could save the country from disappearing behind the Iron Curtain. But when he consulted the US oil companies, Acheson found that they shared Eden's doubts about the feasibility of doing business with Mossadeq. The US ambassador, Loy Henderson, told Mossadeq that once compensation was agreed, the United States would make large immediate payments against future deliveries of oil. As was his habit, Mossadeq kept shifting his position and Henderson's efforts foundered. Eden considered that 'we should be better occupied looking for alternatives to Mussadig [sic] rather than trying to buy him off'.[6]

As it turned out, Eden was vindicated, at any rate in the near term. In February 1953, Mossadeq opened a propaganda attack on the Shah and had to escape from a royalist mob. Eisenhower (who had taken office in January) and Dulles were ready to adopt a tougher attitude towards Mossadeq than the Truman administration had done. In fact, British intelligence now believed there was enough opposition to enable them and the CIA to encourage a coup. But their own operations were handicapped by the expulsion of British diplomatic personnel from Tehran by Mossadeq. So the British offered to make available their network of contacts to the CIA. The CIA effort was led by Kim Roosevelt, grandson of Teddy Roosevelt. With British assistance, they gave active backing and financial help to Mossadeq's opponents. Mossadeq compounded his own problems by dissolving the Iranian parliament, the *Majlis*. He then found himself pressed from the left by the Communists.

In a secret meeting with the Shah, to demonstrate that he had British as well as American support, Roosevelt told him that he would arrange for the BBC announcer on the following evening, instead of saying 'It is now midnight', to say, 'It is now *exactly* midnight'. As Eisenhower wrote in his diary: 'It seemed more like a dime novel than an historical fact.' The Shah was encouraged by Roosevelt to dismiss Mossadeq. When he attempted to do so, the officer carrying the orders was arrested and the Shah had to go hurriedly into exile. Within a few days, however, encouraged by Britain and the United States, the army intervened, jailing Mossadeq and restoring the Shah.

Kim Roosevelt was summoned by Churchill to receive his congratulations. The alternative to Mossadeq for which the British had been looking had been found. A new agreement was worked out with a consortium of American and European oil companies, in which Anglo-Iranian had less than a half interest. This, Acheson claimed, was not as good a deal as they could have got before, but to the British, this was nonsense: Mossadeq had never accepted any of Acheson's proposals. Acheson considered the whole affair an illustration of Oxenstierna's question: 'Dost thou not know, my son, with how little wisdom the world is governed?'[7]

Nevertheless, the balance of power in the Middle East had shifted decisively in favour of the Americans. As the British ambassador in Washington, Sir Roger Makins, pointed out in 1954, they were now firmly established as the predominant foreign influence in Turkey and Saudi Arabia and, increasingly, in Iran. The British wondered if the Americans were 'consciously trying to substitute their influence for ours in the Middle East', whereas the Americans saw themselves as filling the vacuum caused by the decline of British power. The success of the operation to dislodge Mossadeq contributed powerfully to the mystique of the CIA in the 1950s and was to be followed by further successes in toppling left-wing regimes in Central America. The resultant exaggerated notions of what covert action could achieve were to lead in turn to an expensive fiasco eight years later in the Bay of Pigs (Chapter 27).

21

'THE MOST POWERFUL OF THE ANTI-COLONIAL POWERS'

IN MAY 1952, Churchill gave a farewell dinner at 10 Downing Street for Eisenhower, on the eve of his departure as Supreme Allied Commander in Europe to become a candidate in the US presidential election. The dinner was attended by most of the British Service Chiefs from the Second World War. Eisenhower said that, if elected, he would pay just one visit outside the United States – to Britain, to underline the special relationship. Churchill told his advisers that if Eisenhower were elected, he would have another shot at ending the Cold War by means of a meeting of the Big Three.

When Eisenhower won the election in November, however, Churchill lamented that he would have to cut much out of the last volume of his War Memoirs about how the United States, to please Russia, failed to occupy or gave away large areas of Central Europe despite Churchill's pleas for caution. Churchill still blamed Eisenhower for the failure of the Allied forces to occupy Berlin and Prague.

But Churchill's immediate reaction to the US election result was to travel across the Atlantic. He met Eisenhower in New York in January 1953, shortly before his inauguration. Eisenhower was very genial, but proved to have a bee in his bonnet about 'collusion' with the British. He was all in favour of it clandestinely, but not overtly. This was a reaction to the criticism of Acheson from the Republican Right for excessive deference to the Allies, but to the British it came as an unwelcome surprise.

Eisenhower's caution immediately had a practical manifestation. John Foster Dulles arrived to advise Churchill not to return to Washington, as he wished to do, in early February after the inauguration, as that would coincide with an economic conference between the US and Commonwealth governments. Churchill's Private Secretary, Jock Colville, records:

> Dulles said he thought this would be most unfortunate, whereupon [Churchill] sat up and growled. He explained that the American public thought [Churchill] could cast a spell on all American statesmen and that if he were directly associated with the economic talks, the fears of the people and of Congress would be aroused to such an extent that the success of the talks would be endangered.

Churchill took this very badly, saying afterwards some very harsh things about the Republican Party in general and Dulles in particular. He declared that he would have no more to do with Dulles whose 'great slab of a face' he disliked and distrusted.[1] In this judgement Churchill was far from alone, then or later. Eisenhower actually liked Dulles, but in that respect he was virtually unique. Nearly everyone else found Dulles impossibly pompous, priggish and unbearably dull. He loved to give sermons, moralise and monopolise conversations.

Churchill flew on to Washington for a farewell meeting with Truman. After dinner at the British embassy, the President played the piano. It was hard to get the other guests to listen because they were busy with post-mortems on a diatribe in favour of Zionism and against Egypt that Churchill had delivered across the dinner table. Acheson, Marshall and others disagreed, but admitted that the large Jewish vote would have prevented them from saying so publicly.[2]

As a candidate, Eisenhower had appeared to promise a tougher line with the Communists than Truman and Acheson. That reputation was at least in part borne out by his more active consideration of the use of atomic weapons in Korea. Eisenhower also attacked Yalta. But Yalta had given the Americans their occupation rights in Berlin and Vienna and the British warned that if the United States denounced the Yalta agreements, so would the Russians. Eden said bluntly that Britain would never participate in a repudiation. Once President, while Eisenhower attacked the Russians for violating the agreements, he did not denounce them.

In London, meanwhile, in June 1953, at a dinner he was giving for the Italian Prime Minister, Alcide de Gasperi, Churchill suffered a stroke from which it took him months to recover. The seriousness of his illness was so effectively disguised by his entourage that not a word of his stroke appeared in the press until Churchill himself casually mentioned it in a speech in the House of Commons a year later.

By October, Churchill was hankering after a meeting with Eisenhower in the Azores. But the proposal was turned down by Eisenhower, who knew that, if he agreed, he would be confronted by a demand for a conference with the Russians that he was unwilling to accept.

In December, Churchill and Eisenhower did meet in Bermuda, in a conference also attended by the French. Churchill took Eisenhower off for a private lunch in his room, greatly disturbing Dulles and Eden, neither of whom trusted his chief alone. In the conference proper, Churchill suggested that there was a 'new look' in Russia after Stalin, and that the West should respond with increased trade, high-level meetings and so on. Eisenhower shocked the British by responding that to him it looked like the same Soviet street-walker in new clothes. He had already made clear that he would not attend a summit with the Russians unless agreement had been worked out in advance by foreign ministers.

In July, at long last, an armistice had been concluded in Korea. But the British feared that the Americans might use nuclear weapons if the truce broke down. Eden was alarmed about the effect of American attitudes on public opinion in Britain. Eisenhower told Churchill that he attached less weight than the Prime Minister to the distinction between nuclear and conventional weapons. This, the British noted, represented a fundamental difference of view between the United States and Britain. Discussing Eisenhower's 'Atoms for Peace' speech, due shortly to be made at the United Nations, Churchill persuaded him to substitute for the United States being 'free to use the atomic bomb' a phrase about the United States 'reserving the right to use the atomic bomb'. Churchill also persuaded Eisenhower to drop a reference to the 'obsolete colonial mould'. Despite British nervousness, Eisenhower's speech at the UN was well received.[3]

———

John Foster Dulles was convinced that US foreign policy was fundamentally unselfish and, therefore, imbued with a moral superiority which others should acknowledge. The British found this particularly irksome.

In the words of his biographer, Richard Goold-Adams, Dulles 'was not exactly anti-British. But he was always particularly suspicious of them, often profoundly irritated by them, and sometimes despairingly contemptuous of them. The British were apt to be the last people whose views he wished to hear.' He resented the fact that the British claim to special relations with the United States was not matched by British support for his policies when he needed it.[4]

The prime example of this, in his view, was in Indo-China, where Dulles sought to apply his policy of containment by providing the French with financial assistance and arms supplies. In March 1954, the French made a first appeal to the Americans to help the beleaguered garrison at Dien Bien Phu. Admiral Radford, Chairman of the Joint Chiefs of Staff, wanted to respond with an air strike. The army chief, General Ridgway, however, was strongly against committing US land forces. Eisenhower, who was himself extremely cautious about intervention, made clear that he would not authorise air strikes without Congressional approval and support from America's allies, especially Britain. Senator Lyndon Johnson was opposed to US involvement, but indicated that he might reconsider if the British joined in.

In April, Eisenhower warned Churchill of the consequences of abandoning Indo-China. 'It is difficult to see how Thailand, Burma and Indonesia could be kept out of Communist hands. This we cannot afford. The threat to Malaya, Australia and New Zealand would be direct.' As Henry Kissinger notes, Churchill was not persuaded: he perceived more dangers than benefits to be gained in Indo-China, and that the best line of defence was in Malaya. Churchill warned Admiral Radford of the dangers of 'war on the fringes, where the Russians were strong and could mobilize the enthusiasm of nationalist and oppressed peoples'.[5]

Eden believed that support for the French in Indo-China was a lost cause. He did not want the United States to intervene militarily and press Britain to do the same, fearing that this would alienate India and split the Commonwealth. Refusing to be 'hustled into injudicious military decisions', he believed in the possibility of a negotiated solution, in which he saw himself as playing the leading role. But Dulles was instinctively wary of negotiations with the Communists, believing they could never be trusted to honour any agreements entered into.

The British Chiefs of Staff supported Eden. After the long and costly struggle in Korea, they did not want to be drawn into another Asian war. When Dulles convened a meeting in Washington of Commonwealth and other representatives to discuss a new security pact in Southeast Asia, Eden instructed the British ambassador, Roger Makins, not to attend. An irate Dulles considered this a repudiation of earlier understandings between them. Britain was to become a member of the Southeast Asia Treaty Organization when it was set up later in the year, but in April 1954 Eden did not want to do anything that might complicate his diplomacy.

Eden telegraphed to Makins: 'Americans may think the time past when they need consider the feelings or difficulties of their allies. It is the conviction that this tendency becomes more pronounced every week that is creating mounting difficulties for anyone in this country who wants to maintain close Anglo-American relations.'[6]

On 23 April, Dulles told Eden of a final desperate appeal from the French military commanders to help save their forces surrounded at Dien Bien Phu. Eden questioned whether air strikes would save the French, while they certainly would entail an extension of the war. On the following day, Dulles and Admiral Radford declared that they were disposed to try to help the French, but Eden remained opposed. Eden's decision not to support the Americans was endorsed by Churchill and his Cabinet colleagues. There followed a further heated discussion with Dulles in Geneva on 1 May, with Eden arguing that if the Americans intervened militarily in Indo-China, the Chinese would step up their involvement and 'that was in all probability the beginning of the third world war'.

In Washington, Eisenhower vetoed plans to give the French any assistance with ground forces in Indo-China. In reality extremely reluctant to intervene, Eisenhower used the absence of Allied support to explain his refusal to permit the US Air Force to help at Dien Bien Phu, Dulles sanctimoniously told the French that the standing of the United States as the most powerful of the anticolonial powers was 'an asset of incomparable value'. The United States, he said, had to guard its moral position in Indo-China. He also referred to the lack of British support. On 7 May, Dien Bien Phu fell to the North Vietnamese. This drama was to have far-reaching consequences when de Gaulle returned to power in France.[7]

On the day following the fall of Dien Bien Phu, the Geneva Conference on Indo-China opened, with Eden and Molotov in the chair. Eden's efforts to find a diplomatic solution acceptable to the Indians, Russians and Chinese brought him into further conflict with Dulles, who wanted the British to agree on a strategy of combating Communism through military assistance to the anti-Communist forces. Eden felt that this would entail taking over the conduct of the war from the French and running the risk of a conflict with Russia or China. He saw no need to placate Dulles, as some of his officials were urging, and was pleased by press suggestions that he was mediating between the United States and the Communist powers. Eden was intoxicated by his apparent success with the Russians. Molotov, he felt, had 'mellowed'. In the British press he was praised for standing up to the Americans and keeping Britain out of the war in Indo-China. Dulles flew from Geneva in a huff, leaving his deputy, Bedell Smith, to try to bridge the Anglo-American divide.[8]

In June, Churchill and Eden returned to Washington. Churchill's aims were to convince Eisenhower that atomic cooperation must be renewed and that the Americans and British must talk to the Russians in an effort to avert war and gain ten years of 'easement' during which resources could be diverted away from defence spending.

The press were advertising this as a period of almost unparalleled friction in postwar Anglo-American relations. Eden was concerned about the American determination to get rid of the left-wing regime of President Árbenz in Guatemala. Churchill wanted to organise a meeting with the Russians in London, which Eisenhower would attend. Eisenhower appeared to agree but then backtracked under the influence of Dulles. Dulles also rejected Eden's plea to admit China to the UN. Churchill eliminated some Dulles-inspired anti-colonial sentiments from the press statement after the meeting. But the Americans and British did agree that if the proposed European Defence Community failed, Germany must be admitted to NATO and permitted to rearm. On this note, Churchill went on to Canada well-pleased with his reception in Washington. Eden, he considered, was very foolish to quarrel with the Americans about 'petty issues' such as Guatemala.[9]

Sharp differences, however, remained over policy towards Indo-China. Eden extracted agreement from a very reluctant Dulles to the partition of Vietnam; and the British agreed to participate in what was to become the Southeast Asia Treaty Organization (SEATO). In July, the Geneva agreements were signed, partitioning Vietnam, calling for nationwide elections within two years, banning external military supplies and establishing a supervisory commission under Poland, India and Canada. The United States had no confidence in these arrangements – none of which was to prove effective – and refused to sign the accords. Eden's efforts in Geneva, which continued to win such applause in Europe, were criticised in the United States as amounting to appeasement. While Churchill was unhappy about the deterioration in relations with the Americans, Eden believed that his diplomatic triumph had helped to limit – and keep the Americans out of – an extremely dangerous conflict.[10]

In August, the French Parliament, outraged at the failure of the United States to help save Dien Bien Phu, rejected the European Defence Community and the United States moved to bring Germany into NATO with an independent German Army. The Eisenhowers went off for Thanksgiving to Augusta, accompanied by Field Marshal Montgomery, who, Eisenhower claimed, had 'invited himself'.

22

'UNITED STATES POLICY IS EXAGGERATEDLY MORAL, AT LEAST WHERE NON-AMERICAN INTERESTS ARE CONCERNED'

IN APRIL 1955, after a long struggle of wills with Churchill, Eden at last got his wish to become Prime Minister. The Americans, who knew Eden well, had very mixed feelings about him. He was exactly the kind of Englishman they suspected of trying to patronise them.

These suspicions were well-founded. Unlike Churchill and Macmillan, themselves both half American, Eden had no instinctive understanding or sympathy for the United States. He had played relatively little part in Anglo-American relations during the Second World War. That great subject had been left largely to Churchill. In 1942, Eden had observed: 'United States policy is exaggeratedly moral, at least where non-American interests are concerned.' He first met John Foster Dulles in October 1942 and conceived a pretty instant dislike for him. Dulles, like Acheson, did not react well to Eden's habit of addressing his male colleagues as 'my dear'. Eden suspected the Americans of wanting to supplant the British in the Middle East. Churchill, he felt, often was too complaisant towards them. At Tehran he considered that both Roosevelt and Churchill had been too deferential to Stalin. Roosevelt had appeared uninterested in the future frontiers of Poland. On the eve of Yalta, Eden worried about Roosevelt's 'fading powers'. Eden told Colville that 'the Americans had been very weak. The President looked old and ill and had been a hopelessly incompetent chairman.' Roosevelt appeared not to understand Stalin's attitude towards small countries, which had struck Eden as 'grim, not to say sinister'. Eden continued to fear that at Potsdam the Americans would sacrifice European interests to the Russians. He was despondent about American domination of Western diplomacy.[1]

These experiences affected Eden's attitude when he returned to office in 1951. Eden did not believe that British interests lay in Europe. But he continued to have serious doubts about American capacities in international affairs. He and Acheson fell out badly over Iran and Korea. When Eden successfully supported a resolution at the United Nations on Korea put forward by the Indian representative, Krishna Menon, whom the Americans disliked and distrusted, Acheson charged Eden and his deputy, Selwyn Lloyd, with disloyalty, telling Eden that 'one day you will find that it never pays to win victories over your friends'. Acheson and Eden did have a grudging but considerable respect for each other, as Acheson made clear in his memoirs, and there were periods in which they worked well together. Both had strong opinions and volatile temperaments and there was a real element of rivalry. Acheson's affection was never extended to Eden: it was reserved for Ernest Bevin. By the time Acheson left office, relations were very strained. Eden's biographer, Robert Rhodes-James, suggests that matters were not improved by the fact that in his dealings with the Americans, Eden often was proved right, for instance over Iran: 'Acheson found this difficult to forgive.'[2]

Eden realised that Britain was a relatively poor country, its resources grossly overstretched in the postwar world. But he could not resign himself to playing second fiddle. He knew how circumscribed Britain's power was, but, convinced that he was right, believed that he could conduct world affairs better than the United States.

Eden was by no means alone in these opinions. At the end of 1951, Mountbatten recorded in his diary that, at dinner with Churchill on the *Queen Mary*, he had questioned the wisdom of linking Britain irrevocably to American foreign policy, especially if the course followed by the Americans was likely to lead to war. Churchill replied that the only security for Britain was to be found in cooperation with the United States. Mountbatten opined that Americans were charming as individuals 'but, taken as a corporate mass, they were immature, and if they were allowed their own way they would probably take a course which would not only destroy this country but would ultimately end in the destruction of their own system'.

Churchill advised Mountbatten to stay out of politics. Mountbatten denied indignantly that these were political views.[3]

At Churchill's farewell dinner for Eisenhower before he left NATO for the presidential campaign, Eden unwisely advised Eisenhower not to appoint Dulles as his Secretary of State ('I do not think I would be able to work with him'). Eden was surprised when his advice was not followed. He then was disconcerted at the appointment of Winthrop Aldrich as US ambassador to London being announced without consultation with the British government: Dulles had forgotten to inform him.[4]

At the Bermuda Conference in 1953, Eden was appalled when Eisenhower made it clear that he considered nuclear weapons to be merely another form of weaponry, which the United States, if necessary, might have to use in the Far East. Nor was he ever at any pains to disguise his growing personal irritation with Dulles. As the British ambassador at the time, Roger Makins, commented, both were prima donnas, Eden intuitive and instinctive, Dulles legalistic and pedantic. They were temperamentally incapable of getting on.

Dulles had been upset about the British lack of enthusiasm for the proposed European Defence Community (EDC), which the Americans hoped would provide the framework for the Germans to be integrated in a European army. Churchill was not prepared to subordinate British forces to what he derided as a 'sludgy amalgam'. At the Bermuda Conference, Dulles hinted that the United States might not maintain its support for NATO if the matter remained unresolved. He followed this up at a press conference by threatening an 'agonizing reappraisal' of American policy if the EDC should fail. Eden was told that Britain and the United States were approaching a 'parting of the ways with regard to American policy'. If things went badly, Dulles warned, the United States might swing over to a policy of hemispheric defence, with the emphasis on Asia.

Things did go badly and the situation was saved, very largely, by Eden. Following the rejection of the EDC by the French Parliament, Eden convened a conference in London, followed by one in Paris, which admitted West Germany to NATO and at which Britain made the historic pledge to maintain four divisions in Germany. As Eden told his colleagues, this would be an unprecedented commitment for Britain to make, but he saw it as essential to the organisation of an effective system of European defence and to keeping the Americans in Europe.

But within months of becoming Prime Minister, Eden was making clear his intention to end what he regarded as the excessive deference Churchill had paid to the Americans. 'The British should not allow themselves to be restricted overmuch by reluctance to act without full American concurrence and support', he told his Cabinet in October 1955. 'We should frame our own policy in the light of our interests and get the Americans to support it to the extent we can induce them to do so.'[5]

Eden had no particularly high regard for Eisenhower. In that he shared the fashionable prejudices of the time. Most of the foreign press corps in Washington underestimated the President, depicting him as a golf-playing figure-head. Eden was not alone in imagining that the President was not the real decision-maker in US foreign policy. As it was to turn out, he could not have been more mistaken.

As for Dulles, his philosophy was set out in his 1956 interview with *Life* magazine: 'The ability to get to the verge without getting into war is the necessary art ... If you are scared to go to the brink, you are lost.' Dulles resented the way in which over Indo-China in 1954 and the US confrontation with China over Quemoy and Matsu in 1955, Eden had sought to play the role of peacemaker. In doing so, in Dulles's view, he had let down the United States. Yet, in his subsequent dealings with Dulles and Eisenhower, Eden seemed barely to understand how thoroughly he had offended them by the way in which he had conducted his diplomacy over Indo-China.

Eden's near-perpetual state of nervous irritation with the Americans was compounded by the fact that, although only fifty-eight, he was suffering from severe ill-health. To members of his immediate staff, he seemed temperamentally unstable. The operations he had suffered for gallstones in 1953 had not been a success. Damage was done to his bile duct, leaving him liable to sudden fevers and jaundice. He travelled everywhere accompanied by a large supply of pills and painkillers.

––––––––

In February 1953, shortly after his inauguration, Eisenhower had been alarmed by the 'somewhat frightening phraseology' of a letter from Churchill about Egypt. The Americans felt that with the decline of British power in the Middle East, the Foreign Office had been 'tragically incapable of developing a new basis for a satisfactory relationship with the peoples of the area'. The State Department was convinced that the United States must avoid being identified with British and French colonial interests and that it could come to terms with Iranian and Egyptian nationalism. In 1954, to Churchill's disgust, the British and Egyptian governments reached agreement that British troops would leave the Suez Canal Zone within eighteen months. Eden pushed this through after a series of bruising battles with Churchill and was correspondingly sensitive when this major concession failed to improve relations with Nasser.

The British did not share the benign State Department view of Nasser as simply a nationalist. Harold Macmillan as Foreign Secretary telegraphed to Washington on 28 November 1955: 'We are afraid that Nasser, whether innocently or deliberately, is dangerously committed to the Communists. Consequently we believe that it would be advantageous, in any event, to overthrow him if possible.' But the CIA regarded Nasser as a protégé of theirs, with Kim Roosevelt cabling Allen Dulles, the CIA Director, that 'Nasser remains our best, if not our only hope here'.[6]

In September, the British received reports that Nasser had concluded a major arms deal with Russia. Kim Roosevelt and Miles Copeland watched from Nasser's office as the British ambassador's Bentley drove across the bridge over the Nile, carrying Sir Humphrey Trevelyan to protest. The CIA operatives advised Nasser to tell the ambassador that the contract had been made with Czechoslovakia rather than with Russia and that Egypt had no intention of exchanging British for Russian domination.[7]

On 26 September, Macmillan argued with Dulles in New York that they should tell Nasser that the West would not tolerate his action or the Soviet Union becoming the guardian of the Suez Canal: 'We could make life impossible for Nasser and ultimately bring about his fall.' Dulles appeared to agree: 'We did not all work so hard to get a Suez base agreement in order to turn the base over to the Soviets.' Macmillan pointed out that Britain had not yet completed its withdrawal from Suez: if they had US support, they might call the whole thing off.[8]

On 20 October, Eden invited Winthrop Aldrich, the US ambassador in London, to see him on a matter of 'the greatest importance and urgency'. Following the news of the Egyptian arms deal with the Soviet Union, Eden told Aldrich that the Russians had offered to finance the Aswan Dam. It was vital that the Western powers should offer to provide the credits instead. The argument did not appeal to the US Treasury Secretary, George Humphrey, who commented on the proposed partnership with Britain in this affair: 'I asked them on what basis it would be and it was just what I thought: they would take 10 per cent and we would take 90 per cent.' Nevertheless, on 14 December, an Anglo-American offer was made to help meet the foreign exchange costs of the dam.[9] Eden, meanwhile, was finding the presence of Harold Macmillan at the Foreign Office increasingly irksome. As he wanted to run foreign policy himself, he transferred Macmillan to the Treasury, replacing him by Selwyn Lloyd who he felt had a 'safe pair of hands'. In reality, Eden knew that Lloyd could be relied upon to do what he was told.

In February 1956, British prestige in the Middle East suffered a further blow when King Hussein abruptly dismissed the British commander of his armed forces, Sir John Glubb.

In April, Humphrey Trevelyan warned from Cairo that an anti-Nasser campaign was 'quite impossible unless we have not only full American support but active American cooperation in a joint policy'.[10] On 10 April, Dulles told Congressional leaders: 'We believe that unless and until we can bring the UK around to our view, it would be a mistake to identify ourselves too closely with them in the Near East.' The British, he said, 'were in a state of undeclared war with Saudi Arabia and had very bad relations with Nasser'.

But Nasser then infuriated the Americans by deciding to visit China. In June, the Americans informed the British that in the altered climate of American opinion, there was no chance of persuading Congress to put up money for the Aswan Dam. Dulles was no longer sure that it would be a bad thing for the Russians to take on that commitment. Selwyn Lloyd told the British Cabinet on 17 July that the Americans were likely to share the British view that the offer of aid for the building of the dam should be withdrawn.[11] But the British preferred to play for time and not give a definite refusal. Dulles said that he would have preferred this too, but Congress gave him no choice. On 19 July, he told the Egyptian ambassador that the US offer was withdrawn. Eden described Dulles's handling of the issue as a calamity. The British felt that the ensuing crisis was triggered by the way in which the United States had turned down the project.

———————

On 26 July 1956, Nasser precipitated the crisis by announcing that the Egyptians were taking over the Suez Canal Company and control of shipping in the canal. Eden called the Chiefs of Staff to 10 Downing Street and summoned the French ambassador and the US chargé. He made clear his very strong feeling that Nasser must not be allowed to get away with it. The Egyptian dictator could not be permitted to 'have his hand on our windpipe'.[12]

But there were problems with the response. The British Cabinet noted that it would be difficult to argue that Nasser had acted illegally, and Eden was reluctant to go to the UN Security Council because he was uncertain about the US attitude. On 29 July, Eden sent a message to Eisenhower that the Cabinet was agreed that they could not allow Nasser to seize control of the canal in defiance of international agreements. Otherwise 'our influence and yours throughout the Middle East will, we are convinced, be finally destroyed'. He told Eisenhower that the British government had decided, in the last resort, to use force: 'I have this morning instructed our Chiefs of Staff to prepare a military plan accordingly.'[13]

In Washington, the Pentagon wanted to support the British, but the State Department advised that Egypt had acted within its rights and that unless Egyptian operation of the canal turned out to be arbitrary, there was nothing to be done. The French ambassador, Couve de Murville, reported that the Americans appeared to want to mediate. The British ambassador, Roger Makins, was told by Under-Secretary Herbert Hoover Jr that in the absence of more aggressive action by Egypt, military action could not be justified. Hoover left Makins with the impression that the State Department was 'weak and irresolute in the face of this crisis and tepid about taking any vigorous action'.[14]

At the end of July, the US Deputy Under-Secretary of State, Robert Murphy, met Eden in London. Eden appeared to take it for granted that the Americans would endorse his policies, saying that there was no thought of asking the United States for help, 'but we shall rely on you to watch the Bear'. Murphy commented that: 'It seemed impossible for Eden to keep in mind how much Britain's power had diminished in relation to the United States and Russia. Dulles never forgot this.'

After meeting with Eden, Murphy dined with Harold Macmillan and Field Marshal Alexander. Macmillan wrote subsequently: '[We] certainly did our best to frighten him or at least to leave him in no doubt about our determination.' From both Macmillan and Eden, Murphy received the firm message that, in the British view, military action was necessary and inevitable. Macmillan declared that if they had to go down, the government would rather do so on this issue than any other; otherwise 'Britain would become another Netherlands'. Three divisions would be landed in Egypt and there would be little resistance. He did not believe the Russians would intervene. Whatever negotiations and conferences might be undertaken, 'in the end the Government were determined to use force'.[15]

On reading Murphy's report, Eisenhower asked Dulles to go to London to tell the British 'how very unwise their decision is'. Dulles thought there was a chance that an international conference would give general backing for the international operation of the canal, thereby defusing the crisis. Eisenhower feared that military action against Nasser would array the entire Third World against the United States. Dulles believed that he could dissuade the British from their course of action.

Dulles arrived in London on 1 August. He brought with him a letter to Eden from Eisenhower, describing the President's alarm at receiving Murphy's cable 'telling me on a most secret basis of your decision to employ force without delay or attempting any intermediate or less drastic steps'. Eisenhower sought to convey 'the unwisdom even of contemplating the use of military force at this moment'. If force were used without peaceful means having been exhausted, there would be a very sharp public reaction in the United States. This was not, as the British believed, the opinion of Dulles, but that of Eisenhower, who had personally dictated the letter. Eden chose to interpret the exchange as meaning that Eisenhower did not rule out the use of force. Yet the whole tenor of the President's letter was against it.[16]

Dulles agreed that it was intolerable that the Suez Canal should come under the domination of one country without any international control. He told Eden that 'ways had to be found to make Nasser disgorge what he was attempting to swallow'. But Dulles spoke also about the disastrous consequences of military action against Nasser if it were not supported by world opinion and about the dangers of Soviet intervention. If the Russians did not intervene openly, they might send 'volunteers' and supply weapons. The US government would not be able to associate itself with an operation involving force that had not been preceded by genuine efforts to reach a negotiated solution. Dulles commented afterwards on the difference between the two governments: 'While the United States considered that all possible efforts should be made to reach a satisfactory solution by international consultation, the United Kingdom regarded such efforts as a matter of form.'

Selwyn Lloyd reported to the British Cabinet Dulles's statement that Egypt must 'disgorge' the canal, but there must be no premature use of force. Meanwhile Dulles, on returning to Washington, said that some people had suggested an immediate use of force, but that would have been against the principles of the UN Charter. He was convinced that 'by the conference method, we would invoke moral forces which are bound to prevail'. Yet Eden had convinced himself that, in the end, Dulles would go along with the eventual use of force. Eden was subsequently to argue that Dulles had been 'not straight'.[17]

23

'THE US ARE BEING VERY DIFFICULT'

THE BRITISH AND AMERICAN intelligence services had undertaken some contingency planning about ways to counter the increasing Soviet influence in Egypt. Confronted with a memorandum entitled 'Means of Bringing about the Fall of Nasser', Dulles asked that the title should be changed to something more innocuous. An American colleague warned the British that this should not be seen as a title change alone: it was in fact a policy decision. Dulles continued to make clear that so long as there was no interference with navigation in the Suez Canal, there were no grounds for military action.

In public, the British government still was limiting its objectives to the reestablishment of international control over the canal. But Eden did not attempt to disguise his real purpose from Eisenhower: 'I have never thought Nasser a Hitler, he has a no war-like people behind him, but the parallel with Mussolini is close. Nasser's removal and replacement by a regime less hostile to the West must rate highly among our objectives.' He expressed the hope that the conference proposed by Dulles would induce Egypt to accept international operation of the canal. But if Nasser refused:

> You know us better than anyone, and so I need not tell you that our people here are neither excited nor eager to use force. They are, however, grimly determined that Nasser should not get away with it this time because they are convinced that if he does their existence will be at his mercy. So am I.[1]

Meanwhile, on 3 August, the State Department sent a cable to Chip Bohlen, US ambassador in Moscow, instructing him to tell the Russians that the Americans were having great difficulty restraining their friends from taking action in the Middle East. Bohlen queried the wisdom of exposing these differences between the Allies to the Russians, but was told by Dulles to carry out his instructions.

On 8 August, Eden told the British people in a television broadcast that without international control of the canal 'machinery and much of our transport would grind to a halt'. He recalled the costs of giving in to Fascism. Eisenhower, however, believed that Nasser probably would be able to keep the canal open and functioning.

The Pentagon remained sympathetic to British and French views. At a meeting of the National Security Council on 9 August, Eisenhower said that Egypt had gone too far. Even Dulles felt that the United States could not ask the British and the French to accept 'subservient' dependence on Egyptian control of the canal. The Supreme Allied Commander in Europe, General Gruenther, reported that the British Chiefs of Staff would recommend military action. Admiral Radford was puzzled that if the British and French started such action, they thought they could finish it quickly. The US Chiefs of Staff noted subsequently that the British were critically short of landing craft. Admiral Burke suggested making some available to the Allies, but Dulles did not think that would be proper.[2]

Leaving for the conference of the maritime powers in London in mid-August, Dulles told Eisenhower that he would lead the British and French away from precipitate action. But if Nasser rejected reasonable proposals and the British then felt they had to act to protect their interests, the United States should give them moral and economic support. The British and French were saying that they would not expect the Americans to involve themselves militarily. But Dulles did not believe the British and French military establishments were adequate to take on a 'real fighting job of this size'.[3]

At the conference, Dulles sought to give the British and French the impression that he favoured them, while in his private talks with others he sounded hostile to the former colonial powers. Macmillan told Dulles over dinner on 18 August that if Nasser did not accept Dulles's scheme for international control over the canal, Britain would be finished and he would resign if the British government did not deal with the problem. On the following day, Eden said that delay would be fatal: if the conference did not succeed, military action could not be put off indefinitely. Dulles questioned whether the British public would support the use of force. Eden told him that he was wrong: when the time carne, the government would have full backing for military action. Eden asked the US ambassador to tell Dulles that he was convinced that the Labour leader, Hugh Gaitskell, would support the government if force had to be used. On 23 August, Lloyd, showing 'obvious emotional strain', told Dulles that preparations for military action would be set in train in early September. Dulles still believed that he could work out a scheme that might be acceptable to Nasser.[4]

In the Egypt Committee of the Cabinet, Eden was having difficulties with the Defence Minister, Walter Monckton. Alec Douglas-Home warned Eden that some of his colleagues were wavering. They felt that the use of force would 'divide country, party and Commonwealth so deeply that we should never recover'. But the Cabinet generally was agreed that Nasser must not be allowed to get away with it. The Cabinet Secretary, Norman Brook, believed that 'if he succeeds we lose our oil and, with it, our standard of life in this country, not to mention our position in the Middle East and our influence as a world power'.[5]

On 27 August, the Washington embassy was instructed to pass a message to Dulles. Selwyn Lloyd thought that moderate opinion would be shocked at forcible action being taken without any reference to the United Nations. Having praised Dulles for his 'masterly' management of the London conference, he asked for American support in an approach to the UN.

Dulles told the National Security Council that the British and French had gone along with the US plan for the canal very reluctantly and in the hope that Nasser would not accept it. Dulles said that he had found it difficult to take a strong stand against British and French views 'since after all, the British and French would be finished as first rate powers if they didn't somehow manage to check Nasser and nullify his schemes'. But it obviously was impractical for them to try to re-establish what amounted to colonial rule. For the Joint Chiefs, Admiral Radford suggested supporting the British and French military action logistically, though with no participation by US forces. But Eisenhower would not commit himself.[6]

After the meeting, Dulles told Eisenhower that, 'regrettable as it might be to see Nasser's prestige enhanced even temporarily', he did not believe that the situation should be resolved by force:

I could not see any end to the situation that might be created if the British and French occupied the Canal and parts of Egypt. They would make bitter enemies of the entire population of the Middle East and much of Africa. Everywhere they would be compelled to maintain themselves by force and in the end their own economy would be weakened virtually beyond repair and the influence of the West in the Middle East and most of Africa lost for a generation, if not a century. The Soviet Union would reap the benefit.[7]

On 2 September, Eisenhower wrote to Eden: 'I must tell you frankly that American public opinion flatly rejects the thought of using force.' He pointed out that the British economy would not be able to sustain prolonged military operations or the loss of Middle East oil that was likely to follow. Eden replied by referring to the history of the 1930s: if Nasser were permitted to get into a position where he could deny oil to Western Europe, 'we here should be at his mercy'. In reply, Eisenhower warned Eden of the danger of 'making of Nasser a much more important figure than he is'. The use of force would be justified if Nasser actually interrupted oil supplies through the canal, but not otherwise.[8]

On 4 September, Dulles told the British chargé in Washington that the West was in a weak position juridically. The users of the canal should club together and run it themselves. Thus was born the idea of the Suez Canal Users Association. The British were sceptical but went along with the idea in the hope of engaging the Americans against Nasser.

On the following day the Australian Prime Minister, Sir Robert Menzies, leading a delegation to Cairo after the London conference to convey the proposal for international control of the canal, considered his mission to be completely undercut when Eisenhower at a press conference stressed US determination to 'exhaust every feasible method of peaceful settlement', thereby encouraging Nasser to believe that he could safely reject the proposals. The British ambassador in Cairo, Sir Humphrey Trevelyan, was convinced that Nasser would have rejected them anyway.

At a meeting of the British Cabinet on 6 September, it was noted that the use of force probably would entail a run on sterling. Harold Macmillan, Chancellor of the Exchequer, insisted that this was to be preferred to the 'slow strangulation that would follow if Egypt extended her control over the oil-producing countries of the Arab world'.[9]

Sir Edward Bridges, Permanent Secretary to the Treasury, pointed out to Macmillan the 'vital necessity from the point of view of our currency and our economy of ensuring that we do not go it alone and that we have maximum US support'. Macmillan replied: 'Yes, this is just the trouble. The US are being very difficult.'[10] The Treasury view that US support was the only way of avoiding financial disaster did not appear to have been conveyed to his colleagues.

Selwyn Lloyd asked Sir Roger Makins to convey to Dulles his 'grave anxiety at the present state of our consultations and seek to impress upon him the absolute necessity for effective action urgently'. Lloyd felt that he did not know where the US government stood on any of the key issues.[11]

Makins warned Lloyd that there was 'no support in the United States for the use of force in present circumstances and in the absence of further clear provocation by Nasser'. This was not just due to the imminence of the presidential election. 'I do not really know what your personal thoughts are as regards military action but, as it looks from Washington, to attempt it without full American moral and material support could easily lead to disaster.'[12] Selwyn Lloyd, for his part, was worried that having proposed the idea of a Canal Users Association, Dulles would not support the only effective sanction, that is, refusing the payment of fees for the operation of the canal to the Egyptians.

On 12 September, asked if the USA would back Britain and France if they used force, President Eisenhower said publicly that if all peaceful means were exhausted and Egypt interrupted use of the canal, Britain and France might have to be 'more forceful than merely sailing through it'. But, he added: 'I am not going to be a party to aggression if it is humanly possible.'

This was followed by another 'terrible' Dulles press conference. Asked what the United States would do if Egypt resisted his plan, Dulles replied: 'If physical force should be used to prevent passage, then obviously as far as the United States is concerned the alternative, for us at least, would be to send our vessels around the Cape ... We do not intend to shoot our way through.' As Eden wrote in his memoirs, it would be hard to imagine a statement more likely to cause the maximum Allied disunity and disarray.[13] Gaitskell, quoting Dulles, demanded assurances from Eden that Britain also would not use force to secure free passage through the canal.

The second London conference in September was, to the British, a depressing affair. As Eden's press secretary, William Clark, saw it: 'Dulles pulled rug after rug from under us and watered down the Canal Users Association till it was meaningless.' Yet Dulles told Selwyn Lloyd that it was imperative that Nasser should be made to lose. The only question was how. War would make him a hero. He must be made to wither away. The British and Americans should work out a plan to get rid of him in six months.

Immediately on his return to Washington, Dulles was told that Britain and France had decided to go to the UN Security Council. The British claimed that the Russians were planning to get in first and, in any event, 'we must dispel the appearance of indecisiveness'. Dulles complained to Macmillan, who was visiting Washington as Chancellor of the Exchequer. Before they embarked on a confrontation with Egypt, Dulles wanted to know how Britain and France would face the financial consequences of having to divert oil from the canal. Macmillan told Dulles that the detour around the Cape was not a practical possibility for Britain for any length of time. Britain could not afford to borrow more money and already was suffering strong pressure on the reserves as a result of lack of confidence due to Nasser's action.

Dulles told Macmillan privately that he wanted to discuss alternative methods of getting rid of Nasser. An attempt to do so through economic pressure and covert action, Dulles argued, could succeed but would take six months. Macmillan said that if Nasser avoided accepting international control, he would have won and Britain could not afford to wait six months.

According to Macmillan, Dulles said that he realised that Britain might have to use force. He thought the threat of force was vital as pressure on Nasser. But, Macmillan claims, he asked the British to hold off until after the US presidential election on 6 November. Dulles's account is different. He reports Macmillan as having begun the exchange by hoping devoutly that Eisenhower would be re-elected, causing Dulles to say that he hoped the British would do nothing drastic that would affect his chances.[14]

Macmillan went in by the back door to the White House to see his wartime friend, Eisenhower. They appear to have talked mainly about the US elections. Eisenhower telephoned Dulles to say that nothing had been said that need worry him. Macmillan reported to Eden: 'As is usual with Ike, it was rather rambling and nothing very definite.' There does not seem to have been any serious discussion of Suez. Nevertheless, the meeting led Macmillan subsequently to tell his colleagues: 'I know Ike: he will lie doggo.'[15]

On 2 October, Dulles was asked about differences with the French and British governments over the Canal Users plan. In reply he said: 'There is talk that the teeth were pulled out of it. There were no teeth in it.' There were some differences, he added, in the approach to the Suez problem. These related to the fact that the United States, France and Britain were not treaty allies all over the world, but only in parts of it. 'Other problems relate to other areas and touched the so-called problem of colonialism in some way or another. On these problems, the United States plays a somewhat independent role.'

An infuriated Eden despaired, he said, of ever being able to work with the Americans. 'It was I who ended the so-called colonialism in Egypt. And look at what Britain has done all over the world in giving colonies independence.'[16] Dulles apologised.

On 4 October, Dulles lamented privately:

> I know the British and French want us to stand with them, but we do not know where they stand, nor are we consulted … Both the British and French embassies seem to be completely in the dark and we cannot get guidance from them. We do not know and cannot find out whether they want peace or war.

The Europeans, he suspected, wanted a 'more or less blank cheque on the US for economic, military and political support everywhere in the world'.[17]

On the following day, Dulles saw the British and French Foreign Ministers in New York. He asked whether their move to the UN was a genuine attempt at a settlement: or were they going through the motions? The US position was that war would be a disaster. Lloyd said that if other measures failed to solve the problem, force would have to be used. The French Foreign Minister, Christian Pineau, said that if Nasser succeeded over Suez, the French position would collapse throughout North Africa. NATO also would face collapse. Dulles argued that if force were used in violation of the UN Charter, the United Nations would be destroyed. He agreed that the threat of force was useful to keep up pressure on Nasser, but if it had to be used, the West would lose much of the Middle East.

Reading the reports from New York, Eden wrote: 'We must never forget that Dulles' purpose is different from ours. The Canal is in no sense vital to the United States and his game is to string us along at least until polling day.'[18]

On 12 October, Lloyd and the Egyptian Foreign Minister, Mahmoud Fawzi, agreed on various principles for the future operation of the canal, including free and open transit and respect for Egyptian sovereignty. All members of the UN Security Council endorsed the principles. The problem, as Lloyd commented, was how they were to be interpreted. But the Americans now were optimistic about the prospect of a peaceful settlement. Dulles told the National Security Council that the British appeared to favour a compromise, but were concerned how they could square this with their strong public statements. In his relief, Eisenhower unwisely told the press that 'it looks like here is a very great crisis that is behind us'. Lloyd protested strongly, telling Dulles that he was 'disgusted by the way in which our hand is weakened at every stage of this business by what is said over here'.[19] Nevertheless, it seemed at this stage to Eden and his colleagues in London that they would have little option but to postpone the operation intended to seize control of the canal.

On 14 October, following the debate in the Security Council, Lloyd was flabbergasted to be told by Dulles that 90 per cent of the dues collected by the Suez Canal Users Association should be made over to the Egyptian authorities. This marked a crisis in personal relations between Dulles and Lloyd, each writing to the other to justify his point of view. Lloyd could not accept Dulles's tortured explanations and there was by now a complete breakdown of confidence between them.[20]

At this point, the situation was transformed, at any rate in Eden's eyes, by the arrival in London on 14 October of the French Acting Foreign Minister and General Challe, bringing proposals from the French Prime Minister, Guy Mollet. The French wanted to know what action Britain would take if Israel attacked Egypt. It was clear that they had knowledge of a possible Israeli attack. Challe proposed that if Israel invaded the Sinai, Britain and France should order the Egyptians and Israelis to withdraw their forces while an Anglo-French force occupied the canal zone.[21]

Lloyd returned to London on 16 October to be told of the French plan. Eden and Lloyd went into discussions with Mollet and Pineau from which all officials, including the British ambassador to France, Gladwyn

Jebb, were excluded. Mollet enquired whether, in the event of hostilities in the vicinity of the canal, the British would intervene to stop them. Eden agreed with the French that in the event of hostilities, the French and British governments should call on the belligerents to withdraw from the vicinity of the canal. If they did not, Anglo-French forces should intervene 'to ensure the free passage of the Canal'.[22]

On 22 October, the Israeli Prime Minister, David Ben-Gurion, and General Moshe Dayan flew to a secret meeting with the French at Sevres outside Paris. The French promised air support for the Israeli attack. Lloyd arrived from London to join the meeting. He insisted that Israel must attack Egypt alone. But Britain and France then would intervene to safeguard the canal and stop the fighting. Ben-Gurion wanted Anglo-French bombing of the Egyptian airfields to follow within twelve hours of the Israeli attack. Lloyd wanted a longer delay. Dayan proposed a paratroop attack on the Mitla Pass only thirty miles from the canal, offering the pretext for Anglo-French intervention.[23]

Pineau took the plan to London on the following day. Eden agreed that they should serve notice on the parties to withdraw from the canal and threaten them with military intervention if they did not. Consultation with the United States was rejected 'owing to their pre-occupation with the election campaign and the generally unsatisfactory nature of our exchanges with Mr Dulles about US action of any character'.[24]

In the subsequent secret meeting at Sevres on 24 October, at which the British were represented by Sir Patrick Dean and Donald Logan of the Foreign Office, a three-page document, the Sevres Protocol, was produced. This stated that Israel would launch a full-scale attack on the afternoon of 29 October. On the next day the British and French governments would demand that Egypt and Israel cease fire and withdraw from the canal, while Anglo-French forces established a 'temporary occupation'. The inevitable Egyptian refusal would bring an Anglo-French attack early on 31 October. Eden tried to get all three copies of the protocol destroyed, but Ben-Gurion refused.[25]

Eden did not reveal the extent of preplanning with the Israelis to his Cabinet. He informed the Cabinet on 25 October that the Israelis were making military preparations for an attack on Egypt. The French were strongly of the view that intervention would be justified to limit the hostilities. In that event, Britain and France would require the combatants to withdraw and would intervene if they did not. Dissenting members of the Cabinet foresaw that this action would 'cause offence to the US government and might do lasting damage to Anglo-American relations. There was no prospect of securing the support or approval of the US government.'[26] But Eden, bolstered by Macmillan's assessment that the Americans would acquiesce, carried the day. In his memoirs Macmillan admitted a 'heavy responsibility' for the mistake and said, subsequently, that his judgement was wrong: he thought that the Americans did not wish to be informed when the British decided to take action because that would embarrass them, but that they would give support once action was taken.[27]

The Cabinet was told on the following day that the economic situation was so serious that, unless all the reserves were mobilised to maintain the fixed rate against the dollar, it would be necessary to move to a floating exchange rate. That, Macmillan said, would end sterling's role as an international currency and destroy the sterling area. He expected further serious losses in the reserves in November. There would need to be contact with the Americans to prepare the way for substantial loans.[28]

Meanwhile, on 26 October, the Russians began the suppression of the Hungarian uprising. On the same day, Dulles expressed fears that the British, French and Israelis might be on the verge of an attack on Egypt. Meanwhile Eden continued to pursue what the Americans regarded as the 'deliberate British purpose of keeping us completely in the dark'. Dulles telephoned Eisenhower about the Anglo-French military build-up in Cyprus. Eisenhower still could not believe that Britain would be dragged into such an affair.[29]

At this crucial moment the British, deliberately, were without an ambassador in Washington. Roger Makins had been recalled to London to become Permanent Secretary to the Treasury. His successor, Sir Harold Caccia, had been instructed to travel to Washington by sea. The British chargé and the French ambassador denied having any information about Israeli mobilisation. Dulles warned them not to assume that, because they were on the eve of an election, the United States was incapable of taking an anti-Israeli stand.

On the same evening, the US ambassador in London asked Selwyn Lloyd if he knew the reasons for the Israeli mobilisation. The Foreign Secretary claimed to be completely in the dark. But he said that the British had warned the Israelis against attacking Jordan. When Aldrich asked if the Israelis were planning to attack Egypt, Lloyd's denial carried 'sufficient conviction for him to conclude that any UK complicity in such a move is unlikely'.[30] On the following morning, 29 October, the British Chief of Air Staff received feverish calls from Eden asking for news of the 'surprise aggression' that would precipitate British and French intervention.

24

'NOTHING JUSTIFIES DOUBLE-CROSSING US'

ON THE AFTERNOON of 29 October, the Israelis launched their para-troop attack on the Mitla Pass, forty-five miles from the town of Suez. Other Israeli forces crossed the border into Sinai in support. Dulles reacted immediately, telling the British and French chargés that the USA would go to the UN Security Council forthwith with a resolution calling on the Israeli troops to withdraw and on member states to refrain from giving any assistance to Israel.

That evening, Dulles told Eisenhower that the British and French might have concerted their actions with the Israelis and might think that America had no choice but to go along with them. A furious Eisenhower declared that 'nothing justifies double-crossing us'. He told Dulles that he had sent for the British chargé, John Coulson, and intended to behave with him as if he believed that France was playing a lone hand. The British would be told that if they backed the Israelis they could expect to find the USA on the other side, otherwise the way would be open for Russia to enter the scene.[1]

Eisenhower and Dulles still hoped to detach the British from the French. Dulles told the US ambassador at the UN, Henry Cabot Lodge, that the effort to carry the British with them was 'basic and goes to the heart of our relations all over the world'. The US ambassador in London told Selwyn Lloyd that the Americans suspected a prior French arrangement with Israel. Any disharmony between the United States and Britain in the Security Council would create the impression that Britain and France had contrived the Israeli attack to try to get rid of Nasser.[2]

Eisenhower sent a personal message to Eden that began: 'Dear Anthony, I address you in this note not only as head of Her Majesty's Government, but as my long term friend.' He appealed to Eden for help in clearing up exactly what was happening between the USA and its allies. If the UN found Israel to be the aggressor, the Egyptians could well ask the Russians for help 'and then the Mid East fat would really be in the fire'. Britain and America needed to concert their plans.[3]

But that morning (30 October), the British Cabinet already had approved the notes to be addressed by Britain and France to Egypt and Israel. Selwyn Lloyd reported the US determination to ask the Security Council to condemn Israeli aggression. Macmillan said that the gold and dollar reserves were falling at a dangerously rapid rate and 'in view of the extent to which we may have to rely on American economic assistance, we could not afford to alienate the US Government any more than was absolutely necessary'. Eden replied to Eisenhower that Britain could not permit the canal to be closed or lose the shipping in passage through it: 'We feel that decisive action should be taken at once to stop hostilities.' This, he said, could not simply be left to the United Nations.[4]

Eisenhower and Dulles concluded that Britain and France were placing themselves in a position to take military action. The British and French ultimata were presented to the Israelis and Egyptians on the afternoon of 30 October. Egypt, supposedly to safeguard shipping and to separate the belligerents, was asked to accept the temporary occupation by Anglo-French forces of much of the canal zone. A reply was requested within twelve hours. If by that time Israel and Egypt had not undertaken to comply, British and French forces would intervene in whatever strength might be necessary to secure compliance.

The US ambassador in London was given a copy of the ultimatum. He noted that Egypt could not possibly accept these conditions. Dulles, after reading the text over the phone to Eisenhower, said that the ultimatum to Egypt was about as crude and brutal as anything he had ever seen. He considered it utterly unacceptable. Eisenhower sent messages to Eden and Mollet dissociating himself from their action and so informed the press. Britain and France vetoed a resolution supported by the United States at the UN: it was the first time in the history of the UN that Britain had used its veto. In Washington, Dulles told Coulson: 'We have seen the destruction of our trust in each other.' The British government had kept the United

States deliberately in the dark about its plans. Coulson said that he knew nothing about the situation and had no instructions. Coulson reported that 'the Administration, from top to bottom, is both angry and dismayed. You were, no doubt, anticipating a serious reaction but it is even worse than I would have myself expected.'[5]

As the Soviet Union used tanks to crush the uprising in Budapest, Allen Dulles, Director of the CIA, asked his brother Foster: 'How can anything be done about the Russians, even if they suppress the revolt, when our own allies are guilty of exactly similar acts of aggression?' When the National Security Council met on 1 November, Dulles said that for years the United States had been walking a tightrope between the effort to maintain its old and valued relations with the British and French and the attempt to win the friendship of the newly independent countries that had escaped from colonialism: 'Unless we now assert and maintain this leadership, all of these newly independent countries will turn from us to the USSR ... We will be looked at as for ever tied to British and French colonialist policies.'

Britain and France, he pointed out, had acted 'deliberately contrary to the clearest advice we could possibly give them. They have acted contrary both to principle and to what was expedient from the point of view of their own interests ... It is nothing less than tragic.' Harold Stassen alone argued on behalf of the allies, pointing out that the Suez Canal was a vital lifeline for the British. Eisenhower said that Britain and France were 'going down-hill' with the kind of policy they were pursuing, but then asked Dulles if the USA needed to do anything beyond a relatively mild UN resolution.

Eisenhower concluded:

> Of course, no one in the whole world really expected us to break off our long alliance with Great Britain and France. We must not permit ourselves to be blinded by the thought that anything we are going to do will result in our fighting with Great Britain and France. Such a course of action is simply unthinkable.

But Dulles sought Eisenhower's consent to a tough UN resolution.[6]

Eisenhower thought of sending Eden a message that 'the very second you obtain your minimum objectives', the British should call a ceasefire and undertake to evacuate as soon as the Israelis did and the Egyptians agreed to negotiate.[7] In the event, the message was never sent. The British government continued to lie to Parliament, Selwyn Lloyd saying that it was quite wrong to state that Israel was incited to this action by Britain: '[T]here was no prior agreement between us about it.'

On the eve of the crisis, Harold Macmillan had told Treasury officials and the Bank of England that he intended to 'remain firm and see the affair through'. But the Egyptians responded to the Israeli attack and Anglo-French threats by sinking block-ships in the canal. With the Suez Canal blocked and the reserves falling dramatically, Macmillan by now was extremely worried at the US reaction, 'much worse than he had expected'. Eisenhower, meanwhile, was complaining to General Gruenther about Anglo-French folly: 'I do not see the point in getting into a fight to which there can be no satisfactory end and in which the whole world believes you were playing the part of the bully and you do not even have the firm backing of your entire people.' Dulles was infuriated at the damage to the Western case against the Soviet intervention in Hungary, saying of French and British behaviour at the UN: 'It is a mockery for them to come in with bombs falling over Egypt and denounce the Soviet Union for doing something that is not quite as bad.'[8]

While Eden sought to portray the Anglo-French operation as a 'police action', the editor of The Times, William Haley, quoted Churchill in a leader on 2 November: 'I hold it perfectly justifiable to deceive the enemy, even if, at the same time, your own people are for a while misled. There is one thing, however, which one must never do and that is mislead your ally.'

On 3 November, Dulles was taken to hospital suffering from cancer. This left the field free for the Treasury Secretary, Humphrey, who was unwilling to help the British in any way, and for the acting Secretary of State, Herbert Hoover, who was even more resentful about British policy than Dulles.

Eisenhower and other key officials in the administration could not understand why the British, having decided on military action, were so hesitant in carrying it out. Eden noted that the Americans assumed that

> once we had decided on action it would be swift and decisive ... In the event our military plan took far more time to carry through than they had allowed for ... Consequently it no longer seemed practical for the US to stand aside until we had finished the job.[9]

On the afternoon of 4 November, Selwyn Lloyd reported that oil sanctions against Britain, France and Israel were being discussed in New York, causing Macmillan allegedly to exclaim: 'Oil sanctions! That finishes it.' Eden sent a desperate telegram to Eisenhower:

> The future of all of us depends on the closest Anglo-American cooperation. It has, of course, been grave to me to have had to make a temporary breach into it which I cannot disguise, but I know that you are a man of big enough heart and vision to take up things again on the basis of fact.[10]

Meanwhile, the military operations had their own momentum. On 5 November, British paratroopers landed near Port Said. French paratroopers occupied two bridges on the canal and captured Port Fuad. The air-drops were successful, with Egyptian resistance being fairly quickly overcome.

At this stage the Soviet Premier, Bulganin, entered the fray, with notes to Britain, France and Israel hinting at military action and suggesting joint US–Soviet intervention. Eisenhower consulted urgently with his advisers about Soviet intentions. The US ambassador in Moscow, Chip Bohlen, believed that the Russians would not risk war, but he thought that some form of Soviet assistance to Egypt was likely. Eisenhower warned that 'the Soviets are scared and furious, and there is nothing more dangerous than a dictatorship in this state of mind'.[11] He instructed that the Russians should be given a clear warning to stay out of Egypt.

The main Anglo-French landings took place at dawn on 6 November. Port Said was quickly captured. But by the time the main Anglo-French forces were preparing to break out of Port Said to advance to Suez at the southern end of the canal, the British Cabinet already had agreed to a ceasefire, to take effect at 5 p.m. London time.

At the Cabinet meeting that morning, Lloyd argued that it was urgently necessary that Britain should move to bring hostilities to an end, given the state of opinion at the UN. He added that it was 'equally important that we should shape our policy in such a way as to enlist the maximum sympathy and support from the US government'. Ministers favouring a ceasefire were worried about possible Soviet intervention, and that the UN might impose oil sanctions against Britain and France.[12]

In the first few days of November, 5 per cent of the foreign exchange reserves ($85 million) had been lost. The estimated annual additional cost of oil imports resulting from the blockage of the canal was more than $800 million. Eden later noted:

> The fall of sterling … came mainly from New York. Harold [Macmillan] told me that he had no doubt that this was encouraged by Washington. I would also think this so. We were therefore faced with the alternatives of a run on sterling and the loss of our gold and dollar reserves, till they fell well below the safety margin … or make the best we could of a UN 'takeover'.[13]

In fact there was no evidence that the US administration instigated the run on the pound: it was caused by the actions of the British government. All the Americans had to do was fail to support sterling. When Macmillan belatedly tried to withdraw funds from the IMF, Humphrey refused to support the request. The Americans also declined to start diverting oil supplies to Britain.

By the morning of 6 November, Macmillan was in a panic. Humphrey told him that only a ceasefire by midnight would secure US support. Macmillan told Lloyd before the Cabinet that 'in view of the financial and economic pressures we must stop'. He told his colleagues that, without a ceasefire, he could not be responsible for Her Majesty's Exchequer: '[I]f sanctions were imposed on us the country was finished.'[14] The British ambassador in Moscow, Sir William Hayter, warned that the Russians might take some violent independent action and that it was 'vitally necessary to get into step with the US again immediately' to dissuade the Soviet leadership from committing 'dangerous acts of folly'.[15]

The US assessment was that the Russians would not intervene directly. US forces were not put on strategic alert, though Eisenhower did authorise some additional precautionary measures. It was not the Soviet threats but the lack of American support that was critical. If the US Treasury had been more helpful, the Anglo-French forces would have been able to complete the occupation of the canal – though what they would have done thereafter remained an open question.

25

'WE CAN FURNISH A LOT OF FIG LEAVES'

AFTER THE CABINET, Eden told the French Prime Minister that they must get a ceasefire. Mollet argued for two more days to seize the rest of the canal, but Eden said that Britain could not withstand American pressure on the pound.

The Anglo-French commanders learned of the ceasefire from the BBC. Advance patrols that were within twenty-five miles of Suez were recalled. Twenty-three British and ten French soldiers were killed in the two days of fighting, along with several hundred Egyptians. The British commander, General Stockwell, was reprimanded for telling reporters that British and French forces could have taken Suez in forty-eight hours if the ceasefire had not intervened.

Eisenhower called 10 Downing Street to express his pleasure at the news. He assured Eden that if the Soviet Union intervened, Britain would not be alone. Eden, ever a master of self-deception, told Mollet that 'the President of the US called me on his own account. There is no doubt at all that the friendship between us all is restored and even strengthened.'[1]

On 7 November, Eden called Eisenhower to congratulate him on his re-election and to suggest a meeting with the President and Mollet on the Middle East. Eisenhower initially responded positively, but was warned by Hoover and others to ensure that the British agreed to plans for UN forces to take over from them in the canal zone. In a second telephone call, Eisenhower still appeared to agree to a meeting, which Eden proposed to announce in the House of Commons that afternoon. After further

discussion with Hoover, Humphrey and others, however, Eisenhower telephoned Eden again to postpone the meeting: 'I have just had a partial
Cabinet meeting on this and they think our timing is very, very bad.'[2]

The official present with Eden saw his distress as he took the call. He
protested desperately that nothing should prevent friends discussing matters, but Eisenhower cut off further discussion. Eisenhower told Sherman
Adams that turning down Eden's request for a personal talk did not seem
to him the right thing to do. But he was not prepared to overrule his advisers. Dulles also was urging from hospital that no meeting should take place
until British and French troops had been withdrawn from Egypt. For Eden
it was a crushing and politically mortal blow.

There followed a virtual shut-down of communication between the US
government and the Prime Minister. When the new British ambassador,
Sir Harold Caccia, presented his credentials to Eisenhower on 9 November, he reported that the President 'could not personally have been more
friendly or indeed more forgiving'. Eisenhower told Caccia: 'Just because
Britain and the US had had a sharp difference over the attack on Egypt,
there was no thought that we would not keep our friendship over the long
term.' Humphrey, in contrast, was telling the British that for the United
States to offer financial aid in the light of Britain's actions over the past
ten days would be totally unacceptable politically in the USA for a considerable time. In London, Selwyn Lloyd still was denying collusion with
Israel to the US ambassador: 'The British government', he claimed, 'had
no advance knowledge that the Israelis were going to attack Egypt and
had entered into no commitments to Israel.'[3]

Treasury and Bank of England officials in London concluded that only
with a 'friendly and compliant attitude' from the US would Britain be able to
secure the funds from the IMF desperately needed to shore up the reserves.
When Selwyn Lloyd proposed to visit Washington for urgent discussions,
Hoover opposed the idea. On 15 November, Eden still was refusing to
withdraw British troops until a satisfactory agreement was reached to clear
the canal. Lloyd was reduced to making a private visit to Washington, in the
course of which he called on Dulles in the Walter Reed Hospital.

It was on this occasion that, according to Lloyd, Dulles asked: 'Selwyn,
why did you stop? Why didn't you go through with it and get Nasser
down?' The astounded Lloyd told Dulles: 'Well, Foster, if you had so much
as winked at us, we might have gone on.'[4]

This was not just an aberration by Dulles. Five days earlier he had told Eisenhower: 'The British having gone in should not have stopped until they had toppled Nasser. As it was they now had the worst of both possible worlds.' Dulles subsequently told Harold Caccia that for moral reasons he had disapproved of Suez, which was aggression pure and simple. But he had never understood why, once the British had decided to fight, they did not go ahead and win. Caccia told Joe Alsop that he was so angry that 'literally it required a physical effort not to leap up and storm over the desk'.[5]

Reporting to Eden, Lloyd said that Dulles had been friendly, but seemed to want to avoid responsibility in the next phase. Hoover, Lodge and the State Department officials were positively antagonistic.

In London the Lord Privy Seal, Rab Butler, told the US ambassador how deeply he deplored the 'mutual misunderstandings of policy' that had arisen. Macmillan also approached Aldrich, suggesting to him that he should visit Washington as Eden was 'very tired and should have a rest'. Aldrich commented that he could not help wondering 'whether this might not be a hint that some sort of movement is on foot in the Cabinet to replace Eden'.[6]

On the following day, Winthrop Aldrich telephoned the President to report that his guess was correct. Macmillan had come to his residence to say that Eden had had a physical breakdown and would go on a holiday that would lead to his retirement. The first action after Eden's departure would be a step towards withdrawal from Egypt, if the USA could 'give us a fig leaf to cover our nakedness'. Aldrich told Eisenhower that Macmillan wanted to see him as soon as possible. The US Treasury Secretary, George Humphrey, thought that Butler would be the better man to succeed Eden. Eisenhower disagreed: he had always thought highly of Macmillan 'who is a straight, fine man, and, so far as he is concerned, the outstanding one of the British he served with during the War'. Aldrich reported Macmillan's description of the difficulties facing the British government, caused, he claimed, by 'humiliations almost vindictively inflicted upon us at the instance of the United States government'. Eisenhower told Aldrich that 'as soon as things happen we anticipated [i.e., British withdrawal from Suez] we can furnish a lot of fig leaves'. Eisenhower added in the meeting that he could see 'the possibility of some blessings in disguise coming to Britain out of this affair, in the form of impelling them to accept the Common Market'.[7]

Hoover was still very cautious, but Humphrey indicated that he would support a Conservative government without Eden, if only to keep the Labour Party from power. Macmillan, meanwhile, was telling the Cabinet that they might have to let sterling float, with the possible consequence that it would cease to be an international currency. The next morning, Butler and Macmillan assured Aldrich that the Cabinet would approve British withdrawal from the canal.

Eden, who by now had cancelled all public engagements, drafted a last plea to Eisenhower: 'I must tell you frankly that there is a body of opinion here which believes that we have been let down.' The message was never sent. On 23 November, Eden left Britain to recuperate in Jamaica at Goldeneye, home of Ian Fleming. A motion deploring the attitude of the US as gravely endangering the Atlantic Alliance was signed by 130 Conservative MPs. Butler told Aldrich that 'the wave of anti-American feeling in Great Britain … cannot possibly be exaggerated'. If things continued to deteriorate, Butler suggested, the US could be asked to give up its bases in Britain.

Churchill had started by strongly supporting forceful action to undo Nasser's seizure of control over the canal and said so in a message published in the press on 5 November, as British and French paratroopers captured Port Said. But he was horrified at the public breach with the Americans. On 20 November, Jock Colville asked Churchill if he would have done the same as Eden. Churchill replied that he 'would never have dared, and if I had dared, I would never have dared stop'. Colville suggested that he should write to Eisenhower in an attempt to repair relations.[8]

So on 23 November, Winston Churchill, making his last contribution to the 'special relationship', wrote a personal letter to President Eisenhower: 'There is not much left for me to do in this world … But I do believe, with unfaltering conviction, that the theme of the Anglo-American alliance is more important today than at any time since war.' If Anglo-American misunderstandings were permitted to continue, the only beneficiary would be the Soviet Union. 'Whatever the argument produced here and in the United States for or against Anthony's action in Egypt, to let events in the Middle East become a gulf between us would be an act of folly on which our whole civilisation may flounder.'

Eisenhower replied that Britain's action over Suez was 'not only in violation of the basic principles by which this great combination of nations

can be held together, but that even by the doctrine of expediency the invasion could not be judged as soundly conceived and skillfully executed'. But
he hoped that this 'may be washed off the slate as soon as possible and
that we can then together adopt other means of achieving our legitimate
objectives in the Middle East … I shall never be happy until our old time
closeness has been restored.'[9]

Following this exchange, Eisenhower proceeded to overrule Hoover and
others in the State Department who wished to prolong the quarrel with
Britain. Hoover believed that 'it might be necessary to tell Britain that it
looks as though they are through in the area and ask if they want us to
pick up their commitments'. Eisenhower replied that the Anglo-American
partnership was still necessary: 'We should give the British every chance
to work their way back into a position of influence and respect in the
Middle East.'[10]

Dulles was still objecting that 'it was they who double-crossed us and
now try to put the blame on us'. But Eisenhower was determined to restore
relations. On 26 November, the US Treasury Secretary, Humphrey, telephoned Butler to say that provided the British withdrew from Egypt, the
United States would help over loans and oil and would press the Egyptians
on free international use of the canal. Called back to London from New
York on 28 November, Lloyd told the Cabinet: 'If we withdraw the Anglo-
French troops as rapidly as was practicable, we should regain the sympathy of US government.'[11]

Macmillan called for an immediate announcement of withdrawal. On
the following day he told the Cabinet that more than 20 per cent of the
reserves had been lost since September. The Americans still were insisting
on the announcement of a firm date for withdrawal.[12] At a private meeting
with Conservative MPs in late November, Butler, as acting Prime Minister, had the unpleasant task of telling them that Britain, for financial and
economic reasons, had to withdraw her troops from Egypt.

At this stage there was an unwelcome complication. Eden, who was still
Prime Minister, started trying to take an interest in public affairs from his
exile in Jamaica. Macmillan and Butler moved to block the Prime Minister from giving any interviews to the press and to censor the statement
he proposed to make on his return to London: 'There is a growing wish
to end the breach with the US. It is important that your first pronounce-
ment should be in tune with the changed atmosphere.'[13]

Once they knew of the intention to withdraw, the Americans activated the Anglo-American committee to discuss oil supplies. On 3 December, Lloyd announced that British troops would withdraw by mid-December if an effective UN force was in place.

The difficulty now was that Eden, refreshed by Jamaica, did not want to resign as Prime Minister. Humphrey told Foster Dulles that nothing but a change of government would save the pound.

Macmillan met Dulles at a NATO meeting in Paris on 12 December. Dulles reported to Eisenhower that Macmillan recognised:

> There had been a certain loss of confidence on the part of the President, ourselves and others because of the Suez operation and the deception practised in that connection ... He, personally, was very unhappy with the way in which the matter was handled and the timing but ... Eden had taken this entirely to himself and he, Macmillan, had had no real choice except to back Eden. Macmillan did not disguise the fact that he had always favoured strong action.

But, he claimed, he did not like the manner and timing, particularly *vis-à-vis* the USA.[14]

Following a conversation with Humphrey, Macmillan reported to Butler that the Americans would not lift their quarantine on Eden. According to Macmillan, the US Treasury Secretary said: 'It was like a business deal. They were putting a lot of money into the re-organisation of Britain and they would hope very much that the business would be successful.' Macmillan asked Humphrey if he did not trust the board, to which the reply was: 'Well, since you asked me, I think it would be as well if we could deal as much as possible with the directors.'[15]

On 7 January, Eden was told by his doctors that his health would be endangered if he stayed in office. Macmillan describes meeting Eden on 9 January, the day he told the Cabinet that he could not go on: 'I can see him now on that sad winter afternoon, still looking so youthful, so gay, so debonair – the representative of all that was best of the youth that had served in the 1914–18 War.'[16] Lord Salisbury summoned the members of the Cabinet to ask them: 'Which is it to be: Hawold or Wab?' All but three opted for Macmillan.

Suez was a watershed for British influence, not only in the Middle East but throughout the world. Eden's decision to act alone with France and Israel was a final attempt to establish that Britain could act independently from the United States. The contemporary records belie the myth propagated by Eden and others that Dulles privately supported the use of force. While Dulles supported the *threat* of force, he never gave any indication that, in his view, the moment for military action had been reached. But, however much they disliked it, if Anglo-French forces had proceeded quickly to occupy the canal zone, Dulles and Eisenhower would have accepted the *fait accompli*.

The Americans were not asked to support Anglo-French intervention. But they were expected not to oppose it. Macmillan gave Eden a misleading impression of his visit to Washington and conversation with Eisenhower. On the basis of an extraordinary exercise in self-deception, the Prime Minister and his colleagues believed that the Americans would acquiesce. Despite his warnings to the Cabinet, Macmillan was unprepared for the subsequent run on the pound. Humphrey and Hoover blocked any assistance to Britain until political and economic pressures forced agreement to a ceasefire. The British government ended up in the tragic and absurd position of going ahead with an invasion within twenty-four hours of deciding to call it off.

26

'IF ANYTHING GOES WRONG YOU MAY BE SURE THAT MR DULLES WILL PLACE THE BLAME ELSEWHERE'

BRITAIN STILL WAS suffering from the after-shock of Suez, which appeared definitively to have relegated it to the rank of a second-rate power. Macmillan's own role in the crisis had been strongly criticised: 'first in, first out', in the words of Harold Wilson.

But, unlike Eden, Macmillan understood and liked the Americans and was trusted by them. In 1942 Macmillan had been despatched by Churchill as his representative, with the title of Minister Resident, in North Africa. He was greeted coolly by Eisenhower, who had not been told about the appointment by either London or Washington, but had heard about it on the radio. 'You are a Minister, but what sort of Minister are you?' 'Well, General, I said, I am not a diplomatic Minister; I am something worse.' 'There is nothing worse', Eisenhower replied.[1] But he was mollified to discover that Macmillan's mother came from Indiana. Macmillan went out of his way to conciliate Eisenhower and, from the outset, they got on well.

Macmillan attended the meeting between Churchill and Roosevelt in Casablanca. He did not share Churchill's admiration for the President, who, in Macmillan's view, thought he could charm everyone, including Stalin. 'Churchill had a certain naivety in his character ... I don't think he realised how devious FDR could be.'[2] Ironically, in view of the damage the

General was to do him later, Macmillan spent much of his time in Algiers protecting de Gaulle from the wrath of Roosevelt and Churchill.

When Macmillan took over, Eisenhower sent his old wartime friend a warm personal letter, welcoming him to 'new headaches'. On 17 January, Macmillan said on television that 'any partners are bound to have their differences ... we do not intend to part from the Americans and we do not intend to be satellites'.

Nevertheless, as a result of Suez, the 'special relationship' had never been in worse repair. In Britain, anti-American feelings – as Winthrop Aldrich warned – were at a postwar high. In January, Duncan Sandys, the new Minister of Defence, brought this forcibly home to Dulles in Washington. Sandys told Dulles that what Britain most complained of was the way in which she had been misled by Dulles's scheme for the Suez Canal Users Association as a way of bringing pressure on Egypt. Sandys said that the British felt that they had been led up the garden path.

Eisenhower, anxious to get relations on a more even keel, offered a meeting with Macmillan in Bermuda in March. Macmillan felt able to 'revert to our old friendly relations'. Macmillan was determined that Britain should never again permit a basic policy conflict with the United States. But he remained disparaging about American policy in the Middle East.

In Bermuda, Macmillan was gratified to find that

> Eisenhower talked very freely to me – just exactly as in the old days. There were no reproaches on either side but (what was more important) no note of any change in our friendship or the confidence he had in me ... he told me very frankly that he knew how unpopular Foster Dulles was with our people and with a lot of his people.

But, Eisenhower added, Dulles remained indispensable to him.[3]

In the formal meeting, Macmillan said that over Suez: 'Your Government and many of your people think we acted foolishly and precipitately and illegally. Our Government and many of our people think that you were too hard on us – and rather let us down.' Eisenhower in reply took up sharply the point about the British feeling let down. In his memoirs, Eisenhower wrote that Macmillan and Selwyn Lloyd felt a blinding bitterness towards Nasser and were so obsessed with the possibilities of getting rid of him that they were handicapped in searching for any realistic method of operating the canal. Nevertheless, Eisenhower and Macmillan spent much time in private conversation together at the Mid-Ocean Club and both were satisfied by the results.

Agreement was reached that sixty Thor intermediate-range nuclear missiles should be based in Britain. In 1952, Churchill and Truman had agreed that the use of US bases in an emergency would be a matter for 'joint decision'. In the case of the Thor missiles, it was agreed that these should be under joint control. These were the only American nuclear weapons based on British soil to which a dual key system, giving the British as well as the Americans physical control over their use, ever applied. Such a system obviously was impractical for air- or sea-launched weapons. In respect of US aircraft operating from British bases, 'joint decision' meant that political agreement would be required, but, as with US weapons elsewhere in Europe, there was no system of joint control.

Eisenhower observed after the meeting that the British did not like to commit themselves to generalisations, 'no matter how plausible or attractive they may be, but once their signature is affixed to a document, complete confidence can be placed in their performance. French negotiators sometimes seem to prefer to sign first and then to begin discussion.' Macmillan reported to his deputy, Butler, that on Eisenhower's part there was a genuine desire to forget their differences and restore their old relationship. 'But of course he leaves so much to Dulles and neither the Foreign Secretary or I feel so happy about his attitude ... He acts as a brake on the process of rebuilding confidence and help.' Eisenhower wrote at the time that 'Macmillan is, of course, one of my intimate war-time friends and so it is very easy to talk to him on a very frank, even blunt, basis.'[4] Eisenhower counted Bermuda as the most successful international meeting he had attended since the war. The 'special relationship' had been restored at the level of the Prime Minister and President.

On 25 March 1957, while Macmillan was still with Eisenhower in Bermuda, the European Six signed the Treaty of Rome. On 1 January 1958, the European Economic Community came into being. Philip de Zulueta, serving in Macmillan's office at the time, expressed the general British disbelief that the French and Germans would ever bury the hatchet to the extent of getting together to make the Common Market work. Macmillan was incensed by remarks relayed by Adenauer, who claimed that Dulles had told him that 'the British had no foreign policy'.

In August, Macmillan wrote to Dulles about the increasing Soviet influence in Syria. In his opinion Khrushchev might prove more dangerous than Stalin: 'Under his direction we must expect continual Russian pressure but always by subversive tactics; by blackmail, not military operations.' The next stage, in Macmillan's view, was likely to be an attempt to subvert Lebanon and Jordan: 'If we do nothing, both of these countries might easily fall.' He suggested an operation to eradicate Communist influence in Syria, to be undertaken by Syria's Arab neighbours led, if possible, by Iraq. The British ambassador in Washington, Harold Caccia, recorded his impression that 'Mr Dulles is trying to screw up his courage to act. As is his custom, he has allowed himself a great number of escape routes ... If anything goes wrong, you may be sure that Mr Dulles will place the blame elsewhere.'[5]

Britain, meanwhile, had tested its first hydrogen bomb in the Pacific. In Macmillan's view, 'we should prepare against a time when the Americans may no longer need to use the UK as a base'.[6] He wanted to get the Americans to share their information on research and development of nuclear weapons, so as to reduce the strain on Britain's resources. The H-bomb test was followed by the burgeoning in Britain of the Campaign for Nuclear Disarmament. The immediate effect was to split the Labour Party, Aneurin Bevan making an impassioned defence of British nuclear weapons at the Party Conference.

In October, Macmillan, visiting Washington, found the Americans shaken by the successful Russian launch of the sputnik space satellite. Macmillan found his first round of talks with Eisenhower and Dulles discouraging, but on the following day the President astonished the British delegation by producing a directive setting up two joint Anglo-American committees to deal with weapons and nuclear cooperation. This spelt the end of the restrictions imposed by the McMahon Act: Macmillan could scarcely believe that such rapid progress had been made. Earlier in the year a reluctant Admiral Hyman Rickover had been instructed to make available to the British the first nuclear propulsion plant for British submarines.

In return Macmillan promised that Britain would not press for the admission of Communist China to the United Nations. The Americans agreed to regard Hong Kong as a joint defence problem. Although attempts were made by US atomic experts to water down the agreement on nuclear cooperation, the President stood firm. Eisenhower told the British that he regarded the passage of the McMahon Act as 'one of the most deplorable incidents in American history', of which he personally felt ashamed.[7]

The day after Macmillan's departure, Eisenhower suffered a slight stroke. He made a rapid recovery, but admitted to Macmillan privately that he had suffered some loss of speech and memory. The following July, the McMahon Act was replaced by the 'Agreement for Cooperation on Uses of Atomic Energy for Mutual Defence Purposes'. Britain was enabled to receive technical information on the production of nuclear warheads as well as fissile material. No other nation was given this privileged treatment. Andrew Pierre, who served in the State Department, commented that in the case of Britain,

> the creation and continuation of an independent nuclear force can be understood in the context of a once Great Power in decline, attempting to adjust to reduced circumstances ... Though she had become a junior partner of the United States during the course of the war, Britain thought of herself as a small superpower rather than a strong middle power.

He added that the decision 'created an environment in which American trust in the British Government deepened so that American officials discussed a wider range of political and military topics with their British counterparts than with officials from other friendly nations'.[8] The agreement opened the way for future British nuclear tests to be conducted at the US underground nuclear test site in Nevada. The spectre of Suez had been buried. It was one of Macmillan's greatest achievements that he proved able so fully to restore the relationship with the United States.

───────

In May 1958, President Chamoun of Lebanon asked the British and American governments if they would provide military assistance in the event of a Nasser-inspired coup against him. The Cabinet agreed that Britain should join the US in promising help. In July, King Feisal and Nuri al-Said were murdered in Iraq. The Baghdad Pact was effectively destroyed. To Macmillan, this was disastrous news. Chamoun appealed again for help. Eisenhower sent the Sixth Fleet to Beirut, informing Macmillan of his intentions. At the same time, King Hussein of Jordan appealed to Macmillan for British help against the Syrian threat. Macmillan telephoned Dulles twice before deciding to respond with two battalions of paratroopers. Dulles would not promise troops, but said he would give moral and logistic support. The Americans had decided to act independently in Lebanon and to leave Jordan to the British and only support them if they got into trouble. As Harold Caccia had reported two months before, Dulles and others had been going through 'a bout of that chronic American phobia: the fear of being seen alone with the British. They badly want ... a secret liaison. But they are scared stiff that we are going to ask for marriage bells.'[9]

Macmillan expressed to Eisenhower his anxieties about being militarily exposed in Jordan. The Americans did help in getting the Israelis to agree to the necessary overflights, but Macmillan's request for American troops was denied. By November the Anglo-American forces had been withdrawn from both Lebanon and Jordan. Selwyn Lloyd regarded the State Department's attitude to Jordan at the time as defeatist. But the operation was successful in stabilising King Hussein's government there. Eisenhower and Macmillan exchanged messages of congratulations.

The British were worried about American intentions in the Far East. In August 1958, the Chinese Communists resumed their bombardment of the offshore islands of Quemoy and Matsu. In response to earlier threats, Eisenhower had responded with a formal declaration that Taiwan and the islands would be defended by the USA against any attack. The overriding concern for the British was Hong Kong, and Eden had infuriated the Americans by stating that, juridically, the Chinese had a good case to claim the offshore islands. Macmillan agreed, but was of the view that 'if we abandon the Americans – morally I mean, they need no active support, it will be a great blow to the friendship and Alliance which I have done so much to rebuild and strengthen'.[10]

But supporting the USA also had its dangers. In September, Dulles warned that the USA might use nuclear weapons against China if it invaded Quemoy. In a letter to Macmillan on 4 September, Dulles questioned whether if we did intervene we could do so effectively without at least some use of atomic weapons; I hope no more than small air bursts without fallout. That is of course an unpleasant prospect but one I think we must face up to because our entire military establishment assumes more and more that the use of nuclear weapons will become normal in the event of hostilities.[11]

Macmillan was horrified, though he also suspected, or at any rate hoped, that Dulles was bluffing. He wrote to Eisenhower saying that he shared US fears of a Munich in the Far East, but warned of British and Commonwealth reservations about bringing the world to the verge of war over Quemoy and Matsu. He suggested, by way of a compromise, demilitarising the islands. Neither the Americans nor the Chinese showed any interest in this initiative. American deterrence proved successful as, a few months later, the Chinese bombardment ceased.

27

'THEY HAVE COMPLETE CONFIDENCE IN ME'

IN EUROPE, DE GAULLE, having returned to power in 1958 in France, was proposing the replacement of NATO with an Anglo-American-French triumvirate, whose authority should extend beyond the NATO area. Macmillan saw this as 'an attempt by France to claim a special position with Britain and America', and the proposal ran directly counter to the Macmillan/Eisenhower agreement excluding any third country from the bilateral exchanges on nuclear weaponry. Macmillan also thought that it would cause problems with the Germans. De Gaulle, for his part, told Adenauer that Britain should not enter the European Common Market so long as she remained the instrument of America.[1]

Macmillan was more interested in pursuing his idea of some kind of summit with the Russians. He had nostalgic memories of the great wartime set-piece encounters – despite the fact that Tehran and Yalta had yielded such mixed results – and he began formulating a 'perhaps crazy idea of offering to go himself to Moscow' to discuss the agenda for a wider summit with Khrushchev. Macmillan's Moscow plan did not find favour with his Cabinet, but he pursued it anyway. He found the Americans negative and 'almost threatening' about his proposed message to the Russians, with both Dulles and Eisenhower hostile to the idea and with no grounds for thinking it would be successful. But Macmillan felt that there were issues on which he was well-qualified to act as an intermediary between the Americans and the Russians.

In November 1958, Khrushchev had demanded the withdrawal of Allied troops from Berlin. Macmillan wrote to Caccia in Washington, expressing his fears about American plans to keep the road to Berlin open:

> [T]he whole art of dealing with an opponent who is indulging in brinkmanship, consists of not allowing him to get into a position in which he has to choose between war and humiliating retreat. This would be precisely the choice which would be imposed on the Russians under the American plan.

Macmillan expressed the hope that the American attitude might become more flexible, without their thinking that Macmillan was being defeatist.[2]

As he persisted with his plans, Macmillan congratulated himself on the fact that Eisenhower had reacted in friendly terms: 'They say, in effect, that they have complete confidence in me and I must do whatever I think best.'

This was, in fact, by no means the American reaction. On 29 January 1959, Dulles called Eisenhower about Macmillan's plan to visit Russia. Dulles thought it was because Macmillan faced an election and 'wants to be the hero who finds a way out of the Cold War dilemma, particularly about Berlin':

> Neither the President nor the Secretary felt they could ... say 'no' but they pointedly said that of course the Prime Minister would be speaking only for himself, not for the United States, or Germany, or France ... The President said that he doubted that [the British] would be able to make a dent in the granite – and the trip would therefore react adversely.[3]

Macmillan sought to reassure his doubtful allies that the visit represented a 'reconnaissance, not a negotiation'. News of his plan was greeted with enthusiasm by the British press.

In February, Macmillan arrived in Moscow wearing his fur hat (he subsequently wore plus-fours to visit a collective farm near Kiev). It was the first visit by a British Prime Minister or any Western leader to the Soviet Union in peacetime. After talks with Khrushchev, Macmillan reported to Eisenhower that in spite of their power, the Russians still were obsessed by a sense of insecurity. They felt encircled and remained extremely distrustful of the Germans. On the following day, Khrushchev launched into a public attack on Dulles, Eisenhower and Adenauer – but offered a non-aggression pact with Britain. As Khrushchev became increasingly intemperate about Berlin, Macmillan warned that his threats could lead to a Third World War: 'because we shall not give in, and nor will the Americans'. Khrushchev continued the row over Germany and declined to accompany Macmillan to Kiev. Macmillan left with most of his allies feeling that he had achieved nothing. Sir Patrick Reilly, the British ambassador in Moscow, shared the American misgivings. The voyage of discovery, he felt, had been undertaken for the wrong motives – 'with electoral advantage in view'.[4]

But Macmillan returned home more convinced than ever that the only way to head off a confrontation over Berlin was to call a wider summit meeting with Khrushchev. He flew to Washington and, with Eisenhower, visited Dulles, who was dying of cancer in the Walter Reed Hospital. Dulles, characteristically, had warned Eisenhower that Macmillan would be trying to get all the domestic mileage he could out of the visit. Dulles added that he did not mind 'since we do not want to see Bevan win the election'.

Macmillan found that while Eisenhower had 'never much liked business, now he had to rest *before* a meal'. Nor was he impressed with the qualities of his deputy, following a less than satisfactory encounter with Vice-President Richard Nixon, who, over dinner one evening, 'poured out a monologue which extinguished any spark of conversation from whatever quarter it might arise. This spate of banalities lasted three to four hours. We withdrew battered and exhausted.'[5]

Macmillan found Dulles 'against almost everything. He was strongly against the idea of a summit.' Eisenhower was equally lukewarm about Macmillan's proposal to try to draw up an agenda for a summit before any agreement on substance was reached. On the issues of Berlin and a summit, the gap remained wide and Macmillan was hard pressed to dispel American misgivings about what he might have said to Khrushchev. On nuclear testing, he noted, the Americans were very unwilling to abandon anything unless Russian observance of an agreement could be effectively policed.

As Macmillan approached the 1959 election, he was able to give his campaign a boost by engineering a visit by Eisenhower to London. As his biographer, Alistair Home, writes: 'In his exploitation of his closest ally, Macmillan was quite shameless and Eisenhower was fully aware of it, even to the point of some irritation.'[6] Through the spring and summer, Macmillan had angled for Eisenhower to visit London in the course of a world tour.

He had some difficulty persuading the President, but Eisenhower's visit in August was a great success. A large crowd turned out to welcome Eisenhower on the road from the airport. He spent two days at Balmoral with the Queen. At Chequers he spent some time hitting golf balls in the grounds. 'Unhappily', noted Macmillan, 'since the grass was long, a large quantity of balls were struck in proportion to those ultimately recovered.'

Eisenhower hosted a dinner at the American embassy for all his British wartime collaborators. Before departing, he made a joint television appearance with Macmillan at No. 10, stressing their old friendship and the closeness of the 'special relationship'. Macmillan could not get Eisenhower publicly to endorse his summit plans and differences remained over a nuclear test ban. But the visit afforded Macmillan wonderful propaganda on the eve of the election he called a few days later.

In September, Khrushchev made his visit to the United States. Following talks with Eisenhower at Camp David, he suspended his threat against Berlin. In October, after his re-election, Macmillan received a message from Eisenhower proposing a summit meeting of the Western heads of government in Paris. Eisenhower accepted that this should lead on to a summit with the Russians. Commenting to the Queen on the meeting of the Western leaders, Macmillan observed that the fact that Eisenhower did not speak to his brief and forgot most of what he was told by his advisers led many to underrate his fundamental strengths. Frequently he was following his own instinctive judgement: 'In many cases I would think this better than that of the State Department or the Pentagon.'[7] The agreement to a Western summit with Khrushchev – now set for May 1960 in Paris – was seen as a personal triumph for Macmillan. But Eisenhower's conversion had been lukewarm and reluctant. He commented that he had no intention of bickering with Macmillan about this. But he remained full of scepticism about the likely results.

Macmillan made his last visit to Eisenhower in Washington in March. He noted that while Eisenhower seemed disposed to go along with a moratorium on nuclear testing, the Pentagon wanted to continue testing indefinitely. Macmillan's preoccupation was with the development of a new delivery system for the British nuclear deterrent.

The 1958 agreement on nuclear cooperation helped Britain to develop more sophisticated nuclear warheads. The delivery vehicle was intended to be the British-manufactured Blue Streak missile. As the programme had run into technical difficulties and massive cost overruns, Macmillan secured from Eisenhower agreement to purchase the US Skybolt. A long-range air-launched missile, this seemed ideally designed to prolong the life of the RAF's ageing Vulcan bombers.

Part of the Skybolt deal reached in principle during this visit was agreement on the British side to provide a base for the US Polaris submarines in a Scottish loch. Macmillan understood the political risks: 'A picture could well be drawn of some frightful accident which might devastate the whole of Scotland.' He concluded that much depended on whether Britain was simply to provide bases 'more or less as a satellite – or whether we can make it a joint enterprise. Can we get one submarine from US and start to build another?'[8]

Macmillan believed that he had obtained a half-promise from Eisenhower about Polaris. But he continued to worry about the choice, proposed by the Americans, of a site on the Clyde as the US Polaris base. This would place a major nuclear target next to the third largest city in Britain. Macmillan hankered after a site in the Highlands. But in September the Cabinet approved the choice of Holy Loch. Macmillan urged that the existing agreement that Polaris missiles should not be fired from Britain's territorial waters without her consent should be extended to a wider area. Eisenhower gave an assurance that in an emergency the USA would take 'every possible step to consult with Britain and other Allies'.

The prospects for the summit, meanwhile, had suddenly been thrown into jeopardy.

On 1 May, Eisenhower was told that a U-2 photographic reconnaissance aircraft had been lost. Macmillan wrote in his diary: 'The Americans have created a great folly.' He noted that Khrushchev made two 'very amusing and effective speeches, attacking the Americans for spying incompetently and lying incompetently'. In fact U-2s had also been carrying out reconnaissance flights from bases in Britain and Macmillan was relieved that nothing had come out about these. The Americans first denied, then confirmed the mission of the plane. Macmillan was unhappy both about the denial and that, subsequently, Eisenhower personally accepted responsibility for the U-2 flights.

Macmillan arrived in Paris full of forebodings, which soon proved to be justified, as Khrushchev evidently was determined to use the U-2 incident to wreck the meeting. 'The summit', wrote Macmillan, 'on which I had placed high hopes – and for which I had worked for two years – has blown up like a volcano.' He told Eisenhower that they stood together: most of their intelligence work was joint and it was bad luck that the Americans had suffered this setback. But Macmillan was depressed and extremely unhappy with the American handling of the affair. De Gaulle was less perturbed, pointing out to Khrushchev that every day a Soviet satellite passed over France.

Eisenhower, like Macmillan, had hoped that the summit might yield some progress on nuclear testing. He was furious that a government that was itself so deeply involved in spying should lecture him as Khrushchev was trying to do. Macmillan tried desperately to salvage something from the wreckage, visiting each of the other three leaders in turn. Eisenhower asked him to go for a drive with him through Paris in an open car. Macmillan was glad to do so: 'If Khrushchev must break up the summit conference, there is no reason to let him break up the Anglo-American Alliance.'[9]

But the debacle was a shattering setback to Macmillan: 'The disappointment amounted almost to despair.' One of the Americans present noted that it left him in a highly emotional state. The summit had been the most important goal towards which he had worked since becoming Prime Minister. Philip de Zulueta said that he never saw Macmillan so depressed: 'This was the moment he suddenly realised that Britain counted for nothing; he could not move Ike to make a gesture towards Khrushchev and De Gaulle was simply not interested.'

Macmillan continued to believe that some gesture from Eisenhower might have let Khrushchev off the hook. To the Queen, however, he commented that some internal change in the balance of power in Moscow might have caused Khrushchev to retreat from his policy of *détente*. In Washington, Eisenhower was obliged to refute press comment that Macmillan had lost standing with him as a result of the events in Paris.

Macmillan saw Eisenhower again at the United Nations in September. In November, he sent Eisenhower a valedictory message, concluding: 'I cannot, of course, ever hope to have anything to replace the sort of relations we have had.' 'Happily for me,' Macmillan observed later, 'the last sentence proved not to be true.'[10]

28

'IT IS GOING TO BE A COLD WINTER'

MACMILLAN'S EARLY KNOWLEDGE of Senator John Kennedy was not encouraging. He was worried about the Irish connection, about Kennedy's youth and inexperience, and his attacks on British and French colonialism. Like other English politicians of the Second World War generation, he also had unpleasant memories of his father, Joseph Kennedy. As Macmillan said: 'We regarded him with some contempt, as being a man of low character whose view was that Britain was beaten.'[1]

By October, Macmillan suspected that Kennedy would win the election (he never had a high opinion of Nixon). After the election his press secretary, Harold Evans, found Macmillan feeling his age and brooding over cartoons depicting the youthful Kennedy pushing Macmillan in a bath-chair. Macmillan was not encouraged by what he learned from Jock Whitney, Eisenhower's outgoing ambassador, who described Kennedy to him as 'sensitive, ruthless and highly sexed'. At the end of November, Macmillan gave a dinner for Lyndon Johnson, the Vice-President-Elect. He was unimpressed, judging Johnson 'an acute and ruthless politician', but not a man of any intellectual power.

Macmillan, however, did have a family connection with Kennedy. Macmillan's nephew, the Marquess of Hartington, had married the new President's sister, Kathleen (Kick) Kennedy, before he was killed on active service in the war.

Macmillan observed to his Foreign Secretary, Alec Douglas-Home, that with Eisenhower there was always the 'appeal to memories'. With

Kennedy, there would be nothing of that kind to draw on. They must, therefore, try to make contact in the realm of ideas. Macmillan wanted to depict himself as a man who, 'although of advancing years, has young and fresh thoughts'.

He enclosed the kind of letter he proposed to send the new President. This contained a fair number of clichés. Macmillan suggested that the policies of the Alliance were not properly adjusted to the 1960s and that there was a danger that Communism might triumph by seeming to be bringing people more material comforts [*sic*]. He emphasised the importance of the Geneva negotiations on a nuclear test ban. He stressed the 'special ties' afforded by Britain and the Commonwealth. He also set out his thoughts about how to handle de Gaulle and his persistent suspicions of the Anglo-Saxons. He emphasised the importance of his initiative to take Britain into the EEC.

Professor Kenneth Galbraith was summoned to the White House to discuss Macmillan's paper, but Kennedy told him that it could not be found. It was discovered in the nursery of Kennedy's three-year-old daughter.[2] Kennedy felt that he had more urgent matters to attend to. Nevertheless, Eisenhower had told Kennedy that he would find Macmillan a good friend, whose counsel he should listen to.

Macmillan was due to have his first meeting with Kennedy in Washington at the beginning of April and left for a holiday in the West Indies. But Kennedy invited him to an urgent meeting on 26 March at Key West in Florida to talk about Laos. Macmillan commented that it was the first time he had flown 3,600 miles for a hamburger ('not a form of lunch I'm very fond of').

Before leaving London, Macmillan had consulted David Ormsby-Gore, then Minister of State in the Foreign Office, who had been a personal friend of Kennedy's when he was in London with his father, the US ambassador, just before the war. He also consulted Henry Brandon, the *Sunday Times* correspondent in Washington. Macmillan told Brandon that he and Eisenhower belonged to the same generation. They had common experiences 'and now there is this young cocky Irishman ... How am I going to deal with him?' Brandon told Macmillan that Kennedy had a keen interest in British political history. Despite his father, Churchill was his greatest hero, and he had distinguished himself in his service with the US Navy in the war.[3]

At the Geneva Conference in 1954, Eden had achieved a precarious neutrality for Laos. This was now threatened by the Pathet Lao, backed by the Russians and North Vietnamese. The Americans were supporting their champion, General Phoumi, through the CIA. As Soviet support for the Pathet Lao increased, the Americans were under strong pressure to intervene directly and had been trying to get others to join in doing so. Macmillan was resigned to telling the Americans at the end of the day that, whatever decision Kennedy took, he would support them politically. This, he believed, was necessary if he was to have influence in the future with the new administration.

But he sought to influence Kennedy against direct intervention. The options, he said, were to install a puppet government, which would be useless (and which Kennedy rejected as 'imperialism'), or for the Americans to take on the war, or to stay out altogether. Kennedy appeared to Macmillan to share some of his doubts. Under pressure from Kennedy, Macmillan agreed that it might be politically necessary to do something in order not to appear to be 'pushed out by the Russians'. If the Americans judged that limited intervention was necessary, Britain would be supportive but would not participate herself. Macmillan was asked to warn the Russians that if the Pathet Lao did not agree to a ceasefire, US military intervention was likely.

A week later Macmillan made his scheduled visit to Washington. Averell Harriman and General MacArthur also had warned Kennedy against committing US troops to Laos and the Russians showed themselves more disposed to accept a nominal coalition government – confident that Laos in due course would fall into their hands anyway.

Macmillan secured Kennedy's active support for Britain joining the EEC. The Americans believed that British influence in the European Community would be helpful, both politically and economically. Kennedy resisted suggestions that China might be brought into the United Nations. He shared State Department fears that Macmillan was soft on Berlin and he was sceptical about Macmillan's ideas on summitry. He made clear that he was not going to ask Macmillan to act as an honest broker with Khrushchev: Kennedy already had made plans to meet Khrushchev in Vienna. Kennedy was disappointed with Macmillan's lack of support over south-east Asia – though Ormsby-Gore believed that Macmillan's advice on Laos did influence the President. Kennedy gave Macmillan no forewarning of the Bay of Pigs operation launched ten days later by the CIA.

Macmillan felt that he had achieved a degree of personal understanding. He enjoyed the company of Jacqueline Kennedy and the informal atmosphere of the Kennedy White House. In the evenings, he noted, there was 'music and wine and pretty women'. When, just after his return to London, the Bay of Pigs operation was launched, Macmillan commented that he had no great hopes of success and that failure would be a severe blow to American prestige. Though it was an appalling blunder, Macmillan was impressed by the way Kennedy publicly shouldered the blame. In an allusion to Suez, he assured Kennedy that he was not going to attack him in the UN! Publicly, Macmillan showed himself fully supportive of a colleague in difficulty.[4]

On 31 May, Kennedy visited Paris and told de Gaulle that he strongly supported British entry into the EEC. Kennedy told Macmillan, however, that he had decided against assisting France's efforts to create a nuclear weapons capability through the provision of technical information.

Kennedy flew on to his meeting with Khrushchev in Vienna. Over the next two days, Khrushchev was at his most threatening. He said that he intended to sign a peace treaty with East Germany. That would be the end of Allied rights in Berlin. If the USA wanted to go to war over Berlin, 'that is your problem'. Kennedy said that it was Khrushchev and not he who wanted to force a change: 'It is going to be a cold winter.'

The Kennedys arrived in London on 4 June. Kennedy was clearly shaken by his encounter with Khrushchev and was suffering from chronic back trouble. Macmillan waved aside the Foreign Office and State Department advisers and invited Kennedy for a long private talk. Macmillan reported to the Queen that Kennedy had been 'overwhelmed by the ruthlessness and barbarity of the Russian premier'. Kennedy, for the first time, had met someone 'who was completely impervious to his charm'.

From a personal point of view, the meeting was a success. When Kennedy, complaining about the way the press had treated his wife in Vienna, asked how Macmillan would react if someone said 'Lady Dorothy is a drunk', Macmillan's response was: 'I would reply: you should have seen her mother!' Kennedy told Henry Brandon that he felt at home with Macmillan: 'the others are all foreigners to me'.[5]

Macmillan remained worried about Kennedy's advisers (this 'immense collection of egg-heads'). He expressed concern about 'not so much the duplicity but the duality of American policy as it is conducted through the strange complex of power that is distributed between the White House, the State Department and the Pentagon'.

Kennedy's Secretary of State, Dean Rusk, was a Rhodes scholar. But he was disappointed by the lack of support he perceived the US as receiving from Britain in the Far East. Within the State Department, the Under-Secretary, George Ball, and other Kennedy appointees took an unsenti-mental view of Britain. They had no enthusiasm for the British nuclear deterrent and favoured the downgrading of the 'special relationship' and greater attention being paid to relations with the other European allies, particularly Germany.

In Key West, Macmillan had consulted Kennedy about the choice of the next British ambassador in Washington. Kennedy urged the appointment of David Ormsby-Gore, who had known him and Robert Kennedy well in London on the eve of the war. The President's sister, 'Kick' Kennedy, was the widow of Macmillan's nephew, Lord Hartington, and godmother of the Ormsby-Gore's eldest child. Kennedy appointed to London the most distinguished of American ambassadors, David Bruce, who had already served in Paris and Bonn.

On 13 August, the East Germans erected the Berlin Wall. Kennedy told Macmillan that he was reinforcing the Berlin garrison with a battle group of 1,500 men. In terms of what the Russians had available, Macmillan thought that militarily this made little sense, but he agreed to contribute some armoured cars.

In August, while the US and Britain continued to observe a moratorium, Khrushchev resumed nuclear testing in the atmosphere. Over the next two months the Soviet Union carried out thirty high-yield tests, including one of fifty megatons, nearly all in the atmosphere.

On 3 September, Kennedy and Macmillan offered Khrushchev an imme-diate ban on atmospheric nuclear tests. When this appeal met with no response, Kennedy announced the resumption of underground nuclear testing by the USA. The British atomic scientists wanted to use the US underground facilities in Nevada to test the warheads designed for Sky-bolt and later Polaris. Macmillan continued to hanker after a general ban on nuclear testing. The United States offered the use of the facilities in

Nevada for the British, but insisted in return on their right if necessary to use the British territory of Christmas Island in the Pacific for testing in the atmosphere.

In a further meeting with Kennedy in December in Bermuda, Macmillan made an impassioned plea about the need to stop the acceleration of the nuclear arms race. Once again he proposed a summit with Khrushchev, in which he also wanted to be involved, and a major push for disarmament as well, he hoped, as a solution for Berlin. Kennedy was not interested in a summit unless it was properly prepared and there was a chance of success; nor was he prepared to exercise unilateral restraint over nuclear testing. Macmillan claimed to find Kennedy quick and effective in dealing with immediate questions but 'on the wider issues, he seems rather lost'. He wrote again to Kennedy about the need to end the nuclear race 'so fantastic and retrograde, so sophisticated and so barbarous as to be almost incredible'. He argued for one further effort to get Khrushchev to agree to a test ban treaty.[6]

Hugh Gaitskell, leader of the Labour Party, also wrote to Kennedy to suggest that US testing in the atmosphere should not resume until a further effort had been made to get Soviet agreement to a treaty. Kennedy and Rusk agreed to give Khrushchev until April to agree to a comprehensive test ban. When this was rejected by Khrushchev, in April 1962 the USA resumed atmospheric testing on Christmas Island. Macmillan loyally supported Kennedy, but felt the ignominy of US atmospheric tests taking place on a British colonial territory.

Despite these differences, the personal relationship between Macmillan and Kennedy continued to flourish. Kennedy's key aide, Ted Sorensen, wrote that the Western leader whom Kennedy 'saw first, liked best, and saw most often' was Macmillan. They did not always see eye to eye. Macmillan was more eager for summits and less firm on Berlin:

> From time to time, the President had to discourage the Prime Minister's temptation to play the role of peace-maker between East and West ... but no differences of opinion or age prevented the two leaders from getting along famously. Each recognized in the other a keen understanding of history and politics.[7]

Kennedy enjoyed Macmillan's style and his sense of humour.

This friendship with Macmillan was by no means an exclusive one. Kennedy also was on excellent terms with Gaitskell. Shortly after his election as President, he had met Hugh Gaitskell at a lunch arranged by Averell Harriman. Gaitskell admired Kennedy, who had an equally high regard for him and could never understand why Macmillan and Gaitskell, both of whom he liked so much, disliked each other so intensely. When his adviser, Arthur Schlesinger, told him of Gaitskell's death at the beginning of 1963, Kennedy regretted the loss of the opportunity of their working together. Kennedy had become the hero of the social democrats in Europe, ensuring that this was a period when anti-Americanism in Europe was at its lowest ebb.

Macmillan, meanwhile, had found de Gaulle intransigent about Britain and Europe during their meeting at Birch Grove in November 1961. France, said de Gaulle, did not want to change the character of Europe and did not want the British to 'bring their great escort in with them'. Europe, he claimed, would be 'drowned in the Atlantic'. Macmillan noted that his hatred of the Anglo-Saxons was as great as ever: 'He talks of Europe, and means France.'

The following May, Macmillan was warned by Sir Pierson Dixon, the British ambassador in Paris, that de Gaulle had decided to exclude Britain from the EEC. But Macmillan remained more sanguine. He felt that de Gaulle had not definitely made up his mind: 'I think he may still be torn between emotion and reason.' In a further meeting with Macmillan in June 1962, de Gaulle reiterated that British entry would alter the character of the European Community and that Britain was too closely tied to America. On nuclear matters, Macmillan thought that de Gaulle understood that Britain could not part with nuclear secrets shared with the Americans as a result of their collaboration during the war.[8]

29

'THANK GOD THEY'VE TURNED BACK, JUST BEFORE THE PRIME MINISTER GAVE WAY'

ON 21 OCTOBER 1962, Macmillan received an urgent message from Kennedy informing him of 'a most serious situation' and of US plans to meet it. Kennedy said that photographic intelligence had established beyond doubt that the Soviet Union was installing medium-range nuclear missiles in Cuba. The US government had decided to prevent any further build-up by sea 'and to demand the removal of this nuclear threat to our hemisphere'. Kennedy observed that Khrushchev's aim might be to increase his chances in Berlin. If he was counting on US weakness or irresolution, he would find that he had miscalculated.

Macmillan was being *informed*, not consulted, about decisions already taken in Washington. On 1 October, the Foreign Secretary, Alec Douglas-Home, had told Macmillan that Kennedy simply could not understand why Britain would not help the US by joining an embargo on trade with Cuba. Kennedy had warned the Russians publicly of the consequences of introducing offensive weapons into Cuba and Ormsby-Gore alerted the Foreign Office on 19 October about 'an impending crisis, probably about missiles in Cuba'. A delegation of intelligence officers from London had found that meetings with the CIA were curtailed or called off and surmised, correctly, that the reason was Cuba.

Ormsby-Gore was told by Kennedy on Sunday 21 October about the missile photographs and that the options were to order an air strike to destroy the missile sites or to impose a blockade. Ormsby-Gore argued that 'very few people outside the United States would consider the provocation offered by the Cubans serious enough to merit an American air attack ... in any case I could not believe that the missiles so far landed constituted any significant threat to the United States'. Ormsby-Gore, therefore, favoured a blockade, though that too carried the probability of an extreme Russian reaction, perhaps in Berlin. Kennedy told him that in fact that was what already had been decided.[1]

Monday 22 October was recorded by Macmillan in his diary as 'the first day of the world crisis'. The US ambassador, David Bruce, called with a long letter from Kennedy, with detailed evidence about the missiles. Macmillan, having looked at the photographs, observed: 'Now the Americans will realise what we in England have lived through for the past many years.' Macmillan said that he would support the United States in the Security Council, but that he was going to have considerable trouble in Parliament and with the public, because of suspicions that the Americans exaggerated the Castro threat. The pictures, he said, satisfied him but ought to be made public.

Macmillan worried (correctly, as it turned out) about the Americans trading the missiles in Cuba for those in Turkey or elsewhere. But above all he worried that if Khrushchev 'was stopped, with great loss of face, in Cuba, would he not be tempted to recover himself in Berlin? Indeed, might not this be the whole purpose of the exercise?' Macmillan put these points to Bruce and, throughout the crisis, feared that Khrushchev's objective was to swap Cuba for Berlin. British nuclear forces were placed on a heightened state of alert.[2]

De Gaulle, informed at the same time, told Acheson that he accepted the President's word and waved aside the photographic evidence. De Gaulle noted that he was being informed, not consulted, adding that if there was a war, 'France will be with you. But there will be no war.'[3] The Soviet ambassador was sent packing with the words that if there was a war, '*nous mourrons ensemble. Au revoir, Monsieur l'Ambassadeur.*'

Kennedy had not failed to notice the 'element of reserve' in Macmillan's response. Arthur Schlesinger, working for Kennedy, noted the 'peculiar reaction' in Britain. Some questioned whether nuclear missiles were in Cuba. Others suspected this to be an American pretext to invade. Gaitskell questioned the legality of the American 'quarantine'. *The Economist* warned against a showdown on this issue. *The Guardian* suggested that if Khrushchev had really brought in nuclear missiles, he had done so primarily to demonstrate to the US the meaning of American bases close to the Soviet border. A. J. Ayer, A. J. P. Taylor and others attacked the quarantine and advocated British neutrality. Bertrand Russell, who already had denounced Kennedy as 'much more wicked than Hitler', telegraphed to Khrushchev: 'Your continued forbearance is our great hope.'

Macmillan told his colleagues that the American blockade ('quarantine') probably was illegal under international law and that he doubted whether it would achieve anything, but he was careful not to say this to Kennedy. Kennedy telephoned the Prime Minister on Tuesday 23 October to explain more fully how he saw the situation. This was largely a monologue with Macmillan, as his biographer says, contributing 'sympathetic interjections that, read subsequently, sound rather vapid'. Macmillan found Kennedy 'rather excited, but very clear'. He did not know what Khrushchev would do. He was prepared, if necessary, to invade Cuba. The calls were purely informative, not to seek advice. Macmillan was, however, kept more closely informed than others, both directly and through Ormsby-Gore.

Contingency arrangements had been made to take Ormsby-Gore and his family, if necessary, to the safety of the presidential nuclear shelter in the Appalachians. The mood in Washington, he recalled later, '*was* frightening ... We dusted off the Embassy evacuation orders.' Kennedy had come to 'trust David as I would my own Cabinet'. On the evening of 23 October, the Ormsby-Gores had been invited to dine at the White House with the Maharajah and Maharani of Jaipur.

In their private apartment, Jacqueline Kennedy found her husband and Ormsby-Gore squatting on the floor, looking at the missile photographs. Ormsby-Gore suggested to Kennedy that the US 'quarantine' line should be drawn 500, rather than 800, miles off the Cuban coast, so as to give the Russians more time to react. This was a personal initiative by Ormsby-Gore. It was accepted by Kennedy, who telephoned instructions to the Defense Secretary, McNamara. Ormsby-Gore also urged Kennedy to take up Macmillan's suggestion that the photographic evidence should be published and that too was done.[4]

Quite separately the British had been able to help with intelligence from their key agent in Moscow, Colonel Oleg Penkovsky. A senior member of Soviet military intelligence, Penkovsky was the most important agent recruited by the Allies since the war. The British made all the intelligence they received from him, and Penkovsky himself, available to the CIA. Penkovsky was arrested in Moscow on 22 October, the day Kennedy publicly revealed the installation of the missiles in Cuba, and later executed. The intelligence he provided in the run-up to the crisis was felt by both the British and Americans to have been invaluable.

On the evening of 24 October, Kennedy telephoned Macmillan to tell him that some of the Soviet ships were turning around. Ormsby-Gore forewarned Kennedy's National Security Adviser, McGeorge Bundy, that the Prime Minister wanted to propose a Kennedy/Khrushchev summons to a meeting on disarmament in which Macmillan also would be involved, pending which there might need to be a standstill involving 'no import of arms and no blockade'. Having conveyed this proposal, Ormsby-Gore told Bundy that it was not a good idea because the two sides were too far apart and it left no room for the French. Kennedy, he said, 'should make it very plain to the PM that this was not an acceptable position and that the US cannot stand down its blockade without progress towards the removal of the missiles'.

Speaking to Macmillan, Kennedy speculated on whether to invade Cuba or rather to use it as a sort of hostage *vis-à-vis* Berlin. Macmillan thought that nothing should be done in haste. He offered to fly to Washington to see Kennedy. Gently, Kennedy put him off. At this point the news arrived that Soviet ships approaching the 'quarantine' zone were altering course. Denis Greenhill, then serving as Minister in the British embassy in Washington, recalls Ormsby-Gore exclaiming to him: 'Thank God they've turned back, just before the Prime Minister gave way!'[5]

On the following day, Macmillan sent a message advising against invasion: 'You must try to obtain your objectives by other means.' The blockade should be replaced by some system of inspection.

On the evening of Friday 26 October, Macmillan had two further telephone conversations with Kennedy. Macmillan asked if it would help the Russians to save face to offer to immobilise 'the Thor nuclear missiles in Britain while a conference took place'. He emphasised the need to take account of Berlin and was told by Kennedy that was why the US had not done more.

The Russians now offered to trade their missiles in Cuba against the US Jupiter missiles in Turkey – an offer that seemed reasonable to many in Britain. On 27 October, an American U-2 reconnaissance plane was shot down over Cuba. Kennedy gave the Russians forty-eight hours to stop work on the missile sites and agree to withdraw the missiles.

On the Sunday morning (28 October), the British press reflected the Prime Minister's anxieties whether 'these young men' in Washington really knew what they were doing. But Macmillan sent a message supporting Kennedy to Khrushchev, 'while the world held its breath'. At midday the news came that the Russians had agreed to withdraw the missiles provided Kennedy promised not to invade Cuba. The crisis was over.

'We had been on the brink, almost over it,' observed Macmillan. He telegraphed to Kennedy: 'It was indeed a trial of wills and yours has prevailed.' Kennedy replied: 'Your heartening support publicly expressed and our daily conversations have been of inestimable value in these past few days.'[6]

In his diary, Macmillan observed that he had been urged on by 'the frightful desire to do something, with the knowledge that *not* to do anything ... was probably the right answer'. He felt that his government had 'played our part perfectly. We were "in on" and took full part in (and *almost responsibility*) for every American move. Our complete calm helped to keep the Europeans calm.'[7] Ormsby-Gore, subsequently, took a more realistic view: 'I can't honestly think of anything said from London that changed the US action – it was chiefly reassurance to JFK.' But Macmillan's support was of value and he and Ormsby-Gore certainly were treated as Kennedy's primary foreign confidants.

Macmillan remained puzzled why Khrushchev had not made a countermove in Berlin. In the House of Commons he described the crisis as one of the great turning points in history. Both he and Kennedy were irritated by comments from Macmillan's domestic critics that Britain was not consulted, that the 'special relationship' no longer existed, that Britain's possession of nuclear weapons made no difference and that America had risked war regardless of the consequences for Europe. Congratulating Ormsby-Gore on his role in the crisis, Macmillan wrote that it had strengthened ties with the administration. Ormsby-Gore replied that Kennedy's expressions of appreciation were sincere and that he had 'no similar contacts with any other ally. He is furious with newspaper commentators who suggest that recent events have shown that there is little value for the US in the special Anglo-American relationship.'[8]

Macmillan was not informed, then or later, that Robert Kennedy had promised the Soviet ambassador that if their missiles were withdrawn from Cuba, the US missiles subsequently would be withdrawn from Turkey.

30

'THE LADY HAS ALREADY BEEN VIOLATED IN PUBLIC'

THE SKYBOLT CRISIS, in the view of Arthur Schlesinger, one of Kennedy's close advisers at the time, 'compelled the President to choose between those in his own Government whose main interest lay in transforming Western Europe, including Britain, into a unified political and economic entity, and those whose main interest lay in guarding the Anglo-American special relationship and integrity of the deterrent'.

One day in January 1962, Kennedy wondered aloud at a lunch attended by Julian Amery, the British Minister of Aviation, whether Skybolt would work. Amery said that it was the basis of British nuclear defence: if anything happened to the project, that could have far-reaching consequences for Anglo-American relations. Robert McNamara, however, pursuing his cost-effectiveness drive in the Pentagon, concluded that further investment would be a mistake. But as he had difficulties with the US Air Force over the cancellation of other projects, he deferred a decision. When Peter Thorneycroft, British Minister of Defence, visited Washington in September he emphasised the importance of Skybolt to Britain. He got only a guarded response from McNamara.

On 7 November, McNamara formally recommended cancellation to the President. Kennedy, knowing that this would be a blow to the Macmillan government, said that the British should be informed in good time for them to prepare the ground before the decision was announced. McNamara called Ormsby-Gore and Thorneycroft. Ormsby-Gore, startled and appalled, said that this would be political dynamite in London.

Thorneycroft expressed interest in alternatives, especially Polaris. Kennedy afterwards expressed amazement that the British 'did nothing', even though the life of their government was at stake.[1]

In fact, most of Kennedy's advisers wanted to get rid of the British nuclear deterrent. In April 1961, a National Security Council paper had argued: 'We must try to eliminate the privileged British status.' As a minimum, British nuclear weapons should be committed to the NATO stockpile and placed under the control of NATO commanders. This, it was hoped, would help to dissuade the French from proceeding with their nuclear programme and the Germans from seeking to become a nuclear power. Kennedy agreed, commenting that 'it would be desirable for the British in the long run to get out of the nuclear deterrent business, since their activity in this field is a standing goad to the French'.

The Pentagon understood that Polaris was the only real alternative. But the Europeanists in the State Department felt that 'if Skybolt had to go, at least let it carry the special relationship down with it'. This, they believed, would facilitate British entry into Europe and avoid prolonging the British deterrent. George Ball, Walt Rostow and the other policy-planners still were obsessed with their attempts to launch a NATO Multi-Lateral Force, with ships to be manned by sailors from all the European allies, including Germany, carrying nuclear weapons that, however, would remain under sole US control. This they imagined to be a way of satisfying the European allies about participation in nuclear defence. Ball hoped that it would provide the British with an excuse for giving up nuclear weapons. The British were unimpressed. They saw the idea of naval vessels manned by multinational crews as an exercise in gimmickry. McNamara, meanwhile, had annoyed the British and French by a speech in June at Ann Arbor in Michigan in which he condemned all national nuclear forces, except those of the United States, as 'dangerous, expensive, prone to obsolescence, and lacking in credibility as a deterrent'. Macmillan described this as a foolish speech that had enraged the French and put him in domestic difficulty. He told the Foreign Secretary: 'We have an independent deterrent and the French are going to get one; these are facts which the Americans cannot alter.' Macmillan was the more annoyed when McNamara returned to this theme at the NATO meeting in Paris in December.

McNamara visited London on 11 December. On his arrival, he told the press that the last five Skybolt tests had failed. Thorneycroft spelt out the political consequences of cancellation for the British government and for Anglo-American understanding. Those who said that it was impossible to count on the United States would be proved right. Following McNamara's Ann Arbor speech, cancellation would be taken as a deliberate effort to drive Britain out of the nuclear game. It would tear the heart out of the 'special relationship'.

After rejecting other possibilities, Thorneycroft raised Polaris. McNamara cited legal problems. Thorneycroft recalled British agreement to the basing of American Polaris submarines at Holy Loch. The US, he said, was under a moral obligation, if it cancelled Skybolt, to propose another means of sustaining the British deterrent. McNamara offered Polaris as part of the Multi-Lateral Force which would be fully integrated with NATO and remain subject to American control. Thorneycroft rejected this. Following McNamara's comments at the airport and counter-briefing by Thorneycroft, the whole story appeared in the London evening newspapers.

In Washington, George Ball set out the Europeanists' case in a debate before the President. Kennedy listened carefully, but mentioned the British sense of a moral obligation and Macmillan's shaky political position before suggesting the possibility of linking an offer of Polaris to a British readiness to commit their Polaris force to NATO.

Macmillan's problems were compounded by a speech by the former US Secretary of State, Dean Acheson, at the beginning of December in which he stated:

> Great Britain has lost an empire and has not yet found a role. The attempt to play a separate power role – that is, a role apart from Europe, a role based on a 'Special Relationship' with the United States, a role based on being the head of a 'Commonwealth' which has no political structure, or unity, or strength and enjoys a fragile and precarious economic relationship – this role is about played out.

An infuriated Macmillan wrote in his diary that Acheson always was a 'conceited ass' and that 'the failure of Skybolt might be welcomed in some American quarters as a means of forcing Britain out of the nuclear club'.[2]

In his meeting with de Gaulle at Rambouillet before leaving for Nassau, Macmillan said that he was determined to maintain the British deterrent, he hoped on the basis of Polaris, otherwise Britain would have to develop its own system, whatever the cost.

In the meeting, de Gaulle took a very negative view about British entry to the EEC. He argued that the British people were not ready and that the EEC would be fundamentally changed by British entry. Macmillan said that de Gaulle was raising a fundamental objection to Britain's application. If that really was the French view, it should have been made clear from the start. But Macmillan still did not seem fully to understand that de Gaulle was signalling a veto of the British application.[3]

On the plane to Nassau, Ormsby-Gore told Kennedy that while he recognised that the continuation of preferential treatment for Britain on nuclear matters made difficulties for the USA with its other European allies, there would be a storm of anti-Americanism in Britain if the British believed the Americans were letting them down. Kennedy and Ormsby-Gore tried to work out a solution based on the assumption that the British still wanted Skybolt.[4]

Sorensen, another of Kennedy's closest advisers, saw the crisis with Britain over the cancellation of Skybolt as avoidable. The President 'who saw no point to a small independent British deterrent' had not been aware of quite how much was at stake for the British. Later, he wondered aloud why Ormsby-Gore or David Bruce in London or *someone* had not warned him of the political storm. Dean Rusk, after warning Kennedy in November of the potential British reaction, had deferred to McNamara.

In McNamara's view, the British had known for months that Skybolt was in trouble. But Macmillan had presented the Skybolt agreement as the key to the 'special relationship' and had scrapped completely Britain's own missile programme. The British complained 'with some justification', writes Sorensen, 'that the Americans had been tactless, heavy handed and abrupt, that the US was revealing either an insensitivity to an ally's pride and security concerns or a desire to push her out of the nuclear business'.[5]

What had been planned as a largely symbolic meeting between Kennedy and Macmillan in Nassau suddenly took on a crucial importance. Macmillan's diary showed him as being subject to a growing sense of perfidy in Washington. He sent a message to Ormsby-Gore that if agreement with the Americans could not be reached on a realistic way of maintaining the British deterrent, an 'agonising reappraisal' of all British foreign and defence plans would be required.[6]

The British delegation arrived in Nassau in an angry mood. Henry Brandon of the *Sunday Times* reported a 'resentment and suspicion of American intentions' such as he had never experienced in all the Anglo-American conferences he had covered over the past twenty years.[7] Macmillan was described by the Americans as both eloquent and emotional. He traced Anglo-American nuclear cooperation back to the wartime 'Tube Alloys' project. He poured scorn on the idea of the Multi-Lateral Force (to be manned by sailors from all the European allies, including Germany, with the ships carrying nuclear weapons but still under US control). He went through the history of British efforts in two world wars and the crucial importance of the issue for the survival of his government. Did Kennedy want to live with the consequences of sinking him?

Sorensen comments that Kennedy, like Eisenhower, had a soft spot for Macmillan and had already decided that the bipartisan nature of the 'special relationship' with the British required him not to send Macmillan home without some substitute for the missiles Eisenhower had promised. 'Looking at it from their point of view – *which they do almost better than anybody*,' Kennedy commented rather acidly to Sorensen, 'it might well be concluded that ... we had an obligation to provide an alternative.'[8]

Kennedy offered to continue the development of Skybolt, with the British meeting half the costs. But Britain alone would purchase the missile. This was the proposal Kennedy had worked out en route to Nassau with Ormsby-Gore. Macmillan rejected it. The missile was now compromised – or, as Macmillan put it: 'The lady has already been violated in public.'[9] Kennedy offered a joint study on how to fill the gap. Macmillan rejected this. He needed something more definite and cited an angry letter he had received from 137 Conservative MPs. He also rejected an offer to try to adapt the shorter-range Hound Dog air-launched missile. If the United States would not help, Britain would continue on its own at whatever cost. Macmillan had set his heart on Polaris.

Kennedy was unwilling to provide Polaris unconditionally. Little real thought had been given on the US side to a Polaris agreement. For the State Department, George Ball remained strongly opposed. It would be regarded as fresh evidence of pro-British discrimination and would run contrary to the aim of non-proliferation. It would contrast with Kennedy's earlier decision not to aid the French in developing their nuclear forces. It raised the possibility of an ally triggering a nuclear exchange. The French *force de frappe* was regarded as too small to deter the Soviets but large enough to provoke an attack. It would divert resources away from conventional defence and complicate matters *vis-à-vis* the Germans, who had renounced nuclear weapons.

Kennedy was persuaded to override all these objections. He was influenced, Ball commented, by 'one international distress signal recognised by politicians all over the world, and this is the cry of another politician in trouble'.[10] To meet the 'obligation to the British', Kennedy finally offered Polaris missiles (not warheads) on the basis that, normally, they would be assigned to NATO except when 'supreme national interests' were at stake. It was agreed that this should be accompanied by a similar, though not identical, offer to the French. The Nassau agreement showed signs of 'hasty improvisation and high-level imprecision, of decisions taken by the President in Nassau before he was ready to take them in Washington'. Kennedy had simply overruled his subordinates in order to help Macmillan. George Ball noted that Macmillan, earlier, had told the press that he had never fully understood what the 'special relationship' meant – yet had just shown his skill in exploiting it.[11]

The State Department proposals for a Multi-Lateral Force (MLF) formally were preserved, but Macmillan had shown that he had no faith in them and nor, really, did Kennedy. It would be difficult, he commented, to do more than merely provide 'a different facade of United States control'. To Richard Neustadt, he observed: 'There is no Europe ... who's to be my opposite number ... De Gaulle, Adenauer, Macmillan? None of them can speak for Europe.'[12]

No sooner had the President returned to Washington than McNamara announced the first successful firing of Skybolt. Kennedy flew into a rage but, fortunately for him, McNamara was away skiing.

In fact, Polaris was a far more favourable deal for Britain. The British deterrent was preserved for another generation at a cost much less than the French had to pay to develop their nuclear forces and the Nassau agreement led directly on to the subsequent acquisition by Britain of Trident. Though there could hardly have been a stronger political manifestation of the 'special relationship', Nassau was not portrayed as a victory by the British press.

The US offer to the French got nowhere. The French Defence Minister pointed out that they had neither the submarines nor the warheads to match with the Polaris missiles. Macmillan flirted with the idea of securing American agreement to provide the French with warhead technology. But de Gaulle would not have accepted the subordination of his nuclear forces in normal circumstances to NATO and was pursuing a completely different agenda. At his press conference in January, de Gaulle proceeded to reject both the Polaris offer and the MLF and to signal his veto of Britain's entry into the EEC, suggesting that Britain was too closely tied to the US. Instead, he pressed ahead with the Franco-German treaty with Adenauer.

Macmillan had given Kennedy in Nassau the impression that little more than the dispute over agriculture lay between Britain and accession to the EEC. But Kennedy did not believe that it was the Nassau agreement that triggered de Gaulle's subsequent actions, which corresponded to a much deeper determination on de Gaulle's part to go his separate way and to keep Britain out of a Community he wanted France to dominate. In *Le Salut*, published in 1959, de Gaulle had made clear that he 'intended to assure French primacy in Western Europe'. Told after Nassau that he had been soft on Macmillan, Kennedy replied: 'If you were in that kind of trouble, you would want a friend.'[13]

31

'THIS FRIGHTFUL TANGLE OF FEAR AND SUSPICION'

FOLLOWING DE GAULLE'S veto of the British application to join the EEC, Macmillan's problems were compounded by the Profumo affair. The US ambassador in London, David Bruce, kept Kennedy entertained with salacious details of the affair, but warned the President that Macmillan's admission that he did not know what was going on at critical times was 'pitiable and extremely damaging'. He had given the impression that he did not know how to exercise responsibility in a case about which nearly everyone in Parliament appeared better informed. Bruce concluded that the Prime Minister was mortally wounded. In his opinion, no moves would be made to replace Macmillan before President Kennedy's visit, planned for the end of June. But Macmillan's replacement could not be long delayed as he had become an electoral liability.[1]

Macmillan, meanwhile, continued doggedly to pursue his efforts to achieve a test ban treaty. Khrushchev had proposed that all tests should be banned, including underground tests, while adamantly opposing effective monitoring of Soviet compliance. Macmillan refused to believe that modem science could not devise ways to carry out the monitoring without the need for on-site inspection. Kennedy's advisers did not agree. They saw it as very likely that the Soviet Union would continue to carry out underground tests and deny that they had taken place. The US Chiefs of Staff were opposed to a general test ban. The Russians by this stage had offered to accept, in principle, three annual inspections, while the West had reduced its demands from twenty to seven.

But Kennedy suspected that Macmillan's readiness to compromise had encouraged Khrushchev to believe that three inspections might be acceptable. Macmillan continued to argue with Kennedy that a test ban was the most important step that could be taken towards 'unravelling this frightful tangle of fear and suspicion in East–West relations'. If testing continued, he said, Germany eventually would be bound to demand nuclear weapons of its own. He suggested, once again, a summit in Geneva. He also proposed that it might be worth sending an emissary such as Averell Harriman or Robert Kennedy to probe Khrushchev.[2]

Kennedy ruled out a summit, telling Macmillan that memories of Khrushchev's behaviour in Paris in 1960 were very strong in the US. Nor did Kennedy have pleasant memories of his own meeting with Khrushchev. What he did not reveal to Macmillan were the objections of his advisers, who told the President that the French and Germans would be annoyed by Macmillan's presence at a summit, which Macmillan hoped would help him win the British elections. But Kennedy seemed ready to follow up the idea of a special emissary. Macmillan wrote in April to the Queen that Kennedy had behaved very well, overriding the Pentagon and State Department on some points. When Kennedy did agree on a joint approach to Khrushchev, however, Macmillan feared that the White House would present this as an American initiative, with the 'young New Frontiersman in the vanguard and the old British P.M. being dragged reluctantly at his heels'.

Khrushchev sent a very negative reply, withdrawing his offer of inspections by 'Nato spies'. Ormsby-Gore proposed ignoring the rest of Khrushchev's response and concentrating instead on the idea of a special emissary. Macmillan noted that Ormsby-Gore was confident that the President would agree, 'if only to please me'. On 30 May, Macmillan and Kennedy wrote to Khrushchev proposing that American and British emissaries should go to Moscow. To Macmillan's pleasure, Kennedy adopted his idea of sending Averell Harriman. Macmillan said later that Harriman had all the necessary qualities for the task: 'slightly deaf, but not quite so deaf as he appears. A great advantage for a diplomat.' As his representative, Macmillan appointed a senior member of his Cabinet, Lord Hailsham. Macmillan seemed to be trying to promote Hailsham's chances as a possible successor to him. Since Hailsham knew nothing about the subject, the Americans found him a curious choice.[3]

In June, Kennedy made his famous visit to West Berlin, then stayed for several days in Ireland. Despite their friendship, Kennedy was not keen on this occasion on seeing too much of Macmillan. David Bruce continued to advise from London that the Prime Minister did not have much of a future. Macmillan was irritated by stories that Kennedy was snubbing him and they agreed to meet on 29 June at Macmillan's house in Sussex, Birch Grove. Macmillan found Kennedy in poor health, his face puffed up by cortisone treatment for his back. According to Jacqueline Kennedy, the President arrived depressed at the downturn in Macmillan's fortunes. As usual, most of Macmillan's discussions with Kennedy took place in private. As the advisers on both sides felt left out, Macmillan suggested that he and Kennedy should stage a mock conference, with the two protagonists 'facing each other with a circle of their supporters behind ... Since we had already settled all the important points it was necessary to think of a subject.'

The American side, particularly Dean Rusk, was less amused. But the Americans did secure the result they wanted in the discussions on British Guyana. The territory was still a British colony, but with internal self-government, and the governing party were the Communists, led by Dr Cheddi Jagan. They had won 41 per cent of the vote, giving them a narrow majority over the opposition, led by Forbes Burnham, and were now demanding independence. Ormsby-Gore warned Macmillan that the Americans saw Guyana as 'a most vulnerable point where Communism might easily take over and start a landslide in Latin America'. Dean Rusk told the Commonwealth Secretary, Duncan Sandys, that he wanted independence delayed until there was no risk of British Guyana going Communist. Sandys refused to suspend the constitution and reimpose direct rule, as the Americans wished. But, following this discussion at Birch Grove and a general strike in Guyana organised by the anti-Jagan forces, Sandys changed the voting system to proportional representation. Jagan was defeated in fresh elections held on that basis and, three years later, the territory was brought to independence with a non-Communist government.

Macmillan felt he had got what he wanted – full steam ahead on the test ban talks – and in his memoirs described the 'fantastic, even romantic atmosphere' which he felt had prevailed. But Kennedy found it the least satisfactory of his meetings with Macmillan. He also was disappointed that Macmillan had managed to head him off from a meeting with the new Labour Party leader, Harold Wilson, who looked likely to succeed him. Kennedy was conscious that Macmillan had used Eisenhower for domestic political advantage in the 1959 election and of the great help he had given Macmillan in Nassau. But helping to retrieve Macmillan from the Profumo crisis was a different matter. Kennedy asked Macmillan's Private Secretary, Philip de Zulueta, if a test ban treaty would really help the Prime Minister. De Zulueta replied that it would be of some help electorally, but the fundamental issue was the economy. Kennedy agreed. He felt that Macmillan, beneath the flippancy, seemed disconsolate and fatigued.[4]

At the beginning of July, Khrushchev hinted at the possibility of a partial test ban. On 12 July, Harriman visited Macmillan on his way to Moscow. He appeared determined to try to get an agreement of some kind with the Russians. 'The situation is dramatic and vital for me,' Macmillan wrote in his diary. 'If there is any chance of an agreement and a summit meeting afterwards, I will fight on in home politics. If not, I shall feel inclined to throw in my hand.'[5]

Shortly afterwards, Kennedy caused Macmillan some consternation by proposing that, in order to pacify de Gaulle and induce him to sign a test ban treaty, the US might make available information on nuclear technology which hitherto had been withheld from the French. Macmillan felt that if the Americans had armed him with this offer six months before, 'it might have made the whole difference to Britain and to Europe'. Macmillan suggested offering to provide the French with nuclear information and to supply them with fissile material so as to save them time and money and, he hoped, avoid the need for further French tests in the atmosphere. Kennedy agreed, but de Gaulle was determined that France should carry out its own test programme and rely on no one else.

In Moscow, meanwhile, the Americans were finding it difficult to deal with Hailsham, whom they considered to be ignorant of the technicalities and consumed by a desire to get a treaty at almost any cost. Hailsham, in turn, reported that Harriman 'seemed a man very much after his best, tired and becoming a little deaf. The Americans', he added, 'are suspicious of me personally', and in that he was right. Kennedy disliked Hailsham's apparent willingness to sign some sort of non-aggression pact.

Kennedy wanted a test ban agreement alone. Hailsham, Kennedy suspected, wanted to play the role of mediator between the Americans and

Russians. He had more confidence in Harriman's experience of negotiating with the Russians. Macmillan was worried about some of the conditions the Americans were laying down. He was told by Hailsham that they were being obstructive and that he foresaw 'a wrangle and perhaps a breakdown'. David Ormsby-Gore was told to put this to the White House. When he did so, Kennedy had the satisfaction of telling Macmillan by telephone that the agreement banning testing in the atmosphere had just been signed. Macmillan went to tell his wife then, according to his diary, burst into tears.[6]

Macmillan, in fact, had contributed greatly to this outcome. Arthur Schlesinger concluded that the test ban would not have come about without the intense personal commitment of both Kennedy and Macmillan. Macmillan still was disappointed that it was only a partial test ban and that the opportunity to ban all tests had been missed because of Kennedy's supposed 'weakness'. Kennedy regarded the agreement as a step on the way to a wider ban – but only if the Russians would agree to adequate verification.

The meeting between Kennedy and Macmillan at Birch Grove proved to be their last. Kennedy had the sense that he might not be dealing with Macmillan much longer as Prime Minister. On 8 October 1963, on the eve of the Conservative Party Conference, Macmillan went into hospital for a prostate operation. On the following day, he announced his resignation. Six weeks later, Kennedy was shot in Dallas. David Bruce reported from London: 'Great Britain has never before mourned a foreigner as it has President Kennedy.' Macmillan wrote a long and moving letter to Jacqueline Kennedy, who replied recalling 'how full of charity your relations always were with each other even when unforeseen disastrous things like Skybolt happened'.[7] Macmillan continued his correspondence with Jacqueline Kennedy until close to his death.

32

'I DON'T THINK WE ARE IN FOR A VERY HAPPY FOUR DAYS'

IN JANUARY 1963, Hugh Gaitskell died, suddenly and unexpectedly. President Kennedy had formed a high opinion of Gaitskell, not least because of the battles he had fought within the Labour Party against further nationalisation and unilateral nuclear disarmament. His successor, Harold Wilson, had no such reputation. He came from the left of the party. He had been a frequent visitor to the Soviet Union. His position on many of the issues appeared to the Americans, as it did to others, unclear – which was precisely what had helped him to get elected. On winning the leadership he declared himself a supporter of a Western nuclear deterrent, while stating that British nuclear weapons added nothing to the West's defences. Wilson was eager to portray himself as a British Kennedy, but he was not regarded by the Americans in those terms.

In March, he made plans to visit Washington. Macmillan told his ambassador that he hoped the Americans would realise that they should not take Wilson's views too seriously. Ormsby-Gore replied that he had noted a marked lack of enthusiasm for Wilson's visit on the part of the administration. 'Unfortunately, those who have already met him dislike him, and those who have not distrust him. I don't think we are in for a very happy four days.'[1]

Wilson saw Kennedy for an hour on 2 April. Wilson was convinced that the meeting was a success. In fact the President, according to Henry Brandon, 'did not take to him as a person but was impressed by his breadth of knowledge'.[2] Wilson met other senior members of the administration and impressed them as a shrewd politician. Asked if he would repudiate the Nassau agreement on Polaris, Wilson said that he would renegotiate it. With Macmillan's near collapse in June over the Profumo affair, the Americans started to take seriously the prospect that they might soon be dealing with Wilson as Prime Minister.

In March 1964, Wilson returned to Washington to see President Johnson. By this time Alec Douglas-Home had succeeded Macmillan as Prime Minister. He was liked and trusted by the Americans, but they did not believe he could win an election. Johnson was told by Dean Rusk that Wilson was 'not a man of strong political convictions himself ... Somehow, he does not inspire a feeling of trust in many people.' Bundy told Johnson that he would find Wilson 'interesting, affable, persuasive and seemingly sincere'.[3]

President Johnson already was preoccupied with the Communist challenge in south-east Asia. Wilson said that he supported US policy, but was opposed to an invasion of North Vietnam. Wilson told McNamara that one of his first acts as Prime Minister would be to renegotiate the Polaris agreement. The problem was that the issue had become 'highly electoral' and the idea of a British deterrent 'had an emotional appeal to the man in the pub'.

By July 1964, the Americans were more than ever convinced that Wilson would be the next Prime Minister. One of his advisers, Richard Neustadt, wrote a report to President Johnson about the possibilities for taming and domesticating an incoming Labour government. Neustadt knew the British political scene well. His advice was based on conversations with, among others, Harold Wilson and his senior Labour Party colleagues, George Brown, Denis Healey and Roy Jenkins, as well as with senior officials and journalists.

Neustadt wrote that 'when officials get their hands on the new Ministers, Foreign Office briefs presumably will urge affirmative response to us'. Neustadt expected the probable Labour Foreign Secretary, Patrick Gordon Walker, to 'submit with little struggle ... Assuming Denis Healey is Defense Secretary (he seems confident he will be), his own interest in a mission East of Suez (and in sales of British aircraft), his mistrust of continentals, his disdain for MLF, comport well with the bulk of these official views.'

Neustadt recommended that the President should make a fuss of Wilson when he next visited Washington and find ways to massage British *amour propre*. On nuclear issues, there should be talk of Atlantic consultation on strategy and policy 'up to the final decision on the trigger which must remain yours'.[4]

In October 1964, Wilson won the British election, though by a margin far narrower than the Americans had expected. One of his first acts as Prime Minister was to visit Johnson in Washington in December.

Johnson still knew little of Wilson and what he did know made him suspicious. But Wilson badly needed Johnson's help. The Labour government already had begun its long and ultimately unsuccessful struggle against the devaluation of the pound. Before going to Washington, Wilson wrote to Johnson that he had rejected devaluation 'now, and for all time'. Johnson made clear that he expected moral or, preferably, practical support in Vietnam and a continuing British military presence east of Suez. On Vietnam, Wilson promised general support, except for attacks on the North. He agreed to continue a role east of Suez, as part of the price of the 'special relationship'.

Britain continued to fight and eventually to defeat the Communist insurgency in Malaysia and to maintain a presence in the Indian Ocean. As for nuclear weapons, on his return to London Wilson announced 'in the light of information now available to us' that the Labour government had decided not to cancel Polaris on the grounds that the programme was too far advanced to be abandoned.

But no personal rapport had developed between Johnson and Wilson, hard as Wilson tried to cultivate the impression that there was one. George Ball records that Johnson found Wilson 'too ordinary, too much like other politicians with whom LBJ had dealt, and Johnson took an almost instant dislike to him'.[5] In February 1965, Wilson, under pressure from his party, telephoned Johnson to express concern about the first US bombing raids in Vietnam and to propose, as Attlee had over Korea, an urgent visit to Washington. To Wilson's surprise, Johnson let fly with an outburst of Texan temper. He dismissed the idea of a visit by Wilson. Britain, he pointed out, had troops in Korea and did not in Vietnam. 'I won't tell you how to run Malaysia', he added, 'and you don't tell me how to run Vietnam.'

Wilson assured the US ambassador, David Bruce, that Britain 'solidly supported' US policy, though he hoped that military action would be matched by a willingness to negotiate. But he told his Foreign Secretary,

Michael Stewart, that the Americans should be left in no doubt about the strength of feeling in the Labour Party and the difficulties he was facing. 'Should the President try to link this question with support for the pound I would regard this as most unfortunate.' Johnson told Kenneth Galbraith that he recognised Wilson's difficulties: 'What is just as important is that he should recognize ours.'[6]

With no British military involvement, Vietnam was not an issue on which the British government had any real influence on American policy. Because of the country's financial weakness, Wilson knew that the relationship 'was actually a client one, when the Americans had something specific to ask of their client'.[7] Vietnam was not primarily a British problem and Wilson, through his opposition to sending any British forces there, was determined to keep it that way. But he knew or believed that he could not afford to dissociate himself from US policy. His Foreign Secretary, Michael Stewart, doggedly resisted attempts by much of his party to get the Labour government publicly to criticise US actions. Wilson's approach was to give the Americans everything they wanted short of military help.

When Wilson visited Washington in April 1965, Dean Rusk reported to Johnson: 'We have had an excellent degree of understanding and cooperation in crucial foreign policy matters from the Labour Government.' Johnson, according to Wilson, expressed appreciation for his position on Vietnam. Wilson in turn expressed approval for the Australian decision to send a battalion there, even implying that Britain might do the same if priority did not have to be given to Malaysia.

All this produced protests from the left of the Labour Party. At first these were manageable, but as the situation worsened in Vietnam, the pressures on Wilson increased. David Bruce reported to Johnson that the Prime Minister 'must be sorely tempted to buy some political credit at home by criticizing American policy. Wilson has not done so and I do not think he will. If nothing else, self-interest dictates that he must risk no serious split with the Americans.'[8] Instead, Wilson sought to offer himself as an honest broker to end the conflict. Not surprisingly, he was never regarded as such by the Soviet Union, China or the North Vietnamese. The North Vietnamese and their Viet Cong allies in the South would settle for nothing less than the reunification of Vietnam under their control. Johnson was determined to maintain the independence of South Vietnam and found it impossible to believe that the United States could be defeated in combat by a third-rate Asian power. So the scope for mediation was virtually nil, particularly by a country with no real influence in Indo-China. The cracks plastered over by Eden had widened to a point at which they were not susceptible to that kind of treatment again.

Nevertheless, Wilson proposed to the Russians that Britain and the Soviet Union as co-chairmen should reconvene the Geneva Conference on Indo-China. The Russians failed to respond. At the Commonwealth Conference in June 1965, Wilson sought to play to the domestic and international gallery by proposing a Commonwealth mission to explore whether there was any basis for a peaceful solution in Vietnam. Bundy was sceptical: he expected the British to go ahead 'even though no Communists give them the time of day'.[9] The mission was flatly rejected by the North Vietnamese. Wilson then decided to send a junior member of his government, the Bevanite MP Harold Davies, on a mission to Hanoi. Davies was regarded as a friend of the North Vietnamese and Wilson's senior officials were appalled. 'My first reaction was what bloody nonsense,' commented his Private Secretary, Sir Derek Mitchell. As news of Davies's mission leaked, it was seen as a sop by Wilson to the Labour left and another exercise in political gimmickry. Davies got nowhere in Hanoi, but Wilson still believed years later that his idea had been sabotaged.[10]

The Americans were unimpressed. Bundy told President Johnson that they must get it into the heads of the British 'that it makes no sense for us to rescue the pound in a situation in which there is no British flag in Vietnam, and a threatened British thin-out both east of Suez and in Germany'. Wilson declared to Johnson his admiration for the 'careful balance' he had maintained between resistance to aggression and readiness to negotiate. He applauded his 'patient and courageous policy'.[11] In September, the Americans agreed to continue support for the pound, provided Britain maintained its overseas commitments. The Foreign Secretary reported that British requests had been met with reminders from the White House that Britain had not been helpful over sanctions against Cuba and enquiries as to when British troops would arrive in Vietnam.

In December 1965, Wilson met Johnson in Washington. Wilson stressed the extent to which his hands were tied by his party. He read out a telegram from Labour MPs demanding an end to American bombing of North Vietnam and argued for a bombing pause to test if North Vietnam would respond. He sought continuing American support for sterling, which Johnson promised – provided, Wilson told his Cabinet, 'we stood firm on our present position in the Far East'.

Wilson painted to his colleagues a glowing picture of his relationship with Johnson.[12] Johnson remained less euphoric about Wilson and suspicious of his desire to play a diplomatic role in Vietnam while contributing nothing to the fighting there.

Wilson now was concerned that the Americans would extend the bombing to Hanoi and Haiphong. A Colonel Rogers was sent by the Pentagon to convince him of the military necessity for this. Wilson was opposed because of the political repercussions in Britain. In response, Rusk argued against yet another visit by Wilson to Washington unless he was prepared publicly to support the US position. In February 1966, Wilson visited Moscow, where he tried and failed to win Soviet support for a new initiative.

Wilson claimed that there was no connection between his political support for the US in Vietnam and American support for sterling. But in February 1966, he urged his Cabinet to remember that US financial help 'is not unrelated to the way we behave in the Far East: any direct announcement of our withdrawal, for example, could not fail to have a profound effect on my personal relations with LBJ and the way the Americans treat US'.[13]

As the Vietnam conflict worsened, Wilson came under increasing criticism within his party for servility to Johnson. His attempts, meanwhile, to find a solution to the Rhodesia conflict, for which Britain did have responsibility, fared no better than his initiatives over Vietnam. He repeatedly was outmanoeuvred by the Rhodesian leader, Ian Smith, whose determination to maintain white minority rule led him, in November 1965, to declare Rhodesia independent. Wilson's promise that economic sanctions would bring Smith's rebellion to an end in 'weeks not months' undermined his international credibility. In the event, fourteen years were to elapse before the Thatcher government succeeded in resolving the problem.

As Britain's economic position worsened, Wilson fought an increasingly desperate rearguard action in defence of sterling. He recalled the political costs of devaluation to the previous Labour government and feared that a repetition would weaken his position with the United States and the Commonwealth. But the financial situation continued to deteriorate, necessitating cuts in defence expenditure. The Navy Minister, Christopher Mayhew, resigned over the decision of the government not to build a new large aircraft carrier to replace HMS *Ark Royal*. The lack of such a carrier was to cause serious problems later in the Falklands campaign.

In July 1966, Wilson, about to visit Washington, worried about the American reaction to the cuts in overseas expenditure and told his Cabinet that 'they weren't too pleased with us anyway over Vietnam'. Johnson had sent him an urgent personal message shortly before the visit that the Americans would continue to try to help, but asking whether the British could not send even a token force to Vietnam. 'A platoon of bagpipers would be sufficient,' Johnson declared, 'it was the British flag that was wanted.' But Wilson said that this would be politically impossible for him.

To Wilson's relief, his reception was better than he had expected. Johnson had been told that Wilson had gone as far as he could on Vietnam and that he deserved support. In an after-lunch speech at the White House, Johnson referred to Milton, Shakespeare and Churchill, and congratulated Britain on having a leader whose 'enterprise and courage will show the way. Your firmness and leadership have inspired us deeply.'[14]

The reference to Churchill caused some derision and an alarmed Johnson asked an aide exactly what he had said. He was told that there had been no direct reference to Churchill: the two men had not even been mentioned in the same paragraph. But Wilson, naturally, was pleased, the more so as, by this time, he believed that some of his colleagues were planning to replace him. He told those in favour of devaluation that he would raise with the Americans the possibility of 'linking the pound and dollar and then letting them both float'.

Johnson's brief for his meeting with Wilson had urged him to encourage the British in any action that lowered the status of their 'independent' nuclear deterrent. But the Americans found the Labour government as allergic to the idea of a Multi-Lateral Force as the Conservatives had been. Wilson and his Defence Minister, Denis Healey, had become attached to Polaris, Johnson was told in mid-1966: 'The reason is simple. The nuclear deterrent is the most important of the great power symbols still in British possession. Although Wilson is committed to give it up, he has so far shown no disposition to do so.' By this stage Richard Crossman was convinced that Wilson and the Chancellor of the Exchequer, James Callaghan, 'between them have committed us more deeply than any of their predecessors to the Americans'.[15]

In January 1967, Wilson and his Foreign Secretary, George Brown, set off on a tour of European capitals to prepare the way for a renewed attempt to join the Common Market. Johnson promised his support: 'Your entry would certainly help to strengthen and unify the West.' But de Gaulle, towering over his two British visitors, gave them as little encouragement as he had Macmillan. De Gaulle asked whether Britain was willing to follow any policy that was really distinct from that of the United States.

Wilson continued to believe that he had a role to play in Vietnam. 'One thing is certain,' he wrote to Lord Kennet, 'my visit to Moscow [in July 1966] stopped a very dangerous escalation on both sides.' Wilson sought to use the visit to Britain of the Soviet premier Kosygin in February 1967 to launch a new initiative. His aim was to get an extension of the four-day truce declared over the Tet holiday in Vietnam. This was to be achieved through Wilson's influence in Washington and that of Kosygin with Hanoi.

Wilson consulted the Americans. He asked Kosygin to get a definite sign from the North Vietnamese that they would respond to a cessation of the bombing. The CIA sent a representative, Chet Cooper, to confer with the Prime Minister. A plan was concocted whereby the United States would first suspend the bombing, then the Americans and North Vietnamese would gradually restrict their military actions. Cooper failed to clear this with the White House before it was given to Kosygin.

Wilson was not informed that Johnson had already sent a message to Ho Chi Minh that he would end the bombing and freeze the level of US forces in Vietnam when he was assured that no more men and supplies would be sent to the South, that is, that infiltration had stopped. The proposal given to Kosygin offered a bombing halt first in return for good intentions later. When Johnson saw Cooper's report, Wilson was told that infiltration must stop as a condition for the cessation of the bombing.

This produced a furious row in Cooper's presence between Wilson and his Foreign Secretary, George Brown, who accused Wilson of having acted hastily and of having failed to tell him what was going on. Brown made his usual threats of resignation. Wilson believed that he had been close to pulling off the diplomatic coup of a lifetime. 'In the two decades of my diplomatic experience', reported Cooper, 'I had never seen anyone quite so

LEFT *'Columns of flame and smoke ascending through the night…'* Rear-Admiral Sir George Cockburn in Washington, 24 August 1814.
© Corbis Images

BELOW *'Democracy as we conceive it will not survive in Britain and France after the war.'* John F. Kennedy, Ambassador Joseph Kennedy, and Joseph Kennedy Jr in London, 1938. © Corbis Images

'Evidently he had the first quality of the angler, which is not to measure the pleasure by the catch.' FDR and Churchill fishing at Shangri-La, May 1943.
© Franklin D. Roosevelt Presidential Library

'We greatly appreciate the high value you evidently set on our continued survival.' Churchill and FDR on the White House grounds, 24 May 1943.
© Franklin D. Roosevelt Presidential Library

'It would be idle for us to delude ourselves that we saw eye to eye.' FDR, Churchill and Stalin in Tehran, November 1943.
© Franklin D. Roosevelt Presidential Library

'Frustration was the fate of this final conference of the three.' Truman, Churchill and Stalin at Potsdam, July 1945.
© Corbis Images

'It is most distressing that the Americans do not like him.' Portrait of Montgomery by Eisenhower.
© Government Art Collection

'December opened by bringing us a Job's comforter.' Truman, Attlee, Acheson and Marshall in Washington, December 1950.
© Truman Library

'Around the table this evening there was gathered the governance of the world – not to dominate it, mind you, but to save it.' Truman and Churchill on the *Williamsburg*, January 1952.
© Truman Library

'The lady has already been violated in public.' Kennedy and Macmillan in Nassau, December 1962.
© Getty Images

'Somehow he does not inspire an atmosphere of trust.' Lyndon B. Johnson and Harold Wilson.
© Lyndon B. Johnson Presidential Library

ABOVE 'A couple who had been told by everyone that they should be in love.' Nixon and Heath, 20 December 1971.
© Getty Images

LEFT 'Heavens, not another wet' Margaret Thatcher with Alexander Haig on 8 April 1982.
© The Economist

'I felt as if there had been an earthquake beneath my feet.' Ronald Reagan and Margaret Thatcher at Camp David, 18 November 1986. © Rex Features

'Anchor to windward.' Thatcher and Bush, June 1989. © George Bush Presidential Library

'No time to go wobbly.' Bush and Thatcher in Aspen, Colorado, 2 August 1990.
© George Bush Presidential Library

'They felt like old friends.' Tony Blair and Bill Clinton at a NATO summit, 1997. © Reuters

Colin Powell and Donald Rumsfeld exchanging views in front of Condoleezza Rice at the White House, 28 January 2002.
© Getty Images

ABOVE *'The closest relationship I would form with any foreign leader.'* Tony Blair and George W. Bush in Crawford, Texas, 2002. © Paul Morse; George W. Bush Presidential Library & Museum/NARA

BELOW *'Cameron was told that if he wished to preserve the "special relationship", he would need to commit to spending 2 per cent of GDP on defence.'* David Cameron and Barack Obama outside Parliament, 26 July 2008. © AP Photos

angry, but Wilson kept himself very much under control as he explained how embarrassing and damaging the Washington message was.'[16]

Wilson protested to Johnson that he was in a 'hell of a situation'. He could only get out of it by telling Kosygin that he was not in the President's confidence or that there had been a sudden change in Washington, which, as a loyal satellite, he must follow. Johnson replied that there must be an assured stoppage of infiltration. Johnson added that he was always glad to know that Wilson was in his corner, but he would have some difficulty 'in view of my responsibilities and problems here, in giving anyone a power of attorney'. This clarification, or rather reaffirmation, of the American position was handed to Kosygin as he boarded a train at King's Cross.

The Americans claimed that all along they had insisted on an end to infiltration. They were not satisfied with vague promises and, given the intelligence reports on this subject, they were not prepared to give the North Vietnamese the benefit of the doubt. Johnson admitted 'a diplomatic mix-up for which we shared a measure of responsibility'.

In reality, neither Johnson nor his national security adviser, Walt Rostow, had expected the Wilson–Kosygin meeting to make any difference. The Americans had failed in their own direct contacts to persuade the North Vietnamese to agree to stop infiltration in return for an end to the bombing. 'Wilson seemed to feel that he and the Soviet leader could serve as mediators, and bring an end to the war,' said Johnson. 'I doubted this strongly. I believed that if the Soviets thought they had a peace formula Hanoi would accept, they would deal directly with us rather than through a fourth party. But I was willing for our British friends to try.' Cooper concluded that Washington 'had little real interest in the London episode; they regarded it primarily as a side-show'.[17]

Wilson remained convinced that he had been on the verge of success in Vietnam and that he had the 'absolute confidence' of both Johnson and Kosygin. The reality was different. As Cooper pointed out, Wilson did not have peace within his grasp: '[H]e was always overly optimistic about it … The US Administration regarded Wilson at best as marginal, at worst as a nuisance and did not bother to keep him informed of their own thinking even when he thought that he was negotiating on their behalf.'

The London episode caused bitterness on both sides. When Wilson visited Washington in June, his reception was cooler than before, with Johnson concerned about British plans to withdraw from east of Suez.

On behalf of the Labour left, Tony Benn described him as being received 'with all the trumpets appropriate for a weak foreign head of state who has to be buttered up so that he can carry the can for American foreign policy'.[18] In October, when Wilson defended US policy in Vietnam at his party conference, Johnson was glowing in his tributes. Shortly thereafter, Wilson and his wife were jostled by anti-Vietnam demonstrators in Cambridge. The government was in the throes of another sterling crisis. Once again there were urgent appeals to Washington for support.

———

On 8 November 1967, the Governor of the Bank of England told the Americans that only massive US financial assistance could save the pound. Opposition to US policy in Vietnam was increasing within the Labour Party. Wilson complained that Roy Jenkins, then Home Secretary, had been 'brain-washed by the Kennedy group (Galbraith in fact) against LBJ'. James Callaghan, Chancellor of the Exchequer, by now was half-convinced that devaluation was inevitable. Wilson still hoped to stave it off by a visit to Johnson. His idea was to persuade the Americans that if they did not help, British forces would have to be withdrawn from the Far East forthwith. The American ambassador, David Bruce, was called to 10 Downing Street at midnight to be told that Wilson wanted to fly to Washington two days later, on 10 November. As the real reason for the visit could not be given, Wilson said that he needed to talk to the President about Vietnam, though there would be other questions to discuss. The Foreign Secretary, George Brown, doubted whether anyone would believe the Vietnam story.

Johnson replied that, while ready to see Wilson, Vietnam was the one subject he did not wish to discuss. As other pretexts proved hard to invent, Wilson's appeal instead was relayed to the Americans through the British ambassador, Sir Patrick Dean. On 13 November, the Americans replied that, as Wilson put it, 'with reluctance they would have to see us go down'. By 15 November, it was clear that there were 'no serious signs of a cheque book' from the United States. On 18 November, the pound was devalued from $2.80 to $2.40. On the following day, Wilson told the British public that this did not mean that the 'pound in their pockets' was worth less than before.[19]

Denis Healey, as Defence Secretary, was horrified at the necessity for further defence cuts. Withdrawal from east of Suez was brought forward to 1971. Healey came to the verge of resignation over the decision to cancel the order for fifty American F-111 strike aircraft. President Johnson protested to Wilson that this would be regarded as a 'total disengagement from any commitment whatever to the security of areas outside Europe and, indeed, to a considerable extent in Europe as well'. Wilson replied: 'Believe me, Lyndon, the decisions we are having to take now have been the most difficult and the heaviest of any that I, and I think all my colleagues can remember in our public life.' When George Brown was sent to Washington to explain this further round of defence cutbacks, he got a torrid reception. Johnson told Wilson of his dismay at 'this profoundly discouraging news ... tantamount to the withdrawal of Britain from world affairs'.[20]

When Wilson went to Washington in February 1968, he encountered a protocol crisis, as the highlight of the musical entertainment at the White House was to have been a performance of *The Road to Mandalay*, with Kipling's most famous use of the term 'East of Suez' – from which Britain now was withdrawing. It was thought better not to proceed with *The Road to Mandalay* – a fact prominently reported by the Washington press – until Wilson managed to get it reinstated. At the dinner, he warned against a further escalation of the war in Vietnam.[21]

By March, pressure on sterling already had resumed. Britain through this period rarely had more than $2 billion in the reserves. On 8 March, $250 million was lost through the selling of sterling in a single day. The problem this time was the fear that the dollar/gold exchange rate would not hold. Weakened by the financing of the Vietnam War, the dollar was no longer seen as being as good as gold. These fears were soon realised as, at 11 p.m. on 14 March, a request was received from Washington to close the London gold market.

A Privy Council with the Queen was held after midnight at Buckingham Palace to decide the closure of the foreign exchange market for the following day. The Foreign Secretary, George Brown, protesting that he had not been consulted, resigned. Wilson's supporters claimed that Brown, who had serious drinking problems, had been in no condition to be involved. Over the weekend the Americans introduced a dual price for gold, maintaining parity against the dollar for official transactions only.

By the time the markets reopened, Roy Jenkins, who had succeeded Callaghan as Chancellor of the Exchequer, was able to negotiate a $4 billion line of credit from Washington.

Throughout these years of the Wilson government, the relationship was one of greater dependence on the United States than at any other point in peacetime. The causes were Britain's structural economic problems, but also the recurrent crises resulting from the attempt to maintain a fixed exchange rate between the pound and the dollar, necessitating repeated appeals to the Americans to help reduce the pressure by using their reserves to buy sterling. The idea of letting sterling float and find its own level against the dollar was advocated by some members of the Wilson government, but never became policy. If it had done, that would have relieved the tensions without, however, addressing the fundamental issue of the restructuring of British industry, deferred to be dealt with by future governments.

Though Wilson was determined to portray the President as his friend, the British political establishment, which had so admired John Kennedy, never was able fully to come to grips with the formidable, but not easily exportable, personality of Lyndon Johnson. Roy Jenkins in his memoirs gives a graphic description of this unbridgeable cultural gap:

> The President placed himself on a high rocking chair, with me on a low sofa beside him, and leaned over throughout the conversation so that he was constantly gripping my knee, seizing my arm and almost digging me in the ribs. He began by pulling out what seemed to be a well-thumbed piece of paper from which he read a two- or three-minute entirely non-spontaneous encomium of my Budget. Then he spoke about his new grandchild which he threatened to have summoned down for inspection ... and passed from that to his cattle herd in Texas. Neither subject prospered, and I was relieved when the interview subsided to a conclusion after about twenty-five minutes. There was, as I am well aware, a great deal more to LBJ than this, and I was no doubt too susceptible to the contrasting easy flattery of Kennedy's tailor-made conversation.[22]

In February 1968, on the eve of a visit by Wilson to Washington, Dean Rusk called for a review of the 'nature and worth of the "special relationship"'. The review by the Intelligence Bureau stated that 'Britain had never cut a less impressive figure in American eyes'. Wilson's popularity was at 'an abysmal low'. The country had no plan of action that promised future success. A press critic had described the relationship as like being one with the family retainer. The State Department dismissed these gloomy predictions, insisting that Britain remained a valued partner.[23]

33

'WE DO NOT SUFFER IN THE WORLD FROM SUCH AN EXCESS OF FRIENDS'

AT THE END of January 1968, violating a truce they had themselves pledged to observe during Tet, 70,000 North Vietnamese regular soldiers and Viet Cong guerrillas launched their great offensive in South Vietnam. The result was a military defeat for the Communists, from which they took months to recover, but a strategic victory. The offensive showed that the North Vietnamese could match any increase in US forces. It appeared to many in the United States that the war was unwinnable. President Johnson nearly was defeated by the peace candidate, Eugene McCarthy, in the New Hampshire primary. Four days later, Robert Kennedy declared his candidature. On 31 March, Lyndon Johnson announced that he would not seek re-election.

Following Bobby Kennedy's assassination, the Wilson government hoped and assumed that Hubert Humphrey would win the presidency. There was no love lost for Richard Nixon and few in Britain believed he would win. It was in the expectation of a Humphrey victory that Wilson announced the appointment of his former Labour colleague and editor of the *New Statesman*, John Freeman, then High Commissioner in India, as the new British ambassador to Washington.

When Nixon won, this created a problem as in a *New Statesman* article in 1962 Freeman had described him as 'a man of no principle whatsoever except a willingness to sacrifice everything in the cause of Dick Nixon'.

He added that Nixon's defeat for the Governorship of California was 'a victory for decency in public life'.

Nixon suggested through intermediaries that the appointment might be changed. Eisenhower told him that for the British to persist with Freeman's appointment would be an insult. Nixon, preparing for a visit to London, indicated that he might refuse to meet Freeman. The White House suggested that Nixon might not attend Wilson's dinner in his honour if Freeman were included. The US ambassador, David Bruce, cabled in reply: 'Surely the absurdity of telling the British Prime Minister who he can invite to his own home for dinner requires no explanation.'

But Nixon could surprise. In his toast at the dinner the President said that American journalists had written worse things about him than the *New Statesman*. 'Some say there's a new Nixon,' he added. 'And they wonder if there's a new Freeman. I would like to think that's all behind us. After all, he's the new diplomat and I'm the new statesman.' A greatly relieved Harold Wilson wrote Nixon a note of thanks on the back of his menu. 'That was one of the kindest and most generous acts I have known in a quarter of a century of politics.' John Freeman proved an effective ambassador, forging a real friendship with Henry Kissinger, who admired his intelligence and integrity. He also became an admirer of Nixon, at any rate in foreign policy.[1]

Nixon's visit proved memorable in other ways. It began with a meeting in the Cabinet room with Wilson and a few senior members of his government. Roy Jenkins describes the scene:

> Nixon opened with a half-hour informal expose and did it brilliantly. Then coffee was brought in, and mixed up with putting or not putting sugar and milk in his cup the President mysteriously succeeded in picking up a crystal inkwell and pouring its contents over his hands, his papers and some part of the table.
>
> Consternation broke out, particularly on the British side. It was like a Bateman cartoon, with extremes of surprise, horror and sympathy being registered. Sir Burke Trend even poured cream over his own trousers, although it was not clear whether this was because he was so shocked or because he thought the President would feel less embarrassed if carelessness verging on slapstick appeared to be a Downing Street habit. Blotting paper, napkins and towels were

rushed in, and eventually Nixon was taken out to nailbrushes and pumice stones. They were unavailing. After a long interval he came back with his hands still stained. It was a real Lady Macbeth scene, and it completely ruined his concentration. He could do nothing but look at them for the rest of the morning. His brilliance was all gone. The discussion never regained any verve and was adjourned early.

After the dinner at which Nixon had held out his olive branch to John Freeman, Jenkins continues:

The festivities were rounded off by a little post-prandial charade which Wilson had organised in the Cabinet room. All members, those who had not been at dinner as well as those who had, were required to be present and perform for the benefit of the visitors, as though they were taking part in a real Cabinet. Some of us, notably Crosland and I, were I am afraid a little sullen or shy about doing our pirouettes, but we were more than made up for by Crossman and Benn, who put on bravura performances. Crossman at least struck some rather mordant political paradoxes while Benn trilled away about sputniks and Bible readings. The President took up what was perhaps the only possible polite position, looked amazed that 'two little heads could know so much', and expressed suitable admiration to the Prime Minister about the brilliance of his Cabinet.[2]

Henry Kissinger, who was making his debut as national security adviser, provides a different perspective on the visit. There was no welcoming ceremony lest Nixon be accused of junketing while the war continued to rage in Vietnam. This was a rather painful sacrifice for Nixon who loved ceremony, especially in a country that, Kissinger observes,

has raised under-stated pomp to a major art form ... Harold Wilson greeted Nixon with the avuncular goodwill of the head of an ancient family that had seen better times ... [Nixon] tackled head-on the so-called special relationship between Britain and the United States that was so contentious within our government – by referring to it explicitly twice and in most positive terms.

Kissinger gives an amusing account of the horror this caused the State Department:

> The advocates – almost fanatics – of European unity were eager to terminate the 'special relationship' with our oldest ally as an alleged favour to Britain to smooth its entry into the Common Market. They felt it essential to deprive Britain of any special status with us lest it impede Britain's role in the Europe they cherished. They urged a formal egalitarianism, unaffected by tradition or conceptions of the national interest, as the best guarantee of their Grand Design. Even if desirable, which I doubted, this was impractical.

In a briefing to US correspondents before Nixon's departure for Europe, Kissinger said: 'My own personal view on this issue is that we do not suffer in the world from such an excess of friends that we should discourage those who feel that they have a special friendship for us.' The answer to the 'special relationship' with Britain was to raise other countries to the same status, rather than discouraging Britain into a less warm relationship with the United States. Nixon personally believed in the 'special relationship' and settled the issue with his arrival statement.

Kissinger notes that Wilson had the reputation of a wily politician whose penetrating intelligence was flawed by the absence of ultimate reliability. The Johnson administration had considered him too close to the left wing of the Labour Party: this and his vanity were supposed to make him susceptible to Soviet blandishments. In Kissinger's experience these criticisms proved inaccurate. Wilson had to take account of the left wing of his party. He was not the first British Prime Minister to present himself as a peacemaker with the Russians: Harold Macmillan had played the same role. Kissinger found Wilson a sincere friend of the United States: '[H]is emotional ties, like those of most Britons, were across the oceans and not across the Channel.' His generation of Labour leaders was closer to the United States than the leader of the Conservative Party, Ted Heath. The Conservatives, Kissinger noted, seemed to find the loss of pre-eminence to the United States harder to digest, especially after what they considered the US betrayal over Suez.

Despite Wilson's background as an economics lecturer at Oxford, Kissinger found that he had almost no interest in abstract ideas. He was fascinated by the manipulation of political power: longer-range objectives got only the most cursory attention. He saw no sense in planning, confident that his political skills would see him through almost any tight spot. He was personally rather cold, but eager for approval, especially from American presidents. Early on he suggested to Nixon that they should call each other by their first names: 'a fish-eyed stare from Nixon squelched this idea'.

Kissinger was not impressed by Wilson's Foreign Secretary, Michael Stewart. Stewart was a reliable ally. Despite all his doubts, he defended US policy in Vietnam in a debate at the Oxford Union with skill and vigour. But his schoolmasterly manner drove Nixon to distraction.

Wilson said that he was seeking entry into the European Community less for the economic than for the political benefits of a more outward-looking Europe that he hoped to bring about. Nixon pointed out that the Soviet Union was closing the nuclear gap, but found no willingness on the British side to draw the conclusion that European defences needed to be strengthened. The British argued that the Alliance must be seen as a vehicle for *détente*. At the same time they showed anxiety about a US–Soviet condominium. But Nixon, who lunched with the Queen and dined at Chequers ('comfortable but not ostentatious, full of just enough history to remind one of Britain's glorious past'), departed well-pleased with his reception.[3]

In January 1970, Wilson made a return visit to Washington. Much of the discussion was about Biafra. The British were strongly supporting the Nigerian government against the Biafran attempt to secede. Nixon, happy for once to be on the humane side of the argument, wanted to get relief supplies through to the Biafrans direct, though the Americans never succeeded in doing so. Kissinger comments that Wilson succeeded in curbing US interventionist impulses and that, from the point of view of long-term US interests, he was probably right.

In return for being invited to attend the Cabinet meeting in London, Nixon asked Wilson to attend a meeting of the National Security Council. 'Both events were part charade, as obviously no serious debate would occur in the presence of foreign leaders.' The subject chosen for the NSC meeting was US policy towards Europe. The State Department produced an options paper suggesting: (a) maintaining the present course; (b) supporting an 'enhanced Europe' (meaning British entry and closer integration); or (c) US disengagement.

Kissinger noted the classic bureaucratic device of leaving the decision-maker with only one option, which for ease of identification was placed in the middle. Nixon concluded that it was in the interests of the US to have a strong European Community, with the United Kingdom in it. Wilson claimed, rather incredibly, to have found the debate 'fascinating'. In June, he called an election, which he confidently expected to win – an opinion shared by all the key US decision-makers save the President himself, who predicted a Conservative victory.[4]

34

'A COUPLE WHO HAVE BEEN TOLD BY EVERYONE THAT THEY SHOULD BE IN LOVE'

WHEN THE CONSERVATIVE Party won the British general election in June 1970, Nixon was overjoyed. He had been an unabashed partisan of the Tories. Despite the polls and contrary to the opinion of all his advisers and of the US embassy in London, Nixon was convinced that Heath would win. When his prediction came true, he was so elated that he called Kissinger four times in one night in Mexico City to express his satisfaction. 'He wanted nothing so much as an intimate collaboration of a kind he would grant to no other foreign leader,' wrote Kissinger. At last, Nixon thought, there would be a kindred spirit in one other major country.

But the relationship never flourished:

> Like a couple who have been told by everyone that they should be in love and who try mightily but futilely to justify these expectations, Heath and Nixon never managed to establish the personal rapport for which Nixon, at least, longed in the beginning. Both were rather austere personalities, vulnerable and eager for acceptance but incapable of the act of grace that could have bridged their loneliness.

Kissinger regarded Heath as one of the ablest world leaders he had met. But he noted also that he eschewed any claim to personal charm and that his laugh was distinguished by a notable lack of mirth. Heath seemed the most untypical of Britain's postwar leaders. 'He had a theoretical bent closer than the rest to that of the continental Europeans, which gave his ideas an abstract cast sometimes verging on the doctrinaire.' He was the least committed emotionally to the United States, immune to the sentimental ties forged in two wars. Kissinger believed that for most British leaders, whatever the facts of geography, America was closer than 'Europe'. Heath, however, was persuaded that Britain's future was in Europe and that Britain should join Europe 'not reluctantly and calculatingly but with real conviction'. More than half-convinced by the Gaullist argument that a principal obstacle was Britain's relationship with the United States, Heath was ready to sacrifice whatever was special in that relationship to his European ambitions. Heath was content to enjoy no higher status in Washington than any other European leader. Indeed he came close to *insisting* on receiving no preferential treatment.

Kissinger notes the paradox that Wilson, whom Nixon distrusted, was eager for a closer relationship than Heath, whom Nixon, initially, admired. The Conservative Party seemed to feel more bitterly the decline of Britain's power.

Heath had to exert himself to keep Washington at arm's length: he was being offered for nothing the preferred status for which his predecessors had struggled. He chose not to avail himself of the opportunity. There was no early visit to Washington, as Nixon had hoped and as had been sought by every other postwar Prime Minister. There were few telephone calls, even though Kissinger urged British officials to encourage such contact. Heath himself seemed to want to implement what the advocates of European integration in the State Department had urged when Nixon had entered office – the downgrading of the 'special relationship'. Kissinger questioned whether Heath needed to pay this price in terms of intimacy with Washington to establish his European credentials: he felt it a pity that so able a man could have such a blind spot for the importance of intangibles.

In October, during a tour of European capitals, Nixon visited Chequers, to have lunch with the new Prime Minister. Heath, Kissinger believed, wanted to present this to his European colleagues as essentially a courtesy call in which nothing of substance would be agreed. Europe was not discussed, except for Nixon's comment that the United States wanted to be discreetly helpful over Britain's negotiations to join the EC. But Heath impressed his visitors. He agreed that how the United States disengaged from Vietnam would affect the world beyond. If the Russians felt the US to be in full retreat, Heath feared they would intensify their pressures in Europe. Heath's Foreign Secretary, Alec Douglas-Home, whom Nixon 'positively revered', urged greater US activism in the Arab–Israel dispute.

In December, Heath made an official visit to Washington. Heath left the Americans in no doubt about the new priorities in British policy. His overriding goal was Britain's entry into the Common Market. Once in, Britain would play a constructive role *vis-à-vis* the United States. But he could not negotiate European issues bilaterally with the USA. Nor could he act as America's Trojan Horse in Europe. 'No previous British Prime Minister', commented Kissinger, 'would have considered making such a statement to the American President.' Nixon's understanding reply could not obscure the fact that the Americans were witnessing a revolution in Britain's postwar foreign policy.

Kissinger notes that this had its positive aspects. Britain's influence was likely to be helpful in European counsels. Heath stressed the political benefit to the United States of British involvement in Europe.

> Heath was a new experience for American leaders: a British Prime Minister who based his policy towards the United States not on sentimental attachments but on a cool calculation of interest. At the same time his convictions so nearly coincided with ours that close collaboration would result from that self-interest.

In May 1971, Heath and the French President, Georges Pompidou, overcame the remaining obstacles to British entry to the European Community. It was Heath's greatest achievement. In December, Heath and Nixon met again in Bermuda. Heath sought to assure Nixon that European unity would be 'competitive', not confrontational. The Americans did not find this very reassuring. Heath then described his conception of consultation with the United States, which again was very different from that of his predecessors and successors. First, Europe should develop a common policy. Thereafter an effort would be made to coordinate with the United States. This was the antithesis of the 'special relationship' based on prior consultation between Britain and the United States. As Heath spoke more passionately than Pompidou about European defence, Nixon and

Kissinger realised that 'we faced in Heath the curiosity of a more benign British version of De Gaulle'.[1]

On non-European issues, there was more of a meeting of minds. Heath showed understanding for US policy in Vietnam. When the United States resumed the bombing of North Vietnam over Christmas, Heath, alone among the European leaders, refused to criticise it. This, Nixon told him, did not go unnoticed.

In February 1973, the Paris Agreement with the North Vietnamese was concluded. Kissinger was free to turn his attention once again to Western Europe. The Europeans soon found themselves regretting that Kissinger did not still have other preoccupations. On 1 January 1973, Britain had joined the EEC. Jean Monnet urged Kissinger to start treating Europe as a political unit and to force Europe into a system of consultation on that basis. Nixon queried whether this was in US interests, but Kissinger launched a round of aggressive consultations with the Europeans, starting in London:

> That we should choose Britain for the first of these consultations was natural; it was the essence of what was still called the 'special relationship'. For generations successive administrations had synchronized their moves with London, especially over the Atlantic Alliance. The British had fought for this tenaciously. Their way of retaining great-power status was to be so integral a part of American decision-making that the idea of not consulting them seemed a violation of the natural order of things. So able and self-assured were our British counterparts that they managed to convey the notion that it was they who were conferring a boon on us by sharing the experience of centuries. Nor were they quite wrong in this estimate. But this pattern was precisely what Heath was determined to change. He preferred a leading position in Europe to an honoured advisory role in Washington, and he did not consider the two functions compatible.

Heath's personality would have inhibited the 'special relationship' even if his convictions had not. To the Americans he seemed inflexible and doctrinaire. 'Of all British political leaders, Heath was the most indifferent to the American connection and perhaps even to Americans individually.'

Despite some personal friendship, Kissinger found him 'the most difficult British head of government we encountered'. To the Americans, he
appeared to envisage reducing the intimate consultation through which
British and American policies had been coordinated during the postwar
period to formal diplomatic exchanges. 'There was', concluded Kissinger,
'a stubborn, almost heroic, streak to Heath's policy. He sought to alter not
simply a diplomatic pattern but the attitude of his people.' The sympathies of most Britons were with the United States and the Commonwealth.
Europe for them began not in the British Isles but across the Channel. 'To
the majority of the British, entry into Europe reflected at best a distasteful
adjustment to necessity. Heath, on the other hand, not only accepted that
Britain's future lay with Europe, he preferred it that way.'

When Heath came to Washington in February 1973, as a sign of special regard, Nixon took the British Prime Minister to Camp David for
part of their discussions. Small talk was not the forte of either man; both
were better in set-piece discussions across a conference table. When the
presidential helicopter could not land at Camp David because of fog, the
journey had to be completed by car. Kissinger and the British Cabinet Secretary, Burke Trend, in the follow-up vehicle, had trouble imagining how
these two withdrawn men would conduct a social conversation in the back
seat of a car. Kissinger never learned what, if anything, was discussed; all
he got was Nixon's cryptic comment that it had been tough going.

In the discussions, Kissinger found that for Heath, re-designing the
Atlantic Alliance was not a priority. As usual, there was agreement on
world affairs – outside Europe. Kissinger wanted to set up joint study
groups to coordinate goals and strategies but Heath, politely, brushed this
aside. The Americans, initially, ascribed this to the fact that the still flour-
ishing 'special relationship' seemed to make new mechanisms unnecessary.
There were innumerable contacts taking place already, including regular
meetings between Kissinger and Trend.

But Heath's reluctance was based on his idea of how relations between
Europe and the United States should be conducted. He did not seek to dis-
mantle the existing mechanisms of Anglo-US consultation, which he saw as
providing useful early warning about US intentions. But he wanted Europe
as a unit to formulate a response to the Americans: he was determined to
avoid any whiff of Anglo-American collusion. Kissinger notes that Heath's
attitude was partly obscured by Douglas-Home – an instinctive Atlanticist

– and his colleagues in the Foreign Office 'who did their efficient best to hide the Prime Minister's foot-dragging'.

When Kissinger went to London in May, he found that Whitehall could not have been more understanding or more non-committal about his ideas for revitalising the Alliance. It was clear that Britain could not be counted on to take the lead in formulating a European response to Kissinger's initiative or to help in dealing with the French if they objected. No clearer demonstration could have been given of the new priority Heath gave to European over Atlantic relations.

In the course of this largely futile exercise, Nixon was surprised to receive a message from Heath emphasising that in future the nine European member states would share among themselves the information they obtained in bilateral exchanges with the Americans about US relations with the EEC. Kissinger now understood why the British Cabinet Secretary, Burke Trend, had recently been avoiding the kind of private consultations with him that every previous British government had so eagerly sought. Since the war, Britain had prided itself on a relationship based on a preferential position in Washington. But if every communication to London would automatically be distributed to the Nine, the relationship would hardly be 'special' any longer.

The Americans felt that they had been outmanoeuvred by the French. Kissinger did not appear to understand the extent to which the 'Year of Europe' initiative was felt to be misguided, not just by Heath, but also by the senior British officials with whom Kissinger was accustomed to deal. Heath was indebted to Pompidou for opening the way for Britain in Europe and he was determined to continue to nurture his relationship with the French. The British, on the other hand, were just as irritated as the Americans by the intransigence of Pompidou's new Foreign Minister, Michel Jobert.

Nixon sent Heath a reply of unusual coolness. It was, he said, for the Europeans to decide how to conduct their dialogue with the United States. When Trend visited Washington on 30 July, Kissinger had a 'painful session with my wise and trusted friend. We both realised that if these tendencies continued, we were at a turning point in Atlantic relations. For the sake of an abstract doctrine of European unity … something that had been nurtured for a generation was being given up.' Anglo-American relations had thrived on trust and consultation. They were now, Kissinger feared, being put in a straitjacket. Trend 'came as close to showing his distress as the code of discipline of the British Civil Service and his sense of honour permitted'. When the Americans complained at a British failure to consult them before tabling a text on Atlantic relations in NATO, the British replied that they already were in trouble with some members of the EEC over private consultations with the White House: 'We think wherever possible we should go for multilateral discussion from the outset.'

Kissinger by now was so fed up at Heath's insistence on being 'more European than the Europeans' that he decided to send the British a message by suspending intelligence sharing. The National Security Agency (NSA) responded that its relationship with GCHQ was governed by a binding international treaty. The CIA also continued some cooperation. But, for a while, US satellite imagery was withheld from the British, until Kissinger relented.[2] By now, the Watergate scandal was assuming serious dimensions. Kissinger began to tire of the whole exercise. Eventually a new, but not especially significant, Atlantic Declaration was signed. The 'Year of Europe' had run its course.

Kissinger, meanwhile, did seek British advice on some aspects of his dealings with the Soviet Union, in particular about Soviet ideas on the prevention of general nuclear war. The basic Soviet idea was that in the event of a conflict in Europe, nuclear weapons might be used – but only on the territory of each side's allies, not on that of the United States or the Soviet Union itself. Kissinger informed Trend and in August 1972 continued consultations with the leading Soviet expert and head of the Foreign Office, Sir Thomas Brimelow. Brimelow considered that the threat of war affecting their own territory was a key restraining influence on Soviet behaviour. They were trying to drive a wedge between the United States and its allies. Kissinger needed little convincing. In March 1973, he told Brimelow that the Soviet objective was to promote great-power bilateralism while seeking to create an impression of *détente*. Brimelow agreed, but pointed out that the long-term objective was to enmesh the Soviet Union in 'a less competitive relationship, and we cannot get there by telling them to go to hell'.

Brimelow saw his task as not to make American policy, but to seek to steer it in the safest direction. He proposed changing the Soviet proposal into a renunciation of the use of force. His role was an example of the 'special relationship' in action, even when the incumbent British Prime

Minister was not among its advocates: 'There was no other government which we would have dealt with so openly, exchanged ideas with so freely, or in effect permitted to participate in our own deliberations.' Brimelow drafted most of the American reply: and was in fact part-author of the Nixon–Brezhnev 'Agreement on the Prevention of Nuclear War'.[3]

On 6 October 1973, the Egyptians launched their surprise attack across the Suez Canal, while the Syrians drove into the Golan. British involvement in the ensuing crisis was marginal. On 11 October, Heath called Kissinger about the mounting pressure on King Hussein to do something on behalf of his Arab neighbours. Hussein wanted to move an armoured brigade into Syria, ostensibly to help the Syrians, but to be assured that the Israelis would not attack him if he did. The Israelis, not surprisingly, did not agree.

On the following day, Kissinger asked the British ambassador, Lord Cromer, to arrange for Britain to table a ceasefire resolution at the UN. The British were convinced that President Sadat would not accept a ceasefire without an Israeli commitment to withdraw. The Soviet ambassador, Anatoly Dobrynin, encouraged Kissinger to try. Kissinger told Cromer and urged the British to get on with their resolution 'before any of these maniacal parties change their minds'.

On 13 October, Douglas-Home called Kissinger. He was greatly admired by the Americans. Kissinger regarded him as no intellectual, but one of the wisest men he had known. He inspired confidence and was an unconditional friend of the United States. 'There was quite literally no one we trusted more.'

His response, therefore, came as an unpleasant shock. The British proposed a ceasefire in place, an international police force for the occupied territories, followed by an international conference. There was no chance of the Israelis accepting this and Kissinger told Cromer that, if necessary, the Americans would veto it. Dobrynin by now was backtracking and further British consultations with Sadat confirmed that he would not accept a ceasefire without Israeli withdrawal. With both the United States and the Soviet Union rushing arms supplies to their allies, Kissinger told Douglas-Home that events were driving them towards a confrontation.[4]

On 20 October, Kissinger flew to Moscow. Following the Israeli coun-terattack across the Suez Canal, the Egyptians by now were in a hopeless military situation. The UN Security Council adopted a joint US–Soviet proposal for a ceasefire. On his way back from Moscow and Tel Aviv, Kissinger stopped at London Airport to brief Douglas-Home. The British were worried that the ceasefire would not hold: fighting had broken out again on the West Bank of the Canal. Brezhnev held the Israelis respon-sible and Kissinger suspected that he was right. The Egyptian Third Army was completely cut off. Nixon was on the verge of impeachment over Watergate.

At 7 p.m. on 24 October, the Russians told Kissinger they wanted a UN resolution authorising the despatch of Russian – and American – troops to the area. Kissinger told Dobrynin the Americans would veto this and asked Cromer to get the British to join them. Next came a message from Brezhnev that if the Americans would not act jointly, the Russians would do so unilaterally. As Russian transport aircraft were readied to fly to Egypt, Kissinger and the National Security Council decided, as a clear warning to the Russians, to put US forces on a heightened state of alert – DEFCON III. Cromer was told at 1 a.m. of Brezhnev's message and the US response. He also was told that the Americans would be looking for British support in the North Atlantic Council.

Kissinger regarded this as a classical example of the 'special relation-ship' in action – as well as of the limits of Allied consultation. The US shared its information with Britain as a matter of course, despite the fact that the Heath government was doing its utmost to distance itself from the Americans in Europe and had clearly emphasised its different perspec-tive in the Middle East.

No other ally was informed and the French, in particular, reacted with outrage. At 5.40 a.m. the formal American reply was delivered to Dobrynin. It offered American involvement in supervising a ceasefire but made clear that any unilateral action by the Soviet Union would produce 'incalcula-ble consequences'. Cromer told the Americans that the British government took Brezhnev's message in the same way as they did: the British ambassa-dor in Moscow was instructed to warn the Russians strongly against any unilateral military action. The Egyptians, by this time, were proposing an international force, which the Russians accepted. There were further dif-ficulties with the Israelis, who were unwilling to relax their hold on the

Third Army. But by 28 October Kissinger was able to arrange direct military talks between the combatants and the ceasefire held.

The crisis and in particular the nuclear alert left deep bruises among the Allies, unhappy at the willingness of the United States to risk a confrontation with the Soviet Union on behalf of Israel. The French Foreign Minister, Michel Jobert, was most strident in his denunciations of the United States, but there was unhappiness also in Britain, particularly when Kissinger said that countries that were most consulted had proved among the most difficult in their cooperation. Heath told the American correspondents in Britain on 28 November that there had never been a joint understanding between the United States and Europe on the Middle East. He recalled the differences over Suez and that the Middle East was outside the NATO area. Since the 1967 war, he argued, the United States had had ample opportunity to bring pressure on Israel to negotiate and had done nothing. This, he suggested, had made another war inevitable.

The following day, Douglas-Home sought to undo some of the damage in a personal letter to Kissinger. He emphasised that the Alliance was the lynchpin of Britain's foreign and defence policy. But, he said: 'I do not think you would feel us to be of much value as a friend and ally if we support American policy blindly, even when we think it wrong.' Britain, he pointed out, for years had advocated a different policy on the Arab–Israel dispute. The British would firmly support the United States on East–West issues that could lead to serious confrontation. But the Americans must take their friends more fully into their confidence, particularly on the Middle East.

———————

Unlike Heath, Kissinger comments, Douglas-Home did not see Britain's European vocation as requiring a loosening of transatlantic ties. Throughout this difficult period, he had spared no effort to stabilise transatlantic relations. Addressing a meeting of the Pilgrims Society in London on 12 December, Kissinger said that some Europeans had come to believe that their identity should be measured by distance from the United States. Formal consultative machinery could not replace the 'whole network of intangible connections that have been the real sinews of the transatlantic and especially the Anglo-American relationship'. In retrospect, Kissinger recognised that he should have made a greater effort to keep the other allies, and not only the British, more closely informed during the crisis. But there remained a major difference of policy in the Middle East. The British, like most of the other Europeans, perceived their interests as lying mainly with the Arabs. The Arab oil embargo threatened European interests far more than those of the United States. At the same time, as Kissinger's efforts had made embarrassingly clear, only the Americans had any real influence with the parties.[5]

35

'HE WANTED TO ESTABLISH HIS OWN SPECIAL RELATIONSHIP'

ON 28 FEBRUARY 1974, the Heath government was defeated in the British elections. When Kissinger passed through London a month later, the Labour Foreign Secretary, Jim Callaghan, told him that he wanted to put an end to the antagonisms with the United States that had developed under Heath. Callaghan was far from sharing Heath's enthusiasm for the EEC – he was to spend much of his time as Foreign Secretary 'renegotiating' the terms of British entry – and was a committed Atlanticist. Nixon's presidency by now was in its death throes and Wilson, in contrast to his first term, largely left foreign policy to Callaghan.[1]

In July, Kissinger saw Callaghan in London to brief him on the outcome of the last Nixon-Brezhnev summit in Moscow. The British had been worried that the Americans might give way to Soviet demands for the inclusion of British and French nuclear forces in the SALT negotiations. Kissinger reassured Callaghan on that score.

In mid-July, the Makarios government in Cyprus was overthrown in a coup inspired by the Greek military junta in Athens. Makarios escaped with the aid of the RAF. The coup leaders proclaimed the union of Cyprus with Greece. The crisis came at the worst possible time for the United States – Nixon was within days of resigning. Callaghan urged the Americans to use their influence with the Greek colonels to get rid of the coup leader, Nicos Sampson. He recognised that the Americans had far more influence in both Athens and Ankara. Kissinger did not want Sampson to remain in power, but was lukewarm about the return of Makarios.

While this exchange was taking place, Turkish forces invaded Cyprus. Callaghan was telephoned by Kissinger at 4.20 a.m. on 20 July to be told of the attack. During the weekend, he and Kissinger spoke repeatedly on the telephone. Kissinger tried to stop the Turkish offensive, and Callaghan supported his efforts with the Turks, who swiftly occupied the northern third of the island. As the Turks closed in on Nicosia, Callaghan reinforced the garrison in the British military base at the airport and provided it with air support, helping to check the Turkish advance. The Turks having attained their main objectives, a ceasefire was agreed. In Athens, the Greek military government was overthrown. But the Turks continued to pressure the UN and British forces in Nicosia.

At Callaghan's request, Kissinger delivered a further warning to Ankara. Callaghan, concerned about the threat to British troops, wanted him to threaten an American military response. This Kissinger, determined to preserve relations with Turkey, declined to do. But he did make a personal appeal to the Turkish Prime Minister, Bulent Ecevit. Callaghan believed that more forceful intervention by the United States could have prevented the Turkish invasion or deterred the Turks from advancing as far as they did.

Kissinger disagreed. He believed that once the coup leaders had proclaimed union with Greece, Turkish intervention was inevitable. But Kissinger was caught up in the drama of Nixon's last days in office. He told the British ambassador that the crisis in Washington had caused him at times to lose touch with Cyprus developments. He was irritated by British suggestions that he had not exerted himself enough.[2]

But this did not affect his relationship with Callaghan. Learning that Callaghan was to be honoured by the city of Cardiff, Kissinger flew across the Atlantic to join in the celebrations. On the day, Callaghan records, 'it seemed that every demonstrator in the United Kingdom had descended on Cardiff from afar, waving protest banners about Kissinger's various alleged misdemeanours'. Their views, Callaghan notes, did not appear to be shared by the ordinary people of Cardiff, who greeted Kissinger warmly.[3]

While Wilson largely left the conduct of foreign policy to Callaghan, in August 1974 he wrote to commiserate with Nixon on his resignation after Watergate: 'There is a widespread understanding and appreciation in Britain of the courage which this decision required of you.' As the government faced increasing economic problems, in October 1974 Wilson wrote to President Gerald Ford to tell him that he was obliged to make further defence cuts. These included accelerated withdrawal from east of Suez, a reduction of British forces in Germany and a cutback in naval forces assigned to NATO. Ford reacted calmly, but worried about the effect on others and hoped that Britain would retain its capability to act outside Europe: '[F]or obvious reasons the United States should not be the only Western power which is capable of intervening on a world-wide scale.' Wilson replied that 'we can no longer spread our forces around the world on the scale we have hitherto done'. Yet Wilson was convinced that his standing was high in Washington. Relations with the United States were as good as they had ever been, he told the Cabinet after a visit there in February 1975: '[T]he ceremonies of welcome went far beyond anything I have had before.'[4]

Late one evening in February 1976, Wilson's friend, George Weidenfeld, was asked to meet the Prime Minister at 10 Downing Street. Wilson feared that there was an intelligence cabal against him and wanted to discover if the CIA were involved in it. Weidenfeld approached George Bush, newly appointed as head of the CIA, who was disconcerted to receive this enquiry, but undertook to look into it. Having done so, he assured Weidenfeld that nothing was being undertaken against the Prime Minister.[5]

In March 1976, Harold Wilson surprised his colleagues by suddenly resigning and Callaghan became Prime Minister. With sterling again in crisis, the British sought support from President Ford and his Treasury Secretary, but met with a discouraging reply. In September, the Chancellor of the Exchequer, Denis Healey, about to leave for an IMF meeting, was forced to return from the airport by a further collapse of sterling. George Meany, head of the American labour federation, wrote to President Ford urging him to help 'America's oldest and most steadfast friend'. Ford did offer to help – provided the Labour government did not impose restrictions on imports as some members of the party were demanding. But in November he lost the presidential election to Jimmy Carter.

The Americans were adamant that Britain must negotiate a loan with the IMF. When Healey did so, he found, as Callaghan put it, that 'times had changed and the examination of our affairs was much more rigorous'. Callaghan sent a member of his Cabinet, Harold Lever, to Washington to enlist Ford's support in, by now, the dying days of his administration. Neither Ford nor Kissinger could overcome the opposition of Arthur Burns, head of the Federal Reserve Board, who declined flatly to discuss any kind of safety net for sterling until the Callaghan government had reached agreement with the IMF on reductions in public expenditure.[6]

Despite these economic woes, Callaghan was trusted by the Americans as a good friend of the Alliance and of the United States. In February 1977, David Owen succeeded Anthony Crosland as Foreign Secretary. Anxious to forge close contacts with the incoming Carter administration, Owen proposed the replacement of the British ambassador in Washington, Sir Peter Ramsbotham, by Callaghan's son-in-law, Peter Jay. Owen wanted a younger ambassador and one more in touch with his own views. The appointment was controversial, but Jay did establish a good relationship with some key members of the Carter White House.

In March 1977, Callaghan saw the new President in Washington. As his Foreign Secretary, Owen, notes, 'as a dyed-in-the-wool Atlanticist, he wanted to establish his own special relationship with the new President'. He was quickly made to understand that he would be dealing with a very different type of politician. Callaghan described dinner with Carter at the White House at which all those present were invited to clasp hands around the table while the President said grace.[7] When his Vice-President, Walter Mondale, called on Callaghan in London, he was liberally entertained by the Prime Minister. Next morning the British discovered that one of Mondale's staff had taken the wine list back to his hotel and priced it – then told the press that the Labour government lived in a state of decadent luxury that the President would never tolerate in Washington.

Nevertheless, Carter's national security adviser, Zbigniew Brzezinski, pays tribute to Callaghan's skill in cultivating Carter personally:

> I was amazed how quickly Callaghan succeeded in establishing himself as Carter's favorite, writing him friendly little notes, calling, talking like a genial older uncle, and lecturing Carter in a pleasant manner on the intricacies of inter-allied politics. Callaghan literally co-opted Carter in the course of a few relatively brief personal encounters.[8]

Carter was due to attend the economic summit in London in May. Callaghan, who wanted to show him something of modern-day Britain, persuaded Carter to visit Newcastle and Washington New Town on Tyneside. The Downing Street summit was difficult. Carter wanted the German

Chancellor, Helmut Schmidt, and the French President, Valéry Giscard d'Estaing, to halt the export of nuclear reactors to Brazil and Pakistan. After some discussion, a study group was set up to consider what more could be done about nuclear proliferation. The European heads of government argued in vain that the United States should do more to stabilise the dollar.

In February 1978, Callaghan proposed to Carter concerted action by the principal Western governments to revive the world economy. The British hoped thereby to pressure the Americans to support the dollar and the Germans and Japanese to reduce their large payment surpluses. Callaghan visited Washington to pursue this with Carter, who was preoccupied with the effort to broker the Camp David accord between Sadat and the Israeli Prime Minister, Menachem Begin. Callaghan stressed the disadvantages of the depreciation of the dollar, but found the Treasury Secretary, Michael Blumenthal, unimpressed by his suggestion that the aim should be to develop a new reserve currency. Giscard and Schmidt proceeded instead to establish the European Exchange Rate Mechanism, which Callaghan declined to join because of the probable deflationary effects in Britain of tying sterling to the deutschmark.

The British found the Carter administration difficult to deal with in foreign policy, in part because of continuing disagreements between Carter's respected but remarkably unassertive Secretary of State, Cyrus Vance, and Brzezinski, who saw himself as applying a necessary dose of *realpolitik*. David Owen devoted much of his time to working out with Vance Anglo-American proposals to end the war in Rhodesia and bring the country to independence on the basis of one man, one vote. While this served the purpose of locking the Americans into support for the British government's policy in southern Africa, the difficulty with the proposals, as Owen on one occasion observed, was that no one except the British and Americans agreed with them. They were rejected both by the Smith government and by the African liberation movements. Their chances of forming the basis for a settlement suffered a fatal setback when President Carter, without consulting the British, declared that the future army must be based on the liberation forces. This gave Ian Smith and his allies the chance they had been looking for to block all further progress. Vance and Owen toured Africa in vain pursuit of a settlement. They also sought to work out plans for internationally supervised elections in Namibia. Despite the lack of success at the time, Owen did forge a close working relationship and enduring friendship with Vance.

The relationship with the United States continued to be affected by Britain's chronic economic weakness. Callaghan told Carter that the IMF was insisting on draconian actions to curb the deficit. When Carter asked if he could help, Callaghan said no: 'I want them to force me and my government to do what I know is right.'[9]

In January 1979, Callaghan attended a final meeting with Carter, Schmidt and Giscard in Guadeloupe. Callaghan was disappointed that Carter, under the influence of the Joint Chiefs of Staff, had cooled on the idea of a comprehensive nuclear test ban. The Russians were engaged in an aggressive programme of modernisation of their intermediate-range nuclear missiles and clearly were intent on deploying the new and more capable SS20s, targeted on Western Europe. Schmidt had argued in a speech to the London Institute of Strategic Studies in 1977 that the SALT negotiations tended to neutralise the nuclear capacities of the superpowers and that Soviet intermediate-range missile deployments must be matched or dealt with through arms control. These missiles fell into a 'grey area' not covered by SALT. Carter wanted the Western allies to back him when the SALT II treaty went to the Senate for ratification. British and French nuclear forces had again been excluded from the SALT II negotiations, but many Carter officials doubted if they could be excluded from an eventual SALT III or from negotiations on shorter-range nuclear weapons in Europe.

The meeting in Guadeloupe was as informal as the French could make it. Few staff members were present. Carter jogged. Giscard played tennis. Callaghan took Carter to visit a British frigate. To his colleagues, Carter outlined the state of the SALT II negotiations. Callaghan expressed support, but Schmidt was concerned that the agreement could increase European insecurity by rendering it more doubtful that the United States would be prepared to defend Europe with its strategic nuclear arsenal. The SS20s, meanwhile, posed an increased threat to West Germany. Carter said that the United States would be willing to build and deploy Pershing II missiles and ground-launched Cruise missiles to counter the threat and increase the West's negotiating leverage. But this would depend on a commitment from the Europeans to deploy the missiles if negotiations failed. Schmidt said that he would agree to deployment in Germany only if other European countries did the same. Callaghan pointed out that Britain already had US Polaris submarines and nuclear-armed F-111 bombers based on its territory. Giscard would not permit US missiles to be deployed on French territory. He also made clear that the French would not be prepared to see their nuclear forces included in any future SALT agreement.

During his visit to Guadeloupe, Callaghan took the opportunity to speak to President Carter about the future of the British nuclear deterrent. The Polaris submarine forces would remain in service until the late 1990s, but a decision would be required by 1980 if Polaris was to be replaced. Callaghan had commissioned a study of the options and held a preliminary discussion with his Cabinet colleagues at which the conclusion was reached that British studies could not go much further without consultation with the United States. It was agreed that Callaghan should talk to Carter, without commitment, to explore the possible options. The aim was to discover whether and in what form American help would be forthcoming if the British government decided on a successor to Polaris. The Labour Party conference had declared itself against the replacement of Polaris and Callaghan knew that he would have a battle royal ahead within his party. He told his colleagues that if it were decided to replace Polaris, the best option probably would be to negotiate with the Americans to gain access to the successor system – Trident submarines equipped with C4 missiles.

In Guadeloupe, Callaghan walked the few yards across the grass to Carter's hut and found him resting. No one else was present during their talk but, afterwards, Callaghan reported the substance to the Cabinet Secretary. He told Carter about the report he had commissioned and that he could not proceed further until he received some indication of the US attitude. He said that, in his view, the balance of advantage to Britain itself in procuring a successor to Polaris would be marginal. There was a good case to argue that available resources could be used to better effect on the strengthening of Britain's conventional forces. But Britain had a responsibility not only for her own defence, but also for the defence of Europe. Schmidt had told Callaghan that Germany would prefer that France was not the sole European power possessing nuclear weapons; he would feel more comfortable if Britain also were in the field.

Carter said that, like Schmidt, he too was glad that Britain possessed a nuclear deterrent. He hoped that Britain, as well as France, would remain a nuclear power. It was better that there should be a shared responsibility in Europe. Carter asked Callaghan what replacement for Polaris the British government envisaged. Callaghan said that the Labour government was not committed to a successor to Polaris, but he thought the system most likely to meet British requirements, if they decided to go ahead, was Trident. Carter said that he could see no objection to transferring this technology to Britain and this would assist the United States with the unit costs of production. Callaghan said that cost would be a key factor. He had seen a figure of $10 billion mentioned. This would be beyond Britain's resources. Carter said that he thought it would be possible to work out satisfactory terms. Two senior officials, Professor Mason and Sir Clive Rose, were sent to Washington to discuss the technical and financial aspects. Both Callaghan and Owen wanted to maintain the British nuclear deterrent. But the Labour manifesto declared that the party had renounced any intention of moving towards a successor for Polaris. On 4 May 1979, the day after his election defeat, Callaghan wrote a minute summarising his exchanges with President Carter on this subject and authorising this information to be made available to his successor.[10]

36

'YOUR PROBLEMS WILL BE OUR PROBLEMS AND WHEN YOU LOOK FOR FRIENDS, WE WILL BE THERE'

CALLAGHAN'S VISIT TO Guadeloupe did not help his re-election prospects. As Denis Healey recalls, pictures of the Prime Minister in the tropical sun did not improve the temper of ordinary men and women suffering from a series of major public sector strikes through a miserable winter. Exhausted by the battles within his party and with the unions, Callaghan had little confidence in a Labour victory. There were times, he noted, when there was a sea change in politics – a shift in what the public wanted and what it approved of. He suspected that there might be such a sea change and that it was for Mrs Thatcher.[1]

In September 1975, Margaret Thatcher had made her first visit to the United States as leader of the Conservative Party. The main emphasis in her public speeches was on the need to roll back the 'persistent expansion' of the role of the state in the economy. This was a popular theme in the United States, not only among Republicans. She quickly established a particular rapport with American audiences. In the debate in Britain about the relationship with Europe and the United States, there never was any doubt where her loyalties lay.

She had no great regard for President Carter and certainly did not see him as a kindred spirit. She had met him in London in May 1977, when they had disagreed about Rhodesia. As Prime Minister, her first encounter with him was at the economic summit in Tokyo in July 1979. She recorded her impressions of the President:

> It was impossible not to like Jimmy Carter. He was a deeply committed Christian and a man of obvious sincerity. He was also a man of marked intellectual ability with a grasp, rare among politicians, of science and the scientific method. But he had come into office as the beneficiary of Watergate rather than because he had persuaded Americans of the rightness of his analysis of the world around them.
>
> And, indeed, that analysis was badly flawed. He had an unsure handle on economics and was therefore inclined to drift into a futile *ad hoc* interventionism when problems arose ... In foreign affairs, he was over-influenced by the doctrines then gaining ground in the Democratic Party that the threat from Communism had been exaggerated and that US intervention in support of right-wing dictators was almost as culpable. Hence he found himself surprised and embarrassed by such events as the Soviet invasion of Afghanistan and Iran's seizure of American diplomats as hostages ...
>
> In addition to these political flaws, he was in some ways personally ill-suited to the presidency, agonising over big decisions and too concerned with detail. Finally, he violated Napoleon's rule that generals should be lucky. His presidency was dogged with bad luck from OPEC to Afghanistan. What it served to demonstrate, however, was that in leading a great nation decency and assiduousness are not enough. Having said which, I repeat that I liked Jimmy Carter; he was a good friend to me and to Britain.[2]

If Carter had been re-elected, Margaret Thatcher would have found a way to get on with him and in fact, so long as he remained in office, she was more supportive than other European leaders, especially Helmut Schmidt. She received assurances that the SALT II agreement between Carter and Brezhnev in June 1979 would not affect the British nuclear deterrent. Her main objective was to get the United States to agree to provide Britain with the Trident C4 missile system to replace Polaris. Although President Carter told her that he would supply whatever was needed, he was worried that an announcement of his decision would cause him political difficulties. He also worried that the Soviet Union might respond with some action that would increase the difficulties of getting the US Senate to ratify SALT II. Mrs Thatcher showed strong support for the NATO decision to deploy new American Pershing II and ground-launched Cruise missiles (GLCMs) in Western Europe if the Russians did not remove the threat posed by the SS20s.

In December, she made her first visit to Washington as Prime Minister. It was a month after the American hostages had been seized in Tehran. Over economic sanctions against Iran, she stated, the Americans would expect and get nothing less than Britain's full support.

Mrs Thatcher's prestige was helped by the fact that her visit coincided with a British diplomatic success. The first and most pressing external problem with which she had to deal was Rhodesia. The Anglo-American plan pursued by Vance and Owen had failed. She and her Foreign Secretary, Lord Carrington, decided to scrap it and launch a purely British initiative to end the war – for which, however, they still sought American support. The Carter administration was relieved to let the British deal with this intractable problem, but suspicious that Thatcher's sympathies lay with Bishop Muzorewa and the white Rhodesians. When the Rhodesia Conference was convened by Lord Carrington in London in September, they gave it little chance of success. But as the rival parties were coerced into a series of agreements, the Americans became active supporters of the process. There still was a period of tension, towards the end of the conference, when the British sent Lord Soames to Rhodesia as Governor before final agreement was reached and insisted that, to pressurise Nkomo and Mugabe into participating, sanctions should be lifted forthwith. The Carter administration, after some hesitation, did lift sanctions. Final agreement in the conference was reached and announced by Mrs Thatcher at the dinner in her honour at the White House.

The Soviet invasion of Afghanistan killed off the chances of ratification of SALT II. But at this point the Carter administration said that it was reluctant to announce the decision to supply Trident to Britain because it might be seen as an overreaction to events in Afghanistan. It also was worried about the attitude of Chancellor Schmidt. In return for supplying Trident, the Carter administration wanted a British commitment to increase its defence effort and allow the United States to develop its defence facilities in the Indian Ocean at Diego Garcia.

On 2 June 1980, Mrs Thatcher was able to finalise the terms for the acquisition of Trident with the US Defense Secretary, Harold Brown, at a meeting in Downing Street. The British agreed to pay 5 per cent towards the costs of development of the missile and to bear the cost of manning the Rapier air defence system for the US bases in Britain. Mrs Thatcher agreed to increased US use of Diego Garcia.

Despite her success in persuading Carter to supply Britain with Trident – the most advanced strategic nuclear weapon system in the US armoury – Mrs Thatcher hoped that Ronald Reagan would win the presidential election. She had met him in London in 1975 and learned to take him more seriously than most other British politicians deigned to do: 'I knew that I was talking to some-one who instinctively felt and thought as I did.' Reagan, for his part, concluded that 'we were really akin with regard to our view of government and economics and government's place in people's lives'.[3] He met her again in London in 1978 and was among the first to congratulate her on her election victory. On 4 November 1980, Reagan, confounding most of the Washington pundits, won the US presidential election.

Reagan's style of government could scarcely have been more different from that of Thatcher. He worked rather less than half as hard as she did and rarely attempted to master any detailed argument. This led most of his peers to underestimate him, both in Washington and abroad. The Prime Minister did not make that mistake:

> It was easy for lesser men to underrate Ronald Reagan, as many of his opponents had done in the past. His style of work and decision-making was apparently detached and broad-brush – very different from my own. This was in part the result of our two very different systems of government ... He laid down clear general directions for his Administration, and expected his subordinates to carry them out at the level of detail. These objectives were the recovery of the American economy through tax cuts, the revival of American power by means of a defence build-up, and the reassertion of American self-confidence. Ronald Reagan succeeded in attaining these objectives because he had not only advocated them; in a sense, he embodied them.

Reagan, observed Mrs Thatcher, was not shy about using American power or exercising US leadership in the Alliance. But he still had to face a largely sceptical audience at home and particularly among his allies, 'including most of my colleagues in government'.

Reagan made clear that he wanted Margaret Thatcher to be his first major foreign visitor. They met in Washington a month after his inauguration and she was given an exceptionally warm reception. 'It is widely known that I share many of your ideals and beliefs,' Reagan told her at the state dinner at the White House.

Mrs Thatcher was accompanied by the Foreign Secretary, Peter Carrington, who 'did not altogether share my view of the President's policies and was intent on pursuing lines which I knew would in fact be quite fruitless, given the President's unshakable commitment to a limited number of positions'. The Prime Minister declined to press on Reagan Carrington's worries about US policy in Salvador and Namibia: 'There is one principle of diplomacy which diplomats ought to recognise more often: there is no point in engaging in conflict with a friend when you are not going to win and the cost of losing may be the end of the friendship.'[4] She was, unwittingly, echoing Winston Churchill, who had told Anthony Eden how foolish it was to quarrel with the Americans about 'petty issues like Guatemala'.

Despite her recognition of his qualities as a political leader, Mrs Thatcher was disconcerted by the President's total lack of interest in detail. She worried about his intention to cut taxes without regard to the effect this would have on the US budget deficit (described by her press secretary, Bernard Ingham, as a 'constant source of worry to her prudent soul'). But on the White House lawn, she declared her intentions unequivocally: 'The message I have brought across the Atlantic is that we in Britain stand with you … Your problems will be our problems, and when you look for friends we will be there.'

They met again at the Ottawa Summit in July 1981, where Reagan found her an ally in the economic discussions. British support, however, was far more crucial on the nuclear issues. The NATO decision to deploy new missiles in Europe to counter the Soviet SS20s triggered anti-nuclear demonstrations throughout Western Europe. Schmidt said that Germany could not accept the missiles unless other allies did so as well. Only Britain, Belgium and the Netherlands agreed to take them and, given the degree of political resistance, many in the US administration doubted if they would ever be deployed. In a private meeting with Reagan, Mrs Thatcher expressed her concern about the US administration's rhetoric. She urged him to discourage talk of a 'rising tide of neutralism' in Europe: such warnings could prove self-fulfilling.

She feared that a failure of the planned deployment of Cruise and Pershing missiles would wreck the Alliance. As the British pressed the new administration to make an imaginative negotiating offer, Richard Perle, advising Defense Secretary Caspar Weinberger, responded by coming up with one more imaginative than the British had wished. Under the so-called 'zero option', no Pershing IIs and ground-launched Cruise missiles would be deployed in Western Europe – provided the Russians agreed to withdraw *and destroy* all the SS20s. This was thought to be non-negotiable and many suspected that Perle had put it forward precisely for that reason. Demonstrations continued and intensified in the countries due to receive the missiles.

In July 1980, Mrs Thatcher had exchanged letters with President Carter undertaking to buy American C4 missiles for the future British Trident submarine force on favourable terms. Within a few months of coming into office, however, Reagan cancelled further production of the C4, moving instead to a new and more powerful missile, the D5. The British, with Weinberger's strong support, re-negotiated the agreement to enable them to obtain the new missiles. The Americans were alarmed by the cuts in the Royal Navy being made by Thatcher's Defence Secretary, John Nott. They urged the British to reconsider their plans for the early phasing-out of the two amphibious assault vessels – *Intrepid* and *Fearless* – both of which were to play a crucial role in the Falklands. In return, Weinberger offered an agreement which the British regarded as more advantageous than the original Trident terms.

This did not prevent a sharp disagreement breaking out in December 1981 over the response to the Soviet-inspired imposition of martial law in Poland. Reagan imposed sanctions against the Soviet Union, including a ban on the sale of any equipment for the Russian oil and gas pipelines planned to bring gas from Siberia to Western Europe. Mrs Thatcher supported some economic sanctions herself, but reacted strongly to attempts by the Reagan administration to penalise British companies with existing contracts. She did not mind the US administration prohibiting sales by companies based in the US (though she noted that Reagan had exempted the giant US heavy vehicle manufacturer Caterpillar from his own sanctions). But she objected fiercely, then and later, to US attempts to interfere directly with the activities of companies based in Britain and, worse still, to do so with retroactive effect.

Fearing further US measures, in a January 1983 meeting in Downing Street, Mrs Thatcher told Reagan's Secretary of State, Al Haig, that she did not favour pushing Poland into default. Nor did she believe that West Germany would give up the Soviet gas pipeline. The ban on components for the pipeline would be very damaging to a British company, John Brown Ltd. Haig did little to reassure her, indicating that Weinberger and others were pushing for still tougher sanctions.[5]

There also were some fierce disagreements, this time between Carrington and Haig, over the Middle East. The Reagan administration was determined to develop the concept, initiated under Carter, of a Rapid Deployment Force able to intervene, if necessary, in the event of a threat to oil supplies from the Gulf. This caused some alarm in London.

Haig was bent on holding Begin to his agreement under the Camp David accord to return Sinai to Egypt and wanted British participation in a multinational force there. The other Arabs – and the British – were insisting that more must be done for the Palestinians. Carrington's support for a Saudi plan to involve them in the negotiations brought, as he recalls, Anglo-American relations to a 'somewhat chilly condition', with Haig hinting publicly that this kind of behaviour could cause the Americans to think twice about their contribution to European defence.[6]

Haig felt that he had to do the real work of getting Israel out of Sinai while the Europeans sought to curry favour with the Arabs. The *New York Times* cited Haig as referring in a State Department meeting to the British Foreign Secretary as a 'duplicitous bastard'! Haig subsequently apologised to Carrington and in April 1982 the Sinai was returned to Egypt. But the Begin government put the Americans on notice that they intended to deal militarily with the threat to Israel's security from southern Lebanon. In the British and European view, Haig did little to dissuade them.

It was at this stage that there developed, almost out of the blue, a crisis that put the Anglo-American relationship to the most severe test since Suez.

37

'THAT LITTLE ICE-COLD BUNCH OF LAND DOWN THERE'

ON 19 MARCH 1982, a party of Argentine 'scrap metal merchants' landed on the Falklands' dependency of South Georgia without permission from the British authorities and raised the Argentine flag. The Governor of the Falklands suspected that the Argentine intention was to create a permanent presence and a party of Argentine marines subsequently was landed to 'protect' them. Against the strong objections of the Foreign Secretary, Lord Carrington, the British Defence Secretary, John Nott, had announced plans to withdraw the sole British naval vessel, HMS *Endurance*, from the South Atlantic as part of the 1981 defence review marked by swingeing cuts to the Royal Navy. But the ship was now sent to remove the Argentine party from South Georgia.

Argentine expectations earlier had been aroused by the pursuit of the possibility of a transfer of sovereignty accompanied by a 'lease-back' of the islands to the British, favoured by the Foreign Office, but opposed both by the islanders and Conservative backbenchers. Following a breakdown in talks about the Falklands between the British and representatives of the Argentine military junta in New York in February, the Argentines had issued a threatening communiqué, accompanied by a press campaign hinting at unilateral action. The British minister responsible for the talks, Richard Luce, saw the American Assistant Secretary for Latin American Affairs, Thomas Enders, in Washington and urged him to get the Argentines to cool things down. Enders undertook to do so during his visit to Buenos Aires on 6–7 March.

Lord Carrington sent a personal message to the US Secretary of State, Al Haig, via the British embassy in Washington on 8 March. It expressed the British government's increasing concern about the Argentine government's attitude, and the threats in the Argentine press, apparently with government inspiration, to use force if the negotiations did not soon reach a conclusion on Argentine terms. It said that Haig would realise that it was politically impossible to negotiate against such a background, so that anything that Enders could do to bring the Argentines to a more reasonable frame of mind would be appreciated. Carrington expressed the hope that the British government could count on Haig's help in ensuring that the issue was settled peacefully and in accordance with the democratically expressed wishes of the islanders.

In his reply on 15 March, Haig said that Enders had urged the Argentines to continue negotiations. They had been non-committal, but not negative. The Americans would continue to urge a constructive approach with due regard for all the interests at stake.[1]

In mid-March, Foreign and Commonwealth Office ministers received intelligence that Enders had been told during his visit that Argentina planned to mount an international diplomatic offensive if there were no immediate signs of British willingness to bring negotiations to a conclusion within the next year. Enders apparently had indicated that the US government would see no problem with this.

On 25 March, information was received in London about the despatch of Argentine warships to prevent HMS *Endurance* evacuating the Argentine personnel from South Georgia. On the evening of Sunday 28 March, Carrington sent Haig a message that Britain wanted to resolve the problem peacefully, but the continued presence of the Argentines was an infringement of sovereignty. Haig was asked to intervene with the Argentine authorities. On the following day, the British government decided to send a nuclear-powered submarine to support *Endurance*, but the submarine could not reach the islands until mid-April.

The British ambassador in Washington, Sir Nicholas Henderson, saw Haig's deputy, Walter Stoessel, on the afternoon of 29 March. Stoessel relayed Haig's concern that both parties should show restraint and, to Henderson's fury, insistence that the United States would not take sides. Henderson replied that the Americans could surely not be neutral in a case of illegal occupation of sovereign British territory. He left Stoessel in no doubt that, while the British government remained anxious to keep the temperature down, they could not allow Argentina to assert a claim in this way to a British possession.

On the following day, 30 March, Carrington summoned the US *chargé d'affaires*, Ed Streator, to protest at Haig putting the British position on the same footing as that of Argentina. By this stage an Argentine task force, including an aircraft carrier, four destroyers and an amphibious landing ship, was known to be at sea on 'exercises' north of the Falklands. The US ambassador in Buenos Aires reported that he had got nowhere with an offer of American good offices which he had put to the Argentines. Carrington, meanwhile, left on a visit to Israel.[2]

On 31 March, John Nott was briefed about intelligence that the Argentines had decided to take action at dawn on 2 April. Following a meeting with the Prime Minister, a message was drafted and sent to President Reagan. The Prime Minister referred to intelligence indicating that an Argentine invasion of the Falklands might be imminent and said that the British government could not acquiesce in any Argentine occupation. She asked Reagan to talk urgently to President Galtieri and ask for an immediate assurance that he would not authorise any landing, let alone hostilities. She said that the President could tell Galtieri that the British government would not escalate the dispute or start a conflict. Henderson was asked to speak to Haig to ensure a rapid reaction from the White House.

Henderson and I saw Haig at 7 p.m. on 31 March. As Henderson took him through the intelligence reports demonstrating that Argentina was about to take military action, Haig expressed amazement that his own intelligence services had not alerted him to the threat themselves. They soon provided confirmation of the British assessment. Haig instructed the US ambassador in Buenos Aires to warn the Argentines to take no steps that would aggravate the crisis. But Haig still was saying that he thought the United States would have a greater chance of influencing Argentine behaviour if they appeared not to favour one side or the other.[3]

As the American ambassador's efforts proved futile, on 1 April the British urged President Reagan to telephone Galtieri in a last-ditch attempt to dissuade him from proceeding with the invasion. This Reagan attempted to do. For several hours Galtieri refused to take the call and when he did take it, he appeared to have been drinking. Reagan urged in forceful terms that Argentina should not take action against the Falklands, which, he said, the British would regard as a *casus belli*. Galtieri kept saying that the die was cast. He rejected Reagan's offer to send Vice-President Bush to Buenos Aires to help find a solution. Mrs Thatcher was woken up at 4 a.m. by Henderson to tell her that the last effort to prevent the invasion had failed. He found her not at all in a bellicose mood and fully aware of the dangers that lay ahead.[4] A few hours later the Argentines landed overwhelming forces on the islands, capturing and disarming the small British garrison of Royal Marines.

On the evening of 31 March, John Nott had told the Prime Minister about the firm intelligence that Argentina intended to occupy the islands. He added that in the Ministry of Defence's view, they could not be re-taken, advice instantly rejected by her. At this point, salvation appeared in the form of the First Sea Lord, Admiral Sir Henry Leach, who told her that in forty-eight hours he could despatch a task force to re-take the islands. The operation would be fraught with risk but, otherwise, they would henceforth be living 'in another country, whose word will count for little', with which she whole-heartedly agreed. Lord Carrington resigned, replaced as Foreign Secretary by Francis Pym, an unfortunate choice, given the lack of any real rapport or trust between him and the Prime Minister, who later complained that she had exchanged an amusing Whig for a gloomy one.

The task force was assembled and despatched with astonishing speed. From the outset, American cooperation was vital. The Americans were informed that the British would need to make full use of the US air base, leased from Britain, on Ascension Island. The first British request was for large amounts of aviation fuel in US tankers on the high seas to be diverted to Ascension Island. The US Defense Secretary, Caspar Weinberger, was a strong admirer of Mrs Thatcher and a committed Anglophile. As he wrote afterwards: 'We all knew of the enormous military odds against Britain.'[5] He regarded the Argentine action as a clear case of aggression, which should be resisted. He agreed immediately to these and other British requests, paving the way for huge amounts of military equipment to be flown overnight from the Andrews Air Force Base outside Washington to Ascension Island.

But this was not the reaction in the State Department, where a struggle for influence broke out between the Latin American Bureau and the Europeanists, led by the formidable Lawrence Eagleburger. The Argentine military junta had agreed secretly to fund 500 of the American backed 'contras' opposing the Sandinista regime in Nicaragua. The British were infuriated when the US ambassador to the United Nations, Jeane Kirkpatrick, attended a dinner at the Argentine embassy on the evening of the invasion. Haig's deputy, Walter Stoessel, also attended this event. As Henderson observed publicly at the time, it was as if he had dined with the Iranians on the day the American hostages were seized. Kirkpatrick joined Enders in advocating a policy sympathetic to Latin American concerns. She argued that 'if the Argentines own the islands, then moving troops into them is not armed aggression'.

Eagleburger was having none of this: 'I was driven essentially by one very simple argument – an ally is an ally ... we had no choice.' Still more importantly, it was rejected by Cap Weinberger. Weinberger told the Pentagon that all existing requests from the United Kingdom for military equipment were to be honoured at once, and that if the British made any new requests for equipment or other support short of actual US participation in military action, those requests also should be granted immediately. Haig and Weinberger did not get on and Weinberger took these decisions independently of the State Department.

Weinberger was much closer to Reagan than Haig. He told the President privately what he was doing.[6] He was sufficiently concerned about what he knew to be the critical gap in the British armoury, the lack of a large aircraft carrier, to appear one day at the embassy to enquire if we had considered leasing one from the US! Henderson and I thanked him effusively, however impractical the suggestion.

Haig, meanwhile, was pursuing a different policy. Faced with a quarrel between two friends of the United States, he saw the US interest as lying in an attempt at mediation.

President Reagan himself found it difficult to believe that so serious a conflict could break out over what he described as 'that little ice-cold bunch of land down there'. In the Pentagon and in the US intelligence community, many doubted whether Britain had the military capacity to regain control of the islands. The British, it was pointed out, would be operating 8,000 miles from home and 3,000 miles from their nearest base, at Ascension Island. They would have to undertake opposed landings in hazardous weather conditions against numerically superior forces, and to attempt this in the absence of any effective cover except for twenty Sea Harriers on

Britain's two mini-carriers. While the US military chiefs admired Margaret Thatcher's courage, many also thought that she would lose.[7]

Haig was concerned about the damage that would be done to relations with Latin America if the United States openly backed Britain. He accepted the Kirkpatrick/Enders thesis that this would cause Argentina and other Latin American countries to transfer their allegiance to the Soviet Union. When Henderson sought American support, Haig told him that while his sympathy was with the British, he believed that 'the most practical expression of that sympathy would be impartial United States mediation in the dispute. The honest broker must, above all, be neutral.'[8]

In a meeting at the White House on 7 April, Kirkpatrick argued that 'Latin America is the most important place in the world for us', producing an explosion from Admiral Bobby Inman, deputy head of the CIA, who told her that this was rubbish: the US must support Britain. Reagan, as he was leaving the meeting, said that he would love to stay friends with Argentina, but 'I think our first loyalty, if worst comes to worst, is to side with the Brits'.[9]

The first ideas developed in the State Department were based on holding back the British fleet, the withdrawal of Argentine forces from the islands and introducing a peace-keeping force from Canada, the United States and two Latin American nations, to be followed by negotiations to resolve the dispute. Haig tried out these ideas on Henderson on 6 April before leaving for London to see Mrs Thatcher. He was told that there would be no negotiations on the future of the islands until the Argentine forces had withdrawn and British administration had been restored. When Haig said that Galtieri could not survive if Argentine forces were withdrawn, Henderson said that was Galtieri's problem. Haig pointed out that this did not solve the problem of getting the Argentine forces out of the islands.

This exchange did nothing to allay British concern about the American position, while the Argentine Foreign Minister, Costa Mendez, who saw Haig the same day, came away with the impression that American mediation would be favourable to Argentina so far as the dispute over future sovereignty was concerned.

Haig faced the difficulty that the British were prepared to talk only without pre-conditions and when Argentina's forces had left the islands. Argentina was not prepared to withdraw its forces from the islands until it was assured that the question of sovereignty would be settled – in its favour.

Before Haig's departure for London, Henderson and others impressed on his party that in this crisis there must be no repetition of the US performance over Suez. It was the Argentines who had committed aggression. Public opinion in Britain was united in wanting to resist them. The future of the Thatcher government was at stake. Haig was warned by the US embassy in London that Britain was in a 'bellicose mood, more highly strung and unpredictable than we had ever known it'.

As Haig set off for London, Mrs Thatcher was forewarned that he saw himself in the role of a Kissingerian mediator. He was in for a rude awakening. The US team found 'La Thatcher ... really quite fetching' in a velvet two-piece suit. But Haig was told that she considered the issue to be one of dealing with aggression rather than settling a dispute. 'Do not urge Britain to reward aggression, to give Argentina something taken by force that it could not attain by peaceful means.' She had not, she said, despatched the fleet to install some nebulous 'interim authority', but to restore British administration. She referred to the role Chamberlain had played at the time of Munich, before showing Haig the portraits in 10 Downing Street of Nelson and Wellington. 'I think I got the message', was the reaction of General Vernon Walters on his return from his travels with Haig.[10]

Haig was impressed by the Prime Minister's determination: she had, he told Reagan, the bit between her teeth. But Haig was determined to try to mediate and he felt that her new Foreign Secretary, Francis Pym, was readier to compromise. 'Maybe we should ask the Falklanders how they feel about a war,' suggested Pym. This interjection, as Haig observed, was 'not appreciated by the Prime Minister'.

Haig insisted that he was in London to help the British. But he must try to avoid an armed conflict that, he was convinced, would create new opportunities for Soviet influence in Latin America. He emphasised the strength of feeling in Argentina and that, if he were to be persuaded to withdraw, Galtieri must be offered something to save face. Haig talked of an international force to be stationed on the islands, an interim administration and negotiations that would respect the principle of self-determination.

Mrs Thatcher found all this too 'woolly'. It was clear to her that Haig was anxious not only to avoid what he described as 'a priori judgments about sovereignty', but that he was aiming at something other than the British administration that she had pledged in Parliament to restore.

'Interim authority – to do what?' she enquired. Self-determination would simply produce a reaffirmation of British sovereignty. Admiral Lewin, chief of the defence staff, told Haig that the British fleet, once it arrived in the South Atlantic, could not defer action for an extended period.[11]

Haig left London convinced that the Prime Minister was ready to go to war if Argentina would not withdraw, but that other members of her government understood the risks and were readier to compromise.

In Buenos Aires, Haig was greeted by an enormous crowd, which had been urged to show him the 'spirit of Argentina'. He was told that the US position in Latin America would be destroyed if it backed the colonial power. Haig told Galtieri that Mrs Thatcher was a good friend of the United States and he had to get her out of this corner: 'I must be frank. In the United States, the support for Britain is widespread.'

As Galtieri kept talking about his 'honour', Haig realised that the combination of his machismo and Thatcher's 'icy scorn and iron will' was likely to have an unhappy outcome. General Walters was sent by Haig to tell Galtieri privately that the British would fight and that they would win. They had superior technical means and a professional army. When Galtieri said: 'That woman wouldn't dare', Walters replied: 'Mr President, "that woman" has let a number of hunger strikers of her own basic ethnic origin starve themselves to death, without flickering an eyelash. I would not count on that if I were you.'

Haig sought to convince Galtieri that if Argentine forces withdrew, the prospects would be good for a negotiated transfer of sovereignty. Galtieri was unconvinced. He wanted a guarantee that negotiations would conclude with the recognition of sovereignty for Argentina by 31 December 1982.[12]

38

'DOING THE WORK
OF THE FREE WORLD'

HAIG RETURNED TO London with no worthwhile Argentine offer to make
to the British. Reagan's national security adviser, Judge Clark, wondered
if his mission should be called off. But Haig persevered. He continued to
worry away at the ideas of Argentine withdrawal and an interim administration, followed by negotiations to resolve the dispute. He wanted to halt
the British task force, which the Prime Minister rejected ('the fleet must
sail inexorably on'), though she was prepared to consider slowing it down,
or halting it if the Argentines withdrew. Pym suggested that the trauma of
invasion might have changed the attitude of the islanders. Mrs Thatcher
pointed out that they would hardly be softening in a pro-Argentine direction. At each point at which Haig thought he was making progress, he was
told that the Argentine position had hardened again, leaving him stranded.
To keep the negotiations alive, he had continued to suggest to both sides
that the other might be more flexible than was in fact the case.[1]

Nevertheless, in a first major shift, Mrs Thatcher, despite her initially
uncompromising line with Haig, told the Cabinet on 14 April that she
was prepared to accept an interim administration, including Argentine
representation, provided the Americans also were involved, providing
reassurance against further aggression.[2] She tried but failed to interest the
Americans in some form of security guarantee. But she told Parliament that
afternoon that she had made clear to Haig that Argentine withdrawal must
come first, that British sovereignty over the islands was not affected by the
invasion and that their future would be decided as the islanders wished.[3]

By this time the American press was reporting that Britain was receiving intelligence and other assistance in the crisis from the United States. Haig told Galtieri through General Walters that the USA was not providing any military support. The State Department put out a statement that the United States had 'not acceded to requests that went beyond the customary pattern of cooperation based on existing bilateral agreements'.

Haig at this point asked the US intelligence chiefs to limit what they passed on to the British. Admiral Inman told me with a smile that Haig had been assured that nothing was happening beyond the normal pattern of cooperation (which meant extensive intelligence sharing). Haig also wanted to state that British use of US facilities on Ascension Island had been restricted, a phrase he had to drop when confronted in a fiery telephone call by the Prime Minister, telling him: 'For Pete's sake, get that use of Ascension Island out of your statement, because it's our island and we can't exactly invade our island.'

Mrs Thatcher also told him that while she had always supported President Reagan, the United States was not seen at present as supporting her. She did not want to hear any more about even-handedness between a democratic fellow ally in NATO and a military dictatorship in Argentina.[3]

When contacted by Reagan on 15 April, suggesting that Galtieri wanted to avoid a conflict, Mrs Thatcher said that in that case, he should remove his troops from the islands. On the telephone, Reagan agreed in response to a barrage of arguments that he was 'deeply interested in keeping this great relationship we have'.[4]

On 16 April, Haig met Galtieri again in Buenos Aires. He told the Argentines that he wanted a solution based on stopping the British fleet, keeping the Argentine flag flying on the islands, giving them a role in the administration of the islands and guaranteeing that negotiations on the future of the islands would be concluded by the end of the year. Haig sought to create the impression that this would result in early recognition of Argentine sovereignty, a point on which the Argentines were sceptical. They would have to withdraw their forces. But an interim authority would be set up under the United States, Britain and Argentina.

As the Argentines remained intransigent, Haig warned them that once their fleet was in position, the British would attack, and that if it came to war, US opinion would side with Britain. When Admiral Anaya said that he would be proud to have his son die for the Malvinas, Haig replied:

'Let me assure you, Admiral, that you don't know the meaning of war until you see the corpses of young men being put into body bags.'[5]

In the effort to get an agreement, Haig continued to suggest that negotiations inevitably would lead to Argentine sovereignty. Galtieri insisted that it must be clear in advance that negotiations must be concluded by the end of the year, with the islands 'reverting' to Argentina. Argentina needed more than wishful thinking about what the British might agree to, otherwise negotiations would drag on indefinitely with the British in control of the islands.

Haig kept indicating his sympathy for the Argentine position on sovereignty. He realised that if the Argentines were given an unvarnished account of the British position, the negotiations would end forthwith. The United States, he said, was trying to avert a tragedy, but could not do so without greater Argentine flexibility.

Haig by this stage was becoming increasingly exasperated with the junta's negotiating tactics. Each new session began with a hard-line restatement of the Argentine position, ignoring all previous discussion. The Foreign Minister, Costa Mendez, continued to hint at flexibility, which was never forthcoming. The White House again was questioning whether it was worth pursuing the negotiations. It also was starting to worry about Haig's judgement. At the end of the discussions in Buenos Aires Costa Mendez gave Haig a note, to be read only when the party was airborne. This restated that it was an absolute condition that negotiations must be concluded by the end of the year with the recognition of Argentine sovereignty.

Haig did not feel that he could reveal this to the British, so he sent them instead his own ideas, without this addition. The Prime Minister told Parliament that these failed to stipulate that the islanders would decide their own future. The British, she added, would be making proposals of their own.

Mrs Thatcher reacted fiercely to Haig's proposal that the task force should be halted. She had little faith in a negotiated outcome. She was unimpressed by Haig and did not understand why the United States did not simply support Britain. She accepted, however, the overriding need not to alienate the US administration, given British dependence on the Americans for military supplies and other support. Pym was sent to Washington with one concession, which was that an Argentine flag might continue to fly beside the Union Jack during the interim period. There could be negotiations on sovereignty, but the wishes of the islanders would remain paramount.

Before Pym's arrival in Washington, Henderson notified Haig that British naval forces were about to take action to recover possession of South Georgia. He was flabbergasted to be told by Haig that he must forewarn the Argentinians. Some violent remonstrances were required to prevent this happening. Margaret Thatcher, understandably, was 'appalled'.[6]

Haig told Pym that he intended to submit a proposal to both sides. This provided for an interim administration and negotiations, which were intended by the Americans to lead to a transfer of sovereignty. The British declined to accept this unless it was made clear that the islanders would decide their own future. On 22 April the British Cabinet was told that Galtieri was an alcoholic and 'apparently incapable of rational thought'. It was essential that any failure to secure a negotiated settlement occurred in a way that left the United States firmly in support of the British position. Haig, whose intentions were honourable, but who had none of Kissinger's intellectual power, found it difficult to understand that he was trying to bridge an unbridgeable gap.[7]

Pym returned from Washington with American proposals, sent also to the Argentines, for the withdrawal of Argentine land and British naval forces, and an interim administration while negotiations took place, which was supposed to result in a definitive solution by the end of the year. Pym recommended accepting them. Mrs Thatcher found them utterly unacceptable and representing conditional surrender, as they not only ruled out a return to the British administration, on which she was prepared to compromise, but also failed to protect the principle that the wishes of the islanders would be paramount, on which she was not. She was, she told her deputy, Willie Whitelaw, prepared to resign if her colleagues disagreed.

The War Cabinet agreed with her, but both she and they recognised the need to retain US support and to avoid simply rejecting Haig's ideas. Mrs Thatcher told Parliament that they were complex and difficult and inevitably bore the hallmarks of compromise. The British, she said, would cooperate in any solution the islanders could accept and which did not predetermine the outcome of negotiations. At John Nott's suggestion, in what Henderson regarded as a 'finesse worthy of Talleyrand', Haig was asked to put his proposals first to the Argentines. The War Cabinet regarded it as 'virtually inconceivable' that Argentina would agree to withdraw.[8]

On 25 April, British naval forces attacked and reoccupied South Georgia. The Argentine submarine *Santa Fé* was disabled in a helicopter attack and the Argentine garrison, led by the odious Captain Astiz, wanted in both Sweden and France for the murder of citizens of their countries in the course of the military repression in Argentina, surrendered.

The British government, as it had hoped, was spared further difficulty as Haig's ideas were rejected by the junta. To try to meet the British, Haig had included a reference to the wishes of the islanders and was unable to give any guarantee as to what would happen if negotiations stalled with sovereignty unresolved.

Henderson and the British embassy in Washington, meanwhile, had mounted an effective campaign to mobilise American opinion behind the British cause. On 28 April, following a briefing by Haig on his mediation, the Senate voted 79–1 in favour of support for Britain, with only the ultra-right-wing Senator Jesse Helms voting against. Press and television comment also were running overwhelmingly against Argentina. Within the administration, Weinberger had wanted open US support for Britain from the outset.

President Reagan had allowed Haig to pursue his negotiating efforts, but his own sympathies were never in much doubt. He was a friend and admirer of Margaret Thatcher. He needed her help in Europe. She was the United States' staunchest supporter in the struggle to deploy Pershing II and ground-launched Cruise missiles in Europe to offset the threat posed by the Soviet SS20s. The Europeanists in the State Department, led by Eagleburger, were firmly of the view that a failure to support the British would be near fatal for the Alliance. In his diary, as far back as 19 April, Reagan had written that 'I don't think that Margaret Thatcher should be asked to concede any more'. Jeane Kirkpatrick reflected bitterly: 'There wasn't any question about where President Reagan stood on this issue, from start to finish.'[9]

On 29 April, Mrs Thatcher wrote to Reagan that 'I cannot conceal from you how deeply let down I and my colleagues would feel if under these circumstances the US were not now to give us its full support'.

By this stage, Haig, infuriated by the Argentines, had reached the same conclusion himself. Later that day, President Reagan told Mrs Thatcher that he recognised that, while she had fundamental difficulties with the US proposals, she had not rejected them, while the Argentine government had done so. 'We will leave no doubt that Her Majesty's Government worked with us in good faith and was left with no choice but to proceed with military action based on the right of self-defense.' He added, however, that in the end there would have to be a negotiated outcome, to avoid permanent hostility in the South Atlantic.[10]

In the meeting of the National Security Council that morning, Haig had confirmed to his colleagues the Prime Minister's worst suspicions. His proposal, he said, had amounted to a 'camouflaged transfer of sovereignty' to Argentina, but the Argentines had rejected it. Weinberger wanted to get something out of the conflict, namely the benefits of having supported the British. As Richard Aldous observed, while Haig jetted to and fro, Weinberger simply got on with the business of making sure that Britain won the war.[11]

That evening, the United States declared its support for Britain. Haig had to choose his words carefully. There was 'reason to hope', he said, that the British would have considered a solution on the lines he had proposed, but it had been rejected by Argentina. The United States could not accept the use of force to resolve international disputes. The presidential directive added that the United States 'would respond positively to requests for materiel support for British forces', thereby legitimising what Weinberger had been doing from day one of the conflict.

Haig's mediation foundered on the inability of any negotiator to fudge the central issue in the dispute, hard though he tried to envelop it in other elements. The British would not accept any outcome that handed over sovereignty against the wishes of the islanders. The Argentines would not agree to withdraw their forces without a guarantee that, shortly thereafter, sovereignty would be theirs. With a less determined British Prime Minister, it might have been possible to obscure this fundamental point. With Mrs Thatcher, there was never any chance of doing so. To keep the Americans with her, she was ready to agree to changes in the administration of the islands that would have seemed unthinkable a few weeks before. But she would not give way on the central issues of sovereignty and self-determination. Haig kept trying to wrest enough concessions from the British to induce the Argentines to withdraw.

Following Haig's statement, we took forthwith to Weinberger a request for the supply of 105 AIM-9L Sidewinder air-to-air missiles from the US Air Force. This was the very latest version of the Sidewinder, far more accurate than its predecessors, and not yet in service with many of America's own frontline aircraft. Nevertheless, Weinberger decreed that the missiles should be supplied. As Margaret Thatcher was to record in her memoirs, without the latest version of the Sidewinder, 'we could not have re-taken the Falklands'.[12]

Shortly after the American statement, on the morning of 1 May the British began the naval and air bombardment of Argentine forces on the Falklands. On the same day, Francis Pym returned to Washington to see Haig. At lunch on the British embassy terrace, it was disconcerting to see how much strain the jet-lagged Haig appeared to be under, with the Foreign Secretary, not in much better shape, worrying about the Argentine aircraft carrier (sold to them by Britain some years before).

Haig, or rather Enders, meanwhile, had encouraged President Belaúnde of Peru to put forward new proposals that resembled their own. The difference was that third parties would govern the islands temporarily and there would be no direct British role in the new administration. The idea was also to refer to the need to take account of the 'view-points and interests' rather than the wishes of the islanders. Both changes went in the Argentine direction.

To Pym, Haig relayed President Reagan's view that the British were 'doing the work of the free world', but followed this with an ardent plea that the British should avoid a large-scale battle as this would be unnecessary and risky. Pym was told forcefully about the importance Haig attached to the Peruvian plan.

As the task force closed in on the islands, on the morning of 2 May, Admiral Lewin, the chief of defence staff, with the support and at the behest of the naval commanders, Admirals Woodward and Fieldhouse, asked the War Cabinet, in an emergency meeting at Chequers, for permission to extend the existing rules of engagement to allow a British submarine to attack the Argentine cruiser, the *General Belgrano*. On the previous day, an Argentine signal had been intercepted envisaging a naval attack on the British task force. The *Belgrano* carried a powerful radar that could illuminate the task force and along with its two accompanying destroyers was armed with Exocet missiles.

That evening the *Belgrano*, just outside the total exclusion zone, was torpedoed by HMS *Conqueror*, with the loss of over 300 lives. The Argentines had been warned on 23 April that any Argentine forces that posed a threat to the British fleet would be attacked. The decision was taken on entirely military grounds.[13] The War Cabinet had no knowledge at the time of the Peruvian peace proposals; nor would it have made any difference if they had done. The navy also wanted to sink the Argentine aircraft carrier if it ventured out of territorial waters, and was given permission to do so.

Haig was appalled, berating Henderson. The United States, he said, was suffering in Latin America because of its support for Britain. He warned of opinion in the West becoming less favourable: 'People might say that Britain was over-reacting.' Haig questioned whether 'hitting the Argentines was the only thing that brought them to negotiate or whether it made them more inflexible'. Henderson pointed out that they had shown no great flexibility before military action had been taken.

Haig asked for a ceasefire on receipt of an Argentine commitment to withdraw. Later that day, 3 May, Haig saw Henderson again and insisted that military action must be stopped. He feared that the British would sink the whole Argentine fleet (which in fact by now was heading back to port). Henderson said that the British would not agree to an armistice just because the Argentines were now doing badly. Haig worried about Britain driving things too far. He subsequently sent a copy of the Peruvian plan with a suggested ceasefire statement for the British government to make.

On the following day, the British lost the destroyer HMS *Sheffield* in an Exocet attack. Henderson met Haig and offered some amendments to the Peruvian plan. Haig said that these would be rejected by Argentina. He presented instead variations of his own. These latest proposals presented great difficulties for the British government because not only would there now be no return to British administration of the islands, but they no longer referred to the wishes, but only to the 'aspirations and interests' of the islanders, with Reagan commending them to Mrs Thatcher as 'our best hope' to bring the conflict to an end before more lives were lost. Shaken and angry, Mrs Thatcher wrote a personal letter to Reagan, which she toned down before sending, expressing her frustration at constantly being asked to weaken her position.[14]

Nevertheless, the US proposals were accepted, because of the need to retain American support, with Mrs Thatcher remaining convinced that the junta would reject withdrawal. Pym told Parliament on 7 May that a small group of countries would administer the islands in consultation with the islanders' representatives, pending a solution without prejudice to the wishes of the islanders. Belaúnde had told Galtieri that the Americans would oblige the British to accept these proposals, but they were rejected by the junta. Argentina, said Galtieri, had lost faith in the United States and preferred the mediation of the United Nations. In fact, it was at this stage that Galtieri could have secured an outcome favourable to Argentina.

On 11 May, Mrs Thatcher stressed in Parliament the importance of a ceasefire being linked to Argentine withdrawal and not prejudging the outcome of negotiations. She avoided replying to Enoch Powell when he asked whether there would be a return to British administration.

On 13 May, Thomas Enders persuaded Reagan to try again with the Prime Minister. Enders did not lack self-confidence. As Eagleburger observed, 'even though he is six foot eight inches tall, he *still* has a Napoleon complex'.

Reagan had been given the impression that the British and American negotiating positions were now quite close. Mrs Thatcher disabused him. He referred to concerns that the British might be planning attacks on the airfields on the Argentine mainland. She reassured him on that point. He wanted her to hold off military action. She pointed out that the Argentines were continuing their attacks on the British fleet. Reagan suggested that the conflict was being portrayed as one between David and Goliath. The Prime Minister pointed out the serious disadvantages under which the British were operating. She attempted to convince Reagan of the strategic importance of the Falklands if the Panama Canal ever were closed. With rather more success, she sought to persuade him that he had been misinformed about the concessions the Argentines were supposed to have made. It was, as she recorded, a difficult conversation. 'I talked to Margaret,' Reagan concluded, 'but I don't think I persuaded her against further action.' 'I can't see Ronald Reagan getting onto her on the phone again in a hurry' was Henderson's comment.[15]

As the decisive moment of the war was now approaching when the British must attempt their landing on the Falklands, on 17 May the British government worked out its final negotiating position in a meeting with Mrs Thatcher at Chequers attended by Henderson and Sir Anthony Parsons, British ambassador at the United Nations. On 8 May, she had told Parsons that 'it is going to be the most awful waste of young life if we really have to go and take those islands'. This time the emphasis was on appearing to be reasonable to the world in general, rather than primarily the United States. Although, in the meeting, the Foreign Office representatives found themselves under attack for being 'wet, ready to sell out, unsupportive of British interests, etc.', the Prime Minister accepted the idea of a UN administrator for the islands, to act in consultation with the islanders. This was a vast distance from where she had set out; Parsons felt obliged to check that she really understood what she had agreed to. But again it seemed to her improbable even on this basis that the Argentines would agree to withdraw. Henderson observed that the Americans were impressed above all by success: no diplomatic problems would count for much in the event of military success, which Admiral Lewin was confident of achieving.

Margaret Thatcher had been persuaded to move a surprisingly long way in these negotiations, far further than was generally realised at the time, to a point at which, if the revised proposals had been accepted by the Argentines, she would have been in difficulty at home, with no return to British administration and no certainty as to the outcome of future negotiations. Each one of these documents carried within it the certainty of a further deadlock by the end of the year. She had made some extremely unpalatable concessions because of her own realisation that an opposed landing would be an extremely risky operation, with a certainty of serious casualties. She had been prepared to go way beyond what she thought was reasonable because of the need to retain American support. The Americans did not regard the principle of self-determination as paramount for islands with a population of 1,800 people and did not want a long-running dispute in the South Atlantic.

Jeane Kirkpatrick urged the Argentines to accept the proposals or something like them, but they too were rejected by the junta. With no movement on the Argentine side, the UN Secretary-General in turn abandoned his mediation.[16]

At 4 a.m. on 21 May, the British began their landings in San Carlos bay, with very limited air support. That afternoon the frigate *Ardent* was sunk and *Argonaut* and *Brilliant* were badly damaged by Argentine aircraft. *Antelope* and *Coventry* were lost in the next few days, as was the container ship *Atlantic Conveyor*. The Harriers armed with US Sidewinder missiles caused heavy losses among the attacking aircraft.

Soon after the UN Secretary-General's efforts broke down, the State

Department raised the possibility of a further Haig initiative. Through the national security adviser, Judge Clark, Henderson impressed on the President the inappropriateness of such a move now that the British landings were taking place. Haig urged that Britain should seize the first moment of military success to show readiness to negotiate. He warned that, otherwise, after the war Britain would have a large garrison to sustain in hostile circumstances.

On 24 May, Henderson told Haig that the fact that British forces had fought their way ashore was bound to affect the diplomatic position. Britain could not now agree to a withdrawal or to an interim administration. The Argentines would have to agree to withdraw within a fixed time limit. Haig was still thinking of a US–Brazilian interim administration. He sent that evening a message to Pym also proposing a US–Brazilian peacekeeping force. He was told that Britain would now consider a settlement only after British administration had been re-established in the islands.[17]

As British forces advanced across East Falkland, Haig continued to urge on Britain the need to compromise. He accepted that there would now be a British military administration, but this, he proposed, should be under an international umbrella group that also should seek a solution for the future. Before President Reagan left for a Group of Seven meeting in Paris, Jeane Kirkpatrick met him to argue that the US position in Latin America would be undermined by a bloody British military victory at Port Stanley and further damaged if the United States joined Britain in vetoing a ceasefire resolution at the United Nations.

On the eve of his departure with Reagan to the Versailles economic summit, Haig summoned Henderson yet again to urge a halt to the British advance and compromise, quoting Churchill: 'In Victory, Magnanimity.' Henderson replied that Churchill had been talking about magnanimity *once victory was achieved*.

Prompted by Haig, Reagan telephoned the Prime Minister late on 31 May, having talked to the President of Brazil. He congratulated her on what 'you and your young men are doing down there ... you've demonstrated to the whole world that aggression does not pay', but then sought to urge on her that a deal should be struck to avoid 'total Argentine humiliation'. The President was unable to get much beyond the word 'Margaret...' in the rest of the call. 'This is democracy and our islands,' she told him. Having lost valuable British ships and invaluable servicemen's lives to return to the Falklands, there was no longer any question of an interim administration. She was sure he would have reacted in the same way if, say, Alaska had been threatened. He nervously said that Alaska was different, but she did not agree. 'There is no alternative,' she concluded.

The NSC staff felt that in this call, Reagan had sounded like more of a wimp than Jimmy Carter. Reagan recorded afterwards that she had said that too many British lives had been lost for Britain to withdraw without total victory 'and she convinced me'.[18]

Reagan's heart was not really in some of these calls. One of those present in the Oval Office told me afterwards that the President, listening to this harangue, unable to get a word in, held up the phone to his staff. 'Isn't she wonderful?' he said.

A cross Thatcher telephoned Henderson on an open line to say that she was 'dismayed' by the President's attitude, which had 'horrified' her. 'We have lost a lot of blood,' she said, 'and it's the best blood.' He was urged not to mince his words in telling the White House so.

Before leaving for Paris, Reagan made clear that he would not try to impose a negotiated settlement on Britain and congratulated the British for responding to 'a threat that all of us must oppose – and that is the idea that armed aggression can succeed in the world today'. Haig, however, still was dissatisfied, telling Henderson: 'We can't accept intransigence.'[19]

On 4 June, Reagan and Thatcher were together at the G7 summit in Paris. Reagan wisely saw her without Haig. Before their meeting she told Henderson that there would be no more talk of compromise.[20]

As the British forces closed in on Port Stanley, on 4 June Britain and the United States vetoed a resolution in the UN Security Council calling for an immediate ceasefire. There had been doubts up to the last minute about US intentions, with Jeane Kirkpatrick arguing against a veto. No sooner had the vote been taken than an aide brought a new message to Mrs Kirkpatrick, who then stated:

> I have been told that it is impossible for a country to change its vote
> once it has been made known but my Government has asked me
> to put it on record that if it were possible to change votes, I should
> change it from a no to an abstention. Thank you.

This announcement caused a sensation. As Parsons commented:

> Fortunately any odium which might have attached to us for using
> our veto was diverted by the astonishing statement by Mrs Kirk-
> patrick ... This revelation left the Council and the media stunned
> and I was able to escape from the Chamber almost unnoticed by the
> press, the microphones and the television cameras as they engulfed
> Mrs Kirkpatrick.[21]

This fiasco occurred while Reagan and Mrs Thatcher were at Versailles
together, attending an economic summit. Asked by a journalist about
the US attempt to change its vote in the Security Council, President
Reagan, to Mrs Thatcher's amazement, knew nothing about it. The journalist then turned to the Prime Minister. 'I had no intention of rubbing
salt into a friend's wounds, so all I said was that I did not give interviews
over lunch.'[22]

However 'irritating and unpredictable' Mrs Thatcher found the Americans in their public pronouncements during the conflict and her doubts
about Haig, any US government would have been bound to try to play a
peace-making role. For her part, she had never lost sight of the fact that
without US assistance, the war could not have been won. At each critical
stage, she had shown herself prepared to accept the compromises necessary to retain their support.[23]

In his speech to the Houses of Parliament shortly after the Versailles
summit, Reagan aligned himself with the Prime Minister. British soldiers in
the Falklands, he said, were not fighting for mere real estate: 'They fight for
a cause, for a belief that armed aggression must not be allowed to succeed.'

On 13 June, the British forces launched their final assault on the Argentine defences around Port Stanley. The news of the Argentine surrender on
the following day was greeted with cheering in the Operations Room in the
White House. At a heavy cost – one British serviceman killed for every
seventh islander freed – Mrs Thatcher claimed: 'We have ceased to be a
nation in retreat.' Visiting the Falklands after the victory, Denis Thatcher
concluded that the islands consisted of 'miles and miles of bugger all'. For
Margaret Thatcher, what mattered about them was that they were British,
and thanks to her efforts, they had remained so.

The Americans agreed with her. In Al Haig's view, the fatal miscal-
culation of the Argentines was about the character of the British Prime
Minister. She had shown herself to be by far the strongest and shrewdest

player in the game. The British had shown that they were prepared to fight for a principle and to do so supremely well against considerable odds.[24] The Argentine military were discredited and the pressures for democracy strengthened.

Haig's successor, George Shultz, regarded the British decision to go to war for these desolate, scarcely populated islets 8,000 miles from London as an important statement that a free world nation was willing to fight for a principle. The world paid attention to this; the Soviets did too (a view borne out by Christopher Meyer, then in the British embassy in Moscow, who found that nominal support for Argentina was offset by interest in this new tsarina).[25]

When Mrs Thatcher visited Washington on 23 June, Reagan was briefed to argue that the war needed to be followed by a negotiated 'just peace' to avoid further conflict in the South Atlantic. Forewarned by a staffer that 'Thatcher blasted this position to smithereens on two networks this morning', Reagan prudently decided against pursuing the idea with her.[26]

39

'THE FOCUS OF EVIL IN THE MODERN WORLD'

IMMEDIATELY AFTER THE economic summit in Versailles, Reagan visited Britain. The President stayed and went riding with the Queen at Windsor, which he described as 'a fairy tale experience'. It had been suggested that he should address a joint session of Parliament in Westminster Hall, but the Labour Party objected. Reagan remained a highly controversial figure in Britain, with much of the press continuing to depict him as a warmonger and, despite two successful terms as Governor of California, as a B-movie actor. The President instead addressed those Members of Parliament who wished to hear him in the Royal Gallery.

Reagan had thought hard about the rest of his speech, which he saw as encapsulating his philosophy. He saw the world as at a turning point. Marx was right that they were witnessing a revolutionary crisis, in which economic demands were conflicting with those of the political order. But the crisis was happening not in the West, but in the cradle of Marxism. It was the Soviet Union that was running against the tide of history. It was in deep economic difficulty. The advance of freedom and democracy would leave Marxism-Leninism on the ash heap of history. The determinant in this struggle would not be weapons, but the clash of wills and ideas.

The phrase about the 'ash heap of history' was borrowed from Trotsky. The majority of British and American commentators were far too sophisticated to fall for what they regarded as this crude anti-Soviet rhetoric, as were most Cabinet ministers. There was far more interest in his admittedly expert use of a new British invention – the autocue.

Mrs Thatcher's hopes that the Versailles summit in June would produce a solution to the problem of the sanctions applied to John Brown and other British companies over the Soviet gas pipeline were disappointed. Shortly afterwards, in Haig's absence, the National Security Council decided, as recommended by Weinberger and Perle, to intensify sanctions against the Soviet Union. Reagan regarded the imposition of sanctions against the Soviet Union in response to the crackdown on Solidarity in Poland as a matter of principle and found it hard to understand why Mrs Thatcher did not agree.

The Prime Minister was appalled and condemned the decision in public. What she found irritating was 'the way in which the actions the Americans preferred inflicted a good deal more pain on their allies than on themselves' or, in her view, the Communists in Poland and the Soviet Union. She made clear her determination to oppose the attempt to apply US law extra-territorially to British companies operating outside the United States.[1]

Visiting Washington on 23 June, eight days after the victory in the Falklands, Mrs Thatcher lectured the members of the National Security Council, in Reagan's presence, on the unacceptability of this approach. She pointed out that, while imposing sanctions that affected European companies, the US had decided to lift its ban on grain sales to the Soviet Union, which she regarded as hypocritical. When Reagan unwisely mentioned that the Americans had been in touch with John Brown, who seemed to feel that they could live with the sanctions, an angry Thatcher told the note-takers to stop taking notes. 'You deal with *your* companies and I will deal with mine' was her response. The US Treasury also was told of the evils of the budget deficit.

Mrs Thatcher followed up tough talk by acting so as well. On her return to London, she said in Parliament: 'The question is whether one very powerful nation can prevent existing contracts being fulfilled; I think it is wrong to do so.' A month later the British government used its legal powers to prohibit John Brown and US subsidiaries in Britain from complying with the US embargo because of the unacceptable extension of American extra-territorial jurisdiction.

Immediately after Mrs Thatcher's departure from Washington, Haig threatened to resign as Secretary of State. He was disconcerted to find his offer accepted. He was replaced by the reassuring figure of George Shultz, who had served as Treasury Secretary under Nixon. Shultz worked patiently to find a solution to the sanctions problem, which by now risked doing more damage to NATO than to the Soviet Union. In November, Reagan announced that he was ending the attempt to apply extra-territorial sanctions in return for agreement with the Allies on a more restrictive approach to economic dealings with the Soviet Union.

On 4 November 1982, the UN General Assembly voted on a resolution on the Falklands, sponsored by the Latin Americans, which declared that 'the maintenance of a colonial situation is incompatible with the United Nations ideal of universal peace'. To the annoyance of the British, the United States voted in favour. To pre-empt Mrs Thatcher's reaction, Reagan sent her a letter saying that he did not expect her to enter into negotiations, but did not want to rule them out for the future. The British representative at the UN, Sir John Thomson, pointed out that it was absurd to call for negotiations as if the Argentine invasion had never occurred. George Shultz records that his first encounter with the British ambassador, Sir Oliver Wright, was stormy. Mrs Thatcher was furious at the American vote. Sir Oliver, on instructions,

> read me off like a sergeant would a recruit in a Marine Corps boot camp. I felt Mrs Thatcher was wrong to oppose us for taking a reasonable position on a critical issue in our neighbourhood. And Wright was wrong to lay it on so thick. I worried that President Reagan would be alarmed at Margaret Thatcher's reaction, but I found that he, too, was getting a little fed up with her imperious attitude in this matter.[2]

Having supported Britain during the war, the US administration's overriding concern now was to move to repair relations with Latin America.

In December 1982, Shultz visited Mrs Thatcher at Chequers. Shultz was an admirer of the Prime Minister, particularly of her economic philosophy: 'She left me with the feeling that right or wrong, there wasn't a shadow of doubt in her mind about where she was going and why.' But his admiration did not extend to agreeing with her on all points. When she suggested that the Falklands would be strategically important if the Panama Canal were closed, Shultz thought this 'far-fetched, but there was no point arguing about it. I agreed with our decision to support her, but I felt it was time to repair the damage done to our interests in South America'.

At a dinner at 10 Downing Street, her Foreign Secretary, Francis Pym, launched into an economic argument that made no sense to Shultz. Before he could reply, Pym's argument was summarily dismissed by the Prime Minister. Shultz concluded that the special relationship was going to be stronger than ever, because it was underpinned by the Reagan–Thatcher personal relationship 'which was as close as any imaginable between two major leaders'. Shultz also concluded that the best way to deal with a Prime Minister he admired was to 'know what I was talking about, to talk up, and to talk back'.[3]

At the Williamsburg economic summit in May 1983, Mrs Thatcher tried and failed again to persuade Reagan to curb the US budget deficit. The key issue remained the deployment of new US nuclear missiles in Europe to counter the Soviet SS20s. There was tremendous political resistance to the deployment, which, it was suggested, would greatly increase the risk of nuclear war. Mass demonstrations were organised in Germany, while in Britain the Campaign for Nuclear Disarmament took on a new lease of life. Under Michael Foot the Labour Party opposed the deployment to which, under Callaghan, it had agreed. In the United States, there was growing impatience with the Europeans. They appeared on the one hand to want constant reassurance that they would be defended by the Americans, if necessary by nuclear means; on the other, they agonised about the presence and danger of US nuclear weapons on European soil.

European anxieties were compounded by worries about Reagan's attitude to the Soviet Union. On 8 March, Reagan made his 'evil empire' speech, in which he castigated the Soviet Union as the 'focus of evil in the modem world'. Later that month, he announced his intention to proceed with his Strategic Defense Initiative (SDI), which he hoped would improve ballistic missile defences to a point that would render nuclear weapons obsolete. The British had no prior notice of the announcement even though, if the plan could ever be turned into reality, it would have profound implications for the British nuclear deterrent.

On the other side of the Atlantic, arms control experts were horrified, as the Reagan plan would entail tearing up or modifying the Anti-Ballistic Missile Treaty. It also risked having much greater implications for smaller nuclear forces, like those of France and Britain, than for the superpowers.

Margaret Thatcher's reactions were more moderate than those of the other Europeans. She was interested in the development of super-fast computers and the use of lasers to increase the effectiveness of anti-missile defences. She understood that these new technologies over time could provide protection against a limited nuclear attack. She worried about the exaggerated expectations created by Reagan's speech and the implication for British nuclear forces. But she accepted that the United States had a 'bounden duty to try to get the best defence'.

Meanwhile elections in Britain were approaching and so was the moment when, if negotiations failed, the new US nuclear weapons were due to be deployed. The Russians had flatly rejected the 'zero option' under which they would have to destroy all their SS20s. This proposal continued to the regarded by most European foreign ministries as non-negotiable, as it was by many on the American side. The British and others hoped that agreement might be reached on equal numbers of intermediate-range missiles in the European theatre, with the Russians allowed to deploy a hundred or so additional warheads in Asia.

In Britain as elsewhere, a particular point of controversy was the degree of control the British government could exert over US nuclear weapons on British soil. In fact, under the arrangements worked out under Attlee and Truman, British consent was required for the release of US nuclear weapons from British territory. This was a sensitive subject, as similar arrangements did not exist for Germany or other European countries. Hitherto the two governments had talked of a 'joint decision'. But in the run-up to the British election in 1983, the White House agreed that it could be made clear to Parliament that the consent of the British government would be required before US nuclear weapons could be fired from British soil. (This was on the basis, the deputy national security adviser, Bud McFarlane, told me at the time that 'Ronald Reagan would mortgage the Washington Monument, if necessary, to help get Margaret Thatcher re-elected'.) The British government was content with the reaffirmation of the understanding. It did not insist on a dual key system, which, in any event, could not be applied to nuclear-capable aircraft.

The opposition to missile deployment was so intense, particularly in West Germany, that by this stage there were many on the US side who doubted whether it would be possible to proceed. The Reagan administration found Mrs Thatcher a staunch ally in insisting that, if negotiations failed, the new missiles must be deployed. But she too was facing intense political resistance and a permanent demonstration at Greenham Common, where the missiles would be based.

In July 1982, the US negotiator, Paul Nitze, exceeding his instructions from Washington, attempted to reach agreement with his Soviet counterpart, Kvitsinsky, in the so-called 'walk in the woods'. In Nitze's conception, the Russians would be allowed to retain 225 SS20 warheads, to be offset by 300 Cruise missiles on the Western side. Kvitsinsky did not respond to this idea, which also was disavowed in Washington. The British and other allies as well as the State Department continued to believe that the most likely outcome was agreement on equal numbers of intermediate-range missile warheads in the European theatre and not on zero for zero.

The Russians tried to insist that British and French nuclear weapons must be counted in this equation. Reagan at one stage wondered whether the West might not be on the losing side of the argument about this. Mrs Thatcher and François Mitterrand were adamant that theirs were minimum strategic deterrent forces, a tiny fraction of the nuclear arsenals of the superpowers, and should not be included. In November 1983, the new US missiles began to arrive in Britain and Germany. In Britain, they had to be airlifted into Greenham Common to avoid a near blockade by the demonstrators outside. The Soviet Union broke off the negotiations, but the Soviet propaganda offensive had failed to prevent the deployment.

In the same month, NATO conducted one of its annual war exercises, codenamed Able Archer. The British were warned by their key agent in the KGB, Oleg Gordievsky, that the Russians had genuinely believed that this might be the preparation for a first strike on the Soviet Union, causing them to put some of their nuclear-capable aircraft on alert. When Robert Gates, Deputy Director of the CIA, saw the report, he was horrified.[4] On a visit to Washington, Mrs Thatcher used a speech to the Churchill Foundation to get across the message that: 'We have to deal with the Soviet Union ... not as we would like it to be, but as it is. We live on the same planet and we have to go on sharing it.'

––––––––––

On 13 October 1983, the crypto-Marxist government of Maurice Bishop in Grenada was overthrown in a coup. Six days later Bishop was murdered. The Reagan administration had strongly disliked the Bishop regime and its close ties to Cuba, including a significant Cuban military presence and several hundred construction workers helping to build a large new airport. The US administration would dearly have liked to be rid of the Bishop regime, but not in the way that had now happened, for Bishop was overthrown by a group of extreme left-wing thugs, led by General Hudson Austin. The Grenadan Governor and representative of the Queen, Sir Paul Scoon, was powerless to do anything. Several hundred American students were present on the island at the time.

The Americans consulted the Foreign Office as to what should be done. They were told that Grenada was independent. The coup had taken place and there was nothing that could be done about it, despite the unpleasant nature of the regime. This was the Prime Minister's reaction as well.

This was not the view taken by the other Caribbean leaders, who feared that they might be next. The Prime Minister of Barbados, Tom Adams, and the redoubtable Eugenia Charles, Prime Minister of Dominica, appealed to the United States for help and were encouraged by the Americans to do so. US naval vessels were diverted, ostensibly to assist with the evacuation of US citizens, but also to give the President the option, if he chose, to intervene. On Friday 21 October and through the weekend, the State Department was asked by the British about its intentions. It said that the USA was proceeding cautiously. No decisions had been taken. If they were, the British would be forewarned.

On the afternoon of Monday 24 October, the Foreign Secretary, Sir Geoffrey Howe, was asked in the House of Commons about the threat of US intervention. He said that the government was keeping in close touch with the US authorities. He had no reason to believe that intervention was likely. The Americans had said that they were proceeding cautiously.

In fact, President Reagan had been woken at the Augusta golf club in Georgia on the Saturday morning to be told that the Caribbean leaders were asking for US intervention – a request the US had encouraged them to make. He agreed in principle that the US should respond and that planning should be carried forward.[5] Back in Washington on the Sunday morning, the President was told of the Hezbollah attack on the US Marine Corps barracks in Beirut in which 241 Marines were killed. The National Security Council met in full session throughout the morning. Most of the discussion was about Beirut, on which there was a sense of deep frustration at the inability of the USA to take effective reprisals. When the meeting turned to Grenada, Reagan declared himself in favour of intervention. Otherwise, he commented, the American people might as well have re-elected Jimmy Carter.

By the following morning, the British embassy in Washington was convinced that intervention was close. The ambassador, Sir Oliver Wright, saw the Under-Secretary in the State Department, Lawrence Eagleburger, who confirmed that military action was likely. Because of the time difference, the report did not reach Geoffrey Howe before his statements in Parliament. That evening, Mrs Thatcher received a message from Reagan stating that he was seriously considering the request from the Caribbean governments that the US should take military action. She remained strongly opposed to intervention. Reagan tried to contact her, but found that she was out – at dinner with Princess Alexandra and the US ambassador, who knew nothing of his government's intentions. On her return to Downing Street, she received a second message, confirming the US intention to intervene. She replied immediately, opposing intervention in the internal affairs of a small independent nation, 'however unattractive its regime'.

She followed this up with a call to the White House, while the President was briefing the Congressional leaders. Called out of the meeting, Reagan spoke to the Prime Minister for fifteen minutes. She expressed strongly her opposition to US intervention in a territory that was an independent member of the Commonwealth. President Reagan was taken aback, as he had expected her personally to be better disposed, whatever the official position of the Foreign Office. But he was not deterred: he made clear his intention to proceed anyway. The message to the Prime Minister was sent so belatedly because of fears that she might oppose this.

Mrs Thatcher felt dismayed and badly let down: 'At best, the British Government had been made to look impotent; at worst we looked deceitful.' Only that afternoon Geoffrey Howe had told the House of Commons that he had no knowledge of any American intention to invade Grenada. 'Now he and I would have to explain how it had happened that a member of the Commonwealth had been invaded by our closest ally.'[6]

That night, a US Navy Special Forces team was put ashore and managed to reach the Governor, Sir Paul Scoon, whom they found in fear of his life. He signed a letter requesting US military intervention. In the morning, the small US team spent several hours fighting off a Cuban-led attempt to regain control of Government House, while the main US landings took place at the airport. The hastily improvised landings were marked by a fair degree of chaos and reports of much greater Cuban resistance than was in fact the case. Within twenty-four hours, the Americans had gained control of the island.

In the British Parliament, the Labour opposition had a field day. It was obvious that the British government had not been consulted and that the invasion had been decided over the Prime Minister's objections. This was held to be particularly heinous because Grenada was a member of the Commonwealth – even though the Governor supported the US action and the British government had made clear that it was not prepared to do anything about the situation in Grenada. Geoffrey Howe had a torrid time. Asked about the US action, Mrs Thatcher responded with an outburst:

> We in the Western countries, the Western democracies, use our force to defend our way of life. We do not use it to walk into other people's countries, independent sovereign territories ... If you are pronouncing a new law that wherever Communism reigns against the will of the people ... there the United States shall enter, then we are going to have really terrible wars in the world.

The Americans, on the other hand, saw themselves as carrying out responsibilities that Britain hitherto had exercised in the Caribbean. Britain had looked after the security of the small island territories: it was no longer prepared to do so. British moralising about intervention in independent territories did not impress the Americans, who had intervened in territories in their hemisphere before and were to do so again, in Panama and Haiti. The US forces, meanwhile, were welcomed with open arms by the Grenadans, thankful to be rescued from an appalling band of thugs who had seized power illegally.

So far as consultation was concerned, President Reagan did not take the final decision to intervene until the Sunday. The British were told on the following day, a few hours before the invasion took place. They deliberately were not told earlier, partly because of the danger of leaks, but primarily because earlier contacts with the Foreign Office showed that they would oppose the operation.

George Shultz, Secretary of State at the time, found the British reaction puzzling. President Reagan and he felt that on this issue Mrs Thatcher was 'just plain wrong. He had supported her in the Falklands. He was absolutely right about Grenada. She didn't share his judgment at all. He was deeply disappointed.'[7] She was angered at the lack of real consultation, for which Shultz himself was partly responsible, and at US intervention in a former British colony and member of the Commonwealth.

Reagan had hoped to get a better reaction from the Prime Minister and in that he was disappointed. As she was preparing to explain in Parliament what had happened, he telephoned her to try to make his peace. She was uncharacteristically muted in reply. She told her Cabinet that she was convinced that her advice against intervention had been correct. But the United States had taken a different view on an issue that directly touched its national interests: 'Britain's friendship with the United States must on no account be jeopardised.' The fact that the Grenadans so evidently welcomed the US action had its effect on British opinion – and on Margaret Thatcher – over time. Though Geoffrey Howe felt that 'Grenada, rather than the Falklands, offered the best evidence of American instincts', both governments worked to put this episode behind them.[8]

40

'THE OBJECTIVE IS TO HAVE A WORLD WITHOUT WAR'

REAGAN AND MRS THATCHER met again in June 1984 after the President had visited Normandy to commemorate the fortieth anniversary of the Allied landings there. He returned to London for the economic summit. By this time relations had been fully restored. For Reagan to have borne a grudge about Grenada would have been out of character and anyway his policy, in his view, had been vindicated by its success. In this as in previous economic summits, he and the Prime Minister found themselves on the same side of the ideological divide *vis-à-vis* François Mitterrand and the Canadian Prime Minister, Pierre Trudeau. Reagan was upset when Trudeau criticised Mrs Thatcher's style of chairing the meeting. He was reassured by the Prime Minister that she didn't mind: 'Women know when men are being childish.'[1] It was a story Reagan loved telling afterwards. He coasted to re-election in November.

The British continued to express their concern about the US budget deficit, to no avail. Nigel Lawson, Chancellor of the Exchequer at the time, comments that it was virtually impossible to persuade Donald Regan, the US Treasury Secretary, that the deficit was of any importance at all to other countries, 'not that he would have worried unduly even if he had been so persuaded'. Lawson concluded that 'US economic policy is invariably dictated by the domestic considerations of the moment. The only difference between Don Regan and other incumbents was that he made no attempt to conceal this.'[2]

Lawson recalls on the eve of the summit a small dinner party that Mrs Thatcher gave at 10 Downing Street for Reagan:

Reagan was on sparkling form, reeling off the home-spun anecdotes that defined his political philosophies. It was clear that Margaret was somewhat in awe of Reagan, despite his disarming manner. She had no great respect for his intellect and his hands-off approach to government could not have been more different from hers, but she both respected and envied his power. She recognised in the American President a man whose writ far exceeded her own.

Lawson described Reagan as the most unusual political leader he had met.

He had no time for detail, and little for policy in the everyday sense of the term. His mind worked exclusively on two contrasting levels. He had a small number of principles, which he clung to unswervingly and which informed his decisions. Difficulties arose only when two principles came into conflict. That was the higher level. The lower level was that of anecdote, of which he was a master, which he used for a substitute for argument, which he used to communicate and to persuade.[3]

In December, Mikhail Gorbachev made his first visit to Britain. He was thought likely to succeed the ailing Konstantin Chernenko, and Mrs Thatcher invited him to Chequers. After several hours of passionate discussion, she declared him to be a man the West could do business with.

The Americans were by no means convinced, but she had influence on this subject with Reagan because of the strength of her own anti-Soviet credentials. She told Gorbachev, however, that she was not going to act as a go-between and warned that attempts to persuade Reagan to abandon SDI would get nowhere. While concerned herself about the implications for British nuclear forces, she refused to oppose the whole concept. She accepted that the technology was changing and the time was coming when some missiles at least could be intercepted, as subsequently they were in the Gulf War.

This was to be a main subject for discussion when Mrs Thatcher met Reagan at Camp David just before Christmas 1984. She gave Reagan her impressions of Gorbachev, about whom she was enthusiastic. There followed an intense discussion of SDI. The Prime Minister expressed firm support for research on strategic defence. She had told Gorbachev that there could be no wedge-driving on this subject. But she was extremely concerned that the United States might eventually deploy unilaterally a strategic defence system, weakening the defence link between it and Europe. In reply, Reagan criticised the doctrine of 'mutual assured destruction': 'I don't think there's any morality in that at all.' Mrs Thatcher contended that it was this that had preserved the peace of Europe for forty years. To her alarm, Reagan, at his most idealistic, reaffirmed his long-term goal of getting rid of nuclear weapons entirely. He also talked in terms of making SDI available to the Soviet Union. (Fortunately, commented Mrs Thatcher, the Soviets never believed he would.)[4]

Nevertheless, her arguments made some impression. She produced from her handbag a note seeking to encapsulate the main points of agreement.[5] The four points agreed at Camp David were that the US aim was not to achieve superiority, but to maintain balance; SDI-related deployments would, in view of treaty obligations, have to be a matter for negotiations; the aim was to enhance and not to undermine deterrence; East–West negotiation should aim to reduce the levels of offensive weapons on both sides.

The second point was crucial, as it carried with it the commitment that changes to the Anti-Ballistic Missile (ABM) treaty would have to be negotiated.

The proponents of SDI within the administration were dismayed. Margaret Thatcher, however, had pre-agreed the four points with George Shultz, who considered it an excellent statement. The British were determined to make as difficult as possible any unilateral abrogation by the United States of the ABM treaty. The leading advocates of SDI were reduced instead to arguing that the constraints imposed under the treaty should be subject to a 'broad' interpretation.

Nevertheless, Mrs Thatcher was not seeking to oppose the right of the United States to conduct research on anti-missile systems and to deploy them if that could be done without breaking international agreements. On 15 May 1985, the British Foreign Secretary, Sir Geoffrey Howe, made a very critical speech about SDI in which he appeared to be questioning whether the 'supposed technology' would work. He also questioned whether the increased emphasis on anti-missile defences might not create dangerous uncertainty. Would it not simply risk increasing the levels of offensive weapons designed to overcome them? While many of Howe's criticisms proved well-founded, Richard Perle, a leading proponent of SDI, replied publicly that his speech proved 'an old axiom of geometry that length is no substitute for depth'.

On 20 February 1985, Mrs Thatcher visited Washington again to address both houses of Congress. For the occasion, she borrowed President Reagan's autocue and practised until 4 a.m.[6] She was fulsome in her praise of the United States. America, she said, had been the principal architect of the peace in Europe that had lasted forty years: 'For our deliverance from what might have befallen us I would not have us leave our gratitude to the tributes of history … We thank and salute you.'

The previous October, Mrs Thatcher had narrowly escaped assassination in the Brighton bombing at the hands of the IRA. She devoted a significant part of her speech to Northern Ireland. The British and Irish governments, she declared, were united in condemning terrorism.

She received a standing ovation from the members of Congress, but the speech was less well-received in Britain, where she was accused of subservience towards the United States. In fact it is doubtful if any post-war British Prime Minister was more forthright in her private arguments with the Americans, but public differences were limited to Grenada and the attempt to apply sanctions to British companies.

In her speech she emphasised what Europe had suffered in two conventional wars and quoted Churchill in his last address to Congress: 'Be careful above all things not to let go of the atomic weapon until you are sure and more than sure that other means of preserving peace are in your hands.' She pointed to the imbalance in chemical weapons as well as in Soviet conventional capabilities. It was not the SDI programme that alarmed her but what she feared was the illusion that because of SDI it might become possible to dispense with nuclear weapons.

President Reagan responded that this was exactly what he hoped eventually to achieve. Mrs Thatcher described this disagreement over nuclear arms as the only really serious divergence they had. She declared that a world without nuclear weapons was not the objective: '[T]he objective is to have a world without war and at present it is necessary to have nuclear weapons because they are the greatest deterrent to war.' Reagan's view was very different. In his inaugural address in February he had declared that 'we seek the elimination one day of nuclear weapons from the face of the earth'.

In July 1985, Mrs Thatcher joined an arms control seminar in Washington with Reagan, Shultz and Weinberger. Her defence of nuclear deterrence caused Reagan to comment that 'she's not a great listener'. As she very well knew, however, most of the audience agreed with her.

Although Reagan and his key advisers during his election campaign had been very critical of the SALT II treaty, which was never ratified by the US Senate, they continued to abide by the limits on nuclear weapons laid down in the treaty. By May 1985, the treaty was beginning to bite. When a new Trident submarine was commissioned, two older Poseidon submarines had to be retired to keep the United States within the limits. When Weinberger and Perle contested this, Mrs Thatcher urged Reagan to continue to respect SALT II.

When subsequent attempts were made by the advocates of SDI to secure acceptance of a 'broad' – that is to say, flexible – interpretation of the ABM treaty, Mrs Thatcher agreed that it made sense to pursue the SDI programme to a point at which it would be possible to determine whether it would work. But she remained concerned that the ABM treaty should not be revised in such a way as to increase Soviet defensive capabilities to an extent that could reduce the effectiveness of the British nuclear deterrent. The Americans, for their part, tried and failed to convince the British that the Russians already were in serious breach of the ABM treaty through the deployment of phased-array radars at Krasnoyarsk. The Russians subsequently admitted that these radars were indeed a violation of the ABM treaty.

In November 1985, Reagan held an exploratory summit with Gorbachev in Geneva. Reagan's main concern was to find out what kind of man he was dealing with. In preparing for the summit he was influenced by Mrs Thatcher's impressions of Gorbachev as well as the assessment of Oleg Gordievsky, the senior KBG agent who had defected to the British. Shultz was impressed by a remark the Prime Minister made to him: 'Gorbachev thinks there are problems with the way the system works; he thinks he can made changes to make it work better. He doesn't understand that *the system is the problem*.' Reagan 'had to admit – as Margaret Thatcher predicted I would – that there was something likeable about Gorbachev'.[7]

In mid-December, a youthful Colin Powell was exposed to a first encounter with Margaret Thatcher, accompanying Weinberger to a meeting with her in Downing Street. The British had hoped to win a US order for a new battlefield telecommunications system manufactured by Plessey, which was facing competition from the French company, Thomson. It fell to Weinberger to explain that the contract was being awarded to Thomson, whose bid was several hundred millions dollars cheaper. Notwithstanding her admiration for Weinberger, he was told that 'nothing you can say will

convince me that there wasn't dirty work at the crossroads'. The French
had cheated. 'Don't write that down, young man,' she told Colin Powell.
Weinberger remained stoic under this assault.[8]

While this intervention exposed the limits of Mrs Thatcher's influence, it was
followed by a crisis that confronted the Prime Minister with an extremely
difficult decision and put her relationship with Reagan to a severe test.

At 11 p.m. on 8 April 1986, Mrs Thatcher received a message from
the President requesting her agreement to use US air bases in Britain for a
bombing raid on Libya. The Libyan government was held responsible by the
Americans for a series of terrorist outrages, culminating in the bombing in
West Berlin on 5 April of a discotheque frequented by American servicemen.
In the incident, an American soldier was killed and over fifty were injured.

In January, Mrs Thatcher had told American journalists that she did not
believe in retaliatory strikes that were against international law, annoy-
ing Shultz, who contended that the US had the right to act in self-defence.
After consulting the Foreign Secretary, Sir Geoffrey Howe, and her Defence
Secretary, Mrs Thatcher replied, asking the Americans to think further
about this. She emphasised that her basic instinct was to support the
United States, but expressed considerable anxiety about what was proposed. She worried that it might trigger a series of revenge attacks. She
wanted more information as to what sort of targets would be attacked.
The British also asked whether US planes could not fly from bases in the
United States or from aircraft carriers and what would be the legal basis
for the action the United States proposed to take. 'I am deeply troubled
by what you propose,' she declared.

This was not the response the White House had expected. The Prime
Minister felt that 'there was an inclination to precipitate action in the United States, which was doubtless mirrored there by a perception of lethargy
in Europe'. She knew that the political cost of giving permission for the use
of US bases in Britain for a strike against Libya would be high.

The British were satisfied with the evidence from intercepts that the
Libyans had been responsible for the Berlin bombing and Mrs Thatcher
now accepted that, in response to the Libyan attack, the United States
had the right to act in self-defence under Article 51 of the UN Charter.

Shortly after midnight on 9 April, she received Reagan's reply. He did not believe that the action he planned would trigger a new cycle of revenge. That had been started long before through Gaddafi's continuing support for terrorism. The attack would be aimed at Gaddafi's headquarters and security forces. Reagan said that he had no illusions that US action would eliminate the terrorist threat. But it would demonstrate that state-sponsored terrorism would not continue to be without cost. She should understand the effect on US opinion if the US response to terrorist attacks received no support from allies the US was expected to defend.[9]

Reagan clearly was determined to go ahead. Mrs Thatcher was told that the US F-111s based in Britain were more accurate and could stay longer over the targets than strike aircraft based in the United States or at sea. In the early hours of 10 April, she decided that she must support Reagan. His message that terrorism must not go unpunished strongly influenced her. Above all she was convinced that the United States must not be abandoned by its closest ally: 'Whatever the cost to me, I knew that the cost to Britain of not backing American action was unthinkable.'[10]

Mrs Thatcher's first task was to convince her Cabinet colleagues. Howe appeared to her to be opposed to the US action, though he defended it in public. In the words of her foreign policy adviser, Charles Powell:

> Nobody in the government supported the Americans over [Libya], absolutely nobody. She put it to the Cabinet and the only person who was vaguely in favour was Lord Hailsham, who was vaguely in favour on the somewhat eccentric grounds that his mother was American. The Foreign Office were wholeheartedly against it, believing it would lead to all our embassies in the Middle East being burned, all our interests there ruined. But she knew it was the right thing to do and she just said, 'This is what allies are for. If you're an ally, you're an ally. If one wants help, they get help.' It just seemed so simple to her.[11]

Mrs Thatcher told President Reagan that she would support action against targets demonstrably involved in support of terrorist activities and would allow the use of US bases in Britain if the list of targets were circumscribed accordingly. She also expressed concern about avoiding civilian casualties. Reagan replied, seeking to reassure her about the targets, which would, however, include Libyan military headquarters and air defences.

On the Saturday morning (12 April), General Vernon Walters arrived to see the Prime Minister on Reagan's behalf. She told him how appalled she was that the gist of her exchanges with the President had leaked to the US press. They discussed how much of the available intelligence material could be used publicly to justify the attack.

In deciding finally to support the US action, Mrs Thatcher was conscious, above all, of the damage that would have been done to Anglo-American relations by a refusal, of the debt Britain owed the Americans over the Falklands and the fact that she had declined to support Reagan over Grenada. The Americans, meanwhile, were getting no support from the other European allies. The French rejected a request that the US aircraft should be permitted to overfly France. To avoid overflying Spain, they had to fly through the Straits of Gibraltar.

Mrs Thatcher herself was in a state of considerable anxiety. Visiting *The Economist* on the afternoon of the attack (14 April), she must, she commented, have looked like Banquo's ghost. That night the attack was carried out, generally successfully, but some bombs did fall on civilian targets, causing a public outcry in Britain accompanied by emotionally powerful television reporting.

The initial impact on public opinion in Britain was even worse than Mrs Thatcher had feared. There were demonstrations against the American action and opinion polls suggested that only about 30 per cent of those questioned approved of the US bombing raid, while twice as many were opposed. The government was attacked by the Labour Party for subservience to the United States and criticised by many of its own supporters. Several members of Mrs Thatcher's Cabinet clearly were very unhappy. She had to make a statement to a largely sceptical or hostile House of Commons. The ensuing debate, she found 'rank with anti-American prejudice'. Visiting a constituency that weekend, the Prime Minister found people looking at her strangely, as if she had done something terrible. The raid, as she had feared, was followed by the killing of two British hostages by groups supported by Libya in the Lebanon.

It also was followed for a time by a decline in Libyan-backed terrorism. But in December 1988 a bomb exploded on a Pan Am flight over Lockerbie in Scotland, killing 259 people. Three years later, a Libyan intelligence official, Abdelbaset al-Megrahi, was convicted by a Dutch court of responsibility for this crime.

It was believed at the time that Mrs Thatcher would have to pay a considerable political price for this act of solidarity with the Americans. In the United States she won enormous public acclaim as well as the gratitude of the administration. She felt that her action had strengthened the 'special relationship, which will always be special because of the cultural and historical links … but which had a particular closeness for as long as President Reagan was in the White House'. She also felt that she had faced down a modish tide of anti-Americanism.[12]

It was at this stage that Congress had to consider a new extradition treaty under which IRA terrorists could be sent back to stand trial in Britain. An earlier treaty, signed in 1972, stipulated that extradition should not be granted in cases where the offence was of a political nature. The British were determined to close this loophole and in June 1985 a new treaty was signed covering a range of crimes for which extradition would not be denied on political grounds. The treaty had to be approved by the Senate Foreign Relations Committee. President Reagan intervened to help secure its passage. Rejection, he said, would be an affront to Mrs Thatcher, the 'one European leader who, at great political risk, stood shoulder to shoulder with us during our operations against Gadaffi's terrorists'. On 17 April, he telephoned Mrs Thatcher to tell her that the Senate had ratified the treaty. The Anglo-Irish Agreement concluded in November 1986 between the British and Irish governments was to make an important contribution to reducing support in the United States for the IRA and its fundraising branch, Noraid.

In January 1986, the Thatcher government was rocked by the resignation of Michael Heseltine, Secretary for Defence, over the future of the Westland helicopter company. The question was whether Westland should be rescued by an alliance with the American company, Sikorsky, or a European consortium. Heseltine favoured the European solution. Mrs Thatcher preferred the American option. While the business arguments for an alliance with the US company, Sikorsky, were supported by the Chairman and board of Westland, it was clear that the Prime Minister's own instinctive preferences were for collaboration with the Americans in ventures of this kind. The drama had been caused as much by a clash of personalities as by these policy differences.

In October 1986, Reagan met Gorbachev in Reykjavik. To the amazement and dismay of his allies, led by Mrs Thatcher, Reagan proceeded to use the summit actively to pursue his idea of rendering nuclear weapons 'obsolete'. Six months beforehand, aware of what she regarded as his 'naive' and simplistic views on this subject, the Prime Minister had written to point out to him that, while nuclear weapons in theory might be abolished, 'the knowledge of how to make them never will be'.[13] Gorbachev had proposed the elimination of all intermediate-range nuclear missiles (INF) from Europe. Given the mobility of the missiles, the United States countered by insisting on the elimination of all INF, whether they were east or west of the Urals. The US administration, meanwhile, started to float the idea of eliminating all ballistic missiles as the most dangerous and 'destabilizing' nuclear weapons. Before the meeting, Gorbachev warned the politburo that if it failed, they would be drawn into an arms race that they would lose, 'as we are at the limit of our capabilities'.[14]

At Reykjavik, Gorbachev agreed for the first time that the British and French nuclear deterrents should be excluded from the INF negotiations. Reagan and Gorbachev first agreed to reduce their strategic weapons by 50 per cent and no INF in Europe, but Reagan then made an offer to Gorbachev not to deploy a full SDI defensive system for ten years in return for an undertaking to eliminate all US and Soviet nuclear weapons over that period. While this was a personal initiative by Reagan, George Shultz went along with it, to the dismay of his colleagues. The summit broke down because Gorbachev insisted that testing of SDI capabilities must be limited to the laboratory, which Reagan was not prepared to concede.

There was an air of bizarre unreality to these discussions, as China, France, India, Israel and Pakistan all would have been extremely unlikely ever to agree to abandon their nuclear deterrents. When Mrs Thatcher realised what Reagan had offered, neutralising the effectiveness of the Western nuclear deterrent forces *vis-à-vis* the Soviet superiority in conventional forces, she was appalled, as were most of the US administration. The US Chiefs of Staff agreed with her. As Colin Powell and Richard Perle both observed, Reagan had scared his own side rather more than the Russians.[15] The British and French nuclear forces were not mentioned in the American proposal but would have been profoundly affected by it. But when Reagan telephoned her on the day after the meeting, he gave no ground on his long-held ambition to rid the world of nuclear weapons, expressing pride in his proposal and suggesting that NATO had better prospects in a conventional war than was commonly believed. To her alarm, this conviction was based on a new thriller he had been reading – *Red Storm Rising* by Tom Clancy – which he urged her also to read. Reagan understood, however, that Reykjavik had been a watershed, as for the first time for any Russian leader, Gorbachev had been talking in terms of real disarmament, eliminating entire categories of nuclear weapons.

The US officials accompanying Reagan noted that there had been no commitment by Gorbachev to abolish all ballistic missiles, where the Russians had an advantage.

Mrs Thatcher felt 'as if there had been an earthquake under my feet'. She supported Reagan's proposal to cut ballistic missiles by 50 per cent, but certainly not to eliminate them entirely, imperilling the British and (theoretically) the French nuclear deterrents. The American position on this appeared confused both at and after Reykjavik – deliberately so, as the national security adviser, Admiral Poindexter, sought to obfuscate what Reagan had proposed. President Mitterrand visited London at his initiative to meet Mrs Thatcher on 16 October, to express his misgivings.

Mrs Thatcher feared that the whole system of nuclear deterrence, which had kept the peace for forty years, was close to being abandoned. Apart from the threat to Trident, she also had worries that the 'zero option' for INF missiles in Europe could reduce Western deterrence. She had not expected the Russians to accept this but, sensibly, she now decided to welcome it.

Margaret Thatcher's reaction was to head forthwith for Washington, as she had already planned to do. By this time the US newspapers were beginning to publish stories about White House attempts to trade arms for hostages in the Middle East. Mrs Thatcher declined absolutely to comment on these reports. Visiting President Reagan at Camp David on 15 November, she declared that she believed implicitly in the President's integrity, a position she maintained throughout the crisis. Reagan and his Cabinet were duly grateful, though the British suspected and the evidence subsequently showed that Colonel Oliver North and other elements of the administration had indeed tried to exchange arms for hostages.

Meeting Shultz before she saw Reagan, Mrs Thatcher opened with the words: 'George, how could you have allowed the President to get into this position?' As Shultz observed, she gave him 'unshirted hell'.[16]

At Camp David, the Prime Minister and the President set off in a golf cart for a private discussion before lunch, an experience she did not enjoy, due to a lack of confidence in the President's driving on woodland trails. The NSC staff were rightly worried that, once again, she would produce from her handbag a statement that would commit the administration more than some members of it wished. The outcome, which, as before, she had pre-agreed with Shultz, brought reassurance to the Allies, steering the hugely important advances that had been made at Reykjavik in arms control in a precise and practical direction. The President agreed that she could issue a statement that priority was to be given to an INF agreement, a 50 per cent cut in strategic nuclear arms over five years and a ban on chemical weapons. They declared their support for the UK Trident programme and the continuance of SDI research permitted by the ABM treaty.

It was now over four years since the Falklands War. The State Department and the Pentagon wanted to sell the Argentines military equipment, including aircraft. The question was raised by Mrs Thatcher: 'Oh, arms to Argentina,' she said. 'You won't, will you?' 'No,' replied Reagan, reversing the position of the rest of the administration.[17]

Following the raid on Libya, the Labour leader, Neil Kinnock, had denounced Mrs Thatcher as Reagan's poodle. When Kinnock asked for a meeting with Reagan in the run-up to the British elections in June 1987, he was allowed just twenty minutes. He was told that the Labour Party's policy of unilateral disarmament was completely counter-productive in the arms control negotiations with the Soviet Union. Anti-Americanism and unilateral disarmament, which had appeared quite popular themes the year before, proved an insurmountable handicap in the election.

Mrs Thatcher, meanwhile, was visiting Moscow, where she was followed by Shultz, to discuss arms control. Gorbachev no longer was linking the elimination of INF to American concessions on SDI and was now proposing that shorter-range intermediate nuclear forces should also be eliminated. The NATO commander, General Bernard Rogers, and Mrs Thatcher were concerned that this would weaken Western nuclear defences, but she decided that Britain should not resist a solution on these lines.

On 12 June, Mrs Thatcher won a large majority in the British elections.

In July she returned to Washington, where she was asked by Shultz and the US Assistant Secretary of State for Africa, Chester Crocker, to help the administration resist attempts by right-wing Republican Senators to press for US support for the Renamo rebel movement in Mozambique. She had worked with President Machel during the Lancaster House negotiations on Rhodesia. In a meeting with the Senate Foreign Relations Committee, she strongly opposed demands from Senator Helms that the United States should support Renamo.

By this stage, Gorbachev and the West were close to agreement on the elimination and destruction of all intermediate-range nuclear forces (INF). The 'zero option', which had been thought by many to be non-negotiable with the Russians, came close to reality when Gorbachev accepted the need also to destroy the Soviet SS20s based in the Far East. Gorbachev had proposed and the Allies accepted the elimination of other land-based missiles with a range of above 300 miles (shorter-range INF). This was the 'double zero'. Mrs Thatcher and Mitterrand were concerned that there should be no 'third zero', affecting still shorter-range weapons, as they feared this could lead towards the denuclearisation of European defence. At the Venice economic summit Reagan recalled her arguing with the German Chancellor, Helmut Kohl, about the need to modernise the short-range missiles on German soil.[18] For once she did not win Reagan's support. The final agreement on the elimination of INF was reached in November 1987. The Russians agreed to destroy about 1,500 INF warheads already deployed, including all the SS20s. The Allies undertook to destroy the Pershing II missiles in Germany and the Cruise missiles deployed at Greenham Common.

In December, on his way to the summit meeting in Washington to sign the INF treaty, Gorbachev stopped off in Britain to see Mrs Thatcher at the Brize Norton airfield in Oxfordshire. The Prime Minister telephoned Reagan to report before Gorbachev arrived in Washington. She and Reagan had reason to regard the INF agreement as a joint success. It was impossible to see how the elimination of an entire category of nuclear weapons could have been achieved if the Allies had flinched from proceeding with their own deployment.

Although Mrs Thatcher attached great importance to her relations with Reagan, his reputation remained very low with the British public. Most polls suggested that Britons put more confidence in Gorbachev to reduce world tensions and they also showed that a more negative view of Reagan consistently was held in Britain than in France or Germany. After the INF agreement, this perception began gradually to change.

In March 1988, Reagan appeared at his last NATO summit in Brussels. He swapped places with Shultz so as to sit next to Mrs Thatcher. He spoke impromptu and movingly on what NATO had done to preserve the freedom of the countries represented in the room.

Mrs Thatcher shared these sentiments, but was more preoccupied with the business of the meeting. She was concerned that the West should not move from the elimination of INF towards the denuclearisation of Europe. She continued to press the Germans to accept the replacement of American short-range Lance missiles when they became obsolete. The Germans manifestly were resistant to doing so.

Stopping off in London on his way back from Moscow, Reagan invited Mrs Thatcher to Washington in November after the US elections. Just as she had been the first state visitor of his presidency, so he wanted her to be the last. Mrs Thatcher continued to try to use the personal relationship to get her way on policy, but when she sought reassurance again that the United States would not resume arms sales to Argentina, she received an ambiguous response.

Asked at this time whether she had concerns about her relationship with the next President (at this point the Democratic candidate, Michael Dukakis, was well ahead in the polls), Mrs Thatcher expressed the belief that she had established 'a kind of relationship with the American people: I believe it will outlive any changes'.

In September, Mrs Thatcher made her famous speech about Europe in Bruges, denouncing any thought of a European super state exercising dominance from Brussels. Europe, she argued, must be built on the free association of nation states. She opposed any idea of a European federation. The reaction from most of the rest of the European Community was hostile. The growing friction with the European Community did not damage her standing with Reagan, but it did later with James Baker and George Bush.

On 15 November, Mrs Thatcher visited Washington to say goodbye to Reagan. At the State Department, Shultz presented her with what he described as 'the Order of the Handbag'. Whenever a communiqué was required, he explained, she would produce from her handbag a draft 'which invariably becomes the statement we adopt'. The 'special relation-ship' was as strong as ever, he told Reagan, 'and remains of fundamental importance to the foreign policy of both nations'. At the state dinner at the White House, Reagan said that as he prepared to leave office, he took satisfaction from knowing that Margaret Thatcher would be there to offer his successor her friendship, cooperation and advice.[19]

Mrs Thatcher had been able to use her friendship with Reagan to get specific results. On several issues, her interventions with the President were an important factor in the ceaseless battles over policy in Washington. She avoided public criticism of American policy, except over Grenada and the sanctions against John Brown, even when she disagreed with it. In private, in the American view at least, she expressed her views more forcefully than any other foreign leader. In the opinion of Richard Perle, she never approached discussions with the Americans from a position of inferiority: 'Quite the contrary!' Kissinger felt that in this period she had achieved an influence on US policy not seen since Churchill's day.[20]

American awareness of how much influence she had on Reagan, and of how much he disliked disagreements with her, helped to ensure that full account was taken of British views at each stage of the inter-agency process in Washington, because all those involved in it knew that, oth-erwise, there would be a direct appeal from the Prime Minister to the President. While Germany figured increasingly in American thinking, this was a period of enormous expansion of British economic interests in the United States. Following the abolition of exchange control by Geoffrey Howe, British investments in the United States increased to over $100 bil-lion – well ahead of any other foreign investors, including the Japanese. Mrs Thatcher was determined to ensure by both words and action that Britain should continue to be regarded as the United States' closest ally.

41

'NO TIME TO GO WOBBLY'

MARGARET THATCHER BREATHED a sigh of relief when George Bush defeated the Democratic contender in the 1988 presidential election. But with the new team's arrival in the White House she found herself dealing with an administration which saw Germany as its leading European partner, which proclaimed its support for European integration and which also disagreed with her about nuclear defence. 'I felt I could not always rely as before on American cooperation.'

On her visit to Washington to say goodbye to President Reagan, Mrs Thatcher had talks with the President-Elect, of whom she paints the following portrait:

> I had always found Vice-President Bush easy to get on with and I felt that he had performed good service to America in keeping the Reagan Administration in touch with European thinking. He was one of the most decent, honest and patriotic Americans I have met. He had great personal courage, as his past record and his resilience in campaigning showed. But he had never had to think through his beliefs and fight for them when they were hopelessly unfashionable as Ronald Reagan and I had had to do.

Her Foreign Secretary, Geoffrey Howe, noted that Bush and his Secretary of State, James Baker, wanted to escape from the shadows of their predecessors: 'One perceived part of that inheritance, so it was said, was Ronald Reagan's tendency to take almost too serious note of Margaret Thatcher's instincts and anxieties.' He added that Reagan was 'one of the few men

with whom Margaret's tendency to orate was tempered by deference ...
George Bush was deferred to much less often, if at all.'

Mrs Thatcher subsequently learned that Bush at times was exasperated by her habit of talking non-stop on the subjects that interested her.
She could, he observed, be 'tiresome' and he found conversation with
her a one-way street. As Vice-President, he had arrived on one occasion for a stay at Chequers with a set of golf clubs, hoping to play golf
with Denis Thatcher, only to find himself trapped for twenty-four hours
in non-stop discussion of international affairs, with no time allowed
for golf.

Margaret Thatcher also perceived that Bush felt the need to distance
himself from his predecessor: 'turning his back fairly publicly on the special position I had enjoyed in the Reagan Administration's counsel and
confidence was a way of doing that'. By her last year in office they had
established a better relationship: 'By then I had learned that I had to defer
to him in conversation and not to stint the praise.'[1]

Her analysis was correct. Bush and, especially, Baker were determined
to bring a different approach. Reagan had begun his presidency with a
visit from Thatcher. Bush began his with a visit from Kohl. The key issue
in foreign policy was the reunification of Germany and it was the Germans who had the economic and increasing political power. It also was
Germany that would have most influence in Europe on the future development of East–West relations.

These differences became clear at the first NATO summit attended by
Bush in Brussels in May 1989. Mrs Thatcher was continuing to press for
German agreement to the deployment of a successor to the Lance missile
in Germany: otherwise NATO would have no short-range nuclear missiles, while the Soviet Union still had several hundred. While this doctrine
appealed to the US and British Chiefs of Staff, it took no account of what
was happening politically in Germany. Kohl and his Foreign Minister
Hans-Dietrich Genscher believed that they would be committing political suicide if they sought to deploy new nuclear missiles on German soil.

President Bush came down in favour of the Germans and he did so
without close prior consultation with Mrs Thatcher. Encouraged by Baker,
he sought to resolve the dilemma through a proposal to cut conventional
forces to equal levels between East and West in Europe, thereby reducing the conventional imbalance that nuclear weapons were supposed to

redress. The replacement of Lance would be considered only if circumstances changed very much for the worse.

By this initiative Bush resolved a potential NATO crisis. He said that such an outcome could not have been achieved without the 'anchor to windward' Mrs Thatcher represented.

Margaret Thatcher, outmanoeuvred, strongly disliked 'this sleight of hand': 'I had seen for myself that the new American approach was to subordinate clear statements of intention about the Alliance's defence to the political sensibilities of the Germans.'[2] Bush's description of the Germans as 'partners in leadership' appeared to confirm the way American thinking about Europe was going, giving the British press a field day at her expense, though General Scowcroft could not understand what the fuss was about. The phrase, he said, had been intended as simply a rhetorical flourish. The problem was compounded by her resistance to German reunification, which Bush and Baker regarded as both inevitable and desirable.

Nigel Lawson describes meeting George Bush at a small dinner party the Prime Minister gave for him shortly after the NATO meeting at 10 Downing Street. He found him to be as unlike his predecessor as it was possible to be. Reagan, while absolute master of his prepared script, often was in difficulty on unprepared ground. Bush, by contrast, was 'conspicuously lacking in polish and fluency, but quick to grasp any point made to him. It was clear, too, that the strong personal rapport Margaret had enjoyed with Reagan was not present in her relationship with Bush.' President Bush was seen off at the airport by Lawson, because the Prime Minister and the Foreign Secretary had other commitments. Lawson was right to doubt whether Margaret Thatcher would have permitted this to happen in the case of Reagan.[3] She would certainly have not.

While Thatcher long since had become a firm believer in Mikhail Gorbachev as an entirely new kind of Russian leader, the Bush team initially were far from convinced of this. As Gorbachev recorded, he had to rely on her to help to convince them.[4] The national security adviser, Brent Scowcroft, wondered if Gorbachev would not turn out to be Brezhnev 'with a new paint job'. Astonishingly, it was nearly a year after his inauguration before Bush had his first meeting with Gorbachev.

In July 1989, Mrs Thatcher removed Geoffrey Howe from the Foreign Office. It was clear that part of the reason was their difference of view over

Europe. The Bush administration, meanwhile, was professing enthusiasm for European unity. Baker and his immediate associates saw Mrs Thatcher as being out of step and, therefore, less influential with other European countries. At the same time, she was running into political difficulties at home over the management of the economy and the poll tax. In October 1989, her government was further weakened when Lawson resigned as Chancellor of the Exchequer.

The State Department continued to criticise Mrs Thatcher's policies in Europe. In November, she met Bush at Camp David. Although friendly enough, she noted, the President seemed distracted and uneasy. He did not challenge what she said directly, but asked pointedly whether her views had given rise to difficulties with Kohl and about her attitude to the European Community.

This was followed by a NATO meeting in Brussels in December at which Bush called for a 'continued, perhaps even intensified effort' of the European Community to integrate. This was taken as a signal that the President was aligning the United States with the federalist rather than with Margaret Thatcher's view of European development. The following day, Bush telephoned the Prime Minister to say that he had not intended his remarks to cause difficulties for her. Britain appeared no longer to have the specially favoured status it had enjoyed during the Reagan years.

George Bush had developed the habit of sending two US officials she admired – Larry Eagleburger and Bob Gates – to forewarn her of reductions in US forces in Europe. On their second visit to her, in January 1990, they were invited to 'take your usual places'. She said that of course she would support the President and invited them to return, 'but never again on this subject!'[5]

By this stage – 'partly personal chemistry and partly genuine differences of policy' – the relationship had become strained. Mrs Thatcher and Bush met in Bermuda in April 1990 in deliberately contrived 'relaxed' circumstances. She reported her favourable impression of Boris Yeltsin. Bush, still strongly committed to Gorbachev, made clear that the Americans did not share it. This time, Margaret Thatcher was persuaded to let Bush do more of the talking. The meeting ended with Denis Thatcher not enjoying being required to play playing eighteen holes of golf with Bush in torrential rain. The Prime Minister easily defeated the President in a kite-flying contest.

Bush wanted a further NATO summit in London in July. He told Thatcher that there would be no money from Congress to replace Lance short-range nuclear missiles in Germany.

Bermuda did not help much. As the NATO summit approached, the Americans were keen to announce deep cuts in conventional forces in Europe and the nuclear stockpile. In the communiqué they wanted to refer to nuclear arms as 'weapons of last resort'. Mrs Thatcher, who feared that the Allies were on a slippery slope towards the Soviet doctrine of 'no first use' of nuclear weapons, raised objections. The communiqué did refer to a 'new NATO strategy making nuclear forces truly weapons of last resort', but it also stated that NATO was moving away from 'forward defence', a move with which, given the Gorbachev regime in Moscow, she whole-heartedly agreed.

In retrospect Mrs Thatcher acknowledged that Bush handled the emergence of the post-Cold War world with great diplomatic skill. She also noted that if there was one area of foreign policy where she met with 'unambiguous failure', it was her opposition to German reunification. The Americans could scarcely have been expected to support her on this. On the contrary, they worked actively to achieve the goal to which she was so strongly opposed.[6] As Henry Kissinger observed, George Bush 'managed America's predominance with moderation and wisdom'.[7]

On 10 November, Helmut Kohl telephoned her as the Berlin Wall was being torn down. She wanted a cautious Western response to avoid weakening Gorbachev's position in Moscow. She foresaw, as did Mitterrand, that a re-unified Germany would change fundamentally the balance of power within Europe, but Mitterrand saw no option but to reconcile himself to this. Bush, in contrast, looked on German reunification in a wholly positive light: he had decided to back Kohl. In a meeting with Bush at Camp David on 24 November, she feared that German reunification could mean the end for Gorbachev, though they could not oppose it if the Germans insisted on it. At the NATO summit in December, Bush again laid emphasis on European integration. As this was exploited by the press against her, he telephoned her somewhat disingenuously to say that he had meant further economic, not political integration.

As Bush observed, he was not alarmed by the ghosts of Germany's past. By this time Thatcher was resigned to reunification, but not to the Bush/Kohl idea that this should be as part of an 'increasingly integrated

European Community'. She told Bush that she feared they might find they had not attached Germany to Europe, but Europe to Germany!

Scowcroft shared Thatcher's concern that a precipitous move towards German re-unification could mean the end of Gorbachev, as in effect it did in the coup mounted against him after she left office in August 1991.

The State Department were enthusiasts about European monetary union, an opinion not shared by James Baker, who understood the difficulties that would arise for the weaker member states. He was, he told me, wholly in agreement with her refusal to participate in a monetary union.

As the differences with the Bush administration over Europe were highlighted in the press, Mrs Thatcher told her Cabinet that she was not greatly concerned: in the first major crisis, the Americans would find out who their real friends were.

―――――――

This crisis was not long in coming. For several months Saddam Hussein had been threatening Kuwait, while other Arab leaders tried to mediate the dispute. On 24 July 1990, the head of the CIA, William Webster, showed President Bush photographic evidence that the Iraqis had moved two Republican Guard armoured divisions to within a few miles of the Kuwaiti border. On the following day, the US ambassador in Iraq, April Glaspie, was summoned to see Saddam. Ms Glaspie said that the United States had 'no opinion on the Arab–Arab conflicts, like your border disagreement with Kuwait', though she added that the United States could never accept the settlement of disputes by anything other than peaceful means. Saddam told her: 'Yours is a society which cannot accept 10,000 dead in one battle.' But the Americans and the other Arab leaders still believed at this stage that his objective was to blackmail and pressurise rather than to overrun Kuwait. To the British also it seemed to be a case of sabre-rattling.

On 2 August, these illusions were shattered as the Iraqi armoured divisions invaded Kuwait. Resistance was rapidly overcome.

In Washington, the first meeting of the National Security Council was held at 8 a.m. on 2 August. Before the meeting, General Colin Powell, chairman of the Joint Chiefs of Staff, told General Norman Schwarzkopf that he thought the United States would go to war over Saudi Arabia, but he doubted if they would do so over Kuwait. Going into the meeting, President Bush told reporters that they were not discussing or contemplating intervention. He said that there was no evidence that other countries in the Middle East were threatened but he wanted to have the invasion reversed and to get the Iraqis out of Kuwait. He anticipated 'a lot of frenzied diplomatic activity'.

The meeting discussed action at the United Nations, economic sanctions and the fact that, having seized the Kuwaiti oilfields, there was nothing militarily to prevent Saddam Hussein moving south to Dhahran to seize the Saudi fields as well, giving him control over 40 per cent of the West's sources of supply. It was realised that an economic embargo alone probably would not be very effective. General Powell asked the President whether a 'red line' should be drawn at Saudi Arabia.

The meeting ended inconclusively. Powell did not think it was at all clear what the President was going to do or whether he would accept the loss of Kuwait. He knew that Bush was meeting Margaret Thatcher, who would have strong opinions and a strong influence on him. General Scowcroft, the national security adviser, was concerned at the inconclusive outcome and encouraged Bush towards the view that there would need to be a firmer response.[8]

Later that morning, Bush flew to a prearranged meeting with Mrs Thatcher at a conference in Aspen, Colorado. Thatcher was staying at the ranch of the American ambassador in London, Henry Catto. As the Western ally with closer links to the Gulf than any other, Britain's position was of special importance. In a meeting at Catto's house, Mrs Thatcher made clear that she regarded the Iraqi aggression as exactly the same sort of challenge she had faced from Galtieri in the Falklands. She highlighted the threat to the Saudi oilfields. Bush said that President Mubarak and King Hussein were asking for time to try for an Arab solution.

Margaret Thatcher said that if Saddam did not withdraw, they must get the UN Security Council to impose a full trade embargo. They must get Turkey and Saudi Arabia to close down the pipelines through which Iraq exported most of its oil. They could send troops to defend Saudi Arabia, but only if King Fahd requested it.[9]

They then went out to a press conference. Bush was asked if he ruled out the use of force. He said that he and the Prime Minister were 'on exactly the same wave-length'. Standing beside her, he added: 'We are not ruling any options in, but we are not ruling any options out.' The press interpreted this as a strengthening of his position, as indeed it was, though Thatcher had not detected any weakness in it in their meeting.

Bush flew back to Washington to further meetings of the National Security Council. Much of the discussion still was of political action and economic sanctions. But Scowcroft, Eagleburger (deputising for Baker) and the Defense Secretary, Dick Cheney, all were convinced that a stronger response would be needed. Cheney and General Powell were despatched to Riyadh to warn King Fahd of the danger of an attack on the Saudi oilfields and to discuss what could be done to prevent it. Cheney took with him satellite photographs showing the Iraqi armoured divisions by now positioned on the Saudi border, while the Iraqis had poured 140,000 troops into Kuwait. There was no certainty that they would cross the border, but nor was there any certainty that they would not. On 5 August, George Bush declared, 'This will not stand, this aggression against Kuwait,' which Colin Powell felt had a 'Thatcheresque' ring to it.

By 6 August, the Western powers had pushed through the UN Security Council a resolution imposing a complete embargo on Iraq. Mrs Thatcher had left Aspen for a further meeting with Bush at the White House. In the Oval Office, she participated in what was, in effect, a meeting of the National Security Council:

> For all the friendship and cooperation I had had from President
> Reagan, I was never taken into the Americans' confidence more
> than I was during the two hours I spent that afternoon at the White
> House ... The President that day was an altogether more confident
> George Bush than the man with whom I had had earlier dealings.[10]

Bush showed the Prime Minister the photographs of Iraqi tanks on the Saudi border. They discussed the danger that Iraq might attack Saudi Arabia before the King had formally asked for help. It was at this stage that Cheney reported by telephone from Riyadh that the King had agreed to the despatch of the 82nd Airborne Division and US fighter aircraft to Saudi Arabia.

The following day, the United States began moving forces to Saudi Arabia.

Mrs Thatcher was closely associated with all these early decisions. As usual, no one was left in any doubt where she stood. On 5 August, she told her audience in Aspen that the Iraqi invasion of Kuwait defied 'every principle for which the United Nations stands. If we let it succeed, no small country can ever feel safe again. The law of the jungle would take over from the rule of law.'

Bush's thinking already had evolved significantly by the time he met Mrs Thatcher in Aspen. But she underpinned the conclusions he was beginning to reach about the significance of this crisis. In doing so she strengthened the hand of Scowcroft and others who were arguing for a military response.

On her return to London, she met the Foreign Secretary, Douglas Hurd, and the Defence Secretary, Tom King. She spoke to King Fahd, who asked for British as well as American forces to help defend the kingdom. Hurd announced that Britain would contribute forces to a multinational effort to defend Saudi Arabia and the Gulf states and in support of the UN embargo. The British reinforced their naval patrol in the Gulf with minesweepers, support vessels and an extra destroyer. By the end of August, fifty-six Tornado air defence and ground attack aircraft, a squadron of Jaguars and three Nimrod reconnaissance aircraft were deployed to the Gulf.

The meeting with President Bush in the Oval Office also had seen the beginning of a long argument between Mrs Thatcher and Baker about what authority was needed from the UN Security Council for military action, if necessary, against Saddam Hussein. She was unconvinced that any further UN vote was necessary: in her view, all necessary US and British action could be based on helping Kuwait to exercise its right to self-defence under Article 51 of the UN Charter.

On 19 August, two Iraqi oil tankers ignored warning shots by the US Navy and continued on to Aden. On 26 August, Bush telephoned Mrs Thatcher from his house at Kennebunkport. They congratulated each other on the passage of a further Security Council resolution permitting the enforcement of the embargo. They must, Mrs Thatcher said, use these powers to stop Iraqi shipping. This was no time to go wobbly. Scowcroft recalls the President's amusement: 'We used the phrase almost daily after that.'[11]

When Baker met NATO foreign ministers in Brussels on 10 September, he made clear that the urgent need in terms of the build-up of coalition forces in Saudi Arabia was for more tanks. On 14 September, Mrs Thatcher told Bush that the British Seventh Armoured Brigade would be sent to the Gulf. With none of the other European allies showing anything like that kind of support, Bush described this as a 'marvellous commitment'. The French decided later to send forces, though on a smaller scale. The role of Germany and the other European allies was limited to financial and logistic support.

General Sir Peter de la Billière, former commander of the SAS and with vast experience in the Middle East, was given command of the British forces in the Gulf. He found that for the British Army the task of producing one fully operational armoured brigade imposed a considerable strain on resources. To bring the brigade up to the strength needed to fight in the desert, men and equipment had to be taken away from other units in Germany. When they were joined by the Fourth Armoured Brigade, the effectiveness of what remained of the British Army on the Rhine (BAOR) was drastically reduced for the duration of the Gulf conflict.

Joining the coalition headquarters in Riyadh, de la Billière set himself the task of winning the entire confidence of the US commander, General Schwarzkopf: 'He and I were going to have to trust each other completely and tell each other what was going on, even if it meant, on occasion, sharing information which our own governments might have preferred to keep to themselves.' Schwarzkopf agreed, even though they were both aware 'that America was running the show, that Schwarzkopf himself would always be the main source of information and that I stood to gain most from our deal'. De la Billière also found that the French had virtually no say in the central planning as the pro-Iraqi Defence Minister, Chevènement, allowed no delegated authority to the French commander in Saudi Arabia.[12]

Both the British and Americans were preoccupied with the fate of their citizens taken hostage by the Iraqis. By October, 103 Americans and 260 Britons were being held at strategic sites in Iraq. Other countries were trying to bargain for the release of their nationals. The French appealed to Yasser Arafat and on 20 October Saddam Hussein, in an obvious attempt to divide the coalition, announced the release of the French 'guests' in Iraq.

The former British Prime Minister, Edward Heath, and many others made pilgrimages to Baghdad and managed to secure the release of some hostages. Heath warned Saddam that putting hostages in strategic sites would not stop Mrs Thatcher authorising bombing. Gorbachev sent his Middle East expert, Primakov, to the West to explore the scope for negotiations. Thatcher said that she regarded war as inevitable unless the Iraqis withdrew. According to Primakov, he was told that the best thing Russia could do would be to get out of the way!

By late September, the CIA had concluded that in the short or medium term, sanctions would not secure Iraqi withdrawal from Kuwait. Thanks to the blockade, nearly all Iraq's oil exports had been shut off. Imports were continuing via Jordan. The head of the CIA, Judge Webster, testified that Saddam believed that he could outlast international resolve to maintain the sanctions: there was no guarantee that they would cause him to change his policies.

When Mrs Thatcher chided the European allies for their feeble response to the Iraqi aggression, the Spanish Prime Minister criticised her 'warmongering ardour'. In Washington neither Baker nor General Powell was enthusiastic about offensive military options. De la Billière was concerned at reports that Powell was prepared to allow two years for the blockade of Iraq to take effect, while Mrs Thatcher was pressing for much earlier action.[13] Scowcroft remained convinced that force would be necessary to get the Iraqis out of Kuwait and was by now the President's most influential adviser.

On 11 October, Bush was briefed on the offensive options. General Powell was insistent that there should be no 'incrementalism'. If offensive action was decided, the aim must be to attack from the outset with all the force needed to win a decisive victory. On 23 October, briefing the British chief of defence staff for talks with Powell, Mrs Thatcher stressed the need to get the Americans to accept that in all likelihood military action would have to be initiated by the end of the year. On 30 October, Bush took the decision to deploy sufficient additional forces to be able, if necessary, to eject the Iraqis forcibly from Kuwait. The US and British Chiefs of Staff had reached independently the conclusion that if a ground offensive were launched, the correct strategy would be to attack deep into Iraq to envelop the Iraqi forces in Kuwait.

In the United States, most of the Democrats, led by Senator Sam Nunn, reacted badly to Bush's announcement of the doubling of US forces in the Gulf. The polls at this stage showed that only 40 per cent of Americans thought Kuwait worth a war. Announcing this decision, President Bush told Congressmen that he had been reading Martin Gilbert's history of Churchill in the Second World War. The US administration by now was convinced that there could be no confidence that the area would ever be secure again until Iraq's nuclear capabilities were destroyed.

Margaret Thatcher viewed with scepticism talk by Bush of a 'new world order'. But she was adamant that the Iraqi aggression must be defeated and she did not believe this could be accomplished without the use of force. She was not prepared to bargain for the release of hostages, telling David Frost: 'If you allow the taking of hostages, terrible as it is, to determine your own action against a dictator, he has won.'

Nearly all the Democratic Congressional leaders continued to argue that sanctions must be given time to work. Many experts on both sides of the Atlantic warned against military action to deal with what Senator Moynihan described as 'a small disturbance in a distant part of the world'. The risk was stressed of alienating the whole of the Arab world and of making – it was suggested – a martyr of Saddam Hussein. Scowcroft pointed out that if the Allies waited, there would be little left of Kuwait, and that relying solely on sanctions to force Iraqi withdrawal could leave the West dealing with an Iraq armed with nuclear weapons.

The Allied military commanders were fully conscious of the size of the task confronting them. The Iraqis had nearly one million men under arms, organised in sixty-three divisions, including the eight elite Republican Guard divisions. Saddam Hussein's arsenal included Russian T-72 tanks, Mig-29 fighters and SU24 bombers and French Mirage fighters and Exocet missiles.

On 9 November, in a meeting in Downing Street, Baker asked if Britain could contribute a second armoured brigade. His memo to Bush noted the Prime Minister hesitating about such a large reinforcement and that Douglas Hurd 'winced visibly'.[14] On the 10th, de la Billière formally requested a second armoured brigade to enable the British to participate fully in the liberation of Kuwait and in doing so to exert a considerable influence on American strategy. At Mrs Thatcher's last Cabinet on 22 November – the day on which she announced her resignation – the British government took the decision to increase its forces in the Gulf to divisional strength, with the addition of extra artillery and the Fourth Armoured Brigade. Bush hailed this 'wonderful contribution'.

De la Billière was concerned that at this crucial stage of the build-up to the campaign, the government was in crisis. Mrs Thatcher was admired by the American military and by the Saudi and Gulf leaders. According to de la Billière: '[T]hey all had the highest regard for her and simply could not understand how it was possible for a leader of international stature, who had done so much for her country, to be evicted from office ... just as Britain was preparing to fight a major war.'[15]

In terms of Anglo-American relations, the irony was that by this time the strain which had existed earlier in the Prime Minister's relations with Bush had been completely overtaken and she was recognised by the administration and public alike as the staunchest of America's allies.

As George Bush told me, he had never found it easy to deal with Margaret Thatcher, which did not stop him admiring her. Not surprisingly, he found it easier to get on with John Major, both being pragmatists and neither being a devotee of what Bush described as the 'vision thing'. The Gulf crisis brought them together much closer than they had ever been before. She understood his qualities as a great public servant and statesman, but was right that he was not a great political leader. In one memorable encounter in my presence, as we walked into the Oval Office, instead of opening with any pleasantries, she asked George Bush why he did not change his 'stupid' position against abortion, in which she knew he did not really believe and which, by alienating women voters, she feared would cost him the election against Clinton. As Baker, also present, observed to me afterwards, she was absolutely right.

42

'ALL NECESSARY MEANS'

BEFORE LEAVING OFFICE, Mrs Thatcher had continued to argue that no further authority was required from the UN Security Council for the use of force. But George Bush saw further action at the UN as necessary to hold the coalition together and to sustain domestic support in the United States. James Baker told the Soviet Foreign Minister, Edward Shevardnadze, that sanctions alone would not work: Saddam Hussein was prepared to sacrifice the Iraqi population. On 29 November, on US initiative, the resolution was passed authorising members of the United Nations to use 'all necessary means' if Iraqi withdrawal had not been achieved by 15 January.

From 20 November, Saddam started releasing more Western hostages in an attempt first to divide the coalition, then to reduce the *casus belli* against him. On 6 December, to general surprise, he announced the release of the American and British hostages in Iraq and Kuwait.

Just after Thanksgiving, General Schwarzkopf presented his battle plan to de la Billière:

> It was no coincidence that I had gone to him first. Great Britain had been our closest Western ally in the crisis, and he and I had become good friends. I trusted his brains and judgement so much that I asked his advice on even the most sensitive military issues.

The British Seventh Armoured Brigade was assigned to fight with the US Marine Corps facing Iraqi minefields and heavily defended positions astride the coast road to Kuwait. De la Billière decided to ask for the reassignment of the brigade, which, he felt, would be better equipped for the enveloping manoeuvre planned by Schwarzkopf. He also feared that a frontal assault by the Marines on the Iraqi defences could lead to a lot of casualties: 'Strongly as I supported the international crusade against Saddam Hussein, I did not see that this war was worth a lot of British dead.' The Marines were reluctant to lose the armoured brigade, but Schwarzkopf agreed to de la Billière's request (in the event, the Marines lost just one man in breaching the Iraqi defences). The British by this stage had personnel, including intelligence staff, in the American headquarters and took fire-support teams from the Americans into their own headquarters, at all levels, to help call in artillery and air support. 'Altogether the ties between the two forces had become very close.'[1]

Shortly before Christmas, President Bush invited the new British Prime Minister, John Major, to visit him at Camp David. As the weather was bad, they had to drive there from Washington and their first serious discussion of the military plans took place in the car, with their advisers, Charles Powell and General Scowcroft, perched on the jump seats. Bush made clear that if the Iraqis did not withdraw from Kuwait by the UN deadline on 15 January, he intended to order an all-out coalition air attack, to be followed by a ground offensive once Iraqi resistance had been sufficiently reduced to limit Allied casualties.

Bush was relieved to find Major as supportive as Mrs Thatcher had been on how to handle the Gulf crisis. The Americans found no apparent differences between the new Prime Minister and his predecessor. That the transition had taken place so 'seamlessly' in US eyes owed much to the continued presence at 10 Downing Street of Charles Powell, Mrs Thatcher's principal foreign policy adviser, who stayed with the new Prime Minister for the duration of the Gulf War. Powell was in daily touch with Scowcroft on the secure No. 10/White House telephone link and it was not long before Major and Bush themselves were in almost daily telephone contact.

Baker made final efforts to negotiate Iraqi withdrawal. The Iraqis remained intransigent. Unlike the Americans, who wanted a short war, the Iraqi Foreign Minister, Tariq Aziz, declared: 'We are confident that it will be long.' The British continued to try to dissuade the Europeans from attempting to undertake negotiating efforts of their own. There were particular worries about the French. As the French and Italians tried again to appeal to Arafat, the British Foreign Secretary, Douglas Hurd, observed:

'Anyone who suggests that Mr Arafat is going to produce peace out of this problem has a loose grip on reality.' On 14 January, the French made a last-minute proposal for Iraqi withdrawal, linked to a conference to resolve the Arab–Israel problem. This was unacceptable to the Americans and British, both because of the link and because it set no deadline for Iraqi withdrawal. In any event, withdrawal was rejected by Saddam Hussein.

Saddam remained convinced that the United States would not have the political will to sustain a long war or significant casualties. Despite the obvious and fundamental differences, he could scarcely be blamed for believing in the analogy with Vietnam, since that also was being canvassed by so many Western military experts. General Colin Powell and his colleagues had rather more direct experience of Vietnam and the lessons they derived were to be applied to good effect in the liberation of Kuwait. But the British and Americans were fully conscious of the scale of the task they faced, given the enormous build-up in Iraqi military capabilities over three decades. Brigadier Cordingley, commander of the British Seventh Armoured Brigade, warned journalists: 'There are going to be a lot of casualties.'

As Commander-in-Chief, Bush had the power to order an attack without Congressional authorisation. The Democratic leadership in the House of Representatives and the Senate still opposed the war. But Bush was convinced that, to retain wide public support, there must be a vote and that he could win it. On 12 January, 86 Democrats supported the President in the House of Representatives, which voted 250 to 183 in favour of military action. In the Senate the vote was fifty-two to forty-seven in support of the President. Among the Democrats who voted in favour was Senator Albert Gore, later Vice-President.

The coalition by this time had the largest air force ever assembled – nearly 3,000 aircraft – arrayed against Iraq. While the British presence was not numerically significant as compared with the Americans, British forces were able to apply special capabilities and expertise in areas like minesweeping where the Americans had gaps in their own massive armoury. The RAF had just over 3 per cent of the aircraft in the theatre, flying around 5 per cent of the combat missions. De la Billière reports the differences, in the run-up to the war, between American and British rules of engagement, with the British operating under very tight political constraints. The US Air Force commander told de la Billière that RAF aircraft would have to stop flying with the Americans unless they were authorised to take action against Iraqi aircraft showing apparently hostile intent. On 2 January, de la Billière learned that secret documents and a laptop computer containing an outline version of the American war plan had been stolen from the car of a senior staff officer in London. The papers turned up subsequently on a rubbish dump. De la Billière and the British Chief of Defence Staff, Field Marshal Sir Richard Vincent, had to make embarrassed apologies to the Americans.

The deadline for Iraq's withdrawal expired at midnight on 15 January. On the following night, President Bush launched the Allied air attack. It was of unprecedented intensity. For much of the next month Allied aircraft were flying 3,000 sorties a day. De la Billière was impressed at the accuracy of the new US laser-guided weaponry. The apparently formidable Iraqi air defences were overwhelmed by the weight of the attack and superior American technology. The RAF played a significant part through low-level attacks on Iraqi airfields. These were difficult and dangerous missions, resulting in the loss in the first week of five Tornado aircraft, a much higher rate of attrition than for the Americans, who were operating from over 10,000 feet with laser-guided weapons. De la Billière wondered whether 'such very great courage was not being misused, when weighed against the limited success which we were achieving'. The US Air Force commander agreed and from 23 January the Tornados were given different assignments. Despite these losses, the morale of the pilots was extremely high. Ageing Buccaneer aircraft were brought out from Britain to give the Tornados the laser-designation capability that had proved its worth in terms of the accuracy the Americans were achieving.[2]

In this early phase of the war, British SAS teams were engaged in deep reconnaissance operations inside Iraq, hunting for Scud missiles and exploring routes that subsequently were used by the Allied invasion forces.

The ground war began at 4 a.m. on 24 February when the US Marines broke through the minefields into Kuwait and began to fight their way north along the direct route to Kuwait City. The American XVIII Corps, with a French brigade on their left flank, began the enveloping operation deep into Iraq, designed to trap the Republican Guard divisions. The American 101st Airborne Division landed eighty kilometres inside Iraq, while the US Navy shelled the coast as if in preparation for an amphibious landing.

On 25 February, the British First Armoured Division joined the attack. The British had expected to have to fight their way through heavily defended positions. Instead they found themselves driving into Iraq through lanes marked with tape and huge coloured signs bearing the legend: 'Welcome to Iraq, courtesy of the Big Red One' (the US First Mechanized Infantry Division). The US infantrymen waved the British Challenger tanks through into the attack.

As the first enemy tanks began to be engaged, it became clear that two pieces of Allied equipment were war winners – the satellite global positioning system, which told the tank commanders where they were to within fifteen metres, and the thermal optical gunsight, which enabled crews to see in the dark. By picking up heat emissions, the gunsights gave the American and British tank commanders the ability to detect and fire at enemy tanks before they could themselves be targeted. By midnight on 25 February, the British division was engaged in its first, successful tank battle. The engagement continued on the following morning. Brigadier Chris Hammerbeck wrote the following account of the land battle:

> A tank battle at night is a curious affair, since the action is fought entirely on thermal sights and therefore in green, white and black, which removes much of the drama. You cannot see the enemy firing at your own tank, but you are aware that it is happening as a supersonic bang is heard as each round passes close by. A hit on the enemy is simply a black or white spot on the target, followed by a wisp of thermal smoke. In reality, this hides the catastrophic explosion of a tank, with the consequent loss of its crew.

Also in the early morning of 26 February, HMS *Gloucester*, lying close to the Kuwaiti coast, which was being bombarded by the American fleet, detected and shot down with a Sea Dart missile an Iraqi Silkworm missile aimed at the USS *Missouri*.

American close air support was crucial to the success of the Allied tank formations and was a major factor in limiting the casualties they suffered. But on the afternoon of 26 February, as the British forces engaged an Iraqi tank brigade, there occurred the 'friendly fire' incident in which nine British soldiers were killed in an attack by US A10 aircraft. Over twenty Americans already had been killed in fratricidal incidents. De la Billière knew that

> errors of this kind were very difficult to prevent, especially in a
> fluid and fast-moving armoured battle such as we were fighting
> … I also knew that without the magnificent American air support
> which our ground forces were receiving, our own losses would be
> much higher: hundreds of similar missions had been flown with-
> out mishap.

The pilots and ground controllers were operating under intense pressure
and the Allied advance had gone much faster than anyone had predicted.
De la Billière publicised immediately what had happened.[3]

The British division reached its final objective astride the Basra road
half an hour before the suspension of offensive operations was announced,
after a hundred hours of fighting, at 8 a.m. on 28 February. The division had advanced over 300 kilometres, destroyed much of three Iraqi
armoured divisions and taken 7,000 prisoners.

Although the Foreign Secretary, Douglas Hurd, was in Washington at
the time, the British were informed rather than consulted by President
Bush about the decision to end hostilities after just four days of the ground
war. The White House was responding to concern in the United States
that the air attacks on Iraqi columns retreating from Kuwait were turning into a massacre, with the Iraqis no longer able to defend themselves.
It never had been the intention of the American or British governments
to advance towards Baghdad or to occupy any part of Iraq for longer
than was necessary. The political and military objective of the liberation
of Kuwait had been achieved. General Powell consulted General Schwarzkopf and neither objected to the cessation of the offensive operations on
the morning of 28 February.[4]

As a result, however, Iraqi Republican Guard units were able subsequently to withdraw to Basra with a substantial amount of their weapons
and fighting capability intact. On 2 March, elements of one of the Republican Corps divisions fired on soldiers of the US 24th Mechanized Infantry
Division and lost nearly 100 tanks and armoured cars in the ensuing
counter-attack.

On 3 March, de la Billière accompanied General Schwarzkopf to his
meeting with the defeated Iraqi generals. The Iraqis managed to secure
Schwarzkopf's agreement that they could fly helicopters. Saddam's defeat
was followed by uprisings by the Shiites in southern Iraq. The Republican

Guard units that had not been disarmed in the Basra pocket and Iraqi military helicopters subsequently were used to suppress the insurrection by the Shia in southern Iraq.

From a military point of view, a lesson of the operations in the Gulf was the ability of the American and British armed forces to operate together in a more cohesive manner than any other allies could have done, due to long habits of cooperation, integrated command structures and access to the same real-time intelligence. Politically, Britain had displayed from the outset a willingness to share the military risks involved in defeating Iraqi aggression, in contrast to all the other allies except France. Britain's contribution to the victory had been second only to that of the United States. Without the United States, the European allies combined would not have been able to muster the forces needed to defeat Saddam Hussein.

43

'THE WHOLE OF THE BALKANS ARE NOT WORTH THE BONES OF A SINGLE POMERANIAN GRENADIER'

NO SOONER HAD the war in the Gulf been won than fighting broke out between the Serbs and Croats in Yugoslavia. The Bush administration, preoccupied with bringing US troops back from the Gulf, had no intention of turning them around and sending them to the Balkans. It was far from clear that any US interests were at stake, with the Secretary of State, James Baker, reportedly concluding: 'We do not have a dog in this fight.'

Mediating efforts by Lord Carrington were undercut when Germany insisted on EU recognition forthwith of Croatian independence, precipitating a declaration of independence by the Bosnian Muslim majority and war with the Bosnian Serbs.

The UN imposed an arms embargo, which affected only the Muslims, as the Bosnian Serbs were supplied and backed by the Yugoslav Army. In November 1992, Britain sent 1,800 soldiers under UN auspices to help distribute humanitarian supplies, as did France. Mission creep soon turned this into an attempted peace-keeping mission in the absence of a peace to keep. David Owen for the European Community and Cyrus Vance for the UN attempted to get agreement to a complex, patchwork-quilt cantonal solution, with no success. In the US election campaign, Bill Clinton had begun to advocate lifting the arms embargo, to help the Muslims, with possible air strikes against the Serbs.

Bill Clinton, however, once elected President, was determined to focus exclusively on his domestic priorities and to avoid any foreign quagmires. His wife Hillary had given him a copy of *Balkan Ghosts* by Robert Kaplan,[1] describing the 900-year history of conflict in the Balkans. I found the new President trying to quote to me Bismarck's dictum that the whole of the Balkans were not worth the bones of a single Pomeranian grenadier. The new administration, reacting to criticisms of their passivity by David Owen and judging that it was unworkable, disavowed the Vance–Owen plan. Jacques Poos, Luxembourg's Foreign Minister, meanwhile had declared on behalf of the European Community that this was 'the hour of Europe'.

Lifting the arms embargo obviously would endanger the troops on the ground. Douglas Hurd, the Foreign Secretary, caused indignation by saying that this would create a 'level killing field'. The British Chiefs of Staff were adamant in their advice to the Prime Minister, John Major, that a conflict with the Serbs could not be won by air strikes alone: it would require a massive commitment of ground forces.[2] A 'no-fly zone' was declared, backed by the US, but that was the extent of their involvement.

In April 1993, Clinton's Secretary of State, Warren Christopher, made a half-hearted attempt to persuade the Major government to agree to 'lift and strike'. According to the US ambassador in London, Ray Seitz, this message was delivered by Christopher 'with all the verve of a solicitor going over a conveyance deed'.[3] Nor was it helped by the Defense Secretary, Les Aspin, telling me as Christopher set off for London that the Pentagon thought that lifting the arms embargo was a bad idea. Things went from bad to worse in Bosnia, with the UN declaring Bosnian cities and enclaves 'safe areas', only for them then to be shelled by the Serbs. The efforts of the UN representative, Yasushi Akashi, to get them to desist were hopelessly ineffectual.

In February 1994, in response to heavy casualties from shelling in Sarajevo, the UN authorised NATO to bomb the Serbs unless they withdrew their artillery around Sarajevo or put it under UN control. It never was brought under effective control, though the UN commander in Sarajevo certified that it had been. No action was taken against the Serbs, who, later, resumed shelling Sarajevo with the same weapons. The chairman of the US Joint Chiefs of Staff, General Shalikashvili, considered this to have been a dreadful mistake. The Serbs had been allowed to defy a NATO-backed ultimatum and get away with it.

By the spring of 1995, the situation of the UN forces in Bosnia had become critical. A new commander in Sarajevo, General Rupert Smith, believed that no solution was possible without doing more to deter the Serbs. When they intensified the shelling of Sarajevo, he ordered air strikes against Serb ammunition depots. The Serbs responded by shelling other 'safe areas' and taking over thirty British and many other UN soldiers hostage.

By this stage I was asked to warn General Shalikashvili that the UN forces in Bosnia might have to be withdrawn and that, in that event, we were likely to have to ask for US help in extricating them. Shalikashvili responded that he would recommend that, if necessary, the US should help their allies with an airborne division, but he would have to consult the President.

In July there followed the attack by General Mladić on the enclave of Srebrenica, brushing aside the Dutch peace-keeping contingent, who were powerless to stop the Serbs then rounding up and massacring the 7,000 male inhabitants.

The British military contingent, surrounded by Serb forces in the enclave of Gorazde, very clearly were next in line. As the new Foreign Secretary, Malcolm Rifkind, arrived in Washington, I told him that Richard Holbrooke for the State Department and the national security adviser, Tony Lake, agreed that, this time, a very different sort of ultimatum should be given to Mladić about the consequences of attacking Gorazde, not by the hapless Akashi, but by the heads of US Strike Command (in combat uniform), RAF Bomber Command and a French Air Force general.

To help re-inforce the efforts of Holbrooke and Lake, and knowing that by then Hillary Clinton was in favour of action against the Serbs, very exceptionally, I asked to see President Clinton on his own. I said that if we allowed what had happened in Srebrenica to be repeated elsewhere or the Serbs to overwhelm Sarajevo, I did not believe that the reputation of any Western leader would survive. I found that he had reached this conclusion himself, that there was no low-risk policy in relation to Bosnia and that the US must now show decisive leadership.

John Major had taken the courageous decision to send an 1,800-strong rapid reaction force, armed with artillery, to defend Sarajevo. When the Serbs shelled the city again, on 29 August General Smith withdrew the exposed British contingent from Gorazde and NATO launched a general air attack on all Bosnian Serb military targets. The belief that air power could not succeed without combat troops on the ground was confounded in this case by the vast advances the US had made in precision-guided missiles and targeting. Helped by military advances by the Croats, it resulted in an end to the fighting being agreed through forceful diplomacy by Richard Holbrooke in the Dayton peace accords. While European efforts undoubtedly had saved thousands of lives, there never had been any chance of imposing a solution in Bosnia without a whole-hearted effort by the United States.

The divergence of policy between Britain and the United States had resulted for a time in a blame game neither side could win. The faults on the US side – lack of commitment – and on the British – a reluctance to recognise that the policy was failing – in the end had been overcome, resulting eventually in effective intervention and putting an end to one of the most serious transatlantic disagreements since Suez.

44

'THE BRITISH WERE FURIOUS'

APART FROM THE differences over Bosnia, relations between Bill Clinton and John Major had got off to a rocky start as a result of media reports that the Republicans had asked the Home Office in Britain to examine their files to see if Clinton had enquired about British citizenship while at Oxford to avoid the Vietnam draft. Although a Republican consular official had tried to pursue this, the Home Office had not received, still less responded to, any such request and had done their best to squash any speculation of the kind. But there was no way of getting this out of the heads of some of Clinton's staffers and nor was there any doubt that Major and his colleagues would have preferred George Bush to win the election.

In such circumstances, embassies can have their uses. Much as I admired the Bush foreign policy team, the same could not be said of his domestic policy advisers. Nor was the President, a bona fide statesman and great public servant, much of a politician at all. The economy was struggling and the Federal Reserve Board was slow to raise interest rates. When in April 1992 he failed to replace Dan Quayle as his vice-presidential candidate, I became convinced that he could lose the election, with James Baker confiding to me his worries on that score.

The Democratic candidates were known at the time as the 'seven dwarves'. Jonathan Powell, first secretary in the embassy, was assigned to follow the campaign of the only one of them who looked to us to have the potential to become a serious contender, the 'new Democrat' governor of Arkansas, Bill Clinton. He followed Clinton from his bus in New Hampshire all the way to the White House, while I kept in touch with the main figures in his foreign policy team – Warren Christopher, Tony Lake, Strobe Talbott, Richard Holbrooke and Les Aspin.

Bill Clinton thanked me for this when I met him at the dinner in Washington given for him before his inauguration by Katharine Graham. He agreed that he would need John Major's support in dealing *inter alia* with Saddam Hussein and to invite him to Washington shortly after his inauguration. Their meeting was friendly enough, with agreement if necessary on air strikes to maintain the pressure on Saddam, though there was no great personal chemistry: they were very different people.

As Major was soon to find, the new President was a political animal to his inner core. In December 1993, Major and the Irish Prime Minister, Albert Reynolds, published their Joint Declaration setting out the framework for a peace process in Northern Ireland, with the Irish government reaffirming that Irish unity could only come about with the consent of the people of Northern Ireland and, in an effort to propel them into negotiations, lifting its ban on Sinn Féin.

In January 1994, the Sinn Féin leader, Gerry Adams, applied for a visa to visit the United States. No. 10 and I lobbied the White House against granting a visa to Adams unless he personally renounced violence. The State Department advised against, as did the FBI, the CIA and the US embassy in London. But the Irish government lobbied in favour, as did Northern Ireland Social Democrat leader John Hume, Teddy Kennedy, Pat Moynihan and some other senators and Democratic Party Irish American leaders in New York, plus Tony Lake and the NSC staff.

When the visa was granted, with no IRA ceasefire nor any undertakings from Adams, as Clinton acknowledged, 'the British were furious', with Major refusing to take Clinton's phone calls for several days.[1]

While just as annoyed as my colleagues at this decision, it offered the opportunity to demand that the Americans should now put real pressure on Adams to deliver a ceasefire, failing which they would look ridiculous. Nor did I feel that our own record on Irish matters up to that point was so stellar that we could do without the help of others, provided it was channelled in the right way. When, seven months later, the IRA declared a ceasefire, Clinton felt that he had been vindicated.

This very risky decision had been taken by Clinton primarily for domestic political reasons. But, his attention once engaged, he became a passionate student of the politics of Northern Ireland, regarding the peace process as a cause of his own. Despite the understandable misgivings of the Northern Ireland office, it proved possible to get the US positively involved on the basis, however, that there must be no interference in the negotiations, which must remain entirely a matter for the British and Irish governments, a principle meticulously adhered to by Clinton's envoy, Senator George Mitchell. Senator Teddy Kennedy, far more interested in peace in Northern Ireland than his critics gave him credit for, delivered on his promise to me to help in getting a far better hearing in Washington for the moderate unionists David Trimble and Ken Maginnis than they had ever enjoyed before.

With both of them present for a conference in Washington on investment in Northern Ireland in May 1995, I was asked to arrange the first very awkward encounter between Gerry Adams and a member of the British Cabinet: the Northern Ireland Secretary, Sir Patrick Mayhew. It was a meeting neither of them enjoyed, but a further small step on the road towards a peace.

The process also resulted in Bill Clinton developing a newfound admiration for the political courage and sheer grit displayed by John Major, despite his very small parliamentary majority, in the pursuit of peace in Northern Ireland. When he visited Britain and addressed Parliament in November 1995, he paid a sincere tribute to Major's efforts, before making with Hillary a highly emotional visit to Northern Ireland. Switching on the Christmas lights at the city hall in Belfast, the reception they got made a lasting impression on both of them, as did their equally enthusiastic reception in Dublin.[2]

The resumption of violence by the IRA with the Canary Wharf bombings in February 1996 thereby became as much of a setback for the US as for others and was followed by determined efforts by the administration to get the ceasefire reinstated, which eventually it was in July 1997. Clinton's envoy, the shrewd and experienced George Mitchell, played an important role in helping to get the negotiations back under way.

45

'SHE COULD NOT SEE ANY POLICY DIFFERENCES BETWEEN THEM'

DURING HIS VISIT to London in November 1995, Bill Clinton had his first meeting with the 'impressive young opposition leader', Tony Blair, whom he found bent on reviving the Labour Party with an approach remarkably similar to Clinton's 'new Democrat' campaign. Blair's aide Alastair Campbell half-jokingly urged the Clinton team to be a bit less effusive in their praise of John Major.[1]

Blair met Clinton again in Washington in 1996 as he prepared to contest the election in Britain, getting a lengthy and very positive hearing, in contrast to Reagan's dismissive encounter with Neil Kinnock (and Obama's subsequent, almost as brief encounter with Ed Miliband).

In June 1997, the Clintons flew into London to meet Blair immediately following his election victory, finding him 'young, articulate and forceful' and that they shared many of the same political views. Dining with their wives at the Pont de la Tour restaurant on the Thames, they 'felt like old friends'.[2]

In February 1998, the Clintons entertained the Blairs at Camp David and at a state dinner in the White House featuring Stevie Wonder and Elton John. With Clinton already in the throes of the Monica Lewinsky affair, Blair was determined to be completely supportive, describing Clinton as not just a colleague but a friend, helping the President in a very tight corner indeed. He added in an aside to the Foreign Secretary, Jack Straw: 'I hope to God Bill's telling the truth!'

Clinton supported to the hilt Blair's efforts with the Irish Prime Minister,

Bertie Ahern, in the run-up to the Good Friday Agreement in Northern Ireland. This remained a personal cause for him, and for Hillary, and although the British felt that the National Security Council staff nearly always were inclined to the Irish government's point of view, Clinton was more balanced and ready to speak to the party leaders in Belfast whenever he was asked to do so, maintaining steady pressure on Sinn Féin to conclude the agreement. The transcripts of telephone calls at this time between him and Blair show their extraordinarily close personal relationship, with Clinton offering to help whenever he could, wondering where Adams really stood with the IRA and complaining about the Northern Ireland politicians' constant need for time-consuming psycho-therapy.[3]

In August, a dissident fraction of the IRA exploded a car bomb in Omagh, killing twenty-eight people. The Clintons responded by visiting Omagh with the Blairs and George Mitchell to meet the victims of the bombing, with Martin McGuinness of Sinn Féin now declaring that he would oversee an arms de-commissioning process for the IRA.

In November 1998, Saddam Hussein blocked access by the UN weapons inspectors to various sites in Iraq. Clinton agreed with Blair on four days of Anglo-American air and Cruise missile strikes against the suspect facilities and other military targets.

———————

By this stage, however, Blair was more concerned about the conflict in Kosovo, where the Serbs were determined to maintain their control and to defeat the Muslim 'Kosovo liberation army' through killings that amounted to ethnic cleansing. Blair already was developing in his mind the doctrine of humanitarian intervention he was to articulate in a speech to the Chicago Council of Foreign Relations in April 1999, in which he talked of 'a duty to protect' and, tempting fate, suggested that 'in the past we talked too much of exit strategies'. But there was no appetite in the US to get involved in stopping the fighting. As Blair acknowledged, his determination that the West must intervene sooner and more decisively than it had in Bosnia 'put the most colossal strain on my personal relationship with Bill Clinton'.[4]

Blair knew that diplomacy would have no impact on the Serb leader, Slobodan Milošević, unless backed by the threat of force, and that, if it came to air strikes, 85 per cent of these would have to be delivered by the Americans, demonstrating 'the full extent of Europe's impotence'.[5]

By March 1999, the Americans had agreed to air strikes, with British and other NATO support. The British military again were unanimous, however, that 'you can't win this by air power alone'. Blair urged Clinton to consider the use of ground forces. Clinton went through all the objections even to planning for this, as the planning would leak out. The Americans felt that, as with Bosnia, the Europeans had failed to deal with a problem in their own backyard, with Blair now wanting ground forces the great majority of which would have to be American.

In a meeting with Clinton and his senior advisers in Washington at the end of April, the Americans were not to be moved. Clinton said little, chewing on an unlit cigar, while the NSC staff made the counter-arguments.[6] On 7 May, NATO mistakenly bombed the Chinese embassy in Belgrade.

On 18 May, Blair wrote to Clinton proposing a ground offensive with around 150,000 men, with a quarter coming from Britain. A follow-up phone call to Clinton began 'very stickily indeed', as Clinton fulminated about press reports, for which he blamed Alastair Campbell, that the US was being pressured by Blair to commit to ground forces and that Blair was having to stiffen the President's resolve. Listening to one of his calls to Clinton on this subject, his foreign policy adviser, David Manning, was struck by how forcefully Blair made the case that the West must intervene decisively. Blair believed that he was making progress in convincing Clinton of the potential need to commit ground forces, as Clinton himself confirmed.[7] The national security adviser, Sandy Berger, assured the British that a decision was imminent.

These well-publicised exchanges had their effect, helping to achieve a breakthrough on 3 June as, under pressure from the NATO-backed UN negotiator, Martti Ahtisaari, and Yeltsin's representative, Viktor Chernomyrdin, Milošević agreed to the withdrawal of Serb forces from Kosovo.

The drama was not yet over, as Russia stated that its forces would take control of Pristina airport. The NATO commander on the ground, General Mike Jackson, with a contingent of British troops, was ordered by the NATO commander for Europe, General Wesley Clark, to remove them. Jackson declined, saying that he had no intention of starting World War Three. Bill Clinton felt that Jackson had behaved with a lot more common sense than Wes Clark.[8]

Kosovo was the only real upset in the relationship between Bill Clinton and Tony Blair. Both prided themselves on having made their respective parties more modern and electable, periodically holding policy-wonking sessions, one of which was attended by Tony Giddens, author of *The Third Way*, and in which they tried to co-opt Gerhard Schröder, Wim Kok of the Netherlands and others. Hillary Clinton, by now entering the Senate, was a great admirer of Blair, sympathising with him over Kosovo. Between New Democrats and New Labour, she could not see any policy differences – unsurprisingly, as Blair's ambition was to transform Labour into a British version of the Democratic Party: pragmatic, centrist, a party of government. She did, however, suffer something of a reality check when, while staying with the Blairs, she switched on television coverage of the Labour Party conference to find, to her alarm, the delegates referring to one another as 'comrades'.[9]

Following the November 2000 presidential election, the Clintons visited Dublin, then Belfast with the Blairs. It was while staying with the Blairs at Chequers that they heard that the US Supreme Court, dividing five to four on party lines, had rejected Al Gore's plea for a re-count in Florida, thereby confirming George W. Bush as the next President of the United States. Both Clintons were appalled by the decision, but Bill Clinton's advice to Blair was to seek to establish a close relationship with the new President.[10]

46

'THE CLOSEST RELATIONSHIP
I WOULD HAVE WITH ANY
FOREIGN LEADER'

IN HIS FIRST meeting with the new President, shortly after his inauguration, at Camp David in February 2001, Blair found that George W. Bush's priorities were domestic – about education, welfare, tax reform and cutting down on big government as he saw it. Iraq was raised in the context of a new sanctions resolution, but with no great sense of urgency. They got on well, 'but fairly gingerly'. Blair found that George W. had a sense of humour and was self-deprecatory, but he was a dyed-in-the-wool conservative. There were not many social issues on which they agreed, and on climate change, they were poles apart.[1] In the early meetings, there was much about Putin ('one cold dude') and Ariel Sharon ('one mean sonofabitch'), but precious little about Iraq.

Blair managed to contain his political differences with the new President better than his wife. When Bush and his wife stayed with them at Chequers, Cherie spent so long haranguing him about the death penalty that the Blairs' son Euan had to intervene with: 'Give the man a break.'[2]

Bush was a world away from Bill Clinton. One conclusion Blair did reach, however, was that the new President was politically shrewder and more in touch with US opinion than much of the European or Democrat-leaning press seemed to want to realise. In the months that followed, Blair felt that, at this time, he was thinking about Iraq more than Bush. Given the admiration of the new President for Winston Churchill, the British ambassador presented him with a Jacob Epstein bust of Churchill for the Oval Office.

On 11 September 2001, Blair was in Brighton to address the Trade Union Congress. On seeing the television pictures of the attack on the World Trade Center, with the certainty of thousands of casualties, his conclusion was that this was a declaration of war. He denounced 'this new evil in the world' and declared that Britain would stand 'shoulder to shoulder' with the US to defeat and eradicate international terrorism. On the following day, he spoke to President Bush, who wrote subsequently: 'The conversation helped cement the closest relationship I had with any foreign leader. As ... the wartime decisions grew tougher, some of our allies wavered. Tony Blair never did.'[3] Outside Buckingham Palace, the band of the Coldstream Guards played 'The Star-Spangled Banner', causing the normally calm and resilient US national security adviser, Condoleezza Rice, when she saw this on television, to burst into tears.

On 14 September, in a second call to Blair, Bush made clear that the US would be going full force after Osama bin Laden and his allies in Afghanistan. Blair's concern was that if they also targeted Iraq, they would lose Russian and French support: 'My job is to try to steer them in a sensible direction.'[4]

On 20 September, Blair flew to New York. He attended a service at St Thomas's Church on Fifth Avenue with Mayor Giuliani and the families of many of the victims. A message from the Queen included the words: 'Grief is the price we pay for love.' He flew on to Washington for dinner with Bush before his address to Congress that evening. Blair, who agonised over his speeches, found Bush preternaturally calm. Blair concluded that he had found his mission as President, not one he had sought, but which had been thrust upon him.

Bush told Blair of his plans to give the Taliban regime in Afghanistan an ultimatum to hand over the Al-Qaeda leaders or face the consequences. In a written message, Blair had impressed on Bush the importance of concentrating on Al-Qaeda and Afghanistan, and seeking UN and coalition support. Bush had already taken that decision. Iraq was for consideration another day.[5]

Blair listened to the President's speech sitting in the gallery alongside Laura Bush. During his speech, Bush turned to Blair and called him 'our truest friend', resulting in a deluge of applause.

Blair now found himself dealing with an unusual US administration, in extreme circumstances. Differences between the State Department and the Pentagon were a perennial feature of US politics, as was the fact that, within the Pentagon, the military generally were far more cautious about the use of force than the political appointees.

To the dismay of his father, however, who strongly disliked the new appointee ('an arrogant fellow'), Bush had appointed to the Pentagon the hugely opinionated Donald Rumsfeld, who was in every way the polar opposite of the Secretary of State, Colin Powell. The doctrine of Powell's mentor, Cap Weinberger, had been that the US must possess the ability to deploy overwhelming or in any case 'decisive' force, but be extremely cautious about using it. Rumsfeld's view was pretty much the opposite. He was convinced that much smaller forces could prevail in regional conflicts. Also part of the Rumsfeld doctrine was a conviction that the US should not engage in 'nation-building'.

His appointment had been proposed by the Vice-President, Dick Cheney, who was encouraged by Bush to play a far more prominent role than any of his recent predecessors, becoming the most powerful Vice-President in living memory. Cheney consistently aligned himself with Rumsfeld. Colin Powell never was able to establish a close relationship with the President. Powell's deputy, Rich Armitage, another Vietnam veteran, did not bother to disguise his contempt for bellicose civilians in the Pentagon who had no idea what combat was like. The national security adviser, Condoleezza Rice, did not have the authority to cope with the clashing ideas and egos around her, though she was more trusted by the President than any of them.*

As for the circumstances, Blair understood better than others that the US had suffered a trauma every bit as severe as Pearl Harbor, with the casualties even heavier on 9/11, on primetime television in the mainland US. The Pentagon also was struck, resulting in a plume of smoke over

---

* Richard Haass describes a National Security Council meeting at this time: 'Rumsfeld entered the meeting carrying a huge pile of papers, dropped them down with a thud on the table, and announced that he hadn't had time to read them ... Colin sat tight-lipped lest he blow a fuse.'[6]

Washington, with Rumsfeld venturing out to help the rescuers. The White House or the Capitol would have been so as well, but for the passengers who challenged the hijackers of the fourth aircraft, causing it to crash.

The reaction of Bush, Cheney and Rumsfeld was that they were going to do whatever it took to ensure that no such attack could strike the US again. That was to include indefinite detention of suspects at Guantanamo, rendition and water-boarding, with all of them declaring subsequently that they would do the same again to help save American lives, with at the time most Americans agreeing with them.

Within two days, the heads of all three British security agencies (MI5, MI6 and GCHQ) were in Washington to offer their support. In his memoir, George Tenet, head of the CIA, described his dinner with them as the affirmation of a special relationship and, in these circumstances, a moving experience for him.[7]

In the near term, British concerns that the US might respond with some immediate 'ill-considered action' were misplaced: Bush said that he had no intention of firing a $10 million missile at a patch of sand. But, in his speech to the American people, he made clear that, henceforth, the US would make no distinction between the terrorists and those who harboured them. He was articulating a doctrine of pre-emption: threats of this order must be dealt with before further attacks on the US mainland could take place.

———

The Pashtun are always engaged in public or private war. Every man is a warrior, a politician and a theologian. Every large house is a feudal fortress … The numerous tribes and combination of tribes all have their accounts to settle with one another.
—WINSTON CHURCHILL (1897)

The Taliban already had been asked in previous UN Security Council resolutions, 1267 of 15 October 1999 and 1333 of 19 December 2000, to deliver bin Laden to justice for prior Al-Qaeda atrocities. The head of Pakistan's Inter Service Intelligence agency (ISI) saw Mullah Omar to ask the Taliban regime to hand over the Al-Qaeda leaders, a message also given direct to his deputy by the CIA. The Americans doubted if the ISI really pressed them to do so: they had invested so much in building up the Taliban to fight the Soviet occupation that they regarded them as their creation and the main bulwark against Indian influence in Afghanistan.

As they refused, on 7 October the US launched massive air and Cruise missile strikes on Al-Qaeda and Taliban camps and military installations. This was followed by the insertion of CIA and US Special Forces personnel to arm and support the anti-Taliban forces of the Northern Alliance in an offensive to seize Kabul. As the Pashtun leader, Hamid Karzai, returned to Afghanistan to oppose them, the Taliban's main base of Kandahar fell on 7 December. With Afghan militias, but only a handful of US personnel in pursuit, bin Laden escaped via the mountain complex of Tora Bora into Pakistan.

On 22 December, Karzai was sworn in as the new President of a transitional government in Afghanistan. Following the insertion of a small Special Air Service contingent in October, which was involved in a firefight with the Taliban in southern Helmand, in November British troops had helped to secure the main air base at Bagram, as part of a task force that grew to 1,700 men.

The CIA-led military campaign having succeeded brilliantly, and more rapidly than anyone had expected, the UK played the leading role in proposing the creation in December of the International Security Assistance Force (ISAF). Blair persuaded Bush to overrule Rumsfeld's objections to creating a multi-national force to which most of the Western allies eventually contributed small contingents. From December, ISAF, commanded by a British general, John McColl, stabilised the situation in Kabul, McColl thereby becoming a particular favourite of Karzai. The US forces in Afghanistan at this stage amounted to 8,000 men. A presidential election, won by Karzai, was held in October 2004 and legislative elections in September 2005.

By this time, however, the Taliban were re-emerging as a force in southern and eastern Afghanistan. The Pakistan government had been prepared to hand over key Al-Qaeda operatives, but the Afghan Taliban leaders, who were their protégés from the war against the Russians in Afghanistan, were permitted to continue to operate freely from their headquarters in Quetta. Attempts by the Saudis to get them to dissociate themselves from Al-Qaeda had met with no success.* Karzai was unable, and barely tried, to control rampant corruption. Helmand was a major source of the world's opium production. A British-led anti-narcotics programme had aroused the antagonism of the rural community, dependent on the opium poppies as their main cash crop. British troops, when they deployed there, had to try to convince the villagers that they were not part of the poppy eradication programme.

The British insistence on the removal of the corrupt governor of Helmand, Sher Akhundzada, who had been discovered with nine tons of opium at his headquarters, was bitterly resented by Karzai, as the Akhundzada clan had helped to deliver the province to him and continued to have significant influence within it. He was replaced by an unexceptionable civil servant, but who had no local support, with Akhundzada transferring his 3,000-strong militia to the Taliban. British civilian efforts included arranging for a lady from the Department for International Development to give a talk on gender equality to a group of tribal elders whose females were all in purdah.

The British military, dismayed according to Blair at the limits to what they could achieve in Iraq, wanted to switch the emphasis to Afghanistan.[8] At Blair's behest, the NATO summit in Istanbul in June 2004 agreed to expand ISAF's deployment gradually across Afghanistan. Britain then proposed that in 2006 the Allied Rapid Reaction Corps (ARRC) headquarters should be deployed to southern Afghanistan, with troop contributions from all NATO members willing to participate. The creation of the ARRC had been a British initiative in the first place, as a way of adapting NATO to new challenges, and ever since had mainly been commanded by the British. The Canadians, French, Dutch, Norwegians, Czechs, Danes and others signed up, with Germany supplying a non-combatant contingent.

Despite the difficulties the British by then were experiencing in southern

---

* In September 1998, following the Al-Qaeda bombings of the US embassies in east Africa, the Saudis, having supported the Taliban against the Russians, sent their head of intelligence, Prince Turki, to ask Mullah Omar to hand over bin Laden. According to Saudi sources, Omar left the room, only to return soaking wet. He had, he said, been obliged to pour a bucket of water over his head to prevent himself from harming Turki for asking him to surrender 'such an illustrious holy warrior'. For Prince Turki's account, see *Der Spiegel*, 11 August 2004. The Taliban also turned down an American approach to them at this time on the grounds that bin Laden was their 'guest'.

Iraq, Blair and his Defence Secretary, Geoff Hoon, were assured by the Chiefs of Staff that they could manage two deployments at the same time, even if there was a delay in drawing down the forces in Iraq, an assurance also given, in writing, on 19 September 2005 by the chief of defence staff and the army hierarchy to Hoon's successor, John Reid.[9] The Ministry of Defence at the time was envisaging the deployment of only around 3,500 men to Afghanistan.

In autumn 2006, Bush ordered an increase in US troops in Afghanistan, by now 21,000, to 31,000. The British, contributing the second-largest military contingent, agreed to take on what turned out to be the extremely tough and dangerous assignment of security in Helmand, a task that, despite all the history of Afghanistan, their military planners seriously underestimated.

The British would have preferred to deploy to Kandahar, but it was agreed that the Canadians would undertake the deployment there, where they too were engaged in some fierce fighting. Helmand was known to be 'bandit territory' and it was unclear how much of the province was deemed to be of strategic importance. It had only 4 per cent of the population of Afghanistan and 85 per cent of them lived close to the river in central Helmand. The Defence Secretary, John Reid, stated that the British military would be happy to leave after three years without having fired a shot, about as improbable an eventuality as could be imagined. While literally correct, it was an extraordinary statement to make, given the history of Afghanistan.

47

'WE WERE FORTUNATE TO HAVE THEM ON OUR SIDE'

Afghanistan has been less a state in the conventional sense than a geographic expression for an area never brought under the consistent administration of any single authority.
—HENRY KISSINGER

DESPITE THE CONFUSION above them, both military and political, as George W. Bush observed in his memoirs, the British troops engaged in Helmand fought especially bravely in ferocious encounters with the Taliban and suffered serious casualties: 'We were fortunate to have them on our side.'[1]

During the 2008 presidential election campaign, Barack Obama had denounced the Iraq War as having been based on a false premise, but embraced the campaign in Afghanistan as, relatively speaking, a 'good war', to which not enough attention was being paid because of Iraq. Once in office, he found Afghanistan every bit as intractable a problem and, according to his Defense Secretary, Robert Gates, did not want to be there either.[2] He was, however, responsive to the arguments of Gates and Hillary Clinton that the US could not afford to disengage in circumstances that could lead to a return to power by the Taliban on his watch.

The British military soon found that, as in Iraq, they were seriously under-resourced for the task they were called upon to perform and their enemies thought they could outlast them. The House of Commons Defence Committee concluded in July 2011 that the implications of the initial deployment 'were not fully thought through'. The original intention had been to concentrate, at any rate initially, on the protection of central Helmand around the provincial capital of Lashkar Gah. But the officer in charge of the initial British deployment, at the behest of the new governor, who insisted on the need to protect the outlying district centres, in a plan seen by the Chiefs of Staff in London, dispersed the British forces around the province in small contingents, highly vulnerable to Taliban attacks, thereby stirring up a hornets' nest. Blair kept changing defence secretaries. The new incumbent, Des Browne, accepted the dispersal, but realised that it had changed the strategy. By autumn 2006, the number of British troops deployed had doubled to 7,000, peaking at around 10,000 in 2011.

With the arrival of General Richards, a more targeted strategy eventually was pursued, with the US and NATO operations under a single command, and the British forces throughout acquitted themselves with courage and tenacity in their clashes with the Taliban, with far larger and better-equipped US forces having to intervene in support of the British troops in Helmand later in the campaign. When they did so, there was much agonising in Whitehall about the need to avoid this appearing as a setback for the British. The Taliban continued to enjoy safe havens across the border in Pakistan and active support from the Pakistan Inter-Service Intelligence agency (ISI).

As in Iraq, the British troops suffered from critical deficiencies of equipment, above all helicopters, armoured vehicles and mine-clearing equipment. In 2009, the British had just thirty helicopters in support of 8,000 troops. Because of a lack of remote-controlled robots, highly vulnerable foot patrols were having to clear roadside mines.

None of this prevented the troops and their commanders in the field earning admiration for their determination in combat. General Petraeus was impressed by 'the courage, capacity for independent action, skill and exceptional will' of the British troops. They had, he said, been in 'a very tough place ... they have done exceedingly well'. General McChrystal, leading the 'surge' in Afghanistan, regarded the British, however under-resourced, as by far his most effective allies.[3] The Americans, nevertheless, concluded that the British were not going to be able to cope in Helmand without reinforcement by them.

The overall result was a deadlock, with the Taliban unable to advance towards Kandahar, but no one else in effective control of much of Helmand.

The more intelligent military commanders understood that this kind of stalemate was the best that could be achieved and was sufficient to keep the Taliban out of power where it mattered most.

The frustrations of the campaign were epitomised in the fighting around the district centre of Musa Qala. In 2006, a British Pathfinder platoon, subsequently reinforced by a Guards platoon, then by elements of the Royal Irish Regiment, found themselves under repeated Taliban attacks and christening it the 'Alamo'. A truce, leading to their withdrawal, was negotiated by the village elders, only for the Taliban to occupy it a few weeks later. They in turn then were dislodged by British and Afghan forces. There followed a full-bodied assault on Taliban positions in Helmand by US Marines during the American 'surge' in 2008. Musa Qala today is back in the hands of the Taliban, as is much of the rest of Helmand province.[4]

In the same period, British soldiers were besieged for nearly a year in the more important district centre of Sangin, which they christened 'Sangingrad', before they were relieved by the US 82nd airborne division and British commandos in April 2007. Sangin today again is being threatened by the Taliban. General Richards observed that Helmand had seen the fiercest fighting in which British troops were involved since the Korean War.

One British commander described fighting the Taliban in Helmand as like 'mowing the grass'. After each encounter, they would spring back up again. Another concluded that it would have taken a full army division to achieve effective control of Helmand. The British ambassador, Sherard Cowper-Coles, regarded the war as unwinnable without a political solution and many of the military operations as more likely to alienate than to win support.[5] The military, both US and British, felt that if the war could not be 'won', in the sense of a definitive defeat of the enemy, it was important not to lose it either. In the words of a senior British commander, the objective was to reduce the insurgency to a level that was not a strategic threat and could be managed by the Afghan Army, with the US and British in a purely supporting role.[6]

When David Cameron became Prime Minister in 2010, he decided against early withdrawal, letting the Americans and the Afghan government down, but that there must be a term to British combat troops' involvement, which for him was before the next election. Meeting Obama in July 2010, he found him to be on the same wavelength. Obama, to the dismay of the military, had announced publicly that the US troop surge would be followed by a draw down from July 2011, which Gates and Hillary Clinton considered to be an unfortunate message to send to the Taliban, whose entire strategy was based on outlasting their opponents. After their meeting, Cameron declared that British forces would be out of Afghanistan by 2015.

Nearly all coalition combat forces were withdrawn by the end of 2014, with the number of US forces in Afghanistan peaking at around 100,000 in 2011. Britain was the second-largest contributor, with close to 10,000 troops at the height of the US 'surge', many of them heavily engaged in combat operations. A further presidential election, marked by fraud, but with a massive turnout, was held in June 2014, won by the former Finance Minister and World Bank official, Ashraf Ghani, who in an agreement brokered by the US Secretary of State, John Kerry, was able to form a government with his northern rival, Abdullah Abdullah. The outcome has been a government that, to date, has seemed more worthy of support than that of Karzai.

The contention that the coalition 'lost' the war in Afghanistan fails to acknowledge the continued existence, fifteen years on, of a democratically elected pro-Western government currently in control of all the major centres there. The 2014 troop withdrawals resulted inevitably in a resurgent effort by the Taliban, despite the death of Mullah Omar and leadership divisions, including over whether to talk to the Afghan government. It never made sense to announce an inflexible date for the troop withdrawals. Given the manifest need for continuing support, Obama has had to commit to keeping several thousand US troops in Afghanistan beyond his term of office. In 2015, US air strikes helped the Afghan Army to drive the Taliban out of Kunduz. In 2016, a US drone strike inside Pakistan killed Mullah Omar's successor, Akhtar Mansour.

The US and Britain are continuing to support the Ghani government with training, air power and Special Forces, though not with any significant numbers of troops on the ground. ISIS, meanwhile, has sought to establish small footholds on the border with Pakistan and the northern borders, attracting US air strikes and a hostile response from the local Taliban.

The British forces suffered 453 fatalities in Afghanistan (405 of them due to enemy action) and the US 2,259, plus numerous serious injuries.

The Canadians, French and Germans contributed around 4,000 troops each. The Canadians suffered 188 fatalities and the French eighty-eight.

The British Army, in its own pretty unsparing confidential critique of the military campaign, referred to 'a campaign plan kicked way off course', a deployment at variance with planning assumptions and original intent and ambitions unmatched by ways and means. In the latter stages of the campaign, given the high rate of casualties, tactical decisions were being referred to Whitehall, leading to 'creeping risk aversion', as the American commander, Stan McChrystal, also observed. The British chose to fight unsupported by tanks, which were used effectively by the Americans and Canadians. There was a critical lack of mine clearing robots and wheeled armoured vehicles, until the new Mastiffs arrived, greatly reducing casualties. But there had been a 'huge and honourable achievement' in giving Afghanistan a fighting chance of a better future.[7]

The British, led by the Foreign Secretary, David Miliband, kept insisting on the need to 'talk to the Taliban'. Hillary Clinton and Richard Holbrooke agreed and attempted to do so, in particular via Syed Tayyab Agha, who became the Taliban representative in Qatar, though it was unclear what influence he really had.[8] The problem was that the Taliban did not want to talk to them, with the leading CIA analyst, Bruce Riedel, concluding that they were 'not reconcilable'. In 2011, the leading Afghan government negotiator was killed by a Taliban suicide bomber.

If a negotiation is to be engaged with some of the Taliban, it will have to be primarily by the Afghans themselves, as they have been seeking to do. It also would require Pakistan to switch from continuing to give covert support to the Taliban as a hedge against Indian influence in Afghanistan to making a real effort to promote negotiations. A fundamental problem is that there are twice as many Pashtun in Pakistan as in Afghanistan, with an artificial border drawn by the British in 1893 between them, causing any Pakistan government to think in terms of compromises with those purporting to represent them. The Pakistan Army has fought hard against its home-grown version of the Taliban, posing a direct threat to it, but has never been prepared to take action against their allies in Afghanistan. Just as there was no clear military solution in Afghanistan, there was no political solution either, other than to seek to shore up the elected government, with all its imperfections.

The mission succeeded in its primary goal of ensuring no further safe haven for Al-Qaeda in Afghanistan and in denying to the Taliban any return to power in Kabul. In the terminology of Richard Haass, President of the US Council of Foreign Relations and a key adviser at the time to General Colin Powell, Afghanistan was a 'war of necessity', to deny safe haven to Al-Qaeda. Iraq, in contrast, was a 'war of choice'.[9]

48

'I WILL BE WITH YOU, WHATEVER'

AS TONY BLAIR observed in his memoir: 'But for 9/11, Iraq would not have happened.' In their earlier meetings, George W. Bush had been preoccupied with domestic issues. The mindsets of the key figures in the US administration were changed more dramatically than anyone outside America could realise by the attacks on 9/11. No one who visited lower Manhattan in the immediate aftermath of the attack – their lungs full of acrid smoke, with firefighters still staggering from the wreckage, US airspace locked down and 3,000 people killed – was ever likely to forget it for the rest of their lives, and least of all the President.

The greatest fear was that a future attack might be attempted with weapons of mass destruction. Blair saw in the US a belief that the attack was so shocking that 'the world had to be re-made' and in George W. Bush someone who had 'immense simplicity in how he saw the world. Right or wrong, it led to decisive leadership.' Blair agreed with some of this thinking himself. In foreign policy, Blair was a conviction politician. He saw in this virulent form of jihadism a challenge to the core values of Western liberal democracy.[1]

While Bush, in domestic politics, was more astute than his legion of critics gave him credit for, the 'simplicity with which he viewed the world' was based on hardly any experience of the world outside the United States and still less of the Middle East, which he set about transforming, but not in the way he had intended.

The sanctions regime against Iraq had been crumbling as a result of the manipulated evasion of sanctions by the regime under the UN-sponsored oil for food programme. Far from wanting to strengthen 'containment', the French and Russians wanted sanctions removed.

The US and Britain had been continuing to enforce the 'no-fly zones' in Iraq. The no-fly zone in northern Iraq was an initiative by John Major to protect the Kurds. The Americans pointed out that they were going to have to enforce it, but were brought to agree that it was a good idea. The southern no-fly zone was enforced as reassurance to Kuwait and to constrain the regime's military options.

In September 1988, Clinton approved the Iraq Liberation Act, calling for regime change and supported by both sides in Congress, though the Clinton administration had no real intention of giving effect to it. In December, however, in response to Saddam Hussein's expulsion of the UN weapons inspectors, Clinton ordered a major attack, in which the British participated, against Iraqi air defences, suspected weapons sites and command and control centres, under the existing UN resolutions dating from the Gulf War (in particular resolution number 678 authorising 'all necessary means' to terminate the weapons of mass destruction programmes as well as the Iraqi occupation of Kuwait).

Over 400 Tomahawk missiles were fired, plus air strikes, at nearly a hundred targets, severely disabling the Iraqi facilities at this time. Blair said in Parliament that 'it is a broad objective to remove Saddam ... If we can find a way to remove him, we will.' The Foreign Secretary, Robin Cook, in pursuit of his aim of an 'ethical foreign policy', at this time was making similar statements about Saddam.

In February 2001, just after coming into office, the Bush administration launched what it regarded as a routine attack on Iraqi air defences seeking to impede enforcement of the southern no-fly zone.

In the initial National Security Council meeting after 9/11, the only person to raise the idea of an attack on Iraq was the strongly pro-Israeli Deputy Secretary for Defense, Paul Wolfowitz, though fellow 'neoconservatives' like Richard Perle, Chairman of the Defense Policy Board, and Wolfowitz's deputy, Doug Feith, had long been lobbying hard in the same sense, as did Cheney's Chief of Staff, 'Scooter' Libby. On the day after the attacks, the head of the CIA, George Tenet, was astonished to be told by Perle, exiting the White House, that 'Iraq has to pay a price for what happened yesterday'.[2]

In an early telephone call to Blair, Bush suggested that there might be a link between Saddam Hussein and Al-Qaeda, an opinion brushed aside by the British and the US intelligence community and which, after one more suggestion of this kind, he did not pursue. When Blair met Bush in Washington on 20 September, he agreed that Iraq was not the immediate problem. Some members of his team thought differently, but he was the one making the decisions.[3]

The US intelligence assessment, finalised in January 2003, showed no evidence of cooperation between Iraq and Al-Qaeda at the time of the 9/11 attacks. As Al-Qaeda was driven out of Afghanistan, it did, however, show the presence in northern Iraq from May 2002 of a sizeable Al-Qaeda affili-ated group (Ansar al-Islam) led by Abu Musab Zarqawi, trying to establish a new safe haven there and to experiment with low-grade chemical and biological weapons. They appeared to be tolerated by the Iraqi authori-ties, but there was no evidence of Iraqi control. Under interrogation after his capture, Saddam Hussein, whose regime was secular, said that he had no dealings with the Al-Qaeda 'zealots', but the tolerance of the group on Iraqi territory by the regime was by then a real cause of concern.[4]

In November 2001, Bush gave Iraq a stark warning to re-admit the UN weapons inspectors. The US was certain that Saddam Hussein had chemi-cal weapons, which he had used against the Kurds and Iranians, and he consistently had thwarted UN efforts to verify that he had dismantled them. Blair is adamant that there was no decision to go to war at this point. If, as Gaddafi was later to do, Saddam had cooperated fully and openly, war would have been avoided.[5]

In a telephone call to Blair in December, Bush raised the issue of regime change in Iraq, arguing that the threat of Saddam using weap-ons of mass destruction could no longer be tolerated. Blair's focus was on disarming Saddam, but he assured Bush that if getting rid of Saddam was the only way to achieve this, 'we were going to be up for that'.[6] He was far ahead of his Cabinet colleagues and completely out of sympa-thy with most of his party in giving such an assurance.

George W. Bush records that for his first eight months in office, his policy on Iraq had focused on tightening sanctions – as Colin Powell put it, keeping Saddam in his box. September 11, in his view, meant looking at everything again. Saddam's was a thoroughly evil regime, with weap-ons of mass destruction that he was proven to have used. He also had planned, after the Gulf War, to assassinate George Bush Sr during a visit by him to Kuwait, a point to which his son kept returning: 'Through the lens of the post 9/11 world, my view changed.'[7] He was convinced that, if not removed, Saddam would continue to pose a threat, which had to be confronted and if necessary pre-empted.

In November, Bush had asked Rumsfeld and General Tommy Franks to review the contingency plans for war with Iraq. The British were not informed of this. Just after Christmas 2001, Franks told the President that the existing plan envisaged sending 400,000 troops. He was convinced that the mission could be accomplished with far fewer than that. He was asked to continue devising a new plan (which he finally submitted in August 2002). Bush said that they should remain optimistic that diplomacy and international pressure would succeed in disarming the regime: 'But we cannot allow weapons of mass destruction to fall into the hands of terrorists. I will not allow that to happen.'[8] In his State of the Union address on 29 January 2002, Bush alarmed his allies, including the British, by describing the regimes in Iran, Iraq and North Korea as an 'axis of evil'. On 26 February, Richard Dearlove, head of MI6, advised 10 Downing St that the US was drawing up plans for a military campaign later in the year.

This was the background against which the first serious discussion about Iraq with George W. Bush took place, during Blair's visit to the President's ranch at Crawford in Texas in April 2002. Before the meeting, Colin Powell assured the President that Blair 'will be with us', including if it came to military action. On the British side, a Cabinet Office paper on 8 March stated that sanctions were failing and the US had 'lost confidence in containment'.

On 7 March, the British Cabinet had discussed Iraq, but not on the basis of any paper about it and none was forthcoming for months thereafter. Conscious of the divisions within the Labour Party, Blair regarded the subject as so sensitive as not to be suitable for the normal processes. For all her impatience with the bureaucracy, Mrs Thatcher had been meticulous about using Cabinet committees and the Cabinet Office structure in the Falklands conflict. Successive Cabinet secretaries lamented Blair's preference for informal meetings with, at times, no records kept ('sofa government'). No War Cabinet or Cabinet committee was constituted for the conflicts in Afghanistan or Iraq or to oversee postwar stabilisation and reconstruction in Iraq.

On 14 March, Blair's foreign policy adviser, David Manning, told the national security adviser, Condoleezza Rice, that Blair would not budge in his support for regime change, but had to manage a press, Parliament and public opinion very different from anything in the US. On 2 April, a meeting with the Foreign Secretary and the chief of defence staff and other senior military officers concluded that the Americans needed to be told to proceed deliberately 'and, above all, to build a coalition'.[9]

By this stage, Blair had resolved in his own mind that removing Saddam would do the world and the Iraqi people a service. Though he knew that 'regime change could not be our policy', he viewed it as both inevitable and desirable if Saddam failed to comply. In his speech in Chicago in April 1999, he had developed the doctrine that the international community had a 'responsibility to protect', as it had done in Kosovo. He added that 'in the past we have talked too much of exit strategies'. Henry Kissinger had criticised this doctrine as an open-ended invitation to intervene, even when no national interests were at stake. Blair accepted that Saddam could only be removed for non-compliance with UN resolutions, 'not on the basis of tyranny alone'.

The Cabinet were told before Crawford that it was important that the US should not act unilaterally. Blair flatly denies assertions that in Crawford he pledged 'in blood' to support the US, including over regime change, but he accepted that regime change would be the consequence if the regime did not alter its behaviour. A paper written by the British Cabinet Office on 17 July 2002 and Blair himself confirmed that he told Bush at Crawford that 'the UK would support military action to bring about regime change provided certain conditions were met'. Bush and Blair insist that no decision to invade was taken at this time. The intention was first to try 'coercive diplomacy'.

Blair was clear, however, that Saddam had to be made to comply with the UN resolutions on his weapons programme and that Britain must remain 'shoulder to shoulder' with the Americans, the alliance with the US being a vital strategic asset to Britain. The Kosovo experience had shown just how badly Europe needed the US. He 'felt the weight of the alliance and its history ... When they had need of us, were we really going to refuse?'[10]

As the British ambassador in the US at the time, Christopher Meyer, observed, Blair was a 'true believer in the wickedness of Saddam Hussein'.

So, at their press conference in Crawford, Bush and Blair delivered the message: change the regime's attitude on weapons inspection or face the prospect of changing the regime. This, however, was more Blair's message than that of Bush, who told the British TV reporter Trevor McDonald that 'Saddam needs to go'.

On the eve of Blair's visit, and with his strong encouragement, Bush had declared his commitment to a two-state solution for Israel and Palestine. Blair stressed the importance of following through on this, as well as dealing with Saddam. Blair's ambition was to achieve a road map towards a resolution of the dispute, which he saw as key to rendering Arab opinion more favourable to dealing with Saddam. He continued to press for progress on Palestine in his exchanges with Bush, to the irritation of Cheney and others in the administration and probably, at times, as Blair acknowledged, of Bush himself. It was no small ambition, given that the Prime Minister of Israel was Ariel Sharon, given Arafat's leadership of the Palestinians, and given the domestic constraints on Bush and any other US President when it came to dealings with Israel.

Before his meeting with Bush, the Foreign Secretary, Jack Straw, had warned Blair that 'the rewards from your visit to Crawford will be few. The risks are high, both for you and for the Government.' There was no majority among Labour MPs for military action. Iraq was in violation of international law, but the UK must insist on re-admission of the UN weapons inspectors and be sure of the legality of any action to be taken. Iraq had never enjoyed any history of democracy; there was no certainty that a replacement regime would be an improvement.[11] Also, before going to Crawford, Blair had been warned by the British Chiefs of Staff that removing Saddam could be a bloody and protracted fight.

Cheney and Rumsfeld were strongly in favour of removing Saddam. Paul Wolfowitz had a more ambitious agenda. Influenced by the exiled Iraqi opposition leader Ahmed Chalabi, apart from believing that the war would pay for itself and that the Americans would be welcomed with open arms, he saw this as the opportunity to transform the Middle East in a fashion favourable to America and Israel through the introduction of a genuine democracy in Iraq. The problem with the 'neo-conservatives', as Kissinger observed, was that they were not really conservatives at all.

Nevertheless, working at the coalface in Washington, Christopher Meyer saw no linear progression towards a war. The road looked to him at the time 'anything but straight or the destination pre-ordained'.[12] He was concerned, however, that Blair's 'yes, but' risked being interpreted without the 'but' and that, after an abortive visit by Colin Powell to the area, there was no progress on Israel and Palestine, with Powell feeling that his efforts had been undercut by others with stronger pro-Israeli sympathies in the administration.

Aware of the deep fissures within the US administration, Blair's objective was to drive them down a multilateralist route. In the run-up to a meeting with Bush at Camp David in September, Blair insisted on the need to secure a further and stronger UN resolution calling on Saddam to re-admit and fully cooperate with the UN weapons inspectors or face the consequences. Blair saw this as crucial to building an effective international coalition and justifying the legality of military intervention if it became necessary, and as vital also *vis-à-vis* the Parliamentary Labour Party. Bush did not have much faith in the UN, which had passed sixteen resolutions on Iraq to little avail, but agreed to consider this.

This produced the usual split in the Bush team. Cheney and Rumsfeld were strongly against going back to the UN, which they believed would result in interminable delay. In early July, Richard Haass of the State Department was alarmed to find that Condoleezza Rice had become a true believer in the necessity of removing Saddam, telling him that the President had made up his mind.

In July, a memo to the Defence Secretary, Geoff Hoon, advised that there was no convincing case for an early war with Iraq. In a meeting with Blair on 23 July 2002, Dearlove, head of MI6, reported a 'perceptible change' in Washington, where military action was now seen as inevitable. There was no patience with the UN route and little discussion of the aftermath. President Bush wanted to remove Saddam and he suspected that 'the intelligence and the facts were being fixed around the policy' (Dearlove insisted subsequently that he had not said 'fixed' and told Tenet that his concern was based on a conversation with Cheney's Chief of Staff, 'Scooter' Libby, who had tried to insist on a connection between Saddam Hussein and Al-Qaeda).

Straw felt that Bush had made up his mind to take military action, but 'the case was thin', though he believed that Saddam had retained weapons of mass destruction. Britain should work for an ultimatum to Saddam to re-admit the UN weapons inspectors. John Scarlett, head of the Joint

Intelligence Committee, observed that Saddam would not re-admit the inspectors without the threat of military action. By this time Admiral Boyce, chief of the defence staff, was telling Blair that he thought the US had decided on war, barring a major change of heart by Saddam.[13] Blair said that he did not want to look at himself in the mirror in ten years' time, when Saddam had used weapons of mass destruction, and know that he could have prevented it. The meeting concluded that 'we should work on the assumption that we would participate in military action', but no firm decisions were taken.

At the end of July, Blair wrote a private note to Bush that began with the words 'Dear George, I will be with you, whatever'. Blair's foreign policy adviser, David Manning, and his Chief of Staff, Jonathan Powell, both advised against including this phrase, which they saw as giving too unconditional a commitment. Blair agreed that he was saying, in effect, that 'you can count on us'.[14] The remainder of the letter, however, was devoted to urging Bush to go down the UN route.

Despatched to Washington at the end of July, at a dinner on his own with Condoleezza Rice, Manning made clear that if the US wanted British support in action against Iraq, they would have to go through the United Nations, a conversation he subsequently had also direct with the President.[15]

On 15 August, General Brent Scowcroft, national security adviser under George Bush Sr, pointed out in the *Wall Street Journal* that there was 'scant evidence' of any connection between Saddam Hussein and terrorist organisations and that invading Iraq could prove a massive distraction from the fight against terrorism. Cheney replied in a speech that claimed, contrary to CIA views, that Saddam would soon acquire nuclear weapons.

Colin Powell insisted that a new resolution was crucial for the key allies. In August, described by Bush as 'more passionate than I had seen him', he told the President that if the US did attack Saddam, the military campaign would be the easy part. For the US would then 'own' Iraq. They would be responsible for helping a fractured country to re-build. Bush said that he accepted that this was a good reason for hoping that diplomacy would work.[16]

When Blair arrived at Camp David on 7 September, he was told by Bush in the presence of Vice-President Cheney, who said little but clearly did not agree, that the US would go to the UN. Bush agreed that if they got disarmament through the UN, they would have 'cratered' Saddam. But if diplomacy failed, there would only be one option left. Blair said that he did not want to go to war, 'but I will do it'. If it came to war, the UK would take on a significant military role. Bush's response was to tell Alastair Campbell that 'Your man has got *cojones*', adding cheerfully that Campbell could tell the world that Blair had 'pulled the crazed unilateralist back from the brink'.[17] In this meeting, however, it was clear that, while Blair's position was that disarmament might lead to regime change, Bush saw regime change as leading to disarmament.[18]

49

'I HOPE THAT'S NOT THE LAST TIME WE SEE THEM'

IN DEMANDING THE return of and unconditional access for the UN weapons inspectors, both Bush and Blair harboured hopes that a really intrusive inspection regime would shatter Saddam Hussein's authority within Iraq. It was, presumably, precisely for this reason that, to the end, he never really cooperated with the inspectors.

This was the point at which the Blair government published its dossier about the evidence, which undoubtedly was seriously believed, about the continuance of a weapons of mass destruction programme in Iraq. Shortly beforehand, Richard Dearlove, head of MI6, alerted Blair to an important new source confirming an Iraqi biological weapons programme, thereby giving weight to a report that had not been properly evaluated. Blair was not informed that the veracity of this source was being questioned before the invasion or, until long afterwards, that it had been a fabrication.

The dossier was alleged to have been 'sexed up' to suit Blair's arguments, in particular with the improbable claim that Iraq might be able to ready chemical weapons for use within forty-five minutes of an order to do so, but it was prepared by the Joint Intelligence Committee (JIC), with inputs from US and German intelligence, who were equally convinced about the existence of the programme. The JIC earlier had acknowledged that the intelligence was 'sporadic and patchy', a warning that featured nowhere in the public dossier.

The inquiry led by Lord Hutton into the tragic suicide of the leading UK weapons expert, Dr David Kelly, concluded that there had been no deliberate attempt to mislead, but that warnings about a judgment attributed to a single source were ignored. On 30 June, Dr Kelly himself had expressed support for military action to remove Saddam, because he recognised 'from a decade's work the menace of Iraq's ability to further develop its non-conventional weapons programme'.[1]

The Iraq inquiry under Sir John Chilcot also concluded that there had been no deliberate attempt to mislead, but that 'policy on Iraq was made on the basis of flawed intelligence and assessments. They were not challenged and they should have been.' There was an 'ingrained belief' that Saddam Hussein retained weapons of mass destruction. The assessment in the dossier was presented 'with a certainty that was not justified' and without essential caveats about the patchiness of the evidence on which it was based.[2]

The US agencies found themselves under pressure, particularly from Vice-President Cheney's staff, to make the intelligence firmer than it was capable of being. Nevertheless, in October, the US National Intelligence Estimate, reflecting the view across all the US intelligence agencies, was categorical that 'Baghdad has chemical and biological weapons' and, if unchecked, could develop a nuclear weapon by the end of the decade.[3] In October, both houses of Congress voted to give the President authority to use force against Iraq.

The UN Security Council resolution number 1441, passed under Chapter 7 of the UN Charter, giving Saddam a 'final opportunity to comply' and threatening serious consequences if he did not, was passed unanimously in November 2002. In his response, in the UN inspectors' view, Saddam was deemed to have failed to make full disclosure, as the resolution required. He also threatened that any Iraqis who gave interviews to the inspectors would be treated as spies.

The British military at this point was considering participating in a planned invasion of Iraq from the north, via Turkey, in support of the US 4th division, a plan that had to be abandoned when the Turks declined to agree. Blair was given three military options: minimum involvement with only the very limited forces already in theatre; serious British naval and air support; or the commitment also of an armoured division, with the chief of defence staff saying that he would have a real problem with the army if it was not involved. Both Blair and the military favoured the ground forces option, which they felt would give Britain the most influence on events. On 31 October, Blair offered the US significant ground forces for planning purposes.[4]

From December, planning was advanced for the division to operate from Kuwait. On 20 January, the British government announced the despatch of 26,000 troops and a fleet to the Gulf, while stating that no decision to go to war had been taken. Admiral Boyce was warning that he would not order troops into battle without an affirmative opinion from the Attorney General as to the legality of doing so.[5]

By January, US preparations for the military campaign were far advanced and the President's State of the Union speech on 29 January 2003 was a call to arms. At a meeting with Blair in Washington two days later, Bush said that the start of the campaign was pencilled in for 10 March. Bush thought it unlikely that there would be internecine warfare between the different religious groups in Iraq after the invasion, confirming a complete failure at the political level to anticipate that the overthrow of the Sunni regime could precipitate a sectarian war.[6]

The US National Intelligence Committee had produced estimates warning of this, but these were disregarded by the White House. The more prosperous and better-educated Sunni minority had governed Iraq since its inception, courtesy of Winston Churchill, who had carved it out from the Turkish Empire in 1921 (Churchill soon concluded that the British there were sitting on 'an ungrateful volcano!'). Another critical failure, as Blair subsequently avowed, was the inability to understand how the overthrow of the Sunni regime was likely to be exploited by the Iranians to establish their dominance over the Shia militias and most of the Shia political class in Iraq.

By this point, the US military deployment had generated a momentum of its own, having reached a stage at which there was no leeway to argue for the UN inspectors to be given much more time, as Blair, otherwise, would have wished to do. No US President, having despatched 200,000 men to the Gulf, was likely to simply keep them waiting there or bring them back, barring a complete climb-down by the Iraqi regime. A full-scale invasion force of this kind could not easily be flexed down. Yet it was only the threat of an imminent invasion that had induced Saddam Hussein to cooperate with the UN inspectors to the limited extent he had so far shown himself willing to do.

A postponement of the invasion would have needed to be for several months, to get beyond the period of soaring temperatures and sand storms in Iraq. The Bush administration was not prepared to wait that long, though the inspection process was reinforcing containment. The Iraq inquiry was justified in concluding that 'the UK chose to join the invasion of Iraq before the peaceful options for disarmament had been exhausted'. Saddam Hussein did not pose an imminent threat. Military action at the time was not a last resort. The timing was dictated by the military, irrespective of the diplomatic requirements. It was, above all, in this respect that the inquiry concluded that Blair, who sent thirty personal notes to Bush in the course of the crisis, overestimated his ability to influence US decisions on Iraq. He was unable to persuade the Americans to allow the inspectors until April to carry forward their work.[7]

Bush hated the idea of another UN resolution: he had always suspected that a return to the UN might be used to drag out the process indefinitely. But he agreed to try, if this was the only way to help Blair. On 5 February, Colin Powell made his speech at the UN setting out the evidence of infractions by Saddam Hussein, which, despite his best efforts to verify it, turned out to be flawed in several respects.

At the beginning of March, Blair was warned by his Foreign Secretary, Jack Straw, that he might lose the vote in the House of Commons unless there was a further UN resolution authorising the use of force. Without this, Straw suggested, 'the only regime change that will be taking place will be in this room'.[8] Robin Cook, leader of the House of Commons, wanted Britain to stand aside from the conflict as Harold Wilson had done over Vietnam, which Blair was not prepared to contemplate, given his own feelings about Saddam and the consequences for the relationship with the United States.

At this stage, Blair felt himself 'just about as isolated as it was possible to be'. The UN inspectors were producing inconclusive reports. A huge anti-war demonstration was held in London on 15 February. On the morality of getting rid of Saddam, Blair was not giving any ground, but he knew that 'this could be the end politically' for him personally. On 5 March, France, Germany and Russia issued a joint statement against military action, though the US did have majority support elsewhere in Europe. The Cabinet Secretary had started looking into what would need to be done if Blair were voted down by his own party.[9] A declaration by President Chirac that he would veto a new resolution approving the use of force paradoxically reduced the pressure on Blair, by putting an end to this discussion.

The irony was not lost on Blair of a 'centre-left' Prime Minister, as he regarded himself, becoming the closest ally of a conservative Republican President. Within the Labour Party, they could see that he was centrist all right, but struggled to understand in what respect he was leftist. While the intervention in Iraq ever since has been represented as 'Blair's war', this was not the case within the Labour Party leadership at the time. As Jack Straw observed in his memoir, his opposition would have sufficed to prevent Britain participating in the war.[10] But Straw, setting aside the doubts he had continued to express until a very late stage, had allowed himself to become convinced that Saddam Hussein was indeed a threat to international peace and security, a conclusion also reached by Gordon Brown and justified by both of them to the Iraq inquiry.[11]

Brown, who was regarded by most of Labour as much more 'one of us' than Blair, was adamant that there would have been no war if Saddam Hussein had been seen to comply fully with the UN resolutions and that no decision was taken to go to war until March 2003. If either Brown or Straw had reached a different conclusion, it would have been impossible for Blair to carry the Cabinet and Labour Party MPs with him in support of the intervention in Iraq. As Cabinet members repeatedly were assured by the Joint Intelligence Committee that Iraq was pursuing 'a policy of acquiring weapons of mass destruction' and the means to deliver them, they did not have the benefit of hindsight to know that this was mistaken. Given the information available to them at the time, all three had respectable reasons to believe that Britain should support the United States in the Iraq campaign.

In early March, Bush called Blair to say that he would rather have him drop out of the coalition and remain in government than stay in and lose power. He was impressed by Blair's response: 'I said I'm with you ... I absolutely believe in this. I will take it up to the very last.'[12]

Warned by his British counterpart, Geoff Hoon, of the political difficulties in London, to Blair's annoyance, Rumsfeld said publicly that the US might have to manage the invasion without the British. There were many in Blair's party who hoped that he would let them do so. Straw wanted Blair to consider the option of Britain not participating initially, but joining in the later, stabilisation phase, but Blair was having none of this. Admiral Boyce found the US military believing that they would be welcomed as liberators. Boyce expected them very quickly to be regarded as an occupying power.[13]

The British Attorney General, Lord Goldsmith, since October had been expressing his doubts that UN Security Council resolution 1441 provided a sufficient basis to justify military intervention. Sir Jeremy Greenstock, the British representative at the United Nations, advised Goldsmith that the negotiating history of resolution 1441 showed that a further resolution was not required.

There followed a meeting in Washington with the senior State Department legal adviser, who contended that the US would never have sponsored it on the basis that yet another resolution would be required before any action could be taken, particularly as, in their view, they already had the necessary authority under the original resolution 678, passed at the time of the First Gulf War, authorising member states to use 'all necessary means' to deal with the threat to international peace and security posed by Saddam Hussein. The US and British enforcement of the no-fly zones in northern and southern Iraq, including attacks on Iraqi air defences, like those in February 2001, and the attacks on Iraqi military targets ordered by Clinton in response to Saddam's expulsion of the UN weapons inspectors in 1998, all had been conducted under the existing UN resolutions.

On 7 March, Lord Goldsmith delivered his opinion that while 'the safest legal course' would be a further UN resolution, in his view there was a 'reasonable case' that military action would be justified under the terms of the UN Security Council resolution number 1441 and the preceding UN resolutions, in particular resolution 678, an opinion he confirmed in more categorical terms in a one-page paper for the Cabinet meeting that he attended on 17 March.

The Foreign Office legal adviser took a different view, but within the government the Attorney General's view was final. The chief of the defence staff, Admiral Boyce, had demanded again in March a yes-or-no answer on the legality of the war, with no ifs or buts, which finally he was given in a note from the Attorney General's office on 14 March.[14] Lord Goldsmith insisted on being given a categorical statement from the Prime Minister's office that Iraq was in further material breach of its international obligations, thereby at least partially reversing the normal relationship between the Prime Minister and a law officer. The Iraq inquiry expressed no view on the legality of the war, but concluded that the 'circumstances in which it was decided that there was a legal basis for UK military action were far from satisfactory'.[15]

Blair spent the last few days in the countdown to a war seeking to establish a firm US declaration of commitment to a 'road map' towards a peace between Israel and the Palestinians. This was made public by Bush on 14 March and was referred to in the final ultimatum to Saddam Hussein.*

On 16 March, Bush flew to the Azores for a meeting with Blair and the Spanish and Portuguese prime ministers, who also supported the US. President Chirac, having made clear that he would veto a new UN resolution, accused the Eastern Europeans of being 'badly brought up' in following the US rather than France. In the event, a majority of EU countries did support the US and participated in the postwar stabilisation effort in Iraq.

The vote in the House of Commons was due two days later. Blair told Bush that he would resign if the vote failed, meaning that Britain would withdraw from the coalition. As Bush shook hands with Blair and his team on leaving the Azores, Bush's national security adviser, Condoleezza Rice, observed: 'I hope that's not the last time we ever see them.'[16]

In London, Blair reported to the Cabinet, minus Robin Cook who had resigned, that in the Azores Bush had committed to pursue the 'road map' towards an attempt at an agreement between Israel and Palestine. The formal decision to participate in the invasion was not taken until this Cabinet meeting on 17 March 2003. For all the subsequent testimony from various advisers about their doubts at the time, the only one to resign was Elisabeth Wilmshurst, deputy legal adviser in the Foreign Office.

Blair knew by now that he would win the vote in Parliament, given the support of the Conservative opposition. But if he failed to win the support of a majority of his own party's MPs, he would be obliged to resign. Blair made a speech in Parliament that impressed even his critics, winning by 412 votes to 129 and carrying most of his party with him. On the information available to him at the time, Blair believed that it was right to overthrow Saddam Hussein and was prepared to risk his prime ministerial office to do so.

---

* Many of those contending that the war was illegal have based this on the absence of a UN Security Council resolution explicitly authorising the use of force. Whatever may be thought of this as a legal argument in the case of the Iraq War, if accepted as a general doctrine, it would severely constrain the ability to take military action in any circumstances in which this was opposed by Russia or China.

50

'IT WAS, AFTER ALL, THE *CASUS BELLI*'

THE ENSUING MILITARY campaign was a brilliant success, in which the Royal Marines seized the offshore oil installations, while the British 1st armoured division fought a textbook campaign, protecting the flank of the US advance on Baghdad and liberating Basra with a minimum of force. The instinctively unilateralist Donald Rumsfeld declared that 'the job of the American forces would have been infinitely harder without them'. On 5 April, US forces entered Baghdad. By mid-April, the conflict was nearly over, but Baghdad descended into a state of lawlessness, with widespread looting, as Saddam's police melted away.

Blair's main focus was on getting the US to accept UN involvement in the reconstruction of Iraq. Despite opposition from Cheney and Rumsfeld, in a meeting in April at Hillsborough in Northern Ireland, Bush was persuaded to declare that the UN would have a 'vital role' in the reconstruction of Iraq. The Americans, however, had no intention of handing over control to the UN. Sergio Vieira de Mello was appointed the UN special representative in Baghdad, only for him to be killed in August in an Al-Qaeda attack on his headquarters, causing the UN to withdraw.

In Washington, George W. Bush was horrified at the scenes of looting in Baghdad (dismissed by Rumsfeld as 'stuff happens'). In his memoir, more introspective than that of Blair, he concludes that he was badly advised by Rumsfeld and the military to draw down rapidly the 200,000-strong US invasion force, supposedly to avoid antagonising the Iraqis.[1] In the run-up to the war, Rumsfeld had reprimanded the head of the US Army,

General Shinseki, for telling the Senate Armed Services Committee that the stabilisation of Iraq following the invasion would require a force several hundred thousand strong.

In January, Bush had signed a decree putting postwar Iraq firmly under the control of the Pentagon. He appointed an experienced diplomat and counterterrorism expert, Jerry Bremer, as head of the interim regime. Four days after his arrival in Iraq, on 16 May, Bremer, in accord with Doug Feith, Under Secretary of Defense, issued a decree on 'De-Baathification', followed by a further decree disbanding the Iraqi Army. This was in pursuit of the Wolfowitz concept of getting rid of all of Saddam Hussein's Baath party influence in Iraq.

General Jay Garner, briefly in charge of re-construction, and the CIA head of station in Baghdad warned Bremer that the orders were far too sweeping and would drive tens of thousands of Iraqis, with their weapons, into opposition to the Americans, but were overruled.[2] It subsequently was argued that the army had simply melted away. In reality, no effort was made to retain them.

The British were aware of the de-Baathification plan, but not that it would be applied so drastically as to liquidate the Iraqi Army. The US national security adviser, Condoleezza Rice, had no prior notice of the terms of the decree disbanding the army. The coalition had expected Iraq post invasion still to have a functioning civil service. The de-Baathification order had put paid to that notion as well.

This was the kind of US decision that would have sent Mrs Thatcher hotfoot across the Atlantic to get it reversed or modified. But there was no high-level intervention by the British with Bush, who accepts that it was a dreadful mistake: 'Many Sunnis took [Bremer's orders] as a sign that they would have no place in Iraq's future ... Thousands of armed men had just been told that they were not wanted. Instead of signing up for the new military, many of them joined the insurgency.'[3]

Thanks to his mentors in Washington, the de-Baathification programme was to be overseen by the Iraqi exile leader, Ahmed Chalabi, who had cultivated and influenced the neo-conservative members of the Bush administration. Widely believed to be corrupt, he turned out to have little support. Much of the mistaken information about the continuance of weapons of mass destruction programmes had come from exile sources. Though zealously supported by Wolfowitz and Feith, on his return to Iraq, Chalabi soon fell out with the Americans, as he was found to have transferred his allegiance, plus some sensitive information, to the Iranians.[4]

At the outset of his highly controversial year as pro-consul in Iraq, Bremer announced a plan for a protracted transfer of power to the Iraqis in 2005. The first Colin Powell saw of this was when it was published in the *Washington Post*. The leading Shia cleric, the Ayatollah Sistani, denounced the plan, demanding elections before a new constitution was decided. The British favoured an earlier transfer of authority.

The result was sharp friction with the senior British representative in Iraq, Jeremy Greenstock, who told Bremer in Powell's presence that the plan might have to be modified. Bremer was infuriated to be told by Powell's deputy that reports they were receiving from Greenstock 'did not sound good'. When the British commander in the south, General Graeme Lamb, observed that in dealing with oil smuggling, which had become an Iraqi way of life, he had to operate within the law, he was unimpressed to be told by Bremer: 'I am the law.'[5] Greenstock contributed to finessing Sistani's demands on the basis that an interim constitution and government would lead on to elections and a final constitution.

Bremer, meanwhile, had been planning to arrest the Shia extremist leader, Muqtada al Sadr, who had organised the murder of a moderate rival religious leader and also was behind attacks on the British forces in the south. But Bremer's closure of the main Sadrist newspaper had triggered an outbreak of violence in the south and the British feared that Sadr's arrest would lead to worse trouble in Basra. Bremer felt that the British were losing control.

The British Chiefs of Staff were determined to reduce rapidly the force levels in Iraq. By August, these were down to 9,000, yet the British had accepted oversight of stabilisation and reconstruction in an area of Iraq the size of France. A deterioration in the security situation was evident by August 2003, but military planning under the Chiefs of Staff took no account of this. Contingents from several other coalition members were deployed in the south, but they proved to be of uneven military value.

Before the invasion, ministers and the British military had recognised that post-invasion operations were likely to be the strategically decisive phase. The British raised with the Americans their concerns about the lack of any adequate planning for postwar Iraq, but proved even more badly prepared for this themselves. The Iraq inquiry concluded that 'the planning and preparations for Iraq after Saddam Hussein were wholly inadequate'.[6]

Arguably, the task of pacifying postwar Iraq was beyond the power of any occupying force. Christopher Meyer had warned from Washington in September 2002 that 'it will probably make pacifying Afghanistan look like child's play'. Blair's Chief of Staff, Jonathan Powell, had warned at the same time of a 'terrible blood-letting of revenge' once Saddam was overthrown. Blair himself wrote on 2 June 2003: 'The task is absolutely awesome and I am not sure that we are geared for it. This is worse than re-building a country from scratch.'

Yet British force levels were reduced by two thirds within months of the invasion. The Iraq inquiry concluded that the failure to review force levels in southern Iraq despite deteriorating security was a serious omission by the Chiefs of Staff, despite the fact that Iraq was a higher priority for the UK than Afghanistan. The Chiefs of Staff themselves concluded in October 2005 that the campaign could end in 'strategic failure'.

In May 2006, General Mike Jackson, head of the British Army, referred to a perception on the part of the US military that the UK was motivated more by the short-term political gain of early withdrawal rather than by accomplishing the mission. The insistence of the new chief of defence staff, Air Marshal Stirrup, that troop withdrawals should continue irrespective of security conditions, rejection of the offer of US support in Basra and insistence on disengagement from Iraq were sharply criticised by the Iraq inquiry. The inquiry concluded that the UK's most consistent strategic objective in relation to Iraq was to reduce the level of forces deployed there.[7]

While the Americans committed huge resources to the task, this did not happen on the British side. Hilary Synnott, despatched to Basra as the leading civil administrator, was promised personally strong support by Blair, but found getting Whitehall to deliver on that promise a near-impossible task. On arrival in Basra, he found himself without secure communications and with hardly any staff. The Department for International Development, which had been strongly opposed to the war, were extremely reluctant to become involved and Synnott found himself having to beg and borrow resources from the Americans.[8] No formal Cabinet committee was appointed to oversee this task and nor was any minister put in charge of it.

The post-invasion attempts to find chemical and biological weapons in Iraq had proved to be in vain. By the time Blair visited the British troops in

Basra a few weeks after the invasion in May 2003, Rumsfeld had already declared that none might ever be found. Blair felt that this should have been handled more sensitively: 'It was, after all, the *casus belli*.'[9]

Bush was no less concerned at the failure to find the weapons of mass destruction every major Western intelligence agency had been convinced Iraq possessed: 'Nobody was lying. We were wrong.' He was convinced that Saddam would have remained a threat and would have sought to re-develop such programmes. Yet,

> while the world was undoubtedly safer with Saddam gone, the real-ity was that I had sent American troops into combat based in large part on intelligence that proved to be false ... No one was more shocked or angry than I was when we didn't find the weapons. I had a sickening feeling every time I thought about it. I still do.[10]

Following his capture, Saddam Hussein was debriefed by an FBI agent, George Piro, who wanted to know, if he no longer had weapons of mass destruction, why did he not say so? The answer lay in part in a speech Saddam made in 2000, in which he said that it was no use having a sword if his neighbour had a rifle. By 1998, the UN inspectors and US and Brit-ish military actions had dismantled much of the programme. Saddam's priority was to get rid of the remaining sanctions. But 'this is a rough neighbourhood'. It was vital for him that Iran believed that he had chem-ical and biological weapons and that his own army and people did too. He had expected the US action to be a bombardment rather than an invasion.

Piro was clear that, having got sanctions lifted, Saddam's intention was to resume the weapons programmes. The conclusion of the CIA Direc-tor, George Tenet, was: 'We didn't understand that he was bluffing and he did not understand that we were not.'[11] The definitive *ex post facto* study by the Iraq Survey Group concluded that at the time of the invasion, the regime did not possess weapons of mass destruction, but it also reached the less publicised conclusion that Saddam Hussein had the clear intention of resuming such a programme as soon as the opportunity presented itself.

On 17 July, as the United States staunchest ally, Blair was invited to address a joint session of both houses of Congress. This was an honour that had been accorded previously to Churchill and Thatcher, and he received seventeen standing ovations.

51

'THIS ISN'T WORKING'

BREMER HAD PLANNED for a transition extending well into 2005, but by October, to the relief of the British, the White House had asserted stronger National Security Council control. A lack of consultation with the military produced an explosion from Generals Petraeus and Odierno. Bremer's vice-regal days were over. With Bush starting to focus on re-election, the British got a quicker handover than they had bargained for, as Bremer was instructed to transfer power to the Iraqi interim council by mid-2004. In Iraq, meanwhile, the US intercepted a letter from the Al-Qaeda leader Zarqawi declaring his intention to 'bring the Shia into the battle' by igniting a sectarian war.

There was in this period no lack of consultation at a senior political level. Bush and Blair held frequent video conferences, with their advisers. In April 2004, Blair was alarmed at the television images of the first battle between US marines and the insurgents in Fallujah and the fact that the UN Special Representative, Lakhdar Brahimi, was threatening to resign unless it was called off.[1] The offensive was halted and an attempt made to hand over to a Sunni Iraqi military unit, which immediately collapsed, leaving Fallujah in the hands of the insurgents. The marines had to re-take Fallujah at the end of the year.

Post-invasion, relations between the Americans and the British military had got off to a sticky start. The US military, dealing with a full-scale Sunni insurrection in the north, became very tired of the lectures they got from their British counterparts about their prowess in peace-keeping in Northern Ireland and the Americans' supposed 'cultural insensitivity'. British troops had started off in Basra wearing berets and no body armour, a practice that was about to have to be rapidly abandoned.

In June 2004, Bremer handed over authority to the provisional Iraqi government. On 12 November, just after Bush had won re-election, Colin Powell told Bush and Blair in a meeting at the White House, his last before resigning as Secretary of State: 'We don't have enough troops on the ground.' In 2005, nevertheless, despite the continuing violence, elections were held successfully, with a high turnout, for a new national assembly.

In April 2006, Condoleezza Rice, by now Secretary of State, and the British Foreign Secretary, Jack Straw, flew together to Baghdad on Rice's plane. As Straw was feeling queasy, he slept in the bed and Rice on the floor. The aim was to persuade a leading Shia contender to become Prime Minister, Ibrahim al-Jafari, to stand aside as, apart from being chronically indecisive, he was backed by the Iranians and the Sadrists.[2] Another Shia leader, Nouri al Maliki, was chosen instead, but owed his majority initially in part to support from the Sadrists.

Sectarian killings and attacks on US forces were taking place every day. By 2006, the war had become so unpopular in America that it was expected to cost the Republicans control of Congress in the mid-term elections. Bush himself told his national security adviser, Steve Hadley: 'This isn't working.' Under immense pressure to reduce US forces further, to the surprise among others of the British, he decided to do the opposite.[3] To the relief of the US military, Donald Rumsfeld was replaced as Defense Secretary by the highly respected and experienced Robert Gates. General David Petraeus was appointed to the command in Iraq with 20,000 additional troops to 're-take Baghdad'. The US 'surge' took the British by surprise and did not at all mesh with the desire in Whitehall, which was to disengage from Iraq.

US Special Forces under General McChrystal had tracked down and killed Zarqawi in June. After a period of fierce combat, Petraeus was able to exploit the antagonism to Al-Qaeda of the Sunni tribal leaders in Anbar province – the so-called 'Sunni awakening'. By autumn 2007, the level of violence had declined dramatically.

Elements of the British Special Air Service had played a prominent role in the attacks on Al-Qaeda targets around Baghdad, borrowing from McChrystal more advanced US equipment and helicopter support.[4] McChrystal had formed a lasting friendship with General Lamb, former head of the UK Special Forces. He regarded the SAS contingent as 'full-fledged and highly valued members' of his task force, engaged in suppressing the car bomb networks and keeping the insurgent cells in Baghdad under constant pressure. Petraeus asked for General Lamb to be extended as his deputy commander in Iraq, where he played a role in helping to win over tribal leaders in the 'Sunni awakening', and McChrystal then asked for him in Afghanistan.[5]

Lamb believed in the importance of trying to talk to the enemy. He insisted on meeting the main Sunni insurgent leader in the Abu Ghraib prison. Lamb was told that the tribesmen had been brought up to fight against any outsiders and they had done so. But, having observed the American forces' conduct, they had concluded that they did not represent a threat to their way of life, whereas Al-Qaeda did. The Sunni chieftain and his 1,700 men were incorporated in the Iraqi Army.

Elsewhere an unlikely partnership was formed between the towering, highly competent US commander, General Ray Odierno, and a diminutive British female anti-war peacenik, Emma Sky, whom he appointed as his political adviser. Having told the Americans that they were an occupying force and could not be regarded as liberators, she became impressed by the dedication of the US military.

Thanks to the 'surge', the Americans handed over a reasonably stabilised country to the Iraqi government in 2011. But, in Sky's view, they lost the aftermath by permitting Maliki to manoeuvre to continue in power after the 2010 elections, in which he actually fared worse than his main rival, Allawi.[6] Maliki, increasingly in thrall to the Iranians, discriminated systematically against the Sunni leadership and population, thereby feeding the insurrection led by ISIS in Anbar province and losing Mosul to them as well. In 2014, the Shia religious leader Sistani insisted on his replacement by a more moderate Shia politician, Haider al-Abadi.

The Americans were concerned at the paucity of resources allocated to the British mission in southern Iraq and alarmed at the under-equipment of their allies. The British had agreed effectively to assume control of four provinces with shattered infrastructure, which was far beyond their means. The failure to respond in a timely manner to the requirements of the forces in the field for better-protected vehicles, helicopters and surveillance drones was indefensible. When the initial doctrine of 'light touch' peace-keeping was overtaken by the Sadrist insurgency, there were fears that any short-term solution to replace the 'Snatch' Land Rovers the British forces had brought with them from Northern Ireland, which offered protection only against shrapnel and low-velocity rounds, would divert funding from the long-overdue and badly managed future armoured vehicle programme (FRES), of which John Hutton as Defence Secretary was later to say: 'It was hard to imagine a worse procurement shambles.'

In May 2004, the deputy chief of equipment in the Ministry of Defence ruled out buying a stop-gap armoured vehicle for British troops as a 'dead end' that would divert funding from the FRES. Admiral Boyce, chief of defence staff, and Sir Kevin Tebbit, permanent secretary in the Ministry of Defence, told the Iraq inquiry of the desperately tight Treasury constraints under which they were operating.[7] They found that there was a mismatch between Blair's international ambitions and the extent to which the Chancellor was prepared to fund the defence component of them. Appeals to the Prime Minister were met by Blair simply urging them to 'work things out with Gordon', to avoid adding to the friction with his deputy by seeking to do so himself. Faced with the prospect of further Treasury cuts, in 2004 the chief of defence staff, General Walker, threatened to resign. The Treasury regime militated against any leeway or sudden shift in procurement requirements beyond the agreed core equipment funding.

The problem was compounded by the fact that the military hierarchy themselves took time to conclude that new wheeled armoured vehicles were an imperative for the troops in the field. The industrialist Lord Drayson, when put in charge of defence procurement, helped to persuade the Treasury to accept that a major procurement programme for new armoured vehicles could be charged to 'urgent operational requirements' and that, therefore, additional funding could be provided for them. In July 2006, Drayson ordered the procurement of the far better protected Mastiff armoured vehicles. The first Mastiffs, a version of the US Cougar, were delivered in six months, though there still was a long delay before many of these vehicles reached the troops in the field. The other belated solution was the 'Bulldog', an updated version of an armoured vehicle dating from the 1940s. The Iraq inquiry's conclusion that the delay in providing the troops in the field 'should not have been tolerated'[8] was a mild commentary on a fiasco that caused the unnecessary loss of British soldiers' lives.

52

'WE HAD NO IDEA WHAT WE WERE GETTING INTO'

IN *OCCUPATIONAL HAZARDS*, Rory Stewart, ex-British Army and foreign service, provides a dramatic and at times hilarious account of the
attempt to inculcate democratic principles amid the warring and violent
factions in Maysan, a province the size of Northern Ireland and bordering
Iran, with just 1,000 British troops to help police it. His conclusion was:
'We had no idea what we were getting into.'[1]

In Basra from March 2004, the small 5,000- or 6,000-strong British force, in a city of close to two million people, was attacked by the
Shia militia of Muqtada al Sadr, supplied by the Iranians with powerful
roadside bombs. The British contingent had neither the numbers nor the
armoured protection to deal with this threat and nor did Maliki at this
time want a confrontation with the Sadrists, who were his coalition partners in Baghdad. Following the assassination of a Shia religious leader,
the British had permitted the militias to set up checkpoints in Basra. They
also had heavily infiltrated the police. In July 2005, the *New York Times*
correspondent, Steve Vincent, published an article entitled 'Switched off
in Basra', alleging that the British were failing to do anything about militia death squads within the police. Two days later, Vincent himself was
murdered by the police in Basra.

In September 2005, the British arrested the Sadrist leader in Basra,
Ahmed al Fartosi, chief organiser of attacks on British forces. The army
then had to mount an attack on a Basra police headquarters to rescue two
Special Forces operatives captured by them. On his return from a visit

to Basra in October, the head of the army, General Jackson, found the possibility of 'strategic failure' being mentioned in earnest on this visit.[2]

As the militias continued their attacks and most of the violence in the region was directed against them, a feeling had started to spread within the military hierarchy in London that the British force in southern Iraq was 'part of the problem'. The military found themselves caught up in intra-Shia politics. The chief of defence staff, Air Marshal Stirrup, was told by Maliki that he did not want a showdown with the Sadrists at this time. In October 2006, Jackson's successor as head of the army, General Dannatt, declared that the British military presence 'exacerbates the security problem ... and we should get out sometime soon'.[3]

In July 2006, General Shirreff, appointed to command the British forces in Basra, found that there was 'effectively no security at all'. He submitted a plan (Operation Sinbad) to contest the Sadrists' control. The plan was approved, including in Baghdad, but he was able to get only very limited reinforcements and was told by the vice chief of the defence staff, General Houghton, that he did not want a display of 'military testosterone' in Basra. To mobilise forces for Basra, Shirreff had to withdraw from Maysan province, where the British base immediately was overrun and sacked by the locals.

Shirreff's operations made an impact, including neutralising a notorious pro-Sadrist police headquarters, but he found that there was no appetite in London to do any more: 'What Whitehall wanted was an exit strategy.' General Houghton felt that in UK society and politics there was a sense that one of the metrics of success was the reduction in UK force numbers, resulting in 'some policy compromise of our objectives in Iraq'.[4] The US offer of a battalion to reinforce the troops in Basra was turned down because it would look as if the British could not cope. The British military did not have the resources to fight on two fronts and the decision to shift the main effort to Afghanistan was made irrespective of the situation in Iraq.

Regardless of the US 'surge', planning for the withdrawal of British forces from the city of Basra to the airport (Operation Zenith) was proceeding *at the same time* as Shirreff's effort to assert better control was underway. Blair observed in his memoir that 'had we believed more in our mission', the British would have played a full part in the eviction of the Sadrist militia from Basra.[5] The Iraq inquiry found that neither General

Walker nor his successor, Air Marshal Stirrup, made clear to Blair that the mission in southern Iraq would be compromised unless force numbers were increased. But Blair having made the commitment to ramp up in Afghanistan, the military leadership in London wanted an accelerated exit from Basra and Blair himself announced the withdrawal of 3,000 of the 7,000 British troops in southern Iraq in February 2007.

As most of the British forces withdrew to the airport, which was agreed with Maliki's representative, they remained the main target of Sadrist attacks. In a meeting with the US Defense Secretary, Robert Gates, in January 2007, the subsequent British commander, General Shaw, under instructions from Whitehall, sought to persuade the Americans that the withdrawal from Basra was part of a longstanding British plan to hand over in good order to the Iraqis. Gates was unconvinced: he understood that the British were heading for the exit. The US military said that they might as well hoist a Sadrist flag over Basra and suggested that they should take over instead. In February 2007, the US Secretary of State, Condoleezza Rice, asked the British ambassador, David Manning, to 'tell her honestly whether the UK was now making for the exit as quickly as possible'.[6]

The British commander tried again with General Petraeus, arguing that Basra was 'more Palermo than Beirut'. In the US view, however, sections of the Sadrist militia in Basra were controlled by General Qasem Soleimani, commander of the Quds force of the Iranian Revolutionary Guards, chief enforcer of Iranian influence in Iraq and orchestrator of Iranian support for Hezbollah and the Assad regime in Syria. But Petraeus knew that the British were planning to leave and that the US needed them in Afghanistan.

The British military in Basra, at the initiative of the SIS station chief and with authorisation from the military hierarchy in Whitehall, sought to negotiate a *modus vivendi* with the leading Sadrist prisoner in British custody, known to have been responsible for attacks on many British soldiers, Ahmed al Fartosi. This involved the cessation of militia attacks on the British in return for the progressive release of all the Sadrist prisoners and the complete withdrawal of the British troops from the city to the airport. The Americans regarded this agreement, reneged on by the militia as soon as their last prisoner (Fartosi) was released and leaving Basra at their mercy, as a defeat, as did a furious Maliki, who by this time had fallen out definitively with the Sadrists. The British commander felt that in the absence of reinforcements and any political will in London to confront the Sadrists, he had few options.[7]

Bush, meanwhile, had been pressing Maliki to take action against Shia, and not only Sunni, extremist groups. On 25 March 2008, Maliki, exasperated by the Sadrist threat to his authority, ordered the Iraqi Army to attack the Shia militia in Basra in an offensive called the 'Charge of the Knights'. When the attack ran into difficulties, the Americans delivered air strikes and logistics support, helping to drive the Sadrists out of the city.

The defeat of the militia was greeted with jubilation in Basra. The British mechanised brigade, who were not forewarned of the Iraqi offensive, remained camped at the airport until virtually the end of the operation, causing much *ex post facto* heart-searching in the British military hierarchy, for whom Basra had been a serious blow to their reputation. At the Iraq inquiry, senior British military officers still were bewailing the 'perception' that the British were 'bombed out of Basra'.

If the force levels in Basra had been determined by the mission, they would have been reinforced at the time of the American 'surge' and the offer of US reinforcements there would have been accepted as well. Instead, the mission was determined by the force levels and the desire to draw them down.

In Iraq, the British had been very successful in the invasion phase. The Ministry of Defence performed extremely well in mobilising and deploying at short notice a well-equipped armoured division, which fully achieved its military goals. If the British government had decided not to participate in the invasion or to do so only with very limited forces, it still would have come under intense pressure to contribute a 'peace-keeping' contingent thereafter, as many of the European allies agreed to do.

The British had drastically underestimated the tasks, both civilian and military, they were being asked to assume in southern Iraq themselves. There was, in the opinion of one very senior staff officer, a mismatch between Britain's ambitions and the resources made available for the task: 'We simply did not understand the historical forces we were releasing.'[8]

The US military felt that there was a deliberate failure in Whitehall to recognise that the forces deployed in southern Iraq were far too small to carry out their stabilisation mission resulting, in the view of the US General Jack Keane, in 'valiant and well-trained forces' being denied the conditions for them to succeed. Blair was insisting on the need to support the

Americans in Afghanistan. The British military felt that they could have more success there and shifted the balance of forces between the two prematurely, heavily in favour of Afghanistan, with consequent further damage to the effort in Iraq.[9]

As Blair observed to the Iraq inquiry, there was also an extraordinary failure in both Washington and London to anticipate how the Iranians would react to the opportunity presented to them to dominate Iraq through their Shia allies once the Sunni regime was overthrown.

In June 2002, in the run-up to the Iraq War, Bush made a speech supporting a Palestinian state alongside Israel, but calling for new Palestinian leadership. For all Yasser Arafat's denials, the intelligence showed him to be not only corrupt, but also covertly supporting terrorism. Mahmoud Abbas looked to be a much better hope for peace. Following Saddam's overthrow, with Blair's encouragement, Bush announced a 'road map' towards an agreement, holding a meeting in Egypt with Abbas and Ariel Sharon. Despite Hamas taking over in Gaza, Bush tried again in November 2007 with Abbas and the new Israeli Prime Minister, Ehud Olmert. Olmert made a private proposal that would have delivered most of the West Bank to the Palestinians, established a joint capital in Jerusalem and allowed the return of some of the refugees.[10] Abbas was interested, but the initiative foundered when Olmert was forced to resign on corruption charges in Israel. Although by this stage Blair had left office, his influence had been important in persuading Bush to make this effort, however belatedly, which had shown more promise than was generally understood at the time.

The overthrow of the Taliban regime in Afghanistan and, imminently, of Saddam Hussein in Iraq did get the attention of another unpleasant dictator. As the invasion of Iraq was being launched in March 2003, British intelligence received a message from the Gaddafi regime in Libya that they were prepared to consider abandoning their military nuclear programme if the West would then lift sanctions. This was discussed by Bush and Blair a few days later at Camp David. The ensuing negotiation was conducted jointly by the CIA and British intelligence. In September, Gaddafi told them that he wanted to 'clean the file'. In October, US and

British inspectors were shown a huge arsenal of chemical weapons, followed by disclosure of the nuclear centrifuge plans they had purchased from the Pakistani nuclear scientist, A. Q. Khan.[11]

Blair did succeed in influencing US policy on Iraq, in particular in seeking a new UN Security Council resolution – Condoleezza Rice observed that by doing so, Blair had transformed the US approach – and the short-lived UN involvement in reconstruction, as well as the 'road map', but not on the disbanding of the Iraqi Army or allowing the UN inspectors time to reach more definitive conclusions.

Explaining the limited influence Britain was able to exert in the postwar phase, General McColl, deputy commander in Iraq in 2004, pointed out that by this time Britain was contributing less than 5 per cent of the coalition forces in Iraq and a fraction of the financial assistance.[12] That said, though thirty-one countries were involved in the 'stabilisation' phase in Iraq, the American military found their British counterparts more willing to undertake 'hard' peace-keeping and deal with local crises than any of their other allies.

Though Bush and Blair both favoured regime change, both claimed to see the main threat and *casus belli* as Iraqi possession of weapons of mass destruction. If the US and British intelligence assessments had been correct on that issue, the war most likely would not have taken place, and certainly not with Britain involved in it. The Powell team, however, suspected that George W. Bush had taken a more fundamental decision to get rid of Saddam come what may, establishing democracy which he was convinced would be embraced in Iraq and setting an example in the region. Bush, who claimed not to know who the neo-conservatives were, had been largely converted to their agenda.

Bush was not prepared to go after the CIA, which had acted in good faith. Both Bush and Blair set up commissions to try to determine what had gone wrong. Despite a damning report by Lord Butler and his committee on the fragility of the intelligence on which the Iraq dossier was based, Blair refused to authorise a witch-hunt either. The Butler commission declared it to have been a fundamental mistake to require the Joint Intelligence Committee to produce a public report as part of a campaign to justify military action.[13]

The intelligence normally available to the British and American governments has generally been a mix of signals and human intelligence, with the signals intelligence usually predominating and more credence being attached to it. In the case of Iraq's chemical and biological weapons programme, there was no signals intelligence, which of itself might have been seen as a warning. There was, therefore, a special responsibility for the intelligence agencies to verify the typically more fragile and self-interested human intelligence sources.

This SIS (MI6) failed to do. The head of SIS, Richard Dearlove, became a close Blair confidant in the run-up to the war, with unrivalled access to the Prime Minister, constantly assuring him that chemical and biological weapons would be found. At one point, Blair reportedly told him: 'Richard, my fate is in your hands.' The head of the Joint Intelligence Committee, John Scarlett, did not regard it as his job to 'second guess' SIS about the quality of their sources.

The main source for the supposed mobile biological weapons laboratories, a German contact ('Curveball'), was never able to be interviewed by the British and declared subsequently that he had invented evidence to encourage the Americans to overthrow the regime. Unbeknownst to Colin Powell, the Curveball information had been challenged by the group leader in the CIA. The Deputy Chief was alleged to have dismissed concerns about the intelligence on the grounds that the invasion had been decided on anyway.

As the British security coordinator, David Omand, observed, SIS had over-promised and under-performed, with SIS representatives, including Dearlove, still assuring Blair post-invasion that weapons of mass destruction would be found. The Robb/Silberman report in the US was as critical as that of Lord Butler of intelligence analysts 'allowing reasonable suspicions about Iraqi BW activity to turn into near certainty' and failing to communicate this to policy makers, though this was a message some key US policy makers did not want to hear. The report concluded that the US intelligence community was 'dead wrong in almost all its pre-war judgments about Iraq's weapons of mass destruction. This was a major intelligence failure.'[14] Because Saddam Hussein had developed (and used) these weapons before, it was assumed that he *must* be continuing to do so.

It would be a mistake to conclude that this performance was typical of British intelligence or of the CIA. The Security Service (MI5) and GCHQ had no involvement in this fiasco. SIS agents Penkovsky and Gordievsky, out of conviction, played an important part in the Cold War. US National

Intelligence Estimates are required to be free of all political interference and in general they have been. The overheated atmosphere created by the George W. Bush administration contributed to the CIA director allegedly assuring the President that it was a 'slam dunk' that Saddam Hussein had weapons of mass destruction.

While the overthrow of the Saddam regime undoubtedly has benefited the Shia and the Kurds (together representing three-quarters of the population of Iraq), the other main beneficiaries of the conflict to date have been the Iranians, while Iraq has splintered on sectarian lines, with much of Anbar province and Mosul currently in the hands of so-called Islamic State. Asked by Senator John Warner in September 2007 whether the mission in Iraq had made America safer, Petraeus replied: 'Sir, I don't know actually.' The contrast could not be starker with the successful intervention to liberate Kuwait. Blair subsequently was to apologise for the fact that the intelligence received was wrong and for the 'mistakes in our understanding of what would happen when you removed the regime', but not for removing Saddam Hussein.

53

'WHEN WE SAVED THE WORLD'

WHEN GORDON BROWN took over as Prime Minister in June 2007, the Bush administration initially was wary of someone they regarded as having tended to plot against Blair. Brown felt that he had an affinity with the US, on the rather narrow basis of his holidays on Cape Cod and friendship with Teddy Kennedy and members of the Harvard intelligentsia, including Larry Summers, who became a key economic adviser to Obama.

Blair encouraged George W. Bush to make a big effort with Brown, which he did by inviting him to a meeting at Camp David in July. Brown, however, was schizophrenic about Bush, wanting to get on with him but, to safeguard his position in the Labour Party, not to appear to be as pally as Blair. The White House were told to their surprise that Brown wanted no informality at Camp David.

Brown found Bush easier to get on with than he had expected and promised continuing support in Iraq, though the British contingent in Basra had dropped to 3,000 or 4,000 men and Brown wanted to get out as soon as he could. There had long since ceased to be any appetite in Westminster for any forceful action in Iraq, contributing to the fiasco in Basra, which happened on Brown's watch. He and Bush, who believed in personal diplomacy, spoke more frequently than Brown was later able to do with Obama.

Brown's standing with the Americans suffered from his poor relations with the British military, who considered that the only interest he had shown in them as Chancellor had been in cutting their expenditure. The chief of defence staff, Field Marshal Guthrie, highly respected by the Americans and by Blair, held Brown as Chancellor responsible for serious equipment shortages which were to prove costly in Iraq and Afghanistan, with Guthrie warning that these could cost lives and that a lack of funding would risk leading one day to 'operational failure'. Brown countered that he had marginally increased defence expenditure in real terms in every year, a claim he was obliged subsequently to retract. The Ministry of Defence was infuriated when in 2002 £1 billion of expenditure to which it was entitled under the Treasury rules abruptly was clawed back by the Treasury, causing a crisis in the heavily constrained defence budget.

Brown was justified in contending that the Ministry of Defence had proved to be poor at managing major equipment programmes. Chinook helicopters intended for the SAS were unable to be used because they had been modified with dysfunctional software. Brown agreed fully to fund all urgent operational requirements for Iraq and Afghanistan, and never refused any request to do so, but David Cameron was later to claim that, under Brown's accounting rules, the black hole in the Ministry of Defence's finances by 2010 was equivalent to an entire year's budget.[1] The claim was exaggerated, but relentless Treasury pressures plus cost overruns had resulted in serious overstretch in the equipment budget.

In an effort to display resolve, in the course of his first visit to Afghanistan as Prime Minister, to the surprise of his Foreign Secretary, Brown appeared to rule out negotiations with the Taliban. At the NATO summit in Bucharest in April 2008, Brown went along with Bush's insistence, against objections from Angela Merkel, that Ukraine and Georgia should be told that they would be able to join NATO, with no thought apparently given to the consequences of contemplating a defence guarantee for either of these countries.

In the same month, during a visit to Washington, Brown met at the British embassy all three leading candidates to succeed Bush – John McCain, Hillary Clinton and Barack Obama. He had hoped that Hillary, who he knew best, would win, but was impressed by Obama's coolness and self-confidence, reinforced when Obama made a pre-election visit to Britain in July.

As Hillary Clinton observed, Brown was unlucky in his timing in becoming Prime Minister, inheriting an array of problems from his predecessor.

In September, the President and the US Treasury Secretary, Hank Paulson, were dismayed when the UK regulatory authorities, on solid prudential grounds, vetoed a bid for Lehman Brothers by Barclays, pushing

Lehman into bankruptcy.[2] Brown flew to Washington in pursuit of a coordinated international response based on re-capitalisation of the banks and the need for a concerted fiscal stimulus. He found Bush out of his depth on the economic issues and the Treasury Secretary, Hank Paulson, preoccupied with salvaging the situation in the US through the Troubled Assets Relief Program (TARP).

Ben Bernanke, Chairman of the Federal Reserve Board, agreed with the emphasis on the re-capitalisation of the financial sector and TARP funds were used for this purpose. In October, Bernanke persuaded his friend and colleague Mervyn King, Governor of the Bank of England, and Jean-Claude Trichet of the European Central Bank to announce a coordinated cut in interest rates.[3]

Never great practitioners of multilateral diplomacy themselves, the Americans gave Brown full credit and support for his efforts to get a concerted response from other nations through the G20 process, but laughed as heartily as others when he blurted out in Parliament on 10 December 2008: 'When we saved the world...' He meant the world's banking system, still a rather grandiose boast. The principal saviour, in the eyes of the Americans, was Ben Bernanke, student of the Great Depression, who set an example to others by cutting the Federal Reserve lending rate down to zero and launching a massive programme of quantitative easing (fighting deflation by injecting money electronically into the economy to buy mainly government bonds, thereby flooding the financial institutions with liquidity and encouraging them to lend), with the Bank of England taking similar action. He agreed with Brown also on the need for fiscal stimulus, but the US financial community were alarmed to see the UK budget deficit balloon to over 10 per cent of GDP.

To the annoyance of the US Treasury Secretary, Tim Geithner, in November 2009 Brown's team asked Obama's political adviser, David Axelrod, to get the administration to support internationally a tax on financial transactions – the so-called Tobin tax. Geithner was opposed to this 'perennial populist favourite' on the grounds that it would increase costs, especially for retail investors, without, in his opinion, doing anything to promote financial stability. He confirmed his opposition to Brown before the G20 meeting at St Andrews and did so afterwards in an interview with Sky News, only to be berated by Brown for having delivered this put-down on a 'right-wing' news channel.[4]

Brown did not find it easy, and nor at this time did any other foreign leader, to form much of a relationship with the rather cool and aloof new President, Barack Obama. With each change of President in the US (Reagan to Bush and Bush to Clinton), sections of the British press had been wont to forecast a more distant relationship. Unlike others, Obama came into office with no emotional attachment whatever to Britain, rather the reverse, given the origins of his father (whom he hardly knew) in colonial Kenya. The problem of getting close to him, however, was one experienced by every one of his international counterparts, his Senate colleagues and even his staff.

Meeting the new President in March 2009, Brown felt that they had a similar centre-left agenda. He too was asked to address both houses of Congress, though the invitation had come from the Democratic Speaker of the House of Representatives, Nancy Pelosi. He made a very Democratic-sounding speech, emphasising the need to tackle climate change and announcing the award of an honorary knighthood to Teddy Kennedy.

The accompanying British press were upset that there was no formal press conference with the President. When a truncated version was agreed in response to pleas from Brown's staff, Obama was annoyed to find that they only wanted to ask about 'trivia' and not about the substance of their discussions. The White House started to feel that the Prime Minister and his staff were scared of their own press and too 'needy' in relation to the President.

Keen to report any evidence of a snub, the British press discovered that Brown made several requests for a meeting with Obama at the UN General Assembly, in September 2009, with no success. Obama was annoyed with Brown about the release of the Libyan Abdelbaset al-Megrahi (see below). In the event, they had a few minutes' conversation while walking together through the kitchen of the UN headquarters.[5]

As Obama ramped up US forces in Afghanistan, Brown's officials sought to deflect a request by him for more British troops there. Brown, who felt very deeply the casualties the army were suffering in Helmand, reluctantly agreed to pressure from the British military for an increase to 9,000, but insisted that this could only be temporary. He wanted fewer military operations and more emphasis on training the Afghan Army.

Relations were severely strained with the head of the British Army, General Dannatt, who felt that the armed forces were being treated shabbily by the government (on leaving the army, Dannatt became David Cameron's defence adviser in the run-up to the 2010 election). Brown continued to be blamed for the army's lack of crucial equipment. In 2009, the British still were operating in Helmand without properly protected vehicles and with a critical lack of helicopters. When accused of this in Parliament by David Cameron, then leader of the opposition,who had just visited Helmand, Brown stretched credulity by claiming that the brigade commander there had assured him that the 'resources were adequate'.

In February 2010, the British participated in a major US-led offensive in Helmand, as part of the US 'surge'. Against the advice of the British commander, who wanted to concentrate his forces in central Helmand, Brown initially was reluctant to see the British hand over to the Americans responsibility for the hard-fought-over Sangin area of Helmand, fearing that this would look like a defeat. On his last visit to Afghanistan in March 2010, Brown's officials declared that, at long last, 200 new armoured vehicles would be ordered to replace the last of the hopelessly vulnerable 'Snatch' Land Rovers.[6]

In 2003, the Bush administration had cooperated with Blair in negotiating with the Gaddafi regime the abandonment of their effort to develop nuclear weapons. Blair remained in touch with the Libyan regime and several major British companies wanted a normalisation of relations with Libya. The Libyans made clear that this would depend on the release of Abdelbaset al-Megrahi, who had been convicted by a Scottish court of responsibility for the bombing which in December 1988 brought down in Lockerbie the Pan Am flight 103 to New York, killing 259 people on board and eleven in the town below.

In August 2009, al-Megrahi was released by the Scottish Justice Secretary on what he declared to be compassionate grounds, as al-Megrahi was not expected to live for more than another three months (in fact he survived for another two and a half years). The decision was condemned by Obama and Hillary Clinton and brought a furious reaction from the families of those who had been killed. Brown insisted that this was entirely a matter for the Scottish authorities, but was further embarrassed when Megrahi received a hero's welcome in Libya.

Although in a phone call on the eve of the British election he had encouraged Brown to 'kick their ass', the unsentimental Obama insisted on being the first to congratulate his successor, David Cameron, who was to help his cause with the White House by appearing more relaxed and less demanding about his relationship with the President.

54

BRITAIN 'MAY NOT WANT TO PLAY AS CENTRAL A ROLE IN WORLD AFFAIRS'

WHEN, FOLLOWING THE 2010 election in Britain, David Cameron formed a coalition government with the Liberal Democrats, one of his first acts was to conduct a hurried 'Strategic Defence Review', the results of which alarmed the Americans.

The swingeing cuts announced to the armed forces were followed immediately by the crisis in Libya. As Gaddafi's tank forces closed in on the rebels in Benghazi, the French President, Nicolas Sarkozy, took the lead in insisting that the West must intervene. The US Defense Secretary, Bob Gates, was flatly against doing so ('Can't I just finish the two wars we are involved in before starting another?').[1]

As Sir John Sawers, head of MI6, pointed out, this was a humanitarian 'war of choice': it was not clear that British interests were directly involved. But Cameron supported Sarkozy and Hillary Clinton, as Secretary of State, persuaded a very hesitant Obama, who had put off for days taking his principal allies' telephone calls. In the end he agreed, subject to the qualification that after the initial massive US bombardment, the follow-up must be by the European allies, with the US 'leading from behind'.

Given Obama's hesitancy, Sarkozy had suggested that the French and British might be able to conduct the campaign by themselves, but neither had the capacity to deliver the initial bombardment to neutralise the Libyan air defences.

The air campaign was a challenge for the British, with no aircraft carrier to fly from. General Richards, head of the defence staff, felt that there was no clear strategy. The initial effort to protect the civilian population, especially in Benghazi, morphed into a campaign to secure regime change. Despite the lessons of Iraq, no thought was given to what might come after. There was a failure to appreciate the extent to which the resistance was infiltrated and in some areas led by radical Islamists, rather than the more moderate opposition leaders appealing for Western intervention.

Benghazi was saved and Gaddafi overthrown. But, given the experience of 'nation building' in Iraq and Afghanistan, there was no appetite on the part of the countries that had intervened to get heavily involved in helping an alternative government thereafter. Much of the reconstruction effort was handed off to the UN. There was a failure to secure large caches of weapons, which have been used since by ISIS militants in the region, or effectively to help the post-Gaddafi regime establish adequate security. The result has been the fragmentation of Libya, with the country lapsing into a state of anarchy and ISIS establishing a base at Sirte, from which they are now being ousted. Obama subsequently blamed Britain and France for the failure to stabilise Libya post-Gaddafi, a task he chose to see as one for the Europeans, rather than the United States.

While making an effort himself with the Russian President, Dmitry Medvedev, who had swapped posts *pro tem* with Putin, Obama left dealing with the allies mainly to Hillary Clinton, who got on well with her British counterparts. After the disregard for the allies (apart, at times, for Blair) felt to have been shown in the George W. Bush years, David Miliband told her that she had a Herculean task, but he thought she was the right Hercules for it! She had just as good, though rather more formal a relationship with his successor, William Hague. But, given what they saw as a major shift in world power, above all in terms of China, Obama and Hillary advertised a 'pivot to Asia'. (The Chinese, however, did not react well to increased US interest in their activities at the expense of their neighbours in the South China Sea, asking Hillary: 'Why don't you pivot out of here?')

Having learned from mistakes in their dealings with Gordon Brown, the White House rolled out the red carpet for David Cameron, offering a major bilateral meeting (plus a ride on the presidential helicopter) during the G20 meeting in Toronto in June. This was followed by Obama's state visit to Britain in May 2011, when he reminded Parliament that he was the grandson of a Kenyan who had served as a cook in the British Army. At a White House dinner for Cameron in March 2012, Obama described him effusively as 'the kind of partner you want on your side'.

In January 2013, however, the Americans were dismayed by Cameron's announcement of an in/out referendum on British membership of the European Union before the end of 2017. Obama and Hillary, moreover, had no doubt where in Europe real power lay, describing Angela Merkel as 'Europe's greatest leader'. Obama also found that the French, despite their economic travails, were prepared to play more of a role in combating jihadists, through their efforts in the Sahara, than the British initially were prepared to do. When asked during a visit to Washington by President François Hollande about the relationships with Britain and France, Obama said that he had two beautiful daughters: 'They are both gorgeous and wonderful, and I would never choose between them!'

In the run-up to the 2015 British election campaign, the Labour Party leader, Ed Miliband, was granted a meeting with Obama which lasted scarcely longer than Ronald Reagan's dismissive encounter with Neil Kinnock, while Cameron was received very warmly at the White House a few weeks before the election, with Obama describing him as a 'great friend' and lauding the relative economic performance of Britain and the US ('We must be doing something right'). Americans were impressed by the performance of the Cameron-led government in restoring Britain's finances and growth in the British economy. US observers felt that Miliband had far more sympathy and tolerance for the anti-American strain in the Labour Party than previous leaders; in the British election campaign, he prided himself on having stood up to Obama in opposing action in response to the nerve gas attack in Syria.

––––––––––

Yet, in American eyes, serious concerns remained about Britain's reduced defence capabilities. They could see nothing 'strategic' in the 2010 defence review, other than the decision in effect to transfer around £4 billion per annum from the defence to the aid budget, which, unlike defence, was ring-fenced against future cuts.* The decision was taken to build two aircraft carriers, but to mothball one of them, with some extraordinary chopping and changing as to which aircraft and how many would fly from the carrier. They were dismayed at the to them incomprehensible decision that the sea-girt British Isles should seek to dispense with any maritime surveillance capability. The Royal Navy was reduced to just nineteen combatant surface ships (destroyers and frigates), but the cuts to the army, now down to 82,000 troops, caused most alarm in Washington.

The review was conducted at a time when the Cold War was deemed to have ended and no account was taken of the possibility of Russia reverting to the aggressive stance it has adopted under Putin. Russia was not mentioned as a threat at any point in the document, contributing to deep cuts to the air defence and frontline capabilities of the RAF. Of all the defence reviews conducted by British governments, the Americans felt this to be the most ill-considered. They were astonished, as were some key figures on the British side, at the apparent casualness with which decisions were taken affecting Britain's defence and national security for the next twenty years.

The resultant deep cuts in defence spending were far more damaging to Britain's defence capabilities than the expenditure constraints under Gordon Brown. The chief of the defence staff, General Richards, asked himself whether the political leadership understood the value of the British Army.[2] The government, surprisingly, sought to convince itself that the outcome would not affect Britain's standing overseas.

In this, they were mistaken. The outgoing US Defense Secretary, Bob Gates, concluded that Britain would no longer have the full spectrum of military capabilities and the ability to be a full partner of the US it had hitherto. Gates could not believe that a country like Britain could choose to go through this decade without a single aircraft carrier.

The head of the US Army, General Ray Odierno, said that he was very concerned that the defence cuts would limit Britain's ability to participate in future coalition operations. 'In the past, we would have a British Army division working alongside an American division. Now it might be a British brigade inside an American division.'[3] The smaller the force, the

---

* There was nothing wrong with progressively increasing the aid budget, but the sudden, nearly £4 billion hike, with a mandatory requirement to spend it, led to some dysfunctional force-feeding in the disbursement of aid.

more fictional the notion that it would be under independent command, as well as limiting influence on operations.

The defence cuts, followed by the House of Commons vote against taking action in Syria and equivocation over the 2 per cent of GDP commitment to defence spending, led the new US Defense Secretary, Ashton Carter, to say that it would be 'a great loss to the world when a country of that much history and standing ... takes actions which seem to indicate disengagement'.[4] A raft of US pundits bewailed what they saw as Britain's diminished role and ambitions in world affairs. The Brookings Institution referred to fears in Washington that Britain may no longer be in the 'exceptional' category it had once occupied. The respected former Under Secretary and US ambassador to NATO, Nicholas Burns, described Britain as 'until recently, very much our most trusted, dependable and capable ally', but one that may no longer want to play 'as central a role in world affairs'.[5]

The planned response by the US to the nerve gas attack in Syria, in which 1,400 people were killed, was an air and Cruise missile strike on the Republican Guard base from which the missiles were launched, not a wider intervention in the Syrian civil war. The French as well as British were prepared to participate in the action. David Cameron asked for a delay while he consulted Parliament, where he was confident of winning approval. It was a new departure for a British Prime Minister to seek prior approval for a limited, time-sensitive military action: the norm had been to account for such actions to Parliament immediately they had been taken. A meeting with Miliband on 27 August left Cameron believing that he could count on Labour support, only for him to be told that the post-Iraq sentiment in the Labour Party was to oppose military action.

The US Secretary of State, John Kerry, and the Obama national security team regarded it as a major setback when the government lost the vote in the House of Commons, with thirty Conservative MPs joining the Labour Party in voting against, enabling the Russians to intervene to arrange partial destruction of the chemical weapons the Syrians had always denied possessing, with the Assad regime continuing to use chlorine gas against its opponents. The unintended effect was the erosion of Obama's determination to enforce the 'red line' he had drawn against the use of chemical weapons by the Syrian regime, sending a negative signal to Putin about US resolve, appearing to embolden him ever since, while sending a message to the moderate opposition groups who were the main victims of the attack about the apparent lack of any Western resolve.[6] Any other postwar US President would have proceeded without the British but, to the alarm of most of his national security team, Obama backed away as well, denying that his own credibility or that of the US was on the line.

Cameron remained unable for some time to get the agreement of Parliament to extend the campaign against ISIS to Syria. The 'better not' conclusion of the House of Commons Foreign Affairs Committee in October 2015, arguing *inter alia* that British involvement would not make much difference anyway, dismayed the Americans. In September 2015, a drone strike in Syria was authorised by Cameron to kill two ISIS members of British origin believed to be planning terrorist attacks in the UK. A US strike disposed of the British-born Mohammed Emwazi, known as 'Jihadi John', responsible for beheading US prisoners and two British aid workers. Following the ISIS atrocities in Paris, the French and Americans were reassured by the subsequent vote in the British Parliament, when internationalist Labour MPs, led by the shadow Foreign Secretary, Hilary Benn, supported the government taking action against ISIS targets in Syria, realigning the country with its key allies.

George W. Bush's Secretary of State, Condoleezza Rice, contended that 'when the chips are down, the British never go wobbly'. She would be less than reassured by the publicly expressed musings of the chief of the defence staff in September 2015 that a combination of societal pressures, Parliament and the risk of legal challenge could mean that Britain might be unable to take action at all.[7] Serving officers have reacted badly to the demoralising effect of veterans from the Iraq War being sought by the Iraq historical allegations team pursuing mainly mischievous allegations by their former enemies years after the event and with the assistance of a government-funded law firm now found to have been acting improperly.

The Obama administration was concerned that Britain, having urged other allies to spend at least 2 per cent of GDP on defence at the 2014 NATO summit in Wales, declined subsequently to commit to that target itself. Obama raised this at successive meetings with Cameron, in the end telling him that if he wanted to preserve the 'special relationship', Britain must commit to the target and pay its 'fair share'. The British government has responded that it is continuing to spend more on defence than any other countries except the US, Russia, China and Saudi Arabia (and about the same as France), is committed to building four new Trident strategic nuclear submarines and is planning to commission the first large aircraft carrier the Royal Navy has had for decades.

Post-election, the Cameron government reaffirmed its commitment to the 2 per cent of GDP target (subject to a degree of creative accounting) and envisaged a moderate increase in defence expenditure over the next five years. The 2015 defence review sought to undo some of the damage caused by its predecessor, by increasing the planned orders for the F-35 stealth aircraft and ordering Boeing P8 aircraft for maritime surveillance. There was no change in the reduced size of the army and the first aircraft carrier will not have a limited initial operating capability until 2020. The review, nevertheless, was seen in Washington as having a far better focus on Britain's military preparedness than the 2010 defence review.

The outgoing US Defense Secretary, Robert Gates, had a more general worry about what he regarded as the development of a 'two-tier alliance', in which a few countries, notably the US, Britain and France, were expected to deal with conflicts (though the Canadians also fought hard in Afghanistan), while many other European allies, though willing to engage in humanitarian operations, were unwilling to make any significant contribution to their own defence. This he regarded as being liable to impose increasing strains on the Alliance and to promote 'America first' attitudes in the US.[8]

55

THE SPECIAL RELATIONSHIP

AT THE END of the Second World War, Harry Hopkins wrote:

> I know no person in his right mind but that he believes that if this
> nation ever had to engage in another war Great Britain would
> be fighting on our side ... if I were to lay down the most cardi-
> nal principle of our foreign policy, it would be that we must make
> absolutely sure that now and forever the United States and Great
> Britain are going to see eye to eye on major matters of world pol-
> icy. It is easy to say that. It is hard to do, but it can be done and
> the effort is worth it.[1]

It was Winston Churchill who, in his 'Iron Curtain' speech at Fulton, Missouri, advocated

> a special relationship between the British Commonwealth and
> Empire and the United States ... the continuance of intimate rela-
> tionships between our military advisers, leading to the common
> study of potential dangers ... the continuance of the present facil-
> ities for mutual security by the joint use of all naval and air force
> bases in the possession of either country all over the world.

Churchill's was a practical proposal and to a large extent it was put
into effect. The arrangements he urged, in the face of the Soviet threat,
were extended to the North Atlantic Alliance generally. But at the heart
of the Alliance was an especially close relationship between Britain and

the United States, concerned with the management of crises in the post-war world.

On the train back from Fulton, Churchill told Clark Clifford: 'If I were to be born again, I would wish to be born in the United States. Your country is the future of the world. You have the natural resources, the spirit, the youth, the determination, which will steadily increase your global influence. Great Britain has passed its zenith.'[2] Churchill, Clifford notes, wanted to accelerate the process by which the United States would assume leadership in the postwar world and at the same time to preserve a role for Britain as America's special partner. Throughout the war, Churchill perforce had been conscious of the enormous and increasing disparity of power and the extent of Britain's dependence on the United States. 'No lover', he said later, 'ever studied every whim of his mistress as I did those of President Roosevelt.'[3]

As Britain emerged exhausted from the war, the British inability to continue to act as the guarantor of stability in the eastern Mediterranean precipitated the assumption of that mantle by the United States. While the immediate postwar period was one of exceptional achievement in Anglo-American diplomacy, the US ambassador in London was right to note in 1949 that Britain had never before been so completely dependent on another country's decisions: 'Almost every day brings new evidence of her weakness and dependence.'[4]

Despite the precipitous decline in relative power, in 1951 Churchill returned to office intending to continue with the Americans as he had left off and found Truman apparently willing to let him do so. After dinner on the presidential yacht on the Potomac, Churchill asked Dean Acheson if he did not feel that 'around the table this evening there was gathered the governance of the world – not to dominate it, mind you, but to save it'.[5] It came as a disagreeable surprise to Churchill that his wartime colleague Eisenhower should prove, as President, so concerned about overt 'collusion' with the British government. But it was Eisenhower who restored the nuclear collaboration with the British interrupted by the McMahon Act.

At the heart of the 'special relationship' lay this privileged collaboration, dating from the war, which the British enjoyed on defence, nuclear and intelligence issues. From time to time this was threatened on the American side. George Ball, leader of the Europeanists in the State Department, strongly opposed giving Britain the Polaris missile system. Ball, who never lacked confidence, felt that he knew what was good for Britain better than they did themselves:

> It seemed to me we should avoid doing anything that would extend Britain's nuclear deterrent for another generation ... I was very determined to have the British begin to get out of the feeling that they were a great power because they had an Empire, which they no longer had, and they had a nuclear weapon which the others didn't have, and they had a relationship with the United States which nobody else had.[6]

Ball felt that this was unhealthy, even from a British point of view. The British did not see it that way. Although he got no political credit for it at the time, Macmillan used the cancellation of Skybolt to persuade Kennedy to make available the infinitely more capable and long-lasting Polaris system, succeeded subsequently by Trident.

But nuclear weapons or not, in the aftermath of Suez, Macmillan had to confront the painful reality that Britain was no longer a world power. While clear-sighted about the full extent of Britain's wartime dependence on the United States, Churchill had insisted on dealing with Roosevelt and Stalin as an equal, bridging the gap between wishful thinking and reality through his genius and leadership of Britain at war. In the Suez crisis, Eden made a last effort to conduct himself as the head of government of an autonomous great power with a capacity for unilateral action. A quarter of a century later, Margaret Thatcher launched an equally hazardous expedition to recover the Falklands, which, this time, succeeded – but could not have done so without American support.

On the American side, Henry Kissinger in 1964 pointed out that the term 'special relationship' did not have the same psychological significance for the United States as it did for Britain. The memory of Britain's extraordinary wartime effort had faded over time. 'Many influential Americans have come to believe that Britain has been claiming an influence out of proportion to its power.'[7]

His experience as national security advisor and Secretary of State led to some different conclusions. He describes Nixon in 1969 disposing of the argument within the US administration about the 'special relationship' by simply stating flatly his commitment to the concept on his arrival in London. He did so to the dismay of the Europeanists in the State Department, who were eager to terminate the 'special relationship' as a supposed favour to Britain to smooth its entry into the European Community. Kissinger regarded abandoning the concept as both undesirable and impractical: 'For the special relationship with Britain was peculiarly impervious to abstract theories. It did not depend on formal arrangements; it derived in part from the memory of Britain's heroic wartime effort; it reflected the common language and culture of two sister peoples.'

Faced with the loss of real power, the British, in Kissinger's view, succeeded in becoming participants in internal American deliberations to a degree probably never practised before between sovereign states. There developed a pattern of consultation

> so matter-of-factly intimate that it became psychologically impossible to ignore British views. They evolved a habit of meetings so regular that autonomous American action somehow came to seem to violate club rules ... It was an extraordinary relationship because it rested on no legal claim; it was formalised by no document; it was carried forward by succeeding British governments as if no alternative were conceivable ... the 'special relationship' demonstrated the value of intangibles.[8]

When Callaghan became Foreign Secretary in 1974, he made clear his determination to put an end to the friction between the British and American governments that had developed under Heath. An agnostic about European unity, he saw no need for Britain to try to demonstrate its European credentials by distancing itself from the United States. When Carter was elected President, David Owen describes Callaghan's determination 'as a dyed-in-the-wool Atlanticist ... to establish his own special relationship with the new President'.[9] He was largely successful in doing so, eliciting from Carter in 1979 the promise to help Britain replace Polaris by Trident – if the British government decided on that course. Trident was the most advanced US strategic nuclear system and this was an offer that certainly was not going to be made to anyone else.

In his memoirs, Owen wrote:

> Every few years an incident occurs which demonstrates that the

Anglo-American relationship is still very important. I leave to aca-
demics to argue whether or not it is special. Its strength lies in
actions often taken quickly, informally and in an atmosphere of
trust. Those of us who have operated the relationship will have
their own memories of why it matters … The Anglo-American
relationship depends on personal relations at every level, but particularly between US presidents and secretaries of state and their
British counterparts. Down-play or denigrate this relationship and
it will be Europe, not just Britain, that will suffer. The invasion of
Kuwait, the seizure of the Falklands, the bombing of Libya are but
three recent examples in a long list of postwar incidents where it
was tested and not found wanting.[10]

George Shultz observed that, throughout his period as Secretary of State,
the relationship had renewed strength by virtue of the close personal and
political friendship between Margaret Thatcher and Ronald Reagan.[11]
Henry Kissinger described Thatcher's friendship for the United States as
'unqualified and unconstrained'. In his view: 'She achieved an influence
over American decisions, especially with respect to NATO and arms control policy, not seen since Churchill's day.'[12] Thatcher herself recounted the
subsequent strains in her relationship with George Bush, strains which,
however, were overcome by the time of the Gulf War, when the spectacle
of British units fighting alongside US forces and their performance in the
field made a powerful impact on American opinion and seemed to confirm
the continuing strength of an alliance that had endured for half a century.

For Condoleezza Rice, national security adviser, then Secretary of State
under George W. Bush, the 'special relationship' with Britain was 'as solid
as any in international politics' ('There is a kinship and a deep sense of
shared values … It is not that no difference exists, but there *is* a deep feeling that if you cannot count on the Brits, you are really alone').[13] Rice,
who was later to claim that she 'talked to the Brits every day', formed her
own special relationship with her friend the British ambassador, David
Manning. On her fiftieth birthday, going home at the end of a long working day, she was surprised to find her car diverted to the British embassy,

where the President and Cabinet were waiting to celebrate it with her. Hillary Clinton's farewell party as Secretary of State also was celebrated at the embassy.

When Barack Obama took over from George W. Bush, there was speculation on the part of several British commentators that this must mean the end of the 'special relationship'. In his book *Dreams from My Father*, Obama, describing a visit to Kenya to trace his origins, included a critique of the 'folly and conceit' of British colonial rule, rendering understandable the Mau Mau rebellion. His picture was no more flattering of post-colonial Kenya.

The bust of Churchill, treasured by George W. Bush, was removed from the Oval Office. But as he grappled with the problems in Afghanistan, a war that he did not really want to be waging, Obama was as glad as his predecessor to have British troops fighting with the Americans there.

In May 2011, Obama declared that 'the days are gone when Roosevelt and Churchill could sit in a room and solve the world's problems over a glass of brandy', but added that

> the reason for this close friendship doesn't just have to do with our shared history, our shared heritage, our ties of language and culture, or even the strong partnership between our governments. Our relationship is special because of the values and beliefs that have united our people through the ages.

While taking a more detached view of the relationship than any of his recent predecessors, Obama continued to pay rhetorical tribute to it: 'Through the grand sweep of history, through all its twists and turns, there is one constant – the rock-solid alliance between the United States and the United Kingdom' (March 2012).

As this account will have made clear, that there has been an extraordinarily close relationship between Britain and the United States since the desperate summer of 1940 is beyond dispute. The relationship frequently was marked by fierce disagreements, often with good cause, as over Suez, and real clashes of national interest. But to a remarkable extent these were regarded as something akin to family quarrels and, despite the tensions that marked successive prime ministerships – particularly those of Eden, Wilson and Heath – the underlying strength of the relationship always seemed to reassert itself. On the US side, such political opposites as Presidents Carter and Nixon attached value to it. Eisenhower was deeply imbued with it, though remarkably unsentimental about it. It was a reality also to Presidents Reagan and Bush Sr, despite the latter's clear-sighted recognition that Germany not only had much greater economic power but also, and increasingly, greater political importance.

Henry Kissinger observes a fundamental difference between the British and American philosophies of international relations. The British, he contends, do not believe in the perfectibility of mankind – expecting the worst, they are rarely disappointed:

> Whereas Americans have tended to believe that wars were caused by the moral failure of leaders, the British view is that aggression has thrived on opportunity as much as moral propensity, and must be restrained by some kind of balance of power ... In moral matters Britain has traditionally practised a convenient form of ethical egotism, believing that what was good for Britain was best for the rest.[14]

As national security adviser, Kissinger claimed to have kept the British better informed and more closely engaged than he did the State Department.

In economic terms, Britain today ranks fifth among the G7 nations and has impressed the US by achieving higher growth than most of the rest of Europe in recent years. Successive defence cuts have eroded the capabilities, though not the quality, of its armed forces. The ability to project power has dwindled further since the Gulf War, when General de la Billière describes the difficulty of fielding a single fully equipped armoured division.[15] Yet that was far more than any other European ally was prepared to do, and the division distinguished itself in the field, as did the British armoured division and Royal Marines in the operations to overthrow Saddam Hussein.

The United States is bound today to regard Germany as a more important power and far more capable of imposing its views in Europe. German reunification and the creation of the euro has changed the balance not only within Europe, but also across the Atlantic. The German constitution, however, has continued to inhibit cooperation outside the NATO area severely. The Constitutional Court ruled that Germany could play a non-combatant role in multilateral peace-keeping operations, as it did in Afghanistan, but the German contingent were prohibited from playing any part in the fighting there. To the dismay of the Americans, whenever a shot was fired, they returned to barracks and battened down the hatches.

Every American President nevertheless has regarded the relationship with Germany as crucially important to the United States and particularly in 'the role Germany has to play *vis-à-vis* Russia and Eastern Europe'. The relationship with Britain never has looked as special or exclusive to the Americans as to the British.

56

BRITAIN, THE UNITED STATES AND EUROPE

THIS WORK IS published at a time of high drama in the relationship between Britain and Europe, following the British vote on 23 June 2016 to withdraw from the European Union.

While Ernest Bevin played a vital part in the establishment of the Marshall Plan, the British resisted what to the United States was a vital part of the plan – the economic integration of Western Europe. The Americans, from their experience, were great believers in the economies of scale and did not believe that the stricken postwar European economies could revive within Europe's pitifully small national boundaries. All of Truman's key advisers – Dean Acheson, Averell Harriman, John McCloy and David Bruce – set about persuading the Europeans of the necessity of pooling resources, concerting their economic policies, and setting up the Organisation for European Economic Co-operation (OEEC), to which the Americans wanted to give much stronger powers than the British were prepared to accept. In doing so they were strongly influenced by Jean Monnet, well known to them from his service with the British Supply Mission in Washington during the war, but whose ideas on European economic integration were regarded as utopian by his British counterparts.

As part of the implementation of the Marshall Plan, the Americans pressed the idea of a European Customs Union. The Attlee government opposed this, because of its concerns to safeguard access for the Commonwealth and the sterling area. In 1949, the US administrator of the

Marshall Plan, Paul Hoffman, told the European governments that, in the view of the United States, Western Europe's economic ills could not be cured until the narrow national economies were combined into 'a single market within which goods, money and people could freely move and within which all barriers to trade and payments could be swept away'.[1]

When Robert Schuman explained to Acheson the plans he had developed with Monnet to place all French and German production of coal and steel under a joint high authority, which would be open to the participation of other European countries, David Bruce, then American ambassador in Paris, saw this as 'the most imaginative and far-reaching approach that has been made for generations to the settlement of fundamental differences between France and Germany'. Dean Acheson realised the problem Schuman's plan posed for the Labour government's strategy of nationalised control over coal and steel. Despite Acheson's arguments, Britain made 'her great mistake of the postwar period by refusing to join in negotiating the Schuman Plan'.[2]

When, in June 1955, the Foreign Ministers of France, Germany, Italy and the Benelux countries invited Britain to join in their discussions on European economic integration, Harold Macmillan, as Foreign Secretary, replied that there were special difficulties for Britain in a European Common Market, stemming particularly from the relationship with the Commonwealth. In the crucial meetings of the European Foreign Ministers in Messina, Italy, Britain was represented not by Macmillan but by an official from the Board of Trade, Russell Bretherton. In November he declared, on instructions, that Britain would not participate.

Macmillan was in Bermuda, mending fences with Eisenhower after Suez, when, in March 1957, the Six signed the Treaty of Rome. The event, which appeared to pass almost unnoticed by him, was not mentioned in his diaries. Eighteen months later he confided his worries about de Gaulle's opposition to British plans to subsume the Common Market into a European free trade area: 'The French are determined to exclude the United Kingdom. De Gaulle is bidding high for the hegemony of Europe.'

By the time of John Kennedy's election as President, Macmillan had changed his mind. He wrote Kennedy a letter stressing the 'special ties' afforded by Britain and the Commonwealth, but also his intention to take Britain into the EEC. Kennedy, encouraged by George Ball, an ardent proponent of European integration, promised his support.

Macmillan had invested so much in this plan that he found it very difficult to understand, as Harold Wilson did after him, that de Gaulle was
signalling a French veto. Yet Britain's failure to join the Common Market
at the outset had left him in a position of weakness. In November 1961,
de Gaulle told Macmillan that France did not want to change the character of Europe and did not want the British to 'bring their great escort
in with them'. Europe, he claimed, would be 'drowned in the Atlantic'. In
their subsequent meeting at Rambouillet, de Gaulle declared that, within
the Six: 'France could say no against even the Germans; she could stop
policies with which she disagreed ... Once Britain and all the rest joined
the organization, things would be different.'[3]

It was to Edward Heath that it fell at last to take Britain into Europe,
immediately adding a new dimension and also some complications to
Britain's relationship with the United States. To Henry Kissinger, Heath
appeared prepared to sacrifice whatever was special in the relationship
to his European ambitions; indeed, in Kissinger's view, he came close to
insisting on no preferential treatment in Washington.

The subsequent Labour government, especially James Callaghan as
Foreign Secretary, took steps to repair relations with the United States,
but during the attempt to renegotiate the terms of membership of the EC,
Kissinger made clear the US concern that Britain should remain a member.
For the Americans counted on British influence being exerted within the
European Community to make it more outward-looking, resist protection-
ism and preserve a close partnership with the United States, and considered
that therein lay much of the future value of the relationship to them.

———

The former US ambassador to Britain, Raymond Seitz, observed a fairly
general conviction that the end of the Cold War had changed the quality
of the Anglo-American relationship, the essentials of which for fifty years
had rested on meeting that fundamental challenge. Noting the increasing
British preoccupation with Europe, Seitz contended that 'while Britain's
role in the [European] Union is indisputably complicating to our relationship, it is also indispensable to the relationship'.[4]

Seitz felt that policy in the Foreign and Commonwealth Office increasingly was made in a European context. But the relationship with the

United States always had been more of a matter for 10 Downing Street and the Ministry of Defence.

So far as the European debate is concerned, few Americans believe that Britain could turn itself into just another European country even if it wanted to. The United States will remain profoundly ambivalent about European unity – in favour in principle but often disliking the practical manifestations. There was and still is scepticism in the US about the prospects for and effects of the European monetary union, given the manifest differences in economic performance between Germany and several of the other participants. The United States has a monetary union, but it also has a federal government and a fiscal union. What is clear to the Americans, however, is that the core of the monetary union is and will be Germany.

Britain, meanwhile, continued to wrestle with its European destiny. For reasons of politics, history and geography, the country was never going to be at the heart of Europe in the way France, Germany and the Benelux countries are. The Franco-German relationship was and is more important to both countries than the relationship with Britain is to either of them.

The British have remained peculiarly allergic to being governed from outside their own borders, resulting in the populist revolt in the EU referendum. Britain can ill afford to be marginalised in Europe if it is to remain influential in Washington; yet, in some important respects, it is precisely the fact that Britain *is* different from other European countries, and has been willing to act without waiting for a European consensus, that has rendered the relationship valuable to the United States and effective in action.

———————

The Anglo-American 'special relationship' was founded in wartime and continued in peacetime as a response to the threat posed first by Nazi Germany and then by the Soviet Union. That threat was instrumental in cementing the relationship not only between Britain and the United States but also between the USA and Europe. The disappearance of the Soviet threat created a more volatile environment, which, as the Bosnia crisis showed, could lead to a bifurcation between the United States and the European allies. In the view of Henry Kissinger: 'In this period nothing was easier to achieve than to have America turn away from Europe.' US force levels in Europe were reduced to less than divisional strength. The continued presence of US forces even at these levels nevertheless affords a vital guarantee that the defence link between the United States and Europe, the absence of which proved so costly in two world wars, is not about to be broken.

The former Foreign Secretary, David Owen, concluded his account of his unsuccessful diplomacy in the Balkans with the observation that the European Union 'does not know how to exercise power'.[5] The exercise of power requires real unity of purpose and the ability to make credible military threats.

The members of the European Union are committed to the framing of a 'common defence policy which might in time lead eventually to a common defence'. The United States would welcome efforts by the Europeans to become less reliant on it for their defence and more capable of dealing with regional crises themselves. Beyond that, however, European rhetoric about a 'common defence' has been in danger of outstripping reality. Nearly all European countries have been cutting defence spending. Even more than monetary union, an effective common defence policy would require unified central control. It also would require a large increase in defence budgets to give a European entity the sea and airlift and real-time intelligence capabilities that at present are lacking, and a drastic rationalisation of tasks among the participating defence forces. None of these conditions currently have any chance of being met. In the absence of a major increase in European defence spending, the post-Brexit proposal by Jean-Claude Juncker, President of the European Commission, to move ahead with the creation of a 'European army', with a headquarters in Brussels, would risk diverting scarce military resources from NATO, while creating the illusion rather than the reality of an effective European defence system.

As the European Union struggled to affirm its own identity, some European politicians and diplomats started to display once again a tendency to construct systems of collective security based on diplomatic concepts rather than military reality. The British military, rather more firmly than the Foreign Office, kept warning against any new security arrangements that could conflict with or divert resources from NATO. The arrival in the EU and NATO of the East Europeans injected a healthy dose of realism into this debate, while in 2009 the French, in an historic shift under Sarkozy, abandoned four decades of Gaullist anti-NATO prejudice and re-joined the integrated military structure of the Alliance, acknowledging the indispensability of NATO mechanisms in dealing with the crises in, for instance, Libya and Afghanistan.

————

In an essay on Anglo-American relations, Robert Zoellick, former head of the World Bank and a key figure in the administration of George Bush Sr, observed that 'Britain is no longer the mother country. Nor are Britons the wise Greeks who must guide the rustic, untutored Roman Americans.' There was no need for an interpreter between continental Europe and the USA. Yet, he argues, the relationship still matters because the American nation is based on commitment to a set of ideas that have deep British roots: 'The great debates over the past two centuries in both countries reflected a shared body of thought.'

Henry Kissinger also notes that a succession of American leaders of both political parties, 'most of them not known for excessive sentimentality', have considered it natural that on major issues Britain and the United States should seek to cooperate and have a level of consultation that has never been formalised but that has been central to the formation of policy in both countries. The future challenge, he suggests, is to see whether this could be extended to European–American relations, where Britain's influence continues to be counted on to help this to happen.[6]

Zoellick, echoing Kissinger, observed that 'the major foreign policy challenge for the UK today is to help determine the future shape of the European Union and Britain's place within it. Britain's preferences are likely to be positive for the US.' He added that Britain is a 'reluctant Europeanist' and that Americans can comprehend why this is so. They find it easy to understand British resistance to transfers of sovereignty and do not themselves want to see all roads leading to Brussels. Like the British, they see Europe as overregulated, excessively protectionist and pursuing an absurdly costly and trade-distorting agricultural policy. But they counted on Britain to help ensure that the European Union is open to the removal of trade barriers and to strengthening the partnership with North America.[7]

The Brexit vote has upset all these American calculations about the role Britain can play in the world, including seeking to influence the future of the EU and trade negotiations that are of vital interest to the United States, as well as to guard against a divergence between European and Atlantic defence policies. Further dialogue with the British on those subjects will now be far more limited. Many US observers – not only Donald Trump – have sympathy for the British critique of the EU, to the point of wondering how well it will now survive. What is clear to them, however, is that with the vital exception of its defence contribution, Britain henceforth will be a more marginal player in Europe.

57

SPECIAL ANY MORE?

The tumult and the shouting dies;
The Captains and the Kings depart...
Far-called, our navies melt away;
On dune and headland sinks the fire
—RUDYARD KIPLING, 'RECESSIONAL'

IS BRITAIN'S ROLE in the world really quite as reduced as that? And what, post-Brexit, is going to be left of the relationship that has been so permanent a feature of the postwar world?

The unpopularity in Britain (and the US) of the Iraq War has cast a long shadow. Since Saddam Hussein turned out not to have weapons of mass destruction, the better course, self-evidently, would have been to continue the policy of containment. This would not have protected the Shia majority or the Kurds from continuing brutal repression by the regime, but that was not the *casus belli*.

Alongside this obvious conclusion, a debate has raged about how the US and its allies supposedly 'lost' the war in Afghanistan. The rationale for the intervention was to remove the Taliban regime and thereby deny Al-Qaeda safe haven in Afghanistan from which to conduct terrorist attacks worldwide. Those objectives were achieved.

Fifteen years on, despite a resurgent effort by the Taliban, a democratically elected government, in control of the main centres, remains in power in Kabul. The Taliban were enforcing a brutal version of Sharia law, with regular public executions in the Kabul sports stadium. It is impossible to forecast what the future holds for Afghanistan, but on the evidence to date, it is wrong to conclude that this was another case of 'losing small wars'.

———————

The extraordinary history of the Anglo-American relationship since 1940 can lead easily into a tendency to romanticise it. This account will have made clear the roller-coaster nature of the relationship, with the rhetoric about 'shared values' tending to mask the many fierce disagreements and clashes of national interest which also have been a near-constant feature of it. One of the great fallacies in the mythology of US/UK relations is that these have ever been plain sailing. The relationship, over the past seven decades, has had many highs, but also its fair share of lows, and the decision to invade Iraq and then find that there were no weapons of mass destruction there ranks high among them.

In political systems like those of Britain and the US, there are self-correcting tendencies in politics. Over the past fifteen years, Britain has found itself contending first with the overly aggressive instincts of the George W. Bush team and then the relative passivity of the Obama administration. In London, a willingness to take major risks in Iraq and Afghanistan was followed by an understandable degree of risk averseness.

Important lessons that need to be learned from these interventions from a British point of view are the dangers of overreach, of politicians asking very limited numbers of troops to carry out missions beyond their scope, of muddled strategic thinking within the military high command and critical gaps in equipment as a result of relentless Treasury pressures and dysfunctional procurement policies. The US general Jack Keane, part author of the 'surge' in Iraq, attributed many of these difficulties to a failure on the part of the UK military to be more forthright in explaining to their political leaders the limitations of what could be achieved with the limited forces available to be deployed. The British military had neither the numbers nor the equipment to fight on two fronts in Iraq and Afghanistan and failed to make this clear to their political masters.

Yet the British forces, fielding potentially for the last time an armoured division, fought very well in the overthrow of the Iraqi regime, as did the UK Special Forces in the attacks on Al-Qaeda targets around Baghdad and the British troops in Afghanistan. The conclusion of the most successful allied commanders, Generals Petraeus and McChrystal, was that Britain has 'some of the best fighting troops in the world', though seriously under-equipped. The respect in which those troops, though not all their military hierarchy, won unqualified success was in earning once again the admiration of the US military and people as the best allies the US had on its side. In Iraq and Afghanistan, the American commanders – Petraeus, Odierno and McChrystal – earned the highest respect from the British military. As his US counterparts unfailingly responded to requests for help in Iraq and Afghanistan, the conclusion of General Graeme Lamb was: 'As military allies, the Americans do not fail you.'

———————

The United Kingdom needs to understand more clearly than it has in the past the perspective in which it is viewed in Washington. There is admiration for the recent performance of the British economy, but a clear recognition that, from every perspective except military, Germany is a far more important force in Europe and will be still more so post Brexit. The German constitution, however, continues severely to inhibit defence cooperation with the United States, while Germany is continuing to spend just 1.3 per cent of its GDP on defence.

Britain currently has a healthier economy and is spending marginally more on defence than France, but there has been a huge improvement in US–French relations, with the former French Foreign Minister, Laurent Fabius, playing a more prominent role in international affairs than his British counterparts in a period in which British diplomacy has been very little in evidence and preoccupied with the unsuccessful 're-negotiation' with the EU. Reflections from the House of Commons Foreign Affairs Committee suggesting that Britain could afford to sit on the sidelines of the fight against ISIS in Syria were regarded in the US as 'Chamberlainesque'.

Relations between the Foreign and Commonwealth Office, more than ever preoccupied with Europe, and the State Department are far from being as close as they were in the past. In this sense, the relationship has become a more 'normal' one. Rhetorical flourishes from the White House have been regarded by many as masking the fact that Britain today is markedly less influential in Washington than it was in an era when the UK's point of view regularly would be reported to the President alongside those of the major US government agencies and well ahead of that of any other ally.

British support, nevertheless, was important to Obama in Afghanistan and remains so to him and will be to his successor in the struggle against ISIS. While the relationship today is far less important to the United States than it was in the past, there is no sign of any desire on the US side to wind it up.

The euphoria that accompanied the end of the Cold War was celebrated in a book with a particularly inappropriate title: *The End of History*.[1] What we have seen since, in the Middle East, in the Balkans and in Putin's behaviour in Ukraine and Syria, has been the return of history, with a vengeance. The Russian intervention has exposed the hollowness of Western policy in Syria.

The US and its allies today face the prospect of a decades-long campaign against radical Islamists, and not only in Syria and Iraq. The US-led air strikes have inflicted damage on the militia and its commanders and have made a major contribution to the setbacks ISIS have suffered. They have lost a lot of territory and key strongholds in Fallujah and Ramadi. They have been shielded by their control over the civilian populations in Mosul and Raqqa, but risk being cut off and eventually defeated in both centres, though that will not end the struggle against them, which currently is far more threatening to Europe than to the United States.

The British contribution to the campaign against ISIS has remained very limited. But, along with the efforts of the French, and ever more intensive intelligence cooperation, it is important to the US in terms of active allied solidarity in combating the threat, with a pressing need also to counter them in Libya. The decision in December 2015 to extend RAF attacks on ISIS targets from Iraq to Syria brought Britain back into line with the US and France. This was important, given the current debate in America about how much or little the allies at present are contributing to their own and collective defence. Self-evidently, there will be no quick victories in these campaigns. In this new and no less dangerous world, it is hardly the moment to think of weakening any alliances, still less one that has proved as effective as that between Britain and the US.

The past decade has seen two military interventions abroad, both highly controversial. The Iraq War is considered to have been fought on a false premise. The outcome was indeed to transform the Middle East, but for the worse. The campaign in Afghanistan, though more clearly justified, is felt to have gone on too long, with too many casualties.

America's concern about Britain's reduced defence capabilities will be partially addressed when a new large aircraft carrier comes into service from 2020. Despite the anti-Americanism prevalent across much of the left of the political spectrum, the British for the most part will continue to regard the United States as by far their most important ally. They will go on lamenting from time to time that the Americans, in their opinion, can be relied upon to do the right thing in the end, 'having first exhausted the available alternatives', and suggesting that, notwithstanding a couple of hundred years of independence, the British somehow still have greater experience than they do. Americans react tolerantly to these pretensions, but anyone hoping actually to have any influence on the United States needs to start from a different premise.

This narrative will, I hope, have demonstrated how much, in the past seven decades, has been achieved through Anglo-American cooperation in action, which, too often, is taken for granted. The consequences when there has been a breakdown of cooperation, as over Suez or for a time over Bosnia, have been equally striking. It would be naive to imagine that we have seen an end to the crises which forged that alliance, or that the United Kingdom is likely to be able to achieve comparable security by any other route.

US/UK intelligence cooperation has been a lynchpin of the relationship ever since the days when Churchill revealed to Roosevelt the *Ultra* secret and the work of Bletchley Park. Notwithstanding the catastrophic intelligence failure in Iraq, from which those responsible emerged remarkably unscathed, in every other instance it has been one of the ties that bind. The struggle to contain and defeat international terrorism has ensured that, despite different legal frameworks, it has continued unabated. Cooperation with the US in dealing with cyber-attacks is critical to dealing with the challenges of the future.

Those who would like to see Britain distance itself from the United States need to be careful what they wish for. It will remain a crucial objective for any British government to keep the United States engaged in the defence of Europe. The former US Defense Secretary, Robert Gates, did not regard this as set in stone. If Europe continues contributing so modestly to its own defence, Gates considers it only a matter of time before Congress starts insisting that Europe should do more, or the US should do less, predicting a revival of the kind of 'America first' attitudes epitomised by Donald Trump. To Europe's cost, we have already seen this in practice, with the Obama administration choosing initially to regard Syria as a problem mainly for the Europeans, who, however, had had very limited capacity to deal with it themselves. Extremely reluctant to involve the US in Libya, Obama sought to do so on the basis of 'leading from behind' to try to force the Europeans to accept a major share of the effort and risks involved.

As the Trump candidacy for the presidency has reminded us, protectionism and isolationism are recessive genes in the US body politic. If in future the United States is left to grapple with difficult situations with no practical manifestation of European support, then Europe will need to learn to place much less reliance on the US coming to its rescue, as the Americans did in Bosnia and Kosovo. That is a service Britain has rendered to the rest of Europe, without getting much credit for it. But it also is why Britain, though far from being as 'exceptional' as in the past, will continue to be regarded as an important partner for the United States, particularly as Britain and France are seen in Washington as the only allies disposed to be and capable of being of much military help to the US.

The price of influence in Washington always has been relevance and participation. The decision to exit the EU clearly is going to severely limit Britain's future influence in Europe and, therefore, in Washington, representing a structural and irreversible change in the relationship. This does not mean that a 'special' relationship will not survive with, beyond the lip service, some genuine homage being paid to it on both sides of the Atlantic, but it will circumscribe its scope more than ever to defence and the massive cross-investment in each other's economies.

A post-Brexit British government, having burned a lot of bridges in Europe, will be anxious to demonstrate continued closeness to the US and will be humoured by the Americans in doing so. For, today, the relationship still is unique in certain areas – nuclear, defence and intelligence – all dating from the wartime collaboration. Beyond that, it would be extremely unwise to regard it as unique. Britain has influence on American policy to the extent that it is itself perceived as having power and influence in various parts of the world, now seen as being further reduced.

Present-day British political leaders will need to decide whether they are prepared to continue playing the role of America's close ally in helping to deal with international crises, which, hitherto, but no longer today, generally has enjoyed bipartisan support. A refusal to do so would put a swift end to whatever is special about the relationship.

———————

Whatever may be thought of the vagaries of US policy in the past two decades, the United States remains the main guarantor of Britain's security and only effective ally in crises like the Falklands, the Gulf and Bosnia. The United States alone has the capabilities to give effective help to the United Kingdom in any military crisis. Post-Brexit, there will be renewed attempts, led by France and Germany, to increase European defence cooperation, but there is no sign of the European countries giving themselves the real military capabilities that would be necessary to ensure on their own the defence of Europe or enable them in any major or even relatively minor crisis to act independently of the United States.

The demise of the 'special relationship' has been pronounced on many occasions. Yet it has shown remarkable staying power, though not in the mythical form in which it was supposed to have existed in the past. The relationship has been viewed more sanely through American than British eyes. For successive British governments it has appeared to offer some consolation for the loss of real power, leading them to exaggerate the influence they could hope to derive from it. Accordingly, they sought to place upon the concept a weight it will not bear.

The US/UK relationship has been based on a community of interest, but also to some degree on a shared belief that 'for evil to triumph, it is sufficient for good men to do nothing'. The quotation generally is attributed to Edmund Burke, though it is nowhere to be found in his writings. The successive crises in Kuwait, Bosnia, Kosovo, Afghanistan and Libya showed again that, even when united, the UN has little or no enforcement capability, other than through the United States, generally supported by Britain.

In helping to contain and manage threats like those posed by Putin's Russia in Eastern Europe and ISIS in the Middle East, the American role will remain indispensable and they will be looking for Britain's active support, as will those subject directly to those threats. Unless this country were to decide to abdicate any further pretensions to play a significant role in world affairs, it will need to continue to nurture the especially close defence relationship with the United States as crucial to its ability to go on playing an effective part in helping to deal with world crises.

No less vital a feature of the relationship has been the effort to influence US policies and actions. British Prime Ministers frequently have talked a better game than they have played in that regard. The most influential, by a distance, were Churchill and Thatcher, both of whom had fierce disagreements with the United States, despite being accused of being too close to the Americans. Both were effective in ensuring that their views could not be ignored, though that never meant that they necessarily prevailed. Blair was successful in persuading the US to threaten intervention in Kosovo and to seek a new UN resolution on Iraq, but had no real say on the timing of the invasion or the disbanding of the Iraqi Army and civil service.

The Anglo-American relationship self-evidently is today far less intense or influential than it was at the height of the Second World War or the Cold War. While the sense in which it today really is 'special' is limited, there still is an *especially close* relationship between Britain and the United States. That is a product, or at any rate a residue, of habits of cooperation bred over seven decades.

It still has some very practical manifestations. The planned renewal of Trident, extending the British nuclear deterrent for several more decades, rests on the continuance of the military nuclear cooperation between Britain and the United States extending back to the Manhattan Project, and not available to any other ally. Obama's Defense Secretary, Ashton Carter, has supported UK plans to renew Trident as important to NATO deterrence, the 'special relationship' and Britain's standing in the world.[2]

Obama has departed from his predecessors in appearing to resent rather than to accept the notion of the United States as the 'indispensable nation' in dealing with world crises, with Trump representing a different version of America turning inwards. No one, save Obama, and least of all some senior members of his own administrations, believes that the President's refusal to uphold a 'red line' in Syria was not a factor in emboldening

Putin in Ukraine and then in changing the facts on the ground in Syria. As the US foreign policy establishment so disliked by him pointed out, if he did not intend to enforce a red line, he should not have declared one in the first place.

If this tendency to disengage from problems others cannot deal with is to be countered, that will depend on the leading European countries making an effective contribution to tackling them. For the risk otherwise is evident of transatlantic drift, with the US becoming far more selective about the extent to which it is prepared to assist Europe militarily unless US interests are directly threatened.

Whether he or Hillary Clinton is elected the next President of the United States, the questions raised by Donald Trump about disproportionate burden-sharing in defence will not go away, an underlying problem being the very limited contribution still being made by Japan and Germany seventy years after the Second World War. The Abe government in Japan has been doing more to seek to address the problem than Europe has shown much sign of doing. Trump would be an unwelcome outcome for the allies and for America's principal trading partners. So far as the defence relationship with Britain is concerned, however, it has developed sufficiently deep roots within the US and British systems to be in little danger of being uprooted easily and it would be no more in the interests of a Trump than of any other administration to do so.

Beyond the sentiment, beyond the rhetoric, the hard-headed reality is that the US alliance remains as critical as ever to Britain's defence and security. As Churchill declared from bitter experience waiting for the United States to enter two world wars, the only thing worse than fighting with allies is having to fight without them. Because it is one of the ties that have bound Europe and North America, the relationship remains important, and not only to Britain and the United States. Beyond that, it indisputably is the case that it played a major part in the fashioning of the postwar world. There are many on both sides of the Atlantic who will think that the world would have been poorer without it. The world, meanwhile, looks further than ever from having assumed so unthreatening and predictable a form as to render it redundant.

NOTES AND REFERENCES

ABBREVIATIONS

EL   Eisenhower Library, Abilene, Kansas
FRUS Foreign Relations of the United States
PRO   Public Record Office, Kew, London
SWW Winston Churchill, *The Second World War*

FOREWORD
1. PRO, FO 371/38523, 21 March 1944.
2. First published, from a US copy, in 1989 by Louis Krue. Address by Sir David Omand to the Council of Foreign Relations, New York, 17 June 2015.
3. Margaret Thatcher, *The Downing Street Years* (HarperCollins, 1993), p. 226.
4. NSC minutes, 29 April 1982, Reagan library, NSC meeting file, Box 91284.
5. Condoleezza Rice, *No Higher Honor* (Simon & Schuster, 2011), pp. 37–8; Barack Obama, March 2012.
6. Obama interview in *The Atlantic*, April 2016. See also Ben Rhodes interview in the *New York Times*, 8 May 2016
7. Robert Kagan, 'Super-powers Don't Get to Retire', *New Republic*, March 2014.
8. Robert Gates, BBC interview, 16 January 2014; General Ray Odierno, *Daily Telegraph*, 1 March 2015; Ashton Carter, BBC interview, 8 November 2015.
9. General Houghton, BBC interview, 8 November 2015.
10. *The Atlantic*, April 2016.
11. *The Times*, 10 May 2006.

PROLOGUE
1. Richard Rush, cited in J. S. Williams, *History of the Invasion and Capture of Washington* (1857), pp. 274–5.
2. J. W. Taylor, 8 October 1814, quoted in R. Ketcham, *James Madison* (University of Virginia Press, 1990), p. 579.
3. Monroe to Jefferson, 11 January 1807, in S. M. Hamilton (ed.), *The Writings of James Monroe*, Vol. V (G. P. Putnam's Sons, 1898), pp. 1–2.
4. Henry Adams, *History of the United States*, Vol. IV (Charles Scribner's Sons, 1889), p. 182.

5. Henry Adams (ed.), *The Writings of Albert Gallatin*, Vol. I (J. B. Lippincott, 1879), pp. 602–7.
6. Jefferson to Monroe, 24 October 1823, in Hamilton (ed.), *The Writings of James Monroe*, Vol. VI, p. 39.
7. PRO, 30/22/34, 22 May 1860, ff. 138–41.
8. Kenneth Bourne, *Britain and the Balance of Power in North America* (Longman, 1967), p. 219.
9. Henry Adams, *Democracy: An American Novel* (Henry Holt & Co., 1880), pp. 30–31.
10. Susan Mary Alsop, *Lady Sackville* (Doubleday, 1978), pp. 72–5.
11. H. C. Allen, *Great Britain and the United States* (St Martin' s Press, 1995), p. 536.
12. Ibid., p. 539.
13. Edmund Morris, *The Rise of Theodore Roosevelt* (Ballantine, 1979), p. 477.
14. A. T. Mahan, *Lessons of the War with Spain*, cited in Christopher Hitchens, *Blood, Class and Nostalgia* (Chatto & Windus, 1990), p. 74.
15. Hitchens, *Blood, Class and Nostalgia*, p. 80.

1 'YOU MUST NOT SPEAK OF US AS COUSINS'

1. Hitchens, *Blood, Class and Nostalgia*, p. 135.
2. A. S. Link (ed.), *The Papers of Woodrow Wilson*, Vol. I (Princeton University Press, 1969), pp. 393–4.
3. Elting E. Morison (ed.), *The Letters of Theodore Roosevelt*, Vol. VIII (Harvard University Press, 1951–4), pp. 829–30.
4. Charles Seymour (ed.), *The Intimate Papers of Colonel House*, Vol. I (Houghton Mifflin, 1926), p. 296.
5. Ibid., p. 364.
6. Wilson, speech in Philadelphia, 10 May 1915; Patrick Devlin, *Too Proud to Fight* (Oxford University Press, 1975), p. 288.
7. S. Gwynne (ed.), *The Letters and Friendships of Sir Cecil Spring-Rice*, Vol. II (Constable, 1929), pp. 202, 372.
8. Lloyd George, *War Memoirs* (Odhams, 1938), p. 397.
9. Seymour (ed.), *House*, Vol. II, p. 76.
10. Grey of Fallodon, *Twenty-Five Years*, Vol. II (Frederick A. Stokes Company, 1925), pp. 85, 107.
11. Seymour (ed.), *House*, Vol. II, p. 89.
12. Ibid., p. 201.
13. Ibid., p. 256.
14. Woodrow Wilson, Address to the League to Enforce Peace, New York, 27 May 1916; Devlin, *Too Proud to Fight*, p. 490.
15. R. Lansing, *War Memoirs* (Bobbs-Merrill, 1935), p. 172.
16. PRO, FO 371/2796, 205593, 10 October 1916; J. M. Keynes, *Collected Writings*, Vol. XVI (Macmillan, 1971), p. 197.
17. Robert Skidelsky, *John Maynard Keynes: Hopes Betrayed* (Macmillan, 1983), p. 334.
18. Seymour (ed.), *House*. Vol. II, p. 394.
19. Skidelsky, *John Maynard Keynes*, p. 336.
20. Lloyd George, *War Memoirs*, p. 977.
21. Skidelsky, *John Maynard Keynes*, p. 336.
22. Seymour (ed.), *House*, Vol. II, p. 382.
23. Barbara Tuchman, *The Zimmermann Telegram* (Constable, 1959), pp. 175–6.
24. Lloyd George, *War Memoirs*, p. 991.

25. Ibid., p. 994.
26. A. S. Link (ed.), *The Papers of Woodrow Wilson*, Vol. 43. p. 238.
27. Skidelsky, *John Maynard Keynes*, p. 342.
28. W. S. Churchill, *The World Crisis* (Odhams, 1938), p. 1337.
29. Ibid., p. 1334.
30. PRO, CAB 23/43, Imperial War Cabinet (31), 14 August 1918; David Dimbleby and David Reynolds, *An Ocean Apart* (Hodder & Stoughton, 1988), p. 62.
31. J. M. Keynes, *The Economic Consequences of the Peace* (Macmillan, 1920), p. 35.
32. Ibid., p. 50.
33. George C. Marshall, *Memoirs of My Services in the World War* (Houghton Mifflin, 1976), pp. 216–23.
34. Paul Kennedy, *The Rise and Fall of the Great Powers* (Random House, 1987), pp. 227–8.
35. Lloyd George, *War Memoirs*, p. 1057.
36. Seymour (ed.), *House*, Vol. IV, p. 510.

2   'WE WILL GET NOTHING FROM THE AMERICANS BUT WORDS'

1. David Geddes, 'Auckland Geddes in Washington', unpublished biographical study, p. 91.
2. Ibid., pp. 78–9.
3. Dimbleby and Reynolds, *An Ocean Apart*, pp. 79, 82.
4. Ibid., p. 90.
5. B. J. C. McKercher, *The Second Baldwin Government and the United States* (Cambridge University Press, 1984), p. 1.
6. Norman Rose, *Vansittart: Study of a Diplomat* (Heinemann, 1978), pp. 126–7.
7. D. W. Brogan, *The French Nation, 1814–1940* (Hamilton, 1957), p. 267.
8. Sir Alexander Cadogan (ed. David Dilks), *Diaries* (G. P. Putnam's Sons, 1972), p. 53.
9. Sir John Wheeler-Bennett, *King George VI* (Macmillan, 1958), pp. 391–2.
10. W. S. Churchill, *SWW*, Vol. I (Cassell, 1948), p. 345.
11. Ibid., p. 435.
12. Martin Gilbert, *Winston S. Churchill*, Vol. VI (Heinemann, 1975–88), p. 117.

3   'IN THE LONG HISTORY OF THE WORLD THIS IS A THING TO DO NOW'

1. Franklin D. Roosevelt to Winston Churchill, in Warren F. Kimball (ed.), *Churchill and Roosevelt: The Complete Correspondence*, Vol. I (Princeton University Press, 1984), pp. 33–4.
2. Diary of Harold Ickes, 12 May 1940, Library of Congress, Washington, DC.
3. Michael Beschloss, *Kennedy and Roosevelt* (W. W. Norton, 1980), p. 157.
4. Ibid., pp. 186, 197, 204.
5. PRO, CAB 65/7, Imperial War Cabinet, 13 June 1940, ff. 291–7; Gilbert, *Churchill*, Vol. VI, pp. 539–40.
6. Churchill, *SWW*, Vol. II, pp. 167, 172.
7. Churchill to Roosevelt, 15 June 1940, Gilbert, *Churchill*, Vol. VI, pp. 551, 591.
8. Churchill to Lothian, 28 June 1940, *SWW*, Vol. II, p. 201; Gilbert. *Churchill*, Vol. VI, p. 607.
9. John Colville, *The Fringes of Power*, Vol. I (Hodder & Stoughton, 1985), p. 398.
10. PRO, CAB 65/8, WM 231 (40) 1, Imperial War Cabinet, 21 August 1940; Kimball (ed.), *Churchill and Roosevelt*, Vol. I, p. 65.

11. Roosevelt to Churchill, 7 August 1940, in Kimball (ed.), *Churchill and Roosevelt*, Vol. I, pp. 58–9; Gilbert, *Churchill*, Vol. VI, p. 716.
12. Andrew Roberts, *Eminent Churchillians* (Weidenfeld & Nicolson, 1994), p. 48.

4 'YOUR BOYS ARE NOT GOING TO BE SENT INTO ANY FOREIGN WARS'

1. Colville, *The Fringes of Power*, Vol. I, p. 290; Gilbert, *Churchill*, Vol. VI, p. 802.
2. Beschloss, *Kennedy and Roosevelt*, pp. 206–8.
3. J. Leutze (ed.), *The London Observer 1940.25* (Hutchinson, 1972), Chapter III, p. 14.
4. Beschloss, *Kennedy and Roosevelt*, pp. 220–21; Robert Divine, *Foreign Policy and US Presidential Elections* (Franklin Waits, 1974), pp. 82–3.
5. J. R. M. Butler, *Lord Lothian* (Macmillan, 1960), p. 307.
6. PRO, PREM 4/17/1, 28 December 1940; Dimbleby and Reynolds, *An Ocean Apart*, p. 133.
7. Andrew Roberts, *The Holy Fox* (Weidenfeld & Nicolson, 1991), pp. 275, 280.
8. Ibid., pp. 282–3.
9. Robert Sherwood, *Roosevelt and Hopkins* (Harper, 1948), pp. 238, 243, 246.
10. H. Montgomery Hyde, *The Quiet Canadian* (Constable, 1982), p. 37.
11. Ibid., p. 153.
12. Kim Philby, *My Silent War* (MacGibbon & Kee, 1968), p. 54.
13. W. A. Harriman and Elie Abel, *Special Envoy to Churchill and Stalin* (Random House, 1975), p. 31.
14. Cadogan, *Diaries*, p. 393.
15. Sherwood, *Roosevelt and Hopkins*, p. 344.
16. Churchill, *SWW*, Vol. III, p. 387; Gilbert, *Churchill*, Vol. VI, p. 1160.
17. Sherwood, *Roosevelt and Hopkins*, p. 373.
18. Henry Brandon, *Special Relationships* (Atheneum, 1988), p. 4.
19. Gilbert, *Churchill*, Vol. VI, p. 1266.
20. John G. Winant, *Letter from Grosvenor Square* (Hodder & Stoughton, 1947), pp. 198–9; Churchill, *SWW*, Vol. III, pp. 538–9.

5 'THE PRIME MINISTER OF GREAT BRITAIN HAS NOTHING TO HIDE FROM THE PRESIDENT OF THE UNITED STATES'

1. Churchill, *SWW*, Vol. III, pp. 587–8; Sherwood, *Roosevelt and Hopkins*, pp. 442–3.
2. Brandon, *Special Relationships*, pp. 9–11.
3. *US News and World Report*, 2 November 1959, p. 5.
4. Richardson and Ball, pp. 1–2; Winterbotham, p. 86.
5. Sherwood, *Roosevelt and Hopkins*, pp. 511–2; Gilbert, *Churchill*, Vol. VI, pp. 88–9.
6. Arthur Bryant, *The Turn of the Tide* (Collins, 1957), pp. 285–8.
7. Churchill, *SWW*, Vol. IV, pp. 338–9.
8. Margaret Gowing, *Britain and Atomic Energy 1939–45* (Macmillan, 1964), pp. 64–5.
9. Ibid., pp. 96–7; Churchill, *SWW*, Vol. IV, p. 730.
10. Churchill, *SWW*, Vol. IV, pp. 339–40.

6 'THE ONLY WAY IN WHICH WE COULD POSSIBLY LOSE THIS WAR'

1. Bryant, *The Turn of the Tide*, p. 329; Churchill, *SWW*, Vol. IV, pp. 343–7.
2. Sherwood, *Roosevelt and Hopkins*, p. 600; E. Cray, *General of the Army George C. Marshall* (Simon & Schuster, 1990), p. 328.

3. Bryant, *The Turn of the Tide*, p. 341; Churchill, *SWW*, Vol. IV, p. 400.
4. Sherwood, *Roosevelt and Hopkins*, p. 607; Stephen E. Ambrose, *Eisenhower: Soldier and President* (Simon & Schuster, 1990), p. 76; Cray, *General of the Army*, p. 333.
5. Churchill, *SWW*, Vol. IV, pp. 568, 575–6.
6. FRUS, *The Conferences at Washington and Casablanca* (1943), p. 583; Cray, *General of the Army*, pp. 358–9; Harold Macmillan, *The Blast of War 1939–45* (Macmillan, 1967), p. 194.
7. Bryant, *The Turn of the Tide*, pp. 454–5.
8. Churchill, *SWW*, Vol. IV, p. 622.
9. Sherwood, *Roosevelt and Hopkins*, p. 719.
10. Churchill, *SWW*, Vol. IV, p. 713.
11. Cray, *General of the Army*, pp. 386–7.
12. General Ismay, *Memoirs* (Heinemann, 1960), pp. 296–8; Bryant, *The Turn of the Tide*, p. 508.
13. Churchill, *SWW*, Vol. IV, pp. 715–7; FRUS, *The Conferences at Washington and Quebec* (1943), pp. 152–208.
14. Gowing, *Britain and Atomic Energy*, p. 157.
15. Churchill, *SWW*, Vol. IV, p. 723.
16. Bryant, *The Turn of the Tide*, p. 525.

7 'MY GOD! NOW THEY'VE STARTED SHOOTING'

1. Sherwood, *Roosevelt and Hopkins*, p. 733.
2. Churchill, *SWW*, Vol. V, p. 67.
3. H. L. Stimson and McGeorge Bundy, *On Active Service in Peace and War* (Harper, 1947), p. 432; Sherwood, *Roosevelt and Hopkins*, p. 767.
4. Gowing, *Britain and Atomic Energy*, p. 169.
5. FRUS, *The Conferences at Washington and Quebec* (1943), pp. 849–966; Churchill, *SWW*, Vol. V, pp. 76, 81.
6. Cadogan, *Diaries*, p. 559.
7. Arthur Bryant, *Triumph in the West* (Greenwood Press, 1974), pp. 24–5.
8. Ibid., p. 32.
9. Churchill, *SWW*, Vol. V, pp. 193–5.
10. Ibid., p. 226.

8 'THIS IS MUCH THE GREATEST THING WE HAVE EVER ATTEMPTED'

1. Churchill, *SWW*, Vol. V, pp. 254–8; Robert Murphy, *Diplomat among Warriors* (Doubleday, 1964), pp. 208–9.
2. Churchill, *SWW*, Vol. V, pp. 268, 271, 276–7.
3. FRUS, *The Conferences at Cairo and Tehran* (1943), pp. 307–58.
4. Churchill, *SWW*, Vol. V, p. 301.
5. Ibid., pp. 305–6.
6. FRUS, *The Conferences at Cairo and Tehran*, pp. 482–6, 529–33; Churchill, *SWW*, Vol. V, p. 320.
7. Churchill, *SWW*, Vol. V, p. 329.
8. Frances Perkins, *The Roosevelt I Knew* (Viking, 1946), pp. 84–5.
9. Churchill, *SWW*, Vol. V, pp. 339–43.

9 'EVEN SPLENDID VICTORIES AND WIDENING OPPORTUNITIES DO NOT BRING US TOGETHER ON STRATEGY'

1. Bryant, *Triumph in the West*, p. 139; Ambrose, *Eisenhower*, p. 134; Churchill, *SWW*, Vol. V, p. 521.
2. Churchill, *SWW*, Vol. V, p. 555.
3. Bryant, *Triumph in the West*, pp. 181–2.
4. Churchill, *SWW*, Vol. VI, p. 56.
5. Ibid., p. 84.
6. Ibid., pp. 129–30.
7. Roy Harrod, *Life of John Maynard Keynes* (Macmillan, 1951), p. 4.
8. FRUS, *The Conference at Quebec* (1944), pp. 312–28; Murphy, *Diplomat among Warriors*, p. 227.
9. Gowing, *Britain and Atomic Energy*, pp. 341–2.
10. Churchill, *SWW*, Vol. VI, p. 198.
11. Sherwood, *Roosevelt and Hopkins*, pp. 840–42.
12. Churchill, *SWW*, Vol. VI, p. 266.

10 'IKE AND I WERE POLES APART WHEN IT CAME TO THE CONDUCT OF THE WAR'

1. Kay Summersby, *Past Forgetting* (Simon & Schuster, 1974), p. 28.
2. Bryant, *Triumph in the West*, p. 194; Ambrose, *Eisenhower*, pp. 155–6.
3. Ambrose, *Eisenhower*, p. 163.
4. Bryant, *Triumph in the West*, p. 219.
5. Eisenhower papers, cited in Ambrose, *Eisenhower*, p. 167.
6. Bryant, *Triumph in the West*, pp. 279–81; Francis de Guingand, *Operation Victory* (Hodder & Stoughton, 1947), p. 348; Ambrose, *Eisenhower*, pp. 178–9; Montgomery, *Memoirs* (Collins, 1958), p. 289.
7. Colville, *The Fringes of Power*, Vol. II, p. 188; Gilbert, *Churchill*, Vol. VII, pp. 144–5.
8. Churchill, *SWW*, Vol. VI, pp. 298–9; FRUS, *The Conferences at Malta and Yalta* (1945), pp. 460, 540–46.
9. Robert Rhodes James, *Anthony Eden* (McGraw-Hill, 1986), p. 289.
10. Gilbert, *Churchill*, Vol. VI, p. 1175.
11. FRUS, *The Conferences at Malta and Yalta* (1945), p. 617; Churchill, *SWW*, Vol. VI, p. 308.
12. FRUS, *Malta and Yalta*, p. 769; Sherwood, *Roosevelt and Hopkins*, pp. 861–2, 870.
13. Churchill, *SWW*, Vol. VI, pp. 348, 368.
14. Ibid., Vol. VI, p. 399.

11 'THE GREATEST AMERICAN FRIEND WE HAVE EVER KNOWN'

1. Churchill, *SWW*, Vol. VI, pp. 442–3; Omar Bradley, *A Soldier's Story* (Rand McNally, 1951), p. 535.
2. Ambrose, *Eisenhower*, p. 192.
3. Churchill, *SWW*, Vol. VI, pp. 402–5; Bryant, *Triumph in the West*, pp. 339–40.
4. Churchill, *SWW*, Vol. VI, pp. 412–17.
5. Ibid., pp. 422–3, 439.
6. Sherwood, *Roosevelt and Hopkins*, p. 890.
7. Churchill, *SWW*, Vol. VI, pp. 496–502.

8. Herbert Feis, *Churchill, Roosevelt and Stalin* (Princeton University Press, 1957), p. 652; Henry Kissinger, *Diplomacy* (Simon & Schuster, 1994), pp. 430–31.
9. Churchill, *SWW*, Vol. VI, pp. 530, 545–53, 580.
10. Sherwood, *Roosevelt and Hopkins*, pp. 921–2.

12 'ALLIES OF A KIND'
1. Christopher Thorne, *Allies of a Kind* (Oxford University Press, 1978).
2. FRUS, 1942 1 613, CAB 65/25 1942, Transfer of Power No. 294; Thorne, *Allies of a Kind*, p. 235.
3. FRUS, 1942 1 633, 10 March 1942; PREM 4 48–9, 12 April 1942; Churchill, *SWW*, Vol. IV, p. 195; FO 371, 12 August 1942; Roosevelt papers, PSF, box 91, 23 September 1942; Thorne, *Allies of a Kind*, pp. 243–4.
4. FRUS, *The Conferences at Cairo and Tehran*, pp. 482, 485.
5. Barbara Tuchman, *Stilwell and the American Experience in China* (Macmillan, 1990), p. 385.
6. Thorne, *Allies of a Kind*, p. 225.
7. Stilwell diary, 6 January 1942, 29 June, 22 November and 6 December 1943.
8. Cadogan, *Diaries*, p. 586.
9. Hopkins papers, 29 March 1943.
10. Thorne, *Allies of a Kind*, p. 677.
11. PREM 3 143/10 28 July 1943, CAB 6/95; John Masters, *The Road Past Mandalay* (Cassell, 2012); Thorne, *Allies of a Kind*, p. 334.
12. Pownall diary, 14 September 1943.
13. Philip Ziegler, *Mountbatten* (Collins, 1985), pp. 296–7.
14. PREM 3 159/4, 159/10 and 159/14.

13 'I MUST ALWAYS KNOW WHAT IS IN THE DOCUMENTS I SIGN'
1. Harry S. Truman, *Year of Decisions* (Doubleday, 1955), p. 324.
2. Ibid., p. 145.
3. Gowing, *Britain and Atomic Energy*, p. 81; Kenneth Harris, *Attlee* (Weidenfeld & Nicolson, 1982), pp. 277–80.
4. Gowing, *Britain and Atomic Energy*, pp. 107–8; Harris, *Attlee*, pp. 285–6.
5. Harris, *Attlee*, p. 288.
6. Dean Acheson, *Present at the Creation* (W. W. Norton, 1969), p. 320.
7. Clark Clifford, *Counsel to the President* (Random House, 1991), pp. 99–103.
8. Ibid., p. 108.
9. Harris, *Attlee*, p. 292.

14 'THE PATIENT IS SINKING WHILE THE DOCTORS DELIBERATE'
1. Acheson, *Present at the Creation*, pp. 217–23.
2. Ibid., pp. 227–34.
3. Alan Bullock, *Ernest Bevin: Foreign Secretary 1945–1951* (Heinemann, 1963), pp. 405–19.
4. Sir Nicholas Henderson, *The Birth of NATO* (Weidenfeld & Nicholson, 1982), pp. 9, 21–5.
5. Ibid., pp. 12, 36–8.
6. Dimbleby and Reynolds, *An Ocean Apart*, p. 177.

7. Henderson, *The Birth of NATO*, pp. 92–3; Alex Danchev, *Oliver Franks* (Clarendon Press, 1993), p. 104.
8. FRUS, Vol. III (1948), p. 1113.
9. Michael Charlton, *The Price of Victory* (BBC Publications, 1983), p. 61.

15 'THE JEWS ARE A RELIGION, NOT A NATION OR A RACE'

1. Hugh Dalton, *High Tide and After* (Frederick Muller, 1962), p. 147; Acheson, *Present at the Creation*, p. 169; Harris, *Attlee*, p. 391.
2. Bullock, *Ernest Bevin*, p. 277.
3. Acheson, *Present at the Creation*, p. 175.
4. Harris, *Attlee*, p. 396.
5. Bullock, *Ernest Bevin*, p. 366; Harris, *Attlee*, pp. 397–400.

16 'I THINK IT IMPROBABLE THAT THE AMERICANS WOULD BECOME INVOLVED'

1. PRO, FO 371184076.
2. Acheson, *Present at the Creation*, p. 441.
3. Max Hastings, *The Korean War* (Michael Joseph, 1987), p. 59.
4. PRO, CAB 128, 27 June 1950.
5. PRO, CAB 128/17.
6. Hastings, *The Korean War*, pp. 72–4, 91.
7. *Documents on British Policy Overseas*, Series IT, Vol. IV, No. 25 (HMSO, 1991).
8. Hastings, *The Korean War*, p. 118; William Manchester, *MacArthur: American Caesar* (Little, Brown, 1978), pp. 683–8.
9. US National Archives, FR7 1108–9; Hastings, *The Korean War*, p. 148.
10. Harry S. Truman, *Years of Trial and Hope* (Doubleday, 1956), p. 385.
11. PRO, CAB 128/180.

17 'ALL THE PASSION OF A WOODCHUCK CHEWING A CARROT'

1. Acheson, *Present at the Creation*, pp. 478–80.
2. FRUS, Vol. VII (1950), pp. 1348–9, 1361–77; Acheson, *Present at the Creation*, p. 482.
3. PRO, FO 371/83018, 8 December 1950.
4. FRUS, Vol. VII (1950), pp. 1430–32; Acheson, *Present at the Creation*, pp. 483–4.
5. FRUS, Vol. VII (1950), pp. 1449–61.
6. Ibid., pp. 1462–5; Acheson, *Present at the Creation*, pp. 481, 484.
7. Clement Attlee to Ernest Bevin, 10 December 1950, PRO, FO 800/517/US/50/57.
8. PRO, WO 216/836.
9. Hastings, *The Korean War*, pp. 235–40.

18 'THE TIMELY USE OF ATOMIC WEAPONS SHOULD BE CONSIDERED'

1. Philby, *My Silent War*, pp. 137, 151–9; Robert Cecil, *Donald Maclean* (Hodder & Stoughton, 1990), pp. 181–214.
2. Christopher Andrew and Oleg Gordievsky, *KGB* (Hodder & Stoughton, 1990), pp. 331–2.
3. Hastings, *The Korean War*, pp. 313–4.
4. Ibid., p. 393.
5. US National Archives, NSC meeting, 11 February 1953; Eisenhower papers, EL,

31 March 1952; Rosemary Foot, *The Wrong War* (Cornell University Press, 1985), pp. 213–5; Hastings, *The Korean War*, p. 394.

19 'WHAT COULD BE MORE EARTHY THAN COAL OR STEEL?'

1. Acheson, *Present at the Creation*, pp. 382–8, 396–7.
2. Ibid., pp. 578, 592–7.
3. Ibid., pp. 602, 615.
4. Margaret Gowing, *Independence and Deterrence* (Macmillan, 1974), p. 507.

20 'NEVER HAD SO FEW LOST SO MUCH SO STUPIDLY AND SO FAST'

1. Denis Greenhill, *More by Accident* (Wilton, 1992), p. 68.
2. Acheson, *Present at the Creation*, pp. 652–3.
3. Vernon Walters, *Silent Missions* (Doubleday, 1988), p. 250.
4. PRO, CAB 128/20 CM (60).
5. Greenhill, *More by Accident*, p. 70.
6. Acheson, *Present at the Creation*, pp. 510–11, 679–85.
7. Kermit Roosevelt, *Counter-Coup* (McGraw-Hill, 1979); Acheson, *Present at the Creation*, p. 685. See also John Dickie, *Special No More* (Weidenfeld & Nicolson, 1994), Chapter 5.

21 'THE MOST POWERFUL OF THE ANTI-COLONIAL POWERS'

1. Colville, *The Fringes of Power*, Vol. II, pp. 316, 319–21.
2. Ibid., pp. 322–3; Acheson, *Present at the Creation*, p. 767.
3. Colville, *The Fringes of Power*, Vol. II, pp. 347–50.
4. Richard Goold-Adams, *John Foster Dulles: A Re-appraisal* (Weidenfeld & Nicolson, 1962), p. 298.
5. Gilbert, *Churchill*, Vol. VI, pp. 973–4; Kissinger, *Diplomacy*, p. 633.
6. Anthony Eden, *Full Circle* (Cassell, 1960), pp. 98–9.
7. Ambrose, *Eisenhower*, pp. 359–63; Evelyn Shuckburgh, *Descent to Suez* (W. W. Norton, 1986), pp. 170–87.
8. Shuckburgh, *Descent to Suez*, pp. 185–9.
9. Colville, *The Fringes of Power*, Vol. II, pp. 357–61.
10. Anthony Eden, *Full Circle*, pp. 98–9.

22 'UNITED STATES POLICY IS EXAGGERATEDLY MORAL, AT LEAST WHERE NON-AMERICAN INTERESTS ARE CONCERNED'

1. Rhodes James, *Anthony Eden*, pp. 264, 289; Colville, *The Fringes of Power*, Vol. II, p. 200.
2. Rhodes James, *Anthony Eden*, pp. 352–3.
3. Ziegler, *Mountbatten*, pp. 502–3.
4. Rhodes James, *Anthony Eden*, p. 359.
5. PRO, CAB 128/29 CM 34 (55) 8.
6. Keith Kyle, *Suez* (Weidenfeld & Nicolson, 1991), pp. 62, 75.
7. Miles Copeland, *The Game of Nations* (Simon & Schuster, 1969), pp. 159–60.
8. FRUS, Vol. XIV (1955–7), pp. 518–9.
9. Ibid., pp. 632–6; Kyle, *Suez*, p. 83.
10. PRO, FO 371/118861, 5 April 1956.
11. PRO, FO 3711/119055, CAB 128 (30) CM (56) 2, 6 June 1956.
12. FRUS, Vol. XV (1956), pp. 3–5.

13. Eden, *Full Circle*, pp. 427–8.
14. PRO, PREM 11/1098, ff. 346–7.
15. PRO, PREM 11/1098, f. 327; FRUS, Vol. XVI, pp. 60–62; Murphy, *Diplomat among Warriors*, pp. 379–82.
16. FRUS, Vol. XVI, pp. 62–71; PRO, PREM 11/1098, f. 184; Selwyn Lloyd, *Suez 1956* (Jonathan Cape, 1978), p. 98.
17. PRO, PREM 11/1098, ff. 187–8, CM (56); Eden, *Full Circle*, pp. 437–8; Kyle, *Suez*, pp. 162–3.

23 'THE US ARE BEING VERY DIFFICULT'

1. PRO, PREM 11/1098 T352/56, 5 August 1956.
2. FRUS, Vol. XVI, pp. 167–76; Kyle, *Suez*, p. 181.
3. FRUS, Vol. XVI, pp. 185–7, 210.
4. Ibid., pp. 231, 234–5, 281.
5. PRO, PREM 11/1152, ff. 26–41.
6. FRUS, Vol. XVI, pp. 326–30.
7. Ibid., p. 334.
8. Ibid., pp. 356, 431–3; Eden, *Full Circle*, pp. 463–7.
9. PRO, PREM 11/1100 CM (56), 63rd Conclusions, Confidential Annex.
10. PRO, T 236/4188, 7 September 1956; Alistair Horne, *Macmillan*, Vol. I (Macmillan, 1988), pp. 415–6.
11. PRO, PREM 11/1100, ff. 44–5, 8 September 1956.
12. PRO, FO 800/740, f. 33, 9 September 1956.
13. Eden, *Full Circle*, p. 483.
14. PRO, PREM 11/1103, ff. 356–60; FRUS, Vol. XVI, pp. 578, 581; PRO, PREM 11/1102, ff. 302–4.
15. Kyle, *Suez*, p. 258.
16. Iverach McDonald, *History of the Times*, Vol. V (Times Books, 1984), pp. 267–8.
17. Kyle, *Suez*, p. 275.
18. PRO, PREM 11/1102, T 437/56, f. 185, 8 October 1956.
19. PRO, PREM 11/1102, T 472156, f. 17.
20. FRUS, Vol. XVI, pp. 734–40; PRO, PREM 11/1103, ff. 76–7, 15 October 1956; Lloyd, *Suez 1956*, p. 162.
21. Anthony Nutting, *No End of a Lesson* (Constable, 1967), p. 93; Lloyd, *Suez 1956*, p. 164.
22. PRO, FO 800/725; PRO, PREM 11/1126.
23. Lloyd, *Suez 1956*, pp. 181–5.
24. PRO, FO 800/725, 24 October 1956.
25. Lloyd, *Suez 1956*, p. 188; W. Scott Lucas, *Divided We Stand* (Hodder & Stoughton, 1991), p. 248.
26. PRO, CAB 128/30 CM 74 (56).
27. Harold Macmillan, *Riding the Storm* (Macmillan, 1971), p. 157.
28. Kyle, *Suez*, p. 335.
29. Ambrose, *Eisenhower*, p. 424; FRUS, Vol. XVI, pp. 806–7.
30. FRUS, Vol. XVI, p. 818.

24 'NOTHING JUSTIFIES DOUBLE-CROSSING US'

1. FRUS, Vol. XVI, pp. 829–31, 835–40; PRO, FO 800/741.

2. Dulles papers, 30 October 1956, EL; Kyle, *Suez*, p. 335.
3. PRO, PREM 11/1105, ff. 530–32; FRUS, Vol. XVI, pp. 848–50.
4. PRO, CAB 128/30, ff. 632–3 C (56) 75th; FRUS, Vol. XVI, p. 857.
5. FRUS, Vol. XVI, pp. 863, 876; PRO, PREM 11/1105, ff. 476, 327.
6. FRUS, Vol. XVI, pp. 906–14.
7. Ibid., pp. 922–3.
8. PRO, T 236/4188; Eisenhower diaries, Box 20, EL.
9. Lucas, *Divided We Stand*, pp. 282–3.
10. Lloyd, *Suez 1956*, p. 206; PRO, PREM 11/1177, 5 November 1956.
11. FRUS, Vol. XVI, pp. 995, 1001.
12. PRO, CAB 128/30 CM 80 (56).
13. Eden diary, 1957, Avon papers, University of Birmingham; Lucas, *Divided We Stand*, p. 292.
14. Lloyd, *Suez 1956*, pp. 209–11; Hugh Thomas, *The Suez Affair* (Weidenfeld & Nicolson, 1966), p. 146.
15. PRO, FO 371/121867/VY 10338/15.

25 'WE CAN FURNISH A LOT OF FIG LEAVES'

1. PRO, PREM 11/1105, 6 November 1956.
2. FRUS, Vol. XVI, pp. 1045–6.
3. PRO, PREM 11/1106, ff. 514–6; FRUS, Vol. XVI, p. 1098; Lucas, *Divided We Stand*, p. 303.
4. PRO, PREM 11/1106, ff. 266–7; Lloyd, *Suez 1956*, p. 219.
5. FRUS, Vol. XVI, p. 1114; Joseph W. Alsop, *I've Seen the Best of It* (Norton, 1992), pp. 395–6.
6. FRUS, Vol. XVI, p. 1152.
7. Ibid., pp. 1162–3, 1166–8.
8. Ibid., p. 1196; Colville, *The Fringes of Power*, Vol. II, p. 392.
9. Eisenhower papers, International Box 19, EL; Gilbert, *Churchill*, Vol. VIII, pp. 1222–3.
10. FRUS, Vol. XVI, pp. 1194–5.
11. PRO, PREM 11/1106, 26 November 1956; PRO, CAB 128/30 CM 90 (56).
12. PRO, CAB 128/30 CM 91 (56).
13. Lucas, *Divided We Stand*, p. 318.
14. John Foster Dulles papers, General Correspondence, Box I, EL.
15. Horne, *Macmillan*, Vol. I, p. 452.
16. Macmillan diaries, cited in Horne, *Macmillan*, Vol. I, p. 458.

26 'IF ANYTHING GOES WRONG YOU MAY BE SURE THAT MR DULLES WILL PLACE THE BLAME ELSEWHERE'

1. Macmillan, *Blast of War*, p. 173; Horne, *Macmillan*, Vol. I, p. 157.
2. Horne, *Macmillan*, Vol. I, p. 165.
3. Macmillan, *Riding the Storm*, pp. 251–2.
4. Ibid., pp. 253–4; Eisenhower papers, 5 April 1957, EL.
5. Telegram, Sir Harold Caccia to Foreign Office, 29 August 1957, Macmillan papers, cited in Horne, *Macmillan*, Vol. II, p. 42.
6. Horne, *Macmillan*, Vol. II, p. 46.
7. Macmillan, *Riding the Storm*, pp. 322–4.
8. Andrew Pierre, *Nuclear Politics* (Oxford University Press, 1972), p. 303.

9. Macmillan diaries, 22 May 1958; Horne, *Macmillan*, Vol. II, p. 94.
10. Macmillan, *Riding the Storm*, p. 544.
11. Richard Lamb, *The Macmillan Years, 1957–63* (John Murray, 1995), p. 401.

27 'THEY HAVE COMPLETE CONFIDENCE IN ME'

1. Macmillan papers; Horne, *Macmillan*, Vol. II, p. 118.
2. Macmillan papers; Horne, ibid.
3. Eisenhower papers, 20 January 1959, EL.
4. Horne, *Macmillan*, Vol. II, p. 128.
5. Macmillan diaries, 20 March and 7 June 1958; Horne, *Macmillan*, Vol. II, p. 131.
6. Horne, *Macmillan*, Vol. II, p. 146.
7. Ibid., p. 219.
8. Macmillan diaries, 12 June 1960; Horne, *Macmillan*, Vol. II, p. 277.
9. Macmillan diaries, May 1960; Horne, *Macmillan*, Vol. II, p. 225. See also Michael Beschloss, *Mayday: Eisenhower, Khrushchev and the U2 Affair* (Harper & Row, 1986), Chapter 11.
10. Horne, *Macmillan*, Vol. II, p. 231.

28 'IT IS GOING TO BE A COLD WINTER'

1. Horne, *Macmillan*, Vol. II, p. 280.
2. Ibid., pp. 282–6.
3. Brandon, *Special Relationships*, pp. 155–6.
4. Macmillan diaries; Horne, *Macmillan*, Vol. II, pp. 299–300.
5. Horne, *Macmillan*, Vol. II, p. 304; Arthur Schlesinger, *A Thousand Days* (Houghton Mifflin, 1965), pp. 375–6.
6. Harold Macmillan to John F. Kennedy, 5 January 1962; Horne, *Macmillan*, Vol. II, p. 325.
7. Theodore Sorensen, *Kennedy* (Harper & Row, 1965), p. 558.
8. Harold Macmillan, *Pointing the Way* (Macmillan, 1972), pp. 360–80.

29 'THANK GOD THEY'VE TURNED BACK, JUST BEFORE
THE PRIME MINISTER GAVE WAY'

1. Horne, *Macmillan*, Vol. II, pp. 362–4.
2. Macmillan diaries, 22 October 1962; Horne, *Macmillan*, Vol. II, p. 366.
3. Schlesinger, *A Thousand Days*, p. 815.
4. Ibid., pp. 817–18; Sorensen, *Kennedy*, pp. 794–5.
5. Greenhill, *More by Accident*, p. 103.
6. John F. Kennedy Library, T 524/62.
7. Macmillan diaries, 4 November 1962; Horne, *Macmillan*, Vol. II, p. 380.
8. Horne, *Macmillan*, Vol. II, pp. 382, 384.

30 'THE LADY HAS ALREADY BEEN VIOLATED IN PUBLIC'

1. Schlesinger, *A Thousand Days*, pp. 857–60.
2. Ibid., pp. 861–2; Macmillan diaries, 7 December 1962; Horne, *Macmillan*, Vol. II, p. 429.
3. Horne, *Macmillan*, Vol. II, p. 431.
4. Schlesinger, *A Thousand Days*, pp. 863–4.
5. Sorensen, *Kennedy*, pp. 564–5.
6. Horne, *Macmillan*, Vol. II, p. 433.

7. Brandon, *Special Relationships*, p. 164.
8. Sorensen, *Kennedy*, p. 566; Schlesinger, *A Thousand Days*, p. 864; George Ball, *The Discipline of Power* (Little, Brown, 1968), p. 84.
9. Home, *Macmillan*, Vol. II, p. 438.
10. Ball, *The Discipline of Power*, p. 103.
11. George Ball, *The Past Has Another Pattern* (W. W. Norton, 1982), p. 268.
12. Sorensen, *Kennedy*, p. 569.
13. Ibid., p. 559.

31 'THIS FRIGHTFUL TANGLE OF FEAR AND SUSPICION'
1. David Bruce to John F. Kennedy, 18 June 1963, John F. Kennedy Library, Box 171, Folder 14.
2. Horne, *Macmillan*, Vol. II, pp. 506–7.
3. Macmillan diaries, 17 April 1963; Horne, *Macmillan*, Vol. II, pp. 510–11.
4. Horne, *Macmillan*, Vol. II, pp. 515–17; Schlesinger, *A Thousand Days*, p. 810.
5. Macmillan diaries, 12 July 1963.
6. Macmillan diaries, 27 July 1963; Horne, *Macmillan*, Vol. II, pp. 519–22.
7. Horne, *Macmillan*, Vol. II, p. 576.

32 'I DON'T THINK WE ARE IN FOR A VERY HAPPY FOUR DAYS'
1. David Ormsby-Gore to Harold Macmillan, 22 March 1963, Macmillan papers; Horne, *Macmillan*, Vol. II, p. 683.
2. Ben Pimlott, *Harold Wilson* (HarperCollins, 1992), p. 285.
3. Lyndon Johnson Library, NSF file UK, Box 3; Philip Ziegler, *Wilson* (Weidenfeld & Nicolson, 1993), p. 221.
4. Richard Neustadt to President Johnson, July 1964; Hitchens, *Blood, Class and Nostalgia*, pp. 6–7.
5. Ball, *The Past Has Another Pattern*, p. 337.
6. Harold Wilson, *The Labour Government* (Weidenfeld & Nicolson, 1971), p. 80; Johnson Library, NSF memos to the President, Box 3, 9 March 1965.
7. Pimlott, *Harold Wilson*, p. 384.
8. David Bruce to Dean Rusk, 3 June 1965; Ziegler, *Wilson*, p. 224.
9. Johnson Library, NSF memos to the President, Box 3, Vol. II, 23 June 1965.
10. Pimlott, *Harold Wilson*, p. 390.
11. Ibid., p. 386; Ziegler, *Wilson*, p. 226.
12. Wilson, *The Labour Government*, pp. 187–8; Barbara Castle, *Diaries 1964–70* (Weidenfeld & Nicolson. 1974), p. 78:
13. Richard Crossman, *The Diaries of a Cabinet Minister*, Vol. I (Hamish Hamilton, 1975), p. 456.
14. Wilson, *The Labour Government*, pp. 264–5; Ziegler, *Wilson*, p. 229.
15. Dean Rusk to Lyndon Johnson, 27 July 1966, Johnson Library; Crossman, *Diaries*, Vol. II, p. 181; Ziegler, *Wilson*, p. 210.
16. C. L. Cooper, *The Lost Crusade* (MacGibbon & Kee, 1980), p. 362.
17. Pimlott, *Harold Wilson*, p. 464; Cooper, *The Lost Crusade*, p. 368; Robert McNamara, *In Retrospect* (Times Books, 1995), pp. 250–52.
18. Ziegler, *Wilson*, p. 326; Tony Benn, *Out of the Wilderness* (Hutchinson, 1987), p. 501.
19. Wilson, *The Labour Government*, pp. 454–5; Pimlott, *Harold Wilson*, pp. 477–83.
20. Crossman, *Diaries*, Vol. II, pp. 646–7; Ziegler, *Wilson*, pp. 285, 331.

21. Wilson, *The Labour Government*, pp. 497, 500.
22. Roy Jenkins, *A Life at the Centre* (Random House, 1991), p. 262.
23. Richard Aldrich, *The Hidden Hand* (John Murray, 2001), p. 644

33 'WE DO NOT SUFFER IN THE WORLD FROM SUCH AN EXCESS OF FRIENDS'
1. Henry Kissinger, *White House Years* (Little, Brown, 1979), pp. 95–6.
2. Roy Jenkins, *A Life at the Centre*, pp. 262–3.
3. Kissinger, *White House Years*, pp. 89–92.
4. Ibid., pp. 417–19.

**34 'A COUPLE WHO HAVE BEEN TOLD BY EVERYONE THAT
THEY SHOULD BE IN LOVE'**
1. Kissinger, *White House Years*, pp. 932–4, 937–8, 964–5. See also John Campbell, *Edward Heath* (Jonathan Cape, 1993), p. 341.
2. Richard Aldrich, *GCHQ* (HarperPress, 2010), pp. 288–90.
3. Kissinger, *Years of Upheaval* (Little, Brown, 1982), pp. 140–43, 162–3, 189–92, 281–2; Campbell, *Edward Heath*, p. 341.
4. Kissinger, *Years of Upheaval*, pp. 510–11, 516–18.
5. Ibid., pp. 509–3, 720–22, 725; Campbell, *Edward Heath*, pp. 349–50.

35 'HE WANTED TO ESTABLISH HIS OWN SPECIAL RELATIONSHIP'
1. Kissinger, *Years of Upheaval*, p. 933; James Callaghan, *Time and Chance* (Collins, 1987), p. 319.
2. Callaghan, *Time and Chance*, pp. 342–56.
3. Ibid., p. 359.
4. Ziegler, *Wilson*, pp. 459, 461.
5. George Weidenfeld, *Remembering My Good Friends* (HarperCollins, 1995), pp. 352–3.
6. Callaghan, *Time and Chance*, pp. 428, 433.
7. David Owen, *Time to Declare* (Michael Joseph, 1991), p. 282; Callaghan, *Time and Chance*, p. 483.
8. Zbigniew Brzezinski, *Power and Principle: Memoirs of the National Security Adviser, 1977–1981* (Farrar, Straus & Giroux, 1983), p. 291.
9. Jimmy Carter, *A Full Life* (Simon & Schuster, 2015), p. 128.
10. Callaghan, *Time and Chance*, pp. 553–7.

**36 'YOUR PROBLEMS WILL BE OUR PROBLEMS AND WHEN YOU LOOK
FOR FRIENDS, WE WILL BE THERE'**
1. Denis Healey, *The Time of My Life* (Michael Joseph, 1989), p. 463; Owen, *Time to Declare*, p. 313.
2. Margaret Thatcher, *The Downing Street Years* (HarperCollins, 1993), pp. 68–9.
3. Ibid., p. 157; Ronald Reagan, *An American Life* (Simon & Schuster, 1990), p. 204.
4. Thatcher, *The Downing Street Years*, pp. 157–8.
5. Ibid., pp. 251–5.
6. Peter Carrington, *Reflect on Things Past* (William Collins, 1988), p. 344.

37 'THAT LITTLE ICE-COLD BUNCH OF LAND DOWN THERE'
Note: The records of the Thatcher/Reagan and Thatcher/Haig exchanges are now in the public domain on both sides of the Atlantic. Many of the source documents

can most easily be accessed via the Margaret Thatcher Foundation (MTF). Other source documents can be found in the Margaret Thatcher papers at Churchill College, Cambridge (MTCR) and in the Ronald Reagan library, Simi Valley, California. Also now available are Charles Moore's researches into the events of this period in *Margaret Thatcher*, Vols I and II (Allen Lane 2013, 2015).

1. Chairman Lord Franks, *Falklands Islands Review: Report of a Committee of Privy Counsellors*, Cmnd 8787 (HMSO, 1983), pp. 40–42, 46–7.
2. Ibid., pp. 47, 55, 57, 61–4; Nicholas Henderson, *Mandarin* (Weidenfeld & Nicolson, 1994), p. 447.
3. Ibid., pp. 67–8; Henderson, *Mandarin*, p. 448.
4. Nicholas Henderson to the author; Reagan to Thatcher, 1 April 1982 (MTF).
5. Caspar Weinberger, *Fighting for Peace* (Michael Joseph, 1990), pp. 143–4, 146.
6. Weinberger to the author. See also John Lehman lecture on the Falklands War, Royal Navy Museum Portsmouth, May 2012.
7. Weinberger, *Fighting for Peace*, pp. 149–50.
8. James Rentschler, *Falklands Diary*, p. 2 (MTF).
9. Charles Moore, *Margaret Thatcher*, Vol. I (Allen Lane, 2013), p. 686; Interview with James Rentschler.
10. Thatcher, *The Downing Street Years*, pp. 191–2; No. 10 record PREM 19/616, f165; Haig to Reagan 9 April 1982, Reagan Library, NSC records, Falklands War, Box 913365; Alexander Haig, *Caveat* (Weidenfeld & Nicolson, 1984), pp. 272–3; Rentschler, *Falklands Diary*, pp. 3–4; General Walters to the author.
11. Thatcher, *The Downing Street Years*, pp. 192–3; Haig, *Caveat*, pp. 273–4; Rentschler, *Falklands Diary*, p. 4; Haig to Reagan, 9 April 1982 (MTF).
12. Haig, *Caveat*, pp. 279–83; Denis Blair files, Folder UK 1982, Box 90233, Ronald Reagan Library; Rentschler, *Falklands Diary*, p. 9; Vernon Walters, *The Mighty and the Meek* (St Ermin's Press, 2001), pp. 145–6.

38 'DOING THE WORK OF THE FREE WORLD'

1. Thatcher, *The Downing Street Years*, pp. 194–9; No. 10 record, 12 April 1982, PREM 19/617, f227 and f189; Haig, *Caveat*, pp. 283–4; Rentschler, *Falklands Diary*, p. 10; Max Hastings and Simon Jenkins, *The Battle for the Falklands* (Michael Joseph, 1983), p. 109.
2. CAB 148, 14 April 1982; Thatcher, *The Downing Street Years*, p. 203; Cabinet Secretary notes, 14 April 1982.
3. Haig, telephone calls to Thatcher, 14 April 1982, PREM 19/617, f76 and f70.
4. Reagan/Thatcher telecom, 15 April 1982, PREM 19/618, f8.
5. Haig, *Caveat*, p. 288.
6. Henderson telegrams to FCO 1376 and 1381; Thatcher, *The Downing Street Years*, p. 204.
7. CAB 148, 22 April 1982.
8. OD (SA), 24 April 1982 and PREM 19/621, f252; Thatcher, *The Downing Street Years*, pp. 205–8; Thatcher Churchill College papers (THCR), 1/20/3/1.
9. Douglas Brinkley (ed.), *The Reagan Diaries* (HarperCollins, 2007), p. 80; Richard Aldous, *Reagan and Thatcher* (Hutchinson, 2012), p. 89.
10. Reagan to Thatcher, 29 April 1982 (MTF); Thatcher, *The Downing Street Years*, p. 211.
11. NSC minutes, 29 April 1982, Reagan library, NSC meeting file, Box 91284; Aldous, *Reagan and Thatcher*, p. 92; Rentschler, *Falklands Diary*, p. 9.
12. Thatcher, *The Downing Street Years*, pp. 226–7.

13. OD (SA) ad hoc meeting on 2 May 1982; Lawrence Freedman, *Official History of the Falklands Campaign*, Vol. II, Chapter 21.
14. Reagan to Thatcher, 5 May 1982, PREM 19/624, f118; Thatcher to Reagan, 5 May 1982, PREM 19/624 CAB 148; and Armstrong note and Washington tel 1597; Thatcher, *The Downing Street Years*, pp. 217–8.
15. Reagan/Thatcher telecon 13 May 1982; Henderson, *Mandarin*, p. 463; Thatcher, *The Downing Street Years*, pp. 220–21; Brinkley, *Reagan Diaries*, p. 84.
16. Sir Anthony Parsons, 'The Falklands Crisis in the United Nations', *International Affairs*, Vol. 59, No. 2 (spring 1983), pp. 169–78; Thatcher, *The Downing Street Years*, p. 218.
17. Henderson, 'America and the Falklands', *The Economist*, 12 November 1988, p. 58.
18. Reagan/Thatcher telecom, 31 May 1982, PREM 19/633, f161; Ronald Reagan, *An American Life* (Hutchinson, 1990), p. 560; Henderson, *Mandarin*, pp. 464–7; Thatcher, *The Downing Street Years*, pp. 230–32; Rentschler, *Falklands Diary*, p. 34.
19. Henderson, *Mandarin*, pp. 466–7.
20. Henderson to the author.
21. Parsons, 'The Falklands Crisis in the United Nations', pp. 169–78.
22. Thatcher, *The Downing Street Years*, p. 232.
23. Ibid., pp. 226–7.
24. Haig, *Caveat*, pp. 297–8.
25. George Shultz, *Turmoil and Triumph*, p. 153; Christopher Meyer, *DC Confidential* (Weidenfeld & Nicolson, 2005), p. 225.
26. Charles Moore, *Margaret Thatcher*, Vol. I, p. 755.

39 'THE FOCUS OF EVIL IN THE MODERN WORLD'

1. Thatcher, *The Downing Street Years*, pp. 252, 258.
2. George P. Shultz, *Turmoil and Triumph* (Charles Scribner's Sons, 1993), pp. 136, 152.
3. Ibid., pp. 153–4.
4. Robert Gates, *From the Shadows* (Touchstone, 1996), pp 272–3.
5. Shultz, *Turmoil and Triumph*, pp. 323, 329.
6. Thatcher, *The Downing Street Years*, pp. 330–32; Geoffrey Howe, *Conflict of Loyalty* (Macmillan, 1994), pp. 327–36. For an excellent account of the Grenada crisis, see Moore, *Margaret Thatcher*, Vol. II, pp. 118–34.
7. Shultz, *Turmoil and Triumph*, pp. 340–41.
8. Thatcher, *The Downing Street Years*, p. 333; Howe, *Conflict of Loyalty*, p. 337.

40 'THE OBJECTIVE IS TO HAVE A WORLD WITHOUT WAR'

1. Reagan, *An American Life*, p. 354.
2. Nigel Lawson, *The View From No. 11* (Bantam Press, 1992), p. 524.
3. Ibid., pp. 525–9.
4. Thatcher, *The Downing Street Years*, p. 467.
5. Shultz, *Turmoil and Triumph*, p. 509.
6. Thatcher, *The Downing Street Years*, p. 468.
7. Shultz, *Turmoil and Triumph*, p. 568.
8. Colin Powell, *A Soldier's Way* (Hutchinson, 1995), pp 309–10.
9. Reagan to Thatcher, 9 April 1982, Reagan library, Libya Fortier file, Box 91673.
10. Thatcher, *The Downing Street Years*, pp. 443–4.
11. Richard Haass, *The Power to Persuade* (Houghton Mifflin, 1994), p. 107; Howe, *Conflict of Loyalty*, pp. 503–7.

12. Thatcher, *The Downing Street Years*, pp. 445–9; Walters, *The Mighty and the Meek*, pp. 147–8.
13. Thatcher to Reagan, 11 February 1986, Reagan library, NSC PM, Thatcher Box 37 (8591145).
14. Anatoly Chernyaev note of 4 October 1986; Kenneth Adelman, *Reagan at Reykjavik* (HarperCollins 2014), p. 75.
15. Colin Powell and Richard Perle to the author.
16. Shultz interview by Charles Moore, *Margaret Thatcher*, Vol. II, p. 607.
17. Thatcher, *The Downing Street Years*, pp. 471–3; Geoffrey Smith, *Reagan and Thatcher* (W. W. Norton, 1991), pp. 222–4.
18. Reagan, *An American Life*, p. 685.
19. Smith, *Reagan and Thatcher*, pp. 249, 252; Aldous, *Reagan and Thatcher*, p. 265.
20. Kissinger, *New York Times Book Review*, 14 November 1991, pp. 1–2.

41 'NO TIME TO GO WOBBLY'
1. Thatcher, *The Downing Street Years*, pp. 782–3; Howe, *Conflict of Loyalty*, p. 559.
2. Thatcher, *The Downing Street Years*, pp. 788–9; Howe, *Conflict of Loyalty*, p. 565.
3. Lawson, *The View from No. 11*, pp. 946–7.
4. Mikhail Gorbachev, *Memoirs* (Doubleday, 1996), pp. 546–7.
5. Gates, *From the Shadows*, pp 488–9.
6. Thatcher, *The Downing Street Years*, pp. 794–5, 810, 813.
7. Henry Kissinger, *World Order* (Allen Lane, 2014), p. 314.
8. Norman Schwarzkopf, *It Doesn't Take a Hero* (Bantam Press, 1992), pp. 297–8; Bob Woodward, *The Commanders* (Simon & Schuster, 1992), pp. 225–31; Colin Powell, *My American Journey* (Random House, 1995), p. 463.
9. Thatcher, *The Downing Street Years*, pp. 817–9.
10. Ibid., p. 820.
11. James Baker, *The Politics of Diplomacy* (G. P. Putnam's Sons, 1995), pp. 278–9; Thatcher, *The Downing Street Years*, pp. 821, 824.
12. Peter de la Billière, *Storm Command* (HarperCollins, 1992), pp. 26, 39–40, 50–51.
13. Ibid., p. 52.
14. Baker to President Bush, 9 November 1990 (MTF) and George H. W. Bush (Presidential Library).
15. De la Billière, *Storm Command*, p. 126.

42 'ALL NECESSARY MEANS'
1. Schwarzkopf, *It Doesn't Take a Hero*, pp. 385–6; de la Billière, *Storm Command*, pp. 93, 95.
2. De la Billière, *Storm Command*, pp. 141, 175, 179, 181, 230.
3. Ibid., pp. 285, 291.
4. *Triumph without Victory*, US News and World Report (1992), pp. 396–7, 400; Schwarzkopf, *It Doesn't Take a Hero*, pp. 468–71.

43 'THE WHOLE OF THE BALKANS ARE NOT WORTH THE BONES OF A SINGLE POMER-ANIAN GRENADIER'
1. Robert Kaplan, *Balkan Ghosts* (St Martin's Press, 1993).
2. John Major, *The Autobiography* (HarperCollins, 1999), pp. 535, 541.
3. Raymond Seitz, *Over Here* (Weidenfeld & Nicolson 1998), pp. 328–9.

44 'THE BRITISH WERE FURIOUS'

1. Bill Clinton, *My Life* (Arrow Books, 2005), p. 580.
2. Ibid., pp. 686–8; Hillary Clinton, *Living History* (Simon & Schuster, 2003), pp. 426–8.

45 'SHE COULD NOT SEE ANY POLICY DIFFERENCES BETWEEN THEM'

1. Clinton, *My Life*, p. 686; Alastair Campbell, *The Blair Years* (Random House, 2007), p. 95.
2. Clinton, *My Life*, p. 756; Tony Blair, *A Journey* (Hutchinson, 2010), p. 227.
3. Clinton/Blair telephone transcripts released by the Clinton Library to the BBC on 7 January 2016.
4. Blair, *A Journey*, p. 231.
5. Ibid., p. 240; Clinton, *My Life*, pp. 855, 857, 859.
6. Christopher Meyer, *DC Confidential*, pp. 102–3.
7. Blair, *A Journey*, p. 240; Clinton, *My Life*, p. 855.
8. Clinton, *My Life*, p. 859: General Mike Jackson, *Soldier* (Bantam Press, 2007), pp. 271–5.
9. Clinton, *Living History*, pp. 422–8.
10. Clinton, *My Life*, pp. 933–4.

46 'THE CLOSEST RELATIONSHIP I WOULD HAVE WITH ANY FOREIGN LEADER'

1. Blair, *A Journey*, pp. 343, 392–4.
2. George W. Bush, *Decision Points* (Virgin Books, 2010), p. 231.
3. Ibid., p. 140.
4. Alastair Campbell, *Diaries*, Vol. IV (Hutchinson, 2012), pp. 12–13.
5. Meyer, *DC Confidential*, p. 204.
6. Richard Haass, *War of Necessity, War of Choice* (Simon & Schuster, 2010), p. 196.
7. George Tenet, *At the Center of the Storm* (HarperPress, 2007), p. 174.
8. Blair, *A Journey*, p. 470.
9. Iraq inquiry, Tony Blair, 29 January 2010 and 21 January 2011; John Reid, 31 January 2010.

47 'WE WERE FORTUNATE TO HAVE THEM ON OUR SIDE'

1. Bush, *Decision Points*, p. 212.
2. Robert Gates, *Duty* (Knopf, 2014), pp. 377–85, 564–5, 585.
3. House of Commons Foreign Affairs Committee, *Global Security: US/UK Relations*, p. 28; Stanley McChrystal, *My Share of the Task* (Penguin, 2013), pp. 321, 318, 353, 364.
4. For the most vivid account of the fighting in Afghanistan, see Patrick Hennessey, *The Junior Officers' Reading Club* (Penguin Books, 2011).
5. Sherard Cowper-Cowles, *Letters from Kabul* (HarperCollins, 2011).
6. Christina Lamb, *Farewell Kabul* (William Collins, 2015), p. 376.
7. *Operation Herrick Campaign Study*, Ministry of Defence Directorate of Land Warfare, March 2015. Partially redacted. Released under the Freedom of Information Act.
8. Hillary Clinton, *Hard Choices* (Simon & Schuster 2014), pp. 156–9.
9. Richard Haass, *War of Necessity, War of Choice* (Simon & Schuster, 2010).

48 'I WILL BE WITH YOU, WHATEVER'

1. Blair, *A Journey*, pp. 384, 394.
2. Tenet, *At the Center of the Storm*, pp. ix, 302, 306–7, 310, 345–8; Bob Woodward, *Plan of Attack* (Simon & Schuster, 2004), pp. 21–2.
3. *The 9/11 Commission Report* (W. W. Norton, 2004).
4. Tenet, *At the Center of the Storm*, pp. 350–56.
5. Blair, *A Journey*, pp. 400–401.
6. Iraq inquiry, Tony Blair, 21 January 2011.
7. Bush, *Decision Points*, p. 238.
8. Bush, *Decision Points*, p. 235.
9. Iraq Options paper, Cabinet Office, 8 March 2002; Iraq inquiry, Jonathan Powell, 18 January 2010.
10. Blair, *A Journey*, p. 402.
11. Straw memorandum, 25 March 2002.
12. Meyer, *DC Confidential*, p. 238.
13. Iraq inquiry, Sir John Scarlett, 8 December 2009; Jack Straw, memo, January 2010, 8 February 2010; Admiral Sir Michael Boyce, 3 December 2009, 27 January 2011.
14. Iraq inquiry, Sir David Manning, 30 November 2009; Blair, 21 January 2011; Powell, 18 January 2010; Iraq Inquiry Executive Summary (IIES), para 94.
15. Iraq inquiry, Manning, 30 November 2009.
16. Bush, *Decision Points*, pp. 228, 238.
17. Ibid., p. 239; Campbell, Vol. IV, p. 296.
18. Iraq inquiry, Manning, 30 November 2009.

49 'I HOPE THAT'S NOT THE LAST TIME WE SEE THEM'

1. *Hutton Report*, 28 January 2004, p. 26.
2. Iraq Inquiry Report Executive Summary (IIES), paras 326, 330, 536, 540, 806.
3. Tenet, *At the Center of the Storm*, p. 327.
4. Iraq inquiry, Boyce, 27 January 2011; IIES, para 811.
5. Iraq inquiry, Boyce, 21 January 2009, 27 January 2011; Goldsmith, 27 January 2010, 18 January 2011.
6. Iraq inquiry, Manning, 30 November 2009; Bush/Blair meeting, 31 January 2003.
7. IIES, paras 16, 20, 151, 157, 206, 248, 339, 363, 388, 804–5, 830.
8. Jack Straw, *Last Man Standing* (Macmillan, 2012), p. 386; Campbell, *Diaries*, Vol. IV, p. 475.
9. Blair, *A Journey*, pp. 412, 414, 429.
10. Straw, *Last Man Standing*, pp. 409–13.
11. Iraq inquiry, Jack Straw, 2 February 2011; Gordon Brown, 5 March 2011.
12. Bush, *Decision Points*, p. 246.
13. Iraq inquiry, Boyce, 21 January 2009, 27 January 2011.
14. Iraq inquiry, Goldsmith, 27 January 2010 and 17 January 2011; Blair, 29 January 2010, 21 January 2011; Boyce, 21 January 2009, 27 January 2011.
15. IIES, paras 146, 178, 420, 432–5, 468, 473, 810.
16. Bush, *Decision Points*, p. 252; Rice, *No Higher Honor*, p. 203.

50 'IT WAS, AFTER ALL, THE *CASUS BELLI*'

1. Bush, *Decision Points*, pp 258–9, 268.
2. Bob Woodward, *State of Denial* (Simon & Schuster, 2006), p. 194.

3. Bush, *Decision Points*, pp. 259–60.
4. Tenet, *At the Center of the Storm*, pp 397–9, 419–20, 427, 446.
5. Hilary Synnott, *Bad Days in Basra* (I. B. Tauris, 2008); Iraq inquiry, General Sir Graeme Lamb, 6 December 2009; Sir Jeremy Greenstock, 27 November 2009.
6. IIES, paras 592, 594, 626, 631, 634, 814–7, 822, 853, 863, 867.
7. IIES, paras 626, 690, 692–3, 698, 704, 712, 717, 721–3, 747, 756–60, 766, 773–8, 780, 791–2, 816.
8. Synnott, *Bad Days in Basra*.
9. Blair, *A Journey*, p. 452.
10. Bush, *Decision Points*, p. 262.
11. Tenet, *At the Center of the Storm*, p. 332; Saddam Hussein de-briefing by George Piro.

51 'THIS ISN'T WORKING'
1. McChrystal, *My Share of the Task*, p. 131.
2. Woodward, *State of Denial*, p. 458.
3. Bush, *Decision Points*, pp. 355, 364–5, 376–8.
4. For an account of SAS activities against Al-Qaeda in Iraq, see Mark Urban, *Task Force Black* (Abacus, 2011); McChrystal, *My Share of the Task*, pp. 150, 243–5.
5. Iraq inquiry, General Sir Graeme Lamb, 6 December 2009. For the best account of the thinking of the British military hierarchy in this period, see Christopher Elliott, *High Command* (Hurst & Co., 2015).
6. Emma Sky, *The Unravelling* (Atlantic Books, 2011), pp. 345–61.
7. Iraq inquiry, Boyce, 21 January 2009, 27 January 2010; Sir Kevin Tebbit, 3 February 2010.
8. IIES, paras 821, 897

52 'WE HAD NO IDEA WHAT WE WERE GETTING INTO'
1. Rory Stewart, *Occupational Hazards* (Picador, 2006).
2. Iraq inquiry, General Sir Mike Jackson, 28 July 2010 and report of 22 May 2006; Jack Fairweather, *A War of Choice* (Jonathan Cape, 2012), p. 221.
3. *Daily Mail*, 12 October 2006.
4. Iraq inquiry, General Sir Richard Shirreff, 11 January 2010; General Sir Nicholas Houghton, 5 January 2010.
5. Blair, *A Journey*, p. 471.
6. IIES, para. 749.
7. Elliott, *High Command*, pp. 114–25; Iraq inquiry, General Sir Jonathan Shaw, 12 January 2010.
8. Iraq inquiry, General Sir Robert Fry, 16 December 2009.
9. IIES, paras 740, 747, 749, 756, 758–9, 766, 775, 778, 780–81.
10. Bush, *Decision Points*, p. 409.
11. Tenet, *At the Center of the Storm*, pp. 287–97.
12. Iraq inquiry, General Sir John McColl, 8 February 2010; Greenstock, 27 November 2009.
13. Lord Butler of Brockwell and Committee, *Review of Intelligence on Weapons of Mass Destruction*, 14 July 2004.
14. Robb/Silberman, *Commission on the Intelligence Capabilities of the United States Regarding Weapons of Mass Destruction*, 2005.

53 'WHEN WE SAVED THE WORLD'

1. *National Security Strategy and Strategic Defence and Security Review*, 2015, p. 5.
2. Bush, *Decision Points*, pp. 456–7; Hank Paulson, *On the Brink* (Simon & Schuster, 2010), pp. 189, 208–9.
3. Ben Bernanke, *The Courage to Act* (W. W. Norton, 2015), pp. 266, 338, 346–8.
4. Timothy Geithner, *Stress Test* (Random House, 2014), pp. 410–11.
5. Anthony Seldon, *Brown at 10* (Biteback, 2010), pp. 318–9.
6. Jack Fairweather, *The Good War* (Jonathan Cape, 2014), p. 355.

54 BRITAIN 'MAY NO LONGER WANT TO PLAY AS CENTRAL A ROLE IN WORLD AFFAIRS'

1. Gates, *Duty*, pp. 511–3.
2. General David Richards, *Taking Command* (Headline, 2014), p. 280.
3. Robert Gates, BBC interview, 16 January 2014; General Ray Odierno, *Daily Telegraph*, 1 March 2015.
4. Ashton Carter, BBC interview, 1 June 2015.
5. *Financial Times*, 2–3 May 2015.
6. David Kilcullen, *Blood Year* (Hurst & Co., 2016), pp. 79–81.
7. Rice, *No Higher Honor*, p. 203; Address by General Sir Nicholas Houghton at Chatham House, September 2015.
8. Gates, *Washington Post*, 11 June 2011.

55 THE SPECIAL RELATIONSHIP

1. Sherwood, *Roosevelt and Hopkins*, p. 920.
2. Clifford, *Counsel to the President*, pp. 106–7.
3. Colville, *The Fringes of Power*, Vol. II, p. 274.
4. FRUS, Vol. III (1948), p. 1113.
5. Acheson, *Present at the Creation*, p. 763.
6. Dimbleby and Reynolds, *An Ocean Apart*, p. 239.
7. Henry Kissinger, *The Troubled Partnership* (McGraw-Hill, 1965), p. 78.
8. Kissinger, *White House Years*, pp. 90–91.
9. Owen, *Time to Declare*, p. 282.
10. Ibid., p. 79.
11. Shultz, *Turmoil and Triumph*, p. 154.
12. Henry Kissinger, 'The Right to be Right', *New York Times Book Review*, 14 November 1993, pp. 1–2.
13. Rice, *No Higher Honor*, pp. 37–8.
14. Kissinger, *Diplomacy*, p. 598.
15. De la Billière, *Storm Command*, p. 26.

56 BRITAIN, THE UNITED STATES AND EUROPE

1. Charlton, *The Price of Victory*, pp. 69, 92.
2. Acheson, *Present at the Creation*, pp. 382–8.
3. Horne, *Macmillan*, Vol. II, pp. 111, 318, 431–2.
4. Raymond Seitz, speech to the Pilgrims Society, London, 19 April 1994.
5. David Owen, *Balkan Odyssey* (Victor Gollancz, 1995), p. 367.
6. Henry Kissinger, address to Conference on Britain in the World, London, 29 March 1995.
7. Robert Zoellick, 'Britain is Still Special', *Wall Street Journal*, 3 April 1995.

57 SPECIAL ANY MORE?
1. Francis Fukuyama, *The End of History* (Free Press, 1992).
2. Ashton Carter, BBC interview, 13 February 2016.

BIBLIOGRAPHY

Acheson, Dean. *Present at the Creation*. W. W. Norton, 1969.

Adams, Henry. *History of the United States*, Vols I–IV. Charles Scribner's Sons, 1889–96.

— (ed.). *The Writings of Albert Gallatin*, Vol. I. J. B. Lippincott, 1879.

—. *Democracy: An American Novel*. Henry Holt & Co., 1880.

Aldous, Richard. *Reagan and Thatcher*. Hutchinson, 2012.

Aldrich, Richard J. *GCHQ*. HarperPress, 2010.

Allen, Harry C. *Great Britain and the United States*. St Martin's Press, 1955.

Alsop, Joseph W. *I've Seen the Best of It*. W. W. Norton, 1992.

Alsop, Susan Mary. *Lady Sackville*. Doubleday, 1978.

Ambrose, Stephen E. *Eisenhower: Soldier and President*. Simon & Schuster, 1990.

Andrew, Christopher, and Oleg Gordievsky. *KGB*. Hodder & Stoughton, 1990.

Baker, James. *The Politics of Diplomacy*. G. P. Putnam's Sons, 1995.

Ball, George. *The Discipline of Power*. Little, Brown, 1968.

—. *The Past Has Another Pattern*. W. W. Norton, 1982.

Benn, Tony. *Out of the Wilderness*. Hutchinson, 1987.

Bernanke, Ben. *The Courage to Act*. W. W Norton, 2015.

Beschloss, Michael. *Kennedy and Roosevelt*. W. W. Norton, 1980.

—. *Mayday: Eisenhower, Khrushchev and the U2 Affair*. Harper & Row, 1986.

de la Billière, Peter. *Storm Command*. HarperCollins, 1992.

Blair, Tony. *A Journey*. Hutchinson, 2010.

Bourne, Kenneth. *Britain and the Balance of Power in North America*. Longman, 1967.

Bower, Tom. *Broken Vows*, Faber, 2016.

Bradley, Omar. *A Soldier's Story*. Rand McNally, 1951.

Brandon, Henry. *Special Relationships*. Atheneum, 1988.

Bremer, Paul. *My Year in Iraq*. Simon & Schuster, 2006.

Brogan, Denis W. *The French Nation, 1814–1940*. Hamilton, 1957.

Bryant, Arthur. *The Turn of the Tide*. Collins, 1957.

—. *Triumph in the West*. Collins, 1959.

Bryce, James. *The American Commonwealth*, Vols I–III. Macmillan, 1888.

Brzezinski, Zbigniew. *Power and Principle: Memoirs of the National Security Adviser, 1977–1981*. Farrar, Straus & Giroux, 1983.

Bullock, Alan. *Ernest Bevin: Foreign Secretary, 1945–1951*. Heinemann, 1963.

Burk, Kathleen. *Old World, New World*. Little, Brown, 2007.

Bush, George H. W., and Brent Scowcroft. *A World Transformed*, Knopf, 1998.

Bush, George W. *Decision Points*. Virgin Books, 2010.

Butler, James R. *Lord Lothian*. Macmillan, 1960.

Butler Review of Intelligence on Weapons of Mass Destruction, 2004.

Cadogan, Sir Alexander (ed. David Dilks). *Diaries*. G. P. Putnam's Sons, 1972.

Callaghan, James. *Time and Chance*. Collins, 1987.

Campbell, Alastair. *The Blair Years*. Hutchinson, 2010.

—. *Diaries: The Burden of Power: Countdown to Iraq*, Vol. IV. Hutchinson, 2012.

Campbell, John. *Edward Heath*. Jonathan Cape, 1993.

Carrington, Peter. *Reflect on Things Past*. William Collins, 1988.

Castle, Barbara. *Diaries 1964–70*. Weidenfeld & Nicolson, 1974.

Cecil, Robert. *Donald Maclean*. Hodder & Stoughton, 1990.

Charlton, Michael. *The Price of Victory*. BBC Publications, 1983.

—. *The Little Platoon*. Blackwell, 1989.

Cheney, Dick. *In My Time*. Threshold Editions, 2011.

Churchill, Winston S. *The World Crisis*. Odhams, 1938.

—. *The Second World War*, Vols I–VI. Cassell, 1948–54.

Clarke, Michael (ed.). *The Afghan Papers*. RUSI, 2011.

Clifford, Clark. *Counsel to the President*. Random House, 1991.

Clinton, Bill. *My Life*. Arrow Books, 2005.

Clinton, Hillary. *Living History*. Simon & Schuster, 2003.

—. *Hard Choices*. Simon & Schuster, 2014.

Colville, John. *The Fringes of Power*, Vols I and II. Hodder & Stoughton, 1985, 1987.

Cooper, Chester L. *The Lost Crusade*. MacGibbon & Kee, 1981.

Copeland, Miles. *The Game of Nations*. Simon & Schuster, 1969.

Cowper-Coles, Sherard. *Letters from Kabul*. HarperCollins, 2011.

Cray, Edward. *General of the Army George C. Marshall*. Simon & Schuster, 1990.

Crossman, Richard. *The Diaries of a Cabinet Minister*, Vols I and II. Hamish Hamilton, 1975/1976.

Dalton, Hugh. *High Tide and After*. Frederick Muller, 1962.

Danchev, Alex. *Oliver Franks*. Clarendon Press, 1993.

Dannatt, Richard. *Leading from the Front*. Bantam Press, 2010.

Devlin, Patrick. *Too Proud to Fight*. Oxford University Press, 1975.

Dickie, John. *Special No More*. Weidenfeld & Nicolson, 1994.

Dimbleby, David, and David Reynolds. *An Ocean Apart*. Hodder & Stoughton, 1988.

Divine, Robert. *Foreign Policy and US Presidential Elections*. Franklin Waits, 1974.

Eden, Anthony. *Full Circle*. Cassell, 1960.

Elliott, Christopher. *High Command*. Hurst & Co., 2015.

Fairweather, Jack. *A War of Choice*. Jonathan Cape, 2011.

—. *The Good War*. Jonathan Cape, 2014.

Falkland Islands Review: Franks Report. HM Stationery Office, 1983.

Feis, Herbert. *Churchill, Roosevelt and Stalin*. Princeton University Press, 1957.

Foot, Rosemary. *The Wrong War*. Cornell University Press, 1985.

Foreign Relations of the United States. *The Conferences at Washington and Casablanca*. Washington, DC: Department of State, US Government Printing Office, 1943.

—. *The Conferences at Washington and Quebec*. Washington, DC: Department of State. US Government Printing Office, 1943.

—. *The Conferences at Cairo and Tehran*. Washington, DC: Department of State, US Government Printing Office, 1943.

—. *The Conference at Quebec*. Washington, DC: Department of State, US Government Printing Office, 1944.

—. *The Conferences at Malta and Yalta*. Washington, DC: Department of State, US Government Printing Office, 1945.

Freedman, Lawrence, and Virginia Gamba-Stonehouse. *Signals of War*. Faber & Faber, 1990.

Fukuyama, Francis. *The End of History*. Free Press, 1992.

Gates, Robert. *From the Shadows*. Touchstone, 1996.

—. *Duty*. Knopf, 2014

Geithner, Timothy. *Stress Test*. Random House, 2014.

Gilbert, Martin. *Winston S. Churchill*, Vols III–VIII. William Heinemann, 1975–88.

Goold-Adams, Richard. *John Foster Dulles: A Re-appraisal*. Weidenfeld & Nicolson, 1962.

Gowing, Margaret. *Britain and Atomic Energy, 1939–45*. Macmillan, 1964.

—. *Independence and Deterrence*. Macmillan, 1974.

Greenhill, Denis. *More by Accident*. Wilton, 1992.

Grey of Fallodon. *Twenty-Five Years*, Vol. II. Frederick A. Stokes Company, 1925.

de Guingand, Francis. *Operation Victory*. Hodder & Stoughton, 1947.

Gwynn, Stephen (ed.). *The Letters and Friendships of Sir Cecil Spring-Rice*, Vol. II. Constable, 1929.

Haass, Richard. *The Power to Persuade*. Houghton Mifflin, 1994.

—. *War of Necessity, War of Choice*. Simon & Schuster, 2010.

Haig, Alexander. *Caveat*. Weidenfeld & Nicolson, 1984.

Hamilton, Stanislaus M. (ed.). *The Writings of James Monroe*, Vols V and VI. G. P. Putnam's Sons, 1898.

Harriman, W. Averell, and Elie Abel. *Special Envoy to Churchill and Stalin*. Random House, 1975.

Harris, Kenneth. *Attlee*. Weidenfeld & Nicolson, 1982.

Harrod, Roy. *The Life of John Maynard Keynes*. Macmillan, 1951.

Hastings, Max. *The Korean War*. Michael Joseph, 1987.

— and Simon Jenkins. *The Battle for the Falklands*. Michael Joseph, 1983.

Healey, Denis. *The Time of My Life*. Michael Joseph, 1989.

Henderson, Nicholas. *The Birth of NATO*. Weidenfeld & Nicolson, 1982.

—. 'America and the Falklands', *The Economist*, 12 November 1983.

Hennessy, Patrick. *The Junior Officers' Reading Club*. Penguin Books, 2010.

Hitchens, Christopher. *Blood, Class, and Nostalgia*. Chatto & Windus, 1990.

Holbrooke, Richard. *To End a War*. Random House, 1998.

Horne, Alistair. *Macmillan*, Vols I and II. Macmillan, 1988, 1989.

Howe, Geoffrey. *Conflict of Loyalty*. Macmillan, 1994.

Hurd, Douglas. *Memoirs*. Little, Brown, 2003.

Hyde, H. Montgomery. *The Quiet Canadian*. Constable, 1982.

Ismay, Hastings. *Memoirs*. Heinemann, 1960.

Jackson, Mike. *Soldier*. Bantam Press, 2007.

Jenkins, Roy. *A Life at the Centre*. Random House, 1991.

Kampfner, John. *Blair's Wars*. Free Press, 2004.

Kennedy, Paul. *The Rise and Fall of the Great Powers*. Random House, 1987.

Ketcham, Ralph. *James Madison*. University of Virginia Press, 1990.

Keynes, John Maynard. *The Economic Consequences of the Peace*. Macmillan, 1920.

—. *Collected Writings*, Vol. XVI. Macmillan, 1971.

Khalilzad, Zalmay. *The Envoy*. St Martin's Press, 2016.

Kilcullen, David. *Blood Year*. Hurst & Co., 2016.

Kimball, Warren F. (ed.). *Churchill and Roosevelt: The Complete Correspondence*, Vols I–III. Princeton University Press, 1984.

Kipling, Rudyard. *Writings in Prose and Verse*, Vols I–XXXVI. C. Scribner's Sons, 1897–1937.

Kissinger, Henry. *The Troubled Relationship*. Google Books, originally published 1965.

—. *The White House Years*. Little, Brown, 1979.

—. *Years of Upheaval*. Little, Brown, 1982.

—. *Diplomacy*. Simon & Schuster, 1994.

—. *World Order*. Allen Lane, 2014.

Kyle, Keith. *Suez*. Weidenfeld & Nicolson, 1991.

Lamb, Christina. *Farewell Kabul*. William Collins, 2015.

Lamb, Richard. *The Macmillan Years, 1957–63*. John Murray, 1995.

Lansing, Robert. *War Memoirs*. Bobbs-Merrill, 1935.

Lawson, Nigel. *The View from No. 11*. Bantam Press, 1992.

Ledwidge, Frank. *Losing Small Wars*. Yale University Press, 2011.

Leutze, James (ed.). *The London Observer 1940.25*. Hutchinson, 1972.

Link, Arthur S. (ed.). *The Papers of Woodrow Wilson*, Vols I and XLIII. Princeton University Press, 1969.

Lloyd, Selwyn. *Suez 1956*. Jonathan Cape, 1978.

Lloyd George, David. *War Memoirs*. Odhams, 1938.

Lucas, W. Scott. *Divided We Stand*. Hodder & Stoughton, 1991.

McDonald, Iverach. *History of the Times*, Vol. V. Times Books, 1984.

McKercher, B. J. C. *The Second Baldwin Government and the United States*. Cambridge University Press, 1984.

Macmillan, Harold. *The Blast of War*. Macmillan, 1967.

—. *Riding the Storm*. Macmillan, 1971.

—. *Pointing the Way*. Macmillan, 1972.

Mahan, A. T. *The Influence of Sea-Power upon History*. Sampson Low, 1889.

McNamara, Robert S. *In Retrospect*. Times Books, 1995.

Major, John. *The Autobiography*. HarperCollins, 1999.

Manchester, William. *MacArthur: American Caesar*. Little, Brown, 1978.

Marshall, George C. *Memoirs of My Services in the World War*. Houghton Mifflin, 1976.

McChrystal, Stanley. *My Share of the Task*. Penguin, 2013.

Meyer, Christopher. *DC Confidential*. Weidenfeld & Nicolson, 2005.

Montgomery, Bernard L. *Memoirs*. Collins, 1958.

Moore, Charles. *Margaret Thatcher*, Vols I and II. Allen Lane, 2013, 2015.

Morison, Elting E. (ed.). *The Letters of Theodore Roosevelt*, Vols I–VIII. Harvard University Press, 1951–54.

Morris, Edmund. *The Rise of Theodore Roosevelt*. Ballantine, 1979.

Murphy, Robert. *Diplomat among Warriors*. Doubleday, 1964.

Newhouse, John. *Imperial America*. Alfred A. Knopf, 2003.

Nutting, Anthony. *No End of a Lesson*. Constable, 1967.

Obama, Barack. *Dreams from My Father*. Random House, 2004.

Owen, David. *Time to Declare*. Michael Joseph, 1991.

—. *Balkan Odyssey*. Victor Gollancz, 1995.

Parsons, Anthony. 'The Falklands Crisis in the United Nations'. *International Affairs*, Vol. 59, No. 2, spring 1983.

Paulson, Hank. *On the Brink*. Simon & Schuster, 2010.

Perkins, Frances. *The Roosevelt I Knew*. Viking, 1946.

Philby, Kim. *My Silent War*. MacGibbon & Kee, 1968.

Pierre, Andrew. *Nuclear Politics*. Oxford University Press, 1972.

Pimlott, Ben. *Harold Wilson*. HarperCollins, 1992.

Powell, Colin. *My American Journey*. Random House, 1995.

Reagan, Ronald. *An American Life*. Simon & Schuster, 1990.

Renwick, Robin. *A Journey with Margaret Thatcher: British Foreign Policy under the Iron Lady*. Biteback, 2014.

Rhodes James, Robert. *Anthony Eden*. McGraw-Hill, 1986.

Rice, Condoleezza. *No Higher Honor*. Simon & Schuster, 2011.

Richards, David. *Taking Command*. Headline, 2014.

Richardson, Jeffrey T., and Desmond Ball. *The Ties That Bind: Intelligence Cooperation between the UK and USA*. Allen & Unwin, 1985.

Riddell, Peter. *Hug them Close*. Politico's, 2003.

Riedel, Bruce. *Deadly Embrace*. Brookings, 2011.

Roberts, Andrew. *The Holy Fox*. Weidenfeld & Nicolson, 1991.

—. *Eminent Churchillians*. Weidenfeld & Nicolson, 1994.

Roosevelt, Kermit. *Counter-Coup*. McGraw-Hill, 1979.

Rose, Norman. *Vansittart: Study of a Diplomat*. Heinemann, 1978.

Rumsfeld, Donald. *Known and Unknown*. Sentinel, 2011.

Schlesinger, Arthur. *A Thousand Days*. Houghton Mifflin, 1965.

Schwarzkopf, H. Norman. *It Doesn't Take a Hero*. Bantam Press, 1992.

Seitz, Raymond. *Over Here*. Weidenfeld & Nicolson, 1988.

Seldon, Anthony. *Blair*. Free Press, 2004.

— and Guy Lodge. *Brown at 10*. Biteback, 2010.

— and Peter Snowden. *Cameron at 10*. William Collins, 2015.

Seymour, Charles (ed.). *The Intimate Papers of Colonel House*, Vols I–IV. Houghton Mifflin, 1926.

Sherwood, Robert. *Roosevelt and Hopkins*. Harper, 1948.

Shuckburgh, Evelyn. *Descent to Suez*. W. W. Norton, 1986.

Shultz, George P. *Turmoil and Triumph*. Charles Scribner's Sons, 1993.

Simms, Brendan. *Unfinest Hour*. Allen Lane, 2001.

Skidelsky, Robert. *John Maynard Keynes: Hopes Betrayed*. Macmillan, 1983.

Sky, Emma. *The Unravelling*. Atlantic Books, 2014.

Slim, Field Marshal. *Defeat into Victory*. McKay, 1956.

Smith, Geoffrey. *Reagan and Thatcher*. W. W. Norton, 1991.

Sorensen, Theodore. *Kennedy*. Harper & Row, 1965.

Stimson, Henry L., and McGeorge Bundy. *On Active Service in Peace and War*. Harper, 1947.

Stewart, Rory. *Occupational Hazards*. Picador, 2006.

Straw, Jack. *Last Man Standing*. Macmillan, 2012.

Summersby, Kay. *Past Forgetting*. Simon & Schuster, 1974.

Synnott, Hilary. *Bad Days in Basra*. I. B. Tauris, 2008.

Tenet, George. *At the Center of the Storm*. HarperPress, 2007.

Thatcher, Margaret. *The Downing Street Years*. HarperCollins, 1993.

Thomas, Hugh. *The Suez Affair*. Weidenfeld & Nicolson, 1966.

Thorne, Christopher. *Allies of a Kind*. Oxford University Press, 1956.

— (Edited by the staff of US News and World Report). *Triumph without Victory*. Times Books, 1992.

Truman, Harry S. *Year of Decisions*. Doubleday, 1955.

—. *Years of Trial and Hope*. Doubleday, 1956.

Tuchman, Barbara. *The Zimmermann Telegram*. Constable, 1959.

—. *Stilwell and the American Experience in China*. Macmillan, 1970.

Urban, Mark. *Task Force Black*. Abacus, 2011.

Walters, Vernon. *The Mighty and the Meek*. St Ermin's Press, 2001.

Weidenfeld, George. *Remembering My Good Friends*. HarperCollins, 1995.

Weinberger, Caspar. *Fighting for Peace*. Warner, 1990.

Wheeler-Bennett, Sir John. *King George VI*. Macmillan, 1958.

Williams, John S. *History of the Invasion and Capture of Washington*. Harper & Brothers, 1857.

Wilson, Harold. *The Labour Government*. Weidenfeld & Nicolson, 1971.

Winant, John G. *Letter from Grosvenor Square*. Hodder & Stoughton, 1947.

Winterbotham, F. W. *The Ultra Secret*. Weidenfeld & Nicolson, 1974.

Woodward, Bob. *The Commanders*. Simon & Schuster, 1992.

—. *Bush at War*. Simon & Schuster, 2002.

—. *Plan of Attack*. Simon & Schuster, 2004.

—. *State of Denial*. Simon & Schuster, 2006.

—. *Obama's Wars*. Simon & Schuster, 2010.

Ziegler, Philip. *Mountbatten*. Collins, 1985.

—. *Wilson*. Weidenfeld & Nicolson, 1993.

INDEX